Maya E Groups

Maya Studies

UNIVERSITY PRESS OF FLORIDA

Florida A&M University, Tallahassee
Florida Atlantic University, Boca Raton
Florida Gulf Coast University, Ft. Myers
Florida International University, Miami
Florida State University, Tallahassee
New College of Florida, Sarasota
University of Central Florida, Orlando
University of Florida, Gainesville
University of North Florida, Jacksonville
University of South Florida, Tampa
University of West Florida, Pensacola

Maya E Groups

Calendars, Astronomy, and Urbanism in the Early Lowlands

EDITED BY
DAVID A. FREIDEL, ARLEN F. CHASE, ANNE S. DOWD,
AND JERRY MURDOCK

University Press of Florida
Gainesville · Tallahassee · Tampa · Boca Raton
Pensacola · Orlando · Miami · Jacksonville · Ft. Myers · Sarasota

Copyright 2017 by David A. Freidel, Arlen F. Chase, Anne S. Dowd, and Jerry Murdock
All rights reserved
Published in the United States of America

First cloth printing, 2017
First paperback printing, 2020

This book may be available in an electronic edition.

25 24 23 22 21 20   6 5 4 3 2 1

Library of Congress Cataloging-in-Publication Data
Names: Freidel, David A., editor of compilation. | Chase, Arlen F. (Arlen
  Frank), 1953– editor of compilation. | Dowd, Anne S., editor of
  compilation. | Murdock, Jerry, editor of compilation.
Title: Maya E groups : calendars, astronomy, and urbanism in the early
  lowlands / edited by David A. Freidel, Arlen F. Chase, Anne S. Dowd, and
  Jerry Murdock ; foreword by David A. Freidel and Jerry Murdock.
Other titles: Maya studies.
Description: Gainesville : University Press of Florida, 2017. | Series: Maya
  studies | Includes bibliographical references.
Identifiers: LCCN 2017005516 | ISBN 9780813054353 (cloth : acid-free paper)
ISBN 9780813064390 (pbk.)
Subjects: LCSH: Mayas—Belize River Valley (Guatemala and Belize) | Maya
  architecture—Belize River Valley (Guatemala and Belize) | Mayas—Belize
  River Valley (Guatemala and Belize)—Antiquities. | Belize River Valley
  (Guatemala and Belize)—Antiquities.
Classification: LCC F1465.M39 2017 | DDC 972.82—dc23
LC record available at https://lccn.loc.gov/2017005516

The University Press of Florida is the scholarly publishing agency for the State University System of Florida, comprising Florida A&M University, Florida Atlantic University, Florida Gulf Coast University, Florida International University, Florida State University, New College of Florida, University of Central Florida, University of Florida, University of North Florida, University of South Florida, and University of West Florida.

University Press of Florida
2046 NE Waldo Road
Suite 2100
Gainesville, FL 32609
http://upress.ufl.edu

To Murray Gell-Mann, who, through his work and effort, taught the fundamental interconnections between modern and ancient wisdom.

Murray Gell-Mann, the Robert Andrews Millikan Professor Emeritus of Physics at the California Institute of Technology, winner of the 1969 Nobel Prize in Physics, author of *The Quark and the Jaguar,* and a Santa Fe Institute founder. Copyright © 2013, Anne S. Dowd, all rights reserved.

Contents

List of Figures ix
List of Tables xv
Preface: On the Path of the Sun xvii
Acknowledgments xxiii
Abbreviations xxv

Part I. E Groups: Historical Perspectives

1. The Distribution and Significance of E Groups: A Historical Background and Introduction 3
   Arlen F. Chase, Anne S. Dowd, and David A. Freidel

2. E Groups and the Rise of Complexity in the Southeastern Maya Lowlands 31
   Arlen F. Chase and Diane Z. Chase

Part II. The Astronomy and Cosmology of E Groups

3. E Groups: Astronomy, Alignments, and Maya Cosmology 75
   Anthony F. Aveni and Anne S. Dowd

4. The Legacy of Preclassic Calendars and Solar Observation in Mesoamerica's Magic Latitude 95
   Susan Milbrath

5. The E Group as Timescape: Early E Groups, Figurines, and the Sacred Almanac 135
   Prudence M. Rice

6. E Groups, Cosmology, and the Origins of Maya Rulership 177
   David A. Freidel

Part III. The Archaeology of E Groups

7. The Isthmian Origins of the E Group and Its Adoption in the Maya Lowlands   215
   Takeshi Inomata

8. A Tale of Two E Groups: El Palmar and Tikal, Petén, Guatemala   253
   James A. Doyle

9. The History, Function, and Meaning of Preclassic E Groups in the Cival Region   293
   Francisco Estrada-Belli

10. Time to Rule: Celestial Observation and Appropriation among the Early Maya   328
    William A. Saturno, Boris Beltrán, and Franco D. Rossi

11. Ordinary People and East–West Symbolism   361
    Cynthia Robin

12. E Groups and Ancestors: The Sunrise of Complexity at Xunantunich, Belize   386
    M. Kathryn Brown

13. Of Apples and Oranges: The Case of E Groups and Eastern Triadic Architectural Assemblages in the Belize River Valley   412
    Jaime J. Awe, Julie A. Hoggarth, and James J. Aimers

14. The Founding of Yaxuná: Place and Trade in Preclassic Yucatán   450
    Travis W. Stanton

15. Founding Landscapes in the Central Karstic Uplands   480
    Kathryn Reese-Taylor

Part IV. Conclusion

16. More Than Smoke and Mirrors: Maya Temple Precincts and the Emergence of Religious Institutions in Mesoamerica   517
    Anne S. Dowd

17. Epilogue: E Groups and Their Significance to the Ancient Maya   578
    Diane Z. Chase, Patricia A. McAnany, and Jeremy A. Sabloff

List of Contributors   583
Index   591

Figures

0.1. November 6, 2011, Santa Fe Institute Working Group planning session   xxii

0.2. August 26, 2012, Santa Fe Institute Working Group participants   xxii

0.3. August 25, 2013, Santa Fe Institute Working Group participants   xxii

1.1. Chronological overview of the Maya area   4

1.2. Plan of the latest (Early Classic) version of Uaxactún Group E   9

1.3. Isometric reconstruction of the Cenote E Group   11

1.4. Distribution of E Group–type complexes   13

1.5. Reported E Groups from the Maya region   14

2.1. The two variants of the E Group plan   33

2.2. The eastern platform at Uaxactún   42

2.3. Caches from the core of Structure EII at Uaxactún   44

2.4. The plan and section of the eastern platform of the Cenote E Group   46

2.5. E Groups from Caracol, Belize   48

2.6. The Caracol epicentral E Group east platform   51

2.7. The architectural development of the eastern platform of the Caracol E Group   52

2.8. Expanded view and upper and lower plans of SD C8B-3   53

2.9. Distribution of 170 known E Groups   55

2.10. Perspective of the center of Ixtontón   57

2.11. Map of Yaxhá, Guatemala   61

2.12. The founder deities or "triad gods"   62

3.1. Plan of Group E, Uaxactún 77
3.2. Uaxactún Group E plan 78
3.3. Seasonal distribution of rainfall in mid-Petén latitudes and seasonal distribution of E Group–type alignments 81
3.4. Quadripartite pecked cross-circle carved into Temple Court floor 84
3.5. Detail of Chiik Nahb market complex and map of Calakmul showing the Chiik Nahb market complex 86
3.6. Murals showing market scenes 87
3.7. Calamkul Structure IVc north doorjambs at summer solstice sunset 89
3.8. Calakmul Group E–type complex 90
4.1. Takalik Abaj Altar 46 105
4.2. Takalik Abaj Stela 5 110
4.3. Leiden Plaque 115
5.1. Mound ZZ1 and the Operation 1 trench and the site of Nixtun-Ch'ich' 144
5.2. A large fireclouded head, seated female, and head and shoulders of a male with a tied headband 146
5.3. Head with a braided hairdo, head with missing facial features, head with an elaborate two-tier headdress, and Classic period head-variant glyph numerals 147
6.1. GI, One Tooth Person 179
6.2. The Quatrefoil "u yol ahk K'inich Bahlam in the head of the turtle" 183
6.3. Burial 37, King Chak Tok Ich'aak of Waka' as the K'an Nahb Isimte' 185
6.4. The Middle Formative dance platforms at Yaxuná 188
6.5. Olmec-style bearded figure in the birthing pose 190
6.6. East side of Structure 5C-2nd Cerro Maya 192
6.7. West side of Structure 5C-2nd Cerro Maya 193
6.8. Quadripartite Badge, Pakal, and Double-Headed Serpent from the Palenque Sarcophagus 195
6.9. The Celestial Monster on Structure 10L-22, Copán 199

6.10. The Panel of the Cross   201

6.11. Structure 29 at Cerros (Cerro Maya) viewed from the west   204

6.12. Structure 29 at Cerros   204

6.13. Panel of the Sun, Palenque   205

7.1. Map of the Maya area   216

7.2. Map of Ojo de Agua   219

7.3. Maps of MFC-pattern sites with E Groups shaded   221

7.4. Map of Group A of Ceibal   222

7.5. Cache 118 of Ceibal   224

7.6. Cache 138 of Ceibal   225

7.7. Cache 160 of Ceibal   225

7.8. Cache 128 of Ceibal   231

7.9. Cache 103 of Ceibal   232

8.1. Map of major sites near El Palmar and Tikal, map of El Palmar with locations of major excavations, and comparison of Late Preclassic E Groups at El Palmar and Tikal   254

8.2. Map of possible or confirmed Middle Preclassic E Groups in the Central Southern Lowlands   256

8.3. Plan view of excavations in Mundo Perdido Structure 5C-54, Tikal   257

8.4. Early Mamom ceramics from El Palmar Structure E4-1   258

8.5. Tikal Structure 5C-54-2, west elevation   261

8.6. El Palmar Structure E4-1-4th   262

8.7. Tikal Structure 5C-54-3B, west elevation   264

8.8. North profile of Late Preclassic expansion episodes, El Palmar Structure E4-1   268

8.9. Exterior walls of Structure E4-1-2nd, El Palmar   270

8.10. Hypothetical replication of Mundo Perdido plaza dimensions across Tikal, Yaxhá, and Calakmul   274

8.11. Tetrapod cache plates, Structure E4-4, El Palmar   277

9.1. Map of the area surrounding the Cival region   294

9.2. Photo and profile views of the Cival Cache 4   297

9.3. Stela 3 of Cival, depicting a Preclassic Rain God   300

9.4. Map of Cival at the end of the Terminal Preclassic period   301
9.5. Stucco mask on the northern façade of the Cival main E Group's western pyramid   302
9.6. Histogram of sight-line azimuths   305
9.7. Location of the thirteen E Groups in the region surrounding Cival   306
9.8. Histogram of E Group plaza areas at Cival   308
9.9. Maps of eleven E Groups mapped at Cival   310
9.10. Histogram of E–W plaza width   311
9.11. Histogram of length of eastern platform for twelve E Groups at Cival and nearby sites   311
9.12. Histogram of footprint areas of western pyramid at Cival and nearby sites   312
9.13. Histogram of azimuths   313
9.14. Profile of the topography along the Dos Aguadas northern sight line   314
9.15. Profile of the topography of the Cival region   315
9.16. Artistic rendering of Cival Center E Group   321
9.17. Drawing of low-relief carving on Cival Stela 2   322
10.1. Map of San Bartolo   331
10.2. Plan of Pinturas complex and chart of architectural phases of Pinturas   335
10.3. Reconstruction of Sub-5 E Group   336
10.4. Early painted hieroglyphic block from Sub-5 and Maize God from Ixbalamqué doorjamb   337
10.5. Reconstruction of Sub-5 "Hunahpu" radial pyramid   338
10.6. Painted marker on alley floor of Sub-5 "Hunahpu" ballcourt   340
11.1. Map of the Belize River valley   363
11.2. Topography, settlement, and agricultural terraces at Chan   366
11.3. Chan's community center   367
11.4. Profile of central east structure   370
11.5. Profile of west structure   371
11.6. Cache 9 cutout figures   373

11.7. Burial 1   377

12.1. LiDAR hillshade image of Xunantunich with site map overlaid   389

12.2. LiDAR hillshade image of Early Xunantunich   391

12.3. Isometric reconstruction of Structure E-2-2nd   392

12.4. Isometric reconstruction of perishable altar in front of Structure E-2-2nd   394

12.5. Isometric reconstruction of E Group at Early Xunantunich   395

12.6. Photograph of burial chamber in Structure E-2-1st   403

13.1. Map of the Belize River valley   421

13.2. North–south profiles of Eastern Triadic Assemblages at selected Belize valley sites   423

13.3. Plan of Cahal Pech site core   424

13.4. North–south profile of Eastern Triadic Assemblage at Cahal Pech   425

13.5. Plan of Bedran Group at Baking Pot   430

13.6. Plan of Structure BR 180–182 at Barton Ramie, Belize   431

14.1. Map of the Maya area showing sites with E Groups   455

14.2. Maler-convention drawing of the possible E Group at Kabah   456

14.3. Maler-convention drawing of the possible E Group at Santa Rosa Xtampak   457

14.4. LiDAR hillshade image of central Yaxuná   462

14.5. Ceramic vessels and greenstone from the cache in the dance platform at Yaxuná   463

14.6. North profile of the center-line excavation into the plaza in front of Structure 5E-2   465

15.1. Map of Central Karstic Uplands showing sites with E Groups   481

15.2. Map of Yaxnohcah   482

15.3. Map of Yaxnohcah civic precinct   483

15.4. Map of El Zacatal   495

15.5. Map of Brisa E Group and reservoirs   498

16.1. El Palenque temple precinct plan, Oaxaca, Mexico   523

16.2. Structure 20 Plan, El Palenque, Oaxaca, Mexico   524

16.3. Hun Ajaw Itzamnaj/One Maize Crocodile Tree or young Maize God emerging from a turtle carapace   525

16.4. Stela 114, front face   527

16.5. Calakmul's toponym from Structure XIII   528

16.6. Calakmul's Central Plaza view   529

16.7. Calakmul temple precinct, Group E–type Complex   530

16.8. Structure IVa and IVc plan details, Calakmul, Campeche, Mexico, Structure IVb upper level, and Structure IVb lower level   531

16.9. Reconstructed view northeast of Calakmul's Structure IVb   532

16.10. Profile of Calakmul Structure IVb   532

16.11. Lintel 1 found in Calakmul's Structure IVb   533

16.12. Calakmul Structure VII, VI, and V plans   534

16.13. Calakmul's Structure II   536

16.14. *Aj k'uhuun* title from bench in Las Sepulturas Group, 9N-82, Copán, Honduras   540

16.15. Graphs of temple rooms and temple floor area   546

16.16. Relative eastern temple proportions   553

Tables

2.1. E Groups of the Southeastern Lowlands   35

11.1. Chronology chart for the Chan site   364

11.2. Summary of radiocarbon dates from the Chan site   365

13.1. Height measurements of Eastern Triadic Structures in the Belize River valley   422

13.2. Frequency of burials and caches in Eastern Triadic Structures in the Belize River valley   433

14.1. AMS radiocarbon dates mentioned in the text   466

15.1. Yaxnohcah chronology based on ceramic complexes   484

15.2. E Groups in the Central Karst Plateau   487

16.1. Room counts/areas   543

16.2. Relative eastern temple proportions   545

Preface

On the Path of the Sun

Don Regi is a Maya leader intent on educating rising generations in his community into the successful ways of his ancestors regarding subsistence cultivation in a rainforest environment. We met with him to see if he would help us hold a ceremony to bless the enclave of wilderness around the ruins of El Perú, ancient Waka', in northwestern Petén. He agreed to do so. In the spring of 2009 we sat in Don Regi's small office in San Pedro Petén, Guatemala, in conversation with a piece of paper on the desk between us. Jerry Murdock was asking questions about the Feathered Serpent. The Itzá sage drew a picture, a line with feather-like lines coming off of it. He looked at Jerry, pointed to the main line, and said that this was the direct path but that we are often tempted to go down one of the side paths. Whether it is serendipity or determined persistence, or both, our path has taken us directly to this book prologue on the sun path and what the earliest people of southeastern Mesoamerica, the Lowland Maya among them, made of it in their first centers.

Jerry was inspired by this encounter, and his long-term engagement in conversation with the Working Group members, to write down the following:

> My view of what is unique about E Group constructions is that: (1) placement is always along the path of the sun; and (2) they exemplify the Mayas' ability to adapt the language of nature into structural forms. Nature's language, as expressed in the path of the Sun, is itself the articulation of a generatrix as seen by the shadow cast to earth. The Sun's path being a directrix creates new shadow shapes as it moves across the sky and through time. A famous example of this activity would be the appearance of the Feathered Serpent deity on a balustrade of El Castillo pyramid during equinox at Chichén Itzá. E Groups, like sundials, express "time-associated information,"

which was utilized by ancient peoples in many cultures. Keen observers such as the Maya understood that time is woven into the creation process and I believe they sought to replicate this within the built environment.

In this way, E Groups both capture and display time and the creation process as an "integrated whole" just as it is in nature. In nature everything is a reflection of everything else. Everything is integrated into cycles of nature and cycles of time. It is only human logic that separates and compartmentalizes time and turns entire ecosystems into individual objects. Everything we know about the Maya suggests that they accepted nature as inseparable from itself.

E Groups being not only portals and centers of ritual were also the earliest permanent gathering places that were constructed out of the landscape. They were likely to be places that helped shape both cultural and personal identity. E Groups may have functioned as plazas and just like milpas; both were often built utilizing golden rectangles, as found throughout nature's ubiquitous creations. It may be that for the Maya being informed of nature's geometry led them to greater functionality in their architecture and greater integration into the world. Perhaps the feathered serpent, which we know is associated with spirals, *Spondylus* shells, and Venus, is also linked with the process of creation. Golden ratios like 8:5 and 13:8 are mathematical expressions of nature's process of creation. These ratios are also found in the growth patterns of flowers, seeds, petals, pinecones, bones, shells, spirals, fruits, and vegetables and are reflected in Mayan structures of time such as the Haab and Tzolk'in calendars.

Back in Don Regi's tiny office I sat thinking of the process of creation and the feathered serpent as Don Regi drew his straight line between what he said was two large pyramid groups that were representations of Orion and the Pleiades in the central core of El Mirador. Then I recalled a large mural painted on the North Wall at San Bartolo where a red serpent path emerges from a mountain in the west and flows toward the east. Two elaborate scenes of Maya life rich with creation mythology were painted above the baseline of the serpent path dotted with footprints of the ancestors. The mural and the line between the star clusters came together in my mind at that moment, and just like the Sun and its movement along its path, time became something that was both linear and cyclical, integrated with the past and the here and now, because they were concepts that were always present together in nature. Perhaps the "Maya concept of time," like the golden ratio, was seen as an organizing constraint that nature and the concomitant Mayan deities utilized to unfold, transform, and ultimately create the world itself.

The collaboration among the authors of the ensuing chapters has been enabled and inspired by the wonderful hospitality of the Santa Fe Institute and its president, Jeremy A. Sabloff. Murray Gell-Mann, one of the founders, and distinguished archaeologist George Gumerman first invited David Freidel to participate in a working group at the institute, and he met Jerry Murdock in that setting in the fall of 2008. When Jerry asked that David organize a working group on Maya origins and astronomy, David suggested a session on E Groups with the goal of recruiting Tony Aveni. Flanked by Tony's friends and collaborators Susan Milbrath and Anne Dowd, we called him. He generously agreed to come. We continued to be lucky: the two working group sessions brought together the remarkable array of archaeologists and archaeoastronomers represented in this book. It was Arlen Chase, also expert in E Groups, who first suggested that we write such a book and has been an energetic collaborator in seeing it through to completion. The give and take around that table at the Santa Fe Institute was memorable for us and is reflected in the syntheses presented by the participants.

Although Maya archaeologists have been researching E Groups for generations, it turns out to be a topic on the present frontiers of our knowledge, with many recent and exciting discoveries made and reported on by the working group participants. Once E Groups manifest in the Maya Lowlands (the temporal benchmark for this is now 1000 BCE at the site of Ceibal, as described by Takeshi Inomata in Chapter 7 in this volume), there are many ways to situate them in the ensuing development of Maya place-making, time-reckoning, religion, politics, and economics. These discussions are the substance of the book. But Jerry Murdock in correspondence in the fall of 2014 pressed his companions on this path once again to look back over their shoulders to its beginnings. The way back, at least in the Maya Lowlands, leads metaphorically into standing forest with few blaze marks or bent twigs to guide us. There are preceramic Archaic period (7,500–1,000 BCE) remains in some places, but not all (for example, not at Ceibal so far), and these offer few insights into the remarkable developments that follow.

Jerry's big questions about how spiritual leaders and close observers of nature like village shamans gave way to the earliest rulers and their ritual advisors presiding over E Group centers require us to widen our perspective in the Mesoamerican world of the time. When we do that two things become clear: the Maya were not the first to have rulers, but they were participants in a close second that brought in E Groups. The Lowland Maya were not, to our knowledge, the first people to establish monumental centers or material symbol systems that expressed precepts of power, earthly and cosmic. The Olmec center of San Lorenzo Tenochtitlán is earlier by centuries, and the society there is intimately related to other early Preclassic period (1,000 BCE–250 CE) societies to the southeast in Chiapas. Determining the direction of emulation among these early Preclassic communities, and others in Highland Mexico, remains a contentious matter among archaeologists. But no one can contest the ability of the San Lorenzo Olmec to move enormous basalt monuments across swampy riverine terrain from quarries in the Tuxtla Mountains or doubt that the symbol-system expressed on those monuments, as a sophisticated cosmologically grounded one, was deeply influential in subsequent middle Preclassic period (1,000–350 BCE) regional religious practices. Furthermore, the earliest use of polished greenstone celts, a middle Preclassic signature of regional interaction, is currently dated to 1,600 BCE at Laguna Manatee near San Lorenzo in the Olmec heartland, more than half a millennium earlier than in the Maya Lowlands. What Takeshi Inomata now proposes, in his contribution to this book and elsewhere, is that in the two centuries or so between the denouement of San Lorenzo and the florescence of the first Olmec center to have a major pyramid, La Venta to the east, a regional interaction sphere incorporating Ceibal in southwest Petén, and centers in Chiapas emerged with the E Group as a signature expression.

This intriguing period, roughly 1,000–800 BCE, straddles the early and middle Preclassic chronological divide; we have no better nomenclature for it, but it will clearly be featured regularly in future discussions of the origins of civilization in the region. What we can say with Inomata's breakthrough and the work of the other scholars in this book is that the E Group phenomenon began as part of an era of major social change embracing Lowland Maya and other Lowland peoples of southeastern Mesoamerica. On the other side of that temporal divide we have increasing evidence that the Middle Preclassic Lowland Maya peoples participated in the development of formal rulership, what Freidel identified in the 1980s as Divine Kingship by the late Preclassic period (350 BCE–0 CE). It has been affirmed as likely present in the middle Preclassic, notably by William Saturno at San Bartolo and Francisco Estrada-Belli at Cival.

Whatever transpired during these eventful centuries, it involved the E Groups and their ritual uses. Returning to Don Regi and the straight path, for all of the variability that is important to understanding the origins, use, and subsequent development of E Groups, it seems likely that this kind of monumental architecture was first and foremost a means of celebrating the sun cycle, agrarian seasonality, astronomy, and eventually formal time-keeping as recorded in calendars. While it is clear in the archaeological record that domesticated plants shaped the subsistence strategies of Mesoamericans for thousands of years before the middle Preclassic, it also seems increasingly clear that significant reliance on staple maize and other crops was only established in the period of the advent of E Groups. This is a matter of empirical contestation, so naturally we always need more data. But experts like Philip Arnold (2009) and Amber VanDerwarker and Robert Kruger (VanDerwarker and Kruger 2012) are pursuing the matter in the field and the general trend in the evidence suggests such a pattern. The innovation of E Groups, and the celebration of the sun path, was seemingly part of a regional recognition by many and diverse peoples that they lived in a natural world shaped by their subsistence, which they celebrated as a covenantal relationship between themselves and the supernatural beings of their cosmos, the sun principal among them.

David A. Freidel and Jerry Murdock

References Cited

Arnold, Philip J., III
2009 Settlement and Subsistence among the Early Formative Gulf Olmec. *Journal of Anthropological Archaeology* 28(4):397–411.
VanDerwarker, Amber M., and Robert P. Kruger
2012 Regional Variation in the Importance of Maize in the Early and Middle Formative Olmec Heartland: New Archaeobotanical Data from the San Carlos Homestead, Southern Veracruz. *Latin American Antiquity* 23(4):509–532.

Figure 0.1. November 6, 2011, Santa Fe Institute Working Group planning session: (*from left to right*) Jerry Sabloff, Paula Sabloff, Jerry Murdock, Anne Dowd, Susan Milbrath, David Freidel.

Figure 0.2. August 26, 2012, Santa Fe Institute Working Group participants: (*from left to right, back row*) Anne Dowd, Anthony Aveni, Jerry Sabloff, Arlen Chase, Jerry Murdock, Francisco Estrada-Belli; (*front row*) Travis Stanton, David Freidel, Susan Milbrath, Cynthia Robin, William Saturno.

Figure 0.3. August 25, 2013, Santa Fe Institute Working Group participants: (*from left to right, back row*) James Doyle, Takeshi Inomata, David Freidel, Travis Stanton, Francisco Estrada-Belli; (*middle row*) Patricia McAnany, Diane Chase, Arlen Chase, Jerry Murdock, Anne Dowd, Peter Harrison; (*bottom row*) Prudence Rice, Kathryn Brown, Murray Gell-Mann, Kathryn Reese-Taylor.

Acknowledgments

The Santa Fe Institute hosted the Maya Working Group program of convivial and rewarding discussion at its research facility in New Mexico. The free exchange of ideas in such a sustaining and nurturing environment has been a central tenet of the vision of Murray Gell-Mann, one of the founders, and Jeremy A. Sabloff, a former president, who are both, we are proud to say, participants in the Maya Working Group sessions. Each of us is beholden to a wide array of funding institutions, students, colleagues, and family members in the realization of the research presented and analyzed in the following chapters. We have become closer friends and comrades on a shared mission and are honored and privileged to participate in the crafting of knowledge about the ancient Maya in the context of this most special and exemplary retreat.

Jerry, Anne, Arlen, and I have enjoyed the process of bringing together such a talented group of scholars to participate in the Santa Fe Institute working groups held during August 2012 and 2013 and are pleased that this book is the result (Figures 0.1, 0.2, 0.3). We trust that you, the reader, will be interested in our latest thoughts on this fascinating subject.

Abbreviations

CONACULTA	El Consejo Nacional para la Cultura y las Artes de México
IDAEH	Instituto de Antropología e Historia
INAH	Instituto Nacional de Antropología e Historia
NWAF	New World Archaeological Foundation
UNAM	Universidad Nacional Autónoma de México

I

E Groups

Historical Perspectives

1

The Distribution and Significance of E Groups

A Historical Background and Introduction

ARLEN F. CHASE, ANNE S. DOWD, AND DAVID A. FREIDEL

Over the past century, Maya architectural groups composed of a raised eastern platform that supported three structures and faced one western pyramid across a public plaza have come to be recognized as nearly ubiquitous in the Southern Lowlands. These complexes, which are called "E Groups," have been correlated with archaeoastronomical alignments and features related to horizon-based calendar observation, measurement, and seasonal celebration. Similar to the patterning evident in other cultures' city or town centers, the early Maya had an ideal in mind for their main squares, recalling cosmologically based myth and ritual, with permutations or custom designs that made each community's ritual architecture unique and awe-inspiring. Like colonial (1675–1775 CE) New England town squares, where escaped livestock were corralled in a central pasture and a number of the administrative or religious buildings faced this "green," Maya centers were organized around an open plaza with origins in their agricultural community life. This chapter examines the historiography of scholarly work on E Groups, from 1924 onward, in an effort to provide a proper context for the rich and varied data on the distribution and significance of this important architectural type.

E Groups embody far more than simply a record of the sun's solstices, equinoxes, and zenith passages. Research over the last twenty-five years increasingly supports the view that they form the earliest identifiable architectural plan at many Maya centers. Reconnaissance and site survey shows that they are widely distributed throughout the Maya Lowlands. E Groups are distinctly clustered in the traditional Maya heartland of Guatemala's Petén, presaging the Late Classic period (550–800 CE) florescence in this same region (Figure 1.1). The adjacent parts of Mexico north of the Guatemalan border and the frontier lands of Belize to the east of Petén also have

Sequence	Period	Major Events
1958-2000 CE	Post-IGY	International Geophysical Year Earth System Observations
1920-1958 CE	Modern	Carnegie Institution of Washington Research Using Instrumental Observation
1697-1920 CE	Historic	Maya Integrated into Modern Nation-States
1519-1697 CE	Colonial	Colonial Occupation of Maya Region by Euroamericans
1200-1519 CE	Late Postclassic	Northern Lowlands Heavily Occupied
900-1200 CE	Early Postclassic	Florescence of Eastern Yucatán Coastal Sites
800-900 CE	Terminal Classic	Political Collapse in the Southern Lowlands
550-800 CE	Late Classic	Regional Polities are Widespread
250-550 CE	Early Classic	Transition to Stratified Regional Polities, Use of Vaulted Buildings, and Widespread Appearance of Polychrome Ceramics
0-250 CE	Terminal Preclassic	Changes Potentially Reflective of a Mini-collapse
350 BCE-0 CE	Late Preclassic	Large Vertical Monumental Constructions, E Groups Proliferate
1000-350 BCE	Middle Preclassic	Large Horizontal Monumental Constructions, E Groups are Built
2000-1000 BCE	Late Archaic	First Recognizable Maya Peoples
7500-2000 BCE	Middle Archaic	Archaic Lithic Assemblages, Ceramics Rare
11000-7500 BCE	Paleoindian	Paleoindian Lithic Assemblages

Figure 1.1. Chronological overview of the Maya area (after Chase et al. 2014c:14).

important sites with E Groups that are often as ancient and enduring as those found in the heartland. Intriguing outliers exist farther afield, with examples being noted from the Mexican sites of Chiapa de Corzo, Chiapas, and Comalcalco, Tabasco.

This volume is an opportunity for many of the researchers engaged in the study of E Groups and the origins and development of Lowland Maya civic-religious architecture to take comparative stock of what is known and to chart a course for future investigation. This is a rapidly expanding area of inquiry in Maya studies, in part because of a current emphasis on early centers and communities in the Lowlands. This volume represents a renewed effort to systematize and synthesize perspectives on the origins and development of Lowland Maya ceremony and centers. Through an examination of E Groups, it potentially becomes possible to understand how the Maya harnessed their beliefs and insights about the natural world to the tasks of living in increasingly complex societies.

Background

If we look at Frederick Law Olmsted's design for Central Park in New York City (Rogers 1972; Rosenzweig and Blackmar 1992), how many of us recognize its origins in small New England farming towns as a place for loose livestock to be penned up while waiting for their owners to reclaim them? Speaking of New York City, with its streets oriented on a strict grid aligned with the cardinal directions, how many of us have watched the hierophantic sun rise or set along those urban canyons and recalled our Julian system of calendar reckoning and its seasonal links to an agricultural past? Similarly, even archaeologists with the benefit of hindsight grapple with seeing a clear picture of the origins of E Group architecture from the Maya region. For this reason, the researchers represented in this book have all wrestled with a large corpus of literature that is available on Maya ceremony in general and on E Groups in particular. The conscious attempt is to situate these architectural complexes in time and space to communicate their meaning and significance better. This introduction provides a background to E Group investigations and introduces readers to their distribution and significance. First, a section on the historiography of the study of Group E–type architecture is presented, following its initial identification at Uaxactún (Blom 1924:218) and ending with current information on E Group research across the Lowland Maya region. Next, reasons are posited for the significance of these architectural complexes and for their function and meaning within Maya societies. This meaning may have changed over time (a subject treated in greater detail in the chapters that follow).

As the first shared form of Maya public architecture, E Groups must have been important. The centrality of ritual and symbolism in the organization of ancient Maya space is reflected in modern Maya society as well. The Tzotzil Maya speakers of Zinacantán see the small mound in their ceremonial center as the navel of the world or earth, *mishik* or *mixik' balamil* (Hanks 1990; Vogt 1976:7, 13, 33; Tate 1992:26; Zaro and Lohse 2005:93). To a large extent, the earliest E Groups must have represented a similar concept to the ancient Maya who constructed them.

During the nearly one hundred years of scholarship preceding this book, many changes in approaches to the archaeology of the region have taken place. For example, settlement pattern archaeology has given us a wealth of cartography and mapping data as well as detailed information about how the Maya distributed themselves over the landscape (Chase et al. 2014a, 2014b). Yet, ironically, these efforts to document the hinterland have brought us back to a consideration of the public architecture found in Maya centers. We now realize that ancient Maya centers, once described as "vacant" by J. Eric S. Thompson (1954) and others like Gordon Willey (1956) before the 1960s (and reinforced by William Bullard's [1960] original settlement pattern interpretations), were far more complex in their internal composition and variable in terms of their sizes. We also recognize that these centers have undergone developmental changes over time. The majority of larger centers in the Southern Maya Lowlands share a profusion of public spaces that conform to an E Group layout. When tested, this architectural plan is always the earliest public architecture at any given Maya site, in some cases going back to almost 1000 BCE (Inomata et al. 2013, 2015).

This volume has an explicit focus on public architecture, the kind that is usually found in the center of Maya sites. It also urges further research within such venues to increase our knowledge of early Maya civilization. In some ways, this brings the Maya field full circle, for in the 1970s there was a backlash against an exclusive focus on monumental architecture by "new archaeologists," like Kent Flannery (2009:16–24), in favor of household archaeology. With continued work, however, we have realized the importance of returning to the excavation of larger central architecture for a better contextualization of Maya residential groups. While archaeologists have documented the importance of the broader populace in terms of agricultural labor and community infrastructure, further excavation data from public architecture are necessary for a more balanced treatment of ancient Maya societal structure and its development.

When considering differences between those people who exerted power and control over others and those who followed or sustained them, it is logical to think about the social processes that led to Maya formal institutions, such as kingship and state-sponsored religion. What cultural adaptations made it possible to create an anthropogenic landscape filled with agriculture terraces, irrigate vast stretches of raised fields for maize agriculture, trade in semiprecious stones like jadeite (but also more quotidian items like obsidian and salt), and build stone edifices reaching high above the jungle canopy? Mayanists now have an opportunity to speak with authority about exactly how, where, and why civilizations took hold and changed, in order to make fruitful comparisons with other Mesoamerican cultures like the Olmec, the Teotihuacanos, or the Zapotec. The underlying assumption made in this volume is that more than one solution for urban growth or collapse was available to Maya peoples. Furthermore, the study of E Group architecture is pivotal to investigating dynamic change and variability in sociocultural organization, in conjunction with other categories of data, such as those from written records, art, astronomical considerations, settlement patterns, artifacts, architecture, caches, and burials.

Many anthropologists and archaeologists recognize that early states arose in Mesoamerica (Fagan and Durrani 2013). Monte Albán, Oaxaca, home of the Zapotec, was the location of one of these primary or first-generation states (Redmond and Spencer 2012; Service 1975; Wright 1977:383). Elsa Redmond and Charles Spencer (2012:30) argue that the Zapotec state came to fruition somewhere between 300 and 100 BCE. Significant societal inequalities existed in the Oaxacan area by about 1200 BCE, however, and there is evidence between 630 and 560 BCE for the first stone monument with writing (Monument 3 from San José Mogote) in Mesoamerica (Spencer 2003:11186–11187, 2009:152). Once the Monte Albán state emerged, it is likely that it was engaged with other complex societies elsewhere in Mesoamerica.

When states appeared, they would have done so in a milieu that included other peer development. Thus, before the Common era, it is likely that contemporary states were operating not only in Oaxaca but also elsewhere in Mesoamerica (Chase et al. 2009), such as in the Veracruz/Tabasco Lowlands (Clark 2007; Cyphers 1997), in central Mexico (Teotihuacán, presumably by 100 BCE [Nichols 2015]), and in the Maya area (El Mirador, possibly by 300 BCE [Dahlin 1984; Hansen 2001]). Social complexity and development are difficult to define in the archaeological record, and this volume has the potential to contribute important new interpretations to how this was accomplished in the past. Archaeologists have begun to move in new directions on the topic of social complexity to offer a richer appreciation for variable societal groups within or beside complex political groups. Through focusing on E Groups, it is possible to incorporate the nuanced views that agency and other theoretical approaches offer on activities that ran counter to normative trends (McGuire 1983; Pauketat 2007; Yoffee 2005).

A significant goal of this volume is directly to address where and when complex societies emerged in the Maya region, what form they took, their tempo and mode, and how they changed and developed or devolved, while keeping in mind that increased political complexity was not inevitable or necessary. Groups resisting trends existed beside people embracing popular, enforced, or coerced solutions (Inomata et al. 2015). The ancient Maya exhibited great variability, both environmental and social (Chase et al. 2014c). Yet there was cultural standardization centered on the E Group. As the earliest recognized form of public architecture in the Maya area, E Groups had to have been central to the social and political transformations that took place.

The ancient Maya were clearly interested in both history and place. While most hieroglyphic texts generally postdate the earliest E Groups, E Groups are the locus for the erection of the earliest stelae known at Uaxactún (Proskouriakoff 1950; Ricketson and Ricketson 1937) and the only one known at Cenote (Chase 1983). The Maya were firm believers in deep mythic time, as is evident in the inscriptions of both Palenque (Lounsbury 1980) and Naranjo (Grube and Schele 1993). Their fascination with time is also presumably conjoined with their rituals, which would have included the original construction and rebuilding of E Groups (Chase and Chase 2013). Because of the lack of a historical record associated with these early constructions, it remains for archaeologists to illuminate the meaning and importance of this architecture relative to Maya ritual, power, and social integration. Understanding the role that E Group architecture played in ancient Maya society is necessary to frame their path(s) to complexity and their later evolution.

Historiography of E Group Research

1924–1954

Credit for the discovery of the first astronomical observatory among the ancient Maya belongs to Frans Blom (1924, 1926), who was mapping Uaxactún's Group E when he realized that the architectural alignments matched the sun's solstice and equinox points. The Ricketsons' (Ricketson 1928; Ricketson and Ricketson 1937) work excavating the Uaxactún Group E prototype soon followed (Figure 1.2). Karl Ruppert (1977; Ruppert and Denison 1943) identified the thirteen other complexes that exhibited the same plan, as well as six others that varied somewhat. Prior to this, Thompson unknowingly had conducted excavations in two E Groups at Hatzcap Ceel

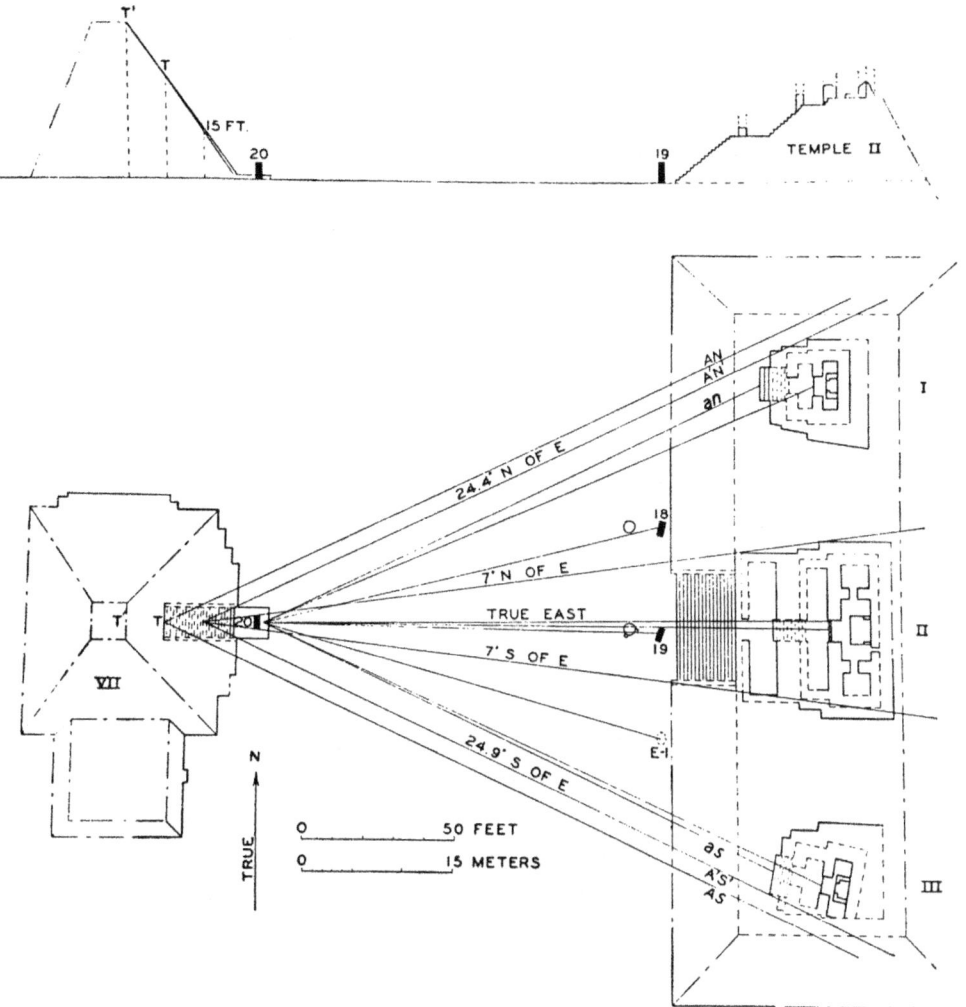

Figure 1.2. Plan of the latest (Early Classic) version of Uaxactún Group E, the prototype for all E Group analysis, showing what Oliver Ricketson and Edith Ricketson (1937:107) referred to as "astronomically important elements."

and Cahal Pichik in 1928 and 1929 (described at length in Chase 1983:90–154, 1985; Chase and Chase 1995; Thompson 1931).

Twenty-five architectural groups resembling Uaxactún's Group E were identified between 1924 and 1954 at twenty-two sites. Most were within a 110 km radius of Uaxactún. Of these known E Groups, four had been excavated (16 percent of the known E Groups at that time). The E Groups that had been excavated prior to 1954 occurred at the sites of Hatzcap Ceel (Belize), Cahal Pichik (Belize), Uaxactún (Guatemala), and San José (Belize) (Aveni and Hartung 1988, 1989; Aveni et al. 2003; Chase 1983:90–154, 1985; Chase and Chase 1995; Ricketson 1927, 1928, Ricketson and Ricketson 1937:107; Ruppert 1934:94, 1977:223, 225, 226, 227, 229, 231; Ruppert and Denison 1943:5–6, 13–23, Plate 61; Smith 1950; Thompson 1931:240, 250, 1939:9). Additional site maps illustrating E Groups (at Acanceh [Mexico], Balakbal [Mexico], and Xunantunich [Belize]) were also presented in a variety of other sources, some of which predate the formal definition of this architectural assemblage (Marquina 1951; Maudslay 1889–1902; Morley 1933, 1937–1938:Plates 218, 191a; Seler 1915; Tozzer 1911, 1913).

1955–1984

Between 1955 and 1984, archaeologists reported E Groups at ten additional sites: Baking Pot (Belize), Caracol (Belize), Ceibal (Guatemala, also spelled Seibal), Cenote (Guatemala), Dzibilchaltún (Mexico), Dzibilnocac (Mexico), El Mirador (Guatemala), Lamanai (Belize), Paxcamán (Guatemala), and Tayasal (Guatemala). Four more E Groups had been excavated: Ceibal in 1970, Cenote in 1971, Lamanai in 1981, and Dzibilchaltún in 1983, making the excavation sample equal to 24 percent of the thirty-four known examples (Andrews 1980:15; Chase 1983; Willey 1970). Not included in this discussion is the early excavation of a triadic shrine at Baking Pot (Bullard and Bullard 1965). Publications that included information relevant to E Groups, either mapped or published, included Robert Carr and James Hazard's (1961:11, 19) Great Plaza Quadrangle (1959) map for Tikal, where the Lost World Complex is recorded; Anthony Aveni (1978) on Uaxactún; Clemency Coggins (1983) and Edward B. Kurjack (1979; Kurjack et al. 1979) on Dzibilchaltún; David M. Pendergast (1981) on Lamanai; and Bruce Dahlin (1984) on El Mirador. Arlen Chase (1983) presented a detailed record of the Cenote E Group excavations and also contextualized this E Group through reanalyzing the data presented in Ruppert's (1977) earlier publication. Chase (1983, 1985; Chase and Chase 1995) defined two specific kinds of E Groups: the Cenote Style E Group (Figure 1.3), an early variant of Preclassic period (1000 BCE–250 CE) date, characterized by a long eastern platform usually supporting a much larger central structure; and the Uaxactún Style E Group, a later architectural variant of Early Classic period (250–550 CE) date, characterized by a shorter eastern platform supporting three structures. Marvin Cohodas (1980) discussed the relationship of E Groups to celebrating agricultural cycles, an idea that was developed

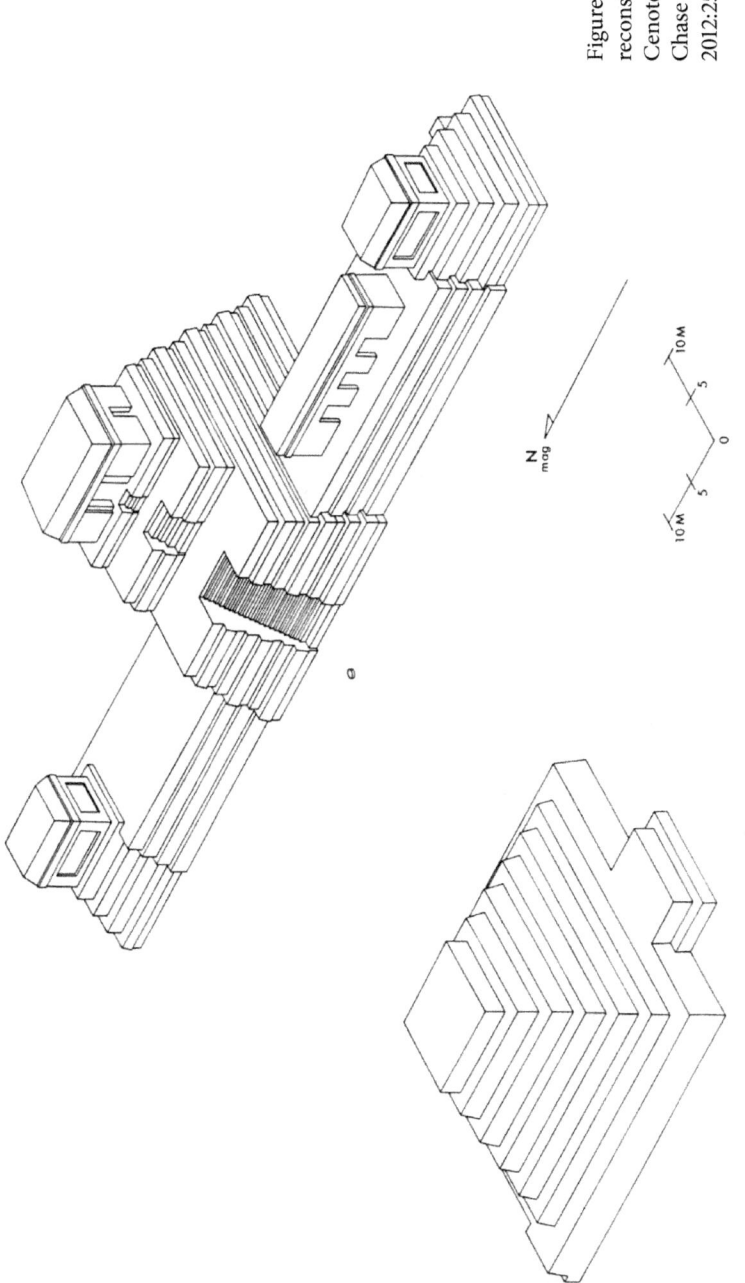

Figure 1.3. Isometric reconstruction of the Cenote E Group (after Chase and Chase 2012:258).

further by James Aimers (1993:171–179), as well as Travis Stanton and David Freidel (2003), who referred to E Groups as "maize theaters." The cosmological landscape of E Groups discussed by Cohodas (1980) has also been viewed as related to origin places for the sun and moon (Chinchilla Mazariegos et al. 2015).

1985–2016

With the explosion in fieldwork that has been carried out in the Maya area between 1985 and 2016, more than 142 additional E Groups have been documented during this time. Many of these E Groups occurred in the southeast Petén and were documented by one project (Laporte 2001:141; Escobedo 2008; see Chapter 2 in this volume). Given the archaeology accomplished to date, at least 34 E Groups have seen some excavation, roughly 20 percent of the known examples (Figures 1.4, 1.5). Calakmul's E Group was excavated and reconstructed in 1994 (Carrasco 1999; Carrasco et al. 1995; Dowd et al. 1995:6; Dowd and Aveni 1998). Other reported E Group assemblages excavated from 1985 through 2014 include Cahal Pech (Belize; Awe 2013), Caracol (Belize; Chase and Chase 1995, 2006), Chan (Belize; Robin et al. 2012), Cival (Guatemala; n = 2; Estrada-Belli 2002, 2003a, 2003b), Nakbé (Guatemala; Hansen 2000), Pacbitún (Belize; Micheletti 2016), and Ceibal (Guatemala; Inomata et al. 2013). Partial excavations of E Groups also have taken place at Nadzca'an (Mexico) in 1994–1995, as well as at Yaxhá (Guatemala; n = 2) and Xunantunich (Belize). The E Group at Dzibilchaltún has also been described (Coggins and Drucker 1988). Tikal's E Group was initially excavated in 1987 (Laporte and Fialko 1987, 1990). Not included in this discussion are two triadic shrines investigated at Cahal Pech (Awe 2013) and Pacbitún (Healy 1990).

Chase's (1985:37) summary pointed out the existence of E Groups at Cenote, Paxcamán, and Tayasal in the area surrounding Lake Petén (Petén-Itzá) in Guatemala. Anthony Aveni and Horst Hartung (1988, 1989) resurveyed Uaxactún's Group E complex to test the hypothesis that it functioned as a solar observatory, with positive results. As of 1989, at least 27 examples had been evaluated for archaeoastronomical alignments (Aveni and Hartung 1988, 1989). Gareth Lowe (1977, 1981, 1989, 1995) and Michael Blake (2013) demonstrated that Middle Preclassic examples of E Groups are known from the upper Grijalva River area in highland Chiapas (Chiapa de Corzo, Finca Arizona, San Isidro), Mexico. The study of E Groups continued unabated in the 1990s with a series of scholars examining this architectural form (Aimers 1993:Figures 13–15 [45 examples]; Becquelin et

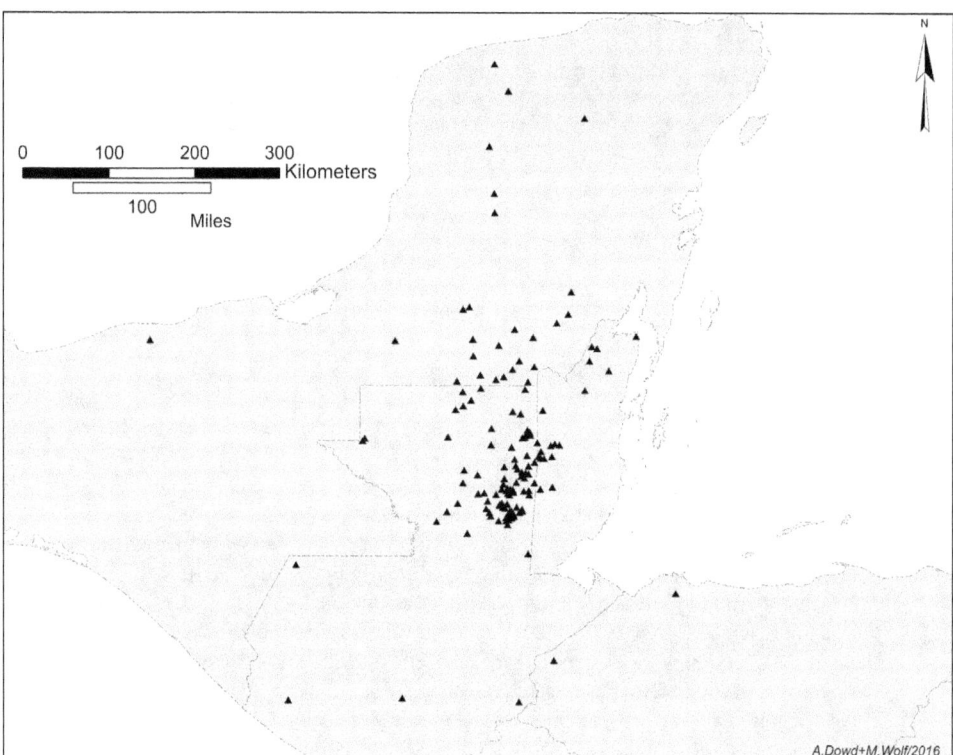

Figure 1.4. Distribution of E Group–type complexes (cartography by Marc Wolf). See Chapter 2 for information on the heavy concentration of E Groups in the southeast Petén.

al. 1997; Carrasco and Wolf 1996; Chase and Chase 1995:90 [34 examples]; Dowd and Aveni 1998:Table 1 [65 examples]; Hansen 1991a, 1991b; Laporte and Fialko 1987, 1990, 1995; and Šprajc et al. 1997). Nicholas Dunning (1992:143–144) further reported on E Groups at Northern Lowland sites such as Yakalxiu, Yaxhom, and Uxmal.

Juan Pedro Laporte (2001:141) mapped a sample of 177 sites from southeast Petén and concluded that 85 percent or 150 of these had Group E complexes present. An additional 13 E Groups occupy the area around the Machaquilá, Cansís, and Pusilhá rivers, bringing his total to 163 known examples from this zone (which may overlap somewhat with the examples that others have mentioned in their publications). Laporte (2001:142) noted that three or more sites had two Group E–type complexes each: Rosario 1, La Unión 1, and Santa Ana–Zamir. While most E Groups occupy the central part of the site ($n = 153$), of the sample that do not ($n = 10$), all are found

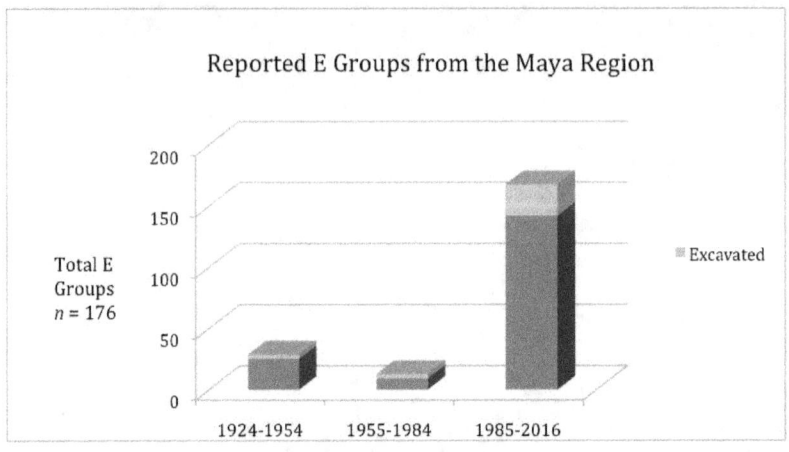

Figure 1.5. Reported E Groups from the Maya region. From 1924 to 1954, E Groups were reported in Belize at Cahal Pichik (excavated 1928–1929), Hatzcap Ceel (excavated 1928–1929), San José (excavated 1939), and Xunantunich (Benque Viejo); in Mexico at Acumal, Balakbal, Calakmul, La Muneca, Oxpemul, Río Bec II, Río Bec III, and Uxul; in Guatemala at El Mirador, El Paraíso, Ixkún, Naachtún, Nakum, Tikal, Uaxac Canal, Uaxactún (excavated 1923–1937, 1993), Ucanal ($n = 2$), Xultún, and Yaxhá ($n = 2$). From 1955 to 1984, E Groups were excavated at Ceibal (1970, 2012–2014), Cenote (1971), and Lamanai (1981, 2002). Other excavated E Groups include Calakmul (1994), Caracol (1985–ongoing), Cival (2011), Cohune (1991), El Mirador (1990, 1998, 2006), El Palmar (2011), Holtún (2010, 2012), Ix Ek' (2007), Ixkún (2005), Ixtontón (1995), K'axob (2004), Mucanncah (2009–2012), Nadzca'an (1994), Nakbé (1992, 1998), Nakum (2002, 2008), Naranjo (2004–2008), Punta de Chimino (1989–1991, 1995–1996, 2004–2005), San Bartolo (2008), Tikal (1995), Wakna (1994), Xunantunich (2013), Yaxhá (2000, 2008), Yaxnohcah (2009–2012), and Yaxuná (2013). Approximately 20 percent ($n = 34$) of known E Groups have seen some excavation. E Group–like architectural complexes have also been excavated in Belize at Chan (see Chapter 11 in this volume) and at Baking Pot, Cahal Pech, and Pacbitún (see Chapter 13 in this volume).

in the periphery of a given site (and 5 of those already have an E Group occupying the site center). Laporte (2001:142) mentioned that many of the sites containing peripheral E Groups were in a relatively constricted zone north of the Salsipuedes River. The 5 sites without central E Groups are El Chilonché, La Amapola, Los Lagartos, El Chal, and Calzada Mopán.

Laporte (2001:142) observed that, besides being centrally located, most E Groups provided the largest open plaza space at a given site, with dimensions ranging from 500 to 5,000 m^2; he further estimated that about 75 examples (about 46 percent) had plazas smaller than 1,000 m^2 and that another 77 (about 47 percent) had plazas between 1,000 to 3,000 m^2. Laporte (2001:143) suggested that a site's location either in hillier regions or in flatter riverine areas affected the plaza size allotted to the E Groups. Another 7 sites (4 percent) contained E Groups with plazas in excess of 3,000 m^2; at least 3 of these sites were more properly parts of larger sites. The remaining 3 percent of his sample lacked size estimates. In the Guatemalan Highlands, sites such as Takalik Abaj also have been noted to have Group E architecture (Estrada-Belli 2012a, 2012b:3; Popenoe de Hatch 2002). Pacific Coast examples have also been noted.

Alignment patterns from 40 E Groups for which good maps were available were analyzed in 2003 (Aveni et al. 2003:162, Table 1). As a result of this analysis, the authors asserted that E Group–type complexes functioned as non-Western observatories and further documented a shift from solstice/equinox to zenith passage dating to within the late part of the Early Classic period or about CE 250–550, attributing the shift to influence from Teotihuacán (Aveni et al. 2003:171). Controversy over the reasons why orientations of other recognized examples of E Group–type structures do not line up with the cardinal directions and/or solstice or equinox positions on the horizon were addressed (Aveni et al. 2003). The authors pointed out that at some sites other periods in the calendar were commemorated, such as 20-day Winals (Maya months) anchored to the zenith and nadir passages of the sun. The precise mode of use changed through time to replace or augment solar solstice/equinox dates with zenith passage dates, meaning that E Group design was tailored to individual site contexts. Regardless, some authors have continued to promote nonastronomical ritual functions for E Groups, a debate that is still evident in the following chapters (Aimers and Rice 2006:82, 86). Rather than being an either/or proposition, both functions are possible simultaneously, and the excavated examples warrant careful study.

Grant Aylesworth (2004:Table 1, 2015) broadened the functional definition of E Group complexes and discussed 50 examples. James Aimers and Prudence Rice (2006: Table 1, 81) reviewed E Group–type complexes and listed 64 examples. Thomas Guderjan (2006:97–103) suggested that there were about 100 examples, citing Gary Savoie (2004), but also discussed 4 "pseudo-E-groups" that lacked a western and a central eastern structure at the Belize sites of Blue Creek, Chan Chich, San José, and Quam Hill. Another possible analog may be at Pusilhá (Structures IV, V, and VII). Recent publications also cover Yaxhá and other sites, like El Mirador (Hansen 1991b; Šprajc et al. 2009).

Current Research

The current volume, resulting from two working sessions at the Santa Fe Institute in August 2012 and August 2013, has produced several insights into the interpretation of E Groups. The earliest known E Groups start by clearing the landscape to bedrock; the bedrock then was modified to produce building-like features that were later encased within rebuilt E Group construction fills (Chase 1983; Estrada-Belli 2002, 2003a, 2003b, 2006, 2011, 2012a:4, 2012b; Robin et al. 2012:Figure 6.3). This focus on bedrock modification is found at other important religious sites throughout the ancient Americas, such as the later Aztec rock sanctuary at Malinalco, Mexico (Jaramillo and Nieto 1998) and the later Inca sites of Quillarumiyoc (Anta Province, Peru) and Saywite (Apurímac Province, Peru) (Aveni 2008). The scraping and shaping of bedrock is part of a long tradition of earth, mountain, or cave (and water) worship in Central and South America (Broda 2015:223–226; Dowd 2015:214).

A second observation was that E Group architecture varied in size and location, possibly cross-cutting several forms of community organization. One E Group variant, a triadic shrine like that found at Chan, Belize (Robin et al. 2012), occurs in a small complex of public architecture that was presumably associated with a single family. Others, like those found at Uaxactún and Calakmul, were parts of larger planned groupings of public architecture that would have served sizable populations; however, later occupation in the immediate region of these plazas precludes fully understanding the size and density of the original communities.

Further insights were also gained about the relationships between E Group locations and trade routes. E Groups tend to be concentrated along trade routes in both the Southern Lowlands (see Chapter 2 in this volume) and the Northern Lowlands (see Chapter 14 this volume). New E Groups continue to be located by researchers (Chase et al. 2014b). Recent excavation of the earliest-known E Group in the Southern Lowlands at Ceibal has raised questions about general Mesoamerican connections in the Middle Preclassic period (1000–350 BCE) (Inomata et al. 2013), calling for more investigation of Middle Preclassic E Groups. Yet our understanding of E Groups has been augmented by the ongoing excavation and analysis carried out at a large number of sites covered within this volume: Calakmul, Mexico (Dowd); Caracol, Belize (Chase and Chase); Ceibal, Guatemala (Inomata and Sabloff); Chan, Belize (Robin); Cival, Guatemala (Estrada-Belli); El Palmar, Guatemala (Doyle); San Bartolo, Guatemala (Saturno, Beltrán, and

Rossi); Tikal, Guatemala (Doyle); Xunantunich, Belize (Brown); Yaxnohcah, Mexico (Reese-Taylor); and Yaxuná, Mexico (Stanton and Freidel). Finally, E Group architectural complexes can be situated in terms of the broader Maya cosmos through framing them with relevant information pertaining to the astronomical, calendrical, ritual, and sociopolitical traditions underlying their construction (Chapters 3, 4, 5, and 6 in this volume; see also Broda 1989; Carlson 1981; Dowd and Milbrath 2015; and Freidel 1986, 2008).

Distribution and Significance of E Group Complexes

The Maya archaeological record provides important information about how E Groups helped to shape societal development. While the original inspiration for E Groups will remain a matter of debate, whether indigenous or borrowed (Clark and Hansen 2001), early versions of these architectural complexes had surely appeared in the Southern Maya Lowlands by 1000 BCE in the Middle Preclassic period (Inomata et al. 2013). By the early part of the Late Preclassic period (350 BCE–0 CE), these layouts were being used to establish a site as a formal Maya place. This can be inferred from the number, spacing, and dating of these groups within the Petén of Guatemala, west-central Belize, and the southern part of the Yucatán Peninsula of Mexico. The idea that these units would have spread along trade routes presumably accounts for their distribution both in the southeastern Petén and in the Yucatán Peninsula.

Time was an important conceptual element for the ancient Maya. It is likely that E Groups were built at auspicious points within the Maya calendar, possibly in concert with events and ceremonies relating to larger temporal cycles that were partitions of the Bak'tun (400-year period). Based on the archaeology and radiocarbon dates, one version of the E Group in the site epicenter at Caracol, Belize, was constructed at the beginning of Bak'tun 8 in 41 CE (Chase and Chase 2006). Given the standardization of the architectural form, it is likely that temporal principles were also incorporated into construction practices elsewhere. Using Caracol as a guide, early special deposits associated with Late Preclassic E Groups appear to have been involved in using elaborate caches to "center" the central eastern E Group structure relative to the Maya cosmos (Chase 1988; Chase and Chase 1998; Freidel et al. 1993).

Several researchers in this book have discovered important expressions of the material symbol-systems deployed by ancient Maya to express what they were doing with early E Groups. Takeshi Inomata and his colleagues (2013) have found the earliest celt caches in the Maya Lowlands defining the sun path at the Ceibal E Group. These caches of precious and labor-intensive greenstone axes anticipate the formally arranged deposits at La Venta and resonate with earlier formal celt caches at Laguna Manatee, both in the Olmec Gulf Coast heartland. David Freidel and F. Kent Reilly (2010) have suggested that such arrangements may reference divination rituals that even today use spatially patterned material tokens among Maya daykeepers. Francisco Estrada-Belli's (2006) project at Cival discovered a remarkably rich later Middle Preclassic cache associated with the E Group there. That cache included the cruciform layout of fine greenstone celts over a bed of greenstone pebbles (Estrada-Belli 2006). Again, as Estrada-Belli suggests in his chapter, the pebbles might represent casting and divining tokens, an artifact category that might prove pervasive in Mesoamerica if we start looking for it (Freidel and Rich 2015). Small stone or shell tokens in conjunction with stick-shaped artifacts were likely used for the calculation of calendar time, especially given the bar and dot positional numeration of Mesoamerica. David Stuart (personal communication, September 16, 2014) reiterates his view that the Maya only used bar and dot numeration for calendar dates and used names for numbers applied to other things like bags of cacao beans. Whether or not the categorical dissociation of bar and dot notation from big number calculation of things other than days proves to be the case, it seems quite possible that the laying out of formal bar and dot inscriptions on public monuments was a way of declaring that the given historical date was also a divination performance anchoring the future to the past on that occasion. Thus, caches associated with Middle Preclassic E Groups might presage such practice.

Public monumental architecture and plazas were places for such ceremony along with more prosaic activities. For all of the contributors to this book who deal with Preclassic material symbols, performance is a thematically central concern. Performance, depicted in the spectacular Pinturas building murals at San Bartolo or implied as in the architecture of the Pinturas Complex (as discussed by Saturno, Beltrán, and Rossi in Chapter 10) or Structure 5C at Cerros, naturally segues to agency: how did the E Group phenomenon bear on the advent and development of rulership? The association of time reckoning with rulership comes as naturally as breathing to Maya archaeologists, and this book is in part a quest for the source of this link. We are some way from consensus on how performance, as manifest in symbols, declared a particular institutional expression of kingship and the relation of kings to gods. Most of the participants in this book accept divine kingship as an institutional reality in the Preclassic Maya world. Some of our colleagues now think that the Maya largely innovated this institution in their own terms, although the iconography of the Late Preclassic Maya Maize God Prototype King is clearly Olmec in stylistic inspiration, as documented at San Bartolo, Cival, Cerros, and elsewhere.

Was Maya kingship always dynastic and based upon principles of primogeniture or some variant of this kin-based method? Simon Martin (2005) is beginning to question this assumption, as have others (Chase et al. 2009; Freidel 2018). In the Preclassic Maya record, there are only a few kings or carved stone monuments depicting kings. While we anchor our premises regarding social development into those that we have, none are associated with genealogical statements such as become common in the Southern Maya Lowlands in the Classic period (250–900 CE). So it is possible that kingship itself evolved significantly in the Late Preclassic–Early Classic transition or the Terminal Preclassic or Protoclassic period at about 0–250 CE in conjunction with E Groups, something potentially reflected in the archaeological record associated with these complexes (Chase and Chase 1995).

With the advent of the Early Classic period, the centering principles were both altered and elaborated. The E Groups that have been excavated demonstrate some of this variability. All three Early Classic buildings situated upon the eastern platform of Uaxactún's E Group appear to have been centered with caches (Ricketson and Ricketson 1937). As human skull caches were used in this centering, it possibly implies a more individualistic aspect than had previously been seen in the associated rituals. Yet the focus on "three" is found elsewhere in Maya art and iconography and may indicate that each eastern building was associated with one of a given site's three founders (Chase and Chase 2012) or with the three items held in the bowl of the Quadripartite Badge (Robertson 1974). Estrada-Belli (2011) discovered three massive postholes, likely the placement of tall posts, organized as a triangle around a Preclassic stela set in front of the eastern range of the E Group at Cival.

Like the Uaxactún E Group, the Cenote E Group was also associated with early Maya monuments, and a skull cache and an elaborate interment were included within the last phase of the central building on the eastern platform in the early part of the Early Classic period (Chase 1983). At Tikal, the E Group goes back to the Middle Preclassic period, but in the early part of the Early Classic period elaborate burials were included in the eastern buildings (Laporte and Fialko 1995). At Caracol, early carved monuments and a late Early Classic tomb were placed in front of the eastern platform; another late Early Classic tomb was included in one of the eastern structures. The association both of early stone monuments and of elaborate early burials in E Groups is suggestive of the conflation of these architectural complexes with dynastic founding and development. Thus, it is likely that E Groups were important places for the establishment of ruling elites at any given site. Even though the buildings in many E Groups were largely left untouched once the dynasties had been established, in an E Group variant found in west-central Belize the three eastern buildings continued to be stocked with important interments throughout the Late Classic period (Awe 2013).

Conclusion

Ancient architectural plans like E Groups are an important form of data that permit an exploration of cultural similarities and differences as well as external connections. When such plans can be joined with their archaeological records, they offer a rich source for interpreting ancient ritual. As the earliest form of public architecture in the Maya area, E Groups facilitate the identification of a shared Maya cultural base; the archaeology of these units provides a window to their ancient ritual world. Recognizing how E Groups both were used and were transformed over a lengthy period permits insight into the changes that occurred in ancient Maya society. E Group plazas are still recognizable at most ancient sites (many largely unchanged in form for nearly two thousand years), which suggests that these complexes must be viewed as cultural hallmarks that held deep evocative meaning to the people who used them and that they can be used to frame our understanding of the ancient Maya.

Acknowledgments

The authors in this volume thank the Santa Fe Institute, Jerry Sabloff, and Jerry Murdock for supporting the sessions that helped to produce these chapters.

References Cited

Aimers, James J.
1993   A Hermeneutic Analysis of the Maya E-Group Complex. M.A. thesis, Department of Anthropology, Trent University, Peterborough, Ontario.

Aimers, James J., and Prudence M. Rice
2006   Astronomy, Ritual, and the Interpretation of Maya "E-Group" Architectural Assemblages. *Ancient Mesoamerica* 17(1):79–96.

Andrews, E. Wyllys, V
1980   *Excavations at Dzibilchaltun, Yucatan, Mexico.* Middle American Research Institute, Publication 48. Tulane University, New Orleans.

Aveni, Anthony F.
1978   Old and New World Naked-Eye Astronomy. *Technology Review* 81(2):60–72.
2008   *People and the Sky: Our Ancestors and the Cosmos.* Thames and Hudson, New York.

Aveni, Anthony F., Anne S. Dowd, and Benjamin Vining
2003   A Statistical Approach to the Astronomical Efficacy of Group E–Type Structures. *Latin American Antiquity* 14(2):159–178.

Aveni, Anthony F., and Horst Hartung
1988   Archaeoastronomy and Dynastic History at Tikal. In *New Directions in American Archaeoastronomy*, edited by Anthony F. Aveni, pp. 1–16. BAR International Series 454. British Archaeological Reports, Oxford, United Kingdom.
1989   Uaxactún, Guatemala, Group E and Similar Assemblages: An Archaeoastronomical Reconsideration. In *World Archaeoastronomy*, edited by Anthony F. Aveni, pp. 441–461. Cambridge University Press, Cambridge.

Awe, Jaime J.
2013   Journey on the Cahal Pech Time Machine: An Archaeological Reconstruction of the Dynastic Sequence at a Belize Valley Maya Polity. *Research Reports in Belizean Archaeology* 10:33–50.

Aylesworth, Grant R.
2004   Astronomical Interpretations of Ancient Maya E-Group Architectural Complexes. *Archaeoastronomy* 18:36–66.
2015   E-Group Arrangements. In *Handbook of Archaeoastronomy and Ethnohistory*, edited by Clive L. N. Ruggles, pp. 783–791. Springer, New York.

Becquelin, Pierre, Dominque Michelet, Charlotte Arnaud, and Eric Taladoire
1997   Proyecto de Investigacion Arqueologica del Clásico Temprano al Clásico Reciente en Balamkú, Mo Hopelchen, Campeche. *Informe de los trabajo de campo realizados del 5 de febrero al 29 de marzo de 1996.* Centro Francés de Estudios Mexicanos y Centroamericanos (CEMCA) y Centre National de la Recherche Scientifique (CNRS) de Francia (Grupo de Investigación 312), Distrito Federal, México.

Blake, Michael
2013   Solar Orientations and Formative Period Site Layouts in SE Mesoamerica: Sunrise and Sunset Alignments during the Equinoxes and Solstices. Paper

presented at the 78th Annual Meeting of the Society for American Archaeology, Honolulu, Hawaii.

Blom, Frans
1924   *Report on the Ruins of Uaxactún and Other Ruins in the Department of Petén, Guatemala.* Carnegie Institution of Washington, Guatemala Expedition, Washington, D.C.
1926   El observatorio más antiguo del continente americano. *Anales de las Sociedad de Geografía e Historia* 2(3):335–338.

Broda, Johanna
1989   Significant Dates of the Mesoamerican Calendars and Archaeoastronomy. In *World Archaeoastronomy*, edited by A. Aveni, p. 494. Cambridge University Press, Cambridge.
2015   Political Expansion and the Creation of Ritual Landscapes: A Comparative Study of Inca and Aztec Cosmovision. *Cambridge Archaeological Journal* 25(1):219–238.

Bullard, William R. J.
1960   Maya Settlement Pattern in Northeastern Peten, Guatemala. *American Antiquity* 25:355–372.

Bullard, William R. J., and Mary R. Bullard
1965   *Late Classic Finds at Baking Pot, British Honduras.* Occasional Paper 8. Royal Ontario Museum, Toronto.

Carlson, John B.
1981   A Geomantic Model for the Interpretation of Mesoamerican Sites: An Essay in Cross-Cultural Comparison. In *Mesoamerican Sites and World Views*, edited by E. P. Benson, pp. 143–215. Dumbarton Oaks, Washington, D.C.

Carr, Robert, and James Hazard
1961   *Tikal Reports.* University Museum, University of Pennsylvania, Philadelphia.

Carrasco Vargas, Ramón
1999   Actividad ritual y objectos de poder en La Estructura IV de Calakmul, Campeche. In *Land of the Turkey and the Deer*, edited by Ruth Guber, pp. 69–84. Labyrinthos, Lancaster, Pennsylvania.

Carrasco Vargas, Ramón, Sylviane Boucher, Anne S. Dowd, Armando Paul, Emyly González, and María Elena García
1995   *Informe sobre el Proyecto Arqueológico de la Biósfera Calakmul.* Consejo de Arqueología, Instituto Nacional de Antropología e Historia, Mérida, Yucatán.

Carrasco Vargas, Ramón, and Marc Wolf
1996   Nadzca'an: Una antigua ciudad en el suroeste de Campeche, México. *Mexicon* 18(4):70–74.

Chase, Arlen F.
1983   *A Contextual Consideration of the Tayasal-Paxcaman Zone, El Petén, Guatemala.* Ph.D. dissertation, University of Pennsylvania, Philadelphia. University Microfilms/ProQuest, Ann Arbor.
1985   Archaeology in the Maya Heartland: The Tayasal-Paxcaman Zone, Lake Peten, Guatemala. *Archaeology* 38(1):32–39.

Chase, Arlen F., and Diane Z. Chase
1995   External Impetus, Internal Synthesis, and Standardization: E-Group Assemblages and the Crystallization of Classic Maya Society in the Southern Lowlands. *Acta Mesoamerica* 8:87–101.
2006   Before the Boom: Caracol's Preclassic Era. *Research Reports in Belizean Archaeology* 3:41–57.
2012   Complex Societies in the Southern Maya Lowlands: Their Development and Florescence in the Archaeological Record. In *Oxford Handbook of Mesoamerican Archaeology*, edited by D. L. Nichols and C. A. Pool, pp. 255–267. Oxford University Press, New York.
2013   Temporal Cycles in the Archaeology of Maya Residential Groups from Caracol, Belize. *Research Reports in Belizean Archaeology* 10:13–24.

Chase, Arlen F., Diane Z. Chase, Jaime J. Awe, John F. Weishampel, Gyles Iannone, Holley Moyes, Jason Yaeger, and M. Kathryn Brown
2014a   The Use of LiDAR in Understanding the Ancient Maya Landscape: Caracol and Western Belize. *Advances in Archaeological Practice* 2(3):208–221.

Chase, Arlen F., Diane Z. Chase, Jaime J. Awe, John F. Weishampel, Gyles Iannone, Holley Moyes, Jason Yaeger, M. Kathryn Brown, Ramesh L. Shrestha, William E. Carter, and Juan Fernández Díaz
2014b   Ancient Maya Regional Settlement and Inter-Site Analysis: The 2013 West-Central Belize LiDAR Survey. *Remote Sensing* 6:8671–8695.

Chase, Arlen F., Diane Z. Chase, and Michael E. Smith
2009   States and Empires in Ancient Mesoamerica. *Ancient Mesoamerica* 20:175–182.

Chase, Arlen F., Lisa J. Lucero, Vernon Scarborough, Diane Z. Chase, Rafael Cobos, Nicholas Dunning, Joel Gunn, Scott Fedick, Vilma Fialko, Michelle Hegmon, Gyles Iannone, David L. Lentz, Rodrigo Liendo, Keith Prufer, Jeremy A. Sabloff, Joseph Tainter, Fred Valdez Jr., and Sander van der Leeuw
2014c   Tropical Landscapes and the Ancient Maya: Diversity in Time and Space. In *The Resilience and Vulnerability of Ancient Landscapes: Transforming Maya Archaeology through IHOPE*, edited by Arlen F. Chase and Vernon L. Scarborough, pp. 11–29. AP3A Paper 24(1). American Anthropological Association, Arlington, Virginia.

Chase, Diane Z.
1988   Caches and Censerwares: Meaning from Maya Pottery. In *A Pot for All Reasons: Ceramic Ecology Revisited*, edited by Luanna Lackey and Charles Kolb, pp. 81–104. Laboratory of Anthropology, Temple University, Philadelphia, Pennsylvania.

Chase, Diane Z., and Arlen F. Chase
1998   The Architectural Context of Caches, Burials, and Other Ritual Activities for the Classic Period Maya (as Reflected at Caracol, Belize). In *Function and Meaning in Classic Maya Architecture*, edited by Stephen D. Houston, pp. 299–332. Dumbarton Oaks, Washington, D.C.

Chinchilla Mazariegos, Oswaldo, Vera Tiesler, Oswaldo Gomez, and T. Douglas Price
2015   Myth, Ritual, and Human Sacrifice in Early Classic Mesoamerica: Interpreting

a Cremated Double Burial from Tikal, Guatemala. *Cambridge Archaeological Journal* 25:187–210.

Clark, John E.
2007 Mesoamerica's First State. In *The Political Economy of Ancient Mesoamerica: Transformations during the Formative and Classic Periods*, edited by Vernon L. Scarborough and John E. Clark, pp. 11–46. University of New Mexico Press, Albuquerque.

Clark, John E., and Richard D. Hansen
2001 The Architecture of Early Kingship: Comparative Perspectives on the Origins of the Maya Royal Court. In *Royal Courts of the Ancient Maya: 2. Data and Case Studies*, edited by Takeshi Inomata and Stephen D. Houston, pp. 1–45. Westview Press, Boulder, Colorado.

Coggins, Clemency
1983 *The Stucco Decoration and Architectural Assemblage of Structure 1-SUB, Dzibilchaltun, Yucatan, Mexico.* Publication 49, Middle American Research Institute. Tulane University, New Orleans.

Coggins, Clemency C., and R. David Drucker
1988 The Observatory at Dzibilchaltun. In *New Directions in American Archaeoastronomy*, edited by Anthony F. Aveni, pp. 17–56. BAR International Series 454. British Archaeological Reports, Oxford, United Kingdom.

Cohodas, Marvin
1980 Radial Pyramids and Radial-Associated Assemblages of the Central Maya Area. *Journal of the Society of Architectural Historians* 39(3):208–223.

Cyphers, Ann M.
1997 *Población, subsistencia y medio ambiente en San Lorenzo Tenochtitlán.* Instituto de Investigaciones Antropológicas y Universidad Nacional Autónoma de México, Mexico City.

Dahlin, Bruce
1984 A Colossus in Guatemala: The PreClassic Maya City of El Mirador. *Archaeology* 37(5):18–25.

Dowd, Anne S. (editor)
2015 Cosmovision in New World Ritual Landscapes. Special Section. *Cambridge Archaeological Journal* 25(1):211–297.

Dowd, Anne S., and Anthony F. Aveni
1998 The Maya Time-Space Continuum: Calakmul's Group E Complex. Paper presented at the 63rd Annual Meeting of the Society for American Archaeology, Seattle, Washington, March 26, 1998.

Dowd, Anne S., Anthony F. Aveni, and Ramón Carrasco V.
1995 Solar Observatory or Allegory? Calakmul's Group E-Type Complex. Paper presented at the 60th Annual Meeting of the Society for American Archaeology, Minneapolis, Minnesota, May 4, 1995.

Dowd, Anne S., and Susan Milbrath (editors)
2015 *Cosmology, Calendars, and Horizon-Based Astronomy in Ancient Mesoamerica.* University Press of Colorado, Boulder.

Dunning, Nicholas P.
1992   *Lords of the Hills: Ancient Maya Settlement in the Puuc Region, Yucatán, Mexico.* Monographs in World Archaeology, No. 15. Prehistory Press, Madison, Wisconsin.

Escobedo, Héctor (editor)
2008   *Registro de sitios arqueológicos del sureste y centro-oeste de Petén.* Monografías Atlas Arqueológico de Guatemala. Dirección General del Patrimonio Cultural y Natural, Guatemala.

Estrada-Belli, Francisco
2002   Archaeological Investigations at Holmul, Peten, Guatemala: Preliminary Results of the Third Season, 2002. http://www.bu.edu/holmul, accessed September 10, 2013.
2003a   Holmul, Peten, Guatemala, 2003 Post-Season Interim Report. http://www.bu.edu/holmul, accessed September 10, 2013.
2006   Lightning Sky, Rain, and the Maize God: The Ideology of Preclassic Rulers at Cival, Peten, Guatemala. *Ancient Mesoamerica* 17(2):57–78.
2011   *The First Maya Civilization: Ritual and Power before the Classic Period.* Routledge, New York.
2012a   Early Human-Environmental Interactions in the Maya Lowlands: Archaeological and Paleoenvironmental Explorations at Dos Aguadas and Holmul, Peten, Guatemala. http://www.bu.edu/holmul, accessed September 10, 2013.
2012b   Investigaciones arqueológicas en la región de Holmul, Péten: Holmul y Dos Aguadas. Informe Preliminar de la Temporada 2012. http://www.bu.edu/holmul, accessed September 10, 2013.

Estrada-Belli, Francisco (editor)
2003b   Archaeological Investigations in the Holmul Region, Peten. Results of the Fourth Season, 2003. http://www.bu.edu/holmul, accessed September 10, 2013.

Fagan, Brian M., and Nadia Durrani
2013   *People of the Earth: An Introduction to World Prehistory.* 14th ed. Pearson, New York.

Flannery, Kent V.
2009   *The Early Mesoamerican Village.* Reprinted. Left Coast Press, Walnut Creek, California. Originally published 1976, Academic Press, New York.

Freidel, David A.
1986   The Monumental Architecture. In *Archaeology at Cerros, Belize, Central America: 1. An Interim Report,* edited by Robin A. Robertson and David A. Freidel, pp. 1–22. Southern Methodist University Press, Dallas.
2008   Maya Divine Kingship. In *Religion and Power: Divine Kingship in the Ancient World and Beyond,* edited by Nicole Brisch, pp. 191–206. Oriental Institute Seminars No. 4. Oriental Institute of the University of Chicago.
2018   Maya and the Idea of Empire. In *Pathways to Complexity: A View from the Maya Lowlands,* edited by M. Kathryn Brown and George J. Bey III, in press. University Press of Florida, Gainesville.

Freidel, David A., and F. Kent Reilly III
2010   The Flesh of God, Cosmology, Food, and the Origins of Political Power in

Southeastern Mesoamerica. In *Pre-Columbian Foodways: Interdisciplinary Approaches to Food, Culture, and Markets in Mesoamerica*, edited by John E. Staller and Michael D. Carrasco, pp. 635–679. Springer, New York.

Freidel, David A., and Michelle E. Rich
2015   Pecked Circles and Divining Boards, Calculating Instruments in Ancient Mesoamerica. In *Cosmology, Calendars, and Horizon-Based Astronomy in Ancient Mesoamerica*, edited by Anne S. Dowd and Susan Milbrath, pp. 249–264. University Press of Colorado, Boulder.

Freidel, David A., Linda Schele, and Joy Parker
1993   *Maya Cosmos: Three Thousand Years on the Shaman's Path*. William Morrow, New York.

Grube, Nikolai, and Linda Schele
1993   *Naranjo Altar 1 and Rituals of Death and Burials*. Texas Notes on Precolumbian Art, Writing, and Culture, No. 54. University of Texas, Austin.

Guderjan, Thomas H.
2006   E-Groups, Pseudo-E-Groups, and the Development of the Classic Maya Identity in the Eastern Petén. *Ancient Mesoamerica* 17:97–104.

Hanks, William F.
1990   *Referential Practice: Language and Lived Space among the Maya*. University of Chicago Press, Chicago.

Hansen, Richard D.
1991a   The Maya Rediscovered: The Road to Nakbe. *Natural History Magazine*, May 8, p. 14.
1991b   *An Early Maya Text from El Mirador, Guatemala*. Research Reports on Ancient Maya Writing, No. 37. Center for Maya Research, Washington, D.C.
2000   Arquitectura e ideología de los antiguos mayas. In *Memoria de la Segunda Mesa Redonda de Palenque*, pp. 72–108. Instituto Nacional de Antropología e Historía, Consejo Nacional Para la Cultura y las Artes, Mexico City.
2001   The First Cities: The Beginnings of Urbanization and State Formation in the Maya Lowlands. In *Maya: Divine Kings of the Rain Forest*, edited by Nikolai Grube, Eva Eggebrecht, and Matthias Seidel, pp. 50–65, Ullmann, Cologne, Germany.

Healy, Paul F.
1990   Excavations at Pacbitun, Belize: Preliminary Report on the 1986 and 1987 Investigations. *Journal of Field Archaeology* 17(3):247–262.

Inomata, Takeshi, Jessica MacLellan, Daniela Triadan, Jessica Munson, Melissa Burham, Kazuo Aoyama, Hiroo Nasu, Flory Pinzon, and Hitoshi Yonenobu
2015   Development of Sedentary Communities in the Maya Lowlands: Coexisting Mobile Groups and Public Ceremonies at Ceibal, Guatemala. *Proceedings of the National Academy of Sciences* 112(14):4268–4273.

Inomata, Takeshi, Daniela Triadan, Kazuo Aoyama, Victor Castillo, and Hitoshi Yonenobu
2013   Early Ceremonial Constructions at Ceibal, Guatemala, and the Origins of Lowland Maya Civilization. *Science* 340:467–471.

Jaramillo Luque, Ricardo, and Rubén Nieto Hernández
1998   Valle de Malinalco. In *Historia general del estado de México: 1. Geografía y ar-*

queología, edited by Yoko Sugiura Yamamoto, pp. 95–117. Gobierno del Estado de México y el Colegio Mexiquense, Mexico City.

Kurjack, Edward B.
1979   Introduction to the Map of the Ruins of Dzibilchaltun, Yucatan, Mexico. Middle American Research Institute Publication 47. Tulane University, New Orleans.

Kurjack, Edward B., George E. Stuart, John C. Scheffer, and John W. Cottier
1979   *Map of the Ruins of Dzibilchaltun, Yucatan, Mexico*. Middle American Research Institute Publication 47. Tulane University, New Orleans.

Laporte, Juan Pedro, and Vilma Fialko C.
1990   New Perspectives on Old Problems: Dynastic References for the Early Classic at Tikal. In *Vision and Revision in Maya Studies*, edited by Flora Clancy and Peter Harrison, pp. 33–66. University of New Mexico Press, Albuquerque.
1995   Re-encuentro con el Mundo Perdido, Tikal, Guatemala. *Ancient Mesoamerica* 6(1):41–94.

Laporte, Juan Pedro, and Vilma Fialko C. (editors)
1987   La cerámica del Clásico Temprano desde Mundo Perdido: Una reevaluación. In *Maya Ceramics: Papers from the 1985 Maya Ceramic Conference*, part 1, edited by P. Rice and R. Sharer, pp. 123–182. BAR International Series 345. British Archaeological Reports, Oxford, United Kingdom.

Laporte, Juan Pedro
2001   Dispersión y estructura de las ciudades del sureste de Petén, Guatemala. In *Reconstruyendo la ciudad maya: El urbanismo en las sociedades antiguas*, edited by A. C. Ruiz, M.J.I. Ponce de León, and M.d.C.M. Martínez Martínez, pp. 136–162. Sociedad Española de Estudios Mayas, Meso Redonda, Valladolid, Spain.

Lounsbury, Floyd G.
1980   Some Problems in the Interpretation of the Mythological Portion of the Hieroglyphic Text of the Temple of the Cross at Palenque. In *Third Palenque Round Table, Part 2*, edited by Merle G. Robertson, pp. 99–115. University of Texas Press, Austin.

Lowe, Gareth W.
1977   The Mixe-Zoque as Competing Neighbors of the Early Lowland Maya. In *The Origins of Maya Civilization*, edited by R.E.W. Adams, pp. 197–248. University of New Mexico Press, Albuquerque.
1981   Olmec Horizons Defined in Mound 20, San Isidro, Chiapas. In *The Olmec and Their Neighbors*, edited by E. Benson, pp. 231–255. Dumbarton Oaks, Washington, D.C.
1989   The Heartland Olmec: Evolution of Material Culture. In *Regional Perspectives on the Olmecs*, edited by Robert Sharer and David Grove, pp. 33–67. Cambridge University Press, Cambridge.
1995   Presencia maya en la cerámica del Preclásico Tardío en Chiapa de Corzo. In *Memoria del Segundo Congreso International de Mayistas*, pp. 321–341. Centro de Estudios Mayas, Universidad Nacional Autónoma de México, Mexico City.

Marquina, Ignacio

1951 *Arquitectura prehispánica.* Instituto Nacional de Antropología e Historia, Mexico City.

Martin, Simon
2005 Of Snakes and Bats: Shifting Identities at Calakmul. *PARI [Precolumbian Art Research Institute] Journal* 6(2):5–13.

Maudslay, Alfred P.
1889–1902 *Biologia Centrali-Americana: Archaeology.* 5 vols. R. H. Porter and Dulau, London.

McGuire, Randall H.
1983 Breaking Down Cultural Complexity: Inequality and Heterogeneity. *Advances in Archaeological Method and Theory* 6:91–142.

Micheletti, George
2016 Excavation of a Triadic Shrine E Group at Pacbitun, Belize. M.A. thesis. Department of Anthropology, University of Central Florida, Orlando.

Morley, Sylvanus G.
1933 *The Calakmul Expedition.* Supplementary Publication No. 6. Carnegie Institution of Washington, Washington, D.C.
1937–1938 *The Inscriptions of Peten.* 5 vols. Publication 427. Carnegie Institution of Washington, Washington, D.C.

Nichols, Deborah L.
2015 Teotihuacan. *Journal of Archaeological Research.* 24:1–74.

Pauketat, Timothy R.
2007 *Chiefdoms and Other Archaeological Delusions.* Altamira, Lanham, Maryland.

Pendergast, David M.
1981 Lamanai, Belize: Summary of Excavation Results, 1974–1980. *Journal of Field Archaeology* 8:29–53.

Popenoe de Hatch, Marion
2002 Evidencia de un observatorio astronómico en Abaj Takalik. In *XV Simposio de Investigaciones Arqueológicas en Guatemala,* edited by Juan Pedro Laporte, Bárbara Arroyo, and Héctor L. Escobedo, pp. 437–458. Museo Nacional de Arqueología y Etnología, Guatemala.

Proskouriakoff, Tatiana
1950 *A Study of Classic Maya Sculpture.* Publication 593. Carnegie Institution of Washington, Washington, D.C.

Redmond, Elsa M., and Charles S. Spencer
2012 Chiefdoms at the Threshold: The Competitive Origins of the Primary State. *Journal of Anthropological Archaeology* 31:22–37.

Ricketson, Oliver G., Jr.
1927 Report on the Uaxactún Project. *Carnegie Institution of Washington Year Book* 26:256–263.
1928 Astronomical Observatories in the Maya Area. *Geographical Review* 18(2):215–229.

Ricketson, Oliver G., Jr., and Edith Bayles Ricketson
1937 *Uaxactún, Guatemala, Group E, 1926–31.* Publication 477. Carnegie Institution of Washington, Washington, D.C.

Robertson, Merle Green
1974   The Quadripartite Badge: A Badge of Rulership. In *Primera Mesa Redonda de Palenque Part 1*, edited by Merle Robertson, pp. 129–137. Robert Louis Stevenson School, Pebble Beach, California.

Robin, Cynthia, James Meierhoff, Caleb Kestle, Chelsea Blackmore, Laura J. Kosakowsky, and Anna C. Novotny
2012   Ritual in a Farming Community. In *Chan: An Ancient Maya Farming Community*, edited by Cynthia Robin, pp. 113–132. University Press of Florida, Gainesville.

Rogers, Elizabeth Barlow
1972   *Frederick Law Olmsted's New York*. Praeger, New York.

Rosenzweig, Roy, and Elizabeth Blackmar
1992   *The Park and the People: A History of Central Park*. Cornell University Press, Ithaca, New York.

Ruppert, Karl
1934   Explorations in Campeche. *Carnegie Institution of Washington Year Book* 33:93–95.
1977   A Special Assemblage of Maya Structures. In *The Maya and Their Neighbors*, edited by Clarence L. Hay, Ralph L. Linton, Samuel K. Lothrop, Harry L. Shapiro, and George C. Vaillant, pp. 222–231. Dover Press, New York. Originally published in 1940 by Harvard University Press, Cambridge, Massachusetts.

Ruppert, Karl, and John Denison
1943   *Archaeological Reconnaissance in Campeche, Quintana Roo, and Peten*. Publication 543. Carnegie Institution of Washington, Washington, D.C.

Savoie, Greg
2004   The Spatial and Temporal Distribution of Maya E-Group Complexes. M.A. thesis, Department of Archaeology, University of Leicester, England.

Seler, Eduard
1915   *Gesammelte Abhandlungen zur Amerikanischen Sprach- un Alterthumskunde*, Vol. 5. A. Asher, Berlin. Reprint 1961 by Akademische Druck und Verlaganstalt, Graz, Austria.

Service, Elman R.
1975   *Origins of the State and Civilization*. Norton, New York.

Smith, A. Ledyard
1950   *Uaxactún, Guatemala: Excavations (1931–1937)*. Publication 588. Carnegie Institution of Washington, Washington, D.C.

Spencer, Charles S.
2003   War and Early State Formation in Oaxaca, Mexico. *PNAS* 100(20):11185–11187.
2009   Testing the Morphogenesist Model of Primary State Formation: The Zapotec Case. In *Macroevolution in Human Prehistory*, edited by Anna M. Prentiss, Ian Kuijt, and James C. Chatters et al., pp. 133–155. Springer, New York.

Šprajc, Ivan, Florentino García Cruz, and Héber Ojeda Mas
1997   Reconocimiento arqueológico en el sureste de Campeche, México: Informe preliminar. *Mexicon* 11(1):5–12.

Šprajc, Ivan, Carlos Morales-Aguilar, and Richard D. Hansen

2009 Early Maya Astronomy and Urban Planning at El Mirador, Peten, Guatemala. *Anthropological Notebooks* 15(3):79–101.

Stanton, Travis W., and David A. Freidel
2003 Ideological Lock-In and the Dynamics of Formative Religions in Mesoamerica. *Mayeb* 16:5–14.

Tate, Carolyn E.
1992 *Yaxchilán: The Design of a Ceremonial City.* University of Texas Press, Austin.

Thompson, J. Eric S.
1931 *Archaeological Investigations in the Southern Cayo District British Honduras.* Field Museum of Natural History Publication 301, Anthropological Series 17(3). Field Museum of Natural History, Chicago.
1939 *Excavations at San Jose, British Honduras.* Carnegie Institute of Washington, Publication No. 58. Carnegie Institute of Washington, Washington, D.C.
1954 *The Rise and Fall of Maya Civilization.* University of Oklahoma Press, Norman.

Tozzer, Alfred
1911 *A Preliminary Study of the Ruins of Tikal, Guatemala.* Memoirs of the Peabody Museum 5(2). Peabody Museum, Harvard University, Cambridge, Massachusetts.
1913 *A Preliminary Study of the Ruins of Nakum, Guatemala.* Memoirs of the Peabody Museum 5(3). Peabody Museum, Harvard University, Cambridge, Massachusetts.

Vogt, Evon Z.
1976 *Tortillas for the Gods: A Symbolic Analysis of Zinacanteco Rituals.* Harvard University Press, Cambridge, Massachusetts.

Willey, Gordon R.
1956 The Structure of Ancient Maya Society: Evidence from the Southern Lowlands. *American Anthropologist* 58(5):777–782.
1970 Type Descriptions of the Ceramics of the Real Xe Complex, Seibal, Peten, Guatemala. In *Monographs and Papers in Maya Archaeology*, edited by William R. Bullard Jr., pp. 313–355. Papers of the Peabody Museum of Archaeology and Ethnology, Vol. 61. Harvard University, Cambridge, Massachusetts.

Wright, Henry T.
1977 Recent Research on the Origin of the State. *Annual Review of Anthropology* 6:379–397.

Yoffee, Norman
2005 *Myths of the Archaic State: Evolution of the Earliest Cities, States, and Civilizations.* Cambridge University Press, Cambridge, Massachusetts.

Zaro, Gregory, and Jon C. Lohse
2005 Agricultural Rhythms and Rituals: Maya Solar Observation in Hinterland Blue Creek, Northwestern Belize. *Latin American Antiquity* 16(1):81–98.

2

E Groups and the Rise of Complexity in the Southeastern Maya Lowlands

ARLEN F. CHASE AND DIANE Z. CHASE

Too often our view of the ancient Maya has been formed by accidents of research history and by our modern predilection to focus on impressive architecture, art, and origins. The investigation of the Group E complex at Uaxactún, Guatemala, was undertaken precisely for these reasons. Perhaps more than any other set of monumental architecture, however, the E Group serves as a proxy for early ceremonialism and its association with the rise of Maya civilization. It provides a framework for interpreting the ancient Maya fascination with time and the cosmos.

At the time of their "discovery" by S. G. Morley (1925) in the first part of the twentieth century, the earliest known dated Maya stelae were located in association with this architectural complex. The site of Uaxactún (Eight Stone) had been named in honor of these stelae. Excavation there was expected to shed light on the development of Maya civilization because of its co-location with an 8th cycle monument. The excavations at Group E in Uaxactún did precisely that: the earliest remains then known from the Maya area were uncovered and defined. In concert with assumptions about the need for the elite to monitor times for planting crops, this architectural complex was related to the Maya observance of solstices and equinoxes (Ricketson and Ricketson 1937), an assumption later ridiculed by cultural ecologists like William Sanders (1979), who, countering arguments for intensive agriculture (Harrison and Turner 1978), argued that any good Maya farmer practicing milpa agriculture knew when to plant without elite oversight. Although the Group E complex was initially dated entirely to the early part of the Early Classic period (278–593 CE or ca. 250–550 CE; Smith 1950:67)—largely based on the associated stelae—the discovery of a radial building arrayed with an impressive series of stucco masks under the western pyramid hinted at an even earlier dating, something implicitly expressed (but not stated) in the architectural plans for this group (Ricketson and Ricketson 1937:Figure 98). Thus, while the temporal dimensions of Uaxactún Group E were never fully fleshed out, this architectural complex came to be correlated with the early crystallization of Maya culture in the Southern Lowlands.

That E Groups are among the earliest Maya architectural assemblages is not in doubt. Deep excavations at Ceibal, Guatemala, have demonstrated the existence of one of these complexes at least as early as 1000 BCE (Inomata et al. 2013). The fully excavated examples of E Groups have one commonality. None of the earliest eastern platforms are associated with central buildings; rather, the extended eastern platform itself is the first hallmark of an E Group. At least at Ceibal and at Tikal, this early platform is also associated with a western pyramidal structure.

Almost fifty years ago, Gareth Lowe (1977:224, Figure 9.4) noted a similar group pattern in the Middle Preclassic settlement of the upper Grijalva River area of Chiapas, where he identified a dozen early sites as having a large western pyramid and a rectangular eastern platform approximately 100 m long. Lowe (1977:226) believed that the pattern was Olmec-derived and indicative of "the steady but more obscure expansion of other and perhaps related peoples into the lowland Maya riverine and water-hole forest regions at about this same time" and that most of these regions "may have had similar advanced organization." Inomata and his colleagues (2013:470) have since shown that the process was far more complex, involving interregional interactions, local Maya innovations, and "shared notions of new social order." The emergence of a standard architectural complex in the form of an E Group has great significance, however, in that the appearance of this architectural complex represents the coalescence of formal Maya communities that shared a unified belief system (Chase and Chase 1995, 2006b; Inomata et al. 2013).

Excavations at the sites of Cenote (Chase 1983; Chase and Chase 1995) and Tikal (Fialko 1988; Laporte and Fialko 1995) in Guatemala have substantially changed our understanding of these architectural complexes. Research at both of these sites demonstrated an early temporal placement for this plaza plan—back to the Middle Preclassic period (1000–350 BCE). Both Cenote and Tikal also evinced a plan different from the Uaxactún Style E Group that has been labeled "the Cenote-style E Group" (Chase 1985:39; Chase and Chase 1995). The majority of the differences between these two styles are found in the eastern platform of the architectural assemblage (Figure 2.1a, b). In the Uaxactún Style, three buildings are located

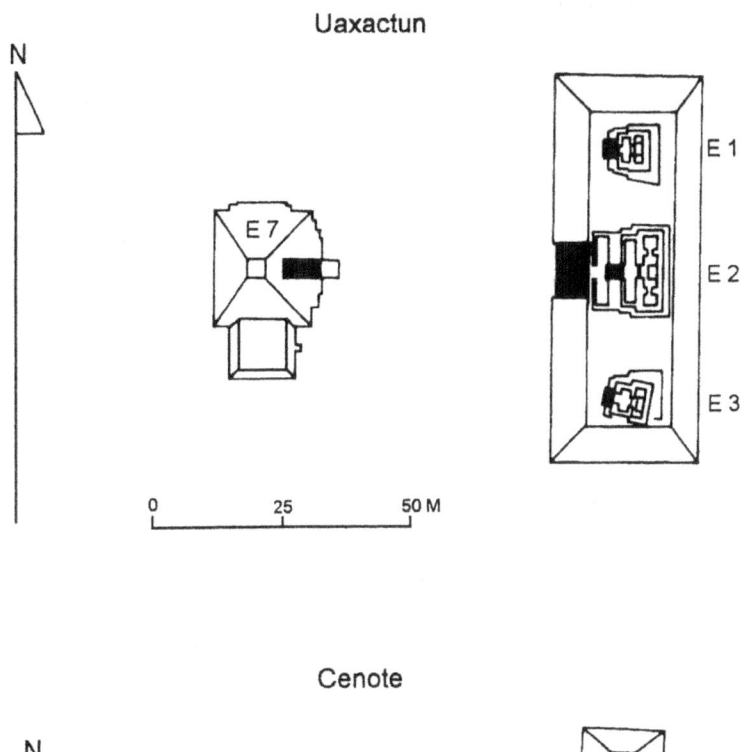

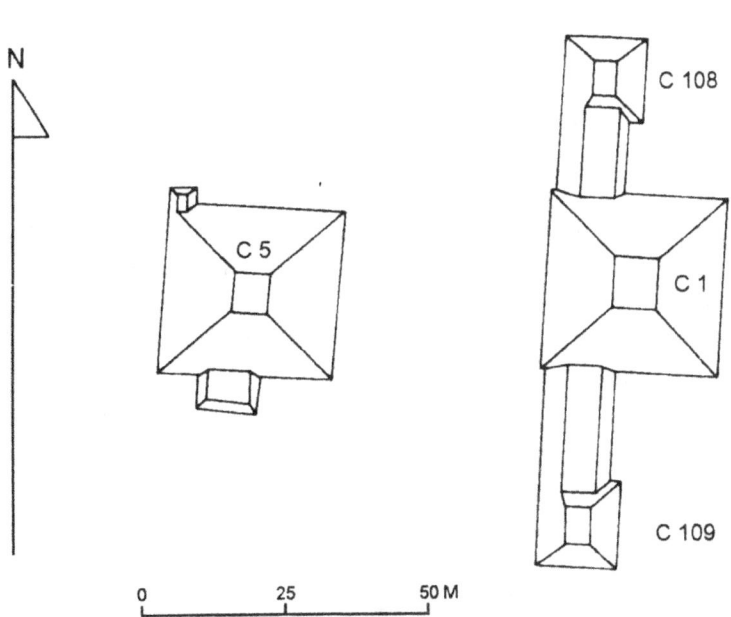

Figure 2.1. The two variants of the E Group plan: (a) Uaxactún, Guatemala; (b) Cenote, Belize (after Chase 1983:1302; Chase and Chase 1995:90) The Cenote variant is always earlier and usually dates to the Middle to Late Preclassic period. The Uaxactún variant is later and dates to the Early Classic period. Excavations have shown the transformation of some Cenote Style E Groups into Uaxactún Style E Groups over time.

upon a single platform that is usually around 70 m in length. In the Cenote Style, the eastern platform usually exhibits a large central pyramid that is offset from the platform to the east and two smaller buildings that may be situated toward the ends of the platform.[1] In the Cenote Style complex, the eastern platform varies in length but can be quite long; the eastern platform of the Cenote Style E Group at Yaxhá, Guatemala, is 172 m in length (Chase 1983:Table 44). Mapping and excavations in the southeast Petén as part of the *Atlas arqueológico de Guatemala* (Escobedo 2008; Laporte and Mejía 2000, 2005b; Laporte et al. 1988) have shown that E Groups are concentrated within the southeastern portion of the Maya Lowlands and that eastern platforms can be as small as 20 m in length. As shown below, there are temporal distinctions between the two styles, with the Cenote Style E Group dating to the Late Preclassic and the Uaxactún Style E Group dating to the Early Classic periods.

Karl Ruppert (1940) noted that almost all known E Groups were within a 110 km radius of Uaxactún and that there appeared to be minimal spacing of approximately 21 km between the occurrences of this architectural complex. Because of this stated spacing, E Groups have been utilized as a size-rank indicator of site status (Rathje 1973; Hammond 1974:326, 1975; Rathje et al. 1978). In the Southeastern Lowlands, however, both the site status and the spacing of these groupings are called into question. Many of the occurrences of this public architecture are much closer, often only 4 to 5 km apart in the southeast Petén—and the plan appears with such frequency as to denote the formal founding architecture of a given Maya community. As shown in this chapter, changes in form and proximity of E Groups over time may be correlated with broader transformations in Maya sociopolitical organization. Thus, while the closely located E Groups of the Lake Petén–Itzá area (Cenote and Paxcamán; Chase 1983:1244) and Mountain Cow region of Belize (Cahal Pichik and Hazcap Ceel; Thompson 1931) were originally thought to be anomalous, the research undertaken for the *Atlas* in the southeast Petén demonstrated a dense clustering of minimally 170 groups evincing the E Group pattern (Table 2.1) and providing archaeological evidence of use during the Late Preclassic era (and some even earlier).[2] This clustering has significance on a number of levels: (1) it permits an analysis of the great variability that is evident in this architectural form, thus allowing for a firmer understanding of its developmental sequence and potential relationships; (2) the location of these groups in association with watersheds that extend from the Usumacinta River to the Belize River is consistent with the existence of one of the most important

Table 2.1. E Groups of the Southeastern Lowlands

Site number & name	E height	E length	#E structures	W height	Other
Río Mopán: Bajo					
157 Buenos Aires Gr 9	?	81 m	none	9 m	E is platform
156 El Camalote	14 m	87 m	none	9 m	central shrine
155 Yok'ol Witz Gr 7	?	37 m	3	?	3 structures platform
154 La Providencia 1	?	113 m	3	?	
163 Dos Hermanos N	9.5 m	56 m	central	14.5 m	
163 Dos Hermanos S	11 m	70 m	central	8.5 m	
151 La Guajira	10 m	43 m	central	5 m	
173 El Cruzadero 1	?	48 m	central	?	
174 El Cruzadero 2	drawing from Yok'ol Wits Gr 7 reused				
Río Mopán: Medio					
94 Ucanal Plaza A	?	ca.160 m	3	?	modified
94 Ucanal Plaza B	4.3 m	55 m	central+S	4 m	
198 Yaltutu/Melchor	3 m	59 m	3	2.5 m	
64 El Calabazal 1	7.7 m	50 m	central	6.6 m	
65 El Calabazal 2	2.05 m	28 m	central	0.75 m	
142 La Vertiente	3 m	23 m	central	0.40 m	
56 Calzada Mopán	3 m	41 m	3	5 m	
57 Agua Blanca	3.4 m	28 m	central	4 m	
58 La Trinidad Plaza A	2.4 m	30 m	3	3 m	shrine/rect. W
58 La Trinidad Gr 8	3 m	48 m	none	4 m	E is platform
59 La Gloria 1	4 m	34 m	3	2.85 m	
61 Miguelon	5.6 m	66 m	3	3.30 m	
62 Las Delicias	4.2 m	28 m	central	5 m	
197 La Gloria 3	4 m	30 m	central	2 m	
63 El Cabro	no information other than it exists				
52 El Rosario 1a	8 m	64 m	3	10 m	
52 El Rosario 1b	5 m	36 m	central	3 m	
132 El Rosario 5a	6 m	35 m	3	?	W platform
132 El Rosario 5b	2.5 m	34 m	central	2 m	
53 El Rosario 4	5 m	63 m	3	3 m	rectangular W
54 El Rosario 2	4 m	23 m	3	?	rectangular W

(continued)

Table 2.1—Continued

Site number & name	E height	E length	#E structures	W height	Other
RÍO MOPÁN: ALTA					
7 Ixtontón	12 m	108 m	3	10.5 m	
8 Moquena	5.3 m	32 m	central	5.3 m	
9 Ix Ak	7 m	49 m	central	3 m	
10 Mopán 2-Oeste	4 m	24 m	central	6.2 m	
19 Ix Kol	6.75 m	28 m	central	5.3 m	
20 Suk Che'	6 m	54 m	3	?	
11 Ixkun	11 m	76 m	central	15.5 m	
12 Mopán 3-Este	11.4 m	77 m	3	11.3 m	
14 Mopán 3-Sureste	5 m	36 m	3	4.4 m	
15 Mopán 3-Oeste	5 m	44 m	3	3 m	rectangular W
17 La Jutera	2.5 m	38 m	3	3 m	
129 El Pedregal 3	?	24 m	central	?	unclear W
128 El Pedregal 2	2 m	22 m	3	1 m	rectangular W
127 El Pedregal 1	2.5 m	23 m	3	2 m	large W platform
29 Sacul Plaza A	5.2 m	35 m	central	4.85 m	Monuments
29 Sacul E of Plaza A	6 m	39 m	3	?	
161 La Gloria/Sacul	?	47 m	3	?	
30 Sacul 4	?	66 m	3	6 m	
31 Sacul 3	5.65 m	74 m	3	8.2 m	
33 Limones	?	37 m	central	5.5 m	
34 El Jutalito	4.5 m	47 m	3	5 m	rectangular W
35 K'ax Ba	4.5 m	62 m	3	6 m	
36 Xa'an Arriba	3 m	70 m	3	9 m	W w/side platforms
37 Canajui	4 m	52 m	3	2.45	pub scale incor
CHIQUIBUL: BAJO Y ALTO					
144 La Cebada	6.8 m	38 m	central	6.8 m	
170 El Ceibo	9 m	55 m	3	12 m	E rebuilding
149 El Mamay	?	63 m	central	16 m	
148 Palestina	>8 m	54 m	central	>8 m	
143 La Rejoya	?	44 m	3	?	
180 Piedra Quebrada	?	39 m	central	?	platform at rear W
146 El Naranjal	?	92 m	3	16 m	shrine front E
241 El Ronron	5 m	30 m	central	?	

Site number & name	E height	E length	#E structures	W height	Other
150 Jinaya	2 m	32 m	central	1.5 m	E projects W
140 Maringa 1	?	48 m	3	?	
135 El Triunfo	?	45 m	central	?	
139 Las Flores Chiquibul	6.5 m	40 m	central	?	
177 San José	8 m	47 m	central	9 m	
134 El Muerto	3 m	30 m	central	1.2 m	rectangular W
121 El Mozote A	?	38 m	central	?	(north)
121 El Mozote B	?	38 m	central	?	(south)

Salsipuedes

Site number & name	E height	E length	#E structures	W height	Other
200 Salsipuedes	6 m	65 m	central	15 m	
93 Los Lagartos	?	57 m	2 (C&N)	?	
91 La Amapola	?	50 m	-	?	E&W platforms
69 El Camalote/Delores	11 m	99 m	central	16 m	
70 La Esperanza	3.10 m	25 m	2 (C&S)	3.5 m	rectangular W
71 La Gloria 2	2 m	28 m	central	3.3 m	shrine?
72 Canija	3.88 m	41 m	3	7.85 m	(north wrong)

Pusilhá–none

Parte Aguas Oriente-Occidente

Site number & name	E height	E length	#E structures	W height	Other
38 Ix Ek'	6 m	37 m	3	6.6 m	(scale? 56 m?)
40 Yaltutu	6 m	32 m	3	5.4 m	
25 Tesik	6 m	33 m	central	1.7 m	(scale? 66 m?)
116 La Pimienta	5 m	39 m	central	?	(scale? 78 m?)

Río Subín

Site number & name	E height	E length	#E structures	W height	Other
278 Rayo de Luz 1	8 m	45 m	3	7 m	
279 Rayo de Luz 2	4 m	39 m	3	2 m	
312 Rayo de Luz 4	2 m	41 m	central	5 m	
205 Subín Arriba	9 m	50 m	3	?	W in acropolis
308 El Tinto	3 m	25 m	central	3 m	
263 Nueva Libertad 1	?	42 m	single range	?	not identified before

Río San Martín

Site number & name	E height	E length	#E structures	W height	Other
208 San Valintín	10 m	70 m	central	8 m	shrine
191 La Guadelupe	3.5 m	47 m	central	5 m	
193 Casas Negras	10 m	52 m	central	5 m	

(continued)

Table 2.1—*Continued*

Site number & name	E height	E length	#E structures	W height	Other
Río San Juan: Bajo					
259 N. Democracia 1	?	38 m	3	1 m	
261 San Juan	?	29 m	central	?	
Río San Juan: Media					
192 Santa Rosa	4.5 m	45 m	central	5 m	late remodeling
189 La Ginebra	9 m	95 m	central	8 m	
103 El Tigrillo	4 m	50 m	3 on plat	3.5 m	shrine
115 Las Flores A	2 m	72 m	3	?	
115 Las Flores B	1 m	?	?	1 m	(not on map)
96 El Edén 1 A	4.8 m	63 m	central	7.6 m	
96 El Edén 1 B	3.4 m	?	?	1.2 m	(not on map)
266 El Edén 3	3 m	35 m	central	4 m	
Río San Juan: Alta					
87 El Chal	7 m	72 m	?	6 m	
88 El Quetzal	4 m	26 m	central	4 m	
89-A Colpetén	6 m	36 m	3	0.3 m	
81 El Ocote 1	2.5 m	30 m	central	2 m	
82 El Ocote 4	?	23 m	central	?	
79 Copoja 1	3.75 m	41 m	3	2.8 m	rebuilt
80 Copoja 2	3.75 m	34 m	2 (C&N)	3.0 m	
76 Santa Cruz 2	4 m	20 m	central	1.9 m	
41 Ix On	7.4	51 m	3	7.8 m	
89 Santa Rosita 1	6.05 m	47 m	3	8.8 m	
47 El Nagual	8 m	46 m	3	7.00 m	scale = 50%?
42 La Unión 1 Cent 1	?	40 m	central	?	
42 La Unión 1 Cent 2	?	40 m	3	?	
43 Ixjuju	4.9 m	34 m	2 (N&C)	?	
77 Santo Torbio 2	4.3 m	32 m	3	4.35 m	
16 Nacim. Moquena	1.5 m	26 m	central	0.60 m	
45 La Unión 2	4.0 m	20 m	3	3.00 m	
44 Sabaneta	4.5 m	26 m	3	0.60 m	
48 Santa Rosita 4	8 m	53 m	3	8.4 m	shrine
49 San Valentín Norte	6 m	30 m	central	6.3 m	
40 Santa Rosita 3	6.05 m	30 m	3	8.8 m	

Site number & name	E height	E length	#E structures	W height	Other
Río Poxte					
97 Nuevas Delicias	2 m	23 m	?	?	(not on map)
5 Pueblito	5 m	50 m	central	5 m	
113 La Lucha	5 m	45 m	central	?	
6 Machaca 2	?	23 m	platform only	?	
51 Santa Rosita 2	4.45 m	43 m	3	?	
4 Poxté 1	6.4 m	42 m	3	?	
39 El Chapayal	4.2 m	29 m	central	2.4 m	
24 Poxté 2	4 m	23 m	3	?	
185 El Tintal 2	3.5 m	18 m	central	3.0 m	
171 El Tintal 1	4 m	24 m	central	0.75 m	
23 Curucuitz	?	58 m	3	?	
26 Ixcoxol 2	5 m	33 m	3	?	
27 Ixcoxol 1	5 m	36 m	2 (C&S)	?	
195 Chaquiux	6 m	50 m	central	5 m	
28-A Nocsos	3.25 m	34 m	central	2.70 m	
Río Machaquilá y Santa Amelia					
209 Esquipulas 1	8 m	80 m	3	6 m	
1 El Achiotal	5.2 m	43 m	central	?	
2 Puente Machaquilá	6.25 m	48 m	3	?	
Central and West Petén					
158 La Pacayera	4.5 m	51 m	central	?	
159 El Bucute	4.0 m	36 m	central	?	destroyed
160 El Juleque	3.5 m	36 m	3	0.5 m	
123 Sajalal	3.0 m	24 m	central	2.3 m	shrine
131 Santa Ana–Zamir A	5.0 m	51 m	3	4.3 m	
131 Santa Ana–Zamir B	4.0 m	?	?	2.0 m	no plan of E
202 La Instancia A	9.0 m	60 m	central	7.0 m	
202 La Instancia B	4.0 m	32 m	?	3.0 m	
280 San Francisco 1	2.0 m	31 m	central	1.0 m	
274 Los Pavos	4.5 m	40 m	central	3.0 m	
288 El Guarumo	2.0 m	29 m	central	?	long west str
237 Ch'ich'a A	12.0 m	91 m	central	?	W remodeled
237 Ch'ich'a B	7.0 m	41 m	central	?	shrine

(continued)

Site number & name	E height	E length	#E structures	W height	Other
Los Lagos					
299 Ts' Unun Witz	1.0 m	41 m	central	3 m	map 90° off
325 K'u Jux 2	5.0 m	52 m	central	7 m	
223 El Sos	2.0 m	22 m	central	?	
221 El Xux	4.0 m	39 m	?	2 m	plan unclear
Eastern Platform, But No West Structure					
167 Casa de Piedra	?	28 m	3	-	no west
155 Yok'ol Wits Gr 1	?	40 m	3	-	no west
153 Los Encuentros	7 m	26 m	none	-	no west
199 Linares 1	6 m	63 m	central	-	no west
138 Sacul 5	?	23 m	central	?	no west
99 El Chilonché	3.5 m	45 m	central	-	no W structure
260 N. Democracia 2	6 m	60 m	central	-	no west
265 El Frijolar	?	40 m	central	-	no west
190 La Pajarera	?	43 m	central	-	no W/rebuilt?
83 El Ocote 3	2.8 m	18 m	central	-	no W/stela
74 Santo Domingo	4.8 m	25 m	3	-	no W
75 Santo Torbio 1	5.5 m	30 m	3	-	no W
291 Chan K'ix	2.0 m	35 m	central	-	no W/Odd Angle
277 El Cosuco	3.5 m	21 m	central	-	no W structure
Identified, But Probably not E Groups					
157 Buenos Aires Gr 1	15 m	?	3	?	separate E strs
172 La Providencia 2	?	34 m	odd	?	juts forward
125 Grano de Oro	?	26 m	central	?	shrine
66 El Bombillo Central	?	23 m	central	-	no west
66 El Bombillo Gr 17	3	10 m	23 m	?	3.30 m
67 El Calabazal 3	7 m	-	3	separate	10 m
60 El Limón	?	47 m	3	?	W is platform
55 El Rosario	2.40 m	22 m	central	1.90 m	
21 Uizil 'Ox	?	19 m	central	?	
22 Ixchen	?	20 m	3	?	W not defined
13 Ek Tzic	7 m	13 m	none	?	W platform
18 Xa'an Abajo	3.7 m	29 m	central	3.2 m	E&W rectangles
147 Chiquibul 2	?	35 m	2 (C&S)	?	rectangular W

Site number & name	E height	E length	#E structures	W height	Other
168 Los Laureles 1	3 m	14 m	none	-	no W/E on platform
169 Los Laureles 2	2.6 m	15 m	central	0.6 m	E on low platform
162 La Ponderosa	3.6 m	22 m	central	0.3 m	rec W/platform E
179 Nueva Armenia	?	26 m	central	6.5 m	no alignment
133 El Llanto	4 m	27 m	2 (C&N)	6 m	rectangular W
234 Camixtun	15 m	32 m	central	4 m	W range/2 E
258 La Reinta	6 m	37 m	3	-	no W/shrine
262 El Botan	6 m	26 m	3	?	rectangular W
119 Buen Retiro	?	29 m	3	?	Triadic?
119 Buen Retiro B	?	29 m	?	?	
124 El Cartucho	3.8 m	23 m	3	?	Triadic?
73 La Puente	10 m	?	?	?	plan unclear
85 San Miguel/Dolores	7.0 m	44 m	platform only	?	W is ballcourt
78 Santa Cruz 1	3.1 m	16 m	central	-	W is quadrangular platform
3 Ixtutz	7 m	23 m	3	?	Triadic?
28 Ixcoxol 3	2.5 m	?	?	?	plan backward
102 Xutilha	4.5 m	-	none	?	3 separate E
285 La Lechuza	?	?	?	?	plan unclear
217 La Benedición 1	3.0 m	21 m	?	3 m	plan unclear
OTHER E GROUPS USED IN CHAPTER					
Caracol epicenter	10 m	95 m	3 (+2)	25 m	remodeling
Caracol Hatzcap Ceel	10 m	96 m	3	10.4 m	
Caracol Cahal Pichik	9.5 m	87 m	3	13 m	
Caracol Ceiba	ca. 7 m	70 m	2 (C&S)	ca. 9 m	
Caracol Cohune	ca. 7 m	54 m	central	ca. 9 m	
Tayasal	ca. 5m	65 m	3 (+1)	rebuilt	
Paxcamán	8 m	96 m	central	7.4 m	
Cenote	8 m	92 m	3 (+1)	9 m	
Yaxhá Cenote Style	?	172 m	3	?	
Yaxhá Uaxactún Style	e	?	65 m	3 m	?

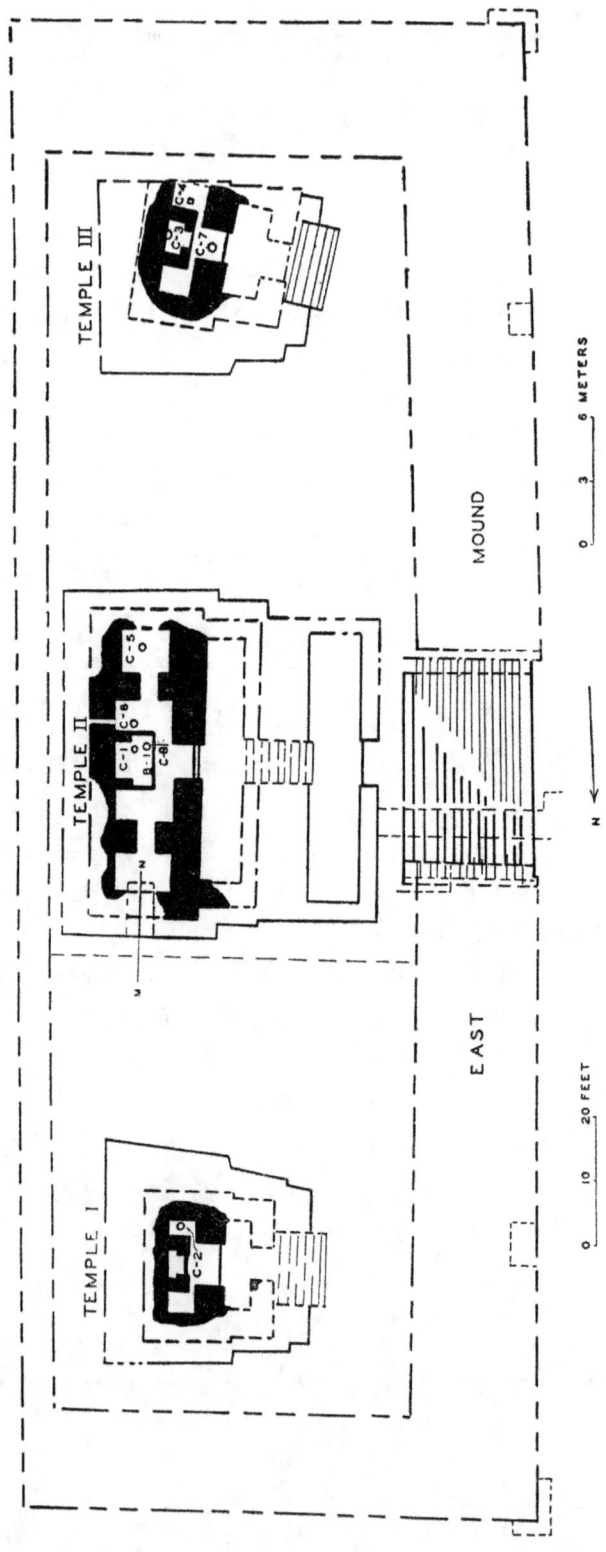

Figure 2.2. The eastern platform at Uaxactún, Guatemala, showing the location of various caches associated with the three buildings, Structures EI-EIII (after Ricketson and Ricketson 1937:48, Figure 8). All three buildings contain a skull cache on the north–south axes.

cross-peninsular Maya trade routes (Chase and Chase 2012); and (3) these E Groups may be used as a partial proxy for understanding the peopling of the Maya Southern Lowlands.

The Archaeology of E Groups

Uaxactún

The Uaxactún Group E (Figure 2.1a and Figure 2.2), from whence the term "E Group" derives, was one of the first major architectural complexes investigated by the archaeologists from the Carnegie Institution program who worked there from 1926 through 1931. These investigations formed the baseline for all other E Group research but were not actually extensive enough to fully document the developmental pattern for this architectural complex. A. V. Smith (1950:63) noted that the latest pottery within all four of the E Group buildings that were investigated by Oliver Ricketson and Edith Ricketson (1937) at Uaxactún dated to Tzakol—or Early Classic (250–550 CE)—times. This dating does not take into account, however, that neither the deeply buried E-VII-Sub (western pyramid) nor the platform supporting the three eastern structures was penetrated. Thus, for the better part of half a century E Groups were dated to the early part of the Early Classic period (for example, Smith 1950:63). The earlier aspects of these archaeological complexes were subsequently documented by research at Cenote (Chase 1983, 1985), Tikal (Laporte and Fialko 1995), Caracol (Chase and Chase 1995), and Mirador and Nakbé (Hansen 1992).

All three of the masonry structures at Uaxactún, which were set astride the summit of the eastern platform, were excavated axially. While the Ricketsons (1937:52) noted that earlier constructions were present in the platform, they did not investigate them: "the additions and refloorings here are very complicated and indicate that the East Mound itself was probably not originally built to its present dimensions." There were minimally three and possibly up to five earlier constructions at this locus (Ricketson and Ricketson 1937:52, Figure 14). Excavations at the base of the eastern platform revealed the presence of several different facings and an inset side panel (Ricketson and Ricketson 1937:Figures 94, 95).

Structure E-I, the northern building, yielded two deposits. Feature 1, dated to Tepeu 1 or 2 times (based on Ricketson and Ricketson 1937:Plate 86, Figure 10), was an intrusive pottery dump placed within the altar of the building. Cist 2 was located south of this altar and consisted of a skull

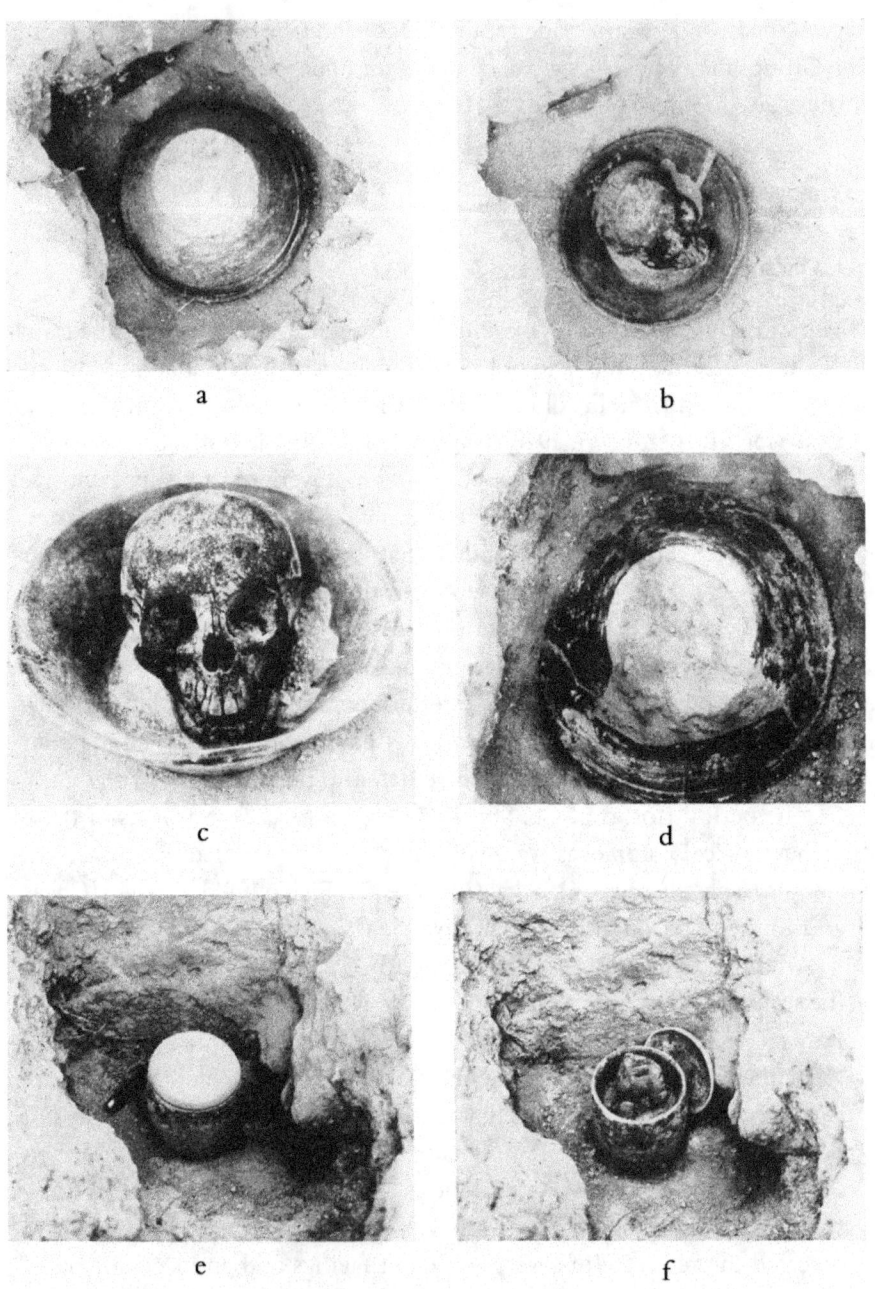

Figure 2.3. Caches from the core of Structure EII at Uaxactún: (a–c) Cist 4; (d) Cist 7; (e–f) Cist 3 (after Ricketson and Ricketson 1937:Plate 23).

set between two Águila Orange bowls (Ricketson and Ricketson 1937:Plate 81a, b) along with twelve jadeite objects; it would appear that Cist 2 was intrusive, based on "a faint line of demarcation in the floor" (Ricketson and Ricketson 1937:49).

Three deposits were uncovered in association with the southern building, Structure E-III. Cist 3, containing an Águila Orange barrel (Ricketson and Ricketson 1937:Plate 81e, f), had been located within the building's altar set against the buried back wall. Cists 4 and 7 each contained a set of Águila Orange dishes that each housed a human skull. Cist 4 was located south of the masonry altar, while Cist 7 was "found in the floor in the doorway between the two galleries" (Ricketson and Ricketson 1937:58).

Three deposits were also recovered from the central eastern building, Structure EII (Figure 2.3a–f), all again on axis and all again associated with Águila Orange dishes (Ricketson and Ricketson 1937:Plate 81d, h, i, l, m). Cist 1 contained one vessel and the bones of a child. The two vessels in Cist 8 encased two obsidian lancets. The two vessels in Cist 6 contained a human skull. Cists 1 and 8 were sealed within the fill of the building and were considered to be nonintrusive (Ricketson and Ricketson 1937:55–56). Yet another deposit, consisting of two very early Early Classic vessels (Ricketson and Ricketson 1937:56, Plate 79j–l), that was not formally recognized by the excavators appears to have been sealed in the fill beneath Cists 1 and 6.

The large western pyramid, Structure E-VII, was also investigated. The later substructure formed a 24.3 m by 24.7 m square that was flanked by stucco masks and had no structure on its summit. Radial stairways were confirmed on its eastern and northern sides and suspected on its southern and western sides (Ricketson and Ricketson 1937:67–68). Three sealed caches (Cists 9, 11, and 12) and one burial (Cist 10) were recovered. The caches contained fifteen Early Classic ceramic vessels—Águila Orange dishes and Balanza Black cylinders (Ricketson and Ricketson 1937:Plates 81n–o, 82a–e, 84a–h). An additional Early Classic polychrome basal-flanged bowl was recovered from the core of Structure E-VII. One other cache (Cist 13) was recovered from the core of the E-VII southern platform and contained sixteen Early Classic vessels (Ricketson and Ricketson 1937:Plates 82g–i, 83a–e, h, i, 85a–g, Figure 190e) and four eccentric flints. Whereas the Ricketsons (1937:93, Figure. 57) argued that Structure E-VII-sub was followed by E-VII-secondary and then by the E-VII-platform, this sequence of construction is inverted, as can be seen in their Figure 57,

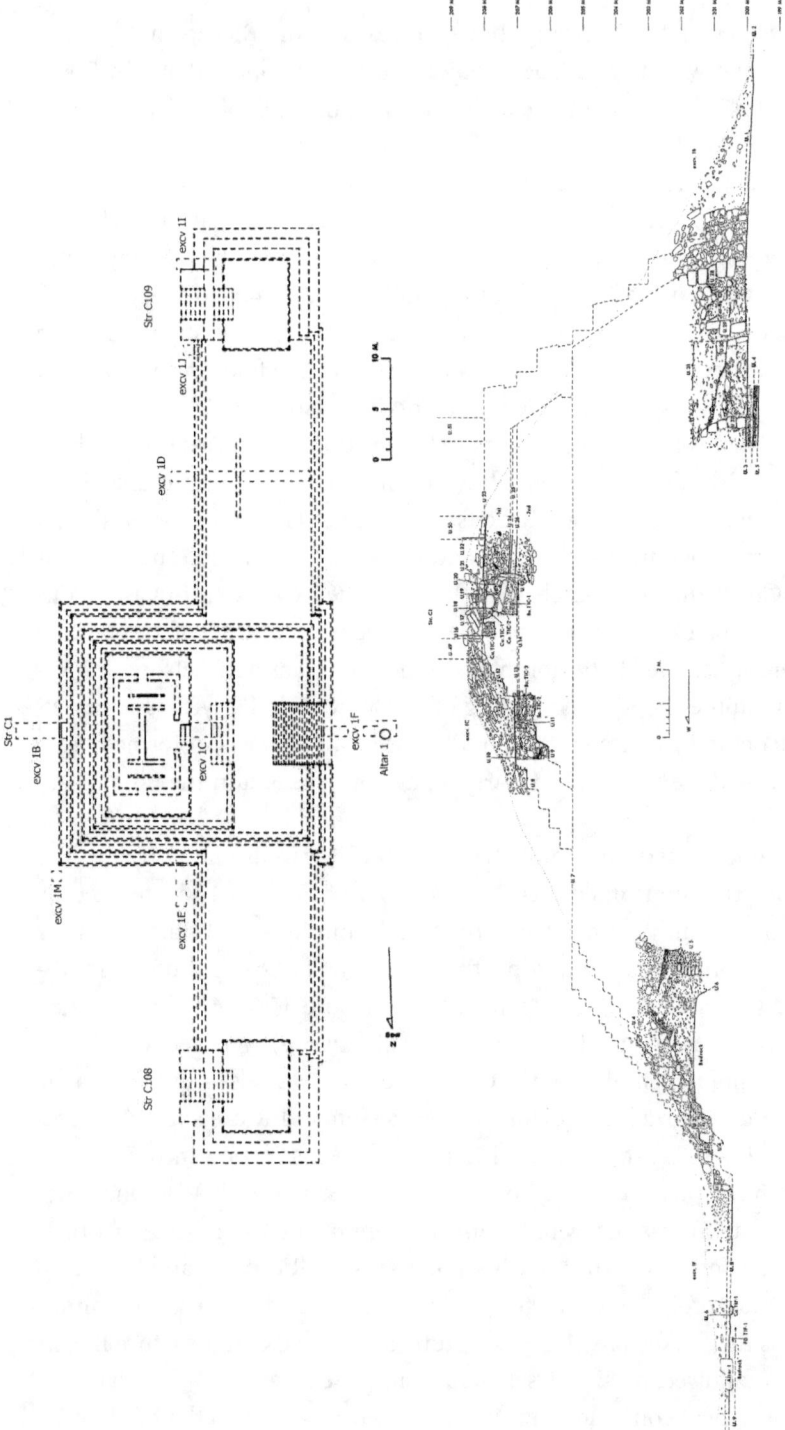

Figure 2.4. The (a) plan and (b) section of the eastern platform of the Cenote E Group, Structures C1, C108, and C109, showing the locations of excavations undertaken in 1971 and the locations of caches and burials associated with the central building. Also shown in the section is the earliest modified bedrock version of the eastern platform (after Chase 1983:298–301).

which correctly shows E-VII-sub followed by E-VII-platform and then by E-VII-secondary.

The reexamination of the Uaxactún E Group investigations reveals three important points. First, the cultural material recovered in association with the western Structure E-VII appears to be of a later Early Classic date than the caches recovered in association with the three buildings atop the eastern platform. Second, the final form of the Uaxactún E Group dates to the Early Classic period but clearly had antecedents in the Late Preclassic period, as the Ricketsons (1937:Figure 98) themselves noted (in spite of no excavations into the earlier version). Finally, the Uaxactún E Group declined in importance in inverse relationship to the development of the Uaxactún Group A acropolis, beginning in the last part of the Early Classic period (Andrews 1975:123; see also Kovic 2011).

Cenote

Three E Groups are noted for the Tayasal-Paxcamán Zone of the central Petén lakes district. A Uaxactún Style E Group of Early Classic date has been documented for the site center of Tayasal, replete with stone stelae; its western pyramid was presumably leveled by subsequent Postclassic period (900–1519 CE) occupation (Chase 1983; see also Pugh et al. 2012:7, Figure 4). Two Cenote Style E Groups are noted, one at the site of Paxcamán and the other at Cenote (Chase 1983:1155). The Paxcamán E Group was mapped in 1977; its eastern platform is 96 m in length, with no lateral structures in evidence; its central east building is 7.4 m in height; its western building is 8 m in height (Chase 1983:1155). The Cenote E Group (Figure 2.1b and Figure 2.4a, b) was excavated in May and June 1971 by the University of Pennsylvania Tayasal Project and formed the type-site for this style variant (Chase 1985). The core of its eastern platform contains materials dating to the Middle Preclassic, and the earliest form of this E Group was constructed of carved bedrock. Under the eastern platform, bedrock was shaped as a stepped platform complete with lower side wings. Under the western platform, bedrock was carved into a small platform. The western pyramid, Structure C5, eventually came to be 8 m in height; it was not, however, a radial pyramid like Uaxactún and did not face to the east in its final form, but rather to the south.

The eastern platform at Cenote was 92 m in length; its central construction, Structure C1, was some 6 m in height by the beginning of the Early Classic period. The two constructions on the end of the platform evinced eastern access. A stone altar was placed on axis to the west of the central

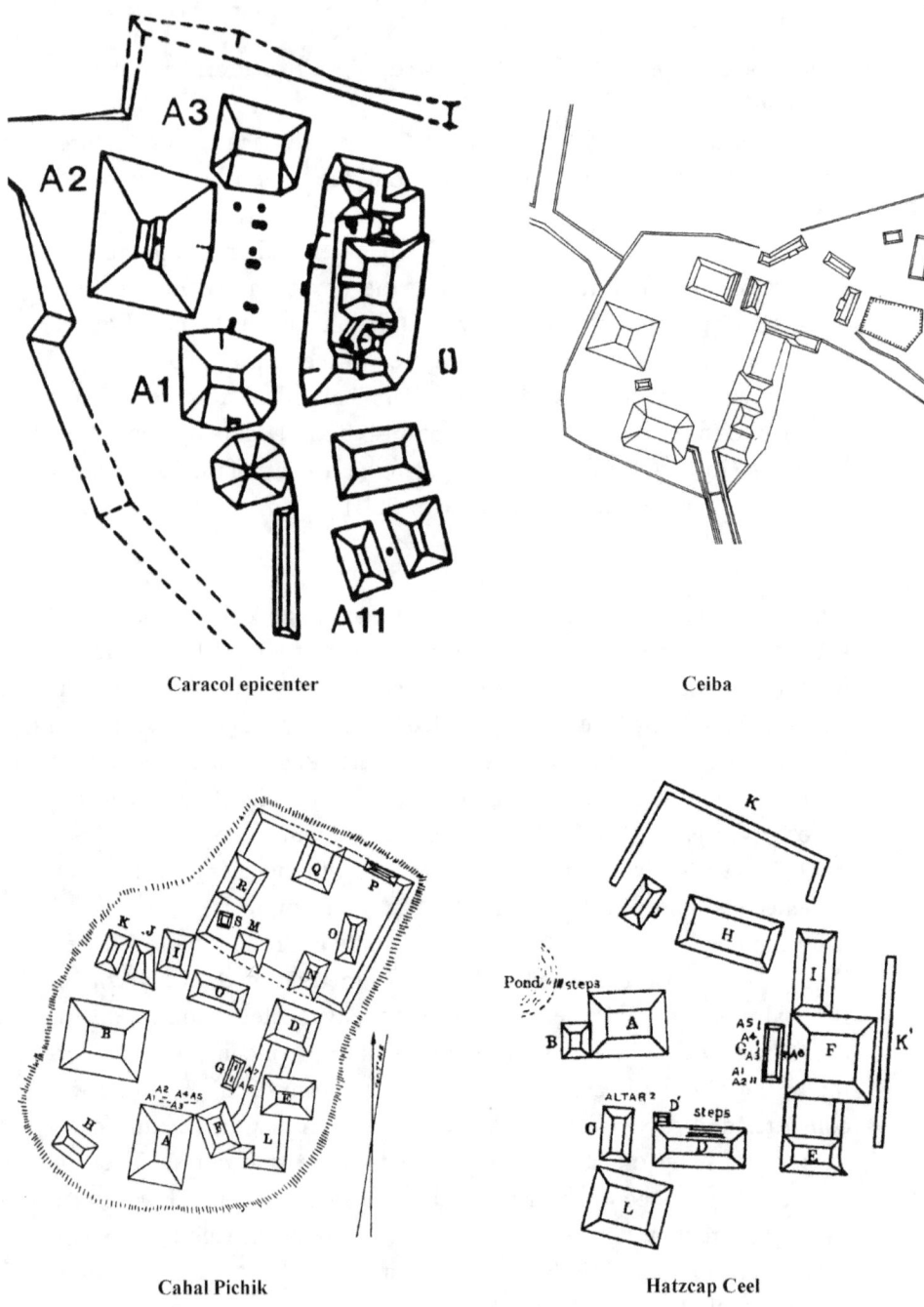

Figure 2.5. E Groups from Caracol, Belize: (a) epicenter (after Chase and Chase 1987:65), (b) Ceiba, (c) Cahal Pichik (after Thompson 1931:240); and (d) Hatzcap Ceel (after Thompson 1931:250).

building and a lip-to-lip cache of black tetrapod vessels was set on bedrock in between the altar and building. What is presumed to have been a corner cache, also consisting of partial tetrapod vessels, was recovered northeast of the latest central building. The latest version of the central construction also was associated with two burials and a series of caches. Sealed within the frontal step was a single supine burial accompanied by two lip-to-lip red cache bowls. Set in the fill above this burial before it was sealed in the construction was another set of lip-to-lip red cache bowls containing a human skull. A second burial was intruded into the floor of the latest building during the transition into the early Early Classic and contained eleven ceramic vessels and two censers. This burial had been disturbed in the early part of the Late Classic, however, but appears to have been reconsecrated with the deposition of four other vessels that likely came from this deposit as a cache through the summit floor and by two other small caches placed in the fill immediately above the redeposited interment. At a much later date, a ritual concentration of broken Terminal Classic vessels appears to have been placed in a shrine on the summit of this building, reminiscent of a similar deposit placed in the northern altar of the Uaxactún E Group (see above) and in a shrine.

Uncovered immediately north of the eastern platform was a small construction, Structure C2, which also faced west. This construction housed an eroded plain stela, and a carved stone was recovered from the platform fill. Two Early Classic burials had been intruded into the building in front of the stela, both sealed by the latest platform floor. A series of three early Early Classic caches had been placed immediately east of this platform. All contained redware bowls. Two caches consisted of single bowls, and the third consisted of a set of these bowls that encased a human skull. These caches are stratigraphically much earlier than the burials. The conjunction of this stela platform with an E Group at Cenote is significant, as it is indicative of the subsequent role of such carved monuments in public ritual.

Caracol

As noted elsewhere (A. Chase and D. Chase 1994, 1996, 1998; Chases et al. 2011), the site of Caracol encompassed almost 200 sq km in the Late Classic period (550–800 CE). Located within this settlement area are the remains of five E Groups (Figure 2.5a–d)—presumably architectural concentrations representing early independent communities within the Caracol landscape. All of the known E Groups in Caracol can be dated to at least as early as the Late Preclassic period. Four of these groups (Hatzcap Ceel, Cahal Pichik,

Caracol, and Ceiba) are linked together by causeways, while one (Cohune) was not formally incorporated into the Late Classic city by roads. Cohune was extensively looted by means of tunnels, but actual excavation data exist for three of the groups (Caracol, Hatzcap Ceel, and Cahal Pichik). All three of the formally excavated groups contain cached deposits that permit both dating and some insight into the broader cosmological functions of these complexes.

Ignored in the early E Group literature (Ricketson and Ricketson 1937; Ruppert 1940; Ruppert and Denison 1943) were the excavations undertaken by Thompson (1931) at the Belizean sites of Hatzcap Ceel and Cahal Pichik in the 1920s. Both the Cahal Pichik and the Hatzcap Ceel E Groups are Cenote Style architectural complexes. The eastern platform at both sites supports three buildings, with two plain stelae set on a smaller platform immediately in front of the eastern platform at Cahal Pichik. The western pyramid at Cahal Pichik, Structure B, is 13 m in height and supported a stone building. A bench was attached to the rear wall of this building, and an earlier bench was found directly below. Thompson (1931:Plate 36) recovered "Votive Cache 4" beneath the back wall of the structure on axis to the bench; this cache consisted of a single large flaring walled dish that contained a single jadeite bead and a shell that had a Maya portrait painted on it. Reconnaissance at the site in 1989 found that Cahal Pichik had been extensively looted, with both the eastern and western pyramids being savagely trenched. Three early barrel caches, stylistically dating to the Late Preclassic, were recovered from the looters' excavations at the summit of the western structure.

On the 3 m high eastern platform of Cahal Pichik, Thompson (1931:243) investigated the 9.5 m high central building, Structure E, which had a western stairway and no formal construction atop the substructure. He also investigated another building, Structure F, associated with the southern extant of the eastern platform, finding a masonry structure that rose 1.5 m above the platform. A refuse dump that produced whole vessels was located under the floor of the rear room of this building; these materials are transitional between the Late Preclassic and the early Early Classic periods (Thompson 1931:Figure 10d).

The plan of the Hatzcap Ceel E Group resembles that at Cahal Pichik, but the eastern platform is actually longer; as at Cahal Pichik, a stela platform is located immediately in front of the eastern platform at Hatzcap Ceel. The western pyramid, Structure A, rose to a height of 10.4 m and supported a formal building; although a stratigraphic sequence of three

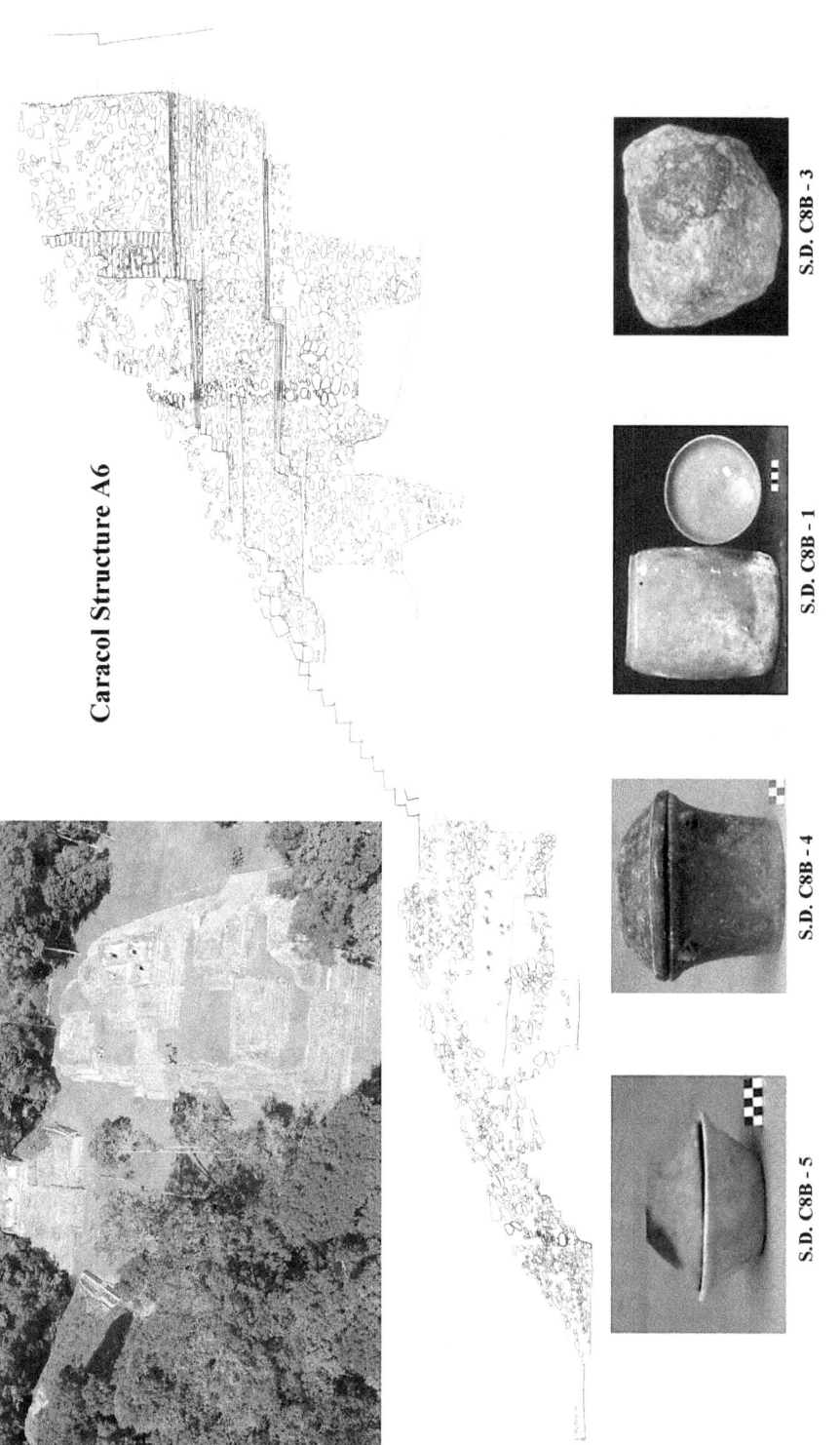

Figure 2.6. The Caracol epicentral E Group east platform, Structure A6, showing (a) an aerial photo of the E Group looking north, (b) the section through the central building of Caracol's east platform, and (c–f) caches associated with the refurbishing of Caracol Structure A6-2nd (SDs 4 and 5) and with the construction of Structure A6-1st (SDs 1 and 3).

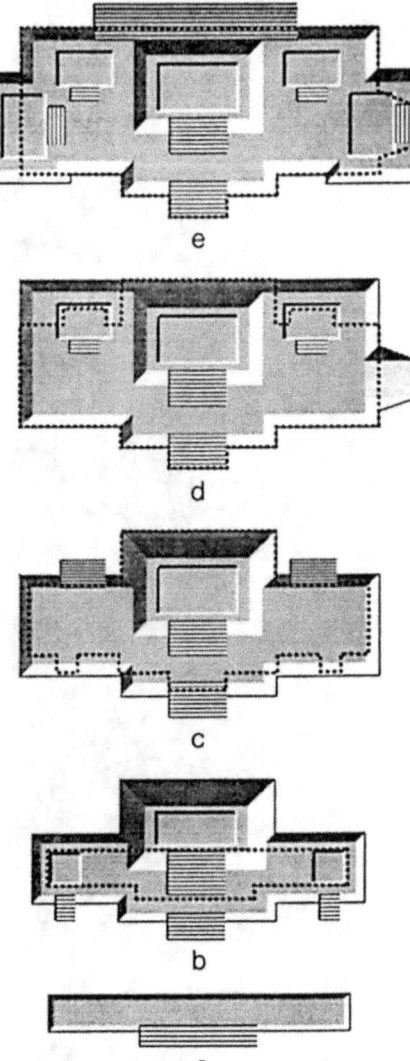

Figure 2.7. The architectural development of the eastern platform of the Caracol E Group based on excavation data: (a) estimated time of construction 360 BCE; (b) estimated time of construction 160 BCE; (c) estimated time of construction CE 41; (d) estimated time of construction CE 440; and (e) estimated time of construction CE 640 (after Chase and Chase 1995:98).

floors was found, no deposits were located (Thompson 1931:260). As at Cahal Pichik, excavation focused on the central and southern buildings of the eastern platform. Investigation of the southern building, Structure E, encountered the remains of two sequent masonry buildings but no associated deposits. The central building on the eastern platform, Structure F, rose to a height of 10 m and supported a single room building at its summit. An earlier red-painted building was located 1.2 m directly beneath the later

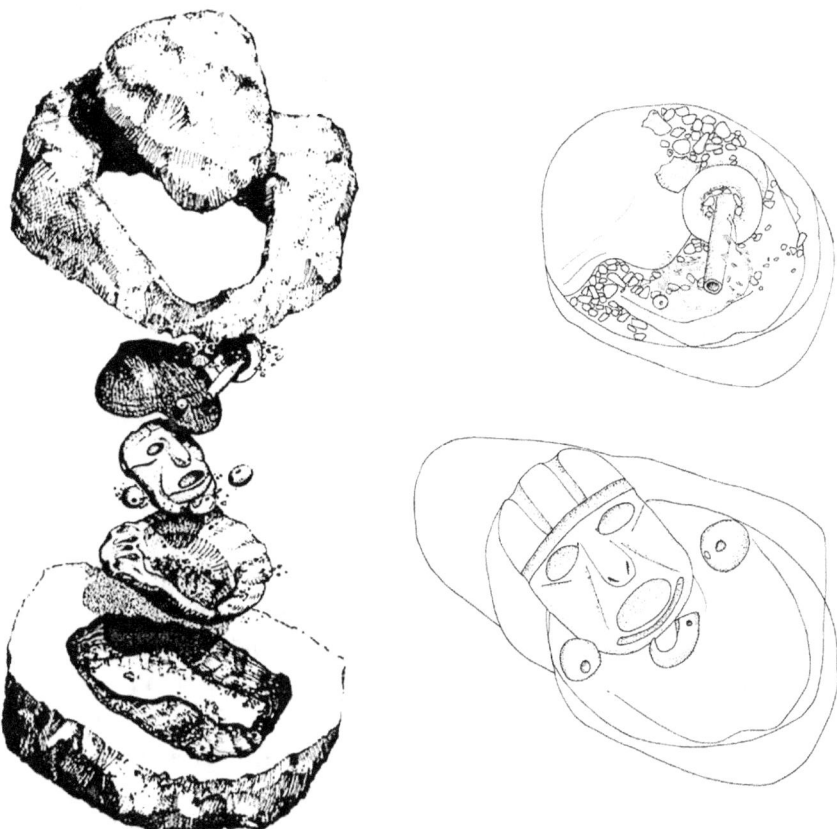

Figure 2.8. Expanded view (after Chase and Chase 1995:96) and upper and lower plans of SD C8B-3. Some 664.7 grams of mercury were found in the bottom of a stone geode. The carved limestone lid was attached to the geode with red bedrock clay. Paired *Spondylus* shells were set above the mercury. Within the *Spondylus* shells was a large jadeite face with a jadeite claw pendant and a jadeite bead and a *Strombus* bead on either side; the items were bedded in malachite chips. A single jadeite earflare assemblage with pearl end was set atop the shells. There were indications that the shells had been wrapped in cloth.

building. Below the floor of this earlier building and centered on its doorway, Thompson (1931:275, Plate 34 left) recovered "Votive Cache 3," which consisted of a red barrel and an unslipped vessel dating to the transition between the Late Preclassic and Early Classic periods. A final plaster floor was found 1.25 m below the earlier building.

The epicentral Caracol E Group has also been investigated extensively. The western pyramid, Structure A1, rises some 25 m above the associated plaza and does not support a formal building. Instead, a 2 m raised platform with side stairways crowns the summit of this building. A carved stela dating to 9.10.10.0.0 is set into the facing of the summit platform between the two stairs and is associated with a Giant Ahau altar that had been placed over the fragments of a partial 8th cycle stela. Three caches were recovered in the summit trench. Within the core of the summit platform was a deposit of obsidian eccentrics, stingray spines, and white calcite balls. East of the summit monuments, set into an upper platform, was a lip-to-lip cache of two large flaring rimmed, redware bowls that contained a host of marine items in the form of shells and coral. A third barrel cache was found deep within the summit core buried within the core of an even earlier construction. This lidded barrel was associated with a number of smaller objects that included stingray spines, coral, jadeite and shell beads, shell "Charlie Chaplin" figures (Lomitola 2012:110), a large jadeite pendant, and a single large jadeite earflare. It is likely that this deposit dates to the Late Preclassic era. Basal excavations were unable to find earlier buried constructions at plaza level.

The eastern platform of the Caracol E Group has also been extensively investigated (Figure 2.6a–f). All of the formal buildings have been excavated and a detailed plan of the development of the eastern platform has been presented (Chase and Chase 1995:98, Figure 60) that extends back to the early part of the Late Preclassic period. As presently understood, the initial construction was a long platform with central steps that did not support structures (Figure 2.7a–e). This platform was eventually engulfed in a Cenote Style E group consisting of an earlier version of the central Structure A6 and at least one deeply buried end-platform structure, the back of one being recovered deep beneath Structure A8. Two caches were recovered sealed in the core of the earlier masonry version of Structure A6. Around CE 41, the final masonry version of Structure A6 was built and the platform was next expanded to its present length and height. This platform evinced rear stairs running east directly beneath where the later Structures A5 and A7 were located.

Two of the most impressive caches recovered at Caracol were included in the construction of the final masonry version of Structure A6, one in a stone geode (Figure 2.8) and one in a large ceramic barrel (Chase and Chase 1995, 2005, 2006a). A tomb was intruded into the platform beneath the locus that was to become Structure A4 between 350 and 400 CE. Another tomb was placed in the plaza to the southern axis of Structure A6 at about the same time; this double-decker chamber had its upper room filled around CE 480. Structures A5 and A7 were constructed around CE 450;

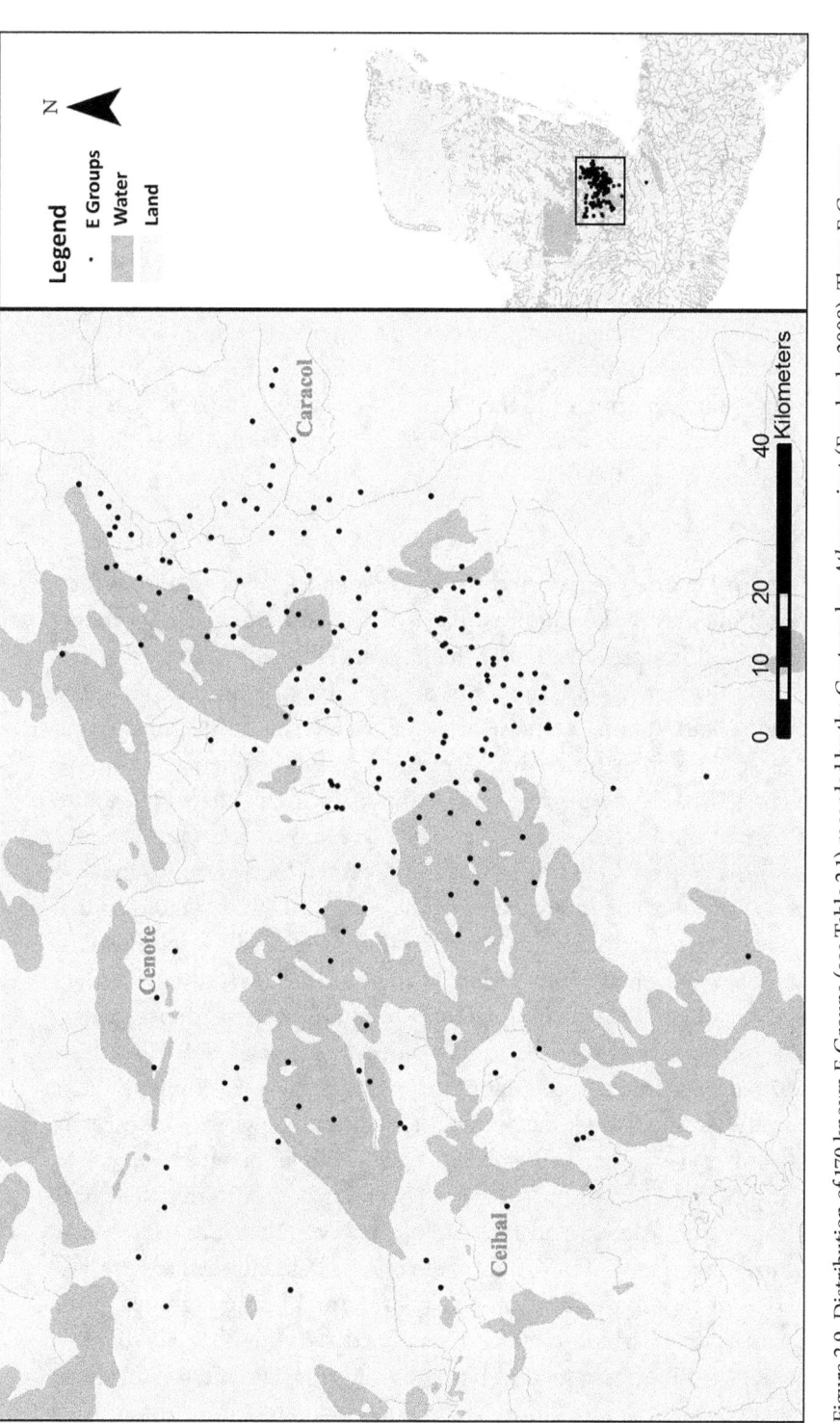

Figure 2.9. Distribution of 170 known E Groups (see Table 2.1) recorded by the Guatemalan *Atlas* project (Escobedo 2008). These E Groups accord well with a major transpeninsular trade route from the Río Pasión to the Caribbean Sea (Chase and Chase 2012; Laporte et al. 2008).

it is suspected that an early version of Structure A8 containing a Charlie Chaplin cache (Lomitola 2012:112) was also constructed about this time. Structure A7 contained a formal tomb with a northern entry that was filled and sealed by 500 CE. Finally, between 550 and 600 CE, Structure A4 was constructed and encased a large tomb. Monuments were erected in front of Structure A4 and eventually were buried in a stelae dump in front of this building in association with a cache. Thus, the eastern platform of Caracol's E Group served as the locus for long-standing concentrated ritual activities that continued throughout Caracol's history, first associated with caching practices in the Preclassic period (1000 BCE–250 CE), then associated with high-status interments in the Early Classic period, and, finally, terminated with burning and trash in the Terminal Classic period (800–900 CE) (Chase and Chase 2000).

Southeast Petén

Juan Pedro Laporte orchestrated a long-term effort to accomplish a total survey of the sites in the southeast Petén of Guatemala in order to understand the political organization of this region (Figure 2.9). This effort ran from 1987 through 2008 (Laporte et al. 1988; Laporte and Mejia 2005a; Escobedo 2008). Among its more important results was the documentation of at least 170 architectural complexes that can be classified as E Groups (Table 2.1). This represents a concentration of E Groups that is not found elsewhere in the Maya area and places the five known E Groups at Caracol within a context where these features are often located only 3 to 5 km apart. While all of the known sites in the southeast Petén were recorded and plotted as to longitude and latitude by the Guatemalans working on the *Atlas* project (Escobedo 2008), most of these sites witnessed only limited excavation, often in the form of test-pits to establish some idea of dating. Significantly, many of these test pits yielded Middle and Early Preclassic sherd materials. Initially, the dating of many of the E Group complexes was not fully understood, much like the situation elsewhere in the Petén. Thus, some were assigned a Late Classic date without being excavated. As the early date of E Groups became better understood (for example, Chase and Chase 1995; Aimers and Rice 2006), however, the *Atlas* project also recognized that many, if not all, of these groups dated to the Late Preclassic period or earlier. By 2008 some forty of the architectural groups in the southeast Petén referred to as E Groups were dated with certainty to minimally the Late Preclassic period based on the associated test excavations (Escobedo 2008).

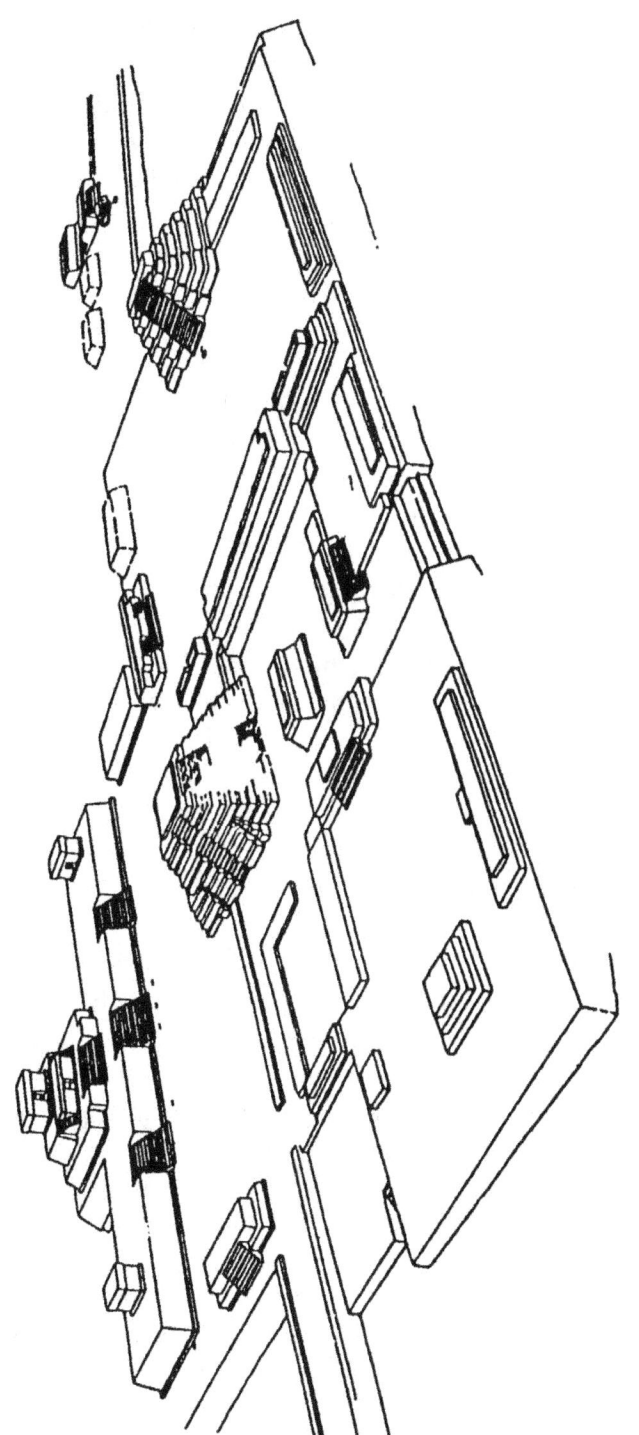

Figure 2.10. Perspective of the center of Ixtontón (*north to the left*) showing a Cenote Style E Group dating to the Late Preclassic period (after Laporte 1994).

Several of the E Groups in the southeast Petén have been investigated in greater detail than a single test excavation, but none have been deeply penetrated and explored. Ixtontón (Figure 2.10) was investigated in the mid-1990s and dated to the Late Preclassic period (Laporte 1994). Other archaeological investigations were undertaken at Ixkún (Laporte and Mejía 2005a) and Ix Ek' (Laporte and Mejía 2007) that confirmed the Late Preclassic dating of these E Groups as well. Cache vessels and burials dating to the Late Preclassic period are reported from a series of sites throughout the southeast Petén (Laporte and Fialko 2007). It is suspected that further work in this region will yield even earlier deposits. Juan Pedro Laporte and Vilma Fialko (2007:60–61) noted that in spite of relatively limited excavation strategies Middle Preclassic occupation could be confirmed at 21 sites and that Late Preclassic occupation was found at minimally 105 sites in the southeast Petén.

In a final publication, Laporte and colleagues (2008) laid out a transpeninsular trade route that ran from the Río Pasión up the Río San Juan and used a portage area to connect to the Río Salsipuedes and Río Mopán and thence to the Belize River and the sea. This was also clearly a route used to settle this part of the Maya area, as is indicated by the ceramic distributions and the E Group distribution. It was also in use during the Late Classic period based on the distribution of Belize Red ceramics (Chase and Chase 2012).

Discussion

Oliver Ricketson (1928) published an early article identifying the Uaxactún E Group as a solar observatory, although the Ricketsons (1937:108–109) felt that the construction of such groups was "more closely associated with geomancy than with observational astronomy." The full publication of the Uaxactún E Group excavations provided great detail and support for the argument for the use of the architectural complex to observe solstices and equinoxes (Ricketson and Ricketson 1937), and the observatory function was applied to all other known E Groups. Given structural variations in the complex across sites, Uaxactún was (and still is) viewed as the earliest and "purest" version of this architectural complex. The Carnegie Project archaeologists' views both on the Early Classic and on Uaxactún as the earliest example of an E Group (Kidder 1950:1) were also later reassessed (Chase and Chase 2005, 2006a).

Ruppert (1940) initially addressed the distribution of E Groups. Ruppert and Denison (1943) mapped a series of these groupings in the northern Petén of Guatemala and in southern Campeche and Quintana Roo, Mexico. Their interpretations went largely unchallenged for more than forty years. Because Uaxactún was considered to be the original E Group, the unclear solar alignments seen in other E Groups were explained as their having become "provincially and decadently . . . merely ritualistic" even though "the obvious similarity in orientation and arrangement suggest [sic] their use for a common function" (Ruppert and Denison 1943:5). Anthony Aveni and Horst Hartung (1989) further demonstrated the variable orientations of these various complexes, but Aveni and colleagues later argued that they all shared a common function in observing and anchoring 20-day Winal intervals around the solar zeniths (Aveni et al. 2003).

The investigation of the Cenote E Group changed our perspectives on both the expected form and date of this complex, resulting in the definition of two distinct variants based on the shape of their eastern platforms: "in the Uaxactun E Group variant, the platform comprises a separate rectangular unit, usually about 70 m in length, supporting three buildings; in the Cenote E Group variant, the platform is much longer and narrower and the three buildings appear to be appended to it" (Chase 1983:191). The investigation of both the Caracol (Chase and Chase 1995) and Tikal (Laporte and Fialko 1995) E Groups established that the Cenote variant was earlier than the Uaxactún variant and that later construction efforts could transform a Cenote variant into a Uaxactún variant (as took place at Caracol). Richard Hansen (1992) recognized the early dating of E Groups in his doctoral dissertation based on archaeological work at Nakbé and elsewhere in the northern Petén and confirmed by excavations at Ceibal (Inomata et al. 2013).

The E Group may therefore be seen as being one of the first hallmarks of Maya public architecture. Its appearance at sites is taken to be indicative of the coagulation of a formal ritual community in which there was broad participation (Chapter 7 in this volume). If the Cenote stratigraphy can be extended to other examples, the earliest complexes were actually carved out of bedrock, with the eastern platform being the most important component of this grouping. In fact, in several cases in the southeast Petén, no western pyramid is in evidence; it either was removed in urban renewal projects or was never in existence (see Chapter 13 in this volume on Belize). Thus, although the western pyramid was a prominent construction in many E Groups (as can be seen in the elaborately decorated E-VII-Sub at Uaxactún), the search for the meaning of such a complex must focus on the eastern platform.

The eastern platforms are usually marked by the presence of three platforms or formal buildings. Often these buildings occur in association with caches and, in later times, burials. At Caracol, four caches line the axis of the central eastern building. The timing and stratigraphy of these caches indicate that they were used to "center" the building during the transition to the 8th cycle (Chase and Chase 2006a), thus ascribing an aspect of temporal ritual to this complex. Prudence Rice (2004; Aimers and Rice 2006) also saw time as being an important element in E Groups both for the celebration of 20-year K'atuns and for the *may* or 256-year cycles. Based on Caracol's archaeology, we would instead see them as important markers for Bak'tuns (400 years) and half-Bak'tun celebrations. Caracol's E Group was presumably founded around 360 BCE (7th cycle); it was remodeled around 40 CE, coincident with the onset of the 8th cycle. Datable burials and remodeling of the central Caracol E Group began around 440 CE with the onset of the 9th cycle. At this time, the Caracol E Group was transformed from a Cenote Style E Group to a Uaxactún Style E Group; the other E Groups within the Caracol metropolitan area did not see similar modification, indicating that 9th-cycle Bak'tun ritual was appropriately centered on the complex in the Caracol epicenter. The west pyramid in Caracol's epicentral E Group was completed in its final form around CE 640, midway between the two cycles, and commemorated with a summit stela that recorded deep mythological history (Grube 1994). While the central building remained relatively unchanged through the 10th cycle, the 10th cycle saw the Caracol epicentral E Group buildings used for caching and for late ceremonies on the west and as a ritual dump on the east. The establishment of Caracol's political presence at Naranjo is memorialized in a hieroglyphic stairway set in that site's E Group around CE 640, also midway between the 9th and 10th cycles. The use of Naranjo's E Group for this act must have been charged with symbolism. Thus, in these archaeologically established examples, the importance of long-term cyclical time is emphasized.

The general development of the more varied-sized Cenote Style E Group into the more regularly shaped Uaxactún Style E Group over time has implications for interpretations based on survey without excavation. Adding the temporal component shows that the Cenote Style E Groups co-occur with greater frequency, particularly in the southeastern Maya Lowlands, where they are often spaced only 3 to 5 km apart. This coagulation of E

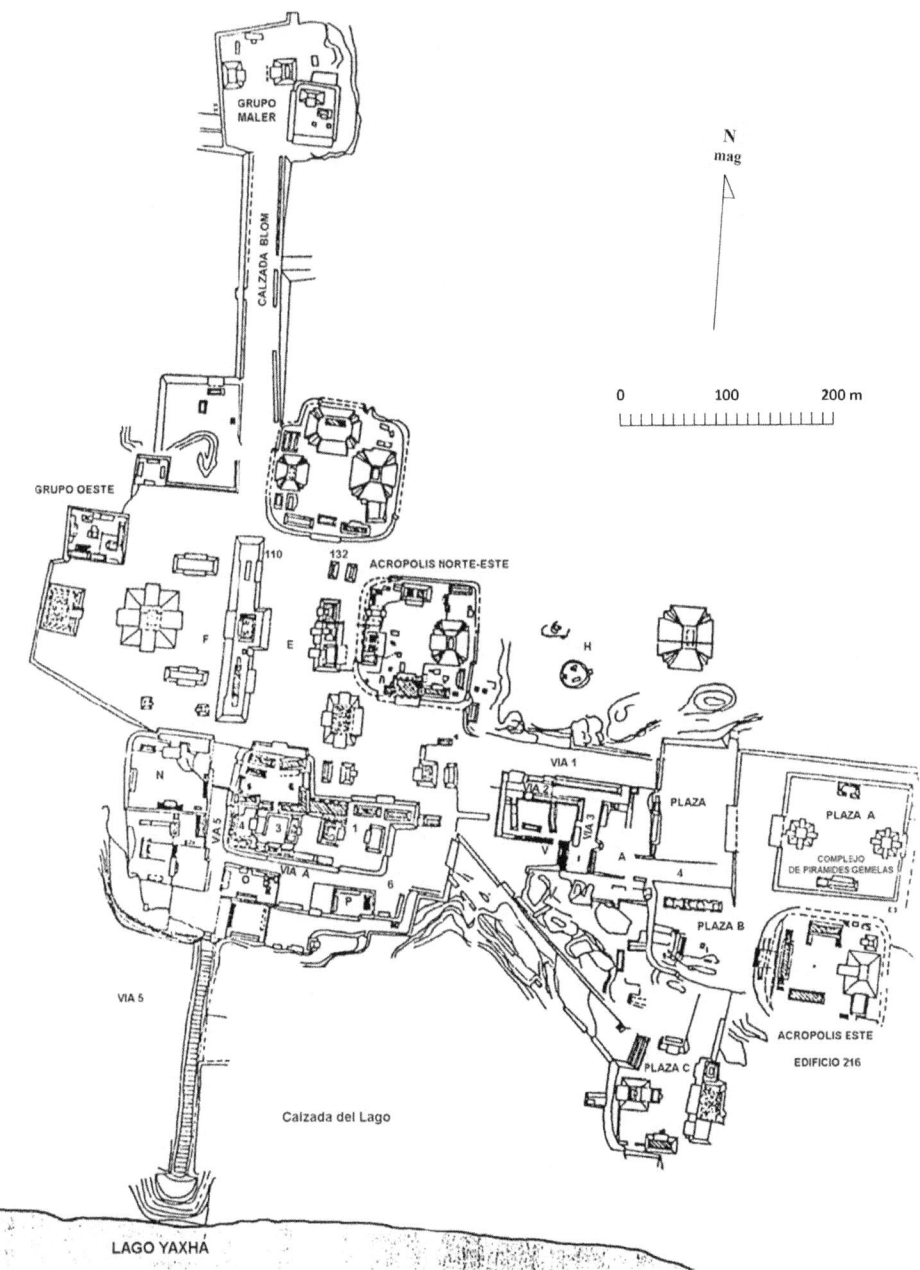

Figure 2.11. Map of Yaxhá, Guatemala, showing a Cenote Style E Group (Plaza F) and a Uaxactún Style E Group (Plaza E). The radial temple in Plaza F is suspected to be a late addition to this E Group complex (map originally published by Hellmuth 1972:149).

Figure 2.12. The founder deities or "triad gods": (*upper*) Palenque; (*middle*) Tikal; (*lower*) Caracol (after Kelley 1976).

Groups suggests a local as opposed to foreign derivation for this form in this part of the Maya world. The Uaxactún Style E Group is far less frequent and more broadly spaced than the Cenote Style E Group (being more consistent with Ruppert's [1940] original spacing of 21 km for these complexes) and is presumably associated to some extent with the differences in Maya polity size and growth between the Late Preclassic and Early Classic periods—and perhaps also with the changing size and composition of the community directly participating in the temporal rituals associated with these buildings.

The emphasis on temporal ritual for the ancient Maya can be seen in several ways within the archaeological record. Stone stelae often mark the ceremonies carried out on 20-year K'atun periods and the caches associated with them reflect Maya cosmological principles related to the Nine Lords of the Night (for example, Coe in Moholy-Nagy and Coe 2008). At Caracol, there was an emphasis on erecting Giant Ahau altars every Katun (Maya 20-year period) (Beetz and Satterthwaite 1981) and "face" caches were also used to mark Katun rituals that were carried out in that site's residential groups (Chase and Chase 2013). At Tikal during the Late Classic period, complete architectural assemblages known as Twin Temple complexes were erected to accompany the stelae erected for the K'atun (Jones 1969). Two of these Twin Temple complexes are known from outside Tikal at the sites of Yaxhá and Ixlú (Rice 2004). Yaxhá presents multiple examples of E Groups (Figure 2.11) and has the longest known eastern platform at 172 m in length

(Chase 1983:1301). Its constructions likely represent three sequent Bak'tun cycles: a Cenote Style E Group constructed for the 8th cycle; a Uaxactún Style E Group immediately east of the early one constructed for the 9th cycle; and a radial pyramid intruded into the original E Group plaza, probably with the onset of the 10th cycle. Other E Groups were modified for the 10th cycle, including the one at Ucanal that had a circular structure placed atop the central building of the eastern platform (Escobedo 2008; Laporte and Mejia 2002). As more extensive archaeological research is undertaken on these complexes, the full temporal complexities of ritual associated with E Groups will be better defined.

Whatever the outcome of the continued debate about their cosmological significance, it is clear that E Groups were key elements in the development of early Maya sites. We have previously proposed that E Groups represented the founding public architecture for sites—something confirmed in the archaeology at sites like Ceibal (Inomata et al. 2013; Chapter 7 in this volume)—and that the three eastern structures may have been associated with the founding deities that are known in the epigraphy of a series of sites (Figure 2.12; see also Chase and Chase 2006b). Palenque, Tikal, Naranjo, Toniná, and Caracol all have records in their hieroglyphic texts of three deities that were important in the mythic foundings of their respective sites (Kelley 1976; Stuart 2005). Because of the detail contained in the texts, the best-known founder deities are those of Palenque (Lounsbury 1985; Schele and Miller 1986; Stuart 2005). Although these founder deities varied by site, they were clearly key in the establishment of any Maya cosmological order and were in our view most likely present at all major centers. The E Groups were also of primary importance in the establishment of a Maya worldview at their respective sites, and ritual deposits associated with these complexes must have represented this cosmological order (see Chapters 6 and 10 in this volume for discussions of architectural decoration and cosmology). At Caracol, the cosmological representation of world order is seen in the placement of objects within the caches associated with the central building of the eastern platform that emphasize layering and directionality (D. Chase and A. Chase 1998). The deposition of three skull caches in each of the eastern buildings in the Uaxactún E Group, possibly in association with the ninth Bak'tun, may have been similarly charged and represented the personalization of the three deity founders in their respective abodes. This is quite possible, as we know that the Maya prepared some of their dead to represent deities. At Caracol, a Protoclassic burial dating to 150 CE was dressed as Ix Chel (Rich Brown 2003) and two Late Classic individuals placed in a Central Acropolis tomb may have represented God K (Chase and Chase 2011). Thus, among any other meanings ascribed to E Group complexes, we would see them as being the physical representation of deep mythical history for any given community.

Finally, the distribution of these E Groups is also reflective of communication and trade. They represent the crystallization of Maya civilization in the Southern Lowlands. While aspects of the architectural form may have antecedents elsewhere in Mesoamerica, it was translated into something that was characteristically Maya; the distribution of E Groups coincides with the core developmental area for Maya civilization. These groups are indicative of a shared culture and shared trade networks. These trade networks minimally go back into the Middle Preclassic period, and it is probably not a coincidence that some of the earliest-known Maya architectural and ceramic expressions occur along the southeastern transpeninsular trade route that extended from Ceibal on the Río Pasión (Inomata et al. 2013) to Cahal Pech and Blackman Eddy on the Belize River (Awe 1992; Garber et al. 2004; Sullivan and Awe 2013). With further excavation, it is likely that similar early occupation will be found throughout the southeastern Petén. The concentration of E Groups in this area likely represents the remnant markers of some of the earliest known Maya. These Maya first occupied the riverine areas of the southeastern Petén and then spread into the drier Southern Lowlands and Vaca Plateau.

Conclusion

The establishment of E Group architectural complexes was clearly foundational and fundamental for the ancient Maya. The distribution of these architectural complexes occurs within the same area that we currently recognize as housing the heartland of Classic Maya civilization in the Southern Lowlands. Thus, E Groups represent the first recognized public architecture of lowland Maya civilization. As such, a consideration of E Groups directly raises questions about the identification and causes of complexity (see Chapters 7 and 8 in this volume). In the example of the Southern Lowland Maya, it would appear that the existence of complex social organization may be recognized through their public architecture and that this architecture was oriented to serve community ritual. The streamlined distribution of E Groups during the Early Classic period correlates with polity growth and increased sociopolitical complexity. Thus, Maya belief systems and religion would have formed the driver for the initial coagulation of Maya societies (see Chapter 16 in this volume). Based on the regularities in form that occurred among early E Group complexes, the underlying belief system was widely shared, deeply held, and persisted for almost 1,400 years.

The development of a subsequent secular order, represented in Maya dynasties as portrayed on their stone monuments, was purposefully located in and conflated with the E Groups. The secular orders, however, neither fully replaced nor destroyed the E Group architectural complexes. Rather, even though the dynastic orders focused on building acropolises and palace compounds, they continued to use the E Groups as ritual locales associated with important long-term Maya temporal cycles and shifts to legitimate their rule. In many instances, as at Caracol and Cenote, the central buildings of E Groups were constructed and then placed in continuous use for 600 to 800 years with only minor changes (that themselves were correlated with broader temporal cycles), indicating that such constructions were presumably imbued with deep religious meaning.

While E Groups have a long history of recognition within Maya studies, it is only comparatively recently that we have recognized the full role that they played in the rise of Maya civilization. These architectural complexes formed the core of early Maya communities, and many continued to be ritually utilized for well over a thousand years. While Belize and the southeastern Petén have always been seen as largely overshadowed by events in the northern Petén, it is clear that early Maya civilization was centered in this region and that many of the central tenets of Maya religion were fully developed here. E Groups serve as a proxy for understanding the spread and nature of the religious foundations that underlay Classic period (CE 250–900) Maya societies of the Southern Lowlands and the long-term changes that took place.

Acknowledgments

This work builds on a long-standing interest in Maya E Groups that started with archaeological work at the site of Cenote, Guatemala, and was later expanded through extensive archaeological work in the E Group at Caracol, Belize. Some of the detailed archaeological discussions related to E Groups are directly derived from the unpublished Ph.D. dissertation of Arlen F. Chase (1983). Sincere appreciation is extended to the Santa Fe Institute for providing funding and support for two sequent sessions that involved over a dozen individuals and permitted an intensive exploration of the meanings that the E Group architectural complexes held for the ancient Maya.

Notes

1. The Uaxactún Style variant has been confused with a triadic eastern building that occurs in western Belize. The triadic eastern buildings in western Belize, such as those that occur at Cahal Pech (Awe 2013:34) and Pacbitún (Healy et al. 2007:19), differ from eastern E Group platforms in that they are agglomerations of three pyramidal structures and not three separate structures set on a platform. They also usually contain a long sequence of important interments that extend into the Late Classic period. Thus, while they may be derivative from E Groups, they are actually quite distinct in both form and archaeological content.

2. The measurements in Table 2.1 are primarily derived from the scaled maps in *Registro de sitios arqueológicos del sureste y centro-oeste de Petén* (Escobedo 2008). In some instances, however, it is clear that the scales are not correct. Where possible, measurements derived from other project publications associated with the *Atlas* project have been used. If anything, the *Atlas* measurements are smaller than they should be. For instance, measuring the map for Ixkún in the *Atlas* (Escobedo 2008:188) yields a measurement of 32 m for the eastern platform. The detailed publications on Ixkún, however, make it clear that this platform is actually 76 m in length (Laporte and Mejía 2005a:42).

References Cited

Aimers, James J., and Prudence M. Rice
2006   Astronomy, Ritual, and the Interpretation of Maya "E Group" Architectural Assemblages. *Ancient Mesoamerica* 17:79–96.

Andrews, George F.
1975   *Maya Cities: Placemaking and Urbanization*. University of Oklahoma Press, Norman.

Aveni, Anthony F., Anne S. Dowd, and Benjamin Vining
2003   Maya Calendar Reform?: Evidence from Orientations of Specialized Architectural Assemblages. *Latin American Antiquity* 14(2):159–178.

Aveni, Anthony F., and Horst Hartung
1989   Uaxactun, Guatemala, Group E and Similar Assemblages: An Archaeoastronomical Reconsideration. In *World Archaeoastronomy*, edited by Anthony F. Aveni, pp. 441–446. Cambridge University Press, Cambridge, United Kingdom.

Awe, Jaime J.
1992   Dawn in the Land between the Rivers: Formative Occupation at Cahal Pech, Belize, and Its Implications for Preclassic Development in the Maya Lowlands. Ph.D. dissertation, Institute of Archaeology, University College of London, London.

2013   Journey on the Cahal Pech Time Machine: An Archaeological Reconstruction of the Dynastic Sequence at a Belize Valley Maya Polity. *Research Reports in Belizean Archaeology* 10:33–50.

Beetz, Carl P., and Linton Satterthwaite
1981 *The Monuments and Inscriptions of Caracol, Belize*. Monograph 45. University Museum, University of Pennsylvania, Philadelphia.

Chase, Arlen F.
1983 *A Contextual Consideration of the Tayasal-Paxcaman Zone, El Peten, Guatemala*. Ph.D. dissertation, Anthropology, University of Pennsylvania, Philadelphia. University Microfilms/ProQuest, Ann Arbor.
1985 Archaeology in the Maya Heartland: The Tayasal-Paxcaman Zone, Lake Peten, Guatemala. *Archaeology* 38(1):32–39.

Chase, Arlen F., and Diane Z. Chase
1987 *Investigations at the Classic Maya City of Caracol, Belize: 1985–1987*. Monograph 3. Pre-Columbian Art Research Institute, San Francisco.
1994 Details in the Archaeology of Caracol, Belize: An Introduction. In *Studies in the Archaeology of Caracol, Belize*, edited by Diane Z. Chase and Arlen F. Chase, pp. 1–11. Monograph 7. Pre-Columbian Art Research Institute, San Francisco.
1995 External Impetus, Internal Synthesis, and Standardization: E Group Assemblages and the Crystallization of Classic Maya Society in the Southern Lowlands. *Acta Mesoamericana* 8:87–101 (special issue edited by Nikolai Grube entitled *The Emergence of Lowland Maya Civilization: The Transition from the Preclassic to Early Classic*).
1996 More Than Kin and King: Centralized Political Organization among the Ancient Maya. *Current Anthropology* 37(5):803–810.
1998 Scale and Intensity in Classic Period Maya Agriculture: Terracing and Settlement at the "Garden City" of Caracol, Belize. *Culture and Agriculture* 20(2):60–77.
2005 The Early Classic Period at Caracol, Belize: Transitions, Complexity, and Methodological Issues in Maya Archaeology. *Research Reports in Belizean Archaeology* 2:17–38.
2006a Before the Boom: Caracol's Preclassic Era. *Research Reports in Belizean Archaeology* 3:41–67.
2006b En medio de la nada, en el centro del universo: Perspectivas sobre el desarrollo de las ciudades mayas. In *Nuevas ciudades, nuevas patrias: Fundación y relocalización de ciudades en Mesoamérica y el Mediterraneo antiguo*, edited by María Josefa Iglesias Ponce de León, Rogelio Valencia Rivera, and Andrés Ciudad Ruiz, pp. 39–64. SEEM, Madrid.
2012 Belize Red Ceramics and Their Implications for Trade and Exchange in the Eastern Maya Lowlands. *Research Reports in Belizean Archaeology* 9:3–14.
2013 Temporal Cycles in the Archaeology of Maya Residential Groups from Caracol, Belize. *Research Reports in Belizean Archaeology* 10:13–23.

Chase, Arlen F., Diane Z. Chase, John F. Weishampel, Jason B. Drake, Ramesh L. Shrestha, K. Clint Slatton, Jaime J. Awe, and William E. Carter
2011 Airborne LiDAR, Archaeology, and the Ancient Maya Landscape at Caracol, Belize. *Journal of Archaeological Science* 38:387–398.

Chase, Diane Z., and Arlen F. Chase
1998   The Architectural Context of Caches, Burials, and Other Ritual Activities for the Classic Period Maya (as Reflected at Caracol, Belize). In *Function and Meaning in Classic Maya Architecture*, edited by Stephen D. Houston, pp. 299–332. Dumbarton Oaks, Washington, D.C.
2000   Inferences about Abandonment: Maya Household Archaeology at Caracol, Belize. *Mayab* 13:67–77.
2011   Ghosts amid the Ruins: Analyzing Relationships between the Living and the Dead among the Ancient Maya at Caracol, Belize. In *Living with the Dead: Mortuary Ritual in Mesoamerica*, edited by James L. Fitzsimmons and Izumi Shimada, pp. 78–101. University of Arizona Press, Tucson.

Escobedo, Héctor (editor)
2008   *Registro de sitios arqueológicos del sureste y centro-oeste de Petén*. Monografías *Atlas Arqueológico de Guatemala*. Dirección General del Patrimonio Cultural y Natural, Guatemala City.

Fialko, Vilma
1988   Mundo Perdido, Tikal: Un ejemplo de complejos de conmenoración astronómica. *Mayab* 4:13–21.

Garber, James F., Kathryn Brown, Jaime J. Awe, and Christopher Hartman
2004   Middle Formative Prehistory of the Central Belize Valley: An Examination of Architecture, Material Culture, and Sociopolitical Change at Blackman Eddy. In *The Ancient Maya of the Belize Valley: Half a Century of Archaeological Research*, edited by James F. Garber, pp. 25–47. University Press of Florida, Gainesville.

Grube, Nikolai
1994   Epigraphic Research at Caracol, Belize. In *Studies in the Archaeology of Caracol, Belize*, edited by Diane Z. Chase and Arlen F. Chase, pp. 83–122. Monograph 7. Pre-Columbian Art Research Institute, San Francisco.

Hammond, Norman
1974   The Distribution of Late Classic Maya Major Ceremonial Centres in the Central Area. In *Mesoamerican Archaeology: New Approaches*, edited by Norman Hammond, pp. 313–334. University of Texas Press, Austin.
1975   Maya Settlement Hierarchy in Northern Belize. *Contributions of the University of California Archaeological Research Facility* 27:40–55.

Hansen, Richard D.
1992   The Archaeology of Ideology: A Study of Maya Preclassic Architectural Sculpture at Nakbe, Petén, Guatemala. Ph.D. dissertation, University of California, Los Angeles.

Harrison, Peter D., and Billie Lee Turner II
1978   *Pre-Hispanic Maya Agriculture*. University of New Mexico Press, Albuquerque.

Healy, Paul F., Christophe Helmke, Jaime J. Awe, and Kay S. Sunahara
2007   Survey, Settlement, and Population History at the Ancient Maya Site of Pacbitun, Belize. *Journal of Field Archaeology* 32:17–39.

Hellmuth, Nicholas M.
1972   Excavations Begin at Maya Site in Guatemala. *Archaeology* 25:148–149.

Inomata, Takeshi, Daniela Triadan, Kazuo Aoyama, Victor Castillo, and Hitoshi Yonenobu
2013   Early Ceremonial Constructions at Ceibal, Guatemala, and the Origins of Lowland Maya Civilization. *Science* 340:467–471.

Jones, Christopher
1969   The Twin-Pyramid Group Pattern: A Classic Maya Architectural Assemblage. Ph.D. dissertation, Anthropology, University of Pennsylvania, Philadelphia.

Kelley, David H.
1976   *Deciphering the Maya Script*. University of Texas Press, Austin.

Kidder, Alfred V.
1950   Introduction. In *Uaxactun, Guatemala: Excavations of 1931–1937*. Publication 588, edited by A. L. Smith, pp. 1–12. Carnegie Institution of Washington, Washington, D.C.

Kovic, Milan
2011   Hiatus en el fin de Preclásico y retorno de los reyes, Uaxactún, Guatemala. *Contributions to New World Archaeology* 3:49–63.

Laporte, Juan Pedro
1994   *Ixtontón, Dolores, Petén: Entidad política del noroeste de las montañas mayas. Atlas Arqueológico de Guatemala No. 2*, pp. 3–142. Dirección General del Patrimonio Cultural y Natural, Guatemala City.

Laporte, Juan Pedro, Jesús Adánez, and Héctor H. Mejía
2008   Entre Cayucos y Caites: Una ruta de interacción entre el Mar Caribe y el Río Pasión. In *XXI Simposio de Arqueologia en Guatemala, 2007*, pp. 744–769. Museo Nacional de Arqueología y Etnología, Guatemala City.

Laporte, Juan Pedro, and Vilma Fialko
1995   Un reencuentro con Mundo Perdido, Tikal, Guatemala. *Ancient Mesoamerica* 6:41–94.
2007   *La secuencia cerámica del sureste de Petén: Tipos, cifras, localidades, y la historia del asentamiento*. Monografía 3. *Atlas Arqueológico de Guatemala*. Dirección General del Patrimonio Cultural y Natural, Guatemala City.

Laporte, Juan Pedro, and Héctor E. Mejía
2000   *Registro de sitios arqueológicos del sureste de Petén*. Report 14. *Atlas Arqueológico de Guatemala*. Dirección General del Patrimonio Cultural y Natural, Guatemala City.
2002   Ucanal: Una ciudad del río Mopán en Petén, Guatemala. *U Tz'ib* 1(2):1–71.
2005a *Ixkún, Petén, Guatemala: Exploraciones en una ciudad del alto Mopán, 1985–2005. Atlas Arqueológico de Guatemala*. Dirección General del Patrimonio Cultural y Natural, Guatemala City.
2005b *La organización territorial y política en el mundo maya Clásico: El caso del sureste y centro-oeste de Petén, Guatemala*. Instituto de Investigaciones Históricas, Antropológicas y Arqueológicas, Escuela de Historia, USAC, Guatemala City.
2007   *Ix Ek': Entidad política del parte Aguas de los Ríos Mopán, San Juan y Poxte, 1990–1997*. Monografía 7. *Atlas Arqueológico de Guatemala*. Dirección General del Patrimonio Cultural y Natural, Guatemala City.

Laporte, Juan Pedro, Rolando Torres, Bernard Hermes, Estela Pinto, Renaldo Acevedo, and Rosa María Flores
1988   *En Reporte 1: Proyecto Sureste de Petén, Segunda temporada, noviembre 1987–julio 1988*. Dirección General del Patrimonio Cultural y Natural, Guatemala City.

Lomitola, Lisa
2012   Ritual Use of the Human Form: A Contextual Analysis of "Charlie Chaplin" Figures in the Maya Lowlands. M.A. thesis, Anthropology, University of Central Florida, Orlando.

Lounsbury, Floyd G.
1985   The Identities of the Mythological Figures in the Cross Group Inscriptions of Palenque. In *Fourth Palenque Round Table, 1980*, edited by Merle Greene Robertson and Elizabeth P. Benson, pp. 45–58. Pre-Columbian Art Research Institute, San Francisco.

Lowe, Gareth W.
1977   The Mixe-Zoque as Competing Neighbors of the Early Lowland Maya. In *The Origins of Maya Civilization*, edited by R.E.W. Adams, pp. 197–248. University of New Mexico Press, Albuquerque.

Moholy-Nagy, Hattula, and William R. Coe
2008   *The Artifacts of Tikal—Ornamental and Ceremonial Artifacts and Unworked Material: Tikal Report 27A*. Monograph 127. University Museum, University of Pennsylvania, Philadelphia.

Morley, Sylvanus G.
1925   The Earliest Mayan Dates. *Compte-Rendu of the 21st ICA* 2:655–667.

Pugh, Timothy W., José Rómulo Sánchez, and Yuko Shiratori
2012   Contact and Missionization at Tayasal, Petén, Guatemala. *Journal of Field Archaeology* 37:3–19.

Rathje, William L.
1973   Trade Models and Archaeological Problems: The Classic Maya and Their E-Group Complex. *XL Congresso Internazionale Degli Americanisti* (Rome) 4:223–235.

Rathje, William L., David A. Gregory, and Fredrick M. Wiseman
1978   Trade Models and Archaeological Problems: Classic Maya Examples. In *Mesoamerican Communication Routes and Culture Contacts*, edited by Thomas A. Lee Jr. and Carlos Navarrete, pp. 147–175. Papers of the New World Archaeological Foundation 40. Brigham Young University, Provo, Utah.

Rice, Prudence
2004   *Maya Political Science: Time, Astronomy, and the Cosmos*. University of Texas Press, Austin.

Rich Brown, Shayna
2003   An Analysis of a Female Protoclassic Costume from the Site of Caracol, Belize. M.A. thesis, Maya Studies, University of Central Florida, Orlando.

Ricketson, Oliver, Jr.
1928   Astronomical Observatories in the Maya Area. *Geographical Review* 8:215–225.

Ricketson, Oliver, Jr., and Edith B. Ricketson
1937   *Uaxactun, Guatemala, Group E, 1926–1931*. Publication No. 477. Carnegie Institution of Washington, Washington, D.C.

Ruppert, Karl J.
1940   A Special Assemblage of Maya Structures. In *The Maya and Their Neighbors: Essays on Middle American Anthropology and Archaeology*, edited by Clarence L. Hay, Ralph L. Linton, Samuel K. Lothrop, Harry L. Shapiro, and George C. Vaillant, pp. 222–231. Dover Publications, New York.

Ruppert, Karl J., and John H. Denison
1943   *Archaeological Reconnaissance in Campeche, Quintana Roo, and Peten*. Publication 543. Carnegie Institution of Washington, Washington, D.C.

Sanders, William T.
1979   The Jolly Green Giant in Tenth Century Yucatan or Fact and Fancy in Classic Maya Agriculture. *Reviews in Anthropology* 6:493–506.

Schele, Linda, and Mary Ellen Miller
1986   *The Blood of Kings: Dynasty and Ritual in Maya Art*. Kimbell Art Museum, Fort Worth, Texas.

Smith, A. Ledyard
1950   *Uaxactun, Guatemala: Excavations of 1931–1937*. Publication 588. Carnegie Institution of Washington, Washington, D.C.

Stuart, David
2005   *The Inscriptions from Temple XIX at Palenque: A Commentary*. Pre-Columbian Art Research Institute, San Francisco.

Sullivan, Lauren A., and Jaime J. Awe
2013   Establishing the Cunil Ceramic Complex at Cahal Pech, Belize. In *Ancient Maya Pottery: Classification, Analysis, and Interpretation*, edited by James J. Aimers, pp. 107–120. University Press of Florida, Gainesville.

Thompson, J. Eric S.
1931   *Archaeological Investigations in the Southern Cayo District, British Honduras*. Publication 301, Anthropological Series Vol. 17(3). Field Museum of Natural History, Chicago.

11

The Astronomy and Cosmology of E Groups

3

E Groups

Astronomy, Alignments, and Maya Cosmology

ANTHONY F. AVENI AND ANNE S. DOWD

"By far the most important discovery was made in Group E, namely, what appears to be an observatory for studying the sun."

Frans Blom 1924:218

In this chapter we trace the historical roots of the scholarship regarding the relationship between Group E–type structures and the Maya solar calendar, leading to the hypothesis that E Group alignments were involved in developing a seasonal calendar motivated by agricultural necessity. It now seems clear than an orientation calendar based on positions of sunrise on the equinoxes and solstices existed in the built environment, at least at Uaxactún, as early as the Terminal Preclassic–Early Classic transition (ca. 278 CE). Though this is difficult to pin down chronologically, statistical evidence from alignment studies suggests that the seasonal basis of the calendar was altered, possibly as a result of Teotihuacán influence (ca. Tzakol Phase: 350–550 CE) to fit with sunrise dates on the first of its two annual overhead (zenith) passages and specifically to mark the 20-day months leading up to that event. This time of year, about May 10 in the Christian calendar, would have offered an opportunity to conduct rituals in anticipation of the rainy season and subsequent crop planting. Finally, we briefly summarize the religious and sociopolitical uses to which such astronomical data might have been put.

Origin of the Group E Astronomical Connection

The intention of Frans Blom in exploring astronomical alignments at Uaxactún during the eighth Carnegie expedition in the Petén after its discovery one hundred years ago (in 1916) had much to do with the intense attention given the calendrical data explored there in the 1920s by Sylvanus Morley

(1937–1938; Lister and Lister 1970), especially the early Bak'tun 8 date recorded on Stela 9, which gave rise to the name meaning "eight stone." Blom (1924) reasoned that if early Maya dynasts were so deeply concerned about keeping precise time, one way to manage it might have consisted in registering the course of celestial events in the architecture. Blom's declaration (1924:218), quoted in our epigraph, initiated the continued association between Group E, Uaxactún, and Maya astronomy.

In his summary of astronomical alignment studies at the Caracol of Chichén Itzá begun in 1925 and those at Group E, Oliver Ricketson (1928a:218) remarks:

> How long the city [Uaxactún] was settled before the Maya carved their dates on stone no one has ventured to guess, much less how long a period must have elapsed before their extraordinary calendric system was finally developed. This system breaks upon our view in full flower, the characters already conventionalized and carved upon stone.

Ricketson (1928a:218) then continues: "We now have at least two bits of evidence as to how the Maya went about making their astronomic observations." The second "bit" refers to the Caracol of Chichén Itzá.

In another work, Ricketson (1928b:433) adds:

> As is well known, their perfection of an accurate and complicated calendric system is an achievement unique among the indigenous races of America. The origin of this system is still shrouded in conjecture, but in two instances it has been found that the Maya erected buildings or markers, the construction and location of which cannot be attributed to any purpose other than the intentional recording of accurate astronomic data. The formulations for the study of these data were first laid by the suggestion of Dr. S. G. Morley that the Department of Terrestrial Magnetism of the Carnegie Institution of Washington cooperate with the Middle American Research expeditions in locating the exact geographic position of certain ruins in the Peten.

Blom (1924) and later Ricketson (1928a, 1928b) were initially attracted by both the N–S axiality of the grouping and the possibility that the three eastern mounds could have marked the extremes (solstices) and midpoint (equinoxes) of the rising sun's course along the horizon throughout the year as viewed from somewhere on Structure E-VII (Figure 3.1). Using a

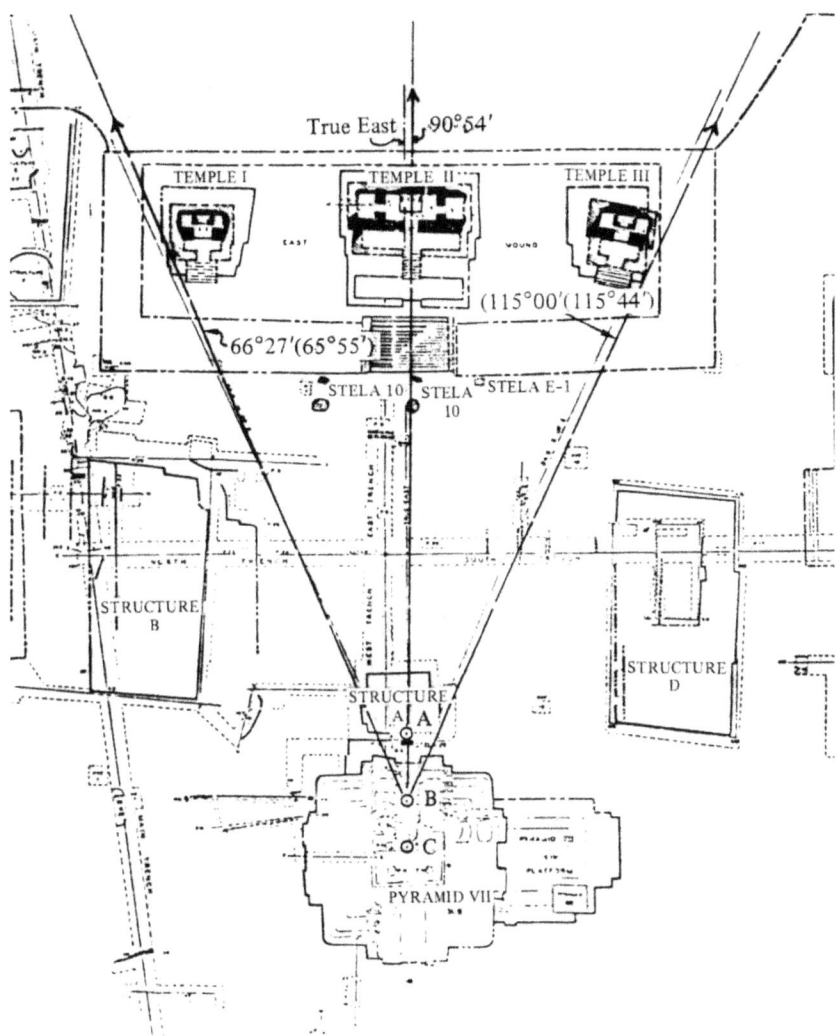

Figure 3.1. Plan of Group E, Uaxactún (after Ricketson and Ricketson 1937:Figure 197), with authors' measurements added. From Aveni and Hartung (1989:Figure 35.2).

Brunton compass, Blom (1924) made several trial measurements from various points on that building (Figure 3.2). After the excavations were complete, measurements were made by his successors with a theodolite. In both cases, the magnetic readings were corrected to true north with the use of tables supplied by the Carnegie Institute of Washington's Department of Terrestrial Magnetism.

In his pre-excavation plan, Blom (1924:218) proposed that the sun had been viewed rising over the eastern mounds, EI–EIII, from Stela 20, not a

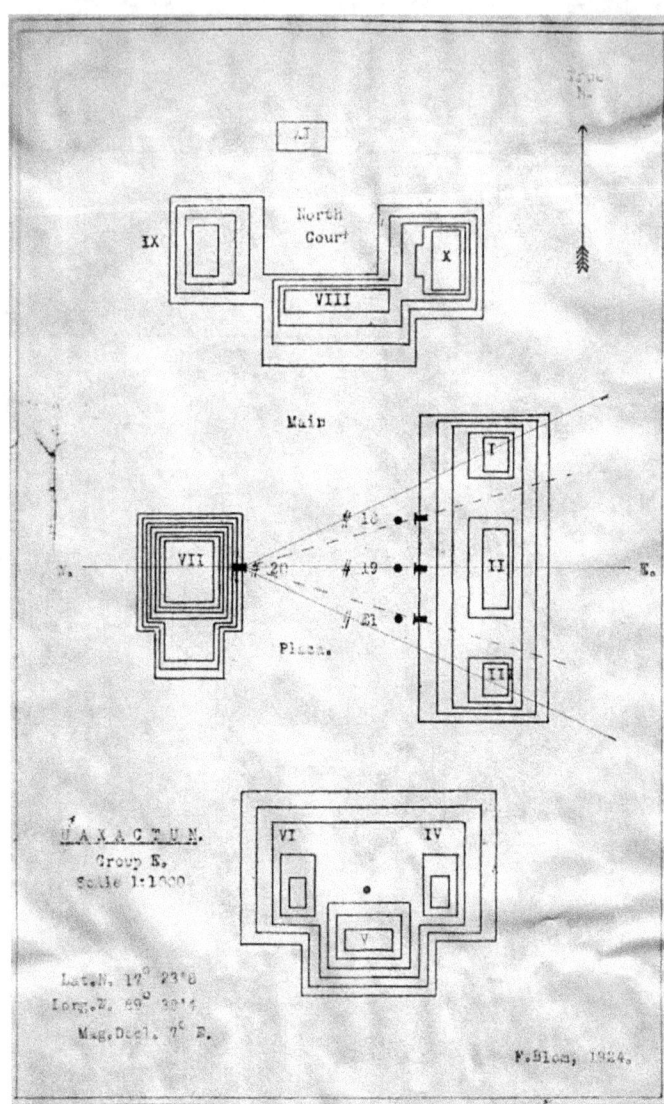

Figure 3.2. Uaxactún Group E plan (illustration by Frans Blom [1924:58]). From Dowd and Milbrath (2015:Figure 3.2). Courtesy of the Peabody Museum of Archaeology and Ethnology, Harvard University.

very convincing location as we see it now. Ricketson (1928a:223), who excavated Group E in 1926–1931, rectified this scheme and presented another plan. He proposed three possible points of observation: (1) in front of Stela 20 (as had Blom), (2) in the middle of the stairway ("fifteen feet above the plaza level"); and (3) at the upper end of the stairway (Ricketson, 1928a:218, Figure 3).

Some of Ricketson's (1928a) selected reference points on E-I and III and on E-VII-Sub remain unconvincing on architectural grounds. Why, for example, would someone observe from the middle of a stairway to the extreme edges of the northern and southern buildings? Evidently, the Ricketsons (1937:134, 135) were well aware of the basic stages of construction of Group E; for example, they tell us that Floor III "is the primary construction" (while E-VII-Sub stands on Floor II), with the East Platform "surely surmounted by primary Temple E-II and possibly by Temples E-I and E-III, though the evidence is negative for these latter two." Both the Ricketsons (1937) and Blom (1924) seem to have become preoccupied with making the most precise fit of solar orientations to the alignments regardless of whether the alignments made much sense architecturally or not.

How Group E Uaxactún Became the Archetype of the Maya Astronomical Observatory

Karl Ruppert (1934) first reported widespread repetition of the Group E arrangement at sites centered on Uaxactún. In a later publication, Ruppert (1940:230) listed thirteen sites where this grouping clearly occurred and concluded that in no case was the "great rigidity to orientation" adhered to as at Uaxactún, likely because whatever ceremony or ritual might have developed with the observations took precedence over the observatory functions.

Having studied and reinterpreted the Chichén Caracol alignments, Horst Hartung and Aveni became interested in Uaxactún, especially when we became aware that in no cases was a precise orientation measure made in the field. In an earlier work Aveni (1975) had demonstrated the wide variation among site orientations acquired via magnetic compass, as opposed to more accurate measurements based on astronomical references, particularly via timed solar fixes, which rendered one capable of extracting orientation data on original walls to at least the accuracy of the capability of Maya builders, about ½ degree.

Other features of Uaxactún architecture that might have been employed in relation to astronomy also attracted our attention, among them three Teotihuacán-type pecked cross-circles, which had been reported at the site (Smith 1950:21–22, Figures 15a, 60–62; also Aveni 2000). Edwin Shook's 1974 restoration of E-VII provided an ideal opportunity to visit the site in 1978 and make our own alignment measurements. Our results (Aveni and Hartung 1989) indicated that a viewer situated at the middle of the second-stage platform of E-VII-Sub (Figure 3.1, Point B) would have seen the sun rise over Structure E-II on the equinoxes and off the northernmost corner of E-I and the southernmost corner of E-III on the June and December solstices, respectively. Moreover, we found the bases of these buildings to be exactly level with these lines of sight as well as with the distant horizon. An observer stationed on the third-stage (top) platform of E-VII Sub would have made slightly less precise observations. Our analysis of the chronology of the group suggested that the East Mound was originally built to the requisite width to encapsulate the annual solar course along the eastern horizon.

We concluded that, at least in its earliest form during the Terminal Preclassic–Early Classic transition period (ca. 278 CE), Uaxactún Group E could have been used to mark significant points in the early Maya annual calendar. Later, when E-VII-Sub was extended and built over, the complex ceased to function astronomically, as the line of sight to the eastern structures from E-VII would have dropped some nine degrees below the horizon (Aveni and Hartung 1989:451). These chronological results were corroborated by Arlen Chase's (1983:1240) reexamination of the archaeological data, which show that E-VII materials postdate those recovered from EI–EIII.

In our 1989 report (Aveni and Hartung 1989:Table 35:3), we extended the list of E Group complexes to 27. Based on the data available at that time, which consisted of fieldwork at a single site, together with analysis of a number of site maps of varying reliability, we tentatively concluded that none of these appeared to have functioned as a precise observatory that registered solstice extremes and equinoxes. We adopted throughout a working definition of the E Group complex based on three criteria: (1) a radial pyramid on the west side of an open plaza, often containing a small altar; (2) a range structure topped by three or more temples on the east; and (3) an imaginary axis connecting the midpoint of the two, which usually appears to lie close to the west–east direction.

In a later study (Aveni et al. 2003) we reported on accurately measured alignments in E Group complexes at twelve additional sites. We also obtained access to accurate site maps secured with total station equipment, bringing the total site sample to thirty and the set of Group E–type architectural complexes to thirty-one, because Yaxhá has two examples. Figure 3.3 plots the distribution of the alignment data with respect to corresponding dates of the seasonal year marked by sunrise. The backsights for each of these alignments are taken to be the top of the stairway of the western structure. The foresights are the northern corners of the structure(s) lying to the north, the southern corners of those lying to the south of the central

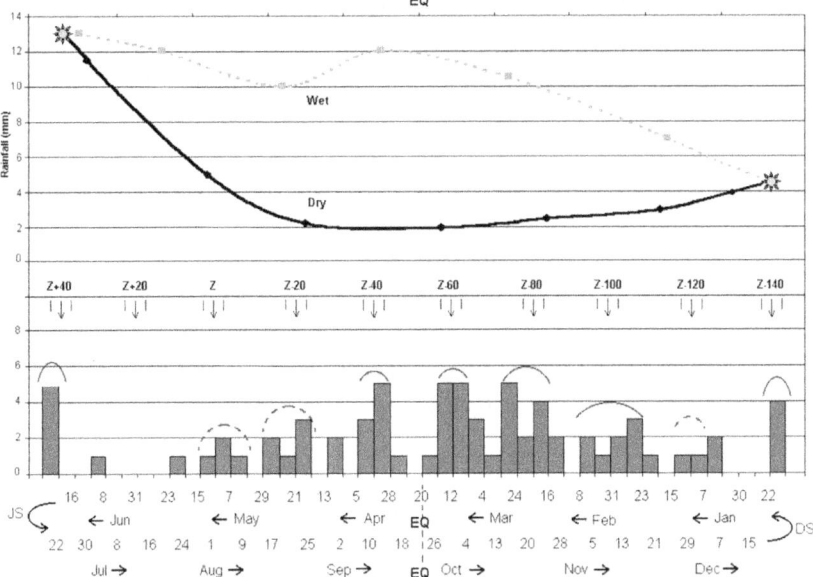

Figure 3.3. (*Top*) seasonal distribution of rainfall in mid-Petén latitudes (World Weather Disc 1988), drawing by Diane Janney; (*bottom*) seasonal distribution of E Group–type alignments, with intervals in days relative to solar zenith passage added. From Aveni et al. (2003:Figure 2).

structure, and the center of the central structure on the eastern side of the plaza. We demonstrated that the alignments are not an artifact of general site orientation.

Concentrations around June 21 and December 21 in Figure 3.3 indicate that the solar horizon extremes were significant with respect to the orientation of E Group complexes taken as a class. In addition, at least three other concentrations appeared in the histogram that had not been disclosed in previous studies. These are centered roughly on the date pairs February 19/October 22, March 11/October 2, and March 31/September 12. These dates correspond to intervals that are whole multiples (four, three, and two, respectively) of 20 days reckoned from the times of the passage of the sun across the zenith (May 10, August 3) in latitude 17½°N, the mean latitude of the sites listed in the table. From an agricultural perspective, the times leading up to the first solar zenith passage (May 10) would have been the most logical points to mark by orientations in specialized groups of buildings where rituals pertaining to the anticipation of the forthcoming crop might have been conducted (Aveni 1991:320). May 10 coincides with preparing the milpa for planting corn by cutting and burning vegetation in the fields.

As the rainfall chart in Figure 3.3 demonstrates, the three aforementioned peaks of the alignment histogram fall precisely in that portion of the year when meteorological conditions would tend to offer the greatest possibility of witnessing sunrises. The gradual onset of the rainy season would have diminished the likelihood of viewing the sun. Although this onset is staggered, depending on the local climatic variation across the geographic distribution of the E Group complexes, cloudy skies would have been the order of the day by the time of solar zenith passage. This would account for the diminution of alignments corresponding to the late April–May upslope in the solid-line portion of the rainfall chart. Though the margin of error in establishing site chronology is substantial, we found the solstice/equinox alignments to favor the Middle Preclassic, 1000–350 BCE, while those related to the zenith generally occurred during the Late Preclassic (LPC) and into the Terminal Preclassic (TPC), 350 BCE–162 CE.

In 1986 we had laid out theoretical arguments and offered supportive evidence from building alignments for an orientation calendar pivoted about the passage of the sun across the zenith and consisting of alignments corresponding to 20- and especially 40-day deviations from that seasonal base date (Aveni and Hartung 1986). Given the autonomous nature of Maya centers of power, we posited that local variants of this form of calendar might have existed. We also pointed out that establishing an empirical solar calendar of this kind would have offered special adaptive advantages owing to peculiar astronomical circumstances pertaining to sun watching in mid-Petén latitudes. Among these is the fact that a whole number of 20-day periods separates the solar zenith passage dates from the solstices as well as from one another; thus, in latitude 17½°N:

$$DS + 7 \times 20 \text{ days} = Z_1,$$
$$Z_1 + 2 \times 20 \text{ days} = JS,$$
$$Z_1 + 4 \times 20 \text{ days} = Z_2.$$

Here DS is the December Solstice, JS is the June Solstice, and Z_1 and Z_2 are the first and second solar zenith passage dates, respectively. These times are among those noted in Figure 3.3. Thus, it would have been both simple and quite natural for the Maya to have gained control of time by taking advantage of celestial symmetries that also brought together the body count of 20 and the zenith, or fifth (up–down) direction, two characteristics of great significance in Maya cosmology.

Were There Local Solar-Based Calendars?

We know that at Uaxactún the Group E form is isolated at the northeasternmost and one of the earliest sections of the site and that it also aligns more closely with the cardinal directions than any of the other complexes at the site (see Aveni and Hartung 1989:Table 35.2). We had demonstrated how astronomically based sight lines, or visual lines, from Group E could be transferred to other building complexes at the site, among them Group A. These "relation lines" (Aveni and Hartung 1989:note 7), while not necessarily implying an act of direct observation, could have been intended to preserve a direction in space held to be significant for purposes related to sacred geography. One example of a relation line might consist in establishing the direction to Mecca for the proper conduct of prayer.

Juan Antonio Valdés and Federico Fahsen (1995) had already demonstrated that Uaxactún's early power center was twice transferred from the locale of Group E and on one occasion, during the Tzakol 2 Phase (300–378 CE), specifically to Group A. As remarked earlier, we had been interested in Group A because of what later would come to be recognized as a Teotihuacán-type pecked cross, an artifact demonstrated to have been connected with both astronomical (solar) orientations and the tallying of calendrical intervals (Aveni 2000; Aveni et al. 1978; Aveni et al. 1982). It is worth noting that a portion of the Ciudadela at Teotihuacán includes an E Group–like set of structures (Laporte and Fialko 1990), though the morphological similarities could be only coincidental. A fuller discussion of the Teotihuacán-Maya calendrical and astronomical connection can be found in Aveni (2000).

In 1978 we measured the orientation of the only extant pecked cross carved in the floor of Structure A-V (Level Ic) (called UAX 1 in the literature, as Smith [1950] had also mentioned, but he provided little information on two other such artifacts) (Figure 3.4). The result, 17½°E of N, is noticeably out of line with the 6½°E of N orientation of the building itself, but it does correspond, within 2°, to the 15°28' E of N skew from cardinal of the Teotihuacán grid orientation. This result seemed surprising at the time because Teotihuacán influence in the Maya area was not generally regarded to be very significant.

Motivated by later evidence establishing a strong Teotihuacán-Maya connection, we reconsidered the Uaxactún alignments and their relation to the pecked cross as well as to the calendar in general (Aveni 2000). Employing the Uaxactún pecked cross as a device for tabulating cylindrical

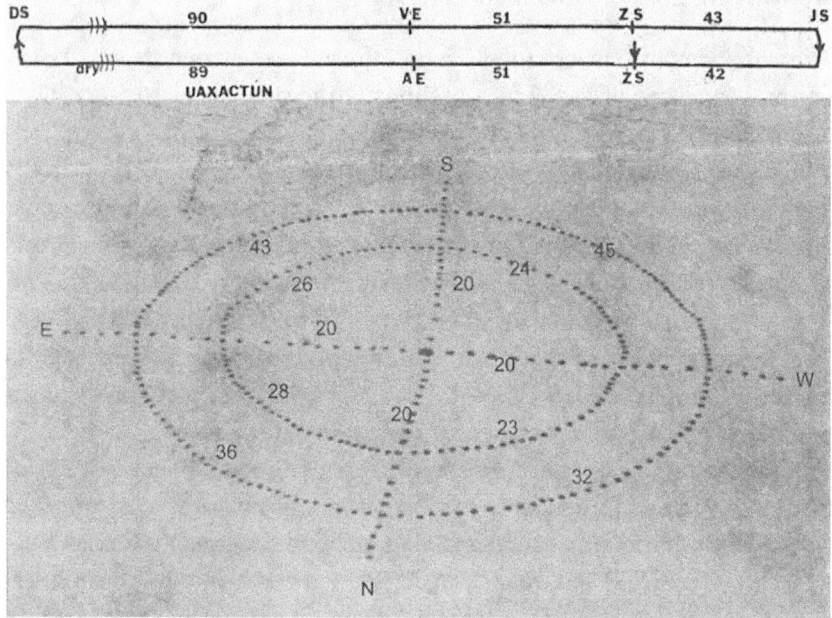

Figure 3.4. Quadripartite pecked cross-circle carved into Temple Court floor (Level Ic) of Structure AV, Uaxactún (after Smith 1950:Figure 15A). The count breakdown along the axes and inner and outer quadrants has been added. From Aveni (2000:Figure 9.2).

intervals, we noted several coincidences in the count of elements that make up the design, especially the asymmetry of their distribution: there are 88 marks on the northern half, as opposed to 68, or 20 less, on the southern half of the outer circle. Each of the axes emanating from the center also has 20 (see Figure 3.4).

Comparing significant intervals that might be reckoned by the sun with the count of elements on various parts of UAX 1, we discovered first that the sum of the inner SE plus SW quadrants (26 + 24), as well as that of the inner NW plus NE quadrants (23 + 28), approximates the number of days between spring equinox and the first of two annual solar zenith passages in the Petén (51 days). Second, the sum of the SE plus SW outer quadrants (43 + 45) equals the observed interval between the autumnal equinox and the December solstice, as well as the interval between the December solstice and the spring equinox (89–90 days), both being components of the solstice-equinox calendar, which we have argued was likely replaced by the 20-day zenith sun-based calendar. Finally, one other set of tallies on the UAX 1 petroglyph signals both the importance of the phenomenon of solar zenith passage as a cylindrical base unit and the Teotihuacán connection: the intervals corresponding to the NW plus NE quadrants of the outer circle (32 + 36) add up to the interval between zenith passages, not at Uaxactún but, rather, at Teotihuacán. These facts about the highly asymmetric arrangement of elements tallied on the UAX 1 feature raise the possibility that the motivation for adopting a new orientation calendar in the Petén may have come from Teotihuacán.

The Uses of Astronomical Knowledge

Having established that many E Group complexes likely served, at least at some time during the course of their development, as devices intended for recognizing solstitially/equinoctially and solar zenith-based time, we can discuss more broadly the ends to which such architecturally based information might have been put. We have long been aware that E Group complexes may have served as social focal points, their open spaces perhaps intended for ritual displays by an emerging theocratic elite (Chase and Chase 1995:100; Dowd et al. 1995:1). Chase (1983:1250) argued that the presence of an E Group complex at a site might be correlated with the onset of widespread organizational principles during the Late Preclassic (350 BCE–162 CE or 350 BCE–0 CE) or Terminal Preclassic (162–278 CE or 0–250 CE). Initially it did not represent a tangential pattern but, rather, provided the central organizational focus for the site. Schemes for mastering time via considerations about the calendar would have constituted one of those organizational principles.

Marvin Cohodas (1980) appears to have been the first to propose a relationship between E Groups and agriculture. As William Rathje (1973) pointed out in his own study of Group E complexes, rigorous scheduling would have lain at the base of any successful market system connecting cities in the Petén core zone. Not only would such seasonal market scheduling have been related to the timekeeping role of E Groups but pilgrimage-fairs, as mentioned by David Freidel (in Sabloff and Andrews 1986:415), could initially have taken place in the plazas themselves, which often provided the largest spaces for congregations of people. At Calakmul, evidence in the form of seventh-century CE murals showing traders with a variety of agricultural products (corn, tobacco) and other goods such as salt and pottery comes from Structure Sub 1-4, dated to 620–700 CE, in the Chiik Nahb complex just to the north of the E Group (Carrasco et al. 2009:19245; Carrasco and Cordeiro 2012:14) (Figures 3.5, 3.6). These depictions suggest

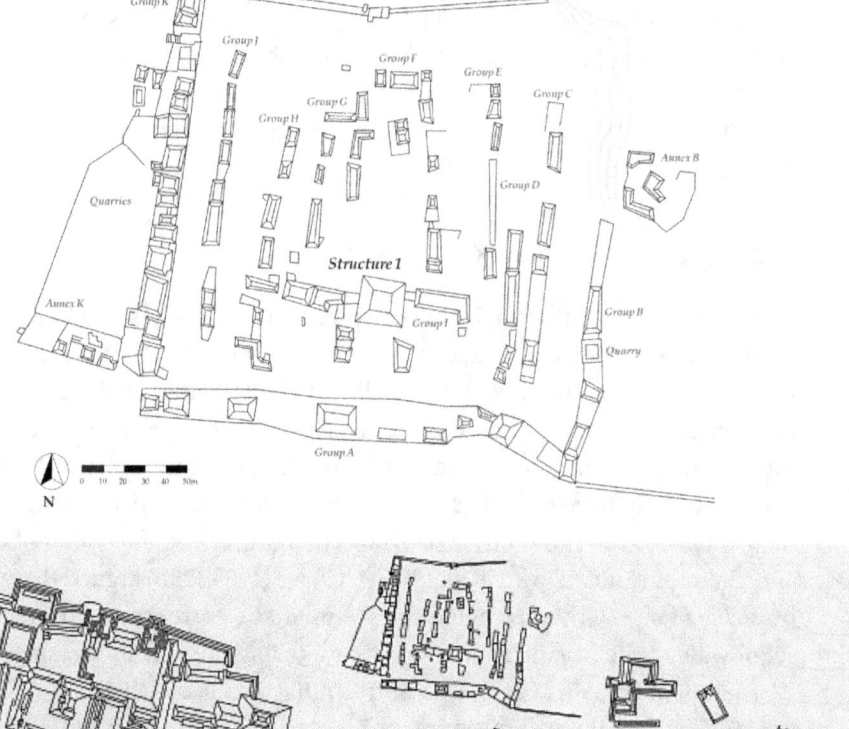

Figure 3.5. (*Top*) detail of Chiik Nahb market complex (after Carrasco and Cordeiro 2012:10); (*bottom*) map of Calakmul showing the Chiik Nahb market complex just north of the main plaza formed by E Group (after Carrasco and Cordeiro 2012:10).

Figure 3.6. Murals showing market scenes on the southeast corner of Structure Sub 1-4 in the Chiik Nahb market complex at Calakmul (after Carrasco et al. 2009). Courtesy of *Proceedings of the National Academy of Sciences*.

that markets may have been located in a complex with easy access to Calakmul's central Group E–type plaza between about 420–820 CE.

But before we can deal further with how E Groups were used by the Maya, we must address the issue of exactly what we mean by an astronomical observatory. In the Western perspective, a Group E solar observatory would consist of architecture intended to view the sun rising along a particular visual line, thus serving as an accurate time marker. James Aimers and Prudence Rice (2006:87) have argued that if E Groups are to be classified as "observatories" in the Western sense they should demonstrate astronomical accuracy; thus, E Groups not correctly "oriented in a functional (i.e., astronomically accurate) sense" may have been constructed and used in ways different from that of a scientific instrument designed for the precise measurement of celestial phenomena. Though it might seem rational to us to associate precisely oriented alignments with calendrical procedures and imprecisely oriented ones with ritual behavior, we (Aveni et al. 2003; Aveni 2010; Dowd 2015) have suggested that any attempt to connect the matter of precision with the issue of intention or purpose on the part of the builders can be misleading. Like Aimers and Rice (2006), we prefer a merging of the ritualistic and scientific perspectives on ancient Maya sky watching, but we are not inclined to make a priori judgments about lack of precision without either excavation data or careful analysis of architectural alignments.

Setting up calendrically timed seasonal rituals triggered by the actual appearance of the sun in the architectural framework makes sense from a religious perspective. We can think of the role of the astronomer as not so much to acquire precise astronomical data in order to set a rigorous schedule but rather to undertake the task of delivering the sun to the appropriate place at the proper time on the architectural stage for all worshippers and celebrants to witness for themselves. These efforts would have been part of prestige technologies, such as writing (Dowd 2015:212; Milbrath and Dowd in Dowd and Milbrath 2015:13; Hayden 1998).

We agree with Aimers and Rice (2006) that E Groups constituted a set of metaphysically linked considerations, among them sacred geography and ritual performance related to seasonality. Opinions vary on the reason for the orientations of other examples of E Group complexes that do not line up even approximately with the cardinal directions or solstice positions on the horizon. Some researchers (for example, Ruppert 1940 and Laporte and Fialko 1990) argued that these are astronomical allegories, commemorative structures in which astronomical function, to a significant degree, has been lost to other interests. In the quarter-century since Laporte and Fialko's article was published, much more information is available on how first solar equinoxes and solstices then later 20-day intervals leading up to the first annual zenith passage, and other key dates or date intervals, may structure horizon-based observations and calendar development and variability.

To carry the association between the astronomical and ritual function of Group E structures further, if group rituals in the open space of the plaza were a part of the design, E Group complexes need not necessarily be conceived as solely facilitating observations, whether accurate or not, made from the radial pyramid on the west by a single individual situated in the correct place. Instead, as we among others (Dowd et al. 1995; Dowd and Aveni 1998; Dowd and Milbrath 2015; Mendez et al. 2005) have suggested and demonstrated photographically, E Group complexes could have also functioned to display a hierophany via the subtle interplay of light and shadow in the architecture (Figures 3.7, 3.8). Such a phenomenon could have served to enhance the drama of ritual. Thus, at Calakmul from the top of Structure IVc at sunset on the summer solstice the doorjamb shadows align perfectly, consequently illuminating the area between the two doorways. To achieve the effect, builders may have found it necessary to offset the interior portal a bit to the south. Similar adjustments might explain

Figure 3.7. Calakmul Structure IVc north doorjambs at summer solstice sunset: view to the east. From Dowd and Milbrath (2015:Figure 3.4). Photograph by Anne S. Dowd, Copyright © 1995, All rights reserved.

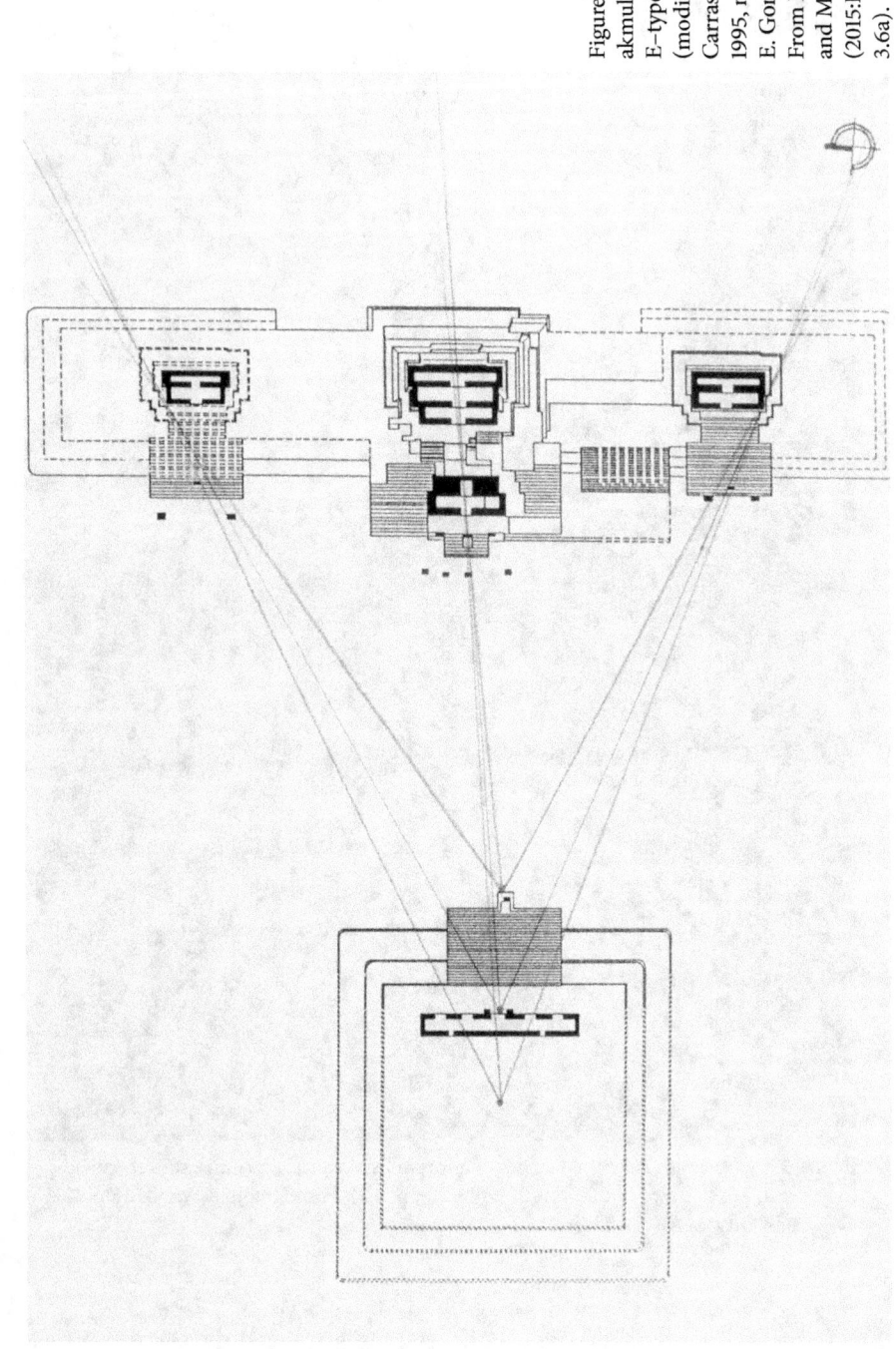

Figure 3.8. Calakmul Group E-type complex (modified after Carrasco et al. 1995, map by E. González). From Dowd and Milbrath (2015:Figure 3.6a).

frequent asymmetries found in the alignments at other E Group complexes (for example, note the clockwise skew of Structure E-III at Uaxactún in Figure 3.1). Scholars have suggested architectural solar hierophanies of this kind elsewhere in the Maya world, such as at Palenque by Linda Schele (1977; Mendez et al. 2014) and at Yaxchilán by Carolyn Tate (1992), who offers dates in the monumental inscriptions as documentary support. Architectural renovations designed to improve hierophantic effects exist both at Calakmul and at Palenque (Dowd in Dowd and Milbrath 2015:62).

Travis Stanton and David Freidel (2003) believe that agents of change influence culture to a greater degree than models that emphasize the dominance of cultural norms. In their study of E Groups they argue that competing religious ideologies that accompanied sedentary agricultural systems during the Formative became locked in at an early date and that these systems exhibited regional architectural and other variations. Following earlier work by Cohodas (1980) and Aimers (1993:171–179), they regard E Groups primarily as maize theaters, that is, places for performing rituals commemorating the rebirth of the Maize God at the beginning of the present creation. The spread of the E Group complex might indicate the innovation and diffusion of this new ritual technology for the assurance of agricultural prosperity in maize production. This view is entirely consistent with the agricultural calendrical function supported by the data that we reported earlier on the solar zenith-based alignments. Whether influenced from within or without, it seems clear that the process of design and development of the widespread phenomenon of E-type groups in the Maya Lowlands included astronomical considerations.

Acknowledgments

We are grateful to two peer referees for their helpful comments.

References Cited

Aimers, James J.
1993   Messages from the Gods: An Hermeneutic Analysis of the Maya E-Group Complex. Master's thesis, Department of Anthropology, Trent University, Peterborough, Ontario.
Aimers, James J., and Prudence M. Rice
2006   Astronomy, Ritual, and the Interpretation of Maya "E-Group" Architectural Assemblages. *Ancient Mesoamerica* 17(1):79–96.

Aveni, Anthony F.
1975   Possible Astronomical Orientations in Ancient Mesoamerica. In *Archaeoastronomy in Pre-Columbian America*, edited by Anthony F. Aveni, pp. 163–190. University of Texas Press, Austin.
1991   The Real Venus-Kukulcan in Maya Inscriptions and Alignments. In *Sixth Mesa Redonda de Palenque 1986*, edited by Virginia M. Fields, pp. 309–321. University of Oklahoma Press, Norman.
2000   Out of Teotihuacan: Origins of the Celestial Canon in Mesoamerica. In *Mesoamerica's Classical Heritage: From Teotihuacan to the Aztecs*, edited by David Carrasco, Lindsay Jones, and Scott Sessions, pp. 253–268. University Press of Colorado, Niwot.
2010   Cosmology and Cultural Landscape: The Late Postclassic Maya of North Yucatán. In *Astronomers, Scribes, and Priests: Intellectual Interchange between the Northern Maya Lowlands and Highland Mexico in the Late Postclassic Period*, edited by Gabrielle Vail and Christine Hernández, pp. 115–132. Dumbarton Oaks, Washington, D.C.

Aveni, Anthony F., Anne S. Dowd, and Benjamin Vining
2003   Maya Calendar Reform?: Evidence from Orientations of Specialized Architectural Assemblages. *Latin American Antiquity* 14(2):159–178.

Aveni, Anthony F., and Horst Hartung
1986   Maya City Planning and the Calendar. *Transactions of the American Philosophical Society* 76 (1):1–87.
1989   Uaxactún Guatemala, Group E, and Similar Assemblages: An Archaeoastronomical Reconsideration. In *World Archaeoastronomy*, edited by Anthony F. Aveni, pp. 444–461. Cambridge University Press, Cambridge, United Kingdom.

Aveni, Anthony F., Horst Hartung, and Beth Buckingham
1978   The Pecked Cross Symbol in Ancient Mesoamerica. *Science* 202:267–269.

Aveni, Anthony F., Horst Hartung, and J. Charles Kelley
1982   Alta Vista (Chalchihuites), Astronomical Implications of a Mesoamerican Ceremonial Outpost at the Tropic of Cancer. *American Antiquity* 47:316–335.

Blom, Frans
1924   Report on the Preliminary Work at Uaxactún, Guatemala. *Carnegie Institution of Washington Year Book* 23:217–219.

Carrasco Vargas, Ramón, Sylviane Boucher, Anne S. Dowd, Armando Paul, María Elena García, and Emyly González G.
1995   *Informe preliminar del Proyecto Arqueológico de la Biosfera de Calakmul*. Instituto Nacional de Antropología e Historia, Mérida, Yucatán, Mexico.

Carrasco Vargas, Ramón, and María Cordeiro Baqueiro
2012   The Murals of Chiik Nahb Structure Sub 1-4, Calakmul, Mexico. In *Maya Archaeology 2*, edited by Charles Golden, Stephen Houston, and Joel Skidmore, pp. 8–59. Maya Archaeology Reports. Precolumbian Mesoweb Press, San Francisco.

Carrasco Vargas, Ramón, Verónica A. Vázquez López, and Simon Martin
2009   Daily Life of the Ancient Maya Recorded on Murals at Calakmul, Mexico. *Proceedings of the National Academy of Sciences* 106(46):19245–19249.
Chase, Arlen F.
1983   *A Contextual Consideration of the Tayasal-Paxcaman Zone, El Petén, Guatemala.* Ph.D. dissertation, Department of Anthropology, University of Pennsylvania, Philadelphia. University Microfilms/ProQuest, Ann Arbor, Michigan.
Chase, Arlen F., and Diane Z. Chase
1995   External Impetus, Internal Synthesis, and Standardization: E Group Assemblages and the Crystallization of Classic Maya Society in the Southern Lowlands. *Acta Mesoamericana* 8:87–101.
Cohodas, Marvin
1980   Radial Pyramids and Radial-Associated Assemblages of the Central Maya Area. *Journal of the Society of Architectural Historians* 39:208–223.
Dowd, Anne S.
2015   Cosmovision in New World Ritual Landscapes: An Introduction. *Cambridge Archaeological Journal* 25(1):211–218.
Dowd, Anne S., and Anthony F. Aveni
1998   The Maya Space-Time Continuum: Calakmul's Group E-Type Complex. Paper presented at the 63rd Annual Meeting of the Society for American Archaeology, Seattle, Washington, March 26, 1998.
Dowd, Anne S., Anthony F. Aveni, and Ramón Carrasco Vargas
1995   Solar Observatory or Allegory? Calakmul's Group E-Type Complex. Paper presented at the 60th Annual Meeting of the Society for American Archaeology, Minneapolis, Minnesota, May 4, 1995.
Dowd, Anne S., and Susan Milbrath (editors)
2015   *Cosmology, Calendars, and Horizon-Based Astronomy in Ancient Mesoamerica.* University Press of Colorado, Boulder.
Hayden, Brian
1998   Practical and Prestige Technologies: The Evolution of Material Systems. *Journal of Archaeological Method and Theory* 5:1–55.
Laporte, Juan Pedro, and Vilma Fialko
1990   New Perspectives on Old Problems: Dynastic References for the Early Classic at Tikal. In *Vision and Revision in Maya Studies*, edited by Flora S. Clancy and Peter D. Harrison, pp. 33–66. University of New Mexico Press, Albuquerque.
Lister, Robert H., and Florence C. Lister (editors)
1970   *In Search of Maya Glyphs: From the Archaeological Journals of Sylvanus Morley.* Museum of New Mexico Press, Santa Fe.
Mendez, Alonso, Edwin L. Barnhart, Christopher Powell, and Carol Karasik
2005   Astronomical Observations from the Temple of the Sun. *Archaeoastronomy* 19:44–73.
Mendez, Alonso, Carol Karasik, Edwin L. Barnhart, and Christopher Powell
2014   The Astronomical Architecture of Palenque's Temple of the Sun. In *Archaeoastronomy and the Maya*, edited by Gerardo Aldana y Villalobos and Edwin L. Barnhart, pp. 37–75. Oxbow Books, Oxford.

Morley, Sylvanus Griswold
1937–1938 *The Inscriptions of Petén*. Publication 427. Carnegie Institution of Washington, Washington, D.C.

Rathje, William L.
1973 Trade Models and Archaeological Problems: The Classic Maya and Their E Group Complex. *Proceedings of the International Congress of Americanists* 4:231–235.

Ricketson, Oliver G., Jr.
1928a Astronomical Observatories in the Maya Area. *Geographical Review* 18:215–225.
1928b Notes on Two Maya Astronomical Observatories. *American Anthropologist* 30:433–444.

Ricketson, Oliver G., Jr., and Edith Bayles Ricketson
1937 *Uaxactún, Guatemala, Group E, 1926–31*. Publication 477. Carnegie Institution of Washington, Washington, D.C.

Ruppert, Karl
1934 Explorations in Campeche. *Carnegie Institution of Washington Year Book* 33:93–95.
1940 A Special Assemblage of Maya Structures. In *The Maya and Their Neighbors: Essays on Middle American Anthropology and Archaeology*, edited by Clarence L. Hay, Ralph L. Linton, Samuel K. Lothrop, Harry L. Shapiro, and George C. Vaillant, pp. 222–231. D. Appleton–Century, New York.

Sabloff, Jeremy A., and E. Wyllys Andrews V
1986 *Late Lowland Maya Civilization: Classic to Postclassic*. School of American Research, Santa Fe, New Mexico.

Schele, Linda
1977 Palenque: The House of the Dying Sun. In *Native American Astronomy*, edited by Anthony F. Aveni, pp. 42–56. University of Texas Press, Austin.

Smith, A. Ledyard
1950 *Uaxactún, Guatemala: Excavations of 1931–1937*. Publication 588. Carnegie Institution of Washington, Washington, D.C.

Stanton, Travis W., and David A. Freidel
2003 Ideological Lock-In and the Dynamics of Formative Religions in Mesoamerica. *Mayeb* 16:5–14.

Tate, Carolyn E.
1992 *Yaxchilan: The Design of a Ceremonial City*. University of Texas Press, Austin.

Valdés, Juan Antonio, and Federico Fahsen
1995 The Reigning Early Dynasty of Uaxactún during the Early Classic. *Ancient Mesoamerica* 6:197–219.

World Weather Disc
1988 *Worldwide Airfield Summaries*. WeatherDisc Associates, Seattle.

4

The Legacy of Preclassic Calendars and Solar Observation in Mesoamerica's Magic Latitude

SUSAN MILBRATH

Study of Preclassic (1000 BCE–250 CE) Maya architecture in relation to developments in the early Maya calendar presents some very interesting patterns that reflect an intertwined history. As the following discussion shows, astronomical observations made in E Groups were most probably used in developing the calendar, because Middle Preclassic E Groups predate the earliest secure evidence of calendar records in Mesoamerica.

Mesoamerica is unified by a unique 260-day calendar combining 20 day signs and 13 numbers, referred to as the sacred calendar or Tzolk'in by Maya scholars, who coined this as the Maya equivalent of Tonalpohualli (count of days), a term recorded in Aztec sources. By the Early Classic, the Maya tracked the annual cycle with the Haab (spelled *h'ab* in most Mayan languages: Stuart 2011:155), a 365-day period formed by 18 "months" of 20 days each plus an added 5-day period (the Uayeb). This 365-day cycle is first documented in Long Count inscriptions recording month patrons on Preclassic inscriptions from Veracruz, but there is evidence that it first developed in the Maya area, as discussed below.

The persistence up to modern times of a sequence of 18-month names among the Maya of Guatemala and Chiapas suggests that the Haab remains an essential component in measuring the year (Edmonson 1988:235–237, Figure 16a). In the Highlands of Guatemala, 34 Maya communities still use the Tzolk'in and the 365-day calendar with a system of yearbearers that links the two cycles to form the Calendar Round (Tedlock 1992:92). This 52-year cycle is quite distinct from the form of the Tzolk'in-Haab Calendar Round used by the Maya in the Classic period, which employed a 52-year cycle of interlocking Haabs (52 × 365) and Tzolk'ins (73 × 260). The yearbearers, rarely noted in Classic Maya texts, become very important in the Postclassic period, especially in the so-called New Year pages of the codices.

The Tzolk'in embodies sets of 20, an intrinsic number in the Mesoamerican calendar shared by most calendar cycles. It is argued here that the division into 20-day sets represents an ancient template of the idealized subdivision of the maize agriculture cycle, which was encoded in architecture at an early time in the Maya area. Solar observations made in early E Groups helped establish a basis for subdivisions of the Maya calendar encoded in the 20-day periods used for both the Haab and the Tzolk'in (Milbrath 2017).

Solar and Stellar Alignments in Early E Groups

During the Middle Preclassic (1,000–350 BCE), specialized architectural complexes were constructed to track the changing seasonal positions of the sun along the horizon. Middle Preclassic linear mound-plus-platform arrangements are found at the Olmec site of La Venta in Tabasco (Structures D1 and D8) and at Chiapa de Corzo (Mounds 11 and 12) in Chiapas (Bachand and Lowe 2011). These Middle Preclassic linear mounds or range structures might have had multiple wooden posts along the platform (or stone markers like the basalt column on La Venta Structure D-8) positioned to mark the solstices, equinoxes, and the zenith sun, when the marker would act as a gnomon and cast no shadow at noon (Aimers and Rice 2006:80, 92; Rice 2007:87, 147). Although archaeological remains of wooden posts on the ranges have not been recorded, crossed sticks or movable stones would not leave a trace if they were used.

The Middle Preclassic E Groups in the Maya area had a pyramid on the west facing a flat range structure to the east, which was probably used to measure the solar trajectory along the horizon at 20-day intervals (Rice 2007:87, 155). The early Lowland Maya E Groups concentrate in what Anthony Aveni (2002:211) has described as the "magic latitude," where the year can be segmented into multiples of 20 days that separate the solstices, equinoxes, and solar zeniths (see also Chapter 5 in this volume). The Ceibal E Group dates as early as 1000 BCE, making it the oldest known example in the Maya Lowlands and possibly the oldest anywhere in Mesoamerica (Inomata et al. 2013:467; but see also Chapter 7 in this volume).

Maya E Groups were widely distributed in the Middle Preclassic at sites such as Caracol, Cival, Nakbé, Takalik Abaj, and Tikal (Aveni et al.

2003:Table 1; Chase and Chase 1995; Clark and Hansen 2001:9, 16; Estrada-Belli 2011:52, 68–69, 74; Hansen 1998:66, 2013; Laporte and Fialko 1990, 1995). Most Maya E Groups in the Middle Preclassic are like the one at Cival, characterized by a pyramid to the west facing an elongated platform that was used to mark solar positions synchronized with the agricultural season, dividing the year in four parts (Estrada-Belli 2006:63, 2011:74, 78–79, 82–83, Figure 4.1). When formal constructions began to be added to the elongated eastern structure, the first phase was usually a single elevated building at the center that may have marked the midpoint of the sun's journey from north to south at the solstices, an approximation of the equinox, as at Tikal and Nakbé (Aveni et al. 2003:Table 1; Hansen 1998:66). The 92° azimuth marked by the central point of the range at Cival (and the post in front of it) would translate into an alignment to the sun's position on March 18, about two days before the equinox (March 20/21).

The equinox orientation of Uaxactún in the Late Preclassic has been linked to Orion (Kováč et al. 2015). This pattern is seen in many early E Groups, which are similarly aligned with the horizon position of Orion (ca. 1000–400 BCE; Aveni et al. 2003:173). And orientations to Orion are also proposed for early architecture in Oaxaca (Peeler and Winter 1992–1993:42).

The three stars in Orion's Belt may have served as a marker for the position of the equinox sunrise in September, when they rose in a vertical alignment just south of due east around midnight. The disappearance interval of Orion was also closely linked with the maize cycle during Preclassic times and later (Milbrath 1999:268, 2016). At dusk in late April, just before planting, the three stars in the belt were aligned in a row just above the horizon in the west, resembling a row of seeds about to be planted in the earth. And when Orion's Belt reappeared in the east, it was rotated in a vertical alignment at dawn on the eastern horizon, like the first maize sprouts in June (the Belt of Orion was invisible from April 23 to June 12 ca. 500 BCE and April 29 to June 17 ca. 0 CE; Aveni 2001:Table 10).

With architectural elaborations of the range structure over time, the alignments of E Groups also changed. Even though Uaxactún's Late Preclassic E Group functioned accurately to mark the solstices and equinoxes, later modifications made the astronomical orientations nonfunctional, but the complex probably retained a commemorative solar function (Aveni et al. 2003:Table 1; Iwaniszewski 2002). By the Classic period, Tikal's E Group had been remodeled repeatedly so that the latest additions to the range structure were aligned to the dates February 8 (5D-85) and April

13 (5D-87), when viewed from the radial pyramid (5C-54), according to calculations published by Aveni et al. (2003:174).[1]

Aveni et al. (2003:162–163, 170–172) do not see E Groups as true observatories but note that sun watching was part of their purpose, so "regardless of whether the Maya were watching it scientifically or ceremonially, the associated architectural complex may be regarded as an observatory" (172). They note that some Maya E Groups marked points on the horizon that seem to define 20-day intervals leading up to the first solar zenith, which anticipated the onset of the planting season. Aveni and his colleagues propose that a calendar reform led to greater emphasis on measuring 20-day intervals leading up to and following the solar zenith date at individual locales.

In the Classic period (250–900 CE), the seasonal cycle was still tracked, but most probably through other forms of architectural orientations, most of which show an interest in 20-day units, and many of these mark a 260/105-day split in the year, according to numerous articles authored and co-authored by Ivan Šprajc (including most recently Sánchez and Šprajc 2015). Classic period architecture continued to be characterized by astronomical alignments at sites like El Mirador and Uaxactún, but instead of emphasizing events such as the solstices and equinoxes important in the early E Group alignments, the most common orientations are to dates in February and October, months that coincide with the initial phases of the agricultural cycle and the beginning of the harvest, and subdivisions of this cycle at 20-day intervals. These 20-day intervals may be seen as subdivisions of the Haab and have been characterized as a Haab form of E Group (Chapter 15 in this volume).

By the beginning of the Early Classic (250/300 CE), continued modifications meant that E Groups did not function in the same manner as earlier versions, but they probably were still used for solar rituals and calendar ceremonies (Aveni et al. 2003; Aimers and Rice 2006:79, 82, 86–87). And some E Groups were apparently modified for use in rituals commemorating the cycle of K'atuns (Aimers and Rice 2006:87, 90–92; Estrada-Belli 2011:79–80). A few E Groups retained some function in terms of solar alignments, as at Late Classic Calakmul, where the E Group shows a specific pattern of light and shadow at the summer solstice (Dowd 2015:Table 3.1, Figure 3.4).

As early as 350 BCE, a number of sites constructed Triadic Groups, a new form of architectural complex representing religious concepts linked with divine kingship (Estrada-Belli 2011:56, 68, 76, 109; Hansen 1998, 2013).

Possibly the triad was linked with the "three hearthstone" stars in Orion, which were important in Classic and Postclassic iconography and survive today in Mayan lore (Freidel et al. 1993; Milbrath 1999:39, 266–268).[2]

In the broadest sense, with or without E Groups, there is evidence of early alignments to the solstices and dates approximating the equinoxes. In Veracruz and Oaxaca, two areas with early calendar inscriptions, Ivan Šprajc and Francisco Sánchez Nava (2015:92–93) conclude that the earliest architectural orientations indicate an interest in the solstices (especially the winter solstice) and the quarter days (March 23 and September 21), marking halfway points between the solstices. It is at this early stage, ca. 1000–800 BCE, that intensive maize agriculture may have inspired a need for a formalized calendar to measure intervals in the agricultural cycle.

The Early Mesoamerican Calendar

The number 20 may ultimately have originated as a count of human digits but very soon a count of 20-day periods developed in relation to the agricultural cycle (Rice 2007). In the Middle Preclassic, 20-day periods were apparently associated with the cycle of maize. It seems likely that a count of 260 days developed to measure the agricultural cycle, tracking the "agrarian year" from the preparation for planting maize to the harvest (Milbrath 1999:15, 2017; Rice 2007:35–36, 2015:271). The 20-day periods subdividing the 260-day count were probably also visualized as 20-day "months" in the 365-day year, well before the Haab was formulated.

By the Late Preclassic (350 BCE–0 CE), the Maya were developing an early form of the Long Count calendar, again using the 20-day intervals they had developed earlier. The vigesimal notation (Winal) allowed the Maya to construct much longer cycles of time that were actually much more precise and easier to work within the large calculations recorded on monuments.

It is noteworthy that E Groups began to decline in importance around the same time that the Long Count appeared in areas surrounding the Maya Lowlands. To understand this process, we need to study how the early Mesoamerican calendar evolved into the highly sophisticated Long Count calendar of the Maya at the beginning of the Classic period. David Stuart (2011:36–37) notes that the widespread distribution of the 260-day calendar suggests that it first developed in the Olmec area, even though Olmec dates in the ritual calendar are not well documented. Scholars have identified some early records of Olmec Tzolk'in dates (Justeson 1989:79; Edmonson 1988; Rice 2007:45). For example, La Venta Stela 13 has a column of glyph-like symbols possibly including the number one (Lacadena 2009).

Linguistic data suggest that Tzolk'in day names were probably used as early as 600 BCE in the Maya area (Justeson 1989:79). This would be contemporary with the earliest Zapotec day name inscriptions and overlap with the range of dates proposed for La Venta Stela 13, which dates to La Venta Phase IV, ending ca. 600–400 BCE (Marcus 1992:41; Milbrath 1979:48, Table 2).[3] The Tzolk'in and yearbearers also appear early, dating to Monte Albán I in Oaxaca (Urcid 2001). At this point it is not possible to be sure which of these three areas had priority in developing the 260-day count, and the same can be said about the year divided into 18 months.

It has been proposed that the Maya month names first developed ca. 550 BCE; the months named for the rainy season months appear to be correlated with the proper season and 0 Pop occurred on the winter solstice (Bricker 1982:102–103). Prudence Rice (2007:47, 57) suggests an even earlier development and notes that the Haab was perhaps as old as 2057 BCE, when 0 Pop coordinated with the winter solstice (as it did in 550 BCE). This date, of course, predates what we identify as the Olmec and Maya cultures. We lack any written records for these formative times, so we can only guess at what was known in the Preceramic period.

It seems likely that by the Middle Preclassic a count of 20 days was recorded with named days that were incorporated in a 260-day calendar. The evidence for this is still somewhat tentative, with the most secure dates coming from Oaxaca. Early written records dating to the Middle Preclassic include the 260-day ritual calendar and a separate cycle recording a 365-day period approximating the solar year in inscriptions with yearbearers dating to the Middle Preclassic in the Valley of Oaxaca.[4] Texts from the Monte Albán IA Phase, ca. 600/500–300 BCE, record Zapotec references to the yearbearers in the 52-year cycle. The possibility of Zapotec month glyphs at Monte Albán, originally proposed by Alfonso Caso and subsequently supported by other scholars (Marcus 1992:38–41; Prem 1971:119), has not been confirmed by more detailed studies of the calendar (Urcid 2001:266–273; Whittaker 1992).[5] Monte Albán Stela 12 and Stela 13 apparently show the earliest evidence of yearbearers (Marcus 1992:40–41).[6] Here a year sign with the yearbearer 4 Wind is paired with the day 8 Water, forming a Calendar Round date somewhat speculatively read as 594 BCE (Edmonson 1988:2).

The yearbearers appear with a year sign (a headdress in early Oaxacan texts) to show that they designate a year, and the date itself is also the day in the 260-day cycle that falls at the beginning or end of the year, depending on the system employed. In the Postclassic Aztec system, the yearbearer dates seem to fall in the last 20-day "month" of the year (Caso 1971; Milbrath 2013:5–10, Table 1.5), whereas in the Postclassic Maya system the Tzolk'in date corresponding to the beginning of the year was the yearbearer (Bricker and Bricker 2011:135–136).

Early Zapotec dates are based on "Type II" yearbearers, according to Edmonson (1988:8–9), who compared them to the yearbearers of the Early Classic Maya (Ik', Manik, Eb, and Caban comparable to Wind, Deer, Grass, and Motion). The Ik', Manik, Eb, and Caban yearbearers are still used by the Quiché to form their Calendar Round (Tedlock 1992:89–92), the same ones used by the Preclassic Maya at San Bartolo, according to David Stuart. He notes that the 3 Ik' yearbearer date in the murals of San Bartolo falls in a 104-year span between 131 and 27 BCE, representing the seating of Pop (0 Pop), the first day of the first of the 18 months in the Maya year (Stuart 2005:4–6, Figure 3). Even though the month glyph is not recorded in this inscription, a link with the annual cycle (18 × 20 + 5) is implicit in interpreting the date as 0 Pop.

Stuart (2011:38) suggests that calendrics in hieroglyphic writing are as old as 300 BCE in the Maya area. This may be confirmed by the early appearance of the K'atun cycle on a stone block associated with the San Bartolo murals complex, recording the K'atun-ending 5 Ajaw (7.5.0.0.0), which would translate into a Long Count date of 255 BCE (Giron-Ábrego 2013:9–10).

Rice (2007:47, 57) suggests that the Calendar Round developed as early as 1650 BCE, pairing the Tzolk'in and Haab to form a cycle of approximately 52 years, a period totaling 18,980 days. Nonetheless, the earliest known records of the 52-year cycle employ the yearbearer type of Calendar Round (first known from Preclassic Oaxaca), instead of the Tzolk'in-Haab form of Calendar Round common among Classic Maya inscriptions. The yearbearer type of Calendar Round is characterized by ambiguity: the yearbearer date actually occurs twice in the year, because after one 260-day cycle was completed 105 days were repeated in the latter part of the 365-day year.

The Preclassic Maya clearly sought greater precision when they developed a Calendar Round formed by the Tzolk'in paired with a month date in the Haab. The earliest known month inscriptions at this point seem to be from the Isthmus area bordering the Maya Lowlands (see below). As discussed below, Maya calendar records initially did not record month glyphs, but by the end of the Late Preclassic the Maya had developed the Tzolk'in-Haab Calendar Round notation as a subset of the Long Count calendar.

Beginning around 300 CE, the Classic Maya used Tzolk'in and Haab dates anchored to Long Count inscriptions that designated a specific date in a cycle 13 Bak'tuns (around 5,128.76 years with each Bak'tun being 144,000 days [$20 \times 20 \times 360$ days]). Months in the Classic Maya Haab were not adjusted to maintain a relationship with the seasons because they were locked into larger cycles in the Long Count. The Long Count calendar combined multiple cycles, most based on 20-day units, including the Bak'tun ($20 \times 20 \times 20 \times 360$ days), the K'atun ($20 \times 20 \times 360$ days), the Tun (18×20 days), and the Winal (20 days).

We can conclude that Tzolk'in records appear earlier than the Haab in the Maya area, but 20-day sets implicit in the Maya Haab most probably developed in tandem with the 20 day signs forming the Tzolk'in. The Haab clearly originated from observations of the solar year, probably first recorded with the same set of 20 day signs used in the 260-day calendar. Initially, the 365-day Haab may have coordinated with the seasonal cycle; but as the Preclassic drew to a close, it became subordinate to the Long Count, which now provided a more precise set of calendar records useful in long-term calculations.

Origin of the Haab and Tzolk'in

To gain a better understanding of the evolution of the early calendar in the Maya area, it is helpful to review some of the theories about the two principal components of the Tzolk'in-Haab form of Calendar Round. Vincent Malmström (1991) originally suggested that the Haab originated in the Maya area at Edzná (19°37' N), where the solar zenith in the Gregorian calendar falls on July 26. In 1566 Friar Landa had noted that the Maya Haab placed the first day of the first month (Pop) as the date of the New Year on July 16 in the Julian calendar (Old Style, abbreviated OS), used prior to the 1582 Gregorian calendar reform (New Style, NS). Malmström proposed that Edzná may have been the geographical "cradle" of the Maya New Year date on 1 Pop around 41 CE (the year ending Cycle 7 of the Long Count). This has proved invalid, because Malmström used the Postclassic (900–1519 CE) New Year date of 1 Pop rather than 0 Pop of the Classic period (also used in the Preclassic). His idea is also considered problematic in the absence of any early calendar inscriptions known from Edzná.

In a later publication, Malmström (1997:64) shifted his focus to 0 Pop. He proposes that this date coincided with the summer solstice (June 22) around 1324 BCE and suggests that the Haab cycle originated prior to Olmec times. As noted previously, others propose that the winter solstice is a more likely starting place for a solar calendar of 365 days, dating the origin to a time when the Haab cycle began on the winter solstice. In the absence of Haab records in the Maya area predating the Late Preclassic, the early dates suggested by these scholars cannot be confirmed.

Although the original basis for the Haab is certainly the solar year, there is considerable debate about the natural cycles that relate to the origin of the 260-day calendar. John Justeson (1989:78) notes that it seems unlikely that the 260-day period approximates any interval in nature and thinks that it is instead simply a permutation of two cycles, the 20 named days and the 13 numerals. Stuart (2011:153) also suggests that the explanation for the 260-day period may be simply numerological, using two meaningful factors: the set of 20 derived from the digits of the human body and the 13 numbers as a cosmological symbol of the core gods of Mesoamerican numerology. Even so, he points out that the 260-day interval between zenith passage dates may play a role, noting that the idea was first proposed by Zelia Nuttall (1904:497–498). In a variation of the geographical model, Clemency Coggins (1982:113) states that the 260-day calendar may have developed in the Early Preclassic as a discontinuous count based on the 260-day interval when the sun moved south of the zenith (August to April) at the latitude of Copán and Izapa. She suggests that later it was carried to other areas of Mesoamerica where it became a continuous count that was no longer a true seasonal interval.

Other intriguing cycles in nature correspond to the 260-day period. The average period that Venus is visible as either morning or evening star ($\approx$263 days) is an interval that could relate to the 260-day period in the calendar (Aveni 2001:144; Peeler and Winter 1992–1993:57). Many scholars note that the human gestation period is very close to 260 days ($\approx$266 days; Aveni 2001:145; Earle and Snow 1985; Tedlock 1992:93). Rice (2007:38) points out that one lasting indication of such a connection is the practice of naming children according to their day of birth in the 260-day calendar (a Mixtec and Aztec practice not recorded among the Lowland Maya). This link with the life cycle of the fetus could also account for the role that the 260-day calendar plays in predictions involving human activities among the Quiché Maya today (Tedlock 1992:127), a form of prognostication also seen in planting almanacs in central Mexican and Mayan codices (Bricker and Bricker 2011; Bricker and Milbrath 2011).

Geographical latitude is considered to be significant in theories about the origin of the Tzolk'in that involve reference to a 260-day interval marked by the solar zenith. Bordering the western limit of the Maya area, Izapa has two annual solar zeniths spaced at 260-day intervals with the second one falling on August 13, a date that Malmström (1997:52–53, Figures 9–10) links to the beginning of the Bak'tun cycle. Malmström (1997) proposes that the Tzolk'in originated in 1359 BCE at Izapa (14°42' N), when the starting point of the Maya Tzolk'in (1 Imix) coincided with the solar zenith on August 13, which he refers to as the calendar creation date because of a presumed connection with the beginning of the Bak'tun cycle on 4 Ajaw 8 Kumk'u (4 Ahau 8 Cumku) in 3114 BCE. Malmström argues that the solar zenith date in the area of Izapa came to be linked with 1 Imix at an early time and a backward projection of the Long Count led the Calendar Round date 4 Ajaw 8 Kumk'u to be selected as the starting point for the Bak'tun because it coordinated with the solar zenith date at Izapa. Again, this seems problematical because of the lack of early calendar records at Izapa, where only a single Tzolk'in date survives (6 Death on Miscellaneous Monument 60; Justeson 1988; Rice 2007:116). Another problem is that only the 584,285 correlation yields August 13, 3114 BCE (NS) as 4 Ajaw 8 Kumk'u (13.0.0.0.0), the zero date of the cycle of 13 Bak'tuns in the Long Count calendar.[7]

Another geographical area of interest for the early calendar is found on the Pacific Slope of Guatemala, bordering the central Lowland Maya area at 14°20' latitude north, where El Baúl and Takalik Abaj (a.k.a. Abaj Takalik) share a zenith passage date on August 15 that divides the year into 106/259 day sets, only one day off the intervals at Izapa (Edmonson 1988:120). Very early inscriptions appear on El Baúl Stela 1 and Takalik Abaj Stela 1, both interpreted as Izapan monuments (Guernsey 2006:46–47, Figures 3.3b, 3.4).

Monuments such as these help us cast a wider net for positing that the calendar originated in the Izapa area, and Takalik Abaj emerges as the most intriguing site. Gerardo Aldana (2007–2008:71) notes that Takalik Abaj Altar 12 has a series of eighteen glyphs around the perimeter that seem to represent solar months associated with star glyphs, which may be an early reference to the Nine Lords of the Night (G1–G9 of the Maya lunar series). Even earlier monuments at Takalik Abaj relate to the Olmec style. In Structure 7, an Olmec monument that is probably contemporary with the

Figure 4.1. Takalik Abaj Altar 46. Photograph by Susan Milbrath.

Middle Preclassic monuments at La Venta (900–400 BCE) is positioned alongside Altar 46, a large, flat stone carved with feet positioned so that they are aligned to the winter solstice sunrise, suggesting an early interest in marking this date in calendar rituals (Figure 4.1; Hatch 2009:999). Other early solstitial orientations have been noted at Takalik Abaj (Abaj Takalik in Aveni and Hartung 2000:Table 1) and Yaxnohcah (Sánchez and Šprajc 2015:Table 2), but it is not clear whether these predate the early solstice alignments in Veracruz and Oaxaca (Šprajc and Sánchez 2015).

Brian Dillon (2013) notes that Takalik Abaj has over 350 Middle Preclassic Olmec and early Maya monuments, more than any other Mesoamerican site. Dillon (2013) proposes that the site may represent a second Olmec "heartland" on the Pacific Slope and argues that the Proto-Maya civilization developed at Takalik Abaj prior to the Izapan style. He points out that Takalik Abaj's proximity to ritually significant volcanoes and its location in the piedmont of Guatemala, a major cacao-producing area characterized by different elevations with growing seasons of varying lengths, are important reasons for its long occupation, spanning from at least 800 BCE to the Conquest period. Although we lack any clear evidence that this site was the origin point of the Tzolk'in, it certainly is an area with early calendar records. Its solar zenith date helps divide the year in two unequal parts, with one segment approximating the 260-day calendar.

The geographical explanation for the origin of the Tzolk'in based on zenith dates at any specific latitude remains controversial. Long ago, J. Eric Thompson (1960:98–99) and other scholars rejected this idea, based on the premise that any natural phenomenon would have to be continuously repetitive and observable in the greater part of the Mesoamerican area in which the sacred almanac was in use (Henderson 1974:542). There is evidence, however, that a fixed 260-day count relates to the maize cycle among the Quiché in the Highlands of Guatemala and the Chortí, living in a territory spanning from Guatemala to Honduras, and also among the Mopán and Tzeltal (Milbrath 1999:15, 2017).

Solar Observations and the 260-Day Agricultural Cycle

The most likely natural counterpart for the cycle of 260 days is one that can be related to the Mesoamerican maize cycle, which was probably significant in developing the Mesoamerican calendar.[8] The 365-day year among the Chortí begins on the same day (February 8), according to Raphael Girard (1962:3–15, 55, 76, 328–342), but there seems to be some flexibility for the beginning date because their calendar year is said to start with the first visible crescent moon.[9] The first 80-day period of agricultural preparation ends with the first solar zenith on May 1, around the onset of the rainy season when the planting period begins.[10] As is the case in most of the Maya area, the rainy season begins in May, around the time of the first solar zenith in the Chortí area (Milbrath 1999:13). A second crop is planted shortly after the ears of the first crop are doubled over to avoid rainfall rotting the maize and also so that birds do not eat the kernels. The second crop is planted in July and cultivated during a period that includes the heaviest rainfall around the fall equinox, but doubling the ears of this second crop is not necessary because the rainy season has come to an end by the time the maize is ready to harvest (Girard 1962:265–268). The harvest begins in October, and the fixed 260-day agricultural count ends around October 25 with a midnight ceremony. The remaining 105 days form a "residual" period of rest that completes the year, ending with a five-day period comparable to the Classic Maya Uayeb, but positioned in February rather than July.

Barbara Tedlock (1992:104, 189–190, Table 4) notes that the Quiché plant mountain maize in March and harvest in December, resulting in a 260-day agricultural cycle. The link between the 260-day count and the agricultural season in two very different areas is intriguing as evidence of an ancient pattern, one encoded in the yearbearer system that divides the year into two sections of 260 and 105 days. The 105-day residual period forms a natural subdivision of the 365-day year, bracketing the 260-day agricultural cycle. This subdivision seems to be preserved in the Aztec system of yearbearers, where the New Year takes place in February (Milbrath 2013:5–10, Table 1.5).

The 260-day agrarian year is also documented in a number of Mesoamerican architectural orientations that focus on dates in February and October, spaced at intervals of 260 days (Aimers and Rice 2006:88; Aveni 2001:228–229; Šprajc 2000:409; Šprajc and Sánchez 2012, 2013b, 2015; Tichy 1991). These orientations define a 260-day period that can be described as an observational calendar related to the agricultural cycle like that surviving today among the Maya. Alignments to the east often seem to mark intervals of 260 and 105 days or, less commonly, in 20-day increments, such as intervals of 240 days and 125 days. A similar pattern has been detected in studies of the 8° west of north orientations at La Venta and early sites in Oaxaca, which seem to designate an alignment that divides the year into 105 and 260-day segments (Peeler and Winter 1992–1993; Šprajc and Sánchez 2015).

This same pattern is noted at Teotihuacán, where the Pyramid of the Sun is aligned to a prominent peak on the eastern horizon that marks the sun's position on February 11 and October 29, indicating a 260-day cycle (Iwaniszewski 2005; Šprajc 2000, 2001:226–229, Tables 5.38, 5.39). These alignments divide up the agricultural season as follows: (1) the initial preparations for planting in early February; (2) the onset of the rains and first planting at the end of April; (3) the first maturing ears of maize in the middle of August; and (4) the beginning of the main harvest at the end of October. The Teotihuacán alignments involve observations of the sun moving along a mountainous horizon. With a flat horizon in the Maya area, the sunrise position on the same seasonal dates yields a 14° south of east orientation, like that found at several large Preclassic Maya sites that have both early E Groups and other architectural constructions that exhibit orientations marking the dates February 12 and October 30 (Šprajc et al. 2009:88–90, Tables 1, 2; Chapter 15 in this volume).

The widespread nature of the 14° orientation in the Maya Lowlands is seen in patterns in Quintana Roo and elsewhere in the Yucatán peninsula. Late Preclassic T'isil, Quintana Roo, has a similar orientation with its main *sacbe* ("white road") aligned to the rising sun on February 14 and the return of the sun to the same horizon position on October 29 (a 14° south of east orientation). Jeffrey Vadala (2009:95–97) notes that this site also has a construction with a 25° south of east orientation to the winter solstice sunrise. Similar alignments, seen later on in Puuc-Maya sites, are distributed along two basic directions, 14° and 25° east of north, with the latter being a winter solstice sunrise for east-facing structures (Aveni 2002:236). The median

14° alignment for sites in the Puuc area was originally interpreted as marking 20-day intervals before and after the solar zenith (Aveni and Hartung 1986:18–19, Table 3), but this orientation would also coincide with dates in February and October used in aligning a 260-day agricultural calendar at a number of Maya Lowland sites. The subdivision of the fixed 260-day period in 20-day sets before and after the solar zenith may be directly linked with timing the onset of the rainy season and planting.

Preclassic "architectural calendars" may be linked with ancient agricultural practices that emphasize certain dates in the maize cycle, established early on by astronomical alignments at Teotihuacán and at sites in Veracruz, Oaxaca, and the Maya area. A fixed count of 260 days, possibly predating the solar calendar cycle of 365 days, was used to reckon time exclusively in the interval when subsistence activities took place (Aveni 2012). Although we have many early orientations emphasizing the solstices and quarter days approximating the equinoxes, the majority of Mesoamerican alignments seem to be aligned to dates in February and October, with many showing a 260-day span overlapping with the agricultural cycle (Sánchez and Šprajc 2015; Šprajc and Sánchez 2012, 2013b, 2015).

Earliest Known Long Count Records

Having established the likely antiquity of the 260-day cycle in relation to the agrarian year, we can return to a more detailed discussion of the development of the calendar. The most ancient Long Count dates are actually found in areas bordering the Lowland Maya area. Numbers arrayed in stacked columns were known by 600–400 BCE in Oaxaca, but they do not record multiples of 20 days (like the Mayan Long Count) and the year is designated by a yearbearer in a cartouche associated with a year sign, making them quite different from Long Count inscriptions (Marcus 1992:40–41). Most of the dates are based on archaeological context rather than secure readings because they are yearbearer dates that can be repeated every 52 years. Although Edmonson (1988) has proposed a specific reading for the dates, the more detailed study of Javier Urcid (2011:Figure 6.11) does not support such specific dates, although it is clear that year glyphs and day names date back to Monte Albán I and the yearbearers implicitly divided the year into 260/105-day segments. This form of reckoning also appears to be early at San Bartolo, as noted previously, and also appears in the Late Preclassic at Chiapa de Corzo (discussed below).

Monuments with Cycle 7 (Bak'tun 7) Long Count dates, the earliest secure dates, are most often found in areas linked with the Mixe-Zoque language. It is presumed that the calendar innovations passed from there on to the Lowland Maya, but it is also possible that the Long Count diffused to the Mixe-Zoque (epi-Olmec) region from the Maya area or the Pacific Slope bordering the Maya area (Justeson et al. 1985:42).

The first known Maya Long Count dates are found on the Pacific Slope of Guatemala. Takalik Abaj Stela 2 may date somewhere between 7.6.0.0.0 and 7.16.0.0.0 in Cycle 7 of the Bak'tun count (as early as 235 BCE; Graham et al. 1978:89–91), but recent high-definition digital photographs suggest the Bak'tun should be read as 8, which would place it hundreds of years later (Milbrath 2017). Takalik Abaj Monument 11 could be Cycle 6. This boulder is carved with a column of glyphs and an inscription possibly dating to Cycle 6 (Middle Preclassic), based on a Tzolk'in date (reconstructed as 11 Ik') that may have an Initial Series glyph attached (Graham and Porter 1989). Other early monuments from the Pacific Slope include El Baúl Stela 1 and Takalik Abaj Stela 5, all bearing rare Long Count texts dating from the second half of the Late Preclassic (Justeson et al. 1985:40). El Baúl Stela 1 preserves the Tzolk'in date 12 Eb, using a Mexican form of day sign that appears above the first part of a Cycle 7 Long Count (7.19), which is reconstructed as 7.19.[15.7.12] 12 Eb, equated to March 2, 37 (NS, March 4 OS) in the 584,283 correlation, approximating the date of the new moon (March 5, 37 OS).

Takalik Abaj Stela 5 records Cycle 8 Long Count dates in two side-by-side glyphic columns (Figure 4.2). John Graham et al. (1978:92) read the date on the right side as 8.2.2.10.5, correlating with August 23, 83 (OS, August 21, 83 NS), but they note that because a dot may have spalled off the right side this inscription could be 8.3.2.10.5 (May 10, 103 OS or May 9, 103 NS), a date which I link to the full moon. They read the better-preserved date on the left side as 8.4.5.17.11, equivalent to June 4, 126 (OS, June 3, 126 NS). Alternatively, the left column could be read as 125 CE, if Justeson (2010:48–49, 2012:834) is correct in suggesting that the Winal was not included.[11] Justeson identifies Stela 5 as the first known monument recording the year ending and argues that the Winal was zero but the zero sign had not yet been invented, so the notation was omitted and the Long Count date was given as a four-digit unit, with the fifth place being used for the numbered coefficient of the T'zolkin. Other glyphs on the monument agree with Maya writing, so this text clearly uses Maya forms of dating (Justeson,

Figure 4.2. Takalik Abaj Stela 5. Photograph by Susan Milbrath.

personal communication, 2014). Like Stela 1 from El Baúl, this early Cycle 8 inscription follows Maya Long Count patterns that place the beginning of the current Bak'tun cycle on 4 Ajaw 8 Kumk'u.

Stela 2 from Chiapa de Corzo has a Long Count date that can be reconstructed as [7.16.] 3.2.13 6 Ben (36 BCE), even though the first two numbers are effaced. The damaged Long Count lacks the top register where the Initial Series Introductory Glyph (ISIG) and month patron would be found, and Haab dates had not yet been introduced in the calendar. The Maya yearbearer glyph should be Ben but more closely resembles the central Mexican yearbearer Reed (Coe 1976:112). Stela 2 has traditionally been dated to December 8, 36 BCE (NS, December 10 OS) in the 584,285 correlation, but more recently it has been argued that it employs an epi-Olmec dating system, which would place the date 20 days earlier than in the 584,285 correlation (Justeson 2010:Table 5.2). According to Justeson (2010:49), the Long Count in the epi-Olmec dating system, using a 584,265 correlation, continued to be used as late as 533 CE at Cerro de las Mesas, but elsewhere it was replaced by the Maya Long Count sometime between 125 and 300 CE.

Tres Zapotes Stela C from southern Veracruz records the oldest well-preserved Long Count date, inscribed as 7.16.6.16.18, equivalent to September 3, 32 BCE (NS, September 5 OS) in the 584,285 correlation, but the date would be 20 days earlier in the 584,265 correlation, falling on August 14, 32 BCE (NS) in the epi-Olmec system (Pool 2007:252, 307 n. 1).[12] There is controversy about whether the epi-Olmec correlation is valid (Houston and Coe 2003; Milbrath 2017), but using this correlation factor does provide a link to a number of specific astronomical events.[13] Justeson's analysis of epi-Olmec texts, using a correlation factor of 584,265, means that 4 Ajaw 8 Kumk'u in the Classic Maya system would have a month inscription that is 20 days earlier in the epi-Olmec texts (Kaufman and Justeson 2001).

On Stela C, for the first time we see the month patron recorded in the ISIG at the top of the inscription. The patron system developed in the Late Preclassic to indicate positions in 365-day cycle at an early time before the Maya Haab was used for Calendar Round dates. As Aldana (2007–2008:69) notes, these Preclassic dates show that the solar year was the leading element; but by the Classic period the month patron became redundant with the Haab inscription at a time the Supplementary Series was introduced, as in the Leiden Plaque discussed below (Figure 4.3). The month patron system clearly developed before the Haab was formalized in inscriptions.

La Mojarra Stela 1, a monument from Veracruz discovered in the Acula

River, has an epi-Olmec Long Count recorded as 8.5.3.3.5 13 Snake (Aveni 2001:Figure 65; Kaufman and Justeson 2001:2.34–2.35; Macri and Stark 1993). The month patron is incorporated in the ISIG with a Tun sign directly below it and the Tzolk'in date appears at the end of the column. Martha Macri and Lauren Stark (1993:43) use the 584,285 correlation to date the monument's inscription at A1-9 to May 21, 143 (NS), whereas Rice (2007:106) uses the 584,283 correlation, resulting in a date of May 19, 143 (NS, May 20 OS). Justeson uses a 584,265 correlation for epi-Olmec texts, however, which makes the date correspond to May 1, 143, in a back-projected Gregorian calendar (NS) or May 2, 143, in the Julian calendar (OS) used by astronomers.[14] This May 2 date is the day of an almost total solar eclipse (83 percent: Aveni 2001:167; Espenak and Meeus 2006). The two Long Count inscriptions (A1-9 and M8-16) are separated by 4,802 days (13.6.2), an interval linking two Venus events, and the interval of 13 years at H3-I4 links a solar eclipse to a lunar eclipse on 8.5.16.3.7. Another interval at I5-J5 leads to the second Long Count inscription (8.5.16.9.7 5 Deer at M8-16) that dates to June 23, 156, correlating with the summer solstice (Kaufman and Justeson 2001:2.37–2.38, 2.71). Of course, the relationship with these specific astronomical events depends on using the 584,265 correlation, which is not used by a number of scholars (Macri and Stark 1993; Rice 2007). The intervals between Venus events remain valid, regardless of the correlation factor, and scholars are generally in accord that the text contains references to Venus (Macri and Stark 1993:43).

The Las Tuxtlas Statuette from Veracruz, identified as a representation of a nocturnal bird commonly known as the boat-billed heron, records another epi-Olmec inscription (Kaufman and Justeson 2001:2.82). The month patron appears in the ISIG just above a Tun inscription, resembling the pattern seen in the La Mojarra texts. The Haab patron would be Kankin using the traditional Classic Maya dating system, but the month closely resembles Mac, the month prior to Kankin, in accord with the epi-Olmec designation (Justeson 1988:7). The Long Count date recorded as 8.6.2.4.17 8 Earthquake has been dated to March 12, 162 CE (NS, March 13, 162 OS), using the 584,283 correlation (Rice 2007:104), but if Justeson's proposed epi-Olmec correlation is used, the date would be 18 days earlier (or 20 days earlier if calculated back from the 584,285 correlation). In any case, there is no clear evidence that this inscription is related to eclipse cycles, but it might be linked with a lunar count, if the 13-day Trecena period is part of an ancient lunar count.

Lunar records may be incorporated in early Trecena cycles. Macri (2005) suggests the head variants of the numbers in Classic inscriptions originated as an early lunar count with the numbers 1–13 designating the 13 days of the waxing moon. In her interpretation, the personified numbers 14–20 represent a 7-day period counting to the waning quarter. Macri (2005) also says that the remaining days of the lunar count are represented by the 9-day cycle of the lunar series (Glyphs G1–G9), which would carry the 29-day count (13 + 7 + 9) through the new moon.

It is possible that the 20-day intervals, used very early on in the Tzolk'in, were integrated with observations of the moon. Certainly the personified numbers could be linked with the moon, as Macri points out, and the 20-day sets in the Winal of the Long Count calendar also have a special connection with the moon on linguistic grounds. "Winal" or "Uinal" is derived from *u* or *uj*, the word for moon (Rice 2007:38) and may also be linked with the word for month (Thompson 1960:143). A similar pattern is in seen central Mexico, where the 20-day months were referred to as *metztli*, meaning moon (Caso 1971:339).

The Early Classic Maya Calendar

Tikal Stela 29 is still considered to be the earliest Maya stela with an ISIG Long Count from a Maya site in the Lowlands.[15] It bears a Long Count date of 8.12.14.8.15 [13 Men 3 Zip], equivalent to July 6, 292 in both the Julian and Gregorian calendars (the associated Calendar Round is now effaced; Jones and Satterthwaite 1982:Figure 29). The ISIG has the T125 superfix and Tun sign, but it lacks the T25 "comb" element (*ka*) that became common later on (Coe 1976:11). The month patron in the ISIG is Zip, indicating a standardized calendar inscription like that of other Classic Maya sites. On Stela 29, we see a Tikal innovation with the first recorded emblem glyph, here represented on a deity head in the ruler's hand, and the event glyph is presumably related to the ruler represented on the front of the monument (Stuart 2011:128). Stela 29 was possibly erected in the Mundo Perdido E Group during the Manik I phase (250–300) at a time when the complex was fully elaborated with a radial pyramid and three buildings on the range structure to the east (Laporte 1987; Laporte and Fialko 1990:46, Figure 3.2).

The Leiden Plaque is an early Maya example of a standardized Long Count with the Haab (1 Eb 0 Yaxkin) and corresponding Haab patron (Yaxkin) in the ISIG at the top of the number column. The ISIG is followed by the Long Count inscription: 8.14.3.1.12, corresponding to September 14, 320 OS (September 15, 320 NS). The Tzolk'in is recorded at the base of the numbers column, just above the Haab date (Figure 4.3; after Milbrath 1999:Plate 2).[16] The symbol for seating the Haab appears on the right, here representing zero, read with Yaxkin in the next row (left) to form the date 0 Yaxkin (Milbrath 1999:4). It also bears an early reference to the 9-day cycle in the lunar series (G5 in Thompson 1960:Figure 34, no. 25). The accession of a ruler sometimes referred to as Jaguar Claw II may be featured on the plaque, presumed to be from the tomb beneath Mundo Perdido Structure 5D-86-6, the central structure on the range (Laporte 1987). This suggests another early dated inscription linked to Tikal's E Group.

The Long Count developed independently from the Haab, but once Maya calendar priests began working with 20-day units to build up longer cycles of time the Haab became a secondary inscription, subordinate to the Long Count. Based on Mixe-Zoque texts, the Haab was first noted in Long Count inscriptions as a month patron in the ISIG at the top of the inscription. After this transitional period, the Haab was further modified by being paired with the Tzolk'in as a Calendar Round notation, and the month patron in the Haab continued to be noted separately in the ISIG.

Some Classic inscriptions record solar events, most notably the solstices (Milbrath 1999:64–65; Šprajc and Sánchez 2013b:334), but generally these events are subordinate to records of historical accounts and more complex astronomical cycles. Time-keeping involving K'atun-endings (approximately every 20 years) became increasingly important. Many Late Classic Maya inscriptions include references to K'atun-endings, designating period-ending rituals in public spaces, like those in Tikal's Twin Pyramid complexes (Aimers and Rice 2006:92). At Tikal, the K'atun monuments were displayed in specialized enclosures with two pyramids flanked by buildings to the north and south (Ashmore 1991; Martin and Grube 2000:51).[17]

Study of the patterning of K'atun-ending records at Tikal suggests that they may be related to planetary observations because the K'atun records on stelae at the site seem to correspond to the retrograde periods of Jupiter and Saturn throughout the Classic period (Milbrath 2004). It is noteworthy that Tikal has more K'atun-ending inscriptions than other sites, and the earliest K'atun notations in the context of the Long Count. The patterning of recorded K'atun-endings seems related to astronomical observations, for they chose to record the K'atun-endings in the Early Classic only at times that these planets were in retrograde. After the "Hiatus Period" at Tikal

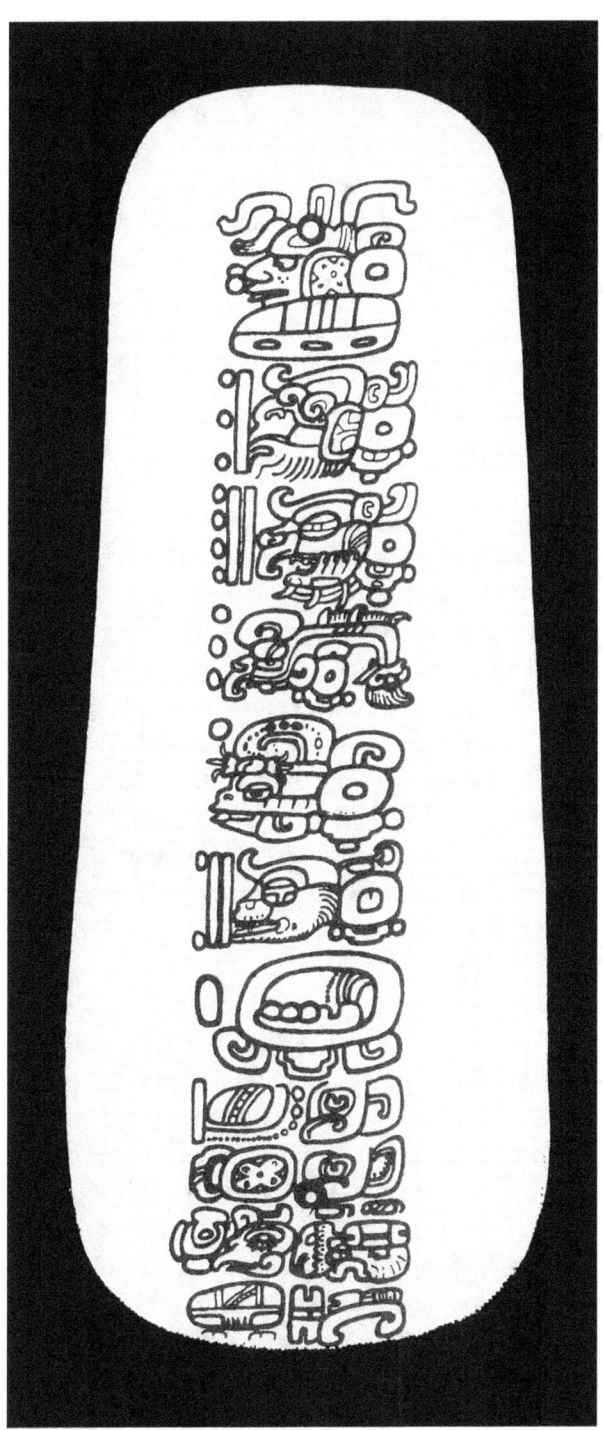

Figure 4.3. Leiden Plaque (modified after Milbrath 1999:Plate 2).

(562–692 CE: Martin and Grube 2000:40), they resumed recording K'atun-endings on monuments precisely at the time that the retrograde of these planets once again coincided with the K'atun end and they stopped recording at the end of the Late Classic when the K'atun end no longer coincided with retrograde of Jupiter or Saturn. These period-ending monuments were erected in Twin Pyramid complexes with radial pyramids (Milbrath 2004). This signals a revival of interest in linking astronomical observations with architecture that included radial pyramids, recalling the pyramids used in Preclassic E Groups and the ones used at later Maya sites in Yucatán (see below).

Terminal Classic Calendar Changes and Solar Alignments

Calendar changes in the Late Classic period are relatively minor until the Terminal Classic (800–900 CE) period, when the Southern Lowlands were in decline and the Long Count ceased to be recorded on monuments. At Tikal, the last Long Count inscription corresponds to 869 CE, and the final date known for the entire Maya area is 909 CE, found at Toniná (Martin and Grube 2000:53, 189). This is contemporary with dates recorded at Uxmal, some written in the Tun-Ajaw format also known from Chichén Itzá, most with Puuc-style Calendar Round dates placing the month's numeral coefficient one day earlier (Kowalski 1987:68–74; Thompson 1937). As Thompson notes, when the Tun-Ajaw dates appear with a Calendar Round, the Long Count equivalent also can be determined with accuracy. An Initial Series date at Chichén Itzá also bears a Tun-Ajaw date, allowing for an accurate correlation between the two calendars (Thompson 1937).

When the Terminal Classic period came to a close, the power center of the Maya had shifted to north to Uxmal and Chichén Itzá, sites with a new form of calendar. Here Calendar Round dates linked to Tun-Ajaw inscriptions recorded the Tun (360-day "year") within the current K'atun, referenced by a K'atun-ending date (always Ajaw). Monuments at Chichén Itzá and nearby sites record a few Tun-Ajaw dates that may be linked with solar events.[18]

In the Terminal Classic at Chichén Itzá there is also a clear focus on solar alignments, especially the solstices and solar zenith (Milbrath 1999:66–68, Figure 3-1a, b; Milbrath and Peraza 2003:17). An interest in 260/105-day intervals dividing the year continued in the Terminal Classic, as evidenced by the April 30/August 13 alignment seen in window 1 of Chichén Itzá's Caracol (Aveni et al. 2004:135). The Castillo, a radial pyramid dating to the

Terminal Classic, and the Early Postclassic Temple of the Warriors both have a west face oriented to the solar zenith sunset, but the Castillo seems more accurate in terms of alignments (Milbrath 1999:66–68; Šprajc and Sánchez 2013a:42). The Castillo reflects an interest in the solar zenith and the solar nadir (six months after the zenith). In addition to the well-known equinox pattern on the balustrades, the orientation of the Castillo creates a solar hierophany with shadow patterns bisecting the building at sunrise on the solar zenith in May and July (Montero et al. 2014).

The Terminal Classic alignments involving seasonal positions of the sun are sometimes also coordinated with horizon positions of Venus, as is the case of the Chichén Itzá's Caracol, an architectural complex that linked astronomical observations of the Sun and Venus (Aveni 2001:274, 285; Milbrath 1999:66–68).[19] Combined observations of the Sun and Venus were useful in coordinating the eight-year Venus almanac with important solar events, a form of almanac apparently imported from central Mexico (Milbrath 2014). Contact between Yucatán and central Mexico may have inspired revived interest in the solar cycle during the Terminal Classic and Early Postclassic.[20] As noted below, there were gradual transformations in the calendar and solar orientations during the Postclassic.

Postclassic Calendar Changes

A change in the beginning of the month from 0 Pop to 1 Pop in the Postclassic indicates a shift from elapsed time to current time in numbering the first day of the first month, a change that Harvey Bricker and Victoria Bricker (2011:85, 135–136) note may be tied to influence from central Mexico. Signs of contact with the Central Highlands of Mexico are also evident in the Dresden Codex, which shows images of central Mexican gods in the context of an eight-year Venus almanac in use in the thirteenth and fourteenth centuries (Bricker and Bricker 2011:Table 8–5; Milbrath 1999:163–177). Long Count dates are lacking in the surviving Maya codices except for the Dresden Codex, where the latest is dated to 1210 CE (Milbrath 1999:5). The Dresden Codex also records the yearbearer cycle in "New Year" pages, a cycle found also in the Madrid Codex (Vail and Bricker 2004). The Codex Madrid, possibly originating from Mayapán (Milbrath and Peraza 2003:28), emphasizes yearbearer dates and Calendar Round dates in the fifteenth century, but similar inscriptions have not been preserved on monuments at Mayapán, which seem to focus instead on the K'atun cycle.

Increasing central Mexican contact is clear during the Late Postclassic in the Madrid Codex (Milbrath 2005; Milbrath and Peraza 2003; Vail and Aveni 2004:19). The Tzolk'in-Haab form of Calendar Round dates in the Postclassic sometimes appeared on the same pages with yearbearer dates, as in the Madrid Codex (Bricker and Bricker 2011; Vail and Bricker 2004). Most of the Calendar Round dates found in the New Year's almanac on Madrid 34–37 cluster between 1460–1512 CE, contemporary with the date of the codex (Vail and Aveni 2004: 6, 18; Vail and Bricker 2004:201). An emphasis on the yearbearer cycle among the Postclassic Maya may relate to central Mexican influence, for this is the principal form of Postclassic Calendar Round known from the Central Highlands. Changes in the Maya calendar during the Postclassic reflect increased contact with central Mexico, where the solar calendar was very important.[21]

The late period at Mayapán was a time of heightened contact with central Mexico (Milbrath 2005; Milbrath and Peraza 2003:29–30). Solar orientations in architecture at Mayapán may reflect an increased emphasis on solar rituals like those seen in Postclassic central Mexico. In the fourteenth century, the latest phase of Mayapán's Castillo (covering the substructure known as Q162a) emphasizes solar orientations and a hierophany on the serpent balustrade on the winter solstice (Aveni et al. 2004; Milbrath and Peraza 2003:17, Figure 12). Other solar dates that seem to be emphasized include alignments from the east and west doorways of the Round Temple (Q152). One diagonal angle in the east doorway aligns to the June solstice sunrise (Aveni et al. 2004:Table 3). The west doorway is aligned to the base of the Castillo's stairway, where the setting sun was seen on April 30 and August 13, a period totaling 105 days that reflects the division of the year into 260/105 day segments. This alignment is also seen in window 1 of Chichén Itzá's Caracol (Aveni et al. 2004:135, Table 3, Figure 6).

Calendar changes also took place during Mayapán's Postclassic occupation. The short count K'atun cycle (around 256 years) seen on stelae appears to be early at Mayapán but apparently ceases to be recorded on monuments at the site later, the last known record being Stela 6, dating to the K'atun-ending in 1283 CE (Milbrath and Peraza 2003:Table 1). Perhaps there were adjustments after the K'atun short count was abandoned at Mayapán so that the 20-day months were more closely tied to the seasons, as they were in Aztec accounts, or perhaps a new form of K'atun count, the 24-year Ajaw K'atun, was introduced to more closely follow the solar year.[22]

With the renovation of Mayapán's Castillo (Q162), an increased emphasis on solstice dates during the fourteenth century may coordinate with changes in the calendar during the late Postclassic (Aveni et al.

2004:131–132). The revival of interest in solar orientations associated with radial pyramids in the Postclassic and Terminal Classic may reflect a return to a focus on the solar cycle, first noted in the designs of Middle Preclassic E Groups.

Changes in the Maya Calendar in Relation to Architecture

Details of the calendar were worked out during a time when the first Maya E Groups were constructed in the Middle Preclassic (1,000–350 BCE). The first known E Groups in Mesoamerica date back to 1000 BCE, well before calendar records were recorded on monumental art. The earliest E Groups probably helped track the sun at 20-day intervals and may also have had added markers for the solstices and quarter days (approximate equinoxes). These E Groups may have been used for observations that helped pin down the dates of important solar events in the agrarian year, contributing to the development of the calendar.

Early E groups may also have been used for observations of Orion, a constellation linked with the maize cycle. The bright star of Orion's Belt reappeared after invisibility at dawn in early June during the Preclassic, in concert with the young shoots of maize as they sprouted; by September when the maize matured, the three "belt" stars were seen rising in a vertical column above the horizon around midnight, suggesting comparison with a mature maize plant. Alignments to Orion have also been noted in Preclassic Oaxaca, where early calendar inscriptions are dated to the Middle Preclassic.

The fixed 260-day count surviving today in the Maya agricultural cycle may have originated in the Middle Preclassic as a subdivision of the 365-day year. The Tzolk'in developed in the Middle Preclassic as a subdivision of the solar year used to codify natural divisions of the agricultural cycle. Mesoamerican calendar priests may have developed the 260-day calendar as a way of marking the length of the agricultural cycle in the context of the solar year. Evidence of orientations encoding the 260-day period is at least as old as the Late Preclassic. An interest in linking specific calendar periods to astronomical orientations in architecture seems to continue in the Classic, but the emphasis appears to be on 20-day units of time and possibly also 13-day units (Aveni et al. 2003; Šprajc 2011:91).

The earliest form of calendar in the Maya area is not entirely clear, but there is evidence of both the K'atun cycle and the yearbearers during the Late Preclassic at San Bartolo. The yearbearers, a facet of the 260-day calendar that designated a split in the year (260 days and 105 days), seem to be earlier in Oaxacan texts dating back to 600 BCE. They appear to be somewhat later in epi-Olmec texts from Veracruz dating to the first century BCE. These texts introduce month patrons that are not apparent in early Oaxacan texts. The month patrons may be the earliest form of designating the 20-day periods of the Haab. The epi-Olmec texts also use a 20-day Winal as the basic subdivision of the 360-day Tun, a format shared by early Maya texts from the Pacific Slope.

The earliest known Long Count inscriptions seem to be Maya texts from an area bordering the Maya Lowlands, although poor preservation does not allow us to determine precise dates. Like the epi-Olmec texts, Cycle 7 and 8 Long Count dates from El Baúl and Takalik Abaj focus on sets of 20 days and a 360-day Tun using multiples of 20 that did not require any form of adjustment to the true tropical solar year. Early dates from the Pacific Slope seem to follow later Maya patterns but lack Haab notations, focusing instead on the Tzolk'in and larger cycles incorporating the Tun. It is noteworthy that Takalik Abaj also has an early E Group and even earlier evidence of solar observations in the solstitial alignment of Altar 46. Clearly, solar events were being tracked at a time that the 360-day civil year was being codified on the Pacific Slope.

The 365-day Haab may have originally coordinated with the seasonal cycles; but as the Preclassic drew to a close, the Haab became subordinate to the Long Count, which was developed to provide a much more sophisticated record of time. At this point, the solar cycle began to take a back seat to the more complex workings of the Bak'tun cycle and lunar series recorded in Mayan texts. By the time the Maya Long Count adopted a standardized format at the beginning of the Early Classic, the Haab was linked with the Tzolk'in as a Calendar Round inscription that could serve as a shorthand reference for the Long Count date. These Calendar Round dates were often used independently of Long Count inscriptions, making the precise date sometimes ambiguous.

During the Classic Maya period, astronomical alignments continued to be important, but architectural orientations most often marked 260 and 105-day divisions of the solar year, and sometimes the solstices or intervals of 20 days before and after the solar zenith.[23] It seems significant that this 260/105-day division of the year is also documented in the calendar at the end of the Classic period, when notations emphasizing the yearbearers surfaced again. Around the time that the political institutions of divine rule associated with the Classic Maya finally began to collapse, and the Long

Count calendar ceased to be recorded on monumental art, the power center shifted to the north during the Terminal Classic period (800–900 CE).

Between 850 and 900 CE, Tun-Ajaw dating was developed in Yucatán, placing a greater emphasis on Tun-endings in the 360-day civil year as an approximation of the solar year. The decline of the Long Count took place at a time when other models of abbreviated notation were favored, such as the Tun-Ajaw at Chichén Itzá and the K'atun short count, well documented in the codices and at Mayapán.

Around this time, architectural assemblages at Chichén Itzá seem to emphasize more precise solar alignments featuring solar dates such as the zenith passages and equinoxes in the Castillo and the Caracol. The Caracol's platform is diagonally aligned to the solstices, while one of its windows helps define the shorter part of the maize cycle with dates late April 30 and mid-August spaced at an interval of 105 days, instead of the more common Classic period orientation emphasizing the 260-day agrarian year (February to October). This pattern continues at Mayapán, but here there is a greater emphasis on the winter solstice, which is the central focus of hierophany seen in the Castillo and the June solstice in the Round Temple. This emphasis on the solstices recalls the patterns in the Preclassic in E Groups that mark the solstices (Milbrath 2017).

At the end of the Early Postclassic, new forms of notation evolved, such as the short count of 13 K'atuns recorded at Mayapán. At a time that the Long Count was no longer in use, an emphasis on the solar calendar may have developed at Mayapán in tandem with solar observations made in the context of Late Postclassic architecture. The intertwined history of the calendar and changes in architectural orientations is a fascinating topic that provides a fertile area for future research.

Acknowledgments

My thanks to John Justeson for reading a previous draft of this paper and commenting to clarify his position on some issues related to the earliest Mesoamerican calendar records. Thanks also to Ivan Šprajc commenting in his area of expertise on a previous draft of this chapter and pointing out that his measurements of Classic period sites indicate a continued interest in solar orientations. And many thanks to our editors, who made this volume possible.

Notes

1. Ivan Šprajc's measurements are different: March 9 and October 4 for 5D-85 and March 12 and October 11 for 5D-87 (Šprajc et al. 2013:1069, Table 1). To the west of the range buildings, Šprajc notes that Structure 5D-54 itself has an orientation to the sunrise on February 24 and October 18, dates that coincide with the agricultural cycle (agrarian year), following a pattern he has observed at a number of sites. Šprajc et al. (2013:1069, 1071–1072) note that the east–west alignment between Tikal 5C-54 (the pyramid) and 5D-86 (the central building on the range structure) is not at 90° as would be expected with an equinox orientation (and a flat horizon) but measures instead 94°30', marking the sunrise dates on March 9 and October 4 and sunset on March 31 and September 12. Šprajc (personal communication, 2014) questions whether E Groups had observational functions to any greater extent than other types of civic and ceremonial structures. He points out that a great variety of orientations are shown in the work of Aveni et al. (2003), and some of these orientations are based on maps that were aligned to magnetic north (Mundo Perdido at Tikal, for example). Nonetheless, Dowd (personal communication, 2015) comments that in their study they routinely corrected to get true north in the maps. Also, it should be noted that the observation point associated with the western pyramid in individual E Groups may vary. For example, an early E Group formed by Structures 1, 2, 3, and 9 at La Milpa seems to be aligned to the equinoxes and solstices, using Stela 18 on Structure 9 as the observation point (Hopkins n.d.).

2. The seasonal position of stars in Orion also relates to images of the turtle constellation (Milbrath 1999:268). Classic Maya imagery shows the Maize God emerging from the split back of the turtle on the famous "Resurrection Vase." Although this turtle image is often referred to as the earth, turtle symbolism is clearly related to later images in Maya art that feature the turtle constellation (Orion), as seen in the murals of Bonampak and the Maya "zodiac" in the Paris Codex (Aveni 2001; Bricker and Bricker 2011; Freidel et al. 1993:80–85; Milbrath 1999:Figure 7.6b). Turtle imagery is especially important in relation to creation cosmology and the three "hearthstone" stars in Orion known from ethnographic accounts (Freidel et al. 1993:68, 79; Milbrath 1999:267).

3. More recently, John Justeson (2012:830) dates La Venta Stela 13 as late as 450–300 BCE, indicating that it is later than the earliest Zapotec Calendar Round records. Zapotec inscriptions with numbered day signs on San José Mogote Monument 3, dated as early as 600 BCE, use a day sign and number to name a slain captive (Marcus 1992:36, Figure 2.9). Even though such an early date for this monument has been questioned, Justeson (2012:831, and personal communication, 2014) offers support for the Middle Preclassic date based on a detailed report on stratigraphy and ^{14}C dates published by Kent Flannery and Joyce Marcus in 2003.

4. Yearbearers are numbered day names found in the 260-day calendar used to name individual years in a cycle of 52 years. Every 20-day period in the 365-day calendar had the same set of 20 day names found in the 260-day calendar, but an extra five-day period was required at year end to round out the solar year, shifting the beginning point for the set of 20 day names five days forward in the next year; hence all the yearbearers were spaced at 5-day intervals. Over the course of four years the shift would amount to 20 days, and in

the fifth year the set of 20 days would once again begin on the same day name as 5 years earlier but now paired with a different number.

5. Glyph W at Monte Albán has been interpreted as a month name because it has a numerical coefficient larger than thirteen in some contexts (Edmonson 1988:22; Marcus 1992:40), but Javier Urcid (2001:273) concludes that Glyph W is not a month glyph even though it might have measured elapsed time because it is associated with year dates (see also Prem 1971:121). Justeson and Kaufman (1995) argue that Glyph W counts days in the lunation, correlating with Glyph D in Maya texts, and that when Glyph W lacks a coefficient it refers to the period of the moon's invisibility. This would suggest an early interest in the lunar cycle in Oaxaca that has not been generally noted by other scholars.

6. Some argue that the earliest records of yearbearers appear among the Olmec, an interpretation that remains highly speculative. Munroe Edmonson (1988:20–21) proposed that symbols on the Olmec Simojovel Axe (Tapijulapa Axe) were components in a Calendar Round date with a yearbearer dating 667 BCE (6.4.2.12.0), interpreting a fire serpent brow as the yearbearer sign Serpent, one of the "type V" yearbearers (Serpent, Dog, Eagle, and Flower). Edmonson (1988) also identified a possible month glyph (Ceh) and a face with dot on the nose as the date 1 Lord. It should be noted, however, that other scholars have taken a more cautious approach (Justeson et al. 1985:33–34; Rice 2007:45). Indeed, what Edmonson identifies as the numeral one more likely represents a nose-bead, a common form of jewelry in Olmec art, as seen in relief figures on La Venta Stela 3 and 13 (Rice 2007:Figures 5.5 and 5.14).

7. Edmonson (1988:119–120) notes that in the correlation preferred by many scholars the Julian Day number 584,283 corresponds to 4 Ajaw 8 Kumk'u, falling on August 11, 3114. Edmonson concludes that using the 584,283 correlation indicates that numerology determined the starting point of the Bak'tun cycle because the Long Count cycle of 13 Bak'tuns was apparently designed to "roll over" on the winter solstice in 2012 CE. Aveni (2012) points out that the August 11, 3114 BCE, could be a solar zenith date in the Central Maya Lowlands, and that the calendar was designed to roll over on the winter solstice in 2012 CE, which means that the system was set up to be in tune with two important seasonal markers. It may also be significant that the date 4 Ajaw 8 Kumk'u was a Tun ending in 7.2.7.0.0, ca. 300 BCE, around the time the Long Count was being developed (Justeson et al. 1985:76, n. 32; for further discussion of the correlation factor, see Bricker and Bricker 2011).

8. Frederick Peterson (1962:186–187; see also Fitchett 1974) first noted that in the zone of Copán (the same latitude as Izapa) the sun passes through zenith twice a year on August 13 and April 30, marking 260- and 105-day intervals, with the 260-day interval from August to April representing a harvesting and devotional period, whereas the growing season is 105 days, spanning from April to August. Nonetheless, if we take into account the complete maize cycle, a longer cycle is evident, one that is still preserved today among some Maya communities, as among the Chortí living near Copán and also among the Quiché (Milbrath 1999:15).

9. According to Girard, this 260-day count has been integrated with a "frozen" 365-day calendar that begins on February 8 among the Chortí, which he coordinates with the day 1 Imix. Clearly this date could fall on February 8 only once every 52 years in the Classic Maya calendar. It is noteworthy that Diego de Landa also speaks about a fixed 260-day

count beginning 1 Imix (Tozzer 1941:151–152). It seems that Girard (1962) traces his idea of a fixed Tzolk'in back to Landa, who may have misunderstood how the system worked in terms of the agricultural cycle. Nonetheless, the fixed 260-day agricultural cycle is also documented in entirely different areas among the Tzotzil in Chiapas and the Quiché in Guatemala, but there is no record of a fixed link with the Tzolk'in. In any individual year, however, a specific Tzolk'in date would not repeat during the 260-day agricultural cycle, so prognostications could be made throughout the cycle.

10. Agricultural practices vary in the Maya area, depending on the altitude, but the onset of rainfall generally determines when the principal maize crop is planted (Iwaniszewski 2002:506; Milbrath 2017; Terán and Rasmussen 1994:205–207). A second crop can be planted in some other Maya areas during the dry season or, more commonly, in the middle of the rainy season (Girard 1962; Estrada-Belli 2011:79; Milbrath 1999:13–14, 2017.

11. In reference to the paired columns of dates on Takalik Abaj Stela 5, Justeson (2010:48, Table 5.3) notes that each column lacks a digit in the month position, but in later positional records the dates would have been represented as 8.3.2.0.10 (left) and 8.4.5.0.17 (right). Justeson (2010) says that the Long Count records just four digits because the stela dates before the development of a zero symbol that would have marked the Winal position. Justeson transcribes the text as 8 Bak'tuns, 3 K'atuns, 2 "years" (Tuns), and 10 days on the day 5 (Coyote), and 8 Bak'tuns, 4 K'atuns, 5 years (Tuns), and 17 days on the day 11 (Earthquake), this last inscription representing the seating of the year in 125 CE.

12. The Tzolk'in date on Tres Zapotes Stela C is debatable. It should be 6 Etz'nab; but as Gerardo Aldana (2007–2008:68) notes, the number is there but the day is ambiguous. Michael Coe (1976:113) says the month patron is Uo, but the feline head lacks the characteristic nose cruller. Others have identified the feline head as the patron of preceding month, Pop, but Justeson (personal communication, 2014) notes that even though the patron is Pop there is a mismatch with the base date of the Long Count, if you use standard correlation factors (584,283 or 584,285). He points out that this discrepancy reflects the fact that epi-Olmec inscriptions use a 584,265 correlation factor, placing the Long Count 20 days earlier than the Classic Maya Long Count. He argues that this epi-Olmec correlation is confirmed by another epi-Olmec text on La Mojarra Stela 1, which has the month patron positioned 20 days earlier (Justeson and Kaufman 1996:22–23).

13. The date August 14, 32 BCE, corresponds to a lunar eclipse that was followed two weeks later by an almost total solar eclipse visible at Tres Zapotes (Malmström 1997:142; Pool 2007:253). This was actually an annular solar eclipse, and because astronomers recognize a zero year, the eclipse date is August 31, 31 BCE (Espenak and Meeus 2006).

14. The date of 159 CE for La Mojarra Stela 1 in Justeson and Kaufman (1993) has been invalidated in light of their more recent interpretation (Kaufman and Justeson 2001).

15. The Hauberg Stela, a small looted monument presumed to be from Tikal, records an ISIG Long Count read as 199 CE, a lunar calendar and a 9-day astronomical cycle that is part of the lunar series. The text referring to 17 lunations was considered to be the earliest evidence of the 18-month lunar synodical period, and Justeson (1989:87) interpreted this text as a reference to 47 + 17 lunations since the last observable eclipse. Justeson (1989) noted that the Hauberg Stela has an unusual sequence, with the Haab preceding the lunar series and the 9-day cycle (G1-G9). The month patron for Xul in the ISIG is correct, but the date is presented in an unorthodox manner: ISIG, then the Haab, and G5 of the lunar

series, followed by an unknown glyph, and closing out with the lunar text (17C) and a Tzolk'in date. Linda Schele (1985:135) noted that the Haab and Tzolk'in are presented in reversed order, and the ISIG lacks a Long Count notation, but both patterns are seen occasionally in Classic period inscriptions. The numerical part of the Haab inscription should be 13 Xul, but 12 Xul is recorded instead, which was presumed to be incorrect by Schele and Mary Ellen Miller (1986:191). They reconstructed the Initial Series date as 8.8.0.7.0, linked to the Calendar Round 3 Ajaw 12 [13?] Xul, and in 584,283 correlation this date would be equated with October 8, 199 (OS; October 7, NS). An alternate date was later proposed (8.7.17.14.4 3 Kan 12 Kankin), but the Brickers (2011:722–723) have rejected reading the month glyph as Kankin. Furthermore, its Preclassic date has recently been called into question, and it is said to be Early Classic but "of uncertain date" (Finamore and Houston 2010:252). If the stela is indeed Preclassic, the original reading could be correct, but that would mean that the Haab falls one day or a half day earlier than standard dates. This is a pattern seen in certain Classic inscriptions that record a time of day when the Tzolk'in had already changed but the Haab had yet not advanced a day (Mathews 2001:406).

16. The standardized Classic Maya Long Count inscriptions are accompanied by Calendar Round dates formed by linking the Tzolk'in and Haab dates in a cycle of approximately 52 years (18,980 days or 4 × 13 × 365) and 73 Tzolk'ins (73 × 260). In the Classic period Calendar Round, Maya months appear with numbers running 0–19 paired with days from the 260-day Tzolk'in with numbers running 1–13.

17. Although Twin Pyramid groups may appear as early as the Protoclassic (0–250 CE) at Tikal, Yaxhá, and possibly Calakmul (Aveni et al. 2003:174), they do not resemble the specialized Twin Pyramid complexes housing K'atun monuments at Late Classic Tikal.

18. Some of Chichén Itzá's Calendar Round dates combined with Tun-Ajaw inscriptions indicate an interest in solar events. Thompson (1960:Figure 38) transcribed a date at Chichén Itzá as 10.1.17.5.13 11 Ben 11 Kumk'u, Tun 18 of K'atun 3 Ajaw (not listed in Krochock 1998), which is equivalent to December 22, 866 CE (NS), a winter solstice date. Also, a date from neighboring Yula may be a "quarter day" close to the spring equinox: 10.2.11.14.1 6 Imix 4 Sek (March 24, 881 NS, also not listed in Krochock 1998).

19. Venus observations were also prominent in the Late Classic period, as is apparent in the orientation of the window of Copán Temple 22 ca. 700 CE and Uxmal's Palace of the Governor, dating ca. 800 CE (Aveni 2001:257–258, 285).

20. Chichén Itzá's architectural alignments emphasizing noteworthy solar dates such as the equinoxes, solstices, and solar zenith come when there are clear architectural parallels with the site of Tula and signs of contact with that central Mexican site starting around 850/900 CE. Chichén Itzá's Temple of the Warriors, constructed between 900 and 1000 CE, shows the strongest link with central Mexico, for it seems to be very similar to the Tula's Early Postclassic pyramid (Edificio B), dating to the Late Tollan subphase, beginning around 950 CE (Kristan-Graham and Kowalski 2007:60, 63).

21. Months of the year (Xihuitl) in central Mexico seem to be independent of the Tonalpohualli and yearbearer cycle and therefore could be coordinated more closely with solar year, perhaps adjusted periodically to keep a specific seasonal relationship (Milbrath 2013:113–114, n. 17). It is possible that by the end of the Postclassic the Maya Haab had also been linked more directly with the seasonal cycle, as it was in Landa's account. In 1566 CE Landa described the "fixed" Haab wherein July 16 (OS) coincided with the beginning of

the year in Pop, and a similar pattern is documented in the Chilam Balam of Chumayel (Milbrath 1999:59).

22. Possibly the 24-year Ajaw K'atun was introduced to emphasize the solar cycle near the end of Mayapán's occupation. John Bolles (1990:87) implies that the Mayapán calendar was keyed to the solar year as early as 1392 CE, the date he proposes for the introduction of the 24-year Ajaw K'atun (Ajaw K'atun 8 Ajaw with 7 Cauac as the yearbearer). Bolles (1990:86–87) says that seasonal correlates for the Yucatecan month names recorded in the sixteenth century indicate that the months were somehow adjusted to stay in tune with the seasons (as may be the case in central Mexico; Milbrath 2013). For example, Bolles (1990) notes that Muan, the name of the month at the beginning of the rainy season, is linked to the Muan bird, a counterpart of the Yucatec screech owl, which is today a sign of the onset of the rains, and Xul ("end") refers to the end of the rainy season in October, while Mol ("gather") in December refers to the harvest. I came to a similar conclusion about the seasonal links for month names when analyzing Landa's data and the books of the Chilam Balam (Milbrath 1999:59), but I could offer no concrete explanation of how the months would have achieved a fixed relationship to the solar year in the Late Postclassic.

23. In the Classic period, the focus is on intervals of 13 and 20 days and crucial days in the agricultural cycle, especially early February and late October. Šprajc (Sánchez and Šprajc 2015:Table 8; Šprajc et al. 2009:82) notes that true equinox orientations are uncommon and that there are actually more orientations to the quarter days, falling halfway between the solstices (Šprajc and Sánchez 2012, 2013b; Šprajc 2015). These quarter days could be useful in subdividing the agricultural calendar, but they do not encode 20-day intervals.

References Cited

Aimers, James J., and Prudence M. Rice
2006 Astronomy, Ritual, and the Interpretation of Maya "E Group" Architectural Assemblages. *Ancient Mesoamerica* 17(1):79–96.
Aldana, Gerardo
2007–2008 Glyph G and the Yohualteuctin: Recovering the Mesoamerican Practice of Time Keeping and Nightly Astrology. *Archaeoastronomy: Journal of Astronomy in Culture* 21:59–75.
Ashmore, Wendy
1991 Site-Planning Principles and Concepts of Directionality among the Ancient Maya. *Latin American Antiquity* 2(3):199–226.
Aveni, Anthony F.
2001 *Skywatchers of Ancient Mexico*. University of Texas Press, Austin.
2002 *Empires of Time: Calendars, Clocks and Cultures*. Revised ed. Basic Books, New York. Originally published in 1989.
2012 Calendars and Archaeoastronomy. In *Oxford Handbook of Mesoamerican Archaeology*, edited by Debra L. Nichols and Christopher H. Pool, pp. 787–794. Oxford University Press, New York.
Aveni, Anthony F., Anne S. Dowd, and Benjamin Vining
2003 Maya Calendar Reform?: Evidence from Orientations of Specialized Architectural Assemblages. *Latin American Antiquity* 14(2):159–178.

Aveni, Anthony F., and Horst Hartung
1986   Maya City Planning and the Calendar. *Transactions of the American Philosophical Society* 76(7):1–84.
2000   Water, Mountain, Sky: The Evolution of Site Orientation in Southeastern Mesoamerica. In *Precious Greenstone, Precious Quetzal Feather: Mesoamerican Studies in Honor of Doris Heyden*, edited by Eliose Quiñones Keber, pp. 55–65. Labyrinthos, Lancaster, California.
Aveni, Anthony F., Susan Milbrath, and Carlos Peraza Lope
2004   Chichen Itza's Legacy in the Astronomically Oriented Architecture of Mayapan. *RES: Journal of Anthropology and Aesthetics* 45:123–143.
Bachand, Bruce R., and Lynneth S. Lowe
2011   Chiapa de Corzo y los olmecas. Las ciudades en Mesoamérica. *Arqueología Mexicana* 107:74–83.
Bolles, John S.
1990   The Mayan Calendar: The Solar-Agricultural Year and Correlation Questions. *Mexicon* 12(5):85–89.
Bricker, Harvey M., and Victoria R. Bricker
2011   *The Dresden Codex*. American Philosophical Society, Philadelphia.
Bricker, Victoria
1982   The Origin of the Maya Solar Calendar. *Current Anthropology* 23(1):101–103.
Bricker, Victoria R., and Susan Milbrath
2011   Thematic and Chronological Ties between Borgia and Madrid Codices Based on Records of Agricultural Pests in the Planting Almanacs. *Journal of Anthropological Research* 67(4):497–531.
Caso, Alfonso
1971   Calendric Systems of Central Mexico. In *Archaeology of Northern Mesoamerica*, part 1, edited by Gordon Ekholm and Ignacio Bernal, pp. 333–348. University of Texas Press, Austin.
Chase, Arlen F., and Diane Z. Chase
1995   External Impetus, Internal Synthesis, and Standardization: E Group Assemblages and the Crystallization of Classic Maya Society in the Southern Lowlands. *Acta Mesoamericana* 8:87–101 (special issue edited by Nikolai Grube entitled *The Emergence of Lowland Maya Civilization: The Transition from the Preclassic to Early Classic*).
Clark, John E., and Richard D. Hansen
2001   The Architecture of Early Kingship: Comparative Perspectives on the Origins of the Maya Royal Court. In *Royal Courts of the Ancient Maya*, edited by Takeshi Inomata and Stephen D. Houston, pp. 1–45. Vol. 2. Westview Press, Boulder, Colorado.
Coe, Michael D.
1976   Early Steps in the Evolution of Maya Writing. In *Origins of Religious Art and Iconography in Preclassic Mesoamerica*, edited by H. B. Nicholson, pp. 107–122. UCLA Latin American Center Publications, Los Angeles.
Coggins, Clemency
1982   The Zenith, the Mountain, the Center, and the Sea. In *Ethnoastronomy and*

Archaeoastronomy in the American Tropics, edited by Anthony F. Aveni and Gary Urton, pp. 111–123. New York Academy of Sciences, New York.

Dillon, Brian D.
2013   Aquí Nació el Mundo: Takalik Abaj and Early Mesoamerican Civilization. In *Fanning the Sacred Flame: Mesoamerican Studies in Honor of H. B. Nicholson*, edited by Matthew Boxt and Brian D. Dillon, pp. 93–136. University Press of Colorado, Boulder.

Dowd, Anne S.
2015   Maya Architectural Hierophanies. In *Cosmology, Calendars, and Horizon-Based Astronomy in Ancient Mesoamerica*, edited by Anne S. Dowd and Susan Milbrath, pp. 37–75. University Press of Colorado, Boulder.

Earle, Duncan Maclean, and Dean R. Snow
1985   The Origin of the 260-Day Calendar: The Gestation Hypothesis Reconsidered in Light of Its Use among the Quiche-Maya. In *Fifth Palenque Round Table, 1983*, edited by Merle Greene Robertson and Virginia M. Fields, pp. 241–244. Pre-Columbian Art Research Institute, San Francisco.

Edmonson, Munro S.
1988   *The Book of the Year: Middle American Calendrical Systems*. University of Utah Press, Salt Lake City.

Espenak, Fred, and Jean Meeus
2006   *Five Millennium Cannon of Solar Eclipses: 1999 to 3000*. NASA/TP-2006-214141. NASA, Hanover, Maryland.

Estrada-Belli, Francisco
2006   Lightning Sky, Rain, and the Maize God: The Ideology of Preclassic Maya Rulers at Cival, Peten, Guatemala. *Ancient Mesoamerica* 17(1):57–78.
2011   *The First Maya Civilization: Ritual and Power before the Classic Period*. Routledge, New York.

Finamore, Daniel, and Stephen D. Houston
2010   *Fiery Pool: The Maya and the Mythic Sea*. Yale University Press, in association with the Peabody Essex Museum, New Haven and London.

Fitchett, Arthur G.
1974   Comment on the Origin of the 260-Day Cycle in Mesoamerica. *Science* 145(4150):542–543.

Flannery, Kent V., and Joyce Marcus
2003   The Origin of War: New ^{14}C Dates from Ancient Mexico. *Proceedings of the National Academy of Sciences* 100(20):11801–11805.

Freidel, David A., Linda Schele, and Joy Parker
1993   *Maya Cosmos: Three Thousand Years on the Shaman's Path*. William Morrow and Company, New York.

Girard, Raphael
1962   *Los mayas eternos*. Libro Mex Editores, Mexico City.

Giron-Ábrego, Mario
2013   A Late Preclassic Distance Number. *PARI Journal* 13(4):8–12.

Graham, John A., Robert F. Heizer, and Edward M Shook
1978   Abaj Takalik 1976: Exploratory Investigations. In *Studies in Ancient Mesoamer-*

ica, III, edited by John A. Graham, pp. 85–110. Contributions of the University of California Archaeological Research Facility, No. 36. Berkeley: University of California, Department of Anthropology.

Graham, John, and James Porter
1989   A Cycle 6 Initial Series?: A Maya Boulder Inscription from the First Millennium B.C. from Abaj Takalik. *Mexicon* 11(3):46–49.

Guernsey, Julia
2006   *Ritual and Power in Stone: The Performance of Rulership in Mesoamerican Izapan Style Art*. University of Texas Press, Austin.

Hansen, Richard D.
1998   Continuity and Disjunction: The Pre-Classic Antecedents of Classic Maya Architecture. In *Function and Meaning in Classic Maya Architecture: A Symposium at Dumbarton Oaks 7th and 8th October 1994*, edited by Stephen D. Houston, pp. 49–122. Dumbarton Oaks, Washington, D.C.
2013   Kingship in the Cradle of Maya Civilization. In *Fanning the Sacred Flame: Mesoamerican Studies in Honor of H. B. Nicholson*, edited by Matthew Boxt and Brian D. Dillon, pp. 139–172. University Press of Colorado, Boulder.

Hatch, Marion Popenoe de
2009   Las cerámicas frente al arte escultórico y su información respecto del cambio social. In *XXIII Simposio de Investigaciones Arqueológicas en Guatemala*, pp. 95–1007. Museo Nacional de Arqueología y Etnología, Guatemala City.

Henderson, John S.
1974   The Origin of the 260-Day Cycle in Mesoamerica. *Science* 145(4150):542.

Hopkins, Stephen C.
n.d.   An E Group in Plaza A at La Milpa, Belize. MS in possession of the author.

Houston, Stephen D., and Michael D. Coe
2003   Has Isthmian Writing Been Deciphered? *Mexicon* 25(6):151–161.

Inomata, Takeshi, Daniela Triadan, Kazuo Aoyama, Victor Castillo, and Hitoshi Yonenobu
2013   Early Ceremonial Constructions at Ceibal, Guatemala, and the Origins of Lowland Maya Civilization. *Science* 340(1126):467–471.

Iwaniszewski, Stanislaw
2002   Los conceptos del tiempo en el discurso ideológico en el Protoclásico Maya: Cerros y Uaxactún. In *Tercer Congreso Internacional de Mayistas: Memoria (9 al 15 de Julio de 1995)*, pp. 503–516. UNAM, Mexico City.
2005   Leer el tiempo: El fenómeno de la sincronicidad en la práctica mántica teotihuacana. In *Perspectivas de la investigación arqueológica: IV Coloquio de la Maestría en Arqueología*, edited by Walburga Wiesheu and Patricia Founier, pp. 93–108. Concultra and INAH, Mexico City.

Jones, Christopher, and Linton Satterthwaite
1982   *The Monuments and Inscriptions of Tikal: The Carved Monuments*. Tikal Report No. 33, Part A. University Museum, University of Pennsylvania, Philadelphia.

Justeson, John S.
1988   The Non-Maya Calendars of Southern Veracruz-Tabasco and the Antiquity of the Civil and Agricultural Years. *Journal of Mayan Linguistics* 6:1–22.

1989   The Ancient Maya Ethnoastronomy: An Overview of Hieroglyphic Sources. In *World Archaeoastronomy: Selected Papers from the Second Oxford International Conference on Archaeoastronomy*, edited by Anthony F. Aveni, pp. 76–129. Cambridge University Press, Cambridge.

2010   Numerical Cognition and the Development of "Zero" in Mesoamerica. In *Archaeology of Measurement: Comprehending Heaven, Earth and Time in Ancient Societies*, edited by Iain Morely and Colin Renfrew, pp. 43–53. Cambridge University Press, Cambridge.

2012   Early Mesoamerican Writing Systems. In *Oxford Handbook of Mesoamerican Archaeology*, edited by Deborah L. Nichols and Christopher A. Pool, pp. 830–844. Oxford University Press, New York.

Justeson, John S., and Terrence Kaufman

1993   A Decipherment of Epi-Olmec Hieroglyphic Writing. *Science* 259:1703–1711.

1995   A Lunar Day Count at Monte Alban. Paper presented at the February meeting of Northeast Mesoamerican Epigraphy Group, February 10, 1995, Albany, NY.

1996   Un desciframiento de la escritura jeroglífica epi-olmeca: Métodos y resultados. *Arqueología Mexicana* 8:15–25.

Justeson, John S., William M. Norman, Lyle Campbell, and Terrence Kaufman

1985   *The Foreign Impact on Lowland Mayan Language and Script*. Middle American Research Institute Publication 53. Tulane University, New Orleans.

Kaufman, Terrence, and John S. Justeson

2001   *Epi-Olmec Hieroglyphic Writing and Texts*. Mesoamerican Languages Documentation Project. http://www.albany.edu/pdlma/EOTEXTS.pdf, accessed December 12, 2014.

Kováč, Milan, Silvia Alvarado Najarro, Tibor Leiskovský, Fátima Tec Pool, Damaris Menéndez, and Mauricio Díaz

2015   Reflexionando sobre el Preclásico de Uaxactun: Resultados de la sexta temporada del Proyecto Arqueológico Regional SAHI-Uaxactún. In *XXVII Simposio de Investigaciones Arqueológicas en Guatemala*, edited by Bárbara Arroyo, Luis Méndez Salinas, and Lorena Paiz, pp. 169–181. Museo Nacional de Arqueología y Etnología, Guatemala City.

Kowalski, Jeff K.

1987   *The House of the Governor: A Maya Palace at Uxmal, Yucatan, Mexico*. University of Oklahoma Press, Norman.

Kristan-Graham, Cynthia, and Jeff K. Kowalski

2007   Chichén Itzá, Tula, and Tollan: Changing Perspectives on a Recurring Problem in Mesoamerican Archaeology and Art History. In *Twin Tollans: Chichén Itzá, Tula, and the Epiclassic to Early Postclassic Mesoamerican World*, edited by Jeff K. Kowalski and Cynthia Kristan-Graham, pp. 13–84. Dumbarton Oaks Research Library and Collection, Washington, D.C.

Krochock, Ruth J.

1998   The Development of Political Rhetoric at Chichen Itza, Yucatan, Mexico. Ph.D. dissertation, Anthropology Department, Southern Methodist University, Dallas.

Lacadena, Alfonso
2009   Escritura y lengua en Takálik Ab'aj: Problemas y prouestas. In *XXIII Simposio de investigaciones arqueológicas en Guatemala*, pp. 1027–1044. Ministerio de Cultura y Deportes/Instituto de Antropología e Historia/Asociación Tikal, Guatemala City, 2010.

Laporte, Juan Pedro
1987   El Grupo 6C-XVI, Tikal Petén: Un centro habitacional del Clásico Temprano. In *Memorias del Primer Coloquio Internacional de Mayistas (August 1985)*, pp. 221–244. Universidad Nacional Autónoma de México, Mexico City.

Laporte, Juan Pedro, and Vilma Fialko C.
1990   New Perspectives on Old Problems: Dynastic References for the Early Classic Tikal. In *Vision and Revision in Maya Studies*, edited by Flora S. Clancy and Peter D. Harrison, pp. 33–66. University of New Mexico Press, Albuquerque.
1995   Un reëncuentro con Mundo Perdido, Tikal, Guatemala. *Ancient Mesoamerica* 6:41–94.

Macri, Martha
2005   A Lunar Origin for the Mesoamerican Calendars of 20, 13, 9, and 7 days. In *Current Studies in Archaeoastronomy: Conversations across Time and Space: Selected Papers from the Fifth Oxford International Conference at Santa Fe, 1996*, edited by John W. Fountain and Rolf M. Sinclair, pp. 275–288. Carolina Academic Press, Durham.

Macri, Martha J., and Laura M. Stark
1993   *A Sign Catalog of the La Mojarra Script*. Pre-Columbian Art Research Institute Monograph 5. PARI, San Francisco.

Malmström, Vincent
1991   Edzna: Earliest Astronomical Center of the Maya. In *Arqueoastronomía y etnoastronomía en Mesoamérica*, edited by Johanna Broda, Stanislaw Iwaniszewski, and Lucrecia Maupomé, pp. 37–47. Universidad Nacional Autónoma de México, Mexico City.
1997   *Cycles of the Sun, Mysteries of the Moon*. University of Texas Press, Austin.

Marcus, Joyce
1992   *Mesoamerican Writing Systems: Propaganda, Myth, and History in Four Ancient Civilizations*. Princeton University Press, Princeton, New Jersey.

Martin, Simon, and Nikolai Grube
2000   *Chronicle of the Maya Kings and Queens*. Thames and Hudson, New York.

Mathews, Peter
2001   The Inscription on the Back of Stela 8, Dos Pilas, Guatemala. In *The Decipherment of Maya Hieroglyphic Writing*, edited by Stephen D. Houston, David Stuart, and Oswaldo Chinchilla Mazariegos, pp. 394–415. University of Oklahoma Press, Norman.

Milbrath, Susan
1979   *A Study of Olmec Sculptural Chronology*. Studies in Pre-Columbian Art and Archaeology 23. Dumbarton Oaks, Washington, D.C.
1999   *Star Gods of the Maya: Astronomy in Art, Folklore, and Calendars*. University of Texas Press, Austin.

2004   The Classic Katun Cycle and the Retrograde Periods of Jupiter and Saturn. *Archaeoastronomy* 18:81–97.
2005   The Last Great Capital of the Maya. *Archaeology* 58(2): 27–30.
2013   *Heaven and Earth in Ancient Mexico: Astronomy and Seasonal Cycles in the Codex Borgia*. University of Texas Press, Austin.
2014   The Many Faces of Venus in Mesoamerica. In *Archaeoastronomy and the Maya*, edited by Geraldo Aldana and Edwin L. Barnhart, pp. 111–134. Oxbow Books, Oxford, United Kingdom.
2017   The Role of Solar Observations in Developing the Preclassic Maya Calendar. *Latin American Antiquity*. In press.

Milbrath, Susan, and Carlos Peraza Lope
2003   Revisiting Mayapan: Mexico's Last Maya Capital. *Ancient Mesoamerica* 14(2):1–47.

Montero García, Ismael Arturo, Jesús Galindo Trejo, and David Wood Cano
2014   El castillo en Chichén Itzá: Un monumento al tiempo. *Arqueología Mexicana* 21(127):80–85.

Nuttall, Zelia
1904   The Periodical Adjustments of the Ancient Mexican Calendar. *American Anthropologist* 6(4):486–500.

Peeler, Damon E., and Marcus Winter
1992–1993 Mesoamerican Site Orientations and Their Relationship to the 260-Day Ritual Period. *Notas Mesoamericanas* 14:37–62.

Peterson, Frederick
1962   *Ancient Mexico: An Introduction to the Pre-Hispanic Cultures*. Capricorn Books, New York.

Pool, Christopher A.
2007   *Olmec Archaeology and Early Mesoamerica*. Cambridge University Press, New York.

Prem, Hans J.
1971   Calendrics and Writing in Mesoamerica. In *Observations on the Emergence of Civilization in Mesoamerica*, edited by Robert F. Heizer and John A. Graham, pp. 112–132. Contributions of the University of California Archaeological Research Facility, No. 11. University of California, Department of Anthropology, Berkeley.

Rice, Prudence M.
2007   *Maya Calendar Origins: Monuments, Mythistory, and the Materialization of Time*. University of Texas Press, Austin.
2015   The "Las Bocas Mosaic" and Mesamerican Astro-Calendrics: "Calculator" or Hoax? In *Cosmology, Calendars, and Horizon-Based Astronomy in Ancient Mesoamerica*, edited by Anne S. Dowd and Susan Milbrath, pp. 265–283. University Press of Colorado, Boulder.

Sánchez Nava, Pedro Francisco, and Ivan Šprajc
2015   *Orientaciones astronómicas en la arquitectura maya de las tierras bajas*. INAH (Colleción Arqueología), Mexico City.

Schele, Linda
1985 The Hauberg Stela: Bloodletting and the Mythos of Maya Rulership. In *Fifth Palenque Round Table, 1983*, edited by Virginia M. Fields, pp. 135–150. Pre-Columbian Art Research Institute, San Francisco.

Schele, Linda, and Mary Ellen Miller
1986 *The Blood of Kings: Dynasty and Ritual in Maya Art*. Kimbell Art Museum, Fort Worth.

Šprajc, Ivan
2000 Astronomical Alignments at Teotihuacan, Mexico. *Latin American Antiquity* 11:403–415.
2001 *Orientaciones astronómicas en la arquitectura prehispánica del centro de México*. Colleción Científica 427. INAH, Mexico City.
2011 Astronomy and Its Role in Ancient Mesoamerica. In *The Role of Astronomy in Society and Culture, Proceedings of the International Astronomical Union Held at the UNESCO Headquarters, Paris, France, January 19–23, 2009*, edited by David Valls-Gabaud and Alexander Boksenski, pp. 87–95. Cambridge University Press, Cambridge.
2015 Pyramids Marking Time: Tony Aveni's Contribution to the Study of Astronomical Alignments in Mesoamerican Architecture. In *Cosmology, Calendars, and Horizon-Based Astronomy in Ancient Mesoamerica*, edited by Anne S. Dowd and Susan Milbrath, pp. 19–36. University Press of Colorado, Boulder.

Šprajc, Ivan, Carlos Morales-Aguilar, and Richard D. Hansen
2009 Early Maya Astronomy and Urban Planning at El Mirador, Peten, Guatemala. *Anthropological Notebooks* 15(3):79–101.

Šprajc, Ivan, Heinz-Dieter Richter, and Pedro Francisco Sánchez Nava
2013 El tiempo registrado en el espacio urbano: alianamientos astronómicos en la arquitectura de Tikal, Petén, Guatemala. In *XXVI Simposio de Investigaciones Arqueológicas en Guatemala, 2012*, edited by Bárbara Arroyo and Luis Méndez Salinas, pp. 1065–1078. Museo Nacional de Arqueología y Etnología, Guatemala City.

Šprajc, Ivan, and Pedro Francisco Sánchez Nava
2012 Orientaciones astronómicas en la arquitectura maya de las tierras bajas: Nuevos datos e interpretaciones. In *XXV Simposio de Investigaciones Arqueológicas en Guatemala, 2011*, edited by Bárbara Arroyo, Lorena Paiz, and Héctor Mejía, pp. 977–996. Museo Nacional de Arqueología y Etnología, Guatemala City.
2013a Astronomía en la arquitectura de Chichén Itzá: Una reevaluación. *Estudios de Cultura Maya* 41:33–60.
2013b Equinoxes in Mesoamerican Architectural Alignments: Prehispanic Reality or Modern Myth? *Anthropological Notebooks* 19 (supplement):319–337.
2015 *Orientaciones astronómicas en la arquitectura de Mesoamérica: Oaxaca y el Golfo de México*. Institute of Anthropological and Spatial Studies, Ljubljana, Slovenia. http://iaps.zrc-sazu.si/sites/default/files/pkc08_sprajc.pdf, accessed September 1, 2015.

Stuart, David
2005 New Year Records in Classic Maya Inscriptions. *PARI Journal* 5(2):1–6.

2011   *The Order of the Days: The Maya World and the Truth about 2012.* Harmony Books, New York.

Tedlock, Barbara

1992   *Time and the Highland Maya.* Revised ed. University of New Mexico Press, Albuquerque.

Terán, Silvia, and Christian H. Rasmussen

1994   *La milpa de los mayas: La agricultura de los mayas prehispánicos y actuales en el noreste de Yucatán.* DANIDA, Mérida, Yucatán, Mexico.

Thompson, J. Eric S.

1937   *A New Method of Deciphering Yucatecan Dates with Special Reference to Chichen Itza.* Contributions to American Archaeology No. 22. Carnegie Institution of Washington, Washington, D.C.

1960   *Maya Hieroglyphic Writing: An Introduction.* 3rd ed. University of Oklahoma Press, Norman.

Tichy, Franz

1991   Los cerros sagrados de la cuenca de México, en el sistema de ordenamiento del espacio y de la planeación de los poblados. In *Arqueoastronomía y etnoastronomía en Mesoamérica,* edited by Johanna Broda, Stanislaw Iwaniszewski, and Lucrecia Maupomé, pp. 447–500. UNAM, Mexico City.

Tozzer, Alfred M.

1941   *Landa's "Relación de las Cosas de Yucatán": A Translation.* Papers of the Peabody Museum of Archaeology and Ethnology, Vol. 18. Peabody Museum, Cambridge, Massachusetts.

Urcid Serrano, Javier

2001   *Zapotec Hieroglyphic Writing.* Studies in Pre-Columbian Art and Archaeology 34. Dumbarton Oaks, Washington, D.C.

Vadala, Jeffrey

2009   Three Dimensional Analysis and Recreation of Preclassic T'isil. M.A. thesis, Department of Anthropology, California State University, Los Angeles.

Vail, Gabrielle, and Anthony F. Aveni

2004   Research Methodologies and New Approaches to Interpreting the Madrid Codex. In *The Madrid Codex: New Approaches to Understanding an Ancient Maya Manuscript,* edited by Gabrielle Vail and Anthony F. Aveni, pp. 1–30. University Press of Colorado, Boulder.

Vail, Gabrielle, and Victoria R. Bricker

2004   Haab Dates in the Madrid Codex. In *The Madrid Codex: New Approaches to Understanding an Ancient Maya Manuscript,* edited by Gabrielle Vail and Anthony F. Aveni, pp. 171–214. University Press of Colorado, Boulder.

Whittaker, Gordon

1992   The Zapotec Writing System. In *Supplement to the Handbook of Middle American Indians,* Vol. 5, edited by Victoria R. Bricker and Patricia A. Andrews, pp. 5–19. University of Texas Press, Austin.

5

The E Group as Timescape

Early E Groups, Figurines, and the Sacred Almanac

PRUDENCE M. RICE

This chapter explores an association between small anthropomorphic figurines of fired clay and their early contexts in Maya E Groups. These figurines date primarily to the Middle Preclassic or Preclassic period in Mesoamerica, but they began to be made earlier in the Late Archaic (2,000–1,000 BCE) and continued briefly into the Late Preclassic (350 BCE–0 CE). Discussion proceeds through an overview of figurines in general, to observations on those from Nixtun-Ch'ich' and Ixlú in central Petén, and then to their apparent association with and possible functions in early ritual areas.

Anthropomorphic Figurines

Worldwide the human body has been a model for conceptualizing and categorizing the organization of natural, social, and cosmic spaces (Csordas 1990, 1994; Mauss 1973). Human representations in Preclassic period Mesoamerica vary from the colossal heads of basalt found only in Gulf coastal Mexico to small portable figurines carved of greenstone and, most abundantly, modeled of clay. Cross-culturally, anthropomorphic and particularly female terracotta figurines are common during the period of transition to sedentary life, horticulture, and emergence of ranked societies.

These early figurines are typically broken and recovered as fragments. Many behaviors account for patterns of artifact breakage and deposition, as revealed in ethnoarchaeological studies of use-lives and site-formation processes (Schiffer 1972, 1976). The interpretive framework here, however, builds on the ideas of John Chapman (2000:23, 2008; Brittain and Harris 2010) about fragmentation and "enchainment": the intentional breakage of objects and exchange of the fragments to create chains of personal relations. Analysis of figurines from several culture areas suggests that their manufacture is designed to facilitate disarticulation and that they were intended to be broken (Chapman 2000:25, 68–69). In addition, embodiment theory holds that human bodies may be considered partible or dividable ("dividual": Strathern 1988) and relational (defined by relations with other people and things). These concepts apply satisfactorily to Classic (250–900 CE) and Postclassic (900–1519 CE) Lowland Maya views of the body (Geller 2012; Houston et al. 2006) and also to Middle Preclassic figurines.

Mesoamerican figurines are typically small (<20 cm), solid (but sometimes hollow and often larger), and modeled by hand rather than mold-made. Occurring by the hundreds or thousands in some areas, they vary stylistically from region to region, and even within sites and contexts, such as individual residences and features (Cheetham 2005, 2009; Coe and Diehl 1980:259–279; Cyphers 1988, 1993; Follensbee 2009; Gillespie 1987; Grove and Gillespie 1992; Lesure 1997, 1999; Marcus 1998; Meissner et al. 2013; Tway 2004; Vaillant 1930). The functions and contexts of manufacture of these artifacts are much debated, but there is general agreement that, because the figurines are recovered primarily in residential settings and burials, they were made by women, primarily represent women, and were made and used in domestic rituals involving ancestors or a "cult of the 'ruler'" (Grove and Gillespie 1984, 2002:15).

Preclassic Mesoamerican figurines display individualized faces, hairstyles, and headdresses. The head is perhaps the most in-"dividual" part of the body of any living creature, and the locus of individual identity. Separation of the head from the body is an important aspect of the breakage of these objects, frequently attributed to ritual termination. Such "decapitation" was an apparently easy, intentional, and common practice cross-culturally with anthropomorphic figurines and is an illustration of bodily partibility.[1]

Perhaps the most puzzling trait of these figurines is their sexual ambiguity. Unlike the Rubenesque "Venus" and "fertility goddess" figurines in many Old World areas, Mesoamerican artifacts generally lack the pendulous breasts, broad hips, and voluptuous abdomen, buttocks, and thighs considered emphases on female fecundity. Instead, the figurines tend to be slender and androgynous, typically lacking breasts and delineation of genitalia, and nude: clothing is rarely modeled in the clay. Anatomical correctness was evidently of little significance to the makers and users, making it difficult to discern not only the sex of the figural representations but also their ages, thus hindering their interpretation. Nonetheless, numerous studies conclude that both males and females and a range of ages are depicted. Adorning the figurines with fabric, fibers, feathers, pigment, or ornaments appropriate to the circumstances in which they were being manipulated may have specified aspects of the age, sex, rank, and social role of the portrayals (Coe and Diehl 1980:260; Marcus 2009:45). Or they might have been given names possibly indicating gender while in use (Joyce Marcus, personal communication, 2013).

Early Maya E Groups and Figurines

Compared with other areas of Preclassic Mesoamerica, Maya Lowland sites have yielded few figurines and fragments, which have not enjoyed comparable levels of scholarly scrutiny (Cheetham 1993; Zweig 2010). Figurines are found primarily in the Southern and Central Lowlands; surprisingly, they are absent in the Northern Lowlands and rare in the east (for example, coastal Belize).[2] In the South-Central Lowlands these objects are recovered from settings deemed residential/private as well as public, such as the fills of civic-ceremonial structures. These secondary contexts are generally ignored and unreported throughout Mesoamerica, presumably under the assumption that the figurines were simply swept up with other domestic refuse or ceremonial trash and dumped into the construction fills (for example, at San Lorenzo: Coe and Diehl 1980:260). But context is crucial to the interpretation of figurines (Bailey 1994:323; Chapman 2000:72; Marcus 1996), especially given these artifacts' sexual ambiguity, and even fills can provide insights into their uses and functions.

Lowland Maya figurines have been recovered in the basal levels of architectural complexes that evolved through time in similar but nonetheless slightly different directions. These complexes include the E Group proper, plus Eastern Triadic Structures and Triadic Groups or Triadic Pyramids.[3] Eastern Triadic Structures are a platform on the east side of a plaza that supports a linear array of three structures. A Triadic Group is an orthogonal arrangement of three buildings—"a central dominant structure flanked by two smaller buildings facing each other" and open to the west—on a large pyramidal platform (Hansen 2000:59). Because test pits and trenches provide minimal exposure of the basal levels underlying these complexes, which often grew to enormous size, we know relatively little about if and how they might have been differentiated—conceptually, architecturally, functionally—at initial "design-and-build." Consequently, I refer to them collectively as Early Ritual Areas. This collective labeling is based on the complexes' shared, tripartite, east-side architectural elaboration, which may be evident only late in their histories, and on an assumption of shared general ritual functions based on that focus. Below I review the occurrence of Middle Preclassic figurines in some of these Early Ritual Areas.

Uaxactún

The "index-fossil" Group E at Uaxactún was constructed in an area of Middle Preclassic occupation that yielded solid and hollow figurine fragments (Hendon 1999; Rands and Rands 1965:536–538; Ricketson and Ricketson 1937:Plate 70). In the plaza of Group E, two deep pits or *chultun*s excavated into bedrock were filled with midden material, including abundant artifacts of shell and Middle Preclassic (Mamom) pottery and also human remains. Pit E-18 had one figurine head plus seven other fragments and Pit E-4 contained twenty-five figurines or fragments, including five possible whistles and one head (Hendon 1999:Tables 1, 2). Low wall-lines of stone were also noted and thought to represent domestic structures.

These pits and structures on bedrock were covered by a stucco floor (Floor 1), upon which three platforms were built and dated to the Middle Preclassic by pottery: possibly cruciform Structure A, elongated Structure D, and rectangular Structure B, forming three sides of a plaza (Hendon 1999:103, 105–106).[4] There is no evidence for the Ricketsons' (1937) expected eastern Structure C in this arrangement, however. Platforms B and D are proposed to have been residential; Structure A, on the west underlying the famous later E-VII-Sub, was concluded to have been "part of household focused religious practice for a household commanding significantly greater resources than its neighbors" (Hendon 1999:117). It is not clear if figurines were associated with these structures.

Thus, the Uaxactún Early Ritual Area began during and perhaps just before the Middle Preclassic period, but it lacked an eastern platform. At some unspecified later date, presumably in the Late Preclassic, Structure E-VII-Sub replaced Structure A and the eastern structure was built (Hendon 1999:116–117), creating the standardized E Group. In the Early Classic (250–550 CE), three period-ending stelae were erected in front of this building: Stelae 18 and 19 (both dated 8.16.0.0.0, 357 CE) and Stela 5 (8.16.10.0.0, 366 CE).

Tikal

The Mundo Perdido E Group is probably the best excavated of these complexes in terms of exposing its architectural development (Laporte and Fialko 1993, 1995; Laporte and Valdés 1993; Chapter 8 in this volume).

Episodes of Middle Preclassic plaza construction were accompanied by massive deposits of ceramic and nonceramic artifacts in large, deep *chultun*s on the east and west peripheries of this sacred space, excavated into bedrock and sealed by Middle Preclassic stucco floors. These deposits consisted of thousands of sherds representing vessels that appeared to have been intentionally broken, plus figurines, whistles, shell, chert, and worked and unworked bone, some burned (Laporte and Fialko 1993).

Two *chultun*s lay just east of the later-constructed eastern platform of the E Group in what became known as the Seven Temples Plaza. Dated by ceramics to the early Eb Phase (pre-Mamom; ~800–700 BCE), each pit held more than 10 m³ of material, including >10,000 sherds (Laporte and Fialko 1995:45–46). The late Eb Phase (early Mamom; ~700–600 BCE) saw considerable activity in the area: two more massive *chultun* deposits, a stucco floor over all four pits, and construction of the basic E Group components, the western (5C-54-1) and eastern (5D-84/88-2) platforms (Laporte and Fialko 1995:47). Two later pit deposits were Tzec (late Mamom; 600–350 BCE) in date. In all, at least one hollow and thirty-eight solid figurines and fragments were recovered in these six pits, including eleven from the earliest ones (Laporte and Fialko 1993:Figures 7–10, 6–18).

Tikal's Mundo Perdido *chultun* deposits resemble (in their association with an early E Group and in the abundance and variety of largely domestic-seeming contents) the pits at Uaxactún. Significantly, however, the Tikal ceramics are described as apparently having been intentionally broken. This suggests that, rather than being accumulations of ordinary domestic refuse, the contents represent large community gatherings involving food and ritual, the remains of which were fragmented and intermingled at the events' end.[5] Unfortunately, we lack a similar quality assessment for the Uaxactún pottery.

Cahal Pech

More than 300 figurines and fragments, including 90 anthropomorphic heads, were found at Cahal Pech in the western Belize Valley. These came primarily from Group B, widely identified as an E Group but more accurately labeled as having Eastern Triadic Structures (Arlen Chase, personal communication, 2013; Chapter 13 in this volume). Occupation of the area that became Plaza B began with an early Preclassic Cunil Phase (prior to BCE 650) residence underlying later Structure B-4, then during the early Middle Preclassic Period Structure B-4 marked the southern edge (southeastern corner) of a plaza (Garber and Awe 2008; Garber et al. 2006; Zweig

2010:46–47). This structure has a total of thirteen sequential platforms, four of which were residential and nine of which are thought to have had public functions; ten of these occurred in the Middle Preclassic, with significant figurine deposition in each. Especially common in Structure B-4 and in the plaza fill itself, figurines were also recovered elsewhere at the site and in small peripheral groups.[6]

Plaza B at Cahal Pech also appears to have been a long-term mortuary ground favored by high-ranking individuals, accompanied by elaborate, layered, cosmic caches (Awe 2013). Middle Preclassic Burial 1 is associated with a large mound with four caches and a headless figurine. Late Preclassic Burial B4-3 included a lip-to-lip cache of Sierra Red vessels, with long bones arranged on the four sides of the vessels and a figurine head placed next to each group of bones.

Chan

Chan is another western Belize site with an Eastern Triadic Structure group, this in the Central Group, constructed in the Late Preclassic period. During the Middle Preclassic, the area that became this complex's plaza was consecrated with numerous caches and a headless burial excavated into bedrock (Robin et al. 2012:126–127; Chapter 11 in this volume). These caches were not the massive deposits of Uaxactún and Tikal but rather smaller accumulations of greenstone, shell, and pottery, frequently in fragments, that more closely resemble the centerline caches in Middle Preclassic Chiapas (see the discussion in note 3).

Of Chan's seventeen figurine fragments, fifteen were from the Central Group and ten of these were from Preclassic contexts (Laura Kosakowsky, personal communication, 2013; Kosakowsky et al. 2012:294). Three came from the Middle Preclassic fills of the northern building in the complex, interpreted—in line with the Maya idea of north as the home of ancestors—as the residence of the site's leading family. Six fragments were found in fills in the Eastern Triadic Structures themselves: two, both faces, were from Late Preclassic contexts, one in a burial. Five other figurine fragments, including three faces/heads, were from Late Preclassic contexts in the western structure of the group; two were in burials.

Other Early Ritual Areas and Figurines

Elsewhere in western Belize, eight figurines were recovered at Pacbitún, a small center with Eastern Triadic Structures (Plaza A) (Zweig 2010:58).

The site of Blackman Eddy, downriver from Cahal Pech, also has Eastern Triadic Structures. Structure B1 on the north side of the complex has a sequence of Middle Preclassic platforms, including a triadic arrangement, constructed over early Preclassic feasting deposits (Brown and Garber 2006). The feasting remains included fragments of vessels that appeared to have been intentionally cut in half (Brown 2003:21). Although E Groups and their variants are rare in Belize, thirteen figurines were recovered at Cuello, nine in Late Archaic and Middle Preclassic contexts (Hammond 1989, 1991:177; South 2001:Table 2.1), and a possible figurine fragment came from K'axob (Bartlett 2004:268, Figure 10.7d). Two heads, one tenoned, were found in a postabandonment midden in Structure E-14 at Altún Ha (Pendergast 1990:Figure 65a, b).

In northeastern Petén, Cival (Estrada-Belli 2006; Chapter 9 in this volume) has both an E Group and an Eastern Triadic Structures Group. The earliest eastern structure of the E Group was "a modified bedrock knoll" (Estrada-Belli 2006:58), in front (west) of which an elaborate Middle Preclassic cosmic cache of pottery and jades was placed into cruciform cut into bedrock (Bauer 2005).

A recent study of figurines from Calakmul, in southeastern Campeche, identified thirty-five Middle Preclassic fragments, including thirteen heads, three of which were of basalt (Martínez 2013). The objects of clay had a red or gray paste; some were slipped and some not; the figurines are nude and both males and females are present. Most were recovered from Structure 1 and the massive Structure 2, a Late Preclassic triadic structure with multiple monuments at its north face (Carrasco 2005:64).

In the Pasión region of southwestern Petén, the earliest E Group in the Maya Lowlands was constructed at Ceibal (or Seibal) around 1000 cal BCE in what is now known as Group A (Chapter 7 in this volume; Inomata et al. 2013). The western structure is represented by modification of bedrock under Structure A-20, and the earliest eastern structure was a low platform built on a knoll about 50 m away, under later plaza fills. Several coeval residential structures were identified under Structure A-24 to the south. Anthropomorphic figurines were recovered in these excavations.[7]

The map of Altar de Sacrificios does not show any E Group variants among the site's final (and late) structural arrangements. The Group A plaza originally might have been so configured, however, and north-facing Structure B1 in Group B, which was covered with lines of mussel shell set into clay surfacing, is thought to have been the earliest structure at the site (Willey and Bullard 1961:83–84). The Harvard project excavations recovered thirty-two figurines: seven in Xe Phase (pre-Mamom, which is equivalent to ca. 1100–900/800 BCE) deposits and twenty-five in San Felix Phase Mamom contexts (Willey 1972:7–14). Six of the Xe figurines were from Plaza B, and the Middle Preclassic ones came from Structures AIII, BI, and BII. A single head is described as female, with a pronounced nose and lips, and the headdress is a turban-like band with punctations and a central ornament. They were found in primarily domestic contexts, but both plazas were locations of period-ending stelae (four erected in Plaza B and dated from 9.1.0.0.0 to 9.4.10.0.0).

The Central Petén Lakes Region

In the eastern lakes, excavations on the Topoxté Islands in Lake Yaxhá yielded three figurine fragments: a hollow figurine, a hollow head, and a solid lower torso (Hermes 2000:207). The islands themselves do not have an E Group, but two of these complexes were constructed at the large site of Yaxhá on the north shore of the lake. In addition, an E Group exists at the small center of Ixtinto, southwest of Lake Yaxhá, which was not excavated but is likely a Middle Preclassic construction (Acevedo et al. 1996). At Yaxhá Hill, another minor center located immediately south of the isthmus between Lakes Yaxhá and Sacnab, testing at Mound 340 (a group of Eastern Triadic Structures) revealed pre-Mamom early Eb (Ah Pam) sherds over bedrock and under the first of four floors. Fills under the three later floors and construction above were dated to the early Mamom Tzec Phase (Rice 1976:435–436). No figurines were recovered in Mound 340. A Triadic Group structure was noted in the minor center of Sacnab, on the southeast shore of Lake Sacnab, but was not excavated. Test units in other structures in this complex yielded Middle Preclassic pottery (Rice 1976:438) but no figurines.

Figurines seem to be relatively more common in the western lakes area around Lake Petén Itzá, although their associations with E Groups and other early constructions are not as clear as elsewhere. An E Group is present at Chachaclun (Chächäklu'um) on the north shore of the lake, but no figurines or Middle Preclassic ceramics were recovered in surface collections (Sánchez 1997) or in a test pit, and construction appears to have begun in the Late Preclassic period (Spensley 2007:222). Two figurine heads were recovered in the center of Flores Island (Chan 1997).

Sites on the Tayasal Peninsula include two E Groups and a Triadic Structure, but very few Middle Preclassic figurines were recovered, suggesting that these complexes might have been Late Preclassic in date. One E Group was constructed at Cenote, where a Middle Preclassic figurine fragment ("probably Kax [Late Preclassic] or earlier") was recovered (Chase 1983:228). To the west, the site of Tayasal has an E Group, but only Structure T100 (the western structure) was excavated and yielded no figurines. A test pit into the Postclassic shrine atop T100 reached Terminal Preclassic or Protoclassic (0–250 CE) material but not bedrock (T. W. Pugh, personal communication, 2013). A massive 270 m-long T-shaped platform in central Tayasal had fills more than 7 m deep in some areas, with the lowest levels including mixed Mamom and Chicanel material. In western Tayasal, two figurine fragments were recovered (in Structure T142 [T27L] and T121 [T19A]; Chase 1983:1332, personal communication, 2013). Farther to the west, in the vicinity of the San Bernabé *congregación*/mission, a large triadic structure (Structures T65–T67) was constructed in the Late Preclassic period.

At Buenavista–Nuevo San José, a small site on the northwest shore of the lake, three Middle Preclassic structures, probably residential, were exposed in an axial trench through the south side of Structure 4, on the north side of a plaza. At least two other Middle Preclassic structures were suggested by pre-Mamom and Mamom ceramics remains in the lowest levels of test pits elsewhere at the site. Thirteen figurine fragments were recovered (Castellanos 2008:Photo 7). At Lake Sacpuy, west of Lake Petén Itzá, an E Group was identified (but not excavated) at the site of Sacpuy 1, south of the northwest end of the lake (Martínez and Laporte 2010).

Figurines at Ixlú and Nixtun-Ch'ich'

Ixlú, occupying the narrow isthmus between the eastern end of Lake Petén Itzá and Lake Salpetén, began to be settled by or during the early Middle Preclassic and flourished through the late Postclassic period (Rice and Rice 2016). Seventeen figurine fragments were recovered, primarily in Middle Preclassic platform fills investigated in a test pit in Plaza B, the central of three small Classic plazas in the Acropolis at the northwest corner of the site. Ixlú does not have an E Group.

Nixtun-Ch'ich' is a large Maya city on the far western mainland edge of Lake Petén Itzá extending southeast over the Candelaria Peninsula (Figure 5.1). Excavations in 2007 focused on Mound ZZ1, a rectangular, 5.7 m high platform on the eastern tip of the peninsula. Mound ZZ1 was salvage-excavated by a 38 m long, 2 m wide trench (Operation 1) over the estimated

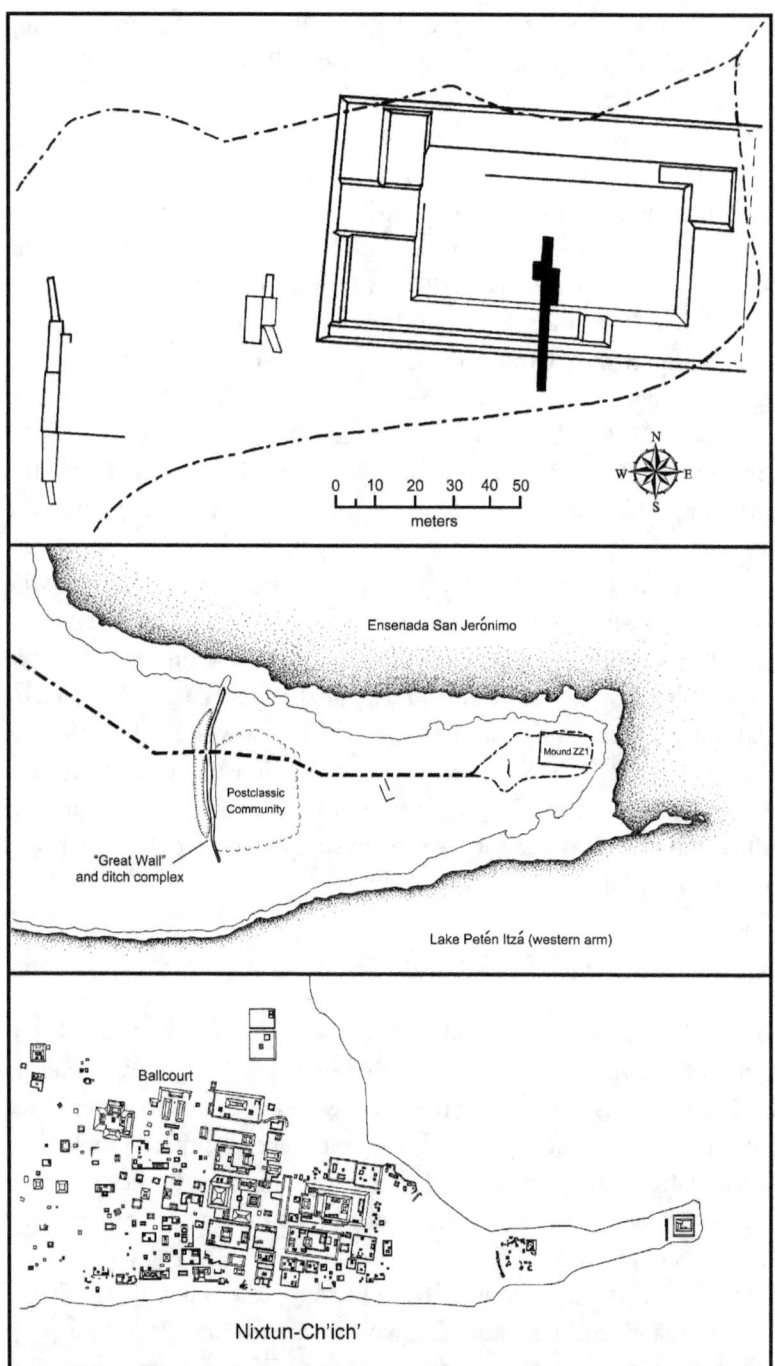

Figure 5.1. Mound ZZ1 and the Operation 1 trench (*top*), on the Candelaria Peninsula (*middle*), and the site of Nixtun-Ch'ich' (*bottom*), on the western edge of Lake Petén Itzá, Guatemala.

north-south centerline of its southern face (Rice 2009), exposing a 1.2 m rise in bedrock (the rise was 1.5–2 m on its bulldozed eastern edge). These excavations yielded seventy Middle Preclassic figurines and fragments of the total of ninety-nine from the site; the other fragments came from eight other locations (Rice n.d.). More recent mapping and excavations have revealed a possible E Group in the site center and recovered additional figurines.

The figurines and fragments in the Operation 1 trench were recovered from three general contexts: primary discard deposits over bedrock (Levels AA, 15, and 16), early platform fills, and later redeposited fills. Level AA was a deposit, 25–70 cm thick, of damp, sandy, light gray-brown soil with small rock and gravel inclusions, exposed in the north part of the trench in three 2 × 2-m units and lateral extensions. Dating to the early Preclassic (two Accelerator Mass Spectrometry [AMS] dates on charcoal with a 2-σ range 1270–920 cal BCE), Level AA yielded a single figurine fragment (an upper leg), plus 3 pieces of obsidian (sourced to El Chayal), 9 chert fragments, 35 shell fragments, and 196 sherds of unslipped pottery (plus 2 slipped sherds). Levels 15 and 16 represent a 20–30 cm deposit over bedrock immediately south of initial platform construction. There 10 figurine fragments, including 5 heads and a torso, were recovered, along with slipped pre-Mamom Eb and early Mamom Tzec pottery and 28 obsidian fragments sourced to San Martín Jilotepeque (Nate Meissner, personal communication, 2013).

Initial platform (ZZ1-sub-8 and -sub-7) construction fills incorporated large quantities of fragments of slipped vessels representing primary breakage, as did fills of Ixlú Plaza B. I interpreted the ZZ1 materials as the remains of community or work-party feasting associated with the building of this platform (see Brown 2003; Follensbee 2009:89; Tway 2004). These levels yielded two nearly complete figurines—a small standing female and a seated figure—plus two heads, one shoulder/torso, and three limbs. In addition, many figurines and fragments were recovered in later Classic period deposits representing construction and remodeling of the raised second tier of Mound ZZ1. This redeposition of Middle Preclassic fills with their sherds and figurines into new constructions and architectural termination/dedicatory deposits "ensouled" and "animated" the new buildings (Mock 1998; Rice 2009:421).

I examined thirty-two Preclassic figurine heads, twenty-five from Nixtun-Ch'ich' and seven from Ixlú. Broad and roundish or squarish in frontal view, the heads are roughly triangular in profile, with a nearly pointed cranium broadening to a variably prognathic jaw plus thickening of the nuchal

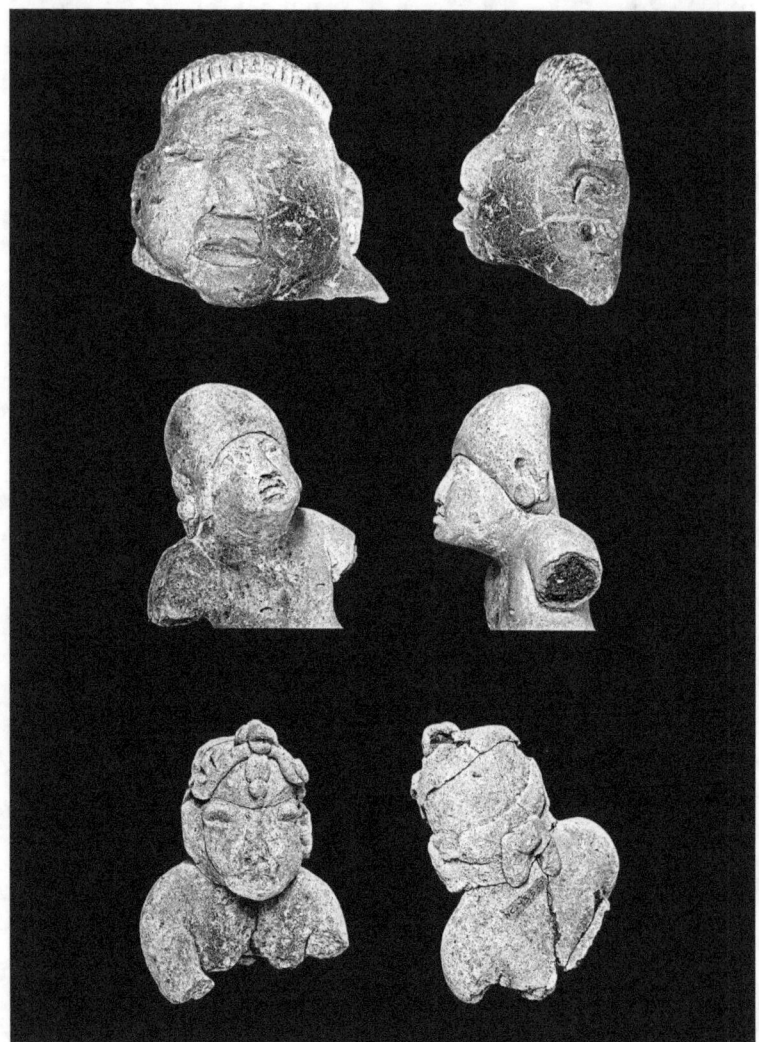

Figure 5.2. (*Top*) a large fireclouded head showing profile and braided band (note: the illustration is intentionally reversed, with the right profile displayed as if it were the left), Nixtun-Ch'ich' Operation 1, Classic level F1, lot 43114; (*middle*) seated female, possibly aged (nasiolabial creases) with "U-helmet" hairdo and round earplugs, with an unidentifiable (cloth?) pendant on the right ear, Nixtun-Ch'ich' Operation 1, Preclassic level U1, lot 43110; (*bottom*) head and shoulders of a male with a tied headband, with an animal (fish?) head atop the head; another ornament, now broken off, was behind it, Nixtun-Ch'ich' Operation 1, Classic level F4, lot 43537.

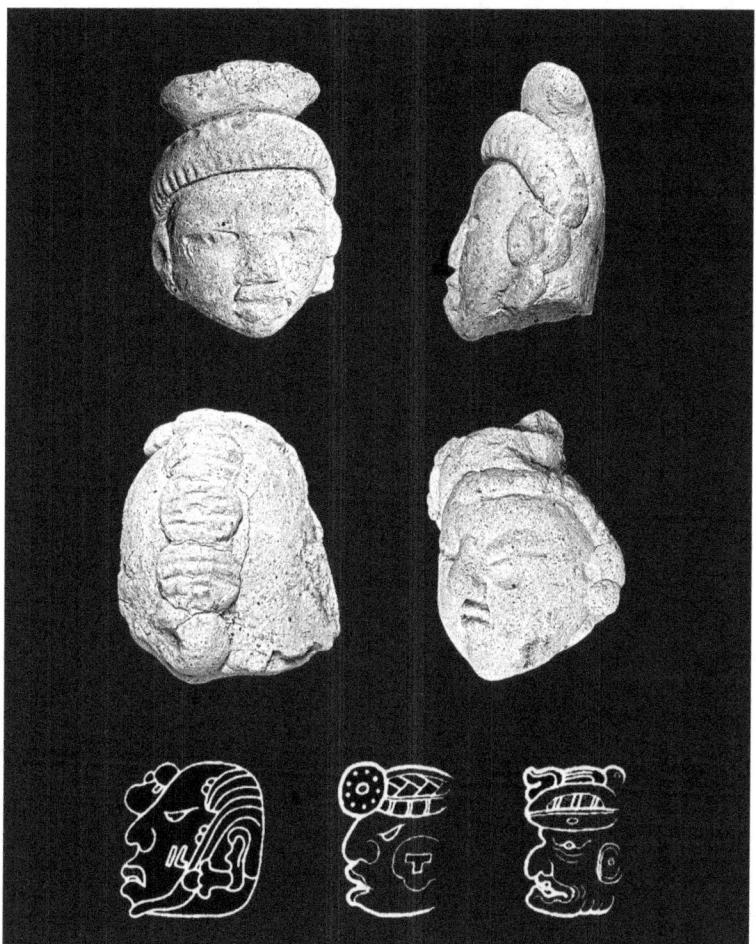

Figure 5.3. (*Top*) head with a braided hairdo and a fan-like element (note the faint incising resembling a "flame eyebrow" over the right eye), Nixtun-Ch'ich' Operation 1, Classic level P, lot 43103; (*middle left*) head with missing facial features and headband featuring seven textured, flattish disks, Nixtun-Ch'ich' Operation 1, Middle Preclassic level 16, lot 43511; (*middle right*) head with an elaborate two-tier headdress (the top behind the band is broken off; six graduated disks or beads extend from above the bridge of the nose to the left ear); Nixtun-Ch'ich' Operation 1, Classic level F4, lot 43097; (*bottom*) Classic period head-variant glyph numerals: (*left*) Number 1 (note hair in front of ear); (*center*) Number 3 (note dotted disk on forehead); (*right*) Number 5 with Tun sign.

area (Figures 5.2, 5.3). They exhibit the "intermediate" form of tabular-erect shaping (Tiesler 2010:Figure 3a), with marked lambdoid flattening seen in figurine heads elsewhere and on many examples of Preclassic figural art in other media, including Olmec sculpture and the San Bartolo murals. Five heads from Mundo Perdido have somewhat elongated crania (Laporte and

Fialko 1993), and nearly half of the heads from Cahal Pech exhibit unusual "concave" foreheads and extreme fronto-occipital thinning (Zweig 2010).

Hairdos and headdresses were semipreserved on twenty-six heads from Nixtun-Ch'ich'. Fourteen displayed variations of headband-like raised fillets at the upper hairline (Figures 5.2, top, and 5.3, top); six of these are ticked on the edges, which may represent braided coiffures on females (Marcus 1998:Figures 10.7, 11.17, 11.28-8) or plaited headbands like those worn by Maya rulers into the Late Classic period (550–800 CE) (Houston 2012). Six heads had a helmet-like coiffure appearing as an inverted U-shape (Figure 5.2, middle), said to be a common female hairstyle also seen in Oaxaca (Marcus 1998:Figure 6.10b), the Gulf Coast (Tway 2004; Weiant 1943:Plates 1–7), and Cahal Pech (Zweig 2010).

One figurine (Figure 5.2, bottom) wore a headband tied in the back. The Maya headband of authority, legendarily of white paper (*sak huunal*), sometimes had three diadems or jewels representing the "Jester God" (Fields 1991; Freidel 1990; Grove 2006:Figure 4; Houston et al. 2006:62; Schele and Miller 1986:53). Heads were often embellished with either (1) an ornament, topknot, or fan-like object (maize vegetation?: Figure 5.3, top; Reilly 2005:33), usually broken off, atop the head ($n = 9$); or (2) an element over the forehead (Figure 5.2, bottom): a lock of hair, a tassel, or beads or "jewels" ($n = 5$). On two heads the embellishments were disks (Figure 5.3, middle).

At Tikal (Laporte and Fialko 1993), two heads wore bands/hairdos like those at Nixtun-Ch'ich': one is braided and one has a topknot. Four have fitted caps or helmets/turbans. Another four, likely females, show the hair with a central tied or braided element on top.

Figurine Heads, the Divinatory Almanac, and Maya Script

In contemplating the Middle Preclassic figurines from Nixtun-Ch'ich' I came to focus (as others have) on the Classic Maya use of anthropomorphic heads in their hieroglyphic script. Martha Macri (1985) and Brian Stross (1985), for example, address the linguistic (phonetic) and rebus components of the head variants, proposing Mayan and Mixe-Zoquean sources, respectively. Tatiana Proskouriakoff (1978:113) addressed the iconography, suggesting that the supernaturals in "Olmec"—or more generally, Middle Preclassic—art are "compositions of signs" abstracted from costumed and masked characters in ritual performances and that these became "standard recognizable signs" over time. My proposal is similar: I suggest that some of the signs were drawn from heads and faces of figurines participating in calendrical rituals in Middle Preclassic Early Ritual Areas; these icons were formalized in Classic script as head-variant glyphs for the numbers and day-names in the Maya 260-day almanac (Rice n.d.). For reasons of length, I summarize only the key points of this proposition.

The Maya Divinatory Almanac and Script

Mesoamerican 260-day divinatory almanacs consist of the concurrent cycling of numbers from 1 to 13 with 20 day-names; the same number-day pairs recur every 260 days. The day-names have been "preserved in oral and written form with remarkable tenacity and conservatism" over the millennia, and 11 are shared among multiple calendars (Edmonson 1988:169). The unusual length of this instrument has been explained by various natural cycles: celestial, which may be solar (days between zeniths), Venusian (visibility), or lunar; and terrestrial, including both an "agricultural year" from February to October and the maize-growing cycle of thirteen 20-day stages (Rice 2007:33–39; Chapter 4 in this volume). Another explanation relates to the 260 days of the gestating human fetus. The sacred almanac is conservatively estimated as "probably in use since Olmec times" (Stuart 2011:67; see also Voss 2000:134). As I have argued (Rice 2007:33, 54–57, 2008:280–281), however, the coinciding day-names suggest earlier origins prior to major Mesoamerican language separations. This prognostic device was likely invented by or during the Archaic (7500–1000 BCE) to Preclassic transition, ca. 3500–2000/1500 BCE; archaeological attestation begins sometime around 600–500 BCE on Monument 3 at San José Mogote, with texts on carved slabs in the gallery of Building L at Monte Albán.

Classic Maya hieroglyphic script, which began during the Late Preclassic period perhaps as a semasiographic system, used several different kinds of signs. One kind, "personifications," consists of left-facing profiled anthropomorphic, zoomorphic, or supernatural heads, called head forms or head variants. The head, besides being a focus of individual identity, is the center of sensory faculties, such as sight, smell, taste, hearing, and vocalization. Among the Maya, breath is the powerful animating essence *ik'* (breath, wind: Taube 2001) and the human voice, especially royal speech or song, is especially precious and powerful (Gossen 1986; Houston et al. 2006:153–156). Key distinguishing elements of heads and faces, visible frontally in three dimensions as on figurines, must be rotated 90° to be recognizable in profile signs. The profile head-variant glyphs typically have large, round or oval heads and large noses, often with a small, receding chin and sloping forehead. In cartouches, the space afforded by the angled forehead and nose is generally filled with a lock of hair or an ornament projecting from the head covering.

The Maya conceived of numbers and units of time as animate, having patron supernatural deities (Thompson 1960) or essences. Thus it is unsurprising that head-glyphs are common among the myriad signs relating to time and its passage, especially numbers but also days, months, and other calendrical periods. Numbers up to 19 have distinct head variants for 1 to 12; compound numbers 13 and higher combine the heads of 3 to 9 with a skeletal mandible or a hand in place of a jaw. A day-name is a single sign in a cartouche, perhaps the name and profile of gods or supernaturals with oversight of the days they represent (Thompson 1962:70) or of revered, maybe royal, ancestors (Marcus 1992:137). Only the *ajaw* ("lord") sign (*aj aw* "he who shouts or proclaims" [Stuart 1995:190–191]), the name for the last and most powerful of the 20 days, is shown with a frontal view of the face.

Iconicity: Preclassic Figurine Heads and Classic Head-Variant Glyphs

The supernatural patrons of Numbers 1 to 13 are male and female, young and old. The patron of 1 is the Moon Goddess; 4 is the Sun God; 8 the Maize God; 9 the Hero Twin Xbalanque; and 13 the Waterlily Serpent (Miller and Taube 1993:125, 184). Although each head glyph varies stylistically from one appearance to another (especially in the eyes and nose), several features are striking (Coe and van Stone 2001:39; Macri 1985; Macri and Looper 2003:Figure 7, 22; Miller and Taube 1993; Thompson 1962:131–137, Table 4, Figures 24, 25; Voss 2000:Figure 202):

- The strand of hair in front of the ear on the head-variant glyph for Number 1, the Moon Goddess (Figure 5.3, bottom left), may represent, in profile, part of the widespread "inverted U-shaped helmet-like" hairdo on Preclassic figurines (Figure 5.2, middle).
- The foreheads of several numerals (except Numbers 2 and 5) are embellished with a lock of hair, a tassel, or jewel(s), as is the Moon Goddess/Number 1. Similar ornaments often appear on the forehead or attached to the headdress of Nixtun-Ch'ich' figurine heads (Figure 5.2, bottom).
- A dotted disk on the forehead of the profile head for Number 3 (Figure 5.3, bottom center) might be analogous to the circles on the heads of two Nixtun-Ch'ich' figurine heads (Figure 5.3, middle).

Number 3 also wears a woven or braided headdress, recalling the braided bands on numerous Petén figurines.
- The upper part of the Maya tied headband of leadership (Figure 5.2, bottom) is topped with a tiny animal head, perhaps a fish(?). The headdress of the glyph for Number 5 has a *tun* (360-day year) sign, sometimes prefixed with what appears to be the knotted *huun* logograph for the paper headband (Figure 5.3, bottom right). Number 13 (generally an avian), also associated with an Olmec Xok (shark) supernatural, said to be a deity of the Olmec and possibly "the basis for the Maya Jester God" (Miller and Taube 1993:152, 153; see also Jones 1991).

The Preclassic figurines and heads from Nixtun-Ch'ich' (and other sites) can be considered icons: likenesses (or effigies) of humans, alive and deceased, that may also represent supernatural creatures and forces. Classic head-variant numerals and day-names in the 260-day divinatory almanac are also icons, painted or carved images of the heads of the figurines. Their iconicity rests in their likeness to these early objects and to actual humans, including the unusually "thick" profiles and headdress/ornament details on the objects from Nixtun-Ch'ich' and Ixlú. Thus, I suggest that these (and other) figurine heads may exemplify developmental relations in these iconic signs (though not necessarily specific prototypes or exact matches). Centuries separate the two media, attributes were likely added, lost, or merged, and a considerably larger corpus will be needed for investigation of such relations.

Early Ritual Areas and Figurines: Possible Functions and Meanings

The spatial distribution of Lowland Maya Early Ritual Areas, especially E Groups, is of considerable interest. E Groups are absent or nearly so in the Northern Lowlands, the Usumacinta drainage, and eastern and northern Belize, where different early structural forms appear (Doyle 2012:357, 370). Likewise, figurines are uncommon in these regions: virtually absent in the Northern Lowlands and scarce elsewhere (see note 2).

E Groups are thought to be early public places central to group identity and cohesion and to ritual performances underlying the emergence of political authority (Doyle 2012; Chapters 7 and 8 in this volume). They were likely sites of varied community activities, as suggested by Juan Pedro Laporte's (1996) label: "Complejo de Ritual Público." One key to understanding the functions of early Maya E Groups is to determine what those activities might have been: probably integrative rituals (initiation ceremonies, rites of passage) and/or cosmic and subsistence-based celebrations (propitiation of supernatural forces controlling rain, maize growth, solar movements), perhaps held at night, and accompanied by feasting; ball-playing and other gaming; oratory and story-telling; music, singing, and dancing; and processions, masked dramas, and other pageantry. Where figurines are recovered in these complexes (including underlying Early Ritual Areas), it is important to understand the uses of these objects. I suggest that their co-occurrence is related to Middle Preclassic development of the Maya version of the 260-day sacred almanac.

Astro-Calendrics

Since the 1920s the Uaxactún Group E has been associated with horizon-based solar astronomy, an interpretation that accorded well with the then-prevailing "star-gazing priests" model of Maya civilization. An observatory role of these complexes, whether empirically functional only in the Middle Preclassic (Rice 2007:155) or also commemoratively in later periods, has continued to be linked to the 365-day solar calendar and vigorously debated (Aimers and Rice 2006; Aveni et al. 2003; Laporte 1996).

The restricted geographical distribution of early Lowland Maya E Groups lends weight to Aveni's suggestion that these complexes are "situated at that 'magic latitude' [~17° N] where the year can be perfectly segmented into multiples of 20 days" separating solstices, equinoxes, and zeniths (Aveni 2002:211; see also Chapter 4 in this volume). Given these intervals, it is not unlikely that Early Ritual Areas and E Groups were settings for celebrations of the 260-day almanac, with its multiples of 13 × 20 days. Early Classic stelae marking K'atun completions with dates in the Long Count, which merges the two calendars, are commonly planted in front of the eastern structures of these E Groups, supporting their interpretation as spaces for time- and calendar-based ritual activities (Rice 2007:177).[8] Figurines, especially if they embodied anthropomorphized units of time, might have been actors in time-related ritual performances as well as mnemonics for the complexities of the temporal intersections. It is easy to envision figurines having functioned in categorical sets, for example, one representing the 13 numbers and the other the 20 days in such ceremonies.

Ancestor Veneration

Some figurines are thought to be portraits of real people considered important by local standards, such as "big" men or women, ritual specialists, and especially ancestors. Ancestors might be the first-comers or founders of a settlement, who typically enjoyed elevated rank and came to be identified with the supernatural as complexity developed (Kopytoff 1987:52–60; Lowe 1977:198; Pauketat 2008). It has been widely speculated that early Maya structures were dedicated to ancestral deities of descent lines (McAnany 1995; Sanders 1973:348). These concepts seem apropos to the interments and figurines found in the Eastern Triadic Structures complexes at Cahal Pech and Chan (Awe 2013; Kosakowsky and Robin 2010; Robin et al. 2012:122). Communal ancestor celebrations in the open plaza areas of Early Ritual Areas would help explain the large *chultun* deposits in Mundo Perdido and Uaxactún. The three structures on the eastern platform of these later E Group and Eastern Triadic Structures complexes might be *wayib'* or *waybil* lineage shrines to the ancestors or supernatural patrons of these locations (Freidel et al. 1993:188).

As in other areas experiencing the subsistence-settlement transformations and emergence of social ranking that characterize Archaic to Preclassic (or Mesolithic–Neolithic) transitions, Preclassic Mesoamerica lacked strong institutions for (re)creating and materializing corporate identities. Figurines, in representing ancestors or other important historical beings, served a "grounding" function for the places where they were used and deposited, as they absorb "the symbolic attributes of the place as much as the place is enhanced by the associations" with these objects (Chapman 2000:33). Likewise, repeated redepositions of early structure fills, as in Mound ZZ1, can be considered acts of "symbolic remembering and forgetting" (Kuijt 2008:171) and "presencing" through enchainment (Chapman 2008:188). They invoke and reincorporate the personages and events of the ancestral founders' past into the present, sacralizing the structures and reinforcing a sense of place-based identity.

Life-Cycle Celebrations

Authors of a study of Jomon period (6000–200 BCE) figurines from Japan proposed that one of their uses—perhaps a major intended use—could have been in community celebrations of the female life cycle and fertility (Chapman 2000:25–26; Cyphers 1988, 1993; Joyce 2008). At the conclusion of the ceremony, the figurines with their "symbolic load of fertility" (Chapman

2000:26) lost their magic powers and were discarded. In the Middle Preclassic Maya Lowlands, the presence of these artifacts in Early Ritual Area construction fills, caches, and burials suggests that these complexes might have been the setting for similar rituals. This explanation becomes more compelling in light of associations among pregnancy or gestation, lunar cycles (Neuenswander 1981), and the 260-day almanac. Pregnant figurines are occasionally present—a broken torso with a protruding belly came from Nixtun-Ch'ich' and another was noted at Tikal (Laporte and Fialko 1993)—but uncommon in these Lowland Early Ritual Areas.[9]

Alternatively, the life cycles being celebrated might not be those of human females but rather those of maize. In the Middle Preclassic, maize cobs were still small with low caloric yields, and in some areas maize may have been an early prestige or luxury food offered at feasts sponsored by aggrandizing individuals as part of competitive displays (Clark and Blake 1994:28; VanDerwarker and Kruger 2012:527).[10] Through time, corn's increased economic importance was reflected in rituals conducted by emerging elites (Estrada-Belli 2006; Freidel 1995; Stross 1994). Complex interrelations among solar zenith, maize agriculture, and the Maize God (whose iconography was often sexually ambiguous [Martin 2003:9]), skull modification, and elite artifacts resulted in a conflationary mimesis of ears of maize, jade celts, and the reshaped human head (Taube 1996, 2006; Taube and Saturno 2008). Thus, commoners' human and agricultural production and reproduction might also have been melded in clay figurine usage (de Borhegyi 1956:345–346). The slim figurines' bodies (particularly pubescent females?) may have been symbolically identified with and embodiments of ears of corn, paralleling greenstone celts possessed by elites. Such associations of the human figure with maize help explain the absence of sexual characteristics of the artifacts.

Figurines might have been originally formed or later bedecked with maize-related adornments for community performances linked to an early version of the Tzeltal maize cycle (Stross 1994:29–31). This cycle consists of 13 stages, each 20 days long; the names of the stages correlate with day-names of the almanac, some of which share similar meanings throughout Mesoamerica. These day-names and their supernatural patrons, illustrated in Classic Maya head-variant glyphs, can be compared to those for numerals (Rice n.d.). The Early Ritual Area settings for such enactments are roughly correlated around 17° N latitude, where such partitioning is easily reckoned.

Exchange and Enchainment

The proposal that E Groups were built to mark calendrical cycles to schedule long-distance trade (Aveni et al. 2003; Doyle 2012:373; Rathje et al. 1978) can be explored with respect to figurines by returning to ideas about fragmentation, partibility, and enchainment. Enchainment is a process of creating social ties through the giving or exchange of fragments of broken objects: "the creation and maintenance of a lasting bond between people or groups, predicated on material culture" (Chapman 2000:226). Fragment enchainment transactions may take place in large gatherings such as those proposed for Early Ritual Areas. Some Japanese Jomon figurine fragments, for example, were taken to other villages rather than discarded on-site (Chapman 2000:26).

Similar fragment enchainment was apparently also pursued in the Maya Lowlands, as evidenced by Instrumental Neutron Activation Analysis (INAA) analyses of the composition of figurines from Nakbé and Uaxactún. Both sites had their own distinct geochemical signatures, established through ceramic analyses. Geochemically, three figurines from Uaxactún were likely manufactured of Nakbé clays (Hansen 2000:52). Of twenty Nakbé figurines, nineteen were similar to that site's Middle Preclassic pottery composition and distinct from those of Uaxactún, but one showed "little tendency to link with anything in the data base" (Ronald Bishop, personal communication, 2013).[11] These data suggest that activities involving Middle Preclassic figurines in Early Ritual Areas were not just community-wide but also had broader regional or even interregional participation and significance.

Enchainment can explain some of the variability in styles and clay pastes among figurines and fragments at a single site as well as the occurrence of figurine fragments at sites outside the core area of E Groups. Possession of a figurine or a fragment from another community may symbolize a valued alliance, including marriages, or memorialize participation in or bearing witness at an event, with its nonlocal or exotic origin conferring prestige (Helms 1988). An analogy might be made to saints' relics in medieval Europe, as a sign of devotion through pilgrimage to a sacred site or location of a critical event (Chapman 2000:38; Geary 1986). For the Middle Preclassic Lowland Maya, this travel might have been to commemorate cosmic or lifecycle transitions relating to maize and ancestors, timed through the calendars. With respect to figurines as ancestor images, the fragment exchanges might trace and help maintain actual or fictive kin relations and genealogies (Wagner 1991:162–165), the fragments being "identity tokens" or "icons of identity" (Schwimmer 1986).

Who, What, When, Why, Where?

The consensus of myriad studies of Preclassic Mesoamerican figurines is that they primarily portray females and were made by women for use in divination and domestic rituals involving family ancestors. I do not disagree with this general premise: the idea that they are individualized representations of ancestors, male and female, does appear to be a reasonable interpretation. But it is insufficient as a functional explanation, and much more can be proposed for figurines in the Maya Lowlands. For example, I am not fully persuaded that it was primarily women who made these objects. Early figurines could have been made and used by multitasking ritual specialists—shamans-daykeepers-curers-diviners; male *or* female "mother-fathers" (Tedlock 1996:349)—who brought the figurines to a dwelling or even made them there, as part of a consultation. In some Preclassic societies, as I have argued (Rice 2007, 2008) and as has Joyce Marcus (1999:90–94), such individuals might have filled increasingly specialized roles, communicating with the supernaturals that controlled time and the future of human enterprises (for example, births, conflicts, maize agriculture) through cosmic forces. They might have been the first record-keepers, predecessors of the later "learned persons" (Maya *itz'aat*) and scribes (*ts'ib, k'uhun*) who were literate and numerate and could be male and female (Coe and Kerr 1998:99).

Part of the reason for continuing debates over the functions of these Middle Preclassic figurines is that their use must be inferred through visual characteristics and contexts of recovery. With respect to appearance, variety occurs primarily in the head and face, and headgear is doubtless an important personal identity signifier. A few Maya figurine heads show a tied headband, as do two colossal heads at San Lorenzo, supporting the likelihood that these human figures represent leaders. Posture, sitting or standing, is also undoubtedly important, as sitting cross-legged on a bench or throne is an iconic position of power in Mesoamerica. With respect to context, Preclassic Southern Lowland Maya figurines are recovered in domestic settings and burials, as elsewhere in Mesoamerica, but in smaller quantities.

Some of the individuals portrayed might have been big-men/big-women; others might have been founding ancestors, shamans, ballplayers, or dancers; still others may have been personifications of earthly or celestial entities and forces (sun, moon, maize, wind, rain), and the numbers and days of the almanac. Indeed, any leaders or would-be leaders in Preclassic society might have adopted these roles at different times in their lives, given that the ballgame, dancing, and oratory were likely part of their public Preclassic responsibilities. Open plazas like those of Lowland Maya Early Ritual Areas would have been effective settings for village- or region-wide gatherings, particularly if founding ancestors were known to have occupied the spaces before and after their deaths. Over the many centuries when figurines were a part of ritual life, they were transformed from ancestors into supernaturals, perhaps patron deities of their communities. Thus, the identities of the figurines were socially mediated as these objects played an active role in the creation of social life, in the constitution of local and regional identities, and in the recursive processes of creating and re-creating meanings in these contexts.

Last Thoughts

The earliest Middle Preclassic Maya figurines were likely made and used in domestic settings, as throughout Mesoamerica. Some settings appear to be compounds of relatively affluent or prestigious households, perhaps heads of kin groups or founders (for example, Chan, Uaxactún). These compounds include open plaza-like areas where the residents evidently sponsored the generous reciprocity and hospitality, displays of food and drink, and entertainment proposed for big-men accumulating prestige and followers in transegalitarian and rank societies (Dietler and Hayden 2001). Early domestic and public rituals likely were "not substantively different," both concerned with collective food supply, group identity, and shared origins (Grove and Gillespie 2002:11). Community celebrations might have been timed to coincide with points in critical solar, rainfall, and maize agricultural cycles and the host possibly the individual charged with the responsibility for maintaining the memory and timing of these cycles, just as lineage heads are daykeepers in Momostenango today (Tedlock 1992:52). Or the gatherings might have involved a feast at the conclusion of communal work efforts to build the Early Ritual Areas that later became the foundations of distinctive monumental civic-ceremonial complexes.

Thus, the lowest basal levels of Early Ritual Areas and E Groups in particular reveal Maya rituals of "place-making": the earliest structuring of the landscape to create and animate public spaces and places. Space produces and is produced by power (Lefebvre 1991). Through that power, spaces become "cult places" (Biehl 2011) that must be understood not only in terms of their physical structures and artifacts but also relative to the landscape in which they are embedded. Landscapes are "simultaneously place, process, and time" (Silverman 2004:4), a characterization that is particularly apt for the Middle Preclassic Maya Lowlands and the observatory functions of its Early Ritual Areas. The transformation of this forested landscape into a network of places—"politicized, culturally relative, historically specific," and created "through praxis" (Rodman 1992:641–642)—began with ritual practices in Early Ritual Areas, where the manipulation of clay figurines in accordance with calendrical rhythms was a key component in the construction of their meaning. Early Ritual Areas and early E Groups are thus timescapes.

Aspects of Preclassic Maya calendrical development and a growing focus on maize-centered ritual are recapitulated and encoded in the Popol Vuh, as argued earlier (Rice 2007:67–74). The structures and plazas of Early Ritual Areas often appear to have re-created the Maya sacred land- and timescape of creation, with heavy loadings of cosmological metaphors. The process began with clearing vegetation from bedrock, often over a small bedrock rise, to expose a clean white surface analogous to that at the moment of creation:[12]

> There is not yet one person, one animal, bird, fish, crab, tree, rock, hollow, canyon, meadow, forest. Only the sky alone is there; the face of the earth is not clear. Only the sea alone is pooled under all the sky. . . . Whatever there is that might be is simply not there. . . . [But with the spoken words of the gods], the earth rose . . . the mountains were separated from the water. . . . By their genius alone . . . they carried out the conception of the mountain-plain. (Tedlock 1996:64–66)

Similarly, the primary contexts of recovery of figurines and fragments, in burials and caches, in these Early Ritual Areas reveal painstaking invocations of the multiple layers of cosmic order as viewed by Middle Preclassic Lowland Maya. For example, the four figurine heads in Burial B4-3 in Cahal Pech Plaza B suggested the Hero Twins taking the decapitated head of their father to the Three Stone Place, where it was resurrected as the Maize God ("First Father") who gives form and sustenance to humans (Awe 2013:39). The four heads may represent the original four humans formed of *masa* (maize dough), perhaps deified ancestors or the four Pawahtuns.[13] It is not unlikely that human figures formed of *masa* (and other perishable materials) accompanied those of fired or unfired clay ("mud-men": Brumfiel and Overholzer 2009) in ritual uses and consumption in the Early Ritual Areas (Joyce 2009:408; Sandstrom 2009).

Moreover, the three structures or monuments on the eastern side of these Early Ritual Area complexes clearly can be read as symbolizing not only the mythological Three Stone Place but also the quotidian three-stone kitchen hearth, where maize is transformed into sustenance for the household. This, in turn, is also symbolized by the stars in the constellation of Orion which, during the Middle Preclassic, rose almost exactly due east (Aveni et al. 2003:173; Freidel et al. 1993:68, 79; Tedlock 1996:236–237).

Just as Catholic saints in rural Latin America symbolize family and community and their veneration establishes a community's ritual calendar (Gudeman 1976), so can we imagine Middle Preclassic deities and celebrations in Early Ritual Areas. The entities and performances that later became the Popol Vuh, and the clay figurines likely used in such enactments provided a "juncture between public symbols and private meanings" and a balance "between the past, remembered and recreated as a series of meaningful events, and the future" (Gudeman 1976:727). At the close of the festivities in the Early Ritual Areas, the Maya ritually smashed ("terminated") their plates and bowls and dumped them, along with figurines, musical instruments, shell ornaments, and other goods, in deep *chultuns* excavated into the bedrock. These pits were then themselves terminated or "sealed" by covering with a layer of plaster or *sascab*, creating another clean white surfacing that archaeologists would later identify as the first formal "floor" of the Early Ritual Area. Analogous deposits of white marl are associated with Classic architectural termination (Wagner 2006) and in mortuary ritual to seal bodies and contain their animating essences (Duncan 2014). Ritually terminating, sealing, and dedicating the Early Ritual Area spaces seem to be the key processes in early re-creations of the sacred landscape and timescape of creation. The Popol Vuh mythic history together with E Groups in general thus represent Maya "memory work" writ large (Mills and Walker 2008; Van Dyke and Alcock 2003).

The association of figurines with Early Ritual Areas (or "prE Groups") is neither exclusive nor perfect. An Early Ritual Area, no matter what kind of complex it later became, may or may not have figurines; if an E Group was first constructed in the Late Preclassic, after initial Lowland place-making was well under way, rather than in the Middle Preclassic, it may lack figurines in its fills. But the association of figurines with the earliest traces of *some* of these significant ritual spaces—or, better said, with the earliest traces of communal ritual spaces in a restricted area of the Lowlands—the south-central area—merits further investigation. To what degree are these associations empirically sound and behaviorally meaningful? Given the substantial volume of excavations into Middle Preclassic contexts in the Northern, Eastern, and Western Lowlands, the relative *absence* of anthropomorphic, fired-clay figurines in these regions seems to be empirically "real" but can be subjected to further testing. The apparent associations of these objects with Early Ritual Areas in southern Campeche, Petén, and western Belize, however, may be a different matter (Rice 2015).

Why do figurines and Early Ritual Areas occur, separately or together, at some sites and not at others, and why did Early Ritual Areas evolve into different but related monumental complexes? I favor an interpretation that incorporates early horizon-based astronomy and maize-based renewal ritual, tied together by the 260-day almanac (Dowd and Milbrath 2015). Early ancestors, both male and female, were apotheosized through mythic identification with and personification of natural or cosmic forces memorialized as patrons of numbers and days in the sacred divinatory almanac of 260 days. This complex process can be considered that of a self-organizing system with "emergent" properties based on the way its components—figurines, celestial observations, and human actors—work together (Damper 2000:815–816; Gell-Mann 1994:99–100). But in terms of historicity, this interpretation is incomplete, as the system's actual emergence began one or two thousand years earlier in oral records of astrocalendrical movements. More complete answers to origin questions may depend on parsing the identities of the earliest fully sedentary residents in the Lowlands and their linguistic, ideological, and cultural affiliations (Ball and Taschek 2003; Lohse 2010; Rice 2007:147–152).

Production of anthropomorphic fired-clay figurines ended in the early Late Preclassic period throughout Mesoamerica. All over the region, the Middle-to-Late Preclassic transition witnessed changes in material culture (Love 1999; Lesure 1999 on use of jade) and "religious practices" (Thompson 1965:340), likely including the development of formal ritual specialists or priests (Chapter 16 in this volume; Joyce Marcus, personal communication, 2013). This transition was also one of intensifying complexity in sociopolitical relations (Blanton et al. 1996:8–9; Marcus 1992:262, 1998:21), including the beginnings of divine kingship in the Maya Lowlands (Freidel and Schele 1988). Significantly, this period also saw the beginnings of formal, material attestation of various scripts and calendars. Maya writing began to emerge in the Late Preclassic period and was "fully developed" by about 300 CE (Fahsen and Grube 2006:75–76; Justeson 1986; Justeson and Mathews 1990; Lacadena 2010:1027; Macri 2008; Macri and Looper 2003:4, 26). Whatever uses figurines served in the Middle Preclassic—as numerical and calendrical mnemonics, ancestor figures, metaphorical maize ears, or symbols of kinship, those needs either no longer existed in the Late Preclassic or the Maya found other ways to meet them.

Acknowledgments

I am grateful to David Freidel and Jerry Sabloff for their generous invitation to join the second Santa Fe Institute Working Group on Maya E Groups and to the members of that group for sharing information on sites with figurines and their recovery locations. Special thanks go to Arlen Chase for advice on several fronts; to Ellen Spensley and Matt Moriarty for information on Chächäklu'um; and to Alma Martínez for sending me her paper on Calakmul figurines. I appreciate the numerous colleagues who kindly slogged through earlier drafts of this essay, patiently answered questions, and/or sent helpful information, including Tony Andrews, Will Andrews, Ron Bishop, Bill Duncan, Norman Hammond, Laura Kosakowsky, Joyce Marcus, Nate Meissner, Don Rice, and Katie South.

Notes

1. Among the figurine fragments from the Gulf coastal Olmec area, for example, 99 percent of the heads had been separated from the bodies (Follensbee 2009:81).

2. A. P. Andrews, personal communication, 2012; E. W. Andrews V, personal communication, 2012. They report no figurines from Komchén and few if any from the many recently explored Middle Preclassic sites in the northwestern peninsula. Two possible Preclassic torso fragments are illustrated from Dzibilchaltún, however (Taschek 1994:Figure 52a, b).

3. There is also the Middle Preclassic Chiapas pattern: an elongated north–south plaza with a tall platform or pyramid in the north, an E Group platform pair at the south, and a small, low platform in the center of the plaza (Clark and Hansen 2001:4, 42–43 nn. 3 and 5). Middle Preclassic Chiapas patterned architectural complexes are particularly common in Chiapas but not restricted to that region.

4. John Clark and Richard Hansen (2001:22) identify Structures A, B, and D as round, but the round platforms are the slightly later Structures E, F, and G (Hendon 1999:105).

5. Three other areas of Middle Preclassic deposits were recovered at Tikal. Particularly interesting are those atop the bedrock rise underlying the massive North Acropolis (Group 5D-2), about 0.5 km northeast of the Mundo Perdido group. There a series of pits and *chultuns* cut into bedrock yielded refuse and burials, one a seated, young adolescent

female wearing a necklace of eight marine shell pendants, three jade beads, and three *Spondylus* beads (Burial 121: Coe 1990:22). One *chultun* (Ch. 5D-4) was a "large, somewhat squared room" with a stepped "bench of sorts hewn from rock" and a plaster floor (Coe 1990:814). Deposit 12P/151 (Unit 223) was a pit into bedrock that contained nearly fifty pounds of (early) Eb pottery, charcoal, *Pomacea flagellata* shells, quantities of flint flakes and debitage, figurines, a fragmentary stamp, a quartzite mano fragment, a marine shell fragment (*Pleuroploca* sp.), and, in its upper levels, a human cranium and mandible (PD 89) (Coe 1990:18, 25, 26). These deposits seem similar to those that I interpret as representing feasting remains; thus this area was very likely an Early Ritual Area, but no postholes were found and any structures that might have existed were destroyed by subsequent construction activity (Coe 1990:814–815). This later activity likely included emptying a cruciform pit (Unit 303) measuring about 1 m N–S, in front (south) of Structure 5D-34 (Coe 1990:Figures 154, 225), which is probably coeval with similar Middle Preclassic pits and cosmic caches at Cival and Ceibal (I could find no discussion of its contents). Four stelae were placed in front of this structure, two plain and two dated: one possibly 8.18.0.0.0 (Stela 4) and the other 9.2.13.0.0 (Stela 2). Note that in multiple places in Tikal Report 14 William Coe (1990) mistakenly refers to Chuen pottery as Middle Preclassic. It is Late Preclassic. Eb material was also found in a *chultun* in residential group 5G-1, a Plaza Plan 2 complex on a slightly raised "peninsula" of land extending east of the main part of the site into the Bajo Santa Fe. *Chultun* 5G-15 (PD 1) included nearly fifty reconstructible Eb vessels along with human bone (Becker 1999:76; Culbert 1993:Figures 116–121; Jones 1999:127).

6. The detailed report on these figurines (Zweig 2010) did not consistently separate anthropomorphic from zoomorphic figurines or ocarinas in the discussion, making it difficult to determine distributions; moreover, reported totals sometimes varied.

7. During the 1960s Harvard-sponsored project at Ceibal, two Middle Preclassic caches, including the famous cruciform Cache 7, in the southern half of Group A contained jade but no figurines (Smith 1982:241–243).

8. The earliest known Long Count date (31 BCE) is at Tres Zapotes; the earliest Maya Long Count date (CE 32) is at Chiapa de Corzo.

9. Some figurines from Kaminaljuyú and Chalcatzingo represent stages of pregnancy or are interpreted in terms of rites of transition associated with puberty, marriage, and pregnancy (Kidder 1965).

10. Three types of maize were recovered in early Preclassic (Swasey/Bladen) Cuello, the smallest cobs estimated to have been about 22 mm in diameter (Hammond 1991:238).

11. Similarly, compositional analyses of early figurines from San Lorenzo and Cantón Corralito (Pacific Chiapas) indicate that some objects at the latter were brought from the Gulf coast (Cheetham 2005).

12. At some sites, occasional seasonal flooding surrounded these elevations. The siting of Nixtun-Ch'ich' Mound ZZ1 is similar: on elevated bedrock at the tip of the peninsula extending 1.5 km into western Lake Petén Itzá. I long suspected that this mound, with its excellent observatory positioning, might have origins as an Early Ritual Area (or prE Group), a function that would help explain the presence of early figurines and conjoinable ceramic fragments. Unfortunately our 2 m-wide Operation 1 axial salvage trench was not suited to recovery of such architecture.

13. Because animal figurines were also common in early Middle Preclassic Mesoamerica, it would be interesting to investigate the kinds and frequencies of these in greater detail. At San Lorenzo, for example, "[f]elines and were-jaguars were conspicuously absent" in the figurine repertoire, but long-beaked avians were "found in every phase" (Coe and Diehl 1980:260). Avians, also widely depicted in iconography on other early media, might represent the prototype of the Principal Bird Deity or Seven Macaw.

References Cited

Acevedo, Reynaldo, Bernard Hermes, and Zoila Calderón
1996   Ixtinto: Rescate arqueológico. In *IX Simposio de Investigaciones Arqueológicos en Guatemala, 1995,* edited by Juan Pedro Laporte and Héctor Escobedo, pp. 207–222. Museo Nacional de Arqueologia, Guatemala City.
Aimers, James J., and Prudence M. Rice
2006   Astronomy, Ritual, and the Interpretation of Maya "E-Group" Architectural Assemblages. *Ancient Mesoamerica* 17(1):79–96.
Aveni, Anthony F.
2002   *Empires of Time: Calendars, Clocks, and Cultures.* Revised ed. University Press of Colorado, Boulder.
Aveni, Anthony F., Anne S. Dowd, and Benjamin Vining
2003   Maya Calendar Reform?: Evidence from Orientations of Specialized Architectural Assemblages. *Latin American Antiquity* 14(2):159–178.
Awe, Jaime J.
2013   Journey on the Cahal Pech Time Machine: An Archaeological Reconstruction of the Dynastic Sequence at a Belize Valley Maya Polity. *Research Reports in Belizean Archaeology* 10:33–50.
Bailey, Douglass W.
1994   Reading Prehistoric Figurines as Individuals. *World Archaeology* 25(3):321–331.
Ball, Joseph W., and Jennifer T. Taschek
2003   Reconsidering the Belize Valley Preclassic: A Case for Multiethnic Interactions in the Development of a Regional Culture Tradition. *Ancient Mesoamerica* 14(2):179–217.
Bartlett, Mary Lee
2004   Artifacts of Fired Clay. In *K'axob: Ritual, Work, and Family in an Ancient Maya Village,* edited by Patricia A. McAnany, pp. 263–273. Monumenta Archaeologica 22. Cotsen Institute of Archaeology, University of California, Los Angeles.
Bauer, Jeremy R.
2005   Between Heaven and Earth: The Cival Cache and the Creation of the Mesoamerican Cosmos. In *Lords of Creation: The Origins of Sacred Maya Kingship,* edited by Virginia M. Fields and Dorie Reents-Budet, pp. 28–29. Los Angeles County Museum of Art, Los Angeles.
Becker, Marshall J.
1999   *Excavations in Residential Areas of Tikal: Groups with Shrines.* Tikal Report 21. University Museum, University of Pennsylvania, Philadelphia.

Biehl, Peter F.
2011 Meanings and Functions of Enclosed Places in the European Neolithic: A Contextual Approach to Cult, Ritual, and Religion. *Archeological Papers of the AAA* 21(1):130–146.

Blanton, Richard E., Gary M. Feinman, Stephen A. Kowalewski, and Peter N. Peregrine
1996 A Dual-Processual Theory for the Evolution of Mesoamerican Civilization. *Current Anthropology* 37(1):1–14.

Brittain, Marcus, and Oliver Harris
2010 Enchaining Arguments and Fragmenting Assumptions: Reconsidering the Fragmentation Debate in Archaeology. *World Archaeology* 42(4):581–594.

Brown, M. Kathryn
2003 Ritual Ceramic Use in the Early and Middle Preclassic at the Sites of Blackman Eddy and Cahal Pech, Belize. *FAMSI: Foundation for the Advancement of Mesoamerican Studies.* http://www.famsi.org/reports/02066/02066Brown01.pdf, accessed September 29, 2016.

Brown, M. Kathryn, and James F. Garber
2006 Preclassic Architecture, Ritual, and the Emergence of Cultural Complexity: A Diachronic Perspective from the Belize Valley. In *Lords of Creation: The Origins of Sacred Maya Kingship*, edited by Virginia M. Fields and Dorie Reents-Budet, pp. 46–51. Los Angeles County Museum of Art, Los Angeles.

Brumfiel, Elizabeth M., and Lisa Overholzer
2009 Alien Bodies, Everyday People, and Internal Spaces: Embodiment, Figurines and Social Discourse in Postclassic Mexico. In *Mesoamerican Figurines: Small-Scale Indices of Large-Scale Phenomena*, edited by Christina T. Halperin, Katherine A. Faust, Rhonda Taube, and Aurore Giguet, pp. 297–326. University Press of Florida, Gainesville.

Carrasco Vargas, Ramón
2005 The Sacred Mountain: Preclassic Architecture in Calakmul. In *Lords of Creation: The Origins of Sacred Maya Kingship*, edited by Virginia M. Fields and Dorie Reents-Budet, pp. 62–66. Los Angeles County Museum of Art, Los Angeles.

Castellanos Cabrera, Jeannette
2008 Buenavista–Nuevo San José, Petén, Guatemala: Another Village from the Middle Preclassic (800–400 BC). *FAMSI: Foundation for the Advancement of Mesoamerican Studies.* http://www.famsi.org/reports/05039/05039Castellanos01.pdf, accessed September 29, 2016.

Chan de Aguilar, Rosa María
1997 Informe del trabajo de campo, Operaciones 06A, 08A, Flores, Petén, Guatemala. In *La Isla de Flores y el Lago Petén Itzá: Estudios de PRIANPEG en el Lago Petén Itzá: Resultados preliminares*, compiled by Richard D. Hansen, no pagination. Report to IDAEH, Guatemala City.

Chapman, John
2000 *Fragmentation in Archaeology: People, Places and Broken Objects in the Prehistory of South Eastern Europe.* Routledge, New York.
2008 Object Fragmentation and Past Landscapes. In *Handbook of Landscape Ar-*

chaeology, edited by Bruno David and Julian Thomas, pp. 187–201. Left Coast Press, Walnut Creek, California.

Chase, Arlen F.
1983   *A Contextual Consideration of the Tayasal-Paxcaman Zone, El Peten, Guatemala*. Ph.D. dissertation, Department of Anthropology, University of Pennsylvania, Philadelphia. University Microfilms/ProQuest, Ann Arbor.

Cheetham, David
1993   A Preliminary Catalogue of Preclassic Figurines: Cahal Pech, Belize. N.p., Belize Valley Archaeological Reconnaissance Project.
2005   Early Olmec Figurines from Two Regions: Style as Cultural Imperative. Online. In *FAMSI: Foundation for the Advancement of Mesoamerican Studies*. http://www.famsi.org/reports/05021/pdf3EarlyOlmec.pdf, accessed September 29, 2016.
2009   Early Olmec Figurines from Two Regions: Style as Cultural Imperative. In *Mesoamerican Figurines: Small-Scale Indices of Large-Scale Social Phenomena*, edited by Christina T. Halperin, Katherine A. Faust, Rhonda Taube, and Aurore Giguet, pp. 149–170. University Press of Florida, Gainesville.

Clark, John E., and Michael T. Blake
1994   The Power of Prestige: Competitive Generosity and the Emergence of Rank Societies in Lowland Mesoamerica. In *Factional Competition and Political Development in the New World*, edited by Elizabeth M. Brumfiel and John W. Fox, pp. 17–30. Cambridge University Press, Cambridge.

Clark, John E., and Richard D. Hansen
2001   The Architecture of Early Kingship: Comparative Perspectives on the Origins of the Maya Royal Court. In *Royal Courts of the Ancient Maya: 2. Data and Case Studies*, edited by Takeshi Inomata and Stephen D. Houston, pp. 1–45. Westview, Boulder.

Coe, Michael D., and Richard A. Diehl
1980   *In the Land of the Olmec: 1. The Archaeology of San Lorenzo Tenochtitlán*. University of Texas Press, Austin.

Coe, Michael D., and Justin Kerr
1998   *The Art of the Maya Scribe*. Harry N. Abrams, New York.

Coe, Michael D., and Mark van Stone
2001   *Reading the Maya Glyphs*. Thames and Hudson, London.

Coe, William R.
1990   *Excavations in the Great Plaza, North Terrace, and North Acropolis of Tikal*. Tikal Report 14, Vols. 1–6. University Museum, University of Pennsylvania, Philadelphia.

Csordas, Thomas J.
1990   Embodiment as a Paradigm for Anthropology. *Ethos* 19:5–47.
1994   Introduction: The Body as Representation and Being-in-the-World. In *Embodiment and Experience: The Existential Ground of Culture and Self*, edited by Thomas J. Csordas, pp. 1–26. Cambridge University Press, Cambridge.

Culbert, T. Patrick
1993   *The Ceramics of Tikal: Vessels from the Burials, Caches, and Problematical De-*

posits. Tikal Report 25, Part A. University Museum, University of Pennsylvania, Philadelphia.

Cyphers Guillén, Ann

1988   Thematic and Contextual Analyses of Chalcatzingo Figurines. *Mexicon* 10(5):98–102.

1993   Women, Rituals, and Social Dynamics at Ancient Chalcatzingo. *Latin American Antiquity* 4(3):209–224.

Damper, R. I.

2000   Emergence and Levels of Abstraction. *International Journal of Systems Science* 31(7):811–818 (editorial for the special issue *Emergent Properties of Complex Systems*).

de Borhegyi, Stephan F.

1956   The Development of Folk and Complex Cultures in the Southern Maya Area. *American Antiquity* 21(4):343–356.

Dietler, Michael, and Brian Hayden (editors)

2001   *Feasts: Archaeological and Ethnographic Perspectives on Food, Politics, and Power*. Smithsonian Institution, Washington, D.C.

Dowd, Anne S., and Susan Milbrath (editors)

2015   *Cosmology, Calendars, and Horizon-Based Astronomy in Ancient Mesoamerica*. University Press of Colorado, Boulder.

Doyle, James A.

2012   Regroup on "E-Groups": Monumentality and Early Centers in the Middle Preclassic Maya Lowlands. *Latin American Antiquity* 23(4):355–379.

Duncan, William N.

2014   Mortuary Sealing among the Maya. In *The Bioarchaeology of Space and Place: Ideology, Power, and Meaning in Maya Mortuary Contexts*, edited by Gabriel D. Wrobel, pp. 255–270. Springer, New York.

Edmonson, Munro S.

1988   *The Book of the Year: Middle American Calendrical Systems*. University of Utah Press, Salt Lake City.

Estrada-Belli, Francisco

2006   Lightning Sky, Rain, and the Maize God: The Ideology of Preclassic Rulers at Cival, Peten, Guatemala. *Ancient Mesoamerica* 17(1):57–78.

Fahsen, Federico, and Nikolai Grube

2006   The Origins of Maya Writing. In *Lords of Creation: The Origins of Sacred Maya Kingship*, edited by Virginia M. Fields and Dorie Reents-Budet, pp. 75–79. Los Angeles County Museum of Art, Los Angeles.

Fields, Virginia M.

1991   The Iconographic Heritage of the Maya Jester God. In *Sixth Palenque Round Table, 1986*, edited by Merle Greene Robertson and Virginia M. Fields, pp. 167–174. University of Oklahoma Press, Norman.

Follensbee, Billie J. A.

2009   Preclassic Period Gulf Coast Ceramic Figurines: The Key to Identifying Sex, Gender, and Age Groups in Gulf Coast Olmec Imagery. In *Mesoamerican Figurines: Small-Scale Indices of Large-Scale Social Phenomena*, edited by Christina T. Halperin, Katherine A. Faust, Rhonda Taube, and Aurore Giguet, pp. 77–118. University Press of Florida, Gainesville.

Freidel, David A.
1990   The Jester God: The Beginning and End of a Maya Royal Symbol. In *Vision and Revision in Maya Studies*, edited by Flora S. Clancy and Peter D. Harrison, pp. 67–78. University of New Mexico Press, Albuquerque.
1995   Preparing the Way. In *The Olmec World: Ritual and Rulership*, edited by Jill Guthrie, pp. 3–9. Princeton University Press, Princeton, New Jersey.

Freidel, David A., and Linda Schele
1988   Kingship in the Late Preclassic Maya Lowlands. *American Anthropologist* 90(3):547–567.

Freidel, David A., Linda Schele, and Joy Parker
1993   *Maya Cosmos: Three Thousand Years on the Shaman's Path*. William Morrow, New York.

Garber, James F., and Jaime J. Awe
2008   Middle Preclassic Architecture and Ritual at Cahal Pech. *Research Papers in Belizean Archaeology* 5:185–190.

Garber, James F., Jennifer L. Cochran, and Jaime J. Awe
2006   Excavations in Plaza B at Cahal Pech: The 2004 Field Season. *Research Reports in Belizean Archaeology* 3:31–40.

Geary, Patrick
1986   Sacred Commodities: The Circulation of Medieval Relics. In *The Social Life of Things: Commodities in Cultural Perspective*, edited by Arjun Appadurai, pp. 169–191. Cambridge University Press, Cambridge.

Geller, Pamela L.
2012   Parting (with) the Dead: Body Partibility as Evidence of Commoner Ancestor Veneration. *Ancient Mesoamerica* 23(1):115–129.

Gell-Mann, Murray
1994   *The Quark and the Jaguar: Adventures in the Simple and the Complex*. Henry Holt, New York.

Gillespie, Susan D.
1987   Distributional Analysis of Chalcatzingo Figurines. In *Ancient Chalcatzingo*, edited by David C. Grove, pp. 264–270. University of Texas Press, Austin.

Gossen, Gary H.
1986   Mesoamerican Ideas as a Foundation for Regional Synthesis. In *Symbol and Meaning beyond the Closed Community: Essays in Mesoamerican Ideas*, edited by Gary H. Gossen, pp. 1–8. Institute for Mesoamerican Studies, State University of New York, Albany.

Grove, David C.
2006   Faces of the Earth at Chalcatzingo, Mexico: Serpents, Caves, and Mountains in Middle Preclassic Period Iconography. In *Olmec Art and Archaeology in Mesoamerica*, edited by John E. Clark and Mary E. Pye, pp. 277–295. Studies in the History of Art 58. Center for Advanced Study in the Visual Arts, National Gallery of Art, Washington, D.C.

Grove, David C., and Susan D. Gillespie
1984   Chalcatzingo's Portrait Figurines and the Cult of the Ruler. *Archaeology* 37(4):27–33.
1992   Ideology and Evolution at the Pre-State Level: Formative Period Mesoamerica. In *Ideology and Pre-Columbian Civilizations*, edited by Arthur A. Demarest and Geoffrey W. Conrad, pp. 15–36. School of American Research Press, Santa Fe.
2002   Middle Preclassic Domestic Ritual at Chalcatzingo, Morelos. In *Domestic Ritual in Ancient Mesoamerica*, edited by Patricia Plunket, pp. 11–19. Cotsen Institute of Archaeology Monograph 46, University of California, Los Angeles.

Gudeman, Stephen
1976   Saints, Symbols, and Ceremonies. *American Ethnologist* 3(4):709–729.

Hammond, Norman
1989   The Function of Maya Middle Preclassic Pottery Figurines. *Mexicon* 11:111–114.

Hammond, Norman (editor)
1991   *Cuello: An Early Maya Community in Belize*. Cambridge University Press, Cambridge.

Hansen, Richard D.
2000   The First Cities: The Beginnings of Urbanization and State Formation in the Maya Lowlands. In *Maya, Divine Kings of the Rain Forest*, edited by Nikolai Grube, pp. 51–65. Könemann, Cologne.

Helms, Mary W.
1988   *Ulysses' Sail: An Ethnographic Odyssey of Power, Knowledge, and Geographical Distance*. Princeton University Press, Princeton, New Jersey.

Hendon, Julia A.
1999   The Pre-Classic Maya Compound as the Focus of Social Identity. In *Social Patterns in Pre-Classic Mesoamerica*, edited by David C. Grove and Rosemary A. Joyce, pp. 97–125. Dumbarton Oaks, Washington, D.C.

Hermes, Bernard
2000   Vasijas de miniatura y figuras de miniatura. In *El sitio maya de Topoxté: Investigaciones en una isla del lago Yaxhá, Petén, Guatemala*, edited by Wolfgang W. Wurster, pp. 205–207. Verlag Philipp von Zabern, Mainz am Rhein.

Houston, Stephen
2012   Diadems in the Rough. Online. *Maya Decipherment: Ideas on Ancient Maya Writing and Iconography*. http://decipherment.wordpress.com/category/aguateca, accessed October 20, 2013.

Houston, Stephen, David Stuart, and Karl A. Taube
2006   *The Memory of Bones: Body, Being, and Experience among the Classic Maya*. University of Texas Press, Austin.

Inomata, Takeshi, Daniela Triadan, Kazuo Aoyama, Victor Castillo, and Hitoshi Yonenobu
2013   Early Ceremonial Constructions at Ceibal, Guatemala, and the Origins of Lowland Maya Civilization. *Science* 340:467–471.

Jones, Christopher
1999   Synopsis. *Excavations in Residential Areas of Tikal: Groups with Shrines*, edited

by Marshall J. Becker, pp. 127–135. Tikal Report 21. University Museum, University of Pennsylvania, Philadelphia.

Jones, Tom
1991   Jaws II: Return of the *Xoc*. In *Sixth Palenque Round Table, 1986*, edited by Merle Greene Robertson, pp. 246–254. University of Oklahoma Press, Norman.

Joyce, Rosemary A.
2008   When the Flesh Is Solid But the Person Is Hollow Inside: Formal Variation in Hand-Modeled Figurines from Preclassic Mesoamerica. In *Past Bodies: Body-Centered Research in Archaeology*, edited by John Robb and Dusan Boric, pp. 37–45. Oxbow Books, Oxford, United Kingdom.
2009   Making a World of Their Own: Mesoamerican Figurines and Mesoamerican Figurine Analysis. In *Mesoamerican Figurines: Small-Scale Indices of Large-Scale Social Phenomena*, edited by Christina T. Halperin, Katherine A. Faust, Rhonda Taube, and Aurore Giguet, pp. 407–425. University Press of Florida, Gainesville.

Justeson, John S.
1986   The Origin of Writing Systems: Preclassic Mesoamerica. *World Archaeology* 17(3):437–458.

Justeson, John S., and Peter Mathews
1990   Evolutionary Trends in Mesoamerican Hieroglyphic Writing. *Visible Language* 29(1):88–132.

Kidder, Alfred V.
1965   Preclassic Pottery Figurines of the Guatemalan Highlands. In *Handbook of Middle American Indians*, Vol. 2, edited by Robert Wauchope, pp. 146–155. University of Texas Press, Austin.

Kopytoff, Igor
1987   The Internal African Frontier: The Making of African Political Culture. In *The African Frontier: The Reproduction of Traditional African Societies*, edited by Igor Kopytoff, pp. 3–84. Indiana University Press, Bloomington.

Kosakowsky, Laura J., Anna C. Novotny, Angela H. Keller, Nicholas F. Hearth, and Carmen Ting
2012   Contextualizing Ritual Behavior: Caches, Burials, and Problematical Deposits from Chan's Community Center. In *Chan: An Ancient Maya Farming Community*, edited by Cynthia Robin, pp. 289–308. University Press of Florida, Gainesville.

Kosakowsky, Laura J., and Cynthia Robin
2010   Contextualizing Ritual Behavior at the Chan Site: Pottery Vessels and Ceramic Artifacts from Burials, Caches, and Problematical Deposits. *Research Reports in Belizean Archaeology* 7:45–54.

Kuijt, Ian
2008   The Regeneration of Life: Neolithic Structures of Symbolic Remembering and Forgetting. *Current Anthropology* 49(2):171–197.

Lacadena García-Gallo, Alfonso
2010   Escritura y lengua en Tak'alik Ab'aj: Problemas y propuestas. In *XXIII Simposio de Investigaciones Arqueológicas en Guatemala, 2009*, edited by Bárbara Arroyo, Adriana Linares, and Lorena Paiz, pp. 1022–1039. Museo Nacional de Arqueología y Etnología, Guatemala City.

Laporte, Juan Pedro
1996   La cuenca del Río Mopán–Belice: Una sub-región cultural de las tierras bajas maya central. In *IX Simposio de Investigaciones Arqueológicas en Guatemala, 1995*, edited by Juan Pedro Laporte and Héctor L. Escobedo, pp. 253–279. Museo Nacional de Arqueología y Etnología and Asociación Tikal, Guatemala City.

Laporte, Juan Pedro, and Vilma Fialko C.
1993   El preclásico de Mundo Perdido: Algunos aportes sobre los orígenes de Tikal. In *Tikal y Uaxactún en el Preclásico*, edited by Juan Pedro Laporte and Juan Antonio Valdés, pp. 9–42. Instituto de Investigaciones Antropológicas, Universidad Nacional Autónoma de México, Mexico City.
1995   Un reencuentro con Mundo Perdido, Tikal, Guatemala. *Ancient Mesoamerica* 6(1):41–94.

Laporte, Juan Pedro, and Juan Antonio Valdés (editors)
1993   *Tikal y Uaxactún en el Preclásico*. Universidad Nacional Autónoma de México, Mexico City.

Lefebvre, Henri
1991   *The Production of Space*. Translated by Donald Nicholson-Smith. Blackwell, Oxford, United Kingdom.

Lesure, Richard G.
1997   Figurines and Social Identities in Early Sedentary Societies of Coastal Chiapas, Mexico 1550–800 B.C. In *Women in Prehistory: North America and Mesoamerica*, edited by Cheryl Claassen and Rosemary A. Joyce, pp. 227–248. University of Pennsylvania Press, Philadelphia.
1999   Figurines as Representations and Products at Paso de la Amada, Mexico. *Cambridge Archaeological Journal* 9(2):209–220.

Lohse, Jon C.
2010   Archaic Origins of the Lowland Maya. *Latin American Antiquity* 21(3):312–352.

Love, Michael
1999   Ideology, Material Culture, and Daily Practice in Pre-Classic Mesoamerica: A Pacific Coast Perspective. In *Social Patterns in Pre-Classic Mesoamerica*, edited by David C. Grove and Rosemary A. Joyce, pp. 127–153. Dumbarton Oaks, Washington, D.C.

Lowe, Gareth W.
1977   The Mixe-Zoque as Competing Neighbors of the Early Lowland Maya. In *The Origins of Maya Civilization*, edited by Richard E. W. Adams, pp. 197–248. University of New Mexico Press, Albuquerque.

Macri, Martha J.
1985   The Numerical Head Variants and the Maya Numbers. *Anthropology Linguistics* 27(1):46–85.
2008   Las lenguas de la Mesoamérica Antigua: ¿Qué es posible saber? In *Olmeca: Balance y perspectivas, Memoria de la Primera Mesa Redonda*, edited by María Teresa Uriarte and Rebecca B. González Lauck, pp. 627–638. UNAM, CONACULTA, INAH, and New World Archaeological Foundation, Mexico City.

Macri, Martha J., and Matthew G. Looper
2003   *The New Catalog of Maya Hieroglyphs: 1. The Classic Period Inscriptions*. University of Oklahoma Press, Norman.

Marcus, Joyce
1992   *Mesoamerican Writing Systems: Propaganda, Myth, and History in Four Ancient Civilizations*. Princeton University Press, Princeton, New Jersey.
1996   The Importance of Context in Interpreting Figurines. *Cambridge Archaeological Journal* 6:285–291.
1998   *Women's Ritual in Preclassic Oaxaca: Figurine-Making, Divination, Death and the Ancestors*. Memoirs of the Museum of Anthropology No. 33. University of Michigan, Ann Arbor.
1999   Men's and Women's Ritual in Preclassic Oaxaca. In *Social Patterns in Pre-Classic Mesoamerica*, edited by David C. Grove and Rosemary A. Joyce, pp. 67–96. Dumbarton Oaks, Washington, D.C.
2009   Rethinking Figurines. In *Mesoamerican Figurines: Small-Scale Indices of Large-Scale Social Phenomena*, edited by Christina T. Halperin, Katherine A. Faust, Rhonda Taube, and Aurore Giguet, pp. 25–50. University Press of Florida, Gainesville.

Martin, Simon
2003   In Line of the Founder: A View of Dynastic Politics at Tikal. In *Tikal: Dynasties, Foreigners, and Affairs of State*, edited by Jeremy A. Sabloff, pp. 3–45. School of American Research Press, Santa Fe, New Mexico.

Martínez, Gerson O., and Juan Pedro Laporte
2010   Laguna Sacpuy en el centro de Petén y su asentamiento arqueológico. In *XXIII Simposio de Investigaciones Arqueológicas en Guatemala, 2009*, edited by Bárbara Arroyo, Adriana Linares, and Lorena Paiz, pp. 441–457. Museo Nacional de Arqueología y Etnología, Guatemala City. http://www.asociaciontikal.com/simposio.php?id=33, accessed September 29, 2016.

Martínez Dávila, Alma
2013   Figurillas preclásicas en la ciudad de Calakmul. Manuscript in possession of the author.

Mauss, Marcel
1973   Techniques of the Body. Translated by B. Brewster. *Economy and Society* 2:70–87.

McAnany, Patricia A.
1995   *Living with the Ancestors: Kinship and Kingship in Ancient Maya Society*. University of Texas Press, Austin.

Meissner, Nathan, Katherine E. South, and Andrew K. Balkansky
2013   Figurine Embodiment and Household Ritual in an Early Mixtec Village. *Journal de la Société des Américanistes* 99(1):7–43.

Miller, Mary Ellen, and Karl A. Taube
1993   *The Gods and Symbols of Ancient Mexico and the Maya: An Illustrated Dictionary of Mesoamerican Religion*. Thames and Hudson, New York.

Mills, Barbara J., and William H. Walker (editors)
2008   *Memory Work: Archaeologies of Material Practices*. School of American Research Press, Santa Fe, New Mexico.

Mock, Shirley B. (editor)
1998   *The Sowing and the Dawning: Termination, Dedication, and Transformation in the Archaeological and Ethnographic Record of Mesoamerica*. University of New Mexico Press, Albuquerque.

Neuenswander, Helen
1981   Vestiges of Early Maya Time Concepts in a Contemporary Maya (Cubulco Achi) Community: Implications for Epigraphy. *Estudios de Cultura Maya* 13:125–163.

Pauketat, Timothy R.
2008   Founders' Cults and the Archaeology of *Wa-kan-da*. In *Memory Work: Archaeologies of Material Practices*, edited by Barbara J. Mills and William H. Walker, pp. 61–79. School of American Research Press, Santa Fe, New Mexico.

Pendergast, David M.
1990   *Excavations at Altun Ha, Belize, 1964–1970*, Vol. 3. Royal Ontario Museum, Toronto.

Proskouriakoff, Tatiana
1978   Olmec Gods and Maya God-Glyphs. In *Codex Wauchope: A Tribute Roll*, edited by Marco Giaradino, Barbara Edmonson, and Winifred Creamer. *Human Mosaic* 12:113–117.

Rands, Robert L., and Barbara C. Rands
1965   Pottery Figurines of the Maya Lowlands. In *Archaeology of Southern Mesoamerica, Part 1*, edited by Gordon R. Willey, pp. 535–560. University of Texas Press, Austin.

Rathje, William, David A. Gregory, and Frederick M. Wiseman
1978   Trade Models and Archaeological Problems: Classic Maya Examples. In *Mesoamerican Communication Routes and Cultural Contacts*, edited by Thomas A. Lee Jr. and Carlos Navarrete, pp. 147–175. New World Archaeological Foundation Papers 40. Brigham Young University, Provo, Utah.

Reilly, F. Kent, III
2005   Olmec Ideological, Ritual, and Symbolic Contributions to the Institution of Classic Maya Kingship. In *Lords of Creation: The Origins of Sacred Maya Kingship*, edited by Virginia M. Fields and Dorie Reents-Budet, pp. 30–36. Los Angeles County Museum of Art, Los Angeles.

Rice, Don S.
1976   Middle Preclassic Settlement in the Central Maya Lowlands. *Journal of Field Archaeology* 3(4):425–445.

Rice, Prudence M.
2007   *Maya Calendar Origins: Monuments, Mythistory, and the Materialization of Time*. University of Texas Press, Austin.
2008   Time, Power, and the Maya. *Latin American Antiquity* 19(3):275–298.
2009   Mound ZZ1, Nixtun-Ch'ich', Petén, Guatemala: Rescue Operations at a Long-Lived Structure in the Maya Lowlands. *Journal of Field Archaeology* 34(4):403–422.
2015   Middle Preclassic Interregional Interactions and the Maya Lowlands. *Journal of Archaeological Research* 23(1):1–47.
n.d.   Anthropomorphizing the Cosmos: Middle Preclassic Maya Figurines and the Sacred Almanac. Manuscript in preparation.

Rice, Prudence M., and Don S. Rice
2016   *Ixlú: A Contested Maya Entrepôt in Petén, Guatemala*. Latin American Archaeological Reports, Center for Comparative Archaeology Memoir 23, University of Pittsburgh.

Ricketson, Oliver G., and Edith B. Ricketson
1937   *Uaxactun, Guatemala, Group E, 1926–1931*. Publication 477. Carnegie Institution of Washington, Washington, D.C.

Robin, Cynthia, James Meierhoff, Caleb Kestle, Chelsea Blackmore, Laura J. Kosakowsky, and Anna C. Novotny
2012   Ritual in a Farming Community. In *Chan: An Ancient Maya Farming Community*, edited by Cynthia Robin, pp. 113–132. University Press of Florida, Gainesville.

Rodman, Margaret C.
1992   Empowering Place: Multilocality and Multivocality. *American Anthropologist* 94(3):640–656.

Sánchez Polo, Rómulo
1997   El territorio de los Kowoj—Proyecto Maya-Colonial: Geografía política del siglo XVII en el centro del Petén, Guatemala. Preliminary report to IDAEH on the 1994 and 1995 field seasons by Don S. Rice, Prudence M. Rice, Rómulo Sánchez Polo, and Grant D. Jones, Guatemala City.

Sanders, William T.
1973   The Cultural Ecology of the Lowland Maya: A Reevaluation. In *The Classic Maya Collapse*, edited by T. Patrick Culbert, pp. 325–365. University of New Mexico Press and School of American Research, Albuquerque.

Sandstrom, Alan R.
2009   The Weeping Baby and the Nahua Corn Spirit: The Human Body as Key Symbol in the Huasteca Veracruzana, Mexico. In *Mesoamerican Figurines: Small-Scale Indices of Large-Scale Social Phenomena*, edited by Christina T. Halperin, Katherine A. Faust, Rhonda Taube, and Aurore Giguet, pp. 261–296. University Press of Florida, Gainesville.

Schele, Linda, and Mary Ellen Miller
1986   *The Blood of Kings: Dynasty and Ritual in Maya Art*. Kimbell Art Museum, Fort Worth.

Schiffer, Michael B.

1972   Archaeological Context and Systemic Context. *American Antiquity* 37(2):156–165.

1976   *Behavioral Archaeology*. Academic Press, New York.

Schwimmer, Eric

1986   Icons of Identity. In *Iconicity: Essays on the Nature of Culture. Festschrift for Thomas A. Sebeok on His 65th Birthday*, edited by Paul Bouissac, Michael Herzfeld, and Roland Posner, pp. 359–384. Stauffenburg Verlag, Tübingen.

Silverman, Helaine

2004   *Andean Archaeology*. Blackwell, Malden, Massachusetts.

Smith, A. Ledyard

1982   *Excavations at Seibal, Department of Peten, Guatemala: Major Architecture and Caches*. Memoirs of the Peabody Museum of Archaeology and Ethnology, Harvard University, Vol. 15, No. 1. Peabody Museum, Cambridge, Massachusetts.

South, Katherine E.

2001   Fired Clay Artifacts from Cuello, Belize. Senior independent work, Department of Archaeology, Boston University, Boston.

Spensley, Ellen

2007   Investigaciones en la sabana Chächäklu'um, 2005. In *Proyecto Arqueológico Motul de San José, Informe #7: Temporada de campo 2005–2007*, edited by Michael D. Moriarty, Ellen Spensley, Jeanette E. Castellanos C., and Antonia E. Foias, pp. 219–225. Report to IDAEH, Guatemala City.

Strathern, Marilyn

1988   *The Gender of the Gift: Problems with Women and Problems with Society in Melanesia*. University of California Press, Berkeley.

Stross, Brian

1985   Maya Head Variant Numerals: The Olmec Case. *Anthropological Linguistics* 27(1):1–45.

1994   Maize and Fish: The Iconography of Power in Late Preclassic Mesoamerica. *RES: Anthropology and Aesthetics* 25:9–35.

Stuart, David

1995   A Study of Maya Inscriptions. Ph.D. dissertation, Department of Anthropology, Vanderbilt University, Nashville.

2011   *The Order of Days: The Maya World and the Truth about 2012*. Harmony Books, New York.

Taschek, Jennifer T.

1994   *The Artifacts of Dzibilchaltun, Yucatan, Mexico: Shell, Polished Stone, Bone, Wood, and Ceramics*. Middle American Research Institute Publication 50. Tulane University, New Orleans.

Taube, Karl A.

1996   The Olmec Maize God: The Face of Corn in Preclassic Mesoamerica. *RES: Anthropology and Aesthetics* 29/30:39–81.

2001   The Breath of Life: The Symbolism of Wind in Mesoamerica and the American Southwest. In *The Road to Aztlan: Art from a Mythic Homeland*, edited by Vir-

ginia M. Fields and Victor Zamudio-Taylor, pp. 102–123. Los Angeles County Museum of Art, Los Angeles.
2006   Lightning Celts and Corn Fetishes: The Preclassic Olmec and the Development of Maize Symbolism in Mesoamerica and the American Southwest. In *Olmec Art and Archaeology in Mesoamerica*, edited by John E. Clark and Mary E. Pye, pp. 265–275. Center for Advanced Study in the Visual Arts, National Gallery of Art, Washington, D.C.

Taube, Karl A., and William A. Saturno
2008   Los murales de San Bartolo: Desarrollo temprano del simbolismo del mito del maíz en la antigua Mesoamérica. In *Olmeca: Balance y perspectivas, Memoria de la Primera Mesa Redonda*, edited by María Teresa Uriarte and Rebecca B. González Lauck, pp. 287–318. UNAM and INAH, Mexico City/NWAF, Brigham Young University, Provo, Utah.

Tedlock, Barbara
1992   *Time and the Highland Maya*. Revised ed. University of New Mexico Press, Albuquerque.

Tedlock, Dennis (translator)
1996   *Popol Vuh: The Definitive Edition of the Mayan Book of the Dawn of Life and the Glories of Gods and Kings*. Revised ed. Simon and Schuster, New York.

Thompson, J. Eric S.
1960   *Maya Hieroglyphic Writing: An Introduction*. 2nd ed. University of Oklahoma Press, Norman.
1962   *A Catalog of Maya Hieroglyphs*. University of Oklahoma Press, Norman.
1965   Archaeological Synthesis of the Southern Maya Lowlands. In *Archaeology of Southern Mesoamerica, Part 1*, edited by Gordon R. Willey, pp. 331–359. University of Texas Press, Austin.

Tiesler, Vera
2010   "Olmec" Head Shapes among the Preclassic Period Maya and Cultural Meanings. *Latin American Antiquity* 21(3):290–311.

Tway, Maria B.
2004   Gender, Context, and Figurine Use: Ceramic Images from the Preclassic Period San Andrés Site, Tabasco, Mexico. M.A. thesis, Department of Anthropology, Florida State University, Tallahassee.

Vaillant, George Clapp
1930   *Excavations at Zacatenco*. Anthropological Papers, Vol. 32, No. 1. American Museum of Natural History, New York.

VanDerwarker, Amber M., and Robert P. Kruger
2012   Regional Variation in the Importance and Uses of Maize in the Early and Middle Preclassic Olmec Heartland: New Archaeobotanical Data from the San Carlos Homestead, Southern Veracruz. *Latin American Antiquity* 23(4):509–532.

Van Dyke, Ruth M., and Susan E. Alcock (editors)
2003   *Archaeologies of Memory*. Blackwell, Melbourne.

Voss, Alexander W.
2000   Astronomy and Mathematics. In *Maya: Divine Kings of the Rain Forest*, edited by Nikolai Grube, pp. 130–145. Könemann, Cologne.

Wagner, Elisabeth
2006   White Earth Bundles: The Symbolic Sealing and Burial of Buildings among the Ancient Maya. In *Jaws of the Underworld: Life, Death, and Rebirth among the Ancient Maya*, edited by Pierre R. Colas, Geneviève LeFort, and Bodil Liljefors Persson, pp. 55–70. Acta Mesoamericana Vol. 16. Verlag Anton Saurwein, Markt Schwaben.

Wagner, Roy
1991   The Fractal Person. In *Big Men and Great Men: Personifications of Power in Melanesia*, edited by Marilyn Strathern and Maurice Godelier, pp. 159–173. Cambridge University Press, Cambridge.

Weiant, Clarence W.
1943   *An Introduction to the Ceramics of Tres Zapotes, Veracruz, Mexico*. Bureau of American Ethnology Bulletin 139, Smithsonian Institution, Washington, D.C.

Willey, Gordon R.
1972   *The Artifacts of Altar de Sacrificios*. Papers of the Peabody Museum of Archaeology and Ethnology, Harvard University, Vol. 64, No. 1. Peabody Museum, Cambridge, Massachusetts.

Willey, Gordon R., and William R. Bullard Jr.
1961   Altar de Sacrificios, Guatemala: Mapa preliminar y resúmen de las excavaciones. *Estudios de Cultura Maya* 1:81–85.

Zweig, Christina L.
2010   The Preclassic Ceramic Figurine Collection from the Site of Cahal Pech, Cayo, Belize. M.A. thesis, Department of Anthropology, University of Wisconsin–Milwaukee, Milwaukee.

6

E Groups, Cosmology, and the Origins of Maya Rulership

DAVID A. FREIDEL

Maya sages are people who craft wisdom from the raw material of observational information and the knowledge that accumulates from observing, contemplating, and discussing these for a long time. As I once put it in "Preparing the Way" (Freidel 1996:3): "Despite the eons of slowly accumulated skills and experience behind them, civilized worlds' mentalities are ultimately invented. They are conjured out of immediate political necessities, combined with special cultural opportunities, in the work of sages." Sages' abilities are no less remarkable or respected by neighbors in Maya communities today than those of other skilled craftspeople. Indeed when the ancient Maya give voice to such notions well into their phase of social and cultural complexity in their Classic inscriptions they have a term for scribe as identified by David Stuart (1986), *itz'aat,* which embraces our notions of creator, artist, and scientist and can be glossed as sage. We can be excused for sensing a primal quality to the idea of *itz'aat* when noting that, in addition to the creator Itzamnaaj, the gods exemplifying *itz'aat* are monkeys, the nearly human beings who, along with the great birds like the Scarlet Macaw, animal avatar of Itzamnaaj, still occupy the canopy of Lowland Maya rainforests.

In the Beginning

This is an inquiry into how the early stages of southeastern Mesoamerica might have invented the rationales of civilization by kneading the knowledge of natural cycles like those of the sun, the seasons, and mortal beings like plants and people into coherent life narratives (Freidel 1996). The proposed narratives, myths, or creeds not only could, I suggest, explain change and continuity but also through such explanations sustain communities and societies. I base their proposed content and structures in iconographic analyses of visual symbol systems defined by many scholars over the last several decades. Importantly, in my view, they likely not only served to provide daily doses of wisdom locally to people in need of it through such means as sayings and proverbs, if analogy to contemporary Maya practices is any guide, but also established a common discourse among the sages of neighboring peoples regarding the nature of the world. For in Mesoamerica we have empirical evidence of such regional interaction from the Archaic period (7,500–1,000 BCE) forward.

The narratives of creation wove together what we in our Western reality would distinguish as natural and supernatural phenomena, material and spiritual things, scientific and religious sensibilities (see Harvey 2013 for a review of animism). Of course this derives not from the lesser intellectual capabilities of Precolumbian Maya but from their universal and manifest observation that human experience is the center and pivot of collective reality and that human experience, like any experience of mindful beings, cannot effectively be reduced to natural and material dimensions. The attribution of an animist understanding, that what is important are the relations between things that are capable of being agentive and that human beings are particularly responsible because they are aware of this connectivity in purpose, is experiencing a revival as an interpretive paradigm in Maya studies (Hendon 2012; Harrison-Buck 2012). In this view the ancient Maya sages, like their contemporary counterparts, engaged in observation and analysis of the exquisite and endlessly fascinating patterns of the natural world as a living web cradling human existence and responding to its performance. In the case at hand, the sun did not mechanically and mindlessly traverse the sky and the underworld but rather did so by its own volition. Stuart (2005) has recently deduced from convincing iconographic and epigraphic analyses that for the Classic Maya the sun in this way brought the rains of the changing seasons (Figure 6.1, GI, in Stuart's decipherment, Hun Yeh Winik) and conversely, I would say, caused them to cease (through K'inich Ajaw, the fiery sun). The relation between the Maya sun gods and the rain gods still needs further elucidation, but one connection is the serpent as a conduit of wind and rain, as observed recently, for example, by Matthew Looper (2003) in the sculptures at Classic Quiriguá and in modern Chortí Maya religion. As he notes, an important double-headed serpent is carried in the mouth of the Principal Bird Deity, avatar of Itzamnaaj, solar deity, and predecessor of GI.

E Groups, Cosmology, and the Origins of Maya Rulership · 179

Figure 6.1. GI, One Tooth Person. Drawings by Linda Schele.

The conceptual tools of ancient Maya sages and their counterparts elsewhere in southeastern Mesoamerica were clearly different from those of modern-day scientists. It is equally important not to overlook the prospects that people can use means other than those guiding modern science in reason-based engagement with the material properties of their world. John Clark and Michael Blake (1994) have already suggested mindful agency as a factor in the processes of the relatively rapid social and cultural change characterizing the Formative period in Mesoamerica in the form of self-aggrandizing leaders. I would further suggest that such ambitious leaders looked to sages for counsel and explanations of how to manage change and that the sages looked to other craftspeople and the experience of food producers for guidance and models of practical success.

Here Comes the Sun in Wide Open Spaces: A Living Theater and Its Main Characters

In his seminal articles outlining models of the origins of agriculture in Mesoamerica and Southwest Asia, Kent Flannery (1973:287) underscored the importance of hunter-gatherer societies, who in settling into their environments learned to schedule their food getting activities to the cycles of plants and animals they consumed, an idea integral also to the thinking of Richard S. MacNeish (1964) in the Tehuacán Valley settlement study. Seasonality in Mesoamerica can be clocked by the cyclical return of the rains following the dry season, but the precise means of anticipating seasonal change is day counting. Just when people in ancient Mesoamerica might have started day counting remains difficult to assess archaeologically. I have recently proposed (Freidel and Rich 2015) that the intriguing discovery by Barbara Voorhies (2012) of possible Archaic period gaming boards designed as arcs of holes in prepared ground surfaces in a settlement on the Pacific coast of Guatemala might have presaged the much later counting surfaces at Teotihuacán and elsewhere proposed by Anthony Aveni (2005) to be calculating devices for day counts. Voorhies (2012) reviews the evidence for the use of such gaming boards with stick dice in both Mesoamerica and North America. Takeshi Inomata (Chapter 7 in this volume) has discovered carefully made small stone balls placed as offerings in Late Preclassic (350 BCE–0 CE) plates at Ceibal. The Archaic and Early Classic (250–550 CE) features, while widely separated in time, share the principle of positional patterning appropriate for the display of tokens, a principle bridged by Inomata's intriguing speculation (Chapter 7 in this volume) that the Ceibal artifacts were divining tokens. The Cerros Project archaeologists found similar small stone balls in the context of a feast preparation also dating to the Late Preclassic period (Garber 1989:32–34). Gaming boards are widespread in the record of the Classic Maya world and in Mesoamerica in later times. The most famous is *patolli*, a rectilinear board game played at the time of the Spanish Conquest. The *patolli* bean was not only a token but also a psychogenic, and it is likely that variants of the game segued into divinatory practices involving the casting and counting of tokens. It also seems likely that some Mesoamericans were both amusing themselves with counting in Late Archaic period (2,000–1,000 BCE) times and counting days as part of their scheduling plans.

We can be certain that Mesoamericans widely used solar calendars at the time of the European encounter and that they used them to calculate the seasonal cycles of the agricultural year. The earliest documented appearance of calendar use is the 260-day sacred almanac using bar (stick dice?) and dot (token?) notation dates are names in Middle Preclassic (1,000–350 BCE) contexts reported by Joyce Marcus (1976) in highland Oaxaca, and the earliest Long Count counts of days appear in epi-Olmec and Maya contexts of the Late Preclassic in the Southeastern Lowlands of Mesoamerica (Chapter 4 in this volume). John Justeson (2009) observes that in the course of these developments calendrical positional notation precedes the actual invention or discovery, as he would prefer it, of the zero. There is no direct correlation between the principle of calendrical positional notation and the positional arrangement of tokens in gaming and calculating surfaces. The earliest examples of calendrical positional notation are carved inscriptions. Spatial positioning is in fact implied in the earliest expression of the concept of zero in that this notion, however, later expressed by the word "lacking," is first expressed at the epi-Olmec site of Chiapa de Corzo as a gap in a sequence of numbers that represent bundles of days counted since creation day. As Aveni (2005) has demonstrated, the Early Classic calculating surfaces were likely used for day counting in tracking seasonal change in the agricultural year.

With the exception of the Archaic period game surfaces we have little to go on in southeastern Mesoamerica regarding the Preclassic or Formative era practice of day keeping and calendar calculation before the middle of the first millennium BCE beyond the E Group phenomenon. Farther west in the mountains, Marcus and Flannery (2004) reprised their arguments regarding the origins of ceremonial architecture in the Valley of Oaxaca, arguing that the cleared and rock-lined space at the site of Geoh Shih dated to the eighth millennium BCE and that it was a performance space for the ad hoc (as opposed to scheduled) ceremonial aggregation of bands in the earliest stages of domesticating plants. They further proposed that the "men's houses" of San José Mogote after 2000 BCE in the Early Preclassic are potentially oriented to solar equinoxes (north 8° east) and presage calendrical calculations that appear later in the Middle Preclassic there. But in southeastern Mesoamerica insofar as a case can be made that E Groups were designed in concert with systematic observation of the sun cycle, and indeed celebrated that cycle, their appearance in light of the Ceibal data and the Chiapas patterns places the formal performance of day counting by sages in public settings at least half a millennium earlier than the earliest inscribed calendar expressions anywhere in Mesoamerica.

James Doyle (Chapter 8 in this volume) suggests that large open plazas preceded the establishment of E Groups at El Palmar and Tikal in central Petén and the data of Francisco Estrada-Belli (Chapter 9 in this volume) for Cival in northeastern Petén support such a notion. I do not conclude as Doyle (Chapter 8 in this volume) does that this might imply a more secular aggregation function for such spaces in emergent Petén centers, such as craftwork and exchange, however, prior to the advent of the E Group buildings. While at Classic period Tikal (Jones 1996) and Calakmul (Martin 2012) there is evidence for specialized central marketplaces, little evidence indicates that the Maya or Mesoamericans more broadly ever divided open plaza public aggregation activities into secular and sacred. Although it is possible, and empirically testable, that open plaza spaces were used for craftwork and market exchange (for example, at Buenavista del Cayo: see Cap 2011), it seems unlikely, and more importantly untestable, that they were ever exclusively used in this fashion. Public spectacle and festival in open spaces, as observed by anthropologists and historians, has combined sacred and secular elements since the Conquest (ca. 1450 CE on), and I see no reason to think the Europeans introduced this practice.

Early open plaza spaces in Petén, as Doyle (Chapter 8 in this volume) notes, bear a resemblance to open agricultural fields and may have had a metaphorical connection to them. In regard to a time much later in the Early Classic, Stanley Guenter (personal communication, 2006) observes that the turning of the 17th K'atun of the 8th Bak'tun at Tikal (376 CE) is recorded retrospectively on Stela 31 there as taking place in the K'ante'el, which he glosses as "the yellow or precious tree grove" and takes as a metaphorical reference to a maize field. It is significant that Tikal Stela 39 records the turning of that K'atun by King Chak Tok Ich'aak I and that the lower half of that stela was reset in the Late Classic (550–800 CE) by King Yik'in Chan K'awiil in the central temple of the eastern range of the Lost World E Group. I return to this field metaphor below, but for now the point is that in order to observe the sky effectively in Petén one must remove the forest canopy or stand above it. No doubt the earliest village centers were cleared at least somewhat and provided some such observational opportunities and agricultural fields likewise provided for sky watching. But the first large open plaza spaces, which were evidently deliberately higher than ambient terrain, must have significantly amplified sky-watching opportunities. These would not only include the daily sun path, to which everyone lacking a modern timepiece is sensitive, but more importantly the complex dynamics of the night sky. My conclusion here is really simple: in a canopied world cleared space is by definition sky-watching space.

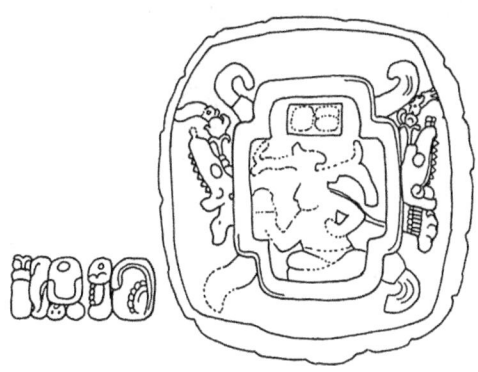

Figure 6.2. The Quatrefoil "u yol ahk K'inich Bahlam in the head of the turtle," Altar 1 El Perú–Waka'. Drawing by Linda Schele.

Open plaza space in ancient Maya thought has a particularly charged significance as sacred landscape, as we can ascertain with the privileged evidence from the Classic period texts and images and extrapolate backward through arguments of iconographic homology and continuity. The Classic Maya referred to plaza space with a quatrefoil glyph that reads *ol* meaning "the heart of" or *hol* meaning "doorway or portal" according to Linda Schele and Peter Mathews (1998:45, Figure 6.2), who note that plazas fill with water in the rains. The stone and waterlily marked quatrefoil glyph is now read *pan-ha* meaning "cavity of water" by Stuart (in Finemore and Houston 2010:87) and so also can define a surface of water. Images of plaza space take this quatrefoil form with vegetation or waterlilies at the corners, and the quatrefoil is a symbol of portal place between this world and the Otherworld going back to the Middle Preclassic at Chalcatzingo in Morelos.

This is another reason to regard open plaza space in Maya centers as intrinsically sacred and commensurate with the aggregation of people that invokes the sacred. The water metaphor of the plaza is reinforced practically by the fact that Maya often designed the impermeable surfaces of open plazas to drain rainwater into reservoirs. When it rains plazas are literally sheeted with water and hence surfaces of water. These metaphors are relevant to the observation of the night sky. Linda Schele, Joy Parker, and I (Freidel et al. 1993) proposed that the night sky represents the revolution of the watery underworld into the sky, and several scholars have elaborated this idea. Along with Milbrath (Chapter 4 in this volume), Stuart (2005), and others (for example, Tate 1992), we identify the Milky Way as a living being glossed as the Celestial Monster. Stuart (2005) argues that this is specifically a variant that he calls the Starry Deer Crocodile and that it not only swims in the night sky but also can serve as the conveyance of the night sun in the underworld. The night sky as a watery place, in this view, is commensurate with the plaza as a watery place. So while early plaza space may have metaphorically connoted the cleared and human ordered fields, it also connoted both the natural open spaces of bodies of water and their human-made extensions in reservoirs.

The primordial resurrection, sprouting, of maize in the Late Classic inscription of the Panel of the Foliated Cross at Palenque took place in the K'an Nahb, "the precious, yellow, pool (or plaza)" according to Stuart's (2006) decipherment, and the image of maize with human heads as ears of corn was the precious pool maize tree emerging from a zoomorphic head, the Waterlily Monster, depicting the animate and maize adorned portal pool. Here then is the yellow or precious plaza, and with its Maize World Tree, the K'ante'el, the yellow grove or maize field represented in the first maize plant in cleared space. The act of sowing implied by the Waterlily Monster head in its earth-marked plane and the consequent act of sprouting are performances in this theatrical setting witnessed by the divine king Kan Bahlam as a boy and as an acceding heir.

These are not abstract concepts detached from real royal practice. In 2006 Juan Carlos Meléndez discovered a sixth-century king at El Perú–Waka' in northwestern Petén laid out with his feet to the west; to the west of them was a large plate with a baseline painted on it (Figure 6.3; Freidel et al. 2013). The K'an Nahb Waterlily Monster head was depicted on the baseline facing up. A cruciform pattern was laid out on this king, with three large *Spondylus* sp. shells along the vertical axis and four small black cylinder vessels perpendicularly arranged across his chest. Three jade jewels adorned his crown. The central jewel depicts the tonsured maize god with an archaic "bib" that has the snout of the crocodile as in the crocodile version of the World Tree. A finely carved jade crocodile head pendant adorned the king as a pectoral. Above the head of this king was a dense scattering of jade jewels and then at the top, in the place of the Principal Bird Deity on the Foliated Cross from Palenque, was a second plate painted with the profile image of a great centipede, Wak, the namesake of the dynasty.

The image of the Foliated World Tree at Palenque, like the bony World Tree on the nearby Panel of the Cross, is embellished, along with symbols of shininess, with squint-eyed and *tau*-toothed faces of animate spirit on the stalk and an upper mask, all expressions of the God C Sun God. God C in the listing of Paul Schellhas (in Taube 1992) is now known to be the glyph for the word *kuh* (god) in Classical Mayan as discerned early on by

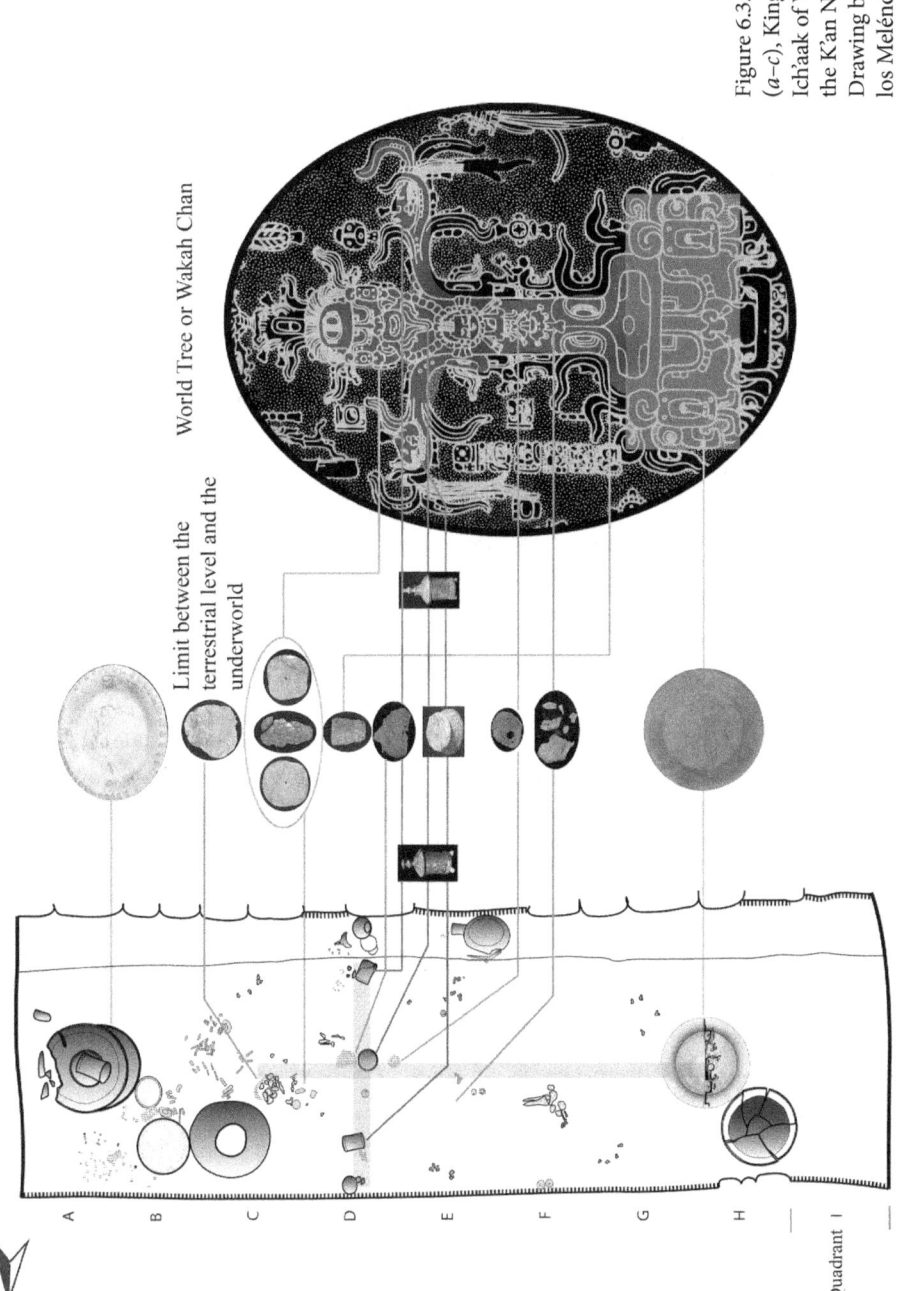

Figure 6.3. Burial 37 (*a–c*), King Chak Tok Ich'aak of Waka' as the K'an Nahb Isimte'. Drawing by Juan Carlos Meléndez.

archaeoastronomer John Carlson (cited as personal communication, 1987, in Taube 1992) among others. So the animate force can be taken to be godlike and sunlike. Here maize is adorned with the jade jewels of Maya divine kings, the pectoral, the earflares, and the collar beads and is marked as divine. The Maize God, the original divine king, performs death and resurrection to become the progenitor of people, who are depicted as maize cob heads on his stalk. Dead Maya kings could be arranged to represent this resurrection.

The Group of the Cross at Palenque is a Triadic Group and in that regard was designed to be an architectural Creation Hearth framing a plaza (Schele and Freidel 1990). I think that some Triadic Groups functioned as death and resurrection performance spaces and as accession spaces, by late Middle Preclassic times based on artifactual and ^{14}C evidence of accession performance platforms at Yaxuná (Stanton 2012). But in this context I focus here on just one other building in the Cross Group. In the Temple of the Cross adjacent to the Foliated Cross and on the northern apex of the group a bony World Tree grows from the skeletal jawed, latch-beaked Quadripartite Badge, which, in Stuart's (2005) analysis, is a symbol of the portal (vagina, anus) of the living world in the east and of the dawning sun.

It is an insignia of GI of the Palenque Triad of tutelary gods of the kingdom. The Temple of the Cross is dedicated to GI of the Palenque Triad (Figure 6.1). In Stuart's (2005) current reading of the Palenque creation stories GI is a deity who experienced rebirth at least at this capital. GI of Palenque is a local tutelary being, but Stuart (2005) proposes that the Maya more broadly associated GI with the rising sun in the east and the returning rains. Archaeologically the dedication of the Temple of the Cross to GI is attested by the discovery of many spectacular giant censer stands depicting this god left abandoned on the terraces of the pyramid. Today in K'ekchi' Maya spring ceremonies at Tikal black smoke rising elicits black rain clouds descending, as depicted, for example, on the West Wall mural of the Pinturas building at San Bartolo.

How icons and elements of such Classic mythology might be traced into the Maya past is addressed below, but generally I suggest that the daily resurrection of the sun, and its ascent, presided over mornings and its descent, death, and sowing over the evenings on open space in the first aggregation plazas of the Maya. In northern and northeastern Petén these plazas were home to the first E Group platforms, places for the observation of celestial and human performance.

Some E Group buildings that are constructed on early leveled and raised plazas in the Lowlands appear to be anchored into, or even literally partially carved from, bedrock. Whether they are or not, they are emergent promontories in a metaphorical pool or celestial space, like the zoomorphic mountains and animate portal places depicted on the Late Classic Palenque panels discussed above and on the Pinturas murals in the Late Preclassic period. Having argued that the plazas themselves evoked solar observation, it follows that such buildings on the plazas, whatever the particulars of their orientations, were keyed to solar observation in diurnal ceremonies filling the plazas with people. But the added advantage of buildings on plazas is that the surfaces higher than about 2 m are above any throng and suitable for spectacle performances. By the middle of the first millennium BCE at the latest, those designing and crafting the buildings were making them enduring stages or frames for spectacles as well as theatrical backdrops.

Building Narratives in the Preclassic

It has been clear to me since the 1978 spring field research at Cerros that some Preclassic public architecture was designed as performance space for public ritual. That is when James Garber excavated the broad landing in the middle of the stairway of first century CE Structure 5C-2nd and found that there was nothing in it at all except construction fill (Freidel 1986). In contrast to mid-stairway landings and platforms on the stairways of Classic period buildings, such as on Structure N9-56 at nearby Lamanai (Pendergast 1981), this space was not used to house remains or offerings but was just a performance platform to frame people within the monumental mask programs on the adjacent terraces. The small but dramatically crafted performance platforms that Charles Suhler (1996) discovered at Yaxuná (Figure 6.4) date to the end of the Middle Preclassic. Although they have lower summits, people performing on those summits would have been observable from a considerable distance and the area around them was never closed off from such access. Those platforms were designed to allow performers to journey into the underworld, represented by subsurface sanctuary rooms, and into the sky, represented by trap-door stairways accessing the summits. Travis Stanton and I (Stanton and Freidel 2003) have hypothesized in print that there were actually three such performance platforms at Yaxuná and that a large pyramid subsequently buried the third one. The Yaxuná archaeologists thought this because the two documented platforms seem to form the southern and eastern points of a triangular triad of buildings. If we eventually prove correct in this matter, it would strengthen the

188 · David A. Freidel

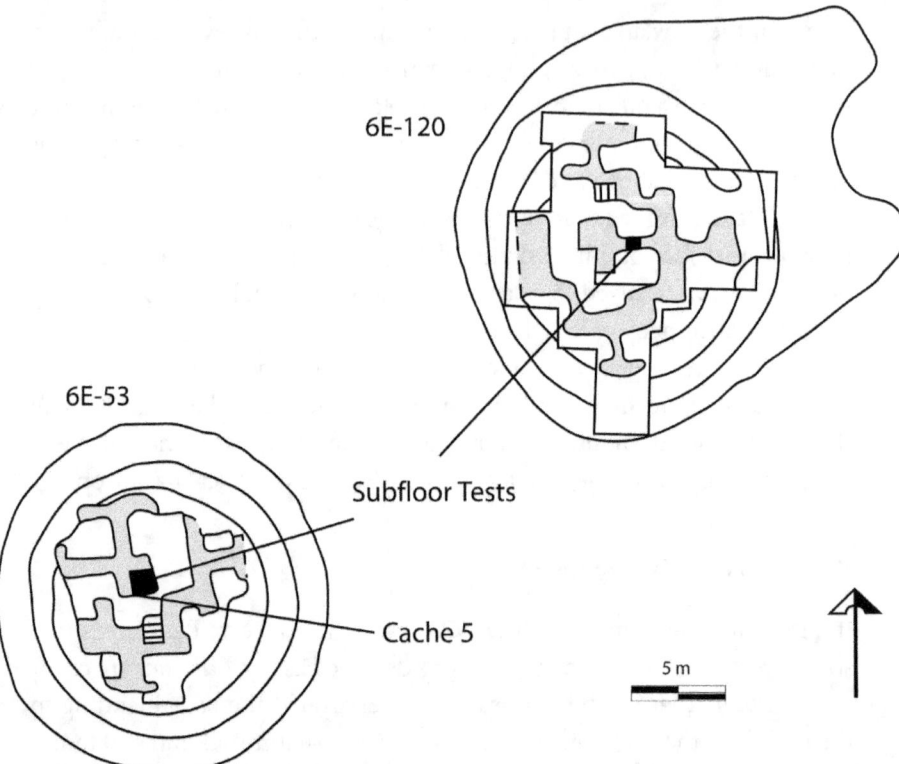

Figure 6.4. The Middle Formative dance platforms at Yaxuná, drawing courtesy of the Selz Foundation Yaxuna Project.

notion that the triadic architectural design, which becomes pervasive in the Late Preclassic Lowlands, was already established in the Middle Preclassic. But whatever the outcome of that inquiry, Preclassic public buildings were designed for performance to be witnessed by congregants. Roy Rappaport (1972) observed that the difference between spectators and congregants is that the latter affirm the truth value of performances by their witnessing.

As cogently outlined by William Saturno, Boris Beltrán, and Franco Rossi (Chapter 10 in this volume) in the context of their research at the Pinturas building in San Bartolo, the design features of E Groups, ballcourts, and Triadic Groups are not only stratigraphically related performance building types there: the discovery of architectural art on these buildings also shows how they are related through material symbol systems. This very privileged data set provides an impressive basis for Saturno, Beltrán, and Rossi's conclusion that the Principal Bird Deity as a solar god was sacrificed and preempted by the Maize God in the course of the Middle Preclassic to

Late Preclassic transition. These authors are part of an emerging consensus of scholars who see an early Lowland Maya solar cult associated with E Group use subsumed and surpassed by a royal cult focused on triadic architecture and on the Maize God.

The Pinturas murals (Saturno 2009; Taube et al. 2010), including important fragments, make a conclusive case for the sequence of worship of the Principal Bird Deity by both the human-form gods that are sons or avatars of the Maize God (and a duck-billed entity who might presage later heroes like Quetzalcoatl in his Ehecatl Wind God aspect) followed by the sacrificial defeat of that god by the Maize God. Sacrifice is a wonderfully complex phenomenon globally, and the southeastern Mesoamericans are no exception in their ritual practices and ideas. Julia Guernsey (2006), in her studies of the Principal Bird Deity iconography at Late Preclassic Izapa, has suggested for a long time that the sacrifice of the bird allows human kings to absorb divine powers. As the Principal Bird Deity is the avatar of the creator Itzamnaaj, the heroes who established kingship absorbed solar powers of the creator. The Pinturas narrative evidently jibes with the Izapa narrative in this regard. Following the sacrifice of the Principal Bird Deity, a personage wearing the white bony head of the Principal Bird Deity is crowning the exemplary human-form king seated in a scaffold throne.

In a fragment of mural painting from the Pinturas building the creator Itzamnaaj is depicted in the quatrefoil portal body of the cosmic world turtle (William Saturno, personal communication, 2012), a place held by the dancing Maize God on the west wall. But it would be a mistake to think that the sacrifice of the Principal Bird Deity results in its diminution or permanent death. On the contrary, the Principal Bird Deity is well featured in the Late Preclassic corpus of monumental art and remains a pervasive living presence in the Classic narratives. It would be safer to suggest that the sacrifice establishes an intimate bond between these gods, transforming agents into objects (for example, severed heads or feathered headdresses) and vice versa, one sustained by their human counterparts, the divine kings.

Before looking at how the partnership between the human form gods, particularly the Maize God, looks at Cerros, it is important to underscore that, while the Late Preclassic Maya Maize God is surely derived from Middle Preclassic Olmec antecedents in Veracruz, the macaw-based Principal Bird Deity evidently is not. There is one headless monumental bird in the Olmec corpus that might be a macaw (Cyphers 1996), but Taube (2000:305) says that the tail feathers are not right for that bird and more likely are those of a quetzal. The supernatural birds in the Middle Preclassic Olmec corpus

Figure 6.5. Olmec-style bearded figure in the birthing pose. Photograph courtesy of the Dallas Museum of Art.

are generally raptors and quite distinct from the macaw and the Principal Bird Deity. The Principal Bird Deity is a major Late Preclassic deity and insignia at Izapa and Kaminaljuyú as well as in the Maya Lowlands, so it is pan-southeastern Mesoamerican. Kent Reilly (personal communication, 2010) suggests that this is an indigenous Maya deity, and I think he is right. A corollary, as Reilly (personal communication, 2010) pointed out to me, is that the creator deity Itzamnaaj is also a Maya deity. There are certainly Olmec-aged deities, so this is a more problematic assertion. I would like to offer a brief sketch of a speculative case that Itzamnaaj is an indigenous Maya deity. In the early 1990s I discovered a small squatting figure in the Dallas Museum of Art and published on it in the Princeton Olmec show (Figure 6.5). To summarize the iconographic argument of that paper (Freidel 1996), this bearded old deity is giving birth to his own raindrop-shaped penis from his vagina. He is the most elementary expression of the Creator. On his buttocks are two large incised circles, which, together with his scrotum, declare the triangular hearth of the creation: the black stone of the figure can be attributed to Highland Guatemala, along with several other Preclassic figurines of similar material also attributed to that region.

The Dumbarton Oaks collection (Taube 2004) contains a greenstone figure in the squatting position that lacks the explicit birth depiction or any genitalia. The personage wears the trefoil insignia of divine kingship on top of his head. This figurine also has a winged mirror crown that could be construed to be an early variant of the flower insignia of Itzamnaaj, according to Kent Reilly (personal communication, 2012). Wherever this figurine is from, it shows a king emulating the old god in the birthing ritual. Returning to the first figurine, the Creator has a beard ornamented with an incised dot in what might be a crescent-shaped jewel. Jewel ornaments are a characteristic of Preclassic Lowland and Highland Maya depictions of rulers and some gods. They are not characteristic of the Gulf Coast Olmec depictions. In fact beards are a more common Preclassic Maya fashion than an Olmec one. The material and the iconography suggest that this black figurine was carved in the Maya area and the depiction suggests that it is Itzamnaaj. The San Bartolo Middle Preclassic figurine from a good context depicts a bearded squatting individual with a shark's-fin headdress. The shark fin, attributed by Taube (1992) to the early Maya rain god Chaak, is actually also associated with the Olmec death shark with its shark's tooth. Both the Sun God (GI) and the Maize God in the Classic Maya corpus are associated with a cosmic shark as a conveyance from death to resurrection. The Preclassic Maya Maize God and the Classic Maya Sun God in his GI aspect are also both associated with the projecting upper tooth.

The general implication of this line of reasoning is that the partnership between the Principal Bird Deity as avatar of the indigenous Itzamnaaj and the Olmec-derived Maize God in the Late Preclassic Maya symbolic system registers syncretism between Middle Preclassic Olmec and Maya religion. The Rain God Chaak is another matter, possibly derived in part from an Olmec feline Rain God. The Maya may have had indigenous serpent Rain Gods, as many Mayan speakers do today, and these may have been incorporated into the imagery of the Principal Bird Deity solar complex, giving rise during the Late Preclassic to the GI Watery Sun.

Magic Birds and Radiant Lords

The partnership between the Principal Bird Deity and the human-form gods is particularly well illustrated in the façade of Structure 5C-2nd at Cerros, where the monumental upper masks depict the Principal Bird Deity and the lower masks depict a feline sun-faced or radiant Maize God. Constructed around 50 CE, in the latter half of the Late Preclassic period, and reverentially buried soon thereafter, the façade program is not didactic like the Pinturas murals but is instead a masterpiece designed for performances to be seen in conjunction with living rulers and their entourages (Figure 6.6). While the Pinturas murals depict key episodes in the

192 · David A. Freidel

Figure 6.6. East side of Structure 5C-2nd Cerro Maya.

narratives defining and legitimizing kingship in which gods and animate beings are central, Structure 5C-2nd literally placed the human agent center stage. The symbols are well enough preserved symbols to be discerned with some clarity and certainty; but their significance continues to change, at least in my mind, as the larger record of Late Preclassic art increases.

What follows is a fairly close reading of the iconography of the façade, focusing on the monumental masks (Figure 6.7). Each mask and its context of panels vary in ways that provide nuance, but the two upper masks clearly have the distinctive broad, projecting and down-curving beak of the Principal Bird Deity, and the western beak has the glyph *ak'bal* ("darkness") on it. Each of the upper masks is wearing the crown of kingship, a headband ornamented with three jewels. The headband on the western mask was ruined beyond further interpretation, but on the eastern headband the right side jewel depicts a cartouched U-glyph. The side jewel depicted on the king's crown on the Pinturas west wall mural is a cartouche. On two other Late Preclassic depictions of the headband, the back of the Dumbarton Oaks Pectoral and the fuchsite bundle mask from Tikal Burial 85, the side jewels are *u*-shaped elements. The Pinturas crown has a chinstrap that is ornamented with a beard with two droplet jewels on it. As this is a profile, we can assume that there are actually three jewels on the beard—as there evidently are on the real beard of the acceding king. Both of the upper masks at Cerros have painted trilobe beards with three dot jewels on them.

Of the depictions of the Principal Bird Deity on the west wall, the one of the bird descending in majesty out of raining clouds definitely has the trilobe beard with three dots. The others do not seem to have this beard. And while the human form gods practicing autosacrifice have beards, these lack the jewels found on the beard of the enthroned king. Suffice to say that the upper masks on 5C-2nd depict the Principal Bird Deities as kings. As a final note on these chin paintings, Karl Taube (2010) has recently identified the trilobed depending element in question as a representation in Preclassic contexts of blood pouring from the necks of severed heads. In light of the red color of these trilobe beards and the dots, which can denote liquid, this is a possible additional meaning referring to the bird as sacrifice, although not an exclusive one, given the very alive depiction of the Principal Bird Deity with such a beard on the San Bartolo West Wall.

With the notable exceptions of the royal crowns and jeweled beards, the Cerros Principal Bird Deity faces are very close in major iconographic features to the Principal Bird Deity images on the west wall of the Pinturas building—paintings that predate Structure 5C-2nd by more than a century and a half. This suggests to me that these two examples of architectural art represent a conservative Late Preclassic canon maintained by master artists and their workshops that spanned the center to the coast of the Southern Lowlands, from which some other known examples stylistically deviate in

Figure 6.7. West side of Structure 5C-2nd Cerro Maya.

various ways, suggesting local artistic traditions and workshops. These facial features include the L-shaped eyes surmounted by medallion brows ornamented with merlons and side scrolls (the symbol used in the early writing system to denote *ajaw*, including in a glyph on the west wall), water lines in the mouth or beak, and breath scrolls flanking the mouth panels.

The Cerros Principal Bird Deity masks lack the snakes in the mouths of the Pinturas Principal Bird Deity images. I think that this is because the snakes in the Cerros composition have been displaced to the bordering panels of the terraces. The heads of the snakes in the west wall depictions display a consistent iconographic program that is almost identical to the profile snakeheads that ornament the flanking panels on the Cerros terrace compositions. As Arthur Miller (1974) showed in the 1970s in his comparison of Izapa and Tulum twisted cord iconography, such snakes can symbolize umbilicus cords pervasively in the southeastern Mesoamerican world. This seems to be unequivocally the case for the West Wall serpents carried by the Principal Bird Deity, as one of the snakeheads has been severed from its body and red blood is gushing down from the neck. In the 1980s (Freidel 1985) I suggested that the iconography of red and black painted imagery on the 5C-2nd composition represents a series of dyadic contrasts, black rain going down, red blood going down, black smoke clouds going up, and red fire going up. I think this program holds pretty well in the case of the Pinturas murals. The snakes in the mouths of the Principal Bird Deity contrast with those accompanying the diving Maize God. These are painted with real snake markings combining both black and red and a realistic snakehead. I speculate that this dying Maize God appears to be flowing down the black body of a cosmic centipede, anticipating the famous Sarcophagus of Pakal the Great, where the king is emerging from the centipede maw of the world at dawn as the Maize God and GI the Watery Sun. The conflation of snakes and centipedes occurs on the 5C-2nd façade. The body of the snake framing the upper west terrace depicts two profile centipede heads. As Taube (2003) has shown, the centipede snake represents the bony maws of serpents linking the Otherworld to this one, as in the case of the famous War Serpent depicted on Yaxchilán Structure 23 Lintel 25.

The snakes are very important as conduits of the sustaining mediums listed above (rain, smoke, blood, fire: see Freidel 1985) and as cords. It is important to underscore that in my interpretation the red medium flowing through the snakes connotes fire as well as blood. The twisted cord carried in the mouth of the Principal Bird Deity also ornaments the face of the human form Fiery Sun God as the cruller insignia of K'inich Ajaw. I remain

Figure 6.8. Quadripartite Badge, Pakal, and Double-Headed Serpent from the Palenque Sarcophagus. Drawing by Linda Schele, courtesy of Los Angeles County Museum of Art and David Schele.

convinced (Freidel 2000) that the ancient Maya made an alliterative connection between two sets of words, one starting with the consonant *k* and meaning sky (*kaan kan*), four, and snake (as elucidated by Houston 2010), and the other with the consonant *k'* (*k'an, k'aan, ka'an*) meaning precious, yellow, and cordage. Snake-headed sky frames are common in Late Preclassic compositions, as in the case of the 5C-2nd terrace panels, and snake-cord frames remain significant throughout later Maya art (as described by Miller 1974). Snakes in trees, a real ecological occurrence when these creatures hunt birds, are also found in both Preclassic and Classic compositions of interest: (1) the Creation Mountain on the north wall of the Pinturas building has a tree with a snake entwined in it (consuming a bird with much blood coming out of it); and (2) the sarcophagus of Pakal at Palenque features a double-headed snake entwined in the cross-shaped World Tree emerging from the Quadripartite Badge Dawn Bowl (Figure 6.8; Freidel et al. 1993). Both snakes and trees serve the Maya as major metaphors of connection and path between existential realms, so their combination is unsurprising.

Both the double-headed serpent creatures carried in the mouth of the Principal Bird Deity frame the upper and lower panels on Structure 5C-2nd, and they have generally comparable earflare assemblages and flanking profile centipede heads adjacent to these flanged crowns. They contrast in other important respects. I identify the lower masks as combinations of multiple deities, mainly the Maize God and the sun. The snarling baby jaguar character of the lower masks, with the blunt and straight alveolar bar with projecting tooth below, certainly ties these masks to the Olmec-inspired Preclassic Maya Maize God. The L-shaped eyes, basically a relief squint eye variant, hark back to the mature jaguarian Olmec Rain God identified by Taube (1992) and contrast with the oval eye that he defines as characteristic of the Olmec Maize God. This oval-eyed variant of the Preclassic Maya Maize God is depicted on a stucco mask on an early building inside Calakmul Structure 2 in addition to the painted examples at San Bartolo and Cival (Hurst 2009), so the eyes of the lower masks at Cerros are an intentional semantic complication that I suggest signals the squint eyes of the fiery Sun God. The lower eastern mask in the Cerros composition definitely has the *k'in* glyph cartouche on its cheek and is therefore sun-faced or radiant.

The lower west mask has a preserved cartouche on one cheek, but the interior of it was not readable, although we presumed from its location that it was also a *k'in* glyph. Schele and Miller (1986) and Schele and I (1990) identified the lower masks as sun gods. In his discussion of GI as a Sun God Stuart (2005) uses this *k'in* cartouche glyph on the cheek as an identifying characteristic. My identification of the lower masks as a combination of the Maize God and a Sun God evolved with the discovery of the Pinturas murals and the decisive iconographic expression of the Preclassic Maya Maize God, much of which fits the lower masks.

A significance of the lower masks as sun deities is that they are human in form. I do not know of earlier possible representations of a human form Sun God in Maya iconography before the Late Preclassic, and these all occur as deities marked with sun cartouches on the cheeks. Other examples include the face glyphs on the Pomona earflare (Freidel et al. 2002) and the stylistically Late Preclassic seated lord found in an Early Classic offering at Uaxactún. The face of this lord resembles a Maize God jade pectoral dating to the Late Preclassic found in Cache 1 at Cerros (Freidel et al. 1993). As

Taube (1985) defined the iconography in his seminal article on the Classic Maya Maize God, the Early Classic Maize God face had evolved away from the Olmec-style Late Preclassic Maize God. In particular, the distinctive alveolar bar and projecting teeth—often curving fangs—became two human upper buckteeth without a snout above. At the same time, the human form Classic Sun God has the *tau*-tooth or shark's tooth that is clearly derived from the Late Preclassic Maize God. The existence of a composite human form Maize-Sun God by at least the final centuries of the Late Preclassic suggests that these radiant lords express the complicated covenant between the creator and his Sun Bird avatar on the one hand and on the other the Maize God and his representatives in the human sphere, the divine kings, on the other. In addition to inspiring the emergence of human form Sun Gods, it also contributed radiance to the divine kings, who also emerged institutionally in the Late Preclassic period. *K'inich* became a royal epithet in the glyphic texts acquired upon accession as king.

This partnership remained complex for the rest of Maya history and at the same time is depicted in a variety of iconographic compositions showing that it continued to evolve. The famous stylistically very early Early Classic monumental mask composition at Kohunlich in southern Quintana Roo to the west of Cerros has been taken popularly to depict K'inich Ajaw, primarily because of the projecting upper tooth in the mouths of these beings. But these masks do not have the squint eyes of K'inich Ajaw, instead having the glyph *winik* ("man") in the eyes, and they lack the twisted cord cruller. Moreover, the composition depicts these lords wearing the flanged crown of kingship with fairly standard earflare assemblages and squint-eyed bulbous snouted zoomorphic chinstrap masks that can be worn by the Classic Sun Gods but also by kings and Maize Gods. Of the four main masks uncovered in this composition, only one has a preserved headdress. It is a zoomorphic mask with a cartouched glyph above. This glyph reads *k'ahk'* ("fire") and could suggest that this is a variant of the fiery Sun God. But the ambiguity of these masks is such that some of them could be Maize God impersonators, and they all appear to be human.

The only mask with the cartouched *k'in* glyph in the Kohunlich composition is the preserved uppermost right side mask, which actually has a total of six panels with human-form masks, three on each side, and presumably two with the cartouched *k'in* glyph images flanking the building platform on the summit. Here a squint-eyed, latch-beaked, skeletal head has the cartouched *k'in* glyph as a headdress. That head, in turn, is resting in a legged bowl. This is a recognizable variant of the skeletal head with a *k'in* marked bowl as a headdress, the head insignia that is the basis of the Quadripartite Badge (Robertson 1974) that Stuart (2005) reads as El K'in ("eastern"). This is the insignia of the Watery Sun of the East in his interpretation. This early version of the Quadripartite Badge is the Principal Bird Deity severed head in an offering bowl, the sun as sacrifice and an object displayed by Classic period kings as an orb of royal power.

Even though the Quadripartite Badge composition shifted the bowl above the head and placed the *k'in* glyph in it, in at least one case (Stela H at Copán) it shows King Waxaklahun Ubah K'awiil performing as the Maize God (Schele and Mathews 1998), carrying in his back rack the Quadripartite Badge with the bowl inverted over the skull and the *k'in* glyph infixed in the forehead of the skull. The Principal Bird Deity as a living being is perched over the back rack in this composition. These examples demonstrate that this image of the sun as a head is not a metaphorical personification of the bowl and *k'in* glyph as an animate being; there are examples of personification heads in Maya iconography, but these are images of the Principal Bird Deity sun as a severed head and a sacrifice. like the Principal Bird Deity dead bird in the Pinturas composition and possibly the upper masks on Structure 5C-2nd. The Quadripartite Badge is an artistic evolution of this severed head image with the significant addition of the El K'in glyphic representation and the three elements surmounting the bowl, but in light of Copán Stela H there is reason to believe that it sustained this original meaning of the sun head as sacrifice. And the position of this head on Stela H is that of a burden, an idea fundamentally linked broadly to office in Mesoamerican thought and specifically an enduring metaphor of office among the Maya.

The Quadripartite Badge occurs in several Classic contexts in addition to those already reviewed. For example, it is also carried as a burden on the back of Chak Chel, the goddess consort of Itzamnaaj in the Classic period, in a well-known looted vase scene as discussed by Taube (1994). So its position on the back rack of the Copán king is only one of several examples of this image as an object. It is a standard headdress for portrayed female rulers wearing a beaded dress and ornamented shell girdle called the Xok Shell girdle, a costume associated with the Moon Goddess but also, sometimes in abbreviated form, with the Classic Maize God. As mentioned previously, Stuart (2005) argues that the Quadripartite Badge when carried on the tail of the Celestial Monster (Figure 6.9) specifically represents a location, the rising place of the dawning sun in the east as an aperture, vagina or anus, of the Celestial Monster. In this Stuart (2005) is following the reasoning of

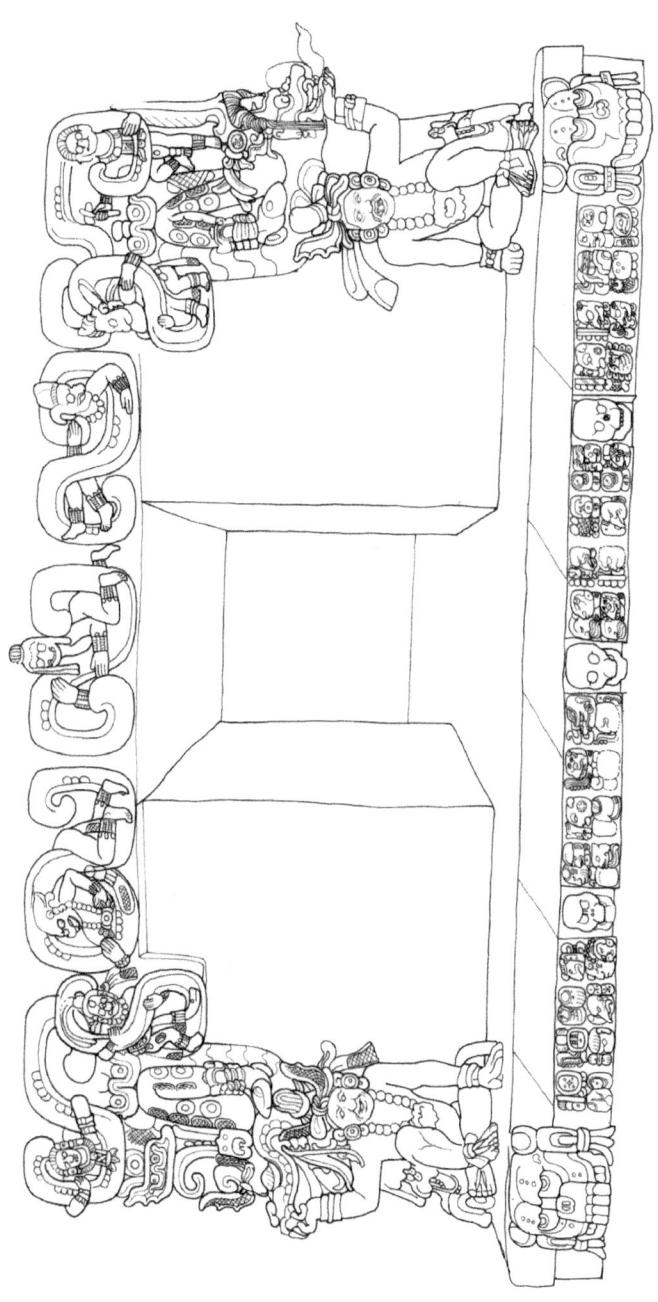

Figure 6.9. The Celestial Monster on Structure 10L-22, Copán. Drawing by Linda Schele, courtesy of Los Angeles County Museum of Art and David Schele.

Carolyn Tate (1992), who noted that the Quadripartite Badge is normally oriented to the east in such depictions. I have already shown that the Classic Maya used plates to designate location in royal tombs.

Linda Schele, Joy Parker, and I (Freidel et al. 1993) made the general argument in *Maya Cosmos* that the Celestial Monster depicts the Milky Way in an east–west conformation in the sky. Stuart (2005) makes a similar case in his recent reading of Palenque mythology. In both of these analyses one particular focus is on the living paths of the major celestial beings, the sun in this case, both through the underworld and through the sky. If we start with the sun as sacrifice, dead bird, and severed skeletal head already found on the Pinturas Murals, this skull bowl becomes a portal for the path of the resurrected sun. Put another way, sacrifice is the means to resurrection. And it is also, as a displayed orb, a symbol of the responsibility and burden, *ikatz* (specifically "jade burden" in Stuart's 2006 reading), of divine kingship. Exemplary of this reality as artifact is the great jade orb of Altún Ha in Belize, an Early Classic royal jewel depicting the severed head of the Principal Bird Deity with the squint eyes of the human form fiery Sun God K'inich Ajaw and the insignia glyph *ajaw* as a diadem.

Another instructive example of this is on the Panel of the Cross (Figure 6.10), dedicated to the birth of GI or the watery sun of the east. Here the boy heir to the throne, Kan Bahlam, is holding the Quadripartite Badge orb that has flowing blood pouring from its jawless skull as an offering. The central image of the panel depicts the Quadripartite Badge as a great severed head and seed poised in the center of a celestial band. From this sun skull seed sprouts a cruciform World Tree with three flowers in the form of profile polymorphs. On the top of this tree is perched the Principal Bird Deity, alive and well, so the tree is a flowery path from death and sacrifice to life again: the path the sun follows daily. The research of William Saturno and his colleagues (see Chapter 10 in this volume) at Xultún has discovered a remarkably preserved Early Classic palace with balustrade masks of the human form fiery sun god with World Trees growing from them, a direct structural substitution of this god's head for the Principal Bird Deity's head expressed in the Quadripartite Badge.

In their study of another Early Classic preserved building in the Diablo complex of El Zotz west of Tikal, Stephen Houston and Edwin Román (in Skidmore 2010) have clear evidence that a myriad of Sun Gods are depicted there. The expedient dichotomy of fiery western sun and watery eastern sun proposed here will eventually give way to a more complex and nuanced narrative than I outline in this brief exploration of relevant symbol-systems.

Figure 6.10. The Panel of the Cross. Drawing by Linda Schele, courtesy of Los Angeles County Museum of Art and David Schele.

But I sense that we are still going to be working with living divine kings who upon accession became radiant like the sun, K'inich, but who were incarnate Maize Gods. The sun is both object and agent in this narrative but distinct from the very human, maize-fleshed, rulers who strove to wield the power of the sun on the one hand and propitiate it to fruitful and prosperous outcomes on the other. What they could in fact control was the count of days, and they and their courtiers became exceptionally good at the mastery of calendar time. But the true nature of the seasons, the patterns of rainy season and dry season, remained the province of the Creator and his avatar, which the rulers had to acknowledge through foresight, planning, and scheduling. Divine kings could be sunlike in their radiance, but they could only hope to wield the power of the sun as agents wielding objects or instruments. Through sacrifice, ritual spectacle, and the careful study of historical patterns revealed in the count of days they could hope to harness that power to wise policy, but they could never truly own it. The realities of economic policy are hard to discern in the language of royal practice, but we are making some progress, as seen in recent studies by epigraphers like Stuart (2006), Houston (2010), and Simon Martin (2012). Elaborations of these insights by archaeologists like Patricia McAnany (2010), Brigitte Kovacevich (2013), and many more means that we will see such ideas as presented here put to the test.

What I have laid out here is one narrative that attempts to accommodate some of the rich material symbol systems now available to us for study. Our term "system" is probably not the best way to think about the complex interplay of the ideas and artifactual expressions under consideration. Claude Lévi-Strauss (1969), in struggling with ways to think about myth, reached for musical analogies, symphonies, as a way to approximate the connections that he was working with. The allusion to performance does make sense: we can start to see how these things work when we have tableaux, spatial arrangements of actors and props as in the Pinturas murals or the Palenque panels. The ancient Maya religion is expressed in such fragments of the sages' own narratives, which will not reduce to simple all-encompassing formulas, even though their visual and verbal components will become increasingly clear to us. I do think that the Maya had a fine sense of both the certainties of their existence as registered in the rhythms of sun cycles and the uncertainties as registered in the weather cycles and the agricultural cycles dependent on them. Divine rulers were exemplary interlocutors between these, and in death they became animate objects and instruments in the propitiation of these forces by successor generations.

Epilogue: An Eastern Triadic Structure at Cerros

Debra Walker, who reviewed our book for the press and served as the second project director at Cerros, now Cerro Maya, in Belize, observed that in this chapter I discussed the iconographic programs of that site but that it does not have an E Group. First of all, Jeffrey Vadala and Susan Milbrath (2014) have made a cogent case for Structure 5C-2nd being an observation place for zenith passage of the sun in the community on May 15. They suggest that this marks the arrival of the rains critical to the agricultural year.

As they note, the interpretation of the symbolism has changed over time, but the building is enduringly associated with celestial symbols and solar imagery (Vadala and Milbrath 2014:10). It is, in brief, a solar commemorative structure that is not on the sun path at all but rather is oriented north–south on the pivot of the rotating sky. Buildings do not have to be on the east–west sun path to celebrate the sun.

In an interesting and substantial critique of the whole idea of E Groups as solar commemorative structures, Jaime Awe, Julie Hoggarth, and James Aimers (Chapter 13 in this volume) propose that such groups in general (which they term Eastern Triadic Assemblages), and solitary Eastern Triadic Structures in particular, could well have served a variety of purposes independent of solar observation and commemoration.

Upon reflection, it is now clear to me that at Cerros we do indeed have a Late Preclassic Eastern Triadic Structure, Structure 29 (Figure 6.11; Freidel 1986:Figure 1.2; Schele and Freidel 1990:Figure 3.23). This large pyramidal structure has three secondary platforms crowding the summit in a row, with the north and south platforms facing inward to the central one that, in turn, faces west. This Eastern Triadic Structure conforms to the type proposed by Awe and associates (see Chapter 13 in this volume) in that it faces a substantial open plaza. The preserved sections of the mask program (Figure 6.12) show that the westward-facing lower mask is a jaguarian creature with a skeletal lower jaw and a massive bifurcated blood scroll pouring out of its mouth. Surmounting that zoomorphic mask is a snarling anthropomorphic mask with the armature for a projecting tooth from below the upper lip. In general this snarling mouth, found also on upper masks of the northern platform, is a trait discussed above in the context of the lower masks on Structure 5C-2nd, except that here the armatures of the snarling mouthed masks seem to indicate angled and projecting singular upper teeth in the jaw. Stuart (2014) has deciphered the name of the deity called GI at Palenque as Hun Yeh Winik, One Tooth Person, and as discussed earlier in this chapter Stuart (2005) makes the case that this is the reborn eastern sun that brings the rains.

That is the focus of the Structure 5C-2nd program as well in the interpretation of Vadala and Milbrath (2014) referenced above. I think that this might well be a productive way to think about the Structure 29 program. But the bloody mouthed jaguarian creature is later associated with the fiery sun, K'inich Ajaw, as seen in the famous Panel of the Sun at Palenque (Figure 6.13). It is possible that this zoomorphic creature in the Preclassic program is actually what Taube (2010) identifies as the saurian crocodilian

Figure 6.11. Structure 29 at Cerros (Cerro Maya) viewed from the west.

Figure 6.12. Structure 29 at Cerros, the preserved mask on the central platform, and one of the preserved masks on the northern platform.

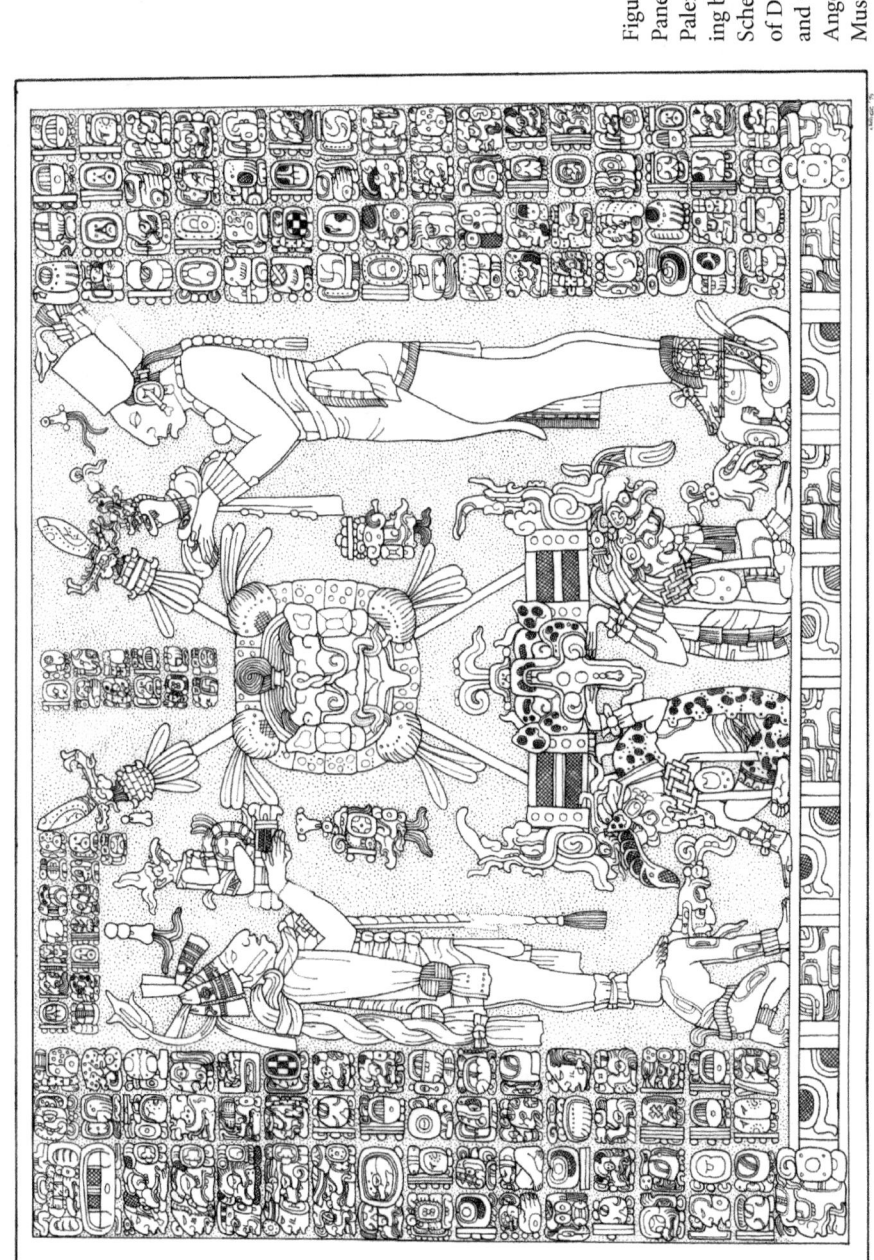

Figure 6.13. Panel of the Sun, Palenque. Drawing by Linda Schele, courtesy of David Schele and the Los Angeles County Museum of Art.

monster that is slain to form the waters of the sea. In that case this would, again, depict the sun emerging from the sea to the east of Cerros.

The masks flanking the stairway on the northern platform both show a different lower entity, one with a wide curving snout. In her study of a Late Preclassic royal bundle temple at the site of El Achiotal in northwestern Petén, Guatemala, Mary Jane Acuña (2013) discovered a well-preserved turtle mask decorating a projecting balk in front of the doorway of the building. That mask has a very similar broad down-curving snout. As discussed above, the turtle as a watery place where the Maize God sojourns in the underworld before rebirth is well attested in the San Bartolo Pinturas Program. With Cerros being at the edge of the Caribbean, and home to deepwater canoe fishers and traders, it would make good sense to celebrate the emergence of the dawn sun from the sea. In sum, the mask program on Structure 29 indicates that it was used for solar commemoration rituals. Relevant to the arguments put forth by Awe and associates, we substantially tested the summit of the central platform and discovered no offerings or burials. We found no offerings or burials at the base of the pyramid either. It is a large building, so perhaps there are internal features, but the evidence at hand does not suggest the kinds of alternative functions for Eastern Triadic Structures that Awe and associates propose (Chapter 13 in this volume).

This is not to say that other Eastern Triadic Structures were necessarily solar commemorative buildings, as Chapter 13 clearly shows that this is not the case. But it does suggest to me that we have a way to go before we can close the book on the many ways in which ancient Maya people, and other Mesoamericans, thought about the relationship between themselves and their world and crafted such visions into material forms.

Acknowledgments

I am especially grateful to Jerry Glick, who has made the long-term research at El Perú–Waka' possible, and to Jerry Murdock, who recruited me to organize the Maya Working Group. That effort would not have been successful without the collaboration of all of my colleagues there, especially Arlen Chase, Anne Dowd, and Susan Milbrath. I also wish to acknowledge the support of PACUNAM (the Foundation for the Maya Cultural and Natural Patrimony of Guatemala), the National Institute of Anthropology and History of Guatemala, the Ministry of Culture of Guatemala, and the National Geographic Society. Portions of research at El Perú–Waka have been also supported by the Alphawood Foundation and the GeoOntological Foundation. All of these institutions and organizations have made my research possible in recent years.

References Cited

Acuña, Mary Jane
2013   Art, Ideology, and Politics at El Achiotal: A Late Preclassic Frontier Site in Northwestern Peten, Guatemala. Ph.D. dissertation, Graduate School of Arts and Sciences, Washington University, St. Louis, Missouri.

Aveni, Anthony F.
2005   Observations on the Pecked Designs and Other Figures Carved on the South Platform of the Pyramid of the Sun at Teotihuacan. *Journal for the History of Astronomy* 36.1(122):31–47.

Cap, Bernadette
2011   Investigating an Ancient Maya Marketplace at Buenavista del Cayo, Belize. *Research Reports in Belizean Archaeology* 8:241–253.

Clark, John, and Michael Blake
1994   The Power of Prestige: Competitive Generosity and the Emergence of Rank Societies in Lowland Mesoamerica. In *Factional Competition and Political Development in the New World*, edited by Elizabeth Brumfiel and John Fox, pp. 17–30. Cambridge University Press, Cambridge.

Cyphers, Ann
1996   San Lorenzo, Veracruz. *Arqueología Mexicana* 4(19):62–65.

Finemore, Daniel, and Stephen D. Houston (eds.)
2010   *Fiery Pool, the Maya and the Mythic Sea*. Peabody Essex Museum in Association with Yale University Press, Peabody, Massachusetts, and New Haven, Connecticut.

Flannery, Kent V.
1973   The Origins of Agriculture. *Annual Review of Anthropology* 2(1):271–310.

Freidel, David A.
1985   Polychrome Facades of the Lowland Maya Preclassic. In *Painted Architecture and Polychrome Monumental Sculpture in Mesoamerica*, edited by Elizabeth Boone, pp. 5–30. Dumbarton Oaks Library, Washington, D.C.
1986   The Monumental Architecture. In *Archaeology at Cerros, Belize, Central America: 1. An Interim Report*, edited by Robin A. Robertson and David A. Freidel, pp. 1–22. Southern Methodist University Press, Dallas.
1996   Preparing the Way. In *The Olmec World: Ritual and Rulership*, pp. 3–9. Princeton University Art Museum, in association with Harry N. Abrams, Princeton, New Jersey, and New York.
2000   Mystery of the Maya Façade. *Archaeology* 53(5):24–28.

Freidel, David A., Hector L. Escobedo, and Juan Carlos Meléndez
2013   Mountains of Memories, Structure M12-32 at El Perú. In *Millenary Maya Societies: Past Crises and Resilience*, edited by M.-Charlotte Arnauld and Alain

Breton, pp. 235–247. http://www.mesoweb.com/publications/MMS/index.html, accessed 2013.

Freidel, David A., Kathryn Reese-Taylor, and David Mora Marín
2002   The Old Shell Game, Commodity, Treasure and Kingship in the Origins of Maya Civilization. In *Ancient Maya Political Economies*, edited by Marilyn A. Masson and David A. Freidel, pp. 41–86. Altamira Press, Walnut Creek, California.

Freidel, David A., and Michelle Rich
2015   Pecked Circles and Divining Boards, Calculating Instruments in Ancient Mesoamerica. In *Cosmology, Calendars, and Horizon-Based Astronomy in Ancient Mesoamerica*, edited by Anne S. Dowd and Susan Milbrath, pp. 249–264. University Press of Colorado, Boulder.

Freidel, David A., Linda Schele, and Joy Parker
1993   *Maya Cosmos: Three Thousand Years on the Shaman's Path*. William Morrow, New York.

Garber, James F.
1989   *Archaeology at Cerros, Belize, Central America*: 2. *The Artifacts*. Southern Methodist University Press, Dallas.

Guernsey, Julia
2006   *Ritual and Power in Stone: The Performance of Rulership in Mesoamerican Izapan-Style Art*. University of Texas Press, Austin.

Harrison-Buck, Eleanor
2012   Architecture as Animate Landscape: Circular Shrines in the Ancient Maya Lowlands. *American Anthropologist* 114(1):64–80.

Harvey, Graham (editor)
2013   *The Handbook of Contemporary Animism*. Acumen, Durham, United Kingdom, and Bristol, Connecticut.

Hendon, Julia A.
2012   Objects as Persons: Integrating Maya Beliefs and Anthropological Theory. In *Power and Identity in Archaeological Theory and Practice, Case Studies from Ancient Mesoamerica*, edited by Eleanor Harrison-Buck, pp. 82–89. University of Utah Press, Salt Lake City.

Houston, Stephen D.
2010   Living Waters and Wondrous Beasts. In *Fiery Pool, the Maya and the Mythic Sea*, edited by Daniel Finemore and Stephen D. Houston, pp. 66–79. Peabody Essex Museum in Association with Yale University Press, Peabody, Massachusetts, and New Haven, Connecticut.

Hurst, Heather
2009   Murals and the Ancient Maya Artist: A Study of Art Production in the Guatemalan Lowlands. Ph.D. dissertation, Department of Anthropology, Yale University, New Haven, Connecticut.

Jones, Christopher
1996   *Excavations in the East Plaza of Tikal*. Vols. 1 and 2. Tikal Report 16. University of Pennsylvania Press, Philadelphia.

Justeson, John S.
2009   Numerical Cognition and the Development of Zero in Mesoamerica. In *The Archaeology of Measurement: Comprehending Heaven, Earth, and Time in Ancient Societies*, edited by Iain Morley and Colin Renfrew, pp. 43–53. Cambridge University Press, Cambridge.

Kovacevich, Brigitte
2013   Craft Production and Distribution in the Maya Lowlands. In *Merchants, Trade, and Exchange in the Pre-Columbian World*, edited by Kenneth Hirth and Joanne Pillsbury, pp. 255–282. Dumbarton Oaks Research Library and Collection, Washington, D.C.

Lévi-Strauss, Claude
1969   *The Raw and the Cooked: Mythologiques*. Vol. 1. University of Chicago Press, Chicago.

Looper, Matthew
2003   *Lightning Warrior: Maya Art and Kingship at Quirigua*. University of Texas, Austin.

MacNeish, Richard S.
1964   The Food-Gathering and Incipient Agriculture Stage of Prehistoric Middle America. In *Handbook of Middle American Indians: 1. Natural Environment and Early Cultures*, edited by Robert Wauchope and Robert C. West, pp. 413–426. University of Texas Press, Austin.

Marcus, Joyce
1976   The Origins of Mesoamerican Writing. *Annual Review of Anthropology* 5:35–67.

Marcus, Joyce, and Kent V. Flannery
2004   The Coevolution of Ritual and Society: New 14C Dates from Ancient Mexico. *Proceedings of the National Academy of Sciences* 101(52):18257–18261.

Martin, Simon
2012   Hieroglyphs from the Painted Pyramid: The Epigraphy of Chiik Nahb Structure Sub 1–4, Calakmul, Mexico. *Maya Archaeology* 2:60–82.

McAnany, Patricia A.
2010   *Ancestral Maya Economies in Archaeological Perspective*. Cambridge University Press, Cambridge.

Miller, Arthur G.
1974   The Iconography of the Paintings in the Temple of the Diving God, Tulum, Quintana Roo, Mexico: The Twisted Cords. In *Mesoamerican Archaeology, New Approaches*, edited by Norman Hammond, pp. 167–186. University of Texas Press, Austin.

Pendergast, David
1981   Lamanai Belize: Summary of Excavation Results 1974–1980. *Journal of Field Archaeology* 8(1):29–53.

Rappaport, Roy
1972   Ritual, Sanctity and Cybernetics. *American Anthropologist* NS 73(1):59–76.

Robertson, Merle Greene
1974   The Quadripartite Badge: A Badge of Rulership. In *Primera Mesa Redonda de*

Palenque, Part 1, edited by Merle Robertson, pp. 129–137. Robert Louis Stevenson School, Pebble Beach, California.

Saturno, William A.
2009   Centering the Kingdom, Centering the King: Maya Creation and Legitimization at San Bartolo. In *The Art of Urbanism: How Mesoamerican Kingdoms Represented Themselves in Architecture and Imagery*, edited by William L. Fash and Leonardo López Luján, pp. 111–134. Dumbarton Oaks Research Library and Collection, Washington, D.C.

Schele, Linda, and David A. Freidel
1990   *A Forest of Kings: The Untold Story of the Ancient Maya*. William Morrow, New York.

Schele, Linda, and Peter Mathews
1998   *The Code of Kings: The Language of Seven Sacred Maya Temples and Tombs*. Scribner, New York.

Schele, Linda, and Mary Ellen Miller
1986   *The Blood of Kings: Dynasty and Ritual in Maya Art*. Kimbell Art Museum, Fort Worth.

Skidmore, Joel
2010   Royal Tomb Discovered in the Diablo Group at El Zotz, Guatemala. http://www.mesoweb.com/reports/ZotzTomb.pdf, accessed 2010.

Stanton, Travis W.
2012   The Rise of Formative-Period Complex Societies in the Northern Maya Lowlands. In *The Oxford Handbook of Mesoamerican Archaeology*, edited by Deborah L. Nichols and Christopher A. Pool, pp. 268–282. Oxford University Press, Oxford.

Stanton, Travis, and David A. Freidel
2003   Ideological Lock-In and the Dynamics of Formative Religions in Mesoamerica. *Mayab* 16:5–14.

Stuart, David
1986   The Classic Maya Social Structure: Titles, Rank and Professions as Seen from the Inscriptions. Paper presented at Maya Art and Civilization: The New Dynamics, a symposium sponsored by the Kimbell Art Museum, Fort Worth, May 1986.
2005   *The Inscriptions from Temple XIX at Palenque*. Pre-Columbian Art Research Institute, San Francisco.
2006   Jade and Chocolate: Bundles of Wealth in Classic Maya Economics and Ritual. In *Sacred Bundles: Ritual Acts of Wrapping and Bundling in Mesoamerica*, edited by Julia Guernsey and F. Kent Reilly, pp. 127–144. Boundary End Archaeology Research Center, Bernardsville, North Carolina.
2014   Four Interesting Logograms. Paper Presented at the Conference Word in Context: Perspectives and Strategies for the Lexicography of Classic Mayan, Nordrhein-Westfälische Akademie der Wissenschaften und der Künste, Düsseldorf, Germany, October 14–15, 2014.

Suhler, Charles K.
1996   Excavations at the North Acropolis, Yaxuna, Yucatan, Mexico. Ph.D. dissertation, Department of Anthropology, Southern Methodist University, Dallas.
Tate, Carolyn E.
1992   *Yaxchilan: The Design of a Maya Ceremonial City.* University of Texas Press, Austin.
Taube, Karl A.
1985   The Classic Maya Maize God: A Reappraisal. In *Fifth Palenque Round Table, 1983*, Vol. 7, edited by Virginia M. Fields, pp. 171–181. Pre-Columbian Art Research Institute, San Francisco.
1992   *The Major Gods of Ancient Yucatan.* Studies in Pre-Columbian Art and Archaeology No. 32. Dumbarton Oaks, Washington D.C.
1994   The Birth Vase: Natal Imagery in Ancient Maya Myth and Ritual. In *The Maya Vase Book*, Vol. 4, edited by Barbara and Justin Kerr, pp. 650–675. Kerr Associates, New York.
2000   Lightning Celts and Corn Fetishes: The Formative Olmec and the Development of Maize Symbolism in Mesoamerica and the American Southwest. In *Olmec Art and Archaeology in Mesoamerica*, edited by John E. Clark and Mary E. Pye, pp. 297–337. Studies in the History of Art 58, Center for Advanced Study in the Visual Arts, Symposium Papers 35. National Gallery of Art, Washington, D.C.
2003   Maws of Heaven and Hell: The Symbolism of the Centipede and Serpent in Classic Maya Religion. In *Antropología de la eternidad: La muerte en la cultura maya*, edited by Andres Ciudada Ruiz, Mario Humberto Ruz Sosa, and María Josefa Iglesias Ponce de León, pp. 405–442. Sociedad Española de Estudios Mayas and El Centro de la Cultura Maya, Madrid and Mexico City.
2004   *Olmec Art at Dumbarton Oaks.* Pre-Columbian Art at Dumbarton Oaks, No. 2. Dumbarton Oaks Research Library and Collection, Washington D.C.
2010   Where Earth and Sky Meet: The Sea and Sky in Ancient and Contemporary Maya Cosmology. In *Fiery Pool: The Maya and the Mythic Sea*, edited by Daniel Finemore and Stephen D. Houston, pp. 202–219. Peabody Essex Museum in Association with Yale University Press, Peabody, Massachusetts, and New Haven, Connecticut.
Taube, Karl A., William A. Saturno, David Stuart, and Heather Hurst
2010   *The Murals of San Bartolo, El Petén, Guatemala, Part 2: The West Wall.* Ancient America 10. Boundary End Research Center, Barnardsville, North Carolina.
Vadala, Jeffrey, and Susan Milbrath
2014   Astronomy, Landscape and Ideological Transmissions at the Coastal Maya Site of Cerros, Belize. *Journal of Caribbean Archaeology* 14:1–21.
Voorhies, Barbara
2012   The Deep Prehistory of Indian Gaming: Possible Late Archaic Game Boards at the Tlacuachero Shellmound, Chiapas, Mexico. *Latin American Antiquity* 24(1):98–115.

III

The Archaeology of E Groups

7

The Isthmian Origins of the E Group and Its Adoption in the Maya Lowlands

TAKESHI INOMATA

Our recent investigations at Ceibal, Guatemala, have revealed the earliest known E Group assemblage in Mesoamerica, dating to roughly 950 BCE, that is, the beginning of the Middle Preclassic period (1000–350 BCE) (Inomata et al. 2013, 2015b). I am not arguing, however, that Ceibal was the place of origin of the E Group. This standardized spatial plan probably emerged through close interactions among diverse groups who lived on the southern Gulf Coast, in central Chiapas, and on the southern Pacific Coast of Mexico, which may be called the Isthmian interaction sphere (Figure 7.1). Groups inhabiting this area had been leading sedentary ways of life longer than the Lowland Maya. In particular, the legacy of the earlier Olmec center, San Lorenzo, was important for the new developments that occurred during this period. Nonetheless, the connection between San Lorenzo and the formation of the E Group is not straightforward. The new spatial plan and architectural form arose after the decline of San Lorenzo around 1150 BCE and before the next Olmec center of La Venta grew as an influential power around 800 BCE (Inomata et al. 2013; Rust 2008). The absence of powerful centers on the Gulf Coast during this interval may have allowed and inspired diverse groups to experiment with new ideas and practices. Among them, communities inhabiting the southern Pacific Coast possibly played a central role in the initial formulation of the new spatial plan.

Located in the southwestern part of the Maya Lowlands, Ceibal was probably at the eastern edge of this interaction sphere. In most parts of the Maya Lowlands besides Ceibal, the E Group assemblage or any other substantial public architectural complexes were not constructed until 800 BCE or even centuries later (Inomata 2016). Thus, in my view, the E Group was not an invention by the Lowland Maya but was not specifically of Olmec origin either. In the long history of the E Group, the associated spatial and

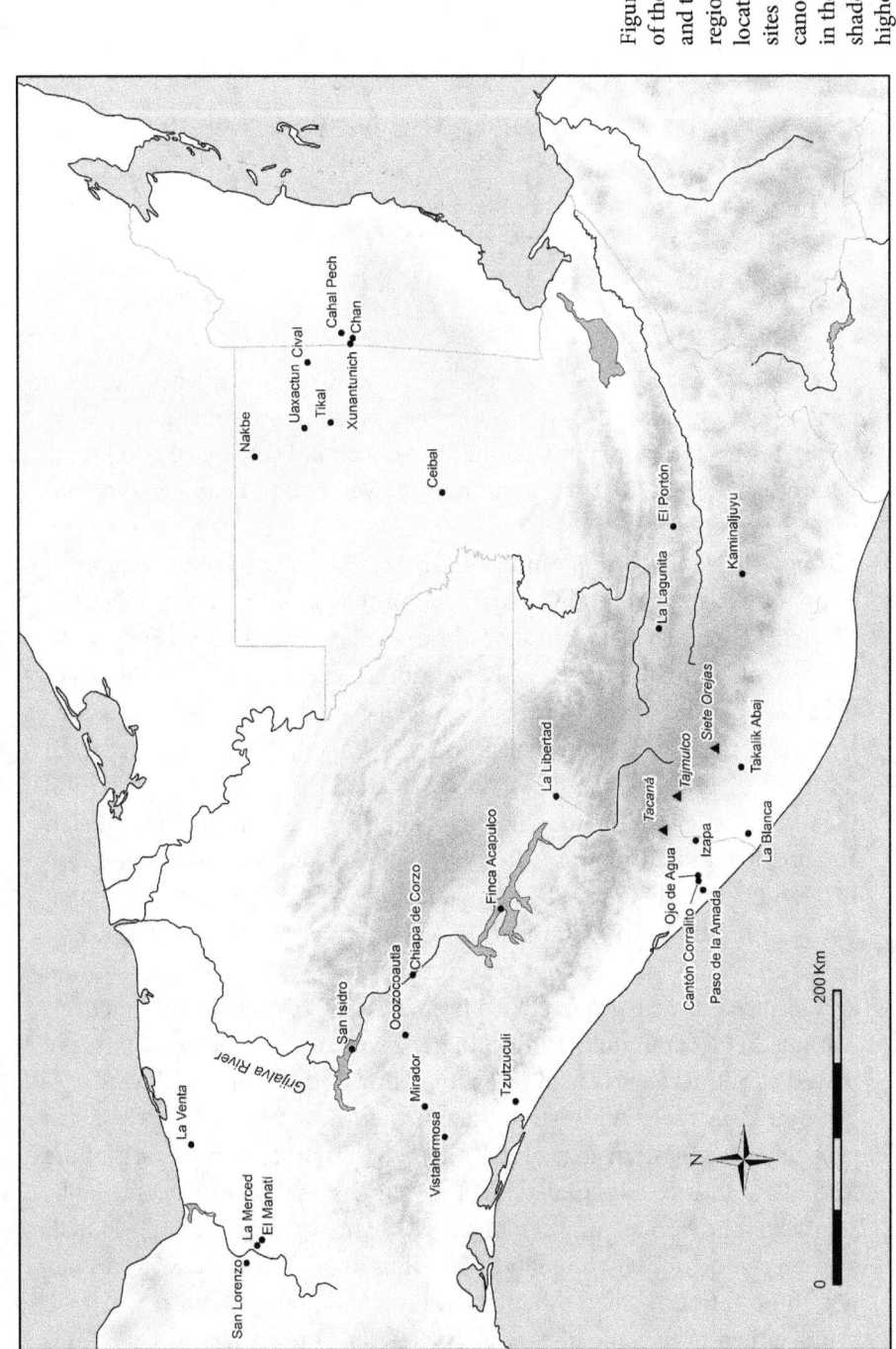

Figure 7.1. Map of the Maya area and the Isthmian region with the locations of the sites and the volcanoes discussed in the text. Darker shades indicate higher elevations.

cosmological notions changed. The symbolism of the early E Group was probably shaped in the local landscape of the Pacific Coast, characterized by the dominant presence of volcanoes and mountains to the north. When it was adopted broadly in the Maya Lowlands, the E Group became more closely tied to the east–west movement of the sun. Data regarding the origins of the E Group are still meager, but the development of this architectural complex appears to have involved a complex process that combined the adoption of preexisting traditions and the inventions of new practices.

Early Preclassic Antecedents

Currently available data suggest that the E Group emerged as part of a broader complex of architecture and ritual practices, including the deposition of greenstone axe caches, mounded buildings, and a highly standardized spatial plan, which John Clark (Clark and Hansen 2001) calls the Middle Formative Chiapas (MFC) pattern (Lowe 1977, 1989; McDonald 1983).

Our understanding of early practices of greenstone axe caching is limited, but important finds include numerous greenstone axes deposited at El Manatí and La Merced, ritual sites associated with springs located in the general San Lorenzo region, but away from major settlements (Ortiz and Rodríguez 1999; Rodríguez and Ortiz 2000, 2010). At the center of San Lorenzo, seven serpentine axes were placed in association with Monument 21, and Monument 8 with axe-shaped slots on its surface also points to the ritual importance of axes (Coe and Diehl 1980:100–103, 313; Freidel and Reilly 2010). These finds show that the tradition of greenstone axe deposits dates back at least to the heyday of San Lorenzo during the Early Preclassic period (1800–1000 BCE). The probable axe offering found under the earliest Locona Phase (1700–1500 BCE) floor of Mound 6 at Paso de la Amada indicates that the inhabitants of the Soconusco region shared this tradition (Blake 1991). During the Cuadros Phase (1350–1200 BCE) of this Pacific coastal region, the occupants of Cantón Corralito also deposited fifteen jade and serpentine axes in Burial 2 (Cheetham 2010:152–153). After 1000 BCE, greenstone axe caches began to be placed along the east–west central lines of E Group assemblages, as documented at Ceibal, San Isidro, and Chiapa de Corzo (Bachand and Lowe 2012; Inomata et al. 2010; Lowe 1981). Thus, the practice of greenstone axe offering was not a new invention during the Middle Preclassic period but the adoption of preexisting practices.

An early tradition of mounded buildings is found on the southern Pacific Coast during the Early Preclassic period. At the community of Paso de la Amada, probable residences were built on raised platforms, which grew in their horizontal and vertical dimensions through successive constructions from the Locona Phase to the Cherla Phase (1700–1350 BCE) (Blake 2011; Blake et al. 2006; Lesure and Blake 2002). Paso de la Amada appears to have been a formal ceremonial center with a public plaza flanked by a possible elite residence (Mound 6) and a ballcourt (Mound 7), although its dimension and the level of formalization are still debated (Clark 2004; Lesure 2011). These buildings loosely conformed to a direction of 35° east of north (Lesure 2011:135), but the center's overall configuration does not resemble the MFC pattern. Bárbara Arroyo et al. (2002) have identified substantial Early Preclassic mounds at San Jerónimo, Escuintla, on the Guatemalan Pacific Coast, but their arrangements are different from the MFC pattern. These architectural traditions of the Pacific Coast contrast with those of the Gulf Coast. Although the space on top of San Lorenzo's enormous artificially raised plateau was apparently organized around multiple plazas during its heyday of the San Lorenzo Phase (1400–1200 BCE), this Olmec center did not have substantial mounds or pyramids (Coe and Diehl 1980; Cyphers 1997; Cyphers and Di Castro 2009; Cyphers and Murtha 2014). Clearly, San Lorenzo was not the place of origin of the MFC pattern. The tradition of mound building on the southern Pacific Coast was disrupted during the Cuadros Phase (1350–1200 BCE), when San Lorenzo's influence on this region became notable. Cantón Corralito, a major settlement with strong evidence of connection with San Lorenzo, did not have mounded buildings dating to this period (Cheetham 2010).

During the Jocotal Phase (1200–1000 BCE), when the influence of San Lorenzo retreated from the Pacific Coast, the inhabitants of the region resumed mound building. Substantial mounds were constructed at sites along estuaries (Lesure 2009; Pye et al. 1999; Rosenswig 2010), but it was at the inland site of Ojo de Agua that the earliest-known pyramids in Mesoamerica were raised (Hodgson et al. 2010). Ojo de Agua's spatial configuration exhibits some resemblance to the E Group and the MFC pattern, equipped with basic components of the later standardized plan: an elongated mound to the east, conical mounds to the west, a large platform to the southwest, and a tall pyramid-like building to the north (see below for the configuration of the MFC pattern; Figure 7.2). This center may have provided a prototype of the MFC pattern. These data on architectural traditions in southern Mesoamerica suggest that the residents of the southern Pacific Coast played a pivotal role in the development of new architectural and spatial forms (Bachand and Lowe 2012; Clark n.d.).

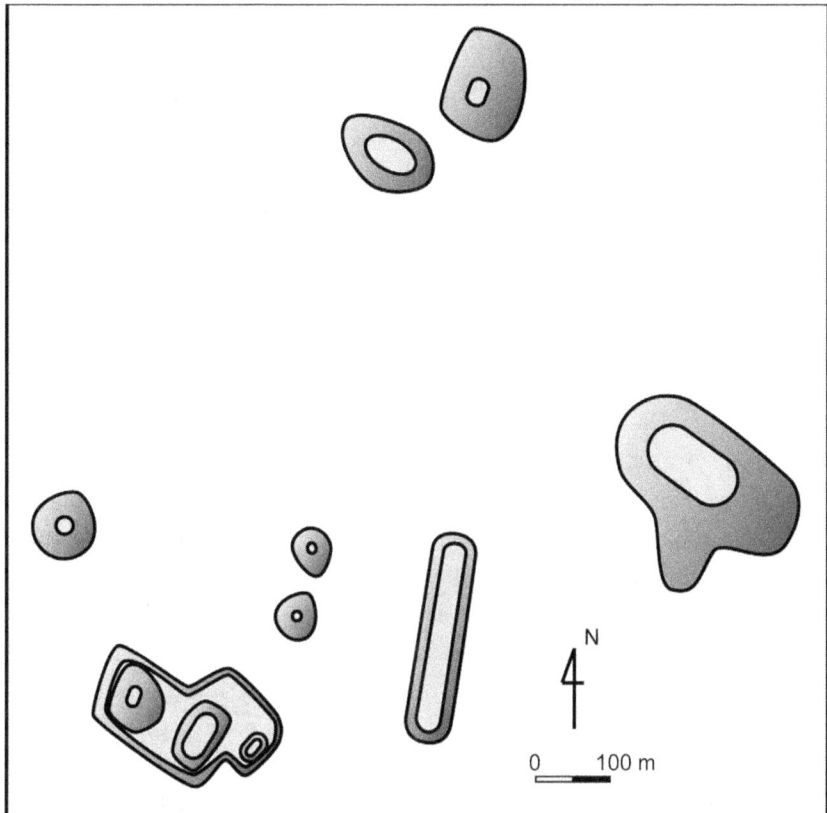

Figure 7.2. Map of Ojo de Agua. Drawing based on Hodgson et al. (2010:Figure 1).

In contrast to these areas to the west and south, no durable buildings predating 1000 BCE have been found in the Maya Lowlands. Settlement patterns of the Maya Lowlands before 1000 BCE remain unclear. Some areas, such as Belize and northern Petén, appear to have been occupied sparsely by mobile horticulturalists, who did not use ceramics (Lohse 2010). Other areas may not have had permanent inhabitants, being visited only occasionally by traders or seasonally by hunter-gatherer-fishers. Thus, the period before 1000 BCE in the Maya Lowlands is commonly called the Archaic period, as opposed to the Early Preclassic period in the rest of southern Mesoamerica. Although the Archaic society in the Maya Lowlands needs to be further examined by future research, it is highly unlikely that the inhabitants of this area provided prototypes for the new architectural innovations of the Middle Preclassic period.

Middle Preclassic Development

After Ojo de Agua was abandoned at the end of the Jocotal Phase, the new center of La Blanca emerged across the Guatemalan border during the subsequent Conchas Phase (1000–700 BCE). Its largest pyramid, Mound 1, reached a height of 25 m, with its substantial bulk built in a single construction episode, which Michael Love (1999, 2013) dates to the Conchas B subphase. In other words, the original version of Mound 1 was probably contemporaneous with or slightly later than the first version of Ceibal's E Group. La Blanca appears to have had a formal site plan oriented 22° east of magnetic north, but it is not clear whether the site had an E Group or a MFC pattern because of modern destruction (Love 1999, 2013; Love and Guernsey 2011:174).

Whereas the southern Pacific Coast appears to be the center of the initial development, it is in the riverine regions, including the Grijalva River Valley in central Chiapas and Ceibal along the Pasión River, that the most elaborate standardized spatial form crystallized. This spatial plan, the MFC pattern, consisted of an E Group assemblage in the center and large platforms arranged along the north–south axis of the complex (Figure 7.3). Our excavations at Ceibal demonstrated that this pattern grew gradually (Figure 7.4). Its first version around 950 BCE consisted of only an E Group assemblage and possibly a southwestern platform. This original configuration loosely resembles the site plan of Ojo de Agua, except for the lack of a northern pyramidal building. The Ceibal residents made a plaza by scraping off humus and carved the earliest E Group buildings out of the natural marl layer. The scraping of humus and the carving of bedrock appear to have been a common practice for the construction of early E Groups or other ceremonial complexes in the Maya Lowlands (Chapters 2, 9, 11, and 12 in this volume; Chase 1983; Estrada-Belli 2006), but the Ceibal example predates other Maya sites by 200 years or more. It is interesting to note that Chiapa de Corzo had been occupied since the Early Preclassic period, but surface soils along with remains of earlier occupation were scraped off at the beginning of the Middle Preclassic period before the construction of MFC-pattern buildings (Bachand and Lowe 2012; Lowe and Agrinier 1960). The removal of surface soils before the construction of an E Group at various sites appears to represent a conscious break from the previous era and the creation of a new social order framed by a new communal space.

For the construction of the western building of the Ceibal E Group (Structure Ajaw), builders placed black soil on top of the carved marl layer

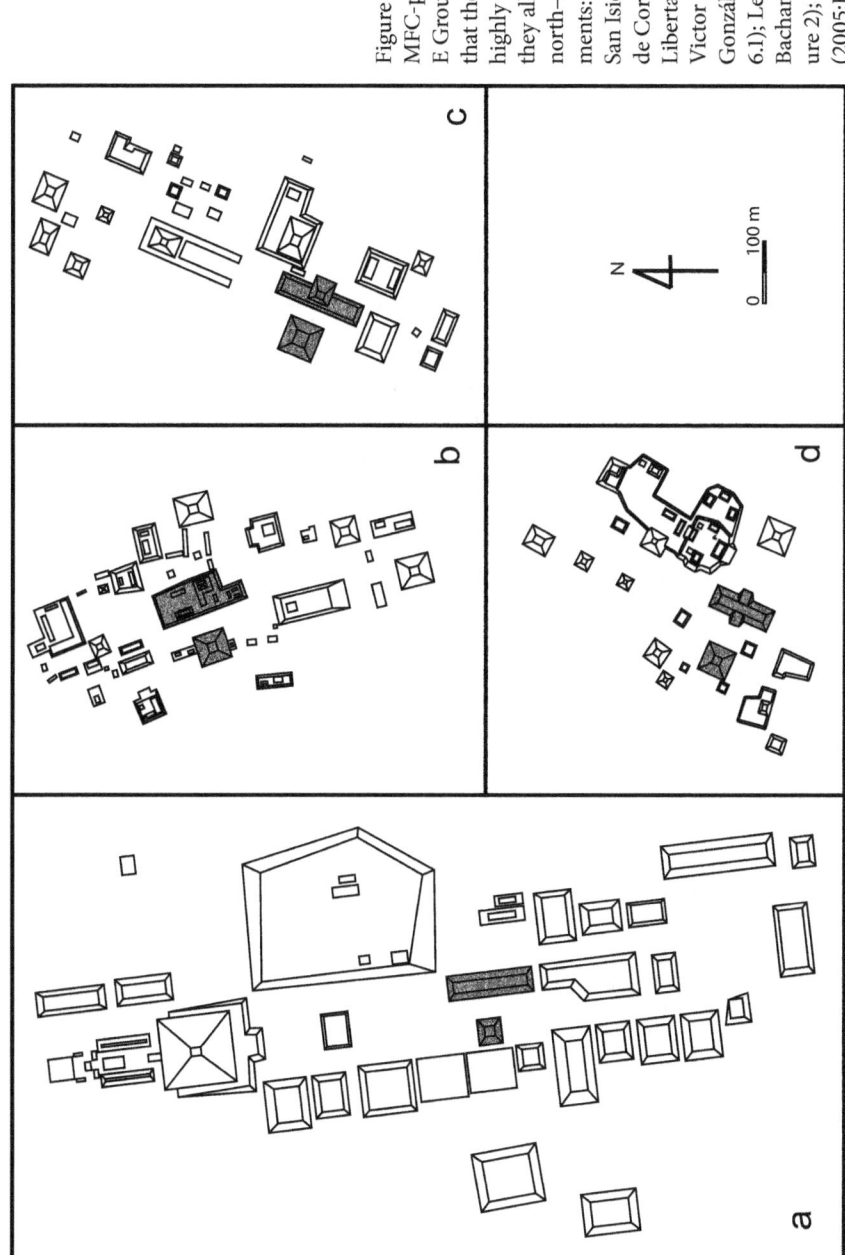

Figure 7.3. Maps of MFC-pattern sites with E Groups shaded. Note that their orientations are highly variable, although they all exhibit general north–south arrangements: (a) La Venta, (b) San Isidro, (c) Chiapa de Corzo; and (d) La Libertad. Drawings by Victor Castillo based on González (2010:Figure 6.1); Lee (1974:Figure 3); Bachand et al. (2008:Figure 2); Bryant et al. (2005:Figure 1.5).

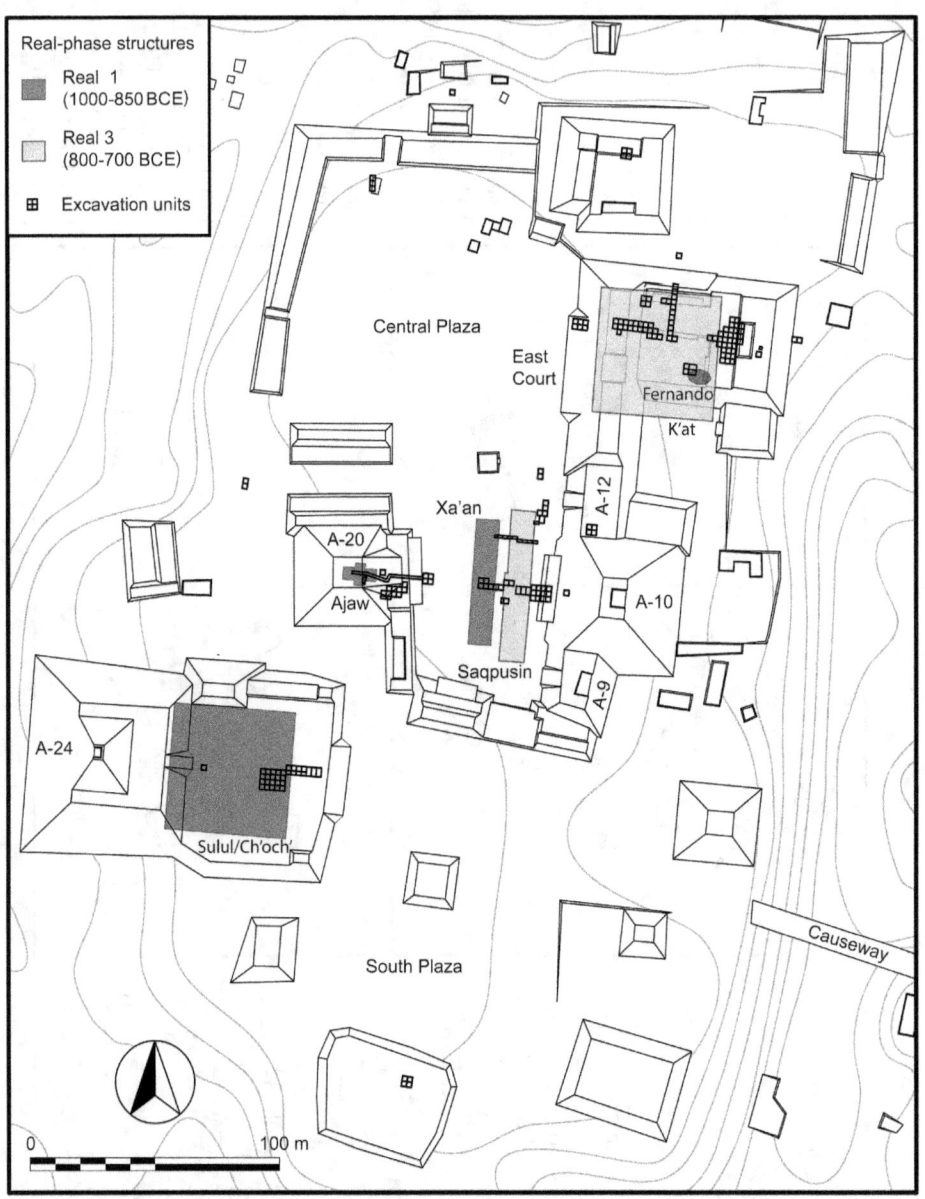

Figure 7.4. Map of Group A of Ceibal with the estimated locations of early buildings.

to raise its height, but its finished form only measured 2.0 m in height and 4.0 m in the east–west dimension at its summit. The central portion of the eastern building (Structure Xa'an) was entirely made of carved marl, but its northern portion, where bedrock sloped lower, included an artificial fill of added soils. The eastern side of this building consisted of a nearly vertical retaining wall measuring 1.0 m in height, which was enforced with limestone blocks. Two steps defined its western side, each measuring 0.1 to 0.4 m in height (Pinzón and De Muylder 2014). The summit of Structure Xa'an was flat, and it apparently did not support any superstructures. As such, the eastern building in its original form looked more like a raised edge of the plaza rather than a well-defined platform. By 800 BCE the western building had grown into a pyramidal shape through renovations. As this building expanded into the plaza space, the Ceibal residents amplified the plaza by covering Structure Xa'an with a plaza floor and by building a new version of the eastern building (Structure Saqpusin) further to the east. Structure Saqpusin was a clearly defined platform, with its western retaining wall consisting of three courses of overhanging limestone blocks, reaching a total height of 0.5 m. Like its predecessor, this platform did not have any signs of superstructures on its summit. On the eastern side of its central portion, excavators found a stairway descending to a flat area 2.0 m below. This means that the main access to Structure Saqpusin was apparently from east rather than from the plaza. A similar pattern was found in the eastern building of the Xunantunich E Group (Chapter 12 in this volume). The ceremonial complex of Ceibal continued to grow throughout the Middle Preclassic period. A northeastern platform was added around 800–700 BCE, and a fully developed MFC pattern with more platforms was established around 700–600 BCE.

From the onset, the E Group plaza was the focus of communal ceremonies, as indicated by the numerous caches deposited there, mostly along its east–west axis. In early caches at Ceibal dating to 1000 to 800 BCE, greenstone axes were commonly placed in parallel horizontal positions, flower-petal forms, or vertical positions, in manners similar to those of the Early Preclassic caches from El Mantí and La Merced (Figures 7.5 and 7.6). The early cruciform cache (Cache 160) was placed between 1000 and 800 BCE, but this arrangement did not become prevalent until the Real 3 Phase (800–700 BCE; Figure 7.7). Although Harvard researchers originally dated the cruciform Cache 7 to around 900 BCE (Smith 1982), our refined ceramic chronology indicates that black-slipped jars placed in this cache belong to the Real 3 Phase (800–700 BCE) or the Real-Escoba transition

Figure 7.5. Cache 118 of Ceibal dating to ca. 1000 BCE. Greenstone axes are placed in horizontal positions.

(around 700 BCE; see below for the discussion of their symbolism). Another elaborate cruciform cache (Cache 171) also dates to the Real-Escoba transition.

The Grijalva River Valley is the area where the most MFC-pattern sites have been identified (Clark and Hansen 2001; Lowe 1977), but the process of architectural development in this area is less clear. Finca Acapulco with substantial Early Preclassic occupation may have been the first center in central Chiapas to develop an initial form of the MFC pattern (Clark n.d.; Lowe 2007). Victor Castillo (2013) notes that the central complexes of Finca Acapulco and Tzutzuculi, another probable early MFC-pattern site located on the Chiapas Pacific Coast, include a large platform located to the southwest of the E Group, in an arrangement similar to that of Ceibal. I should note, however, that the construction history of Finca Acapulco, now submerged under a dammed lake, is poorly known. At Tzutzuculi, limited excavations of the E Group and the southwestern platform did not confirm the presence of constructions dating to the early Middle Preclassic, although possible ceremonial constructions of this period were found around the northern pyramid (Mound 4; McDonald 1983). Although these

Left: Figure 7.6. Cache 138 of Ceibal dating to 1000–850 BCE. Greenstone axes are placed in a flower-petal-like arrangement.

Below: Figure 7.7. Cache 160 of Ceibal dating to 800–700 BCE. Greenstone axes are placed in a cruciform pit.

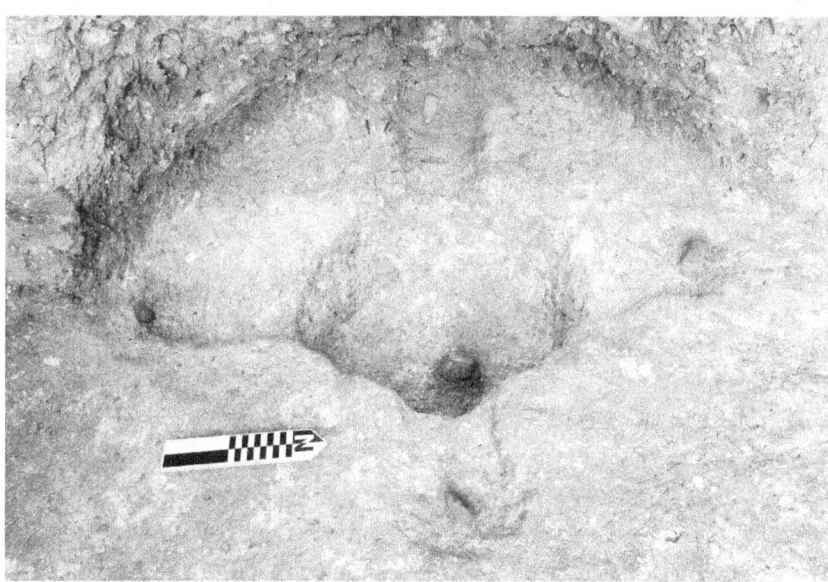

ambiguities remain, it is probable that an early version of the MFC-pattern in Chiapas consisted of an E Group, a southwestern platform, and a northern pyramidal building, resembling the roughly contemporaneous plan of Ceibal, except for the addition of a northern building. These configurations of the early Middle Preclassic Chiapas centers may have developed directly from the earlier template of Ojo de Agua.

When a more developed form of the MFC pattern with the northeastern platform emerged after 800 BCE, this standardized spatial plan was adopted at various communities across the Isthmian area, including Chiapa de Corzo (Bachand and Lowe 2012; Hicks and Rosaire 1960; Lowe 1962; Lowe and Agrinier 1960; Mason 1960), Ocozocoautla (McDonald 1999:61–62), San Isidro (Lowe 1981), La Libertad (Miller 2014), Mirador (Agrinier 1975, 2000), and possibly Vistahermosa (Treat 1986) (Figure 7.3). These later MFC-pattern sites lacked a southwestern platform but prominently featured a northeastern platform and the north–south arrangement of additional platforms. The results of recent research at Izapa by Robert Rosenswig et al. (2013) suggest that this Chiapas Pacific piedmont center may also have had a MFC pattern during the Middle Preclassic period, with Mounds 71 and 73 possibly forming an E Group. Although this center apparently lacked southwestern and northeastern platforms, its northern complex called Group B and the probable E Group assemblage exhibited a clear north–south alignment. The addition of another complex named Group A to the west during the Late Preclassic period marked Izapa's divergence from the MFC pattern (Lowe et al. 1982; Rosenswig et al. 2014). While many of these centers in the Chiapas Grijalva River Valley and on the Pacific Coast possessed a northern pyramid, San Isidro, like Ceibal, lacked this northern component (see the discussion below).

An important community that may have adopted the MFC pattern was the Olmec center of La Venta, located on the Gulf Coast (Figure 7.3). Gareth Lowe (1977) and John Clark and Richard Hansen (2001) originally suspected that La Venta was the source of this standardized spatial plan, but a refined chronological evaluation suggests otherwise. Although the chronology of La Venta is still a vexing problem, significant sets of radiocarbon dates and ceramic data have been provided through settlement excavations by William Rust (2008), excavations at the La Venta core by Rebecca González (1990), settlement excavations in the La Venta peripheries by Christopher Von Nagy (2003), by Kevin Pope et al. (2001), and by Mark Raab et al. (2000), and the survey of the Chontalpa region to the east by Edward Sisson (1976). In addition to the evaluation of ceramic cross-dating, I applied Bayesian statistics to radiocarbon dates from La Venta to refine the chronology of this center (Inomata et al. 2013). Although the construction dates and sequence of its ceremonial core need to be determined by future research, these studies suggest that La Venta did not become an influential center with a large population until 800 BCE. In addition, this center lacked a southwestern platform and conspicuously featured the northeastern platform, the Stirling Acropolis. This arrangement conformed to the well-developed version of the MFC pattern, dating after 800 BCE. Thus, La Venta was among the multiple communities that participated in the development of the MFC pattern but not its sole origin. More likely, La Venta may have adopted the MFC pattern after its developed format was established elsewhere, roughly contemporaneously with the wide spread of this configuration in Chiapas around 800 BCE.

Importantly, at least some of these centers shared similar caching practices, in which greenstone axes were placed in the E Group plazas, mostly along their east–west axes. Some of these caches, such as San Isidro Cache 11 (Lowe 1981) and Chiapa de Corzo Massive Offerings 1 and 2 and Feature 3 (Bachand and Lowe 2012), were in cruciform arrangements. Although the E Group of La Venta remains largely unexplored, the intensive excavation of its Complex A revealed numerous caches with greenstone axes and other objects, including those in cruciform patterns, such as Offering 10 (Drucker et al. 1959). Thus, the closely resembling spatial formats of Ceibal, the Chiapas centers, and La Venta resulted not from a superficial borrowing of built forms but from close interactions among different groups that shared common ritual concepts and practices. The similarities in caches, in particular, suggest that some individuals from those communities visited other centers on occasions of ceremonies and participated in their rituals. In other words, the MFC pattern, the E Group, and related ritual practices did not originate from a single center but resulted from interactions across wide areas (Inomata et al. 2013). They were not the inventions of the Olmec alone; neither can the Lowland Maya claim exclusive credit for them.

Ceibal is the only Lowland Maya site where the presence of an E Group prior to 800 BCE has been confirmed (but see Chapter 14 in this volume for another potentially early example). It is not clear whether this community located near the southwestern edge of the Maya Lowlands can be characterized as culturally Maya before 800 BCE. Early architecture at Ceibal was made primarily of clay, exhibiting strong similarities to construction techniques used in areas to the west and south. These methods contrast with the more abundant use of stone that characterized later Lowland Maya architecture. I should add that Ceibal's ceramics resemble contemporaneous materials from other parts of the Maya Lowlands, while they also share considerable commonalities with Chiapan ceramics. Because evidence for human occupation in Ceibal's vicinity before 1000 BCE is scarce or nonexistent, it appears likely that a significant number of people migrated to the area during the Early–Middle Preclassic transition. Given the ceramic similarities, I suspect that a majority of them were descendants of the Archaic period (pre-1000 BCE) populations in the Maya Lowlands (Cheetham 2005; Clark and Cheetham 2002; Lohse 2010), but a considerable number of migrants may also have come from Chiapas (Andrews 1990; Lowe 1977; Willey 1977).

After 800 BCE the inhabitants of the central Maya Lowlands selectively adopted a component of the MFC pattern, namely, the E Group assemblage. Other elements of this plan, such as greenstone axe caches and platforms arranged along the north–south axis, were largely disregarded. Cival's E Group, dating between 800 and 700 BCE, is the earliest-documented example of this spatial format in the Maya Lowlands after Ceibal. The excavation of this site by Francisco Estrada-Belli (2006, 2011, 2012, Chapter 9 in this volume) revealed a greenstone axe cache in a cruciform pattern. The Mundo Perdido complex at Tikal represents the next earliest E Group confirmed in the Maya Lowlands, which I would date to around 700 BCE. Extensive excavations of this complex by Juan Pedro Laporte and his colleague (Laporte and Fialko 1995) failed to uncover greenstone axe caches. No similar caches have been found in other well-studied E Groups, including those at Uaxactún and Nakbé. Investigations at Mundo Perdido did show that the basic architectural form of the E Group found at Ceibal around 950 BCE was replicated at Tikal two centuries later. The earliest version of Tikal's E Group consisted of a low, wide platform on the west and an elongated platform without superstructures on the east (Chapter 8 in this volume). The eastern platforms of early E Groups at La Venta and in Chiapas also appear to have had flat summit surfaces without superstructures (Lee 1989), indicating that this form represented the original architectural format of early E Groups (Aimers and Rice 2006).

There was an important difference, however. Tikal's E Group consisted of masonry constructions from its inception, whereas contemporaneous complexes on the Gulf Coast, in Chiapas, and on the Pacific Coast were largely made of earth. The extensive use of masonry techniques, often along with lime stucco, became a hallmark of Lowland Maya architecture (Chapter 8 in this volume; Laporte and Fialko 1995; Ricketson and Ricketson

1937). Builders at Ceibal around this time still used earthen fills for most structures but began to apply stone blocks on the outer surfaces of buildings more extensively. This pattern at Ceibal likely represents a gradual shift from the Chiapas-like construction methods to those of the Maya Lowlands. It is also interesting to note that some buildings at La Venta employed stone-block surfaces over earthen fills. The process of interregional interaction as well as the implications of the La Venta buildings need to be further examined; but the general trend is clear: the Lowland Maya were neither the sole inventors of the E Group nor passive recipients of external influence. They actively selected specific elements and integrated them into their own system of cultural practices.

During the late Middle Preclassic period after 600 BCE the deposition of greenstone axe caches became rare at Ceibal, while this practice persisted in central Chiapas and at La Venta. Ceibal was now developing closer affinity with the rest of the Maya Lowlands. It is probable that the E Group in the Lowlands began to serve as the Lowland Mayas' own cultural symbol rather than as an allusion to the connection with the western neighbors. Once adopted by the Lowland Maya, the E Group became the central arena and media for the creation of collective identity for many Maya communities (Aimers and Rice 2006; Chase and Chase 1995; Doyle 2012; Chapters 1, 6, 8, and 10 in this volume).

Late Preclassic Transformation

At the end of the Middle Preclassic period around 400 or 350 BCE, La Venta collapsed, and centers in the Chiapas Grijalva River Valley and beyond appear to have experienced political decline or reorganization (Clark and Hansen 2001; Inomata et al. 2013; Rust 2008). Finca Acapulco appears to have been deserted roughly a century earlier, and La Libertad and Tzutzuculi were abandoned roughly contemporaneously with La Venta's fall (Bryant et al. 2005; Lowe 1977, 2007; McDonald 1983; Miller 2014). Occupation at Chiapa de Corzo, Ocozocoautla, and San Isidro continued, but the closely shared ceramic similarities of the former period broke down, and Chiapa de Corzo appears to have shifted its cultural and political affinities to the Maya Lowlands. The site sizes of some centers may have decreased (Clark n.d.; Clark and Hansen 2001; Lowe 1977). With this change, the tradition of E Groups on the Gulf Coast, in Chiapas, and on the Pacific Coast declined. Although surviving centers retained their E Groups, social and symbolic emphasis appears to have shifted to other architectural complexes, as seen in the construction of Group A at Izapa. During the following Late Preclassic period, the Lowland Maya became the most avid builders of E Groups in Mesoamerica, while this spatial format may also have been adopted by the new highland center of Kaminaljuyú and nearby communities (Murdy 1990:355–356; Valdés 1995:74). Numerous E Group assemblages, including Uaxactún Group E, were built during this period (Chapter 2 in this volume; Ricketson and Ricketson 1937; Rosal et al. 1993). The high concentrations of E Group complexes in the Southern Maya Lowlands, particularly in northeastern Petén and southeastern Campeche, led some Maya archaeologists to argue that the architectural format originated in this region. Nonetheless, a substantial portion of the E Groups in this area were most likely constructed during the Late Preclassic period, and their high density cannot be used as evidence for their origin.

In place of the simple elongated platform of the previous period, the Lowland Maya began to build eastern structures in more complex forms by adding superstructures. A common form during the Late Preclassic period appears to have been what Arlen Chase and Diane Chase (1995, Chapter 2 in this volume) termed the Cenote style E Group, which was characterized by the central building or pyramid larger than those on the two wings. A new type of monumental architectural complex, commonly called the Triadic Group, emerged during this period, but E Groups continued to serve as important symbolic centers of growing communities (Chase and Chase 1995; Hansen 1998; Chapters 1, 6, and 8 in this volume). At Ceibal, the spatial pattern of the MFC arrangement was retained, but its original use had been mostly lost. The eastern building of its E Group was again moved farther to the east, in the locations of Structures A-9, A-10, and A-12, and took the form of the Cenote style E Group. This format of the eastern building was replicated at multiple minor temple groups at Ceibal and in its surroundings, including at the satellite center of Anonal (Tourtellot 1988). In some cases, as at the minor center of Caobal (Munson 2012), however, these eastern buildings were not paired with a western pyramid. In addition, the use pattern of the large platforms of Ceibal changed. They originally supported multiple structures and possibly served as residential complexes of emerging elites in a manner similar to those at Chiapan centers (Agrinier 2000; Clark and Hansen 2001). At the end of the Middle Preclassic period, these platforms at Ceibal were converted to flat, open spaces. In addition to the near cessation of greenstone axe caching during the late Middle Preclassic, these architectural transformations during the Late Preclassic indicate that the residents of Ceibal had nearly abandoned the original use pattern of the

Figure 7.8. Cache 128 of Ceibal dating to 50–125 CE. It contained roughly 145 vessels.

MFC plan and the E Group and possibly their original symbolic contents as well. This also means that new social functions were probably attached to these buildings. I suspect that E Groups now implied a connection to the distant past rather than a reference to distant places, while triadic groups represented relatively recent achievements.

The Ceibal inhabitants, however, appear to have retained some memory of the connection with the Isthmian region in the past, which was associated with the E Group. During the latter part of the Late Preclassic period, or the Protoclassic period, around 1–250 CE, numerous caches were deposited in the eastern part of the E Group plaza at Ceibal. Unlike the greenstone axe caches of the earlier period, these Protoclassic caches contained numerous complete and broken ceramics, in one case as many as 145 vessels (Figure 7.8). Inside or next to some vessels were numerous limestone spheres (Figure 7.9). Caching of small stone spheres during this period is not absent but is rare in the Maya Lowlands (Götting 2011; McAnany 2004:72; 14; Źrałka et al. 2011; Chapter 14 in this volume). These artifacts in caches are more common in the Guatemala Highlands, in central Chiapas, and on the southern Pacific Coast, including at the sites of El Portón (Sharer and Sedat 1987), La Lagunita (Ichon and Arnauld 1985), Kaminaljuyú (Cheek 1977), Chiapa de Corzo (Hicks and Rosaire 1960), and Takalik Abaj (Schieber 2002; Schieber and Orrego 2010). Significantly, these caches

Figure 7.9. Cache 103 of Ceibal dating to 50–125 CE. Limestone spheres are placed in and around ceramic vessels.

at Ceibal were sequential deposits; some caches cut into older ones. Similar sequential deposits of caches with ceramic vessels and stone spheres were also documented in the massive offerings at Takalik Abaj, dating roughly to the same period (Schieber 2002; Schieber and Orrego 2010). The specific meaning of these caches and stone spheres is only a matter of speculation. Nonetheless, it is tempting to think that stone spheres are related to counting and divination and that the caches were deposited according to calendrical cycles. If so, the E Group of Ceibal, as well as of those at many other sites in the Maya Lowlands, may have come to be tied more closely to calendrical cycles during the Late Preclassic period (Aimers and Rice 2006; Aveni et al. 2003; Aveni and Hartung 1989; Chapters 2, 3, 4, 5, 6, 10, and 15 in this volume.

Changing Symbolism

This history of the E Group suggests that the symbolic values and social roles of these architectural complexes most likely changed through time as diverse groups adopted them and reworked them. The analysis of this process may highlight the different roles that the inhabitants of diverse regions played.

Maize Agriculture

It is likely not a coincidence that the formalized E Group, along with other elements of the MFC pattern, was established around 1000 BCE, when maize agriculture was becoming a dominant form of subsistence in Mesoamerica (Arnold 2009; Blake 2015; Blake et al. 1992; Clark et al. 2007; Rosenswig 2010). In this sense, I agree with the authors who argue that the E Group was associated with the symbolism of maize agriculture (Aimers and Rice 2006; Cohodas 1980; Doyle 2012; Stanton and Freidel 2003; Chapters 6, 8, 10, and 14 in this volume). We should also pay attention to the fact that various elements incorporated in the E Group formulation, however, such as greenstone axe deposits and mounded complexes, were originally developed in Early Preclassic societies, which primarily relied on gathering, fishing, and hunting, along with maize cultivation that occupied a relatively small portion of subsistence. The symbolisms of these early elements probably referred not specifically to maize agriculture but more broadly to the general notions of fertility, water, and earth. Even after 1000 BCE, populations maintaining heavy reliance on hunting, gathering, and fishing and relatively mobile ways of life possibly coexisted with those that fully adopted maize agriculture (Inomata et al. 2015a, 2015b; Lohse 2010; Rosenswig 2010, 2011). E Groups and the rituals held in them probably reflected experiences and interests of those diverse groups. Thus, as the early symbols are integrated in the E Group complex, some aspects of their broad, unspecified references were possibly retained.

Directional Concepts of the Earth and the Sky

Along with the increasing importance of maize symbolism, another aspect of the symbolic change associated with the E Group may be a shift from the cosmology tied to the earth, water, and other features on the ground to the one more closely associated with celestial bodies and cardinal directionality. I should note that Mesoamerican worldviews integrate earthly and celestial domains inseparably and that such shifts are never clear-cut. Still, we can recognize a certain trend in which the weight of references tilted from earthly entities toward celestial ones through time. This trend can be seen in the orientations of MFC plans and E Groups. Early MFC site plans at La Venta, Chiapan centers, as well as Tzutzuculi and Izapa on the Pacific Coast exhibited widely different orientations; and at first glance solar alignments do not appear to have been incorporated in their designs

(Figure 7.3). Recent studies by Michael Blake (2013), however, suggest the tantalizing possibility that they represent a compromise between earthly and celestial references. His analysis demonstrates that the MFC arrangements of some sites, including Chiapa de Corzo and Izapa, are oriented toward topographic landmarks, such as hills and volcanoes. In those cases, the center axis of the E Group may not be aligned with the equinox solar orientation. Instead, according to Blake, the center axis may be oriented toward a solstice line and the equinox line may fall around the northern or southern end of the eastern mound.

If Blake is correct, this finding presents important implications. The combination of references to both earthly and celestial elements implies that, while sharing highly standardized spatial templates, the specific designs of these sites were formed in the local setting of each community, significantly affected by the configurations of the surrounding mountain ranges and other topographic features. Their specific symbolic contents and narratives probably varied from one place to another. In these designs, their solar alignments were never precise, which indicates that early E Groups in the Isthmian region served primarily as generalized representations of cosmological symbolisms and as spaces of related rituals rather than as devices for precise solar observations.

Moreover, the strong emphasis on the north–south axis in the early MFC pattern, as well as other related complexes in the Isthmian region, is at odds with the broadly held cosmology of Mesoamerica, which privileges the east–west orientation. Abundant ethnographic data show that the modern Maya view the east–west direction as the primary axis corresponding to the sun's path and the north–south axis as the sideways perspective of this principal line (Bunzel 1952:265; Gossen 1974:31–32; Hanks 1990:338; Vogt 1969:603–604; Watanabe 1983; Wisdom 1940:427). This cognitive model of space may be conditioned partially by movements of celestial bodies observed in lower latitudes (Watanabe 1983:717; see also Aveni 2001:55). In those areas, stars appear to move from east to west in parallel, nearly vertical arcs (14 to 15 degrees off the perpendicular on the southern Pacific Coast). The Pole Star may not be a prominent directional reference in these areas because its position as the pivotal point of celestial motion is less obvious than in mid-latitude areas and because it is located low, close to the horizon, and trees and other obstacles can easily block its view. The primacy of the east–west axis can most likely be traced back to the Prehispanic times and found among other Mesoamerican groups who painted codices and maps with east at the top (Brotherston 1976; Palka 2002; Stuart 2002; Chapter 11 in this volume).

So the emphasis on the north–south axis in the Isthmian site plans was likely rooted in specific local conditions different from astronomically based cardinal directionality. Such settings may be found primarily on the southern Pacific Coast, where a range of volcanoes and other high mountains loom in the northern to northeastern skyline, shaping people's daily experience of space. The Chiapas Grijalva River Valley may be another candidate, but the views of mountains to the northeast appear less impressive in many parts of this region. The inhabitants of the southern Pacific Coast aligned the central axes of their ceremonial centers to dominant volcanoes or mountains: Izapa with the Tacaná volcano (Blake 2013), La Blanca with the Tajumulco volcano (Love and Guernsey 2011:174), and Takalik Abaj with the Siete Orejas volcano (Schieber, personal communication, 2015; Figure 7.1). In many cases, the primary axis was clearly marked by a pyramidal building placed to the north of the E Group, which provided a silhouette overlapping with the mountain behind it. The eastern linear mounds of the E Groups may also have emphasized the alignment of its longitudinal (north–south) axis with these peaks in the skyline, while the general alignments to solar directions viewed from the western mound may have been simultaneously incorporated, as indicated by Blake's (2013) research. At some sites, the direction of sunrise on the summer solstice may also have corresponded to the sight line to a high mountain, as in the case of the Tajmulco volcano for Izapa (Malmström 1978), but this line should probably be considered as a secondary direction different from the primary north–south axis.

These observations point to the central role that southern Pacific coastal societies played in the initial development of the symbolism associated with the E Group and the MFC pattern. This interpretation accords with the presence of earlier mound-building traditions in this area, including the mounded complex of Ojo de Agua. The importance of volcanoes and mountains continued into later societies on the coast and in the nearby Highlands, as seen in stone monuments or other iconographic media of these regions that emphasized the symbolism of mountains (Henderson 2013, 2015; Inomata and Henderson 2016).

When the MFC pattern developed during the Middle Preclassic period through interaction in a wide area beyond the southern Pacific Coast, the emphasis on the north–south directionality persisted. By then the spatial format had become more standardized and probably came to represent more generalized cosmological notions, not necessarily framed in the localized experience of the Pacific coastal landscape. Many centers in the Grijalva River Valley appear to have been aligned to hills to the north rather than to those to the south (Blake 2013). Among them, San Isidro presents a unique case because it lacked a northern pyramid. It is tempting to think that the spatial plan of San Isidro was affected by its location near the northwestern ends of mountain ranges where higher mountains are visible to the southeast rather than to the north. La Venta, situated in the Gulf Coast plain, however, featured a northern pyramid (Complex C) conspicuously along with other elements of the MFC pattern: an E Group (Mounds D-1 and D-8), a northeastern platform (Stirling Acropolis), and the north–south axis. Obviously, La Venta's architectural complex was not aligned to any clearly visible landmark; to the north are a flat alluvial plain and the open sea. These considerations may provide an important clue to La Venta's role in the development of the MFC pattern. It seems unlikely that the occupants of La Venta invented this spatial format of the northern alignment marked by a northern pyramid, with its conical shape resembling volcanoes found in the Sierra Madres along the Pacific Coast. Although the Tuxtla Mountains might have presented such landmarks for the Gulf Coast people, their symbolic role needs to be explored through their relations to the site layouts of the region. As noted earlier, La Venta's spatial plan conforms to the fully developed format of the MFC pattern rather than to its early version, which also indicates that the builders of La Venta borrowed this template from the southern neighbors when the pattern was well established. Currently available ceramic and radiocarbon data mentioned above appear to accord with this interpretation.

The area around Ceibal presents a comparable physical setting in some aspects. Located in the Maya Lowlands, it lacks prominent landmarks in the skyline. This community actively participated in the development of the MFC pattern from its inception, but its western and southern neighbors likely inspired the north–south directionality of this center. As at San Isidro, the residents of Ceibal did not incorporate a northern pyramid in their ceremonial complex, a decision probably not unrelated to the lack of high mountains in this region. Various lines of epigraphic and iconographic evidence from later periods show that the symbolism of hill was important for the Lowland Maya, but their experience of the landscape cannot be equated with those of the inhabitants of the Pacific Coast. Whereas the northern pyramids at the Pacific coastal sites may have represented the mountain symbolism from the onset, the earliest version of Ceibal's E Group buildings were low, broad platforms dissimilar to mountains. At the beginning, these buildings at Ceibal may have been perceived primarily as ceremonial stages associated with the plaza. Their symbolic identification as mountains probably emerged only through a series of renovations that resulted in pyramidal shapes (see Joyce 2004).

If the Middle Preclassic inhabitants of the Maya Lowlands privileged the east–west axis in a manner similar to the modern Maya, this north–south directionality of Ceibal without a prominent referent point in the landscape may not have been congruent with a spatial concept and cosmology broadly held by the members of the society. This may be why other communities in the Maya Lowlands mostly disregarded the north–south arrangement of the overall site plan when they adopted the E Group format after 800 BCE (Ashmore and Sabloff 2002; Clark and Hansen 2001). E Groups of these Lowland Maya communities tended to conform more closely to the solar directionality than the Chiapan and Pacific coastal examples, although their solar alignments were not necessarily precise (Aveni et al. 2003; Aveni and Hartung 1989; Ruppert 1940). This observation, however, does not mean that earthly references were discarded. Earthly features, such as caves, hills, and bodies of water, continued to play important roles in Maya cosmology. Deviations from solar directions found at various Lowland Maya sites imply that symbolisms associated with topographic features were still incorporated in the designs of E Groups and other aspects of the site planning (Aimers and Rice 2006; Brady 1997; Carlson 1981; Ricketson 1928). The examples that Francisco Estrada-Belli (Chapter 9 in this volume) discusses present particularly intriguing cases in this regard.

In this process of adoption of the E Group assemblage, the Lowland Maya probably merged it with the preexisting local concepts of space. Earlier spatial formats of the Maya Lowlands are poorly known, but they may have included open plaza spaces. Excavations in the ceremonial cores of Cahal Pech and Chan in the Belize River Valley showed that the initial arrangement at each of these sites included a single building on the eastern side (Chapters 11 and 13 in this volume). In my view, these complexes, at least in their original forms, should not be regarded as E Groups. They possibly represented local spatial symbolism different from that of the early E Group associated with the MFC pattern. Recent excavations at Actuncán in Belize suggest the presence of an eastern building roughly contemporaneous with Structures Ajaw and Xa'an at Ceibal (LeCount and Mixter 2016), but it will not be known whether this building had a western pair until the western side of the plaza is excavated. As communities in the Belize River Valley and other parts of the Maya Lowlands adopted the E Group template, its underlying symbolisms and associated practices were merged with the preexisting local ones. The resulting symbolism may have diverged from those associated with the early Middle Preclassic E Groups of MFC sites in some aspects. Despite this qualification, the stronger emphasis on celestial references suggests that people began to emphasize more homogeneous symbolic representations and narratives across different communities that superseded variations and idiosyncrasies in local settings.

Symbolisms in Caches

This general shift from earthly references to astronomical ones can also be observed in ritual deposits: from those associated with springs and mountains to cruciform deposits that were more closely connected with cardinal directionality defined by celestial motion. Early Preclassic deposits of greenstone axes at El Manatí and La Merced were apparently not placed in cruciform arrangements (Ortiz and Rodríguez 1999; Rodríguez and Ortiz 2000). These early deposits associated with natural springs appear to have been closely tied to water, fertility, and other earthly notions framed in the specific local setting of each location. Most of the early caches of Ceibal dating before 800 BCE exhibited arrangements of greenstone axes similar to those of El Mantí and La Merced. These early caches of Ceibal probably retained some aspects of the Early Preclassic symbolism. Nonetheless, their reference to earthly features may have become less direct than in the case of Early Preclassic examples. Although the finds from the southern Pacific Coast suggest that the practices of depositing greenstone axes in residential areas existed in earlier periods, their placement in the artificial landscape of plazas became a prevalent mode during the Middle Preclassic. While plazas and associated built forms may have served as metaphors for the broader cultural and natural world, the earthly symbolism of these caches became more abstract and generalized, with their ties to concrete landmarks weakened.

After 800 BCE an even clearer symbolic change occurred. Cruciform caches, clearly tied to cardinal directionality, became common at Ceibal and at other centers, including Cival, San Isidro, Chiapa de Corzo, and La Venta. The spread of cruciform caches and other representations of cardinal directionality in the Isthmian region indicates that this shift in symbolic emphasis occurred across broad areas beyond the Maya Lowlands. Many Maya communities that emerged after 600 BCE do not appear to have practiced the deposit of axe caches, but the use of quadripartite motifs in cache offerings and site plans with specific orientations indicate that the symbolism tied to cardinal directionality continued to be important (Ashmore 1991; McAnany 1995:85; Schele and Freidel 1990).

The earlier symbolism of greenstone axes associated with water and other earthly notions, however, was not lost. As noted earlier, the deposition of greenstone axes in watery features continued during the Middle Preclassic period, as in the case of Arroyo Pesquero and the upper layers of La Merced. Since the discoveries of such deposits in springs and rivers are largely fortuitous, we cannot deny the possibility that comparable offerings will be found in the Maya Lowlands in the future. An important understanding that emerged at the Santa Fe Institute (SFI) meetings was that Middle Preclassic greenstone axe deposits, and the E Group assemblage by extension, represented water symbolism along with celestial references (Chapters 6, 9, and 12 in this volume). This symbolism is most directly indicated by water jars placed in cruciform caches, including Ceibal Cache 7 and Cival Cache 4, as well as recently uncovered Ceibal Cache 171 (Pinzón and De Muylder 2014). This water symbolism of the plaza continued to be notable even during the Classic period (CE 250–900) (Schele and Mathews 1998:43–44).

More importantly, we need to question whether the cosmology dating after 800 BCE that was tied to cardinal directions can be equated with the modern Western notion of directionality, which views cardinal directions as absolute orientations determined in the objective, universal space. John Watanabe (1983) argues that the modern Mam understand directions in relation to the movements of the sun; the east is associated with the notion of "the sun moving in," the west with "out," the north with "up," and the south with "down." Similar concepts are found among other Maya groups (Ashmore 1991). These differences in qualities and dimensions between the north–south and east–west directions were probably present in the cosmology associated with the MFC pattern, at least in its incipient form. Thus, to the degree that the original conceptualizations of this site plan, possibly rooted in the local experience of space on the Pacific Coast, were retained in its later derivatives, and to the degree that the underlying privileging of the east–west axis persisted, the emphasis on cardinal directionality should be not understood in the same manner as in the modern Western model of space.

Conclusion

The early history of the E Group is still poorly understood, and we need more excavation data on early architectural remains for a better understanding of its origins. Still, the foregoing review suggests that, contrary to the perception of many Maya archaeologists, the initial development of the E Group took place mostly outside of the Maya Lowlands (Clark and Hansen 2001; Lowe 1977; McDonald 1983). The primary stage of this cultural and social innovation was a wide area, including the southern Gulf Coast, Chiapas, and the southern Pacific Coast, which I call the Isthmian interaction sphere. Ceibal was probably located at the eastern edge of this sphere. The architectural format of the E Group appears to have been established around 1000 BCE as an element of a broader ritual-spatial complex, including greenstone axe deposits and the standardized spatial formulation named the Middle Formative Chiapas (MFC) pattern. This formal spatial plan possibly resulted from the selective adoption of earlier traditions, the reformulation of them, and the creation of new practices through interactions among the occupants of this sphere. An earlier tradition of greenstone axe deposits can be found primarily on the Gulf Coast, while the residents of the southern Pacific Coast also shared the practice. The earlier roots of architectural forms may be traced back mostly to the Pacific coastal region (Bachand and Lowe 2012; Clark n.d.). The mounded complex of Paso de la Amada there dates back to 1700–1500 BCE, and a more formalized compound at Ojo de Agua (1200–1000 BCE) may have provided a prototype of the MFC pattern.

The development of the E Group reviewed here provides important implications. First, we should not uncritically project back the patterns and symbolisms of the E Group from later periods to their earlier versions. The original E Groups were probably created with intentions and narratives much different from those of the later periods. Our task is to examine this historical process carefully rather than assume continuity a priori. Second, these processes of change were inevitably political, which involved negotiation among diverse groups across wide areas and within individual communities. New physical forms and their symbolic representations gain their social and political meanings in their historical contexts. Particularly important political effects possibly emerged when new forms and symbols succeeded to create a sense of timeless presence (Hobsbawm and Ranger 1992). This may be the case for E Groups in the Maya Lowlands during the Late Preclassic period. Third, for the residents of the Maya Lowlands before

700 BCE, E Group assemblages probably signaled their participation in the pattern of cultural practice shared across wide areas, possibly by different language groups. E Groups in the Maya Lowlands around 700 BCE were increasingly tied to celestial symbolism that superseded local settings of individual communities, although their original association with earthly symbolism was never lost. At the height of their constructions during the Late Preclassic period, Lowland Maya E Groups possibly represented their ties to the distant past more strongly, which were probably differentially claimed, embraced, and tolerated by diverse groups, including growing elites, ritual specialists, and commoners. Thus, the history of the E Group represents not a timeless, unchanged worldview but the process of constant invention and re-creation of new traditions.

Acknowledgments

I thank the organizers of the SFI conferences, David Freidel, Arlen Chase, and Anne Dowd, for the kind invitation, as well as Jeremy Sabloff and Jerry Murdock for their support and hospitality. Debra Walker, James Aimers, and Rebecca Mendelsohn provided thoughtful comments on an earlier draft.

References Cited

Agrinier, Pierre
1975 *Mounds 9 and 10 at Mirador, Chiapas, Mexico.* Papers of the New World Archaeological Foundation, No. 39. Brigham Young University, Provo, Utah.
2000 *Mound 27 and the Middle Preclassic Period at Mirador, Chiapas, Mexico.* Papers of the New World Archaeological Foundation, No. 58. Brigham Young University, Provo, Utah.

Aimers, James J., and Prudence M. Rice
2006 Astronomy, Ritual, and the Interpretation of Maya "E-Group" Architectural Assemblages. *Ancient Mesoamerica* 17:79–96.

Andrews, E. Wyllys, V
1990 Early Ceramic History of the Lowland Maya. In *Vision and Revision in Maya Studies*, edited by Peter Harrison and Flora Clancy, pp. 1–19. University of New Mexico Press, Albuquerque.

Arnold, Philip J., III
2009 Settlement and Subsistence among the Early Formative Gulf Olmec. *Journal of Anthropological Archaeology* 28:397–411.

Arroyo, Bárbara, Hector Neff, Deborah Pearsall, John Jones, and Dorothy Freidel
2002 Últimos resultados del proyecto sobre el medio ambiente antiguo en la Costa

del Pacífico. In *XV Simposio de Investigaciones Arqueológicas en Guatemala, 2001*, edited by Juan Pedro Laporte, Héctor Escobedo, and Bárbara Arroyo, pp. 376–364. Museo Nacional de Arqueología y Etnología, Guatemala City.

Ashmore, Wendy
1991 Site-Planning Principles and Concepts of Directionality among the Ancient Maya. *Latin American Antiquity* 2:199–226.

Ashmore, Wendy, and Jeremy A. Sabloff
2002 Spatial Orders in Maya Civic Plans. *Latin American Antiquity* 13:201–215.

Aveni, Anthony F.
2001 *Skywatchers: A Revised and Updated Version of Skywatchers of Ancient Mexico*. University of Texas Press, Austin.

Aveni, Anthony F., Anne S. Dowd, and Benjamin Vining
2003 Maya Calendar Reform? Evidence from Orientations of Specialized Architectural Assemblages. *Latin American Antiquity* 14:159–178.

Aveni, Anthony F., and Horst Hartung
1989 Uaxactun, Guatemala, Group E and Similar Assemblages: Archaeoastronomical Reconsideration. In *World Archaeoastronomy*, edited by Anthony Aveni, pp. 441–461. Cambridge University Press, Cambridge.

Bachand, Bruce R., Emiliano Gallaga Murieta, and Lynneth S. Lowe
2008 *The Chiapa de Corzo Archaeological Project: Report of the 2008 Field Season*. Report presented to the Instituto Nacional de Antropología e Historia, Mexico City.

Bachand, Bruce R., and Lynneth S. Lowe
2012 Chiapa de Corzo's Mound 11 Tomb and the Middle Formative Olmec. In *Arqueología reciente de Chiapas: Contribuciones del Encuentro Celebrado en el 60° Aniversario de la Fundación Arqueológica Nuevo Mundo*, edited by Lynneth S. Lowe and Mary E. Pye, pp. 45–68. Papers of the New World Archaeological Foundation, No. 72. Brigham Young University, Provo, Utah.

Blake, Michael
1991 An Emerging Formative Chiefdom at Paso de la Amada, Chiapas, Mexico. In *The Formation of Complex Society in Southeastern Mesoamerica*, edited by William L. Fowler, pp. 27–46. CRC Press, Boca Raton, Florida.
2011 Building History in Domestic and Public Space at Paso de la Amada: An Explanation of Mounds 6 and 7. In *Early Mesoamerican Social Transformations: Archaic and Formative Lifeways in the Soconusco Region*, edited by Richard G. Lesure, pp. 97–118. University of California Press, Berkeley.
2013 Solar Orientations and Formative Period Site Layouts in SE Mesoamerica: Sunrise and Sunset Alignments during the Equinoxes and Solstices. Paper Presented at the Annual Meeting of the Society for American Archaeology, Honolulu.
2015 *Maize for the Gods: Unearthing the 9,000-Year History of Corn*. University of California Press, Oakland.

Blake, Michael, John E. Clark, Barbara Voorhies, Michael W. Love, and Brian S. Chisholm
1992 Prehistoric Subsistence in the Soconusco Region. *Current Anthropology* 33:83–94.

Blake, Michael, Richard G. Lesure, John E. Clark, Warren D. Hill, and Luis Barbar
2006   The Residence of Power at Paso de La Amada, Mexico. In *Palaces and Power in the Americas: From Peru to the Northwest Coast*, edited by Jessica J. Christie and Patricia J. Sarro, pp. 191–210. University of Texas Press, Austin.

Brady, James E.
1997   Settlement Configuration and Cosmology: The Role of Caves at Dos Pilas. *American Anthropologist* 99:602–618.

Brotherston, Gordon
1976   Mesoamerican Description of Space II: Signs for Direction. *Ibero-Amerikanisches Archiv* NS 2(1):39–62.

Bryant, Douglas B., John E. Clark, and David Cheetham
2005   *Ceramic Sequence of the Upper Grijalva Region, Chiapas, Mexico.* Papers of the New World Archaeological Foundation, No. 67. Brigham Young University, Provo, Utah.

Bunzel, Ruth L.
1952   *Chichicastenango: A Guatemalan Village*. University of Washington Press, Seattle.

Carlson, John B.
1981   A Geomantic Model for the Interpretation of Mesoamerican Sites: An Essay in Cross-Cultural Comparison. In *Mesoamerican Sites and World-Views*, edited by Elizabeth P. Benson, pp. 143–215. Dumbarton Oaks Research Library and Collections, Washington, D.C.

Castillo, Victor
2013   Interregional Patterns and Local Developments of Early Elite Platforms at Ceibal, Guatemala. M.A. thesis, University of Arizona, Tucson.

Chase, Arlen F.
1983   *A Contextual Consideration of the Tayasal-Paxcaman Zone, El Petén, Guatemala.* Ph.D. dissertation, University of Pennsylvania, Philadelphia. University Microfilms/ProQuest, Ann Arbor.

Chase, Arlen F., and Diane Z. Chase
1995   External Impetus, Internal Synthesis, and Standardization: E-Group Assemblages and the Crystallization of Classic Maya Society in the Southern Lowlands. *Acta Mesoamericana* 8:87–101 (special issue edited by N. Grube entitled *The Emergence of Lowland Maya Civilization: The Transition from the Preclassic to Early Classic*).

Cheek, Charles
1977   Excavations at the Palangana and the Acropolis, Kaminaljuyu. In *Teotihuacan and Kaminaljuyu: A Study in Prehistoric Culture Contact*, edited by William T. Sanders and Joseph W. Michels, pp. 1–204. Pennsylvania State University Press, University Park.

Cheetham, David T.
2005   Cunil: A Pre-Mamom Horizon in the Southern Maya Lowlands. In *New Perspectives on Formative Mesoamerican Cultures*, edited by Terry G. Powis, pp. 27–38. BAR International Series, Vol. 1377. British Archaeological Reports, Oxford.

2010   America's First Colony: Olmec Materiality and Ethnicity at Canton Corralito, Chiapas, Mexico. Ph.D. dissertation, Arizona State University, Tempe.

Clark, John E.
2004   Mesoamerica Goes Public: Early Ceremonial Centers, Leaders, and Communities. In *Mesoamerican Archaeology: Theory and Practice*, edited by Rosemary A. Joyce and Julia A. Hendon, pp. 43–72. Blackwell, Malden, Massachusetts.

n.d.   Western Kingdoms of the Middle Preclassic. Manuscript on file, Department of Anthropology, Brigham Young University, Provo, Utah.

Clark, John E., and David Cheetham
2002   Mesoamerica's Tribal Foundations. In *Archaeology of Tribal Societies*, edited by W. A. Parkinson, pp. 278–339. Archaeological Series, Vol. 15. International Monograph in Prehistory, Ann Arbor.

Clark, John E., and Richard D. Hansen
2001   Architecture of Early Kingship: Comparative Perspectives on the Origins of the Maya Royal Court. *Royal Courts of the Ancient Maya: 2. Data and Case Studies*, edited by Takeshi Inomata and Stephen D. Houston, pp. 1–45. Westview Press, Boulder.

Clark, John E., Mary E. Pye, and D. C. Gosser
2007   Thermolithics and Corn Dependency in Mesoamerica. *Archaeology, Art, and Ethnogenesis in Mesoamerican Prehistory: Papers in Honor of Gareth W. Lowe*, edited by Lynneth S. Lowe and Mary E. Pye, pp. 23–42. Papers of the New World Archaeological Foundation, No. 68. Brigham Young University, Provo, Utah.

Coe, Michael D., and Richard A. Diehl
1980   *In the Land of the Olmec*. University of Texas Press, Austin.

Cohodas, Marvin
1980   Radial Pyramids and Radial Associated Assemblages of the Central Maya Area. *Journal of the Society of Architectural Historians* 39:208–223.

Cyphers, Ann
1997   Olmec Architecture at San Lorenzo. In *Olmec to Aztec: Settlement Patterns in the Ancient Gulf Lowlands*, edited by Barbara L. Stark and Philip J. Arnold III, pp. 96–114. University of Arizona Press, Tucson.

Cyphers, Ann, and Anna Di Castro
2009   Early Olmec Architecture and Imagery. In *Art of Urbanism: How Mesoamerican Kingdoms Represented Themselves in Architecture and Imagery*, edited by William L. Fash and Leonardo López Luján, pp. 21–52. Dumbarton Oaks Research Library and Collection, Washington, D.C.

Cyphers, Ann, and Timothy Murtha
2014   Early Olmec Open Spaces at San Lorenzo, Veracruz. In *Mesoamerican Plazas: Arenas of Community and Power*, edited by Kenichiro Tsukamoto and Takeshi Inomata, pp. 71–89. University of Arizona Press, Tucson.

Doyle, James
2012   Regroup on "E-Groups": Monumentality and Early Centers in the Middle Preclassic Maya Lowlands. *Latin American Antiquity* 23:355–379.

Drucker, Philip, Robert F. Heizer, and Robert H. Squier
1959   *Excavations at La Venta, Tabasco.* Bureau of American Ethnology Bulletin, Vol. 170. Smithsonian Institution, Washington, D.C.

Estrada-Belli, Francisco
2006   Lightning Sky, Rain, and the Maize God: The Ideology of Preclassic Maya Rulers at Cival, Peten, Guatemala. *Ancient Mesoamerica* 17:57–78.
2011   *The First Maya Civilization: Ritual and Power before the Classic Period.* Routledge, London.
2012   Early Civilization in the Maya Lowlands, Monumentality, and Place Making: A View from the Holmul Region. In *Early New World Monumentality*, edited by Richard L. Burger and Robert M. Rosenswig, pp. 198–230. University Press of Florida, Gainesville.

Freidel, David A., and F. Kent Reilly
2010   The Flesh of the God: Cosmology, Food, and the Origins of Political Power in Ancient Southeastern Mesoamerica. In *Pre-Columbian Foodways: Interdisciplinary Approaches to Food, Culture, and Markets in Mesoamerica*, edited by John E. Staller and Michael D. Carrasco, pp. 635–680. Springer-Verlag, New York.

González Lauck, Rebecca
1990   The 1984 Archaeological Investigations at La Venta, Tabasco, Mexico. Ph.D. dissertation, University of California, Berkeley, Berkeley.
2010   The Architectural Setting of Olmec Sculpture Clusters at La Venta, Tabasco. In *The Place of Stone Monuments: Context, Use, and Meaning in Mesoamerica's Preclassic Tradition*, edited by Julia Guernsey, John E. Clark, and Bárbara Arroyo, pp. 177–205. Dumbarton Oaks Research Library and Collection, Washington, D.C.

Gossen, Gary H.
1974   *Chamulas in the World of the Sun: Time and Space in a Maya Oral Tradition.* Harvard University Press, Cambridge, Massachusetts.

Götting, Eva
2011   Excavaciones en el Edificio H-XVI (Operación 12). *Proyecto Arqueológico SAHI-Uaxactun Informe no. 2: Temporada De Campo 2010*, edited by Milan Kováč and Ernesto Arredondo Leiva, pp. 479–504. Report presented to the Instituto de Antropología e Historia de Guatemala, Guatemala City.

Hanks, William F.
1990   *Referential Practice: Language and Lived Space among the Maya.* University of Chicago Press, Chicago.

Hansen, Richard D.
1998   Continuity and Disjunction: The Pre-Classic Antecedents of Classic Maya Architecture. In *Function and Meaning in Classic Maya Architecture*, edited by Stephen D. Houston, pp. 49–122. Dumbarton Oaks Research Library and Collection, Washington, D.C.

Henderson, Lucia R.
2013   Bodies Politic, Bodies in Stone: Imagery of the Human and the Divine in the Sculpture of Late Preclassic Kaminaljuyú, Guatemala. Ph.D. dissertation, Department of Art and Art History, University of Texas, Austin.
2015   Donde hay humo, hay fuego: La búsqueda de la imaginería de volcanes en las tierras altas y la costa sur. In *XXVIII Simposio de Investigaciones Arqueológicas en Guatemala, 2014*, edited by Bárbara Arroyo, Luis Méndez Salinas, and Lorena Paiz, pp. 731–746. Museo Nacional de Arqueología y Etnología, Guatemala City.

Hicks, Frederick, and Charles E. Rosaire
1960   *Mound 13, Chiapa de Corzo, Chiapas, Mexico*. Papers of the New World Archaeological Foundation, No. 10. Brigham Young University, Provo, Utah.

Hobsbawm, E. J., and T. O. Ranger
1992   *The Invention of Tradition*. Cambridge University Press, Cambridge.

Hodgson, John G., John G. Clark, and Emiliano Gallaga Murrieta
2010   Ojo de Agua Monument 3: A New Olmec-Style Sculpture from Ojo de Agua, Chiapas, Mexico. *Mexicon* 32:139–144.

Ichon, Alain, and Marie-Charlotte Arnauld
1985   *Le Protoclassique à La Lagunita, El Quiché, Guatemala*. Centre National de la Recherche Scientifique, Institut d'Ethnologie, Paris.

Inomata, Takeshi
2016   The Emergence of Standardized Spatial Plans in Southern Mesoamerica: Chronology and Inter-Regional Interactions Viewed from Ceibal, Guatemala. *Ancient Mesoamerica*. In press.

Inomata, Takeshi, and Lucia R. Henderson
2016   Time Tested: Revised Thoughts on Chronology, Sculptural Traditions, Interaction, and Social Change in Preclassic Southern Mesoamerica. *Antiquity* 90(350):456–471.

Inomata, Takeshi, Jessica MacLellan, and Melissa Burham
2015a   The Construction of Public and Domestic Spheres in the Preclassic Maya Lowlands. *American Anthropologist* 117:519–534.

Inomata, Takeshi, Jessica MacLellan, Daniela Triadan, Jessica Munson, Melissa Burham, Kazuo Aoyama, Hiroo Nasu, Flory Pinzon, and Hitoshi Yonenobu
2015b   Development of Sedentary Communities in the Maya Lowlands: Coexisting Mobile Groups and Public Ceremonies at Ceibal, Guatemala. *Proceedings of the National Academy of Sciences of the United States of America* 112(14):4268–4273.

Inomata, Takeshi, Daniela Triadan, Kazuo Aoyama, Victor Castillo, and Hitoshi Yonenobu
2013   Early Ceremonial Constructions at Ceibal, Guatemala, and the Origins of Lowland Maya Civilization. *Science* 340(6131):467–471.

Inomata, Takeshi, Daniela Triadan, and Otto Rodrigo Román
2010   La transformación y continuidad de ritos durante el período Preclásico en Ceibal, Guatemala. *El ritual en el mundo maya: De lo privado a lo público*, edited by Andrés Ciudad Ruiz, María Josefa Iglesias Ponce de León, and Miguel Sorroche, pp. 29–48. Sociedad Española de Estudios Mayas, Madrid.

Joyce, Rosemary A.
2004   Unintended Consequences?: Monumentality as a Novel Experience in Formative Mesoamerica. *Journal of Archaeological Method and Theory* 11:5–29.

Laporte, Juan Pedro, and Vilma Fialko
1995   Reencuentro con Mundo Perdido, Tikal, Guatemala. *Ancient Mesoamerica* 6:41–94.

LeCount, Lisa J., and David W. Mixter (editors)
2016   *Actuncan Archaeological Project: Report of the 2015 Field Season*. Report submitted to the Belizean Institute of Archaeology, Belmopan.

Lee, Thomas A., Jr.
1974   *Mound 4 Excavations at San Isidro, Chiapas, Mexico*. Papers of the New World Archaeological Foundation, No. 34. Brigham Young University, Provo, Utah.
1989   Chiapas and the Olmec. In *Regional Perspectives on the Olmec*, edited by Robert J. Sharer and David C. Grove, pp. 198–226. Cambridge University Press, Cambridge.

Lesure, Richard G.
2011   Paso de la Amada as Ceremonial Center. In *Early Mesoamerican Social Transformations: Archaic and Formative Lifeways in the Soconusco Region*, edited by Richard G. Lesure, pp. 119–145. University of California Press, Berkeley.

Lesure, Richard G. (editor)
2009   *Settlement and Subsistence in Early Formative Soconusco: El Varal and the Problem of Inter-Site Assemblage Variation*. Cotsen Institute of Archaeology, UCLA, Los Angeles.

Lesure, Richard G., and Michael Blake
2002   Interpretive Challenges in the Study of Early Complexity: Economy, Ritual, and Architecture at Paso de la Amada, Mexico. *Journal of Anthropological Archaeology* 21:1–24.

Lohse, Jon C.
2010   Archaic Origins of the Lowland Maya. *Latin American Antiquity* 21:312–352.

Love, Michael W.
1999   Ideology, Material Culture, and Daily Practice in Pre-Classic Mesoamerica: A Pacific Coast Perspective. In *Social Patterns in Pre-Classic Mesoamerica*, edited by David C. Grove and Rosemary A. Joyce, pp. 127–153. Dumbarton Oaks Research Library and Collection, Washington, D.C.
2013   La Blanca and the MFC Architectural Pattern. Paper presented at the annual meeting of the Society for American Archaeology, Honolulu.

Love, Michael, and Julia Guernsey
2011   La Blanca and the Soconusco Middle Formative. In *Early Mesoamerican Social Transformations: Archaic and Formative Lifeways in the Soconusco Region*, edited by Richard G. Lesure, pp. 170–188. University of California Press, Berkeley.

Lowe, Gareth W.
1962   *Mound 5 and Minor Excavations, Chiapa de Corzo, Chiapas, Mexico*. Brigham Young University, Provo, Utah.
1977   The Mixe-Zoque as Competing Neighbors of the Early Lowland Maya. In *The

    Origins of Maya Civilization, edited by Richard E. W. Adams, pp. 197–248. University of New Mexico Press, Albuquerque.
1981   Olmec Horizon Defined in Mound 20, San Isidro, Chiapas. In *The Olmec and Their Neighbors*, edited by Michael D. Coe and David Grove, pp. 231–256. Dumbarton Oaks Research Library and Collection, Washington, D.C.
1989   The Heartland Olmec: Evolution of Material Culture. In *Regional Perspectives on the Olmec*, edited by Robert J. Sharer and David C. Grove, pp. 33–67. Cambridge University Press, Cambridge.
2007   Early Formative Chiapas: The Beginnings of Civilization in the Central Depression of Chiapas. In *Archaeology, Art, and Ethnogenesis in Mesoamerican Prehistory: Papers in Honor of Gareth W. Lowe*, edited by Lynneth S. Lowe and Mary E. Pye, pp. 63–108. Papers of the New World Archaeological Foundation, No. 68. Brigham Young University, Provo, Utah.

Lowe, Gareth W., and Pierre Agrinier
1960   *Mound 1, Chiapa de Corzo, Chiapas, Mexico*. Papers of the New World Archaeological Foundation, No. 8. Brigham Young University, Provo, Utah.

Lowe, Gareth W., Thomas A. Lee, and Eduardo Martínez E.
1982   *Izapa: An Introduction to the Ruins and Monuments*. Papers of the New World Archaeological Foundation, No. 31. Brigham Young University, Provo, Utah.

Malmström, Vincent H.
1978   A Reconstruction of the Chronology of Mesoamerican Calendrical Systems. *Journal of the History of Astronomy* 9:105–116.

Mason, J. Alden
1960   *Mound 12, Chiapa de Corzo, Chiapas, Mexico*. Papers of the New World Archaeological Foundation, No. 9. Brigham Young University, Provo, Utah.

McAnany, Patricia A.
1995   *Living with the Ancestors: Kinship and Kingship in Ancient Maya Society*. University of Texas Press, Austin.

McAnany, Patricia A. (editor)
2004   *K'axob: Ritual, Work and Family in an Ancient Maya Village*. Monumenta Archaeologica, Vol. 22. University of California Los Angeles, Cotsen Institute of Archaeology, Los Angeles.

McDonald, Andrew J.
1983   *Tzutzuculi: A Middle-Preclassic Site on the Pacific Coast of Chiapas, Mexico*. Papers of the New World Archaeological Foundation, No. 47. Brigham Young University, Provo, Utah.
1999   Middle Formative Pyramidal Platform Complexes in Southern Chiapas, Mexico: Structure and Meaning. Ph.D. dissertation, University of Texas, Austin.

Miller, Donald E.
2014   *Excavations at La Libertad, a Middle Formative Ceremonial Center in Chiapas, Mexico*. Papers of the New World Archaeological Foundation, No. 64. Brigham Young University, Provo, Utah.

Munson, Jessica
2012   Building on the Past: Temple Histories and Communities of Practice at Caobal, Petén, Guatemala. Ph.D. dissertation, University of Arizona, Tucson.

Murdy, Carson
1990   Tradiciones de arquitectura prehispánica en el Valle de Guatemala. *Anales de la Academia de Geografía e Historia de Guatemala* 64:349–397.

Ortiz C., Ponciano, and María del Carmen Rodríguez
1999   Olmec Ritual Behavior at El Manatí: A Sacred Space. In *Social Patterns in Pre-Classic Meosamerica*, edited by David C. Grove and Rosemary A. Joyce, pp. 225–254. Dumbarton Oaks Research Library and Collection, Washington, D.C.

Palka, Joel W.
2002   Left/Right Symbolism and the Body in Ancient Maya Iconography and Culture. *Latin American Antiquity* 13:419–443.

Pinzón, Flory María, and Sebastién De Muylder
2014   Excavaciones en la Plaza Central: Operaciónes CB203K y CB203L. Proyecto Arqueológico Ceibal-Petexbatún: Informe de la Temporada de Campo 2014, edited by Flory M. Pinzón and Takeshi Inomata, pp. 7–28. Report presented to the Instituto de Antropología e Historia de Guatemala, Guatemala City.

Pope, Kevin O., Mary E. D. Pohl, John G. Jones, David L. Lentz, Christopher L. Von Nagy, Francisco J. Vega, and Irv Quitmyer
2001   Origin and Environmental Setting of Ancient Agriculture in the Lowlands of Mesoamerica. *Science* 292(5520):1370–1372.

Pye, Mary E., Arthur A. Demarest, and Bárbara Arroyo
1999   Early Formative Societies in Guatemala and El Salvador. In *Pacific Latin America in Prehistory: The Evolution of Archaic and Formative Cultures*, edited by Michael Blake, pp. 75–88. Washington State University Press, Pullman.

Raab, L. Mark, Matthew A. Boxt, Katherine Bradford, Brian A. Stokes, and Rebecca B. González Lauck
2000   Testing at Isla Alor in the La Venta Olmec Hinterland. *Journal of Field Archaeology* 27(3):257–270.

Ricketson, Oliver G., Jr.
1928   Notes on Two Maya Astronomic Observatories. *American Anthropologist* 30:434–444.

Ricketson, Oliver Garrison, and Edith Bayles Ricketson
1937   *Uaxactun, Guatemala. Group E—1926–1931*. Carnegie Institution of Washington Publication, Vol. 477. Carnegie institution of Washington, Washington, D.C.

Rodríguez, María del Carmen, and Ponciano Ortiz C.
2000   A Massive Offering of Axes at La Merced, Hidalgotitlán, Veracruz, Mexico. In *Olmec Art and Archaeology in Mesoamerica*, edited by John E. Clark and Mary E. Pye, pp. 155–167. National Gallery of Art, Washington, D.C.
2010   Plates 49–51. In *Olmec: Colossal Masterworks of Ancient Mexico*, edited by Kathleen Berrin and Virginia M. Fields, pp. 140–143. Fine Arts Museums of San Francisco and Los Angeles County Museum of Art, San Francisco.

Rosal, Marco A., Juan Antonio Valdés, and Juan Pedro Laporte
1993   Nuevas exploraciones en el Grupo E, Uaxactún. In *Tikal y Uaxactún en el Pre-*

clásico, edited by Juan P. Laporte and Juan A. Valdés, pp. 70–91. Universidad Nacional Autónoma de México, Mexico City.

Rosenswig, Robert M.
2010   *The Beginnings of Mesoamerican Civilization: Inter-Regional Interaction and the Olmec*. Cambridge University Press, Cambridge.
2011   An Early Mesoamerican Archipelago of Complexity. In *Early Mesoamerican Social Transformations: Archaic and Formative Lifeways in the Soconusco Region*, edited by Richard G. Lesure, pp. 242–271. University of California Press, Berkeley.

Rosenswig, Robert M., Ricardo López-Torrijos, and Caroline E. Antonelli
2014   LiDAR Data and the Izapa Polity: New Results and Methodological Issues from Tropical Mesoamerica. *Archaeological and Anthropological Sciences*. http://link.springer.com/article/10.1007/s12520-014-0210-7#, accessed on September 20, 2015.

Rosenswig, Robert M., Ricardo López-Torrijos, Caroline E. Antonelli, and Rebecca R. Mendelsohn
2013   LiDAR Mapping and Surface Survey of the Izapa State on the Tropical Piedmont of Chiapas, Mexico. *Journal of Archaeological Science* 40(3):1493–1507.

Ruppert, Karl
1940   A Special Assemblage of Maya Structures. In *Maya and Their Neighbors: Essays on Middle American Anthropology and Archaeology*, edited by Clarence L. Hay, Ralph L. Linton, Samuel K. Lothrop, Harry L. Shapiro, and George C. Vaillant, pp. 222–231. D. Appleton-Century, New York.

Rust, William F.
2008   A Settlement Survey of La Venta, Tabasco, Mexico. Ph.D. dissertation, University of Pennsylvania, Philadelphia.

Schele, Linda, and David A. Freidel
1990   *A Forest of Kings: The Untold Story of the Ancient Maya*. Morrow, New York.

Schele, Linda, and Peter Mathews
1998   *The Code of Kings: The Language of Seven Sacred Maya Temples and Tombs*. Scribner, New York.

Schieber de Lavarreda, Christa
2002   La ofrenda de Abaj Takalik. In *XV Simposio de Investigaciones Arqueológicas en Guatemala, 2001*, edited by Juan P. Laporte, Héctor L. Escobedo, and Bárbara Arroyo, pp. 459–473. Museo Nacional de Arqueología y Etnología, Ministerio de Cultura y Deportes, Asociación Tikal, Guatemala City.

Schieber de Lavarreda, Christa, and Miguel Orrego Corzo
2010   Preclassic Olmec and Maya Monuments and Architecture at Takalik Abaj. In *The Place of Stone Monuments: Context, Use, and Meaning in Mesoamerica's Preclassic Tradition*, edited by Julia Guernsey, John E. Clark, and Bárbara Arroyo, pp. 177–205. Dumbarton Oaks Research Library and Collection, Washington, D.C.

Sharer, Robert J., and David W. Sedat
1987   *Archaeological Investigations in the Northern Maya Highlands, Guatemala: Interaction and the Development of Maya Civilization*. University Museum

Monograph, Vol. 59. University Museum, University of Pennsylvania, Philadelphia.

Sisson, Edward B.
1976   Archaeological Survey of the Chontalpa Region, Tabasco, Mexico. Ph.D. dissertation, Harvard University, Cambridge, Massachusetts.

Smith, A. Ledyard
1982   *Excavations at Seibal, Department of Peten, Guatemala: Major Architecture and Caches.* Memoirs of the Peabody Museum of Archaeology and Ethnology, Vol. 15, No. 1. Gordon R. Willey, series editor. Harvard University, Cambridge, Massachusetts.

Stanton, Travis W., and David A. Freidel
2003   Ideological Lock-In and the Dynamics of Formative Religions in Mesoamerica. *Mayab* 16:5–14.

Stuart, David
2002   Glyphs for "Right" and "Left"? http://www.mesoweb.com/stuart/notes/RighLeft.pdf, accessed on September 22, 2015.

Tourtellot, Gair, III
1988   *Excavations at Seibal, Department of Peten, Guatemala: Peripheral Survey and Excavation, Settlement and Community Patterns.* Memoirs of the Peabody Museum of Archaeology and Ethnology, Vol. 16. Gordon R. Willey, series editor. Harvard University, Cambridge, Massachusetts.

Treat, Raymond
1986   *Early and Middle Formative Sub-Mound Refuse Deposits at Vistahermosa, Chiapas.* Notes of the New World Archaeological Foundation, No. 2. Brigham Young University, Provo, Utah.

Valdés, Juan Antonio
1995   Desarrollo cultural y señales de alarma entre los mayas: el Preclásico Tardío y la transición hacia el Clásico Temprano. In *Emergence of Lowland Maya Civilization: The Transition from the Preclassic to the Early Classic*, edited by Nikolai Grube, pp. 71–85. Acta Mesoamericana, Vol. 8. Verlag Anton Saurwein, Möckmühl, Germany.

Vogt, Evon Z.
1969   *Zinacantán: A Maya Community in the Highlands of Chiapas.* Belknap Press of Harvard University Press, Cambridge, Massachusetts.

Von Nagy, Christopher L.
2003   Of Meandering Rivers and Shifting Towns: Landscape Evolution and Community within the Grijalva Delta. Ph.D. dissertation, Tulane University, New Orleans.

Watanabe, John M.
1983   In the World of the Sun: A Cognitive Model of Mayan Cosmology. *Man* NS 18:710–728.

Willey, Gordon R.
1977   The Rise of Classic Maya Civilization: A Pasión Valley Perspective. In *Origins of Maya Civilization*, edited by Richard E. W. Adams, pp. 133–157. University of New Mexico Press, Albuquerque.

Wisdom, Charles
1940 *The Chorti Indians of Guatemala*. University of Chicago Press, Chicago.
Źrałka, Jarosław, Wiesław Koszkul, Simon Martin, and Bernard Hermes
2011 In the Path of the Maize God: A Royal Tomb at Nakum, Petén, Guatemala. *Antiquity* 85:890–908.

8

A Tale of Two E Groups

El Palmar and Tikal, Petén, Guatemala

JAMES A. DOYLE

During the Preclassic period (1000 BCE–250 CE), generations of residents at two neighboring Maya Lowland communities, within sight of one another, centered themselves on large gathering spaces of similar dimensions and building configurations. Residents of both places practiced local traditions of architectural and material production, perhaps subject to wider ideational trends, shared over time through a similar language and symbolic inventory. With their gathering spaces, perhaps they were consciously connecting or making a statement to each other. They clearly shared something, visible in common social trajectories, but marked with a spatial separation that suggests political autonomy. Stark similarities within the construction of the communities' main plazas raise two important questions about the nature of building trends, First, were grander designs at work, such as the replication of cosmic concepts as tangible and visible things? Second, did peoples' movement incite collaboration or mimicry by the builders of each public space?

Building on prior arguments that these two communities, Tikal and El Palmar, Petén, Guatemala, likely lived similar daily experiences through the activities in their centers, organized around their respective E Group architecture (Doyle 2012), this chapter explores in depth the chronological relationships between the major buildings at both sites (Figure 8.1). The main objective in elaborating the temporal sequence is to suggest that two multigenerational communities with shared culture can shed light on the development of Preclassic lifeways intricately related with evolving Maya monumentality. Additionally, Tikal, which later became one of the greatest Maya royal capitals, and El Palmar, which was abandoned and sparsely occupied after about 100 CE, create a stark comparison of how some communities resisted social rupture more than others at the end of the Late

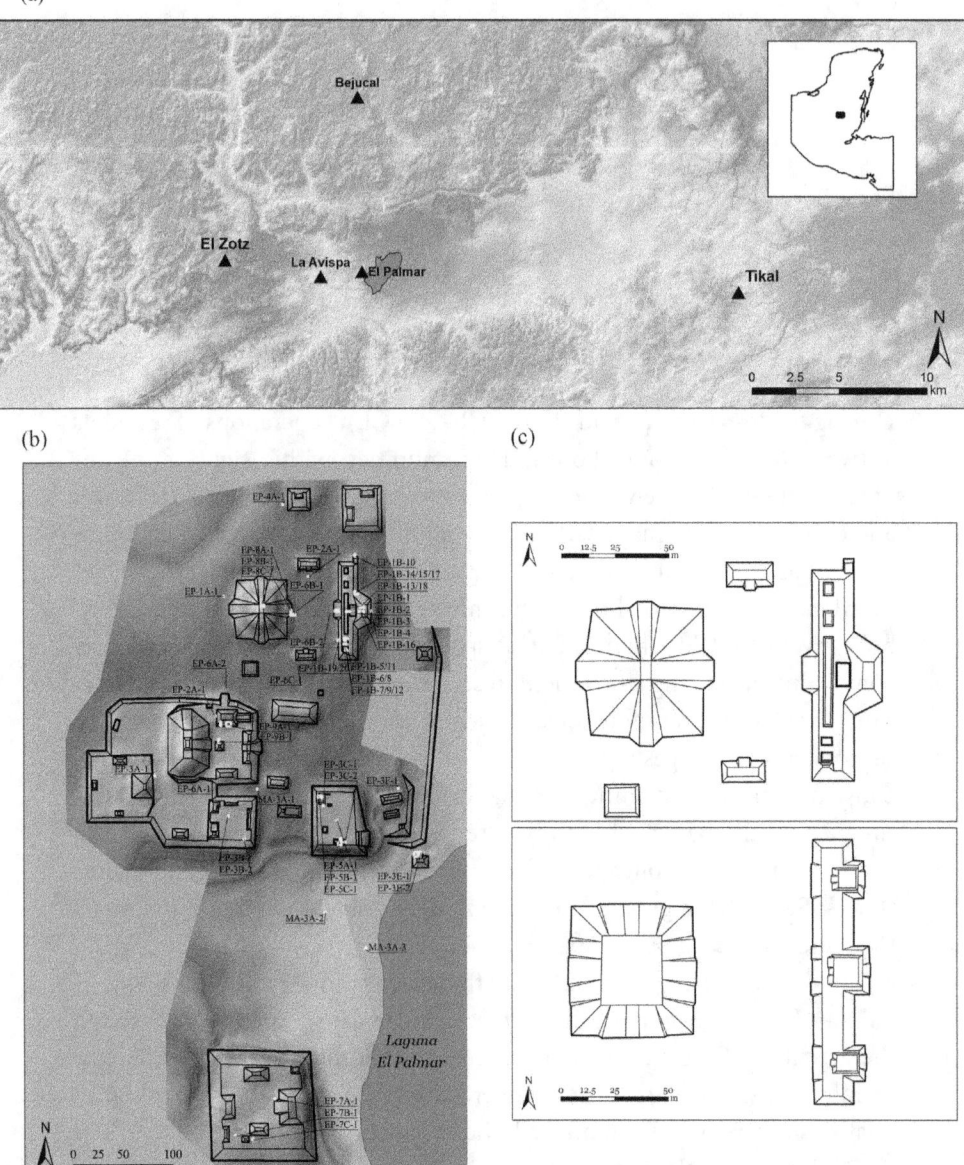

Figure 8.1. (a) Map of major sites near El Palmar and Tikal; (b) map of El Palmar with locations of major excavations; (c) comparison of Late Preclassic E Groups at El Palmar (*above*) and Tikal (*below*).

Preclassic. The evidence supports the claim that autonomous communities expressed wider cycles during the Middle and early Late Preclassic periods, probably along a solar-calendrical-agricultural spectrum, through similar spatial arrangements and periodic expansions. The combinations of environmental change and shifts in the political landscape at the end of the Preclassic period undermined the social connections in certain homelands, however, and caused new relationships to recombine around more desirable new places.

The Mamom Effect in the Central Lowlands

As Takeshi Inomata and colleagues (Inomata et al. 2013; Chapter 7 in this volume) have shown, the Middle and Late Preclassic Maya adopted the E Group as a conceptual community center after 800 BCE. I have argued that the specific spots on the landscape chosen for Middle Preclassic E Groups could have been those places with optimal sight lines or vistas of the surrounding landscape: it was important to "perceive the limits of one's community in relation to neighboring settlements" and to "create and maintain distance from others" (Doyle 2012:370). Moreover, the E Group was a "civic requirement for sociopolitical units, a space and monumental architectural formation necessary for settlers to interact with one another" (Doyle 2012:369; see also Ashmore 2005:40). Interaction played a vital role in this model of Middle Preclassic communities with E Groups, both in intracommunity daily life within the plaza spaces and in the buzz of people periodically journeying to various E Groups near their homes. Many confirmed and possible Middle Preclassic E Group centers are similar in scale to Tikal and El Palmar (Figure 8.2).

It is clear that that the spread of Mamom-type ceramic forms and finishes among potters at different communities is related to the seemingly contemporaneous spread of Lowland Maya E Groups. It is a bit of a chicken-and-egg situation due to the imprecise chronologies of most sites apart from Ceibal, but in general the architectural and ceramic patterns converge between 700 and 400 BCE. At present, it is clear that Tikal has Early Eb ceramics that date from 1000/900–700 BCE, but extensive work did not find architecture associated with these early remains (Inomata n.d.). Late Eb ceramics, dating between 700 and 600 BCE and sharing features with early Mamom ceramics (Inomata n.d.), were recovered in the earliest phase of the Mundo Perdido E Group. In the present chapter, I compare the architectural techniques and chronology of Structure 5C-54 of Mundo

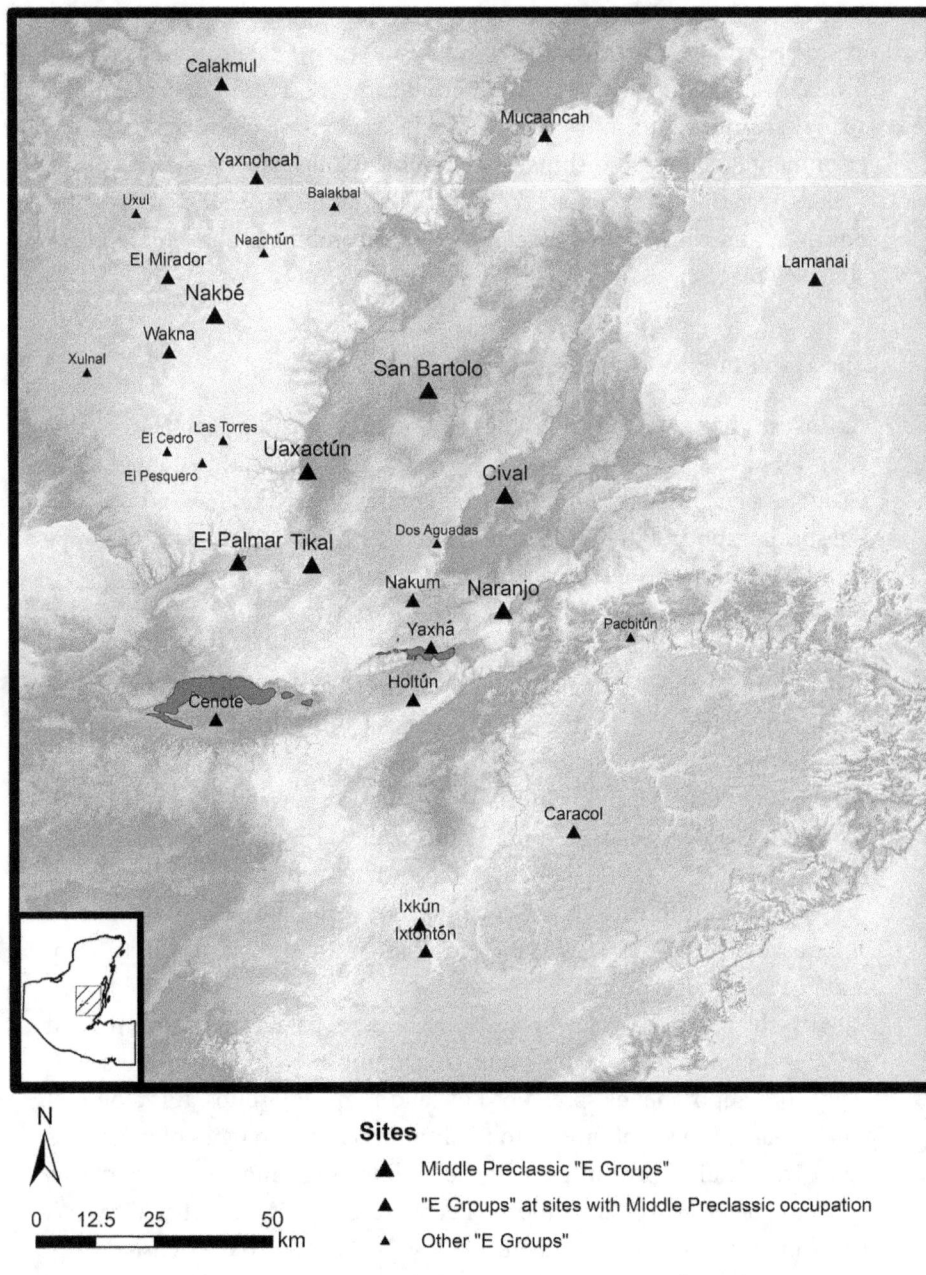

Figure 8.2. Map of possible or confirmed Middle Preclassic E Groups in the Central Southern Lowlands.

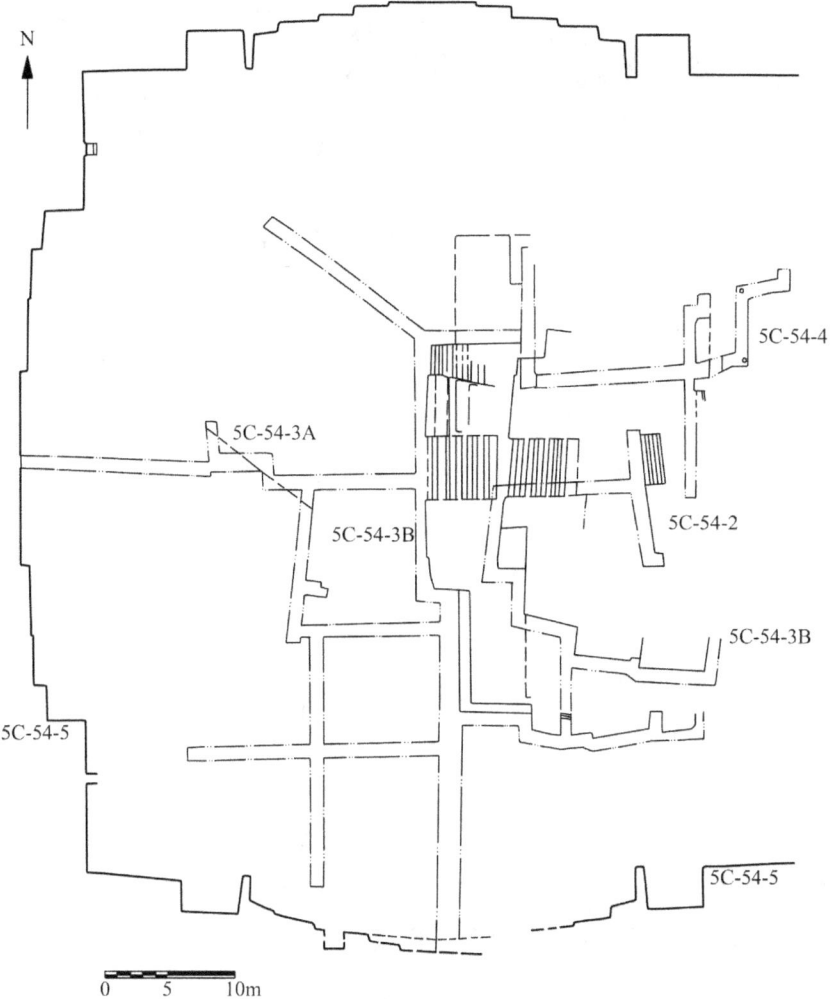

Figure 8.3. Plan view of excavations in Mundo Perdido Structure 5C-54, Tikal. Redrawn after Laporte 1983; see also Laporte 1997:Figure 2.

Perdido, Tikal, and Structure E4-1 of the E Group at El Palmar (Figure 8.3). These two buildings, the respective western radial E Group pyramids at each site, present sealed archaeological contexts in well-preserved architectural phases that facilitate chronological comparison.

The earliest ceramics from El Palmar correspond to this Late Eb or Early Tzec Phase, known as early Mamom sphere in the Uaxactún sequence (Figure 8.4). I have divided the Middle Preclassic ceramics from El Palmar based on stratigraphy into Early Mamom and Late Mamom. From the

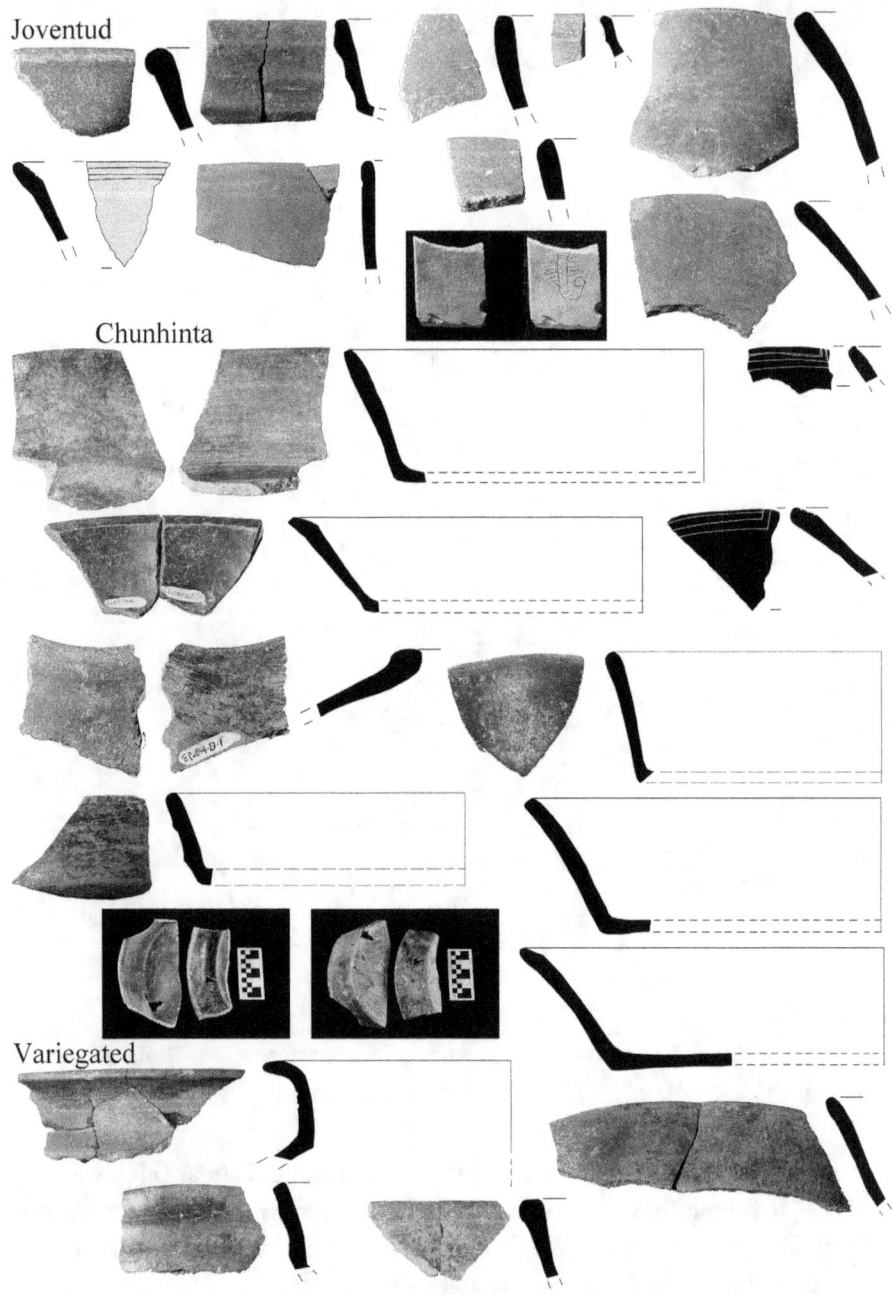

Figure 8.4. Early Mamom ceramics from El Palmar Structure E4-1, Units EP-8A-12/13/14/15.

radial E Group pyramid, Structure E4-1, several suggestive patterns about the earliest ceramics at El Palmar emerged. Although the sample is small (1,509 sherds), the groups represented are Achiotes unslipped (360 sherds, 23.86 percent), Chunhinta Black (136 sherds, 9.01 percent), Joventud Red (117 sherds, 7.75 percent), Pital Cream (38 sherds, 2.52 percent), Savanna Orange (7 sherds, 0.46 percent), and Variegated Indeterminate (80 sherds, 5.30 percent); eroded sherds (580, 38.44 percent) and sherds left for future residue analysis (191, 12.66 percent) made up roughly half the sample. Overall, the average wall thickness (<1 cm) and bowl radii (13.47 cm) were lower than subsequent ceramic phases. These ceramics come from strata within Structures E4-1-4th and E4-1-5th.

One clear feature of early Mamom ceramics at El Palmar is a prevalence of the variegated or mottled color palette. What this suggests to the modern observer is either intentional variation of the firing environment to produce the differential slip colors or a lack of control of the firing environment. For example, the potters of two semicomplete bowls with similar slip mottling seem to have intended a mostly black slip, but are the cream to red areas mistakes or part of a purposeful aesthetic? In the radial pyramid sample and other parts of El Palmar, early Mamom surface treatments include postfire incisions, chamfering, shallow fluting, and bichrome rim treatments (for example, red-on-cream) (Figure 8.4). Although not found in high frequency, chamfered plates (13 sherds) are more common in early Mamom at El Palmar, as noted in other Lowland samples (Takeshi Inomata, personal communication, 2013).

Early Mamom or Late Eb/Early Tzec architecture at Tikal and El Palmar is strikingly similar. Juan Pedro Laporte (1997) provided the original description of the earliest phase of the Mundo Perdido radial pyramid, Structure 5C-54. Although it was published in the proceedings of the annual Guatemalan Symposium in 1997, I have gone back to the report of field investigations on file with the Centro de Investigaciones Regionales de Mesoamérica (CIRMA), which includes details in text and figures that did not appear in the published version. As Laporte (1983: 1-20–1-23) noted, the earliest phase of the Mundo Perdido radial pyramid (Structure 5C-54-1) included block construction, *bajo* (wetland) mud, and rudimentary or damaged stucco deposits. At El Palmar, the earliest structure (E4-1-6th) encountered was known from a corner of the façade or staircase made out of hard limestone blocks constructed above bedrock. This structure was built very close to bedrock, suggesting that it was one of the earliest, if not the earliest, version of the western pyramidal platform, corresponding to the Mundo Perdido Structure 5C-54-1. A possible posthole, filled with dark mud that included a polished biface reduction flake of blue jade (Zachary Hruby, personal communication, 2011), perhaps held a superstructure associated with the earliest phase.

This flake is consistent with the "blue" jadeite common in other Middle Preclassic deposits and contexts (Estrada-Belli 2006:59). The blue jade flake hints at similar symbolic deposits found at Ceibal and Cival, although more evidence is needed. The fact that the flake (presumably kept and polished rather than discarded as debitage) lacked any sort of perforation indicative of other use is suggestive of its value based solely on the source material rather than on function.

The following construction phases at Mundo Perdido (5C-54-2A and 2B) and at El Palmar (E4-1-5th) share very similar sequences of construction fill that encased the earliest building (Figure 8.5). Laporte (1983:1-18-1-20) described 5C-54-2A and 2B as having four tiers created on a fill with "an abundance of small stones with low levels of dark soil in slanted layers, it is loose and prone to settling; this filling is covered by a filling of dark soil and crushed limestone with a large quantity of medium and large stones."[1] Like 5C-54-2, El Palmar Structure E4-1-5th displayed a substantial increase in volume from the prior structure and consisted of a sandy, tightly packed fill and stone-lined platforms and staircase. Although scant materials were found within the construction fill, the few sherds show production techniques similar to early Mamom Complex materials from elsewhere in the Lowlands, which tentatively dates this phase to approximately 600 BCE. Fill was tightly packed and yielded the earliest waxy-slipped Mamom ceramics from El Palmar. One semicomplete bowl mentioned above was perhaps cached as a dedicatory offering on the east–west axis while builders constructed the tamped-earth floor. A notable lack of plaster coatings from the earliest two phases suggests that builders at El Palmar in the Middle Preclassic did not yet incorporate plaster into the façades, which differs from the way in which Laporte (1983) describes Tikal. This is consistent with the early constructions at Cuello and other early sites, indicating that plaster at this time was strictly reserved for use surfaces such as floors, stairs, and other architectural features.

The middle to late Mamom Phase architecture represents a noteworthy advance in architectural practice at El Palmar and Tikal. The following phase of El Palmar, Structure E4-1-4th, was the final enlargement of the pyramid in the Middle Preclassic, in a style similar to Middle Preclassic buildings encountered in Nakbé (Hansen 1998:59, Figure 6, 62, Figure 9).

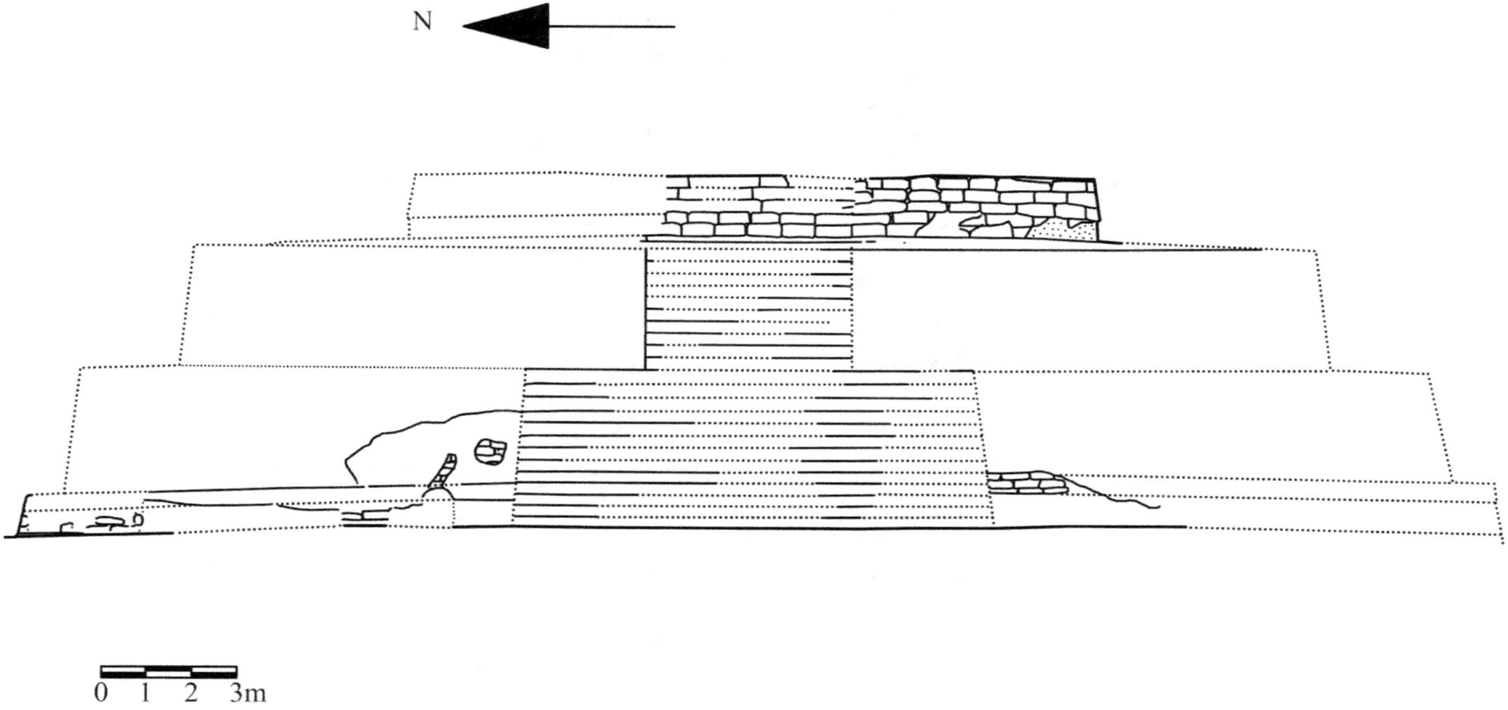

Figure 8.5. Tikal Structure 5C-54-2, west elevation. Redrawn by the author after Paulino Morales in Laporte 1983.

Figure 8.6. El Palmar Structure E4-1-4th.

The building contained an intricate façade composed almost entirely of long, flat cut stones (Figure 8.6). The dark mud fills of this structure, discussed in detail in prior publications (for example, Doyle 2012), included large quantities of Mamom Complex ceramics, figurines (Chapter 5 in this volume), and early stage stone tool production debitage and yielded radiocarbon dates for the organic sediment, likely from the nearby laguna, deposited originally between 1800 and 1600 BCE. The stratigraphy of this layer and the exceptional preservation of the ceramics could suggest that the artifacts were included in the fill as the builders covered Structure E4-1-5th, rather than being refuse that ended up in the mud before extraction. Flat stones were vertically stacked and filled with a masonry mortar, including possible stucco at the corner seams. A layer of thick white stucco not evident on the façade covered the Middle Preclassic staircase. After encasing E4-1-5th in the dark mud, builders deposited a layer almost entirely composed of chert flakes and nodules. Excavators noted similar layers in the Ventanas pyramid at San Bartolo (Urquizú and Saturno 2004:611) and other sites.

Excavations at Mundo Perdido Tikal reported similar layers during this later Mamom Phase (Tzec-Chuen) architecture, most notably the dark soil with few stone inclusions. Laporte (1983:1-17–1-18) reported that the building "presents a good quality construction technique, with a compact and uniform fill composed of dark and light soil without stone inclusions."[2] The following phase at Mundo Perdido, divided into 5C-54-3-A and 5C-54-3-B, however, bears features more similar to El Palmar Structure E4-1-4th (Figure 8.7; translated from Laporte 1983: 1-14–1-17):

> They are fills of compacted soil and rocks of all sizes, with good consistency; only some sectors contain looser fills. Retention walls were detected. Also there are construction walls in the lower tiers, marking the limit or plan of the structure and its core. The exterior walls are composed of larger stones, cut and placed in brick form . . . The building presents a coarse finish.[3]

Late Mamom ceramics in E4-1 were recovered in the fills of Structure E4-1-3rd, which covered Structure E4-1-4th completely. From a total of 883 sherds, groups represented included Achiotes unslipped (72 sherds, 8.15 percent), Chunhinta black (178 sherds, 20.16 percent), Joventud Red (79 sherds, 8.95 percent), Pital cream (69 sherds, 7.81 percent), Savana Orange (1 sherd, 0.11 percent), Sierra Red (2 sherds, 0.23 percent), and Variegated indeterminate (68 sherds, 7.70 percent); eroded sherds (414) made up 46.89

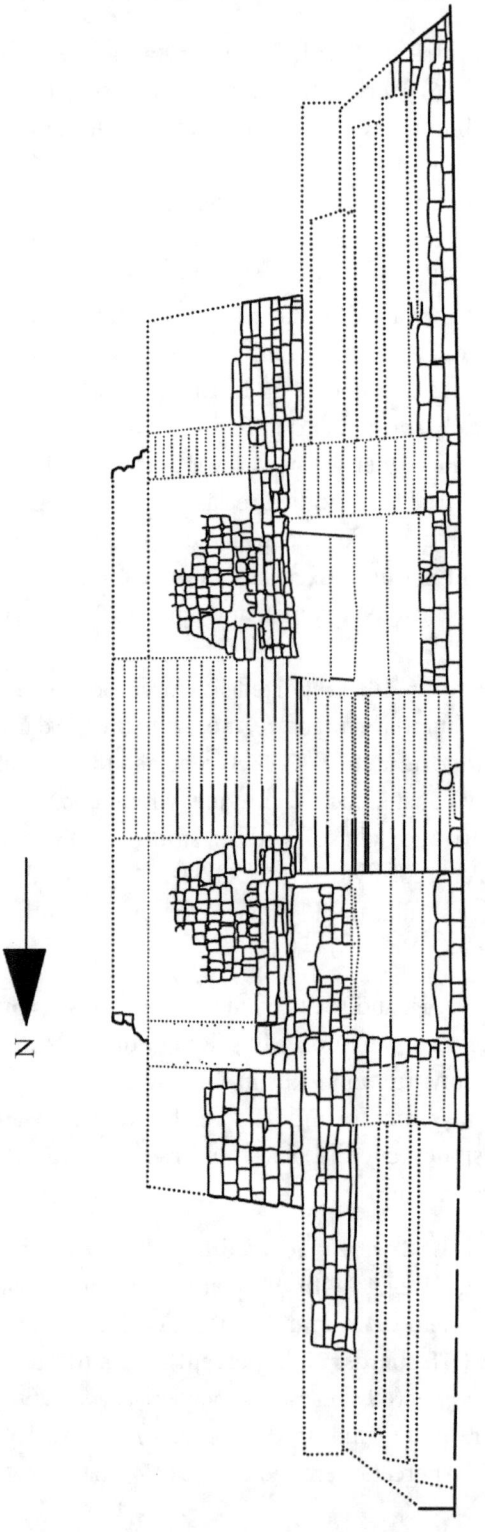

Figure 8.7. Tikal Structure 5C-54-3B, west elevation. Redrawn by the author after Paulino Morales in Laporte 1983.

percent of the Late Mamom sample. The average bowl radius from the late Mamom ceramics, 14.74 cm, represents an increase of more than a centimeter from the earlier materials. A general increase in vessel thickness was observed, with many examples approximately 1 cm in thickness.

In the Tikal collection from the North Acropolis, T. Patrick Culbert (1999:64) comments that there were more plates with shallower walls in the Tzec Phase than in the subsequent ceramic phase, Chuen. Furthermore, Culbert (translated from 1999:64) also remarks on the change in plate form from Tzec to Chuen, in which "the specific plate forms that marked the Tzec Complex disappear and the plate most characteristic of Chuen, the plate with fluted rim, is an innovation that does not appear before." Juan Pedro Laporte and Vilma Fialko (1993:25) note that Tzec ceramics (based on a sample of 5,880 sherds) tend to have reddish pastes, but there are fine-inclusion paste varieties such as Chunhinta Black: Fine Inclusions. Laporte and Fialko (1993) also observed relatively higher frequencies of Savana Orange and Reforma Incised ceramics in the Tzec collection, consistent with Middle Preclassic collections at other sites.

Although they are certainly not identical in construction technique or decoration, there are certain similarities between the Mamom or Late Eb/Tzec buildings at El Palmar and Tikal. Given such similarities, what are some possible models of how these two sites conceived of each other and interacted with one another? Is it possible that we are seeing the actions of autonomous political units—communities of people that identified with the E Group center through their social lives? Are people, as I have previously proposed (Doyle 2012:370), engaging in monumental building that coincided with their "desire to create and maintain distance from others over the landscape"? The likelihood is low that two communities so relatively close to each other independently innovated techniques, such as the noted fills composed of dark clayey soils layered with stones and crushed limestone.

There are several hypotheses about how information traveled among builders. First, the two places could be influenced by each other, or by a third authority, during the Middle Preclassic. Little evidence indicates that any one site held any sway over another, although we have few, if any, explicit statements of royal authority from this time, much less any statements of political hierarchy as known from Classic period (250–900 CE) inscriptions. The same lack of evidence holds true if we consider that Tikal, a well-known Classic period power, might directly have influenced the building at El Palmar by enforcing standards of some sort.

Considering that these building patterns exist at other sites in the area, two hypotheses for these similar architectural trends seem more plausible than those emphasizing a dominant political authority. One major question is: how many people lived near the E Groups at this time? It is highly possible that people lived in dispersed settlements between and around El Palmar and Tikal, visiting and contributing to the E Groups at either or both at any time. This is similar to a pilgrimage model (Stanton and Freidel 2003:8). A final option that may be borne out with more iconographic or textual evidence is that of a shared mythology, dictating periodic renewals according to cycles of deep time (see Chapters 2, 3, 4, and 6 in this volume). When considering the episodic expansions in the Late Preclassic, that possibility becomes more and more likely as the starting point for future investigations.

Putting the Chic in Chicanel

The social mechanisms at work during the Middle Preclassic, which allowed for the seemingly rapid and pervasive spread of Mamom-sphere production technology, became ingrained in Lowland Maya society. In other words, over the 300–400 years that we associate with Mamom-type ceramics, the interaction between communities continued and perhaps intensified over time. Again, we know very little about the people who actually lived in or near these E Group communities during this period. I would contend that the transition from the Middle to Late Preclassic remains largely unknown in terms of political organization and is an important research topic for the coming years (Hammond 1986:402).

The Chuen Complex at Tikal "was marked by the appearance of plates and bowls with flanges, considered one of the most clearly identifying markers to recognize all Late Preclassic complexes" (translated from Culbert 1999:65). Culbert (1999:65) observes that the labial flange was more common in the Chuen Complex and that fewer archaic forms were repeated from prior periods. Laporte and Fialko (1993:30) reported finding 1,234 Chuen Phase sherds from the fill of 5C-54-4, consistent with other finds from the initial part of the Late Preclassic at Tikal.

Early Late Preclassic ceramics from a total of 684 sherds from Structure E4-1 at El Palmar show similarities with the Chuen-Cauac complexes at Tikal. Distinguished from the other phases, these vessels show generally wider vessel walls, with the majority reaching 1 cm or greater. Bowl radii also increase, with a new variety of forms, such as wide, deeply fluted rims and labial flanges. Although eroded sherds made up 53.65 percent of the early Late Preclassic sample from the radial pyramid, the major groups represented were Achiotes unslipped (92 sherds, 13.45 percent), Chunhinta Black (3 sherds, 0.44 percent), Flor Cream (27 sherds, 3.95 percent), Polvero Black (36 sherds, 5.26 percent), Sierra Red (100 sherds, 14.62 percent), Indeterminate (39 sherds, 5.70 percent), and Variegated Indeterminate (20 sherds, 2.92 percent).

Ceramic changes are relatively less pronounced than architectural changes between the Middle and Late Preclassic periods. Whereas the voluminous investments of the early Middle Preclassic pertained to the leveling of hilltops and the creation of plaza gathering spaces (Estrada-Belli 2012, Chapter 9 in this volume), the E Group centers in the early Late Preclassic expanded the buildings on a massive scale. The clearest evidence of this is seen in the western radial pyramids at Tikal and El Palmar, but the eastern platforms also received ample facelifts. Investigations in looters' trenches in the eastern platform, El Palmar Structure E4-4, demonstrated at least three major phases of architectural investment and renovation. The penultimate phase of the long platform, dated to 390–190 BCE (2-sigma cal), was augmented greatly to include a central building that extended eastward from the original long platform, very similar to the Chuen Phase modifications of the equivalent building at Mundo Perdido (400–200 BCE: Laporte and Fialko 1995:Figure 3; Chase and Chase 1995, Chapter 2 in this volume). The best-preserved mask in the Mundo Perdido was found in the corresponding building (Structure 5D-86) in the Cauac Phase (150 BCE–200 CE) architecture (Laporte and Fialko 1995:Figure 14), which likely represents a version of Chahk, the rain god, often shown with *Spondylus* earspools (Doyle and Houston 2012; García Barrios 2008; Henderson 2013).

At least two major Late Preclassic expansion episodes showed up in excavations at El Palmar, along with a possible third phase that had been destroyed (Figure 8.8). These phases correspond to Structures 5C-54-4 and 5C-54-5 at Mundo Perdido Tikal (translated from Laporte 1983:1-11–1-14).[4] One final detail that Laporte (translated from 1983:1-45) notes is that this phase of the radial pyramid "was constructed on the same floor that was newly utilized for the construction of 54-5. It seems that 54-4 only had one floor, because there were no other traces encountered, except for a layer of lime on top of the same, but it does not represent another floor level but possibly only a remodeling or recovering of the existing one."

At El Palmar, the exterior walls of E4-1-2nd were composed of very large-sized stones (approximately 0.50 m^3) and a cap of stucco of the highest

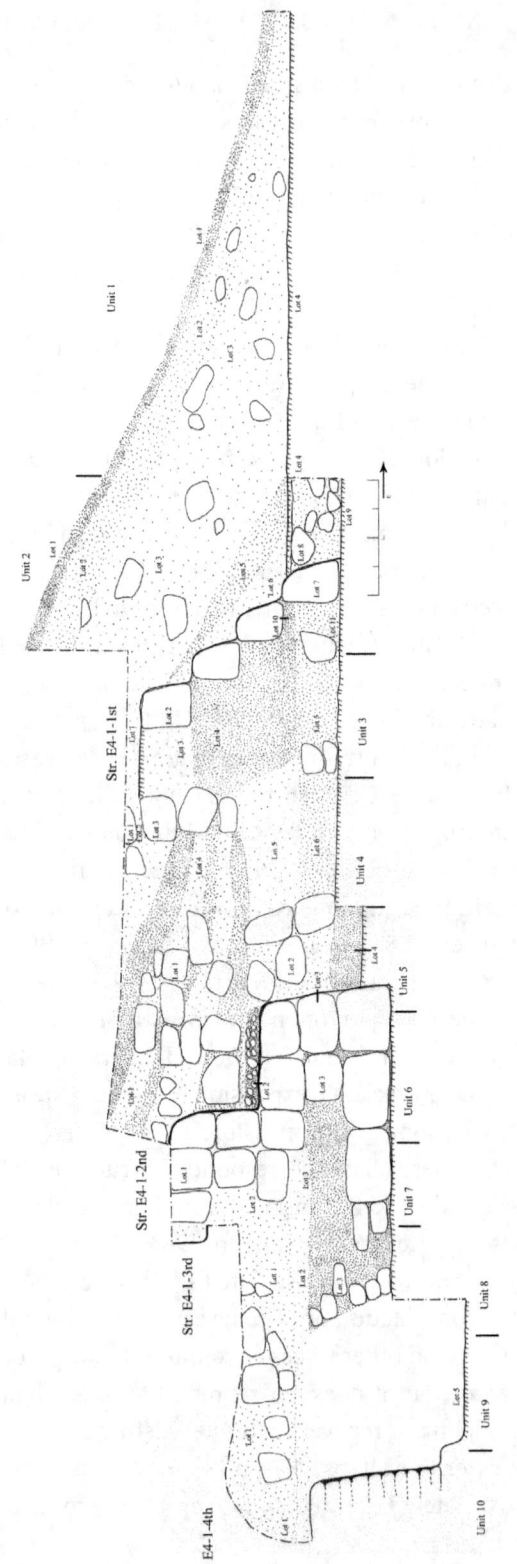

Figure 8.8. North profile of Late Preclassic expansion episodes, El Palmar Structure E4-1.

quality, similar to some described during the Late Preclassic in Mundo Perdido (Figure 8.9). In contrast to the comparable structure at Tikal, it seems that Structure E4-1-2nd had at least two floors (Figure 8.8). A stuccoed portion of a possible precursor to Structure E4-1-2nd was designated E4-1-3rd, but the scope of excavation did not allow for a clarification of the relationship between the two phases.

The differences between the ceramics of the early and late Late Preclassic period are slight, "with few typological changes," and "the majority of Chuen types continue in Cauac" (translated from Culbert 1999:67). Culbert (1999:67) cites Sapote Striated, Sierra Red, and other monochrome types as the most common wares in the Cauac Phase, with decorated wares representing less than 1 percent of the total sample. Flanges in the Cauac Phase tend to be more medial than labial, a distinguishing point between Cauac and Chuen (Culbert 1999:67). Compounding the lack of major differences between early and late Late Preclassic types, however, Laporte and Fialko (1993:31) note that there were few pure Cauac Phase deposits at Mundo Perdido, despite the evidence for intense construction during that time.

Late Chicanel ceramics at El Palmar were largely eroded, unfortunately, with the majority of the sample yielding no diagnostic information (584 sherds, 59.17 percent). The vessel wall depths and bowl radii tended to be consistent with early Late Preclassic wares, greater than in Middle Preclassic times. The group from the radial pyramid that appeared at the highest frequency in investigations was Sierra Red (127 sherds, 12.87 percent), followed by Achiotes unslipped (99 sherds, 10.03 percent), Polvero Black (52 sherds, 5.27 percent), Flor Cream (50 sherds, 5.07 percent), Variegated Indeterminate (44 sherds, 4.46 percent), and Indeterminate (29 sherds, 2.94 percent); 2 sherds (0.20 percent) were classified as Águila Group.

Excavations at the E Group at El Palmar did not yield any stucco masks, but the buildings are highly likely contemporaries of E-VII-Sub at Uaxactún or 5D-86 at Tikal. Evidence from an extensive topographical survey in 2008 indicates the likely presence of large masks on either side of the primary eastern staircase through distinct, symmetric elevated areas facing the east (Nelson and Doyle 2008). Architecture in the three final phases of the E Group at El Palmar is consistent with the large block construction and heavily stuccoed façades as noted at many other sites. As mentioned, the earliest Late Preclassic building, E4-1-3rd, was perhaps cut or partially destroyed to construct the penultimate phase, E4-1-2nd. The practice of dismantling prior buildings in the Late Preclassic also existed in Tikal (Laporte and Fialko 1995:50).

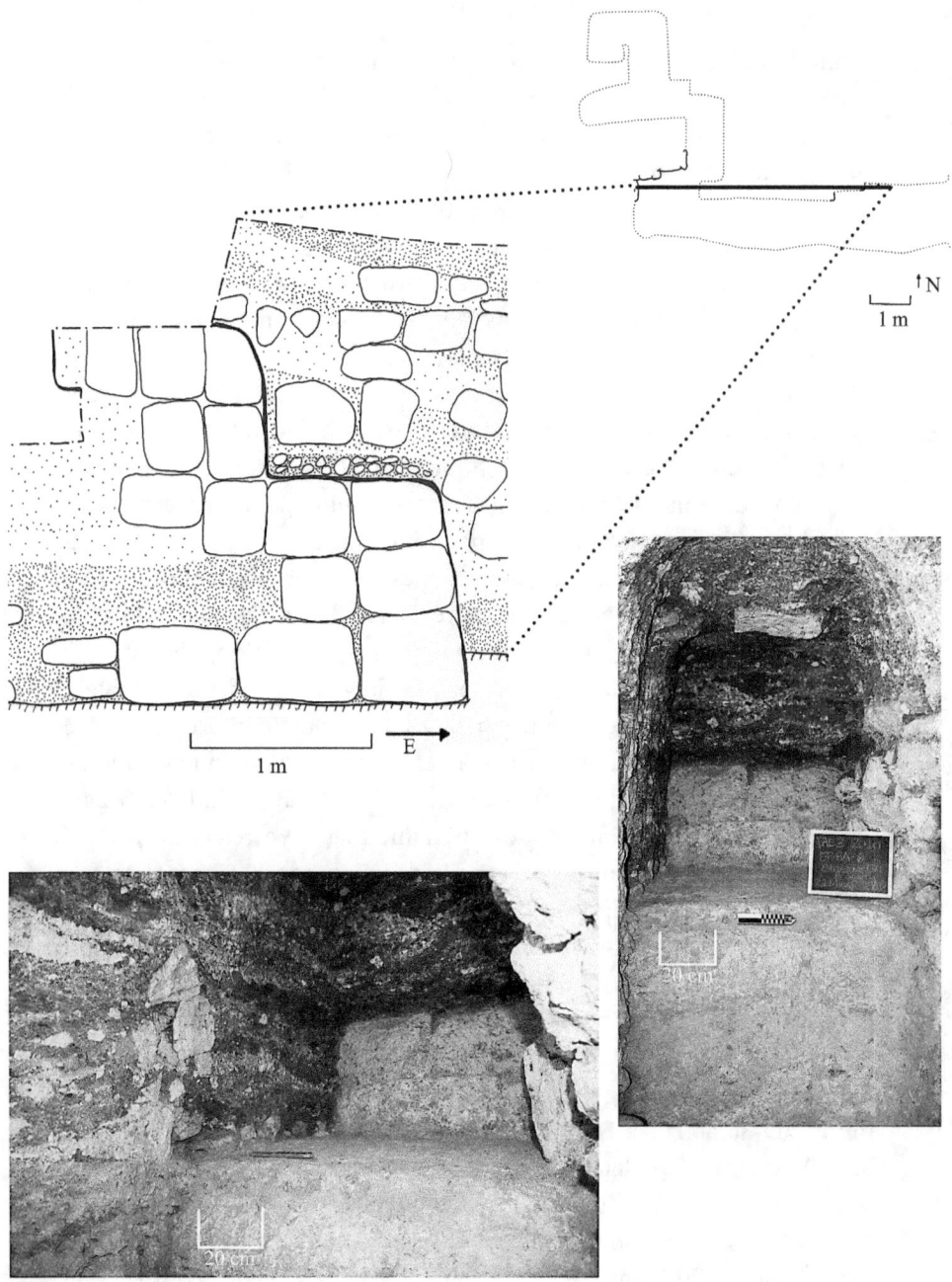

Figure 8.9. Exterior walls of Structure E4-1-2nd, El Palmar.

The most thoroughly investigated version of Tikal Structure 5C-54 was the final expansion (see Figure 8.3), the one visible today to visitors to the park (translated from Laporte 1983:1-08-1-11):

> As expected, the most investigated was Structure 5C-54-5, which corresponds to the exterior facet, or the ultimate construction phase.[5] It presents itself in a lamentable state of conservation, as there now exist parts that are completely collapsed. It is considered natural that this happened, as the fill employed for the building is very poor. It is composed of dark, sandy soil and few inclusions of large stones; furthermore, the system employed architecturally suffers tremendous weaknesses, as the stones used for its construction do not bear any mortar in the wall intersections but only attach one to the other, which does not give sufficient resistance to this enormous construction.
>
> Structure 54-5 is composed of ten tiers that present different dimensions, in both the height and width of their platforms. Its base measures 61.30 meters in length from the northwest corner to the southwest corner; and 56.25 meters from the southwest corner to the extreme southeast. But if we take the measurement in the axis, we find 72 meters north–south and 66.5 meters east–west; this is taking into consideration the protruding corners of the building. The height of the building is 30.70 meters.[6]
>
> The north and south sides were designed in the same way, the most curious part being the existence of "incoming walls" or "niches" located at floor level and repeating in an ascending straight line, but with different dimensions, until the fourth tier. These are located close to their respective corners, or, both in the east and west ends. The west side presents true decorative niches close to the north and south ends. These were encountered on the first four tiers, just as also on the eighth tier, so it is believed that these were present on the entire building façade. These do not go in a straight line but approach the center of the structure, coinciding with the reduction of size in the structure's tiers. The rest of its base on this side is composed only of inset corners that present different dimensions.
>
> Central staircases were located on the four sides, revealing that neither the north nor south staircase reaches the upper surface; they only ascend to the eighth tier. In the east side the situation has not been defined due to the destruction produced in the year 1979, but it could be similar to the west sector, in which the central staircase goes up to the

top of the structure, with an incline of 45 degrees and approximately 86 stairs. This staircase is flanked with enormous *tableros*, of which only the north was present in good condition, as well as by masks that could be reminiscent of some of the Preclassic structures of the North Acropolis or E-VII-Sub of Uaxactún.

In the upper part of this building, no remains of any stone building were encountered; only remains of stucco were found. Nor is it thought that a temple constructed of perishable material existed, because if that were so there would have been mounds or remains of collapse on top of the floors or some sign or impression of the posts that supported it; on the contrary, the surface was encountered with no type of collapse that covered it; the upper floor only presented remains of the gravel that served as its foundation, showing that it was exposed to the elements for a long time. Therefore, the upper surface of the structure did not support any type of temple and its platform was smooth.

On the south side were located auxiliary staircases, one in the base of the structure and another in the middle part, its function remains unknown; both were located to the west of the central staircase.

Structure 54-5 suffered remodeling acts during the Early Classic that can be seen on the west side to the south of the central staircase, in which an auxiliary staircase was eliminated, just as in the northeast corners of the sixth and seventh tiers in which some rounded ones were substituted to result in straight corners with insets.[7]

The final enlargement of the El Palmar radial pyramid (Structure E4-1-1st) involved a heavy investment in architectural fill (2-sigma cal 350 to 300 and 210 to 40 BCE), primarily cut blocks and *bajo* mud (Figure 8.8). The builders first created a retaining wall (Unit 5, Lots 2 and 4) to cover the first tier of Structure E4-1-2nd then laid out the foundational floor for E4-1-1st. This floor, excavated in a separate unit from the main tunnel, represented a heavy investment with more stone inclusions in the fill and a cap of stucco that was 5–7 cm thick, the largest Late Preclassic floor encountered in the E Group.

On the summit in the final phase of the E4-1 pyramid was a building with at least two narrow rooms, probably constructed during the Late Preclassic period. At least three floors in the eastern room represent perhaps a very long use for the building, with resurfacing occurring at least twice. The lack of cultural material from the summit excavations makes these remodeling events difficult to date, but eroded sherds on the surface suggest a possible Early Classic date for the final use of the structure.

Plaza Politics: E Group Roles in Late Preclassic Site Planning and Classic Engagement

A great deal of planning and engineering went into the expansion of the E Group buildings in the Late Preclassic period. I have argued that the nature of site planning at El Palmar and El Mirador in the Late Preclassic was governed by both astronomical and geometric conventions (Doyle 2013a). El Palmar builders used the same proportions to lay out the final E Group plaza to construct the final version of the Triadic Group (Doyle 2013a:Figure 4). In practice, the model I proposed could lead to broader discussions of idiosyncratic proportions (unique to each site and/or political regime) used in Maya planning. Although I have pointed out that Tikal has considerable Classic period overburden that inhibits a thorough study of Preclassic planning at present, certain possibilities are borne out by applying the same analysis to Tikal as El Palmar and El Mirador.

The application of the methods used for El Palmar and El Mirador to Tikal shows certain correlations with wide platforms and spaces and the proportions of the Mundo Perdido plaza between the radial pyramid and long platform. As Laporte and Fialko (Laporte 1997:346; Laporte and Fialko 1995:48) have pointed out, these dimensions were important to the builders of Mundo Perdido and were finalized during the Late Preclassic expansion of the settlement. Notably, it seems that double the width of the E Group plaza is repeated in the Temple IV basal platform, the basal dimensions of the South Acropolis, the Great Plaza, and other spaces (Figure 8.10a). The largest twin pyramid complexes, which have been compared to E Groups in function (Aimers and Rice 2006; Laporte 1997), seem to measure twice the width of the E Group plaza. Yaxhá, too, conforms to the proposed model (Figure 8.10b). Although it is speculative, the same is true also for the large city of Calakmul, wherein the proportions of the central plaza seem to repeat for basal platforms and other plaza spaces in the same fashion (Figure 8.10c). It is possible that a wider study might show major investments in Preclassic architectural platforms and seem to lay out plans proportionally based on the E Group plaza.

Clearly, these and other sites from the Central Lowlands cultural tradition share a similar inventory of architecture and measurement convention; however, no two E Groups are alike. Many consider the regularities

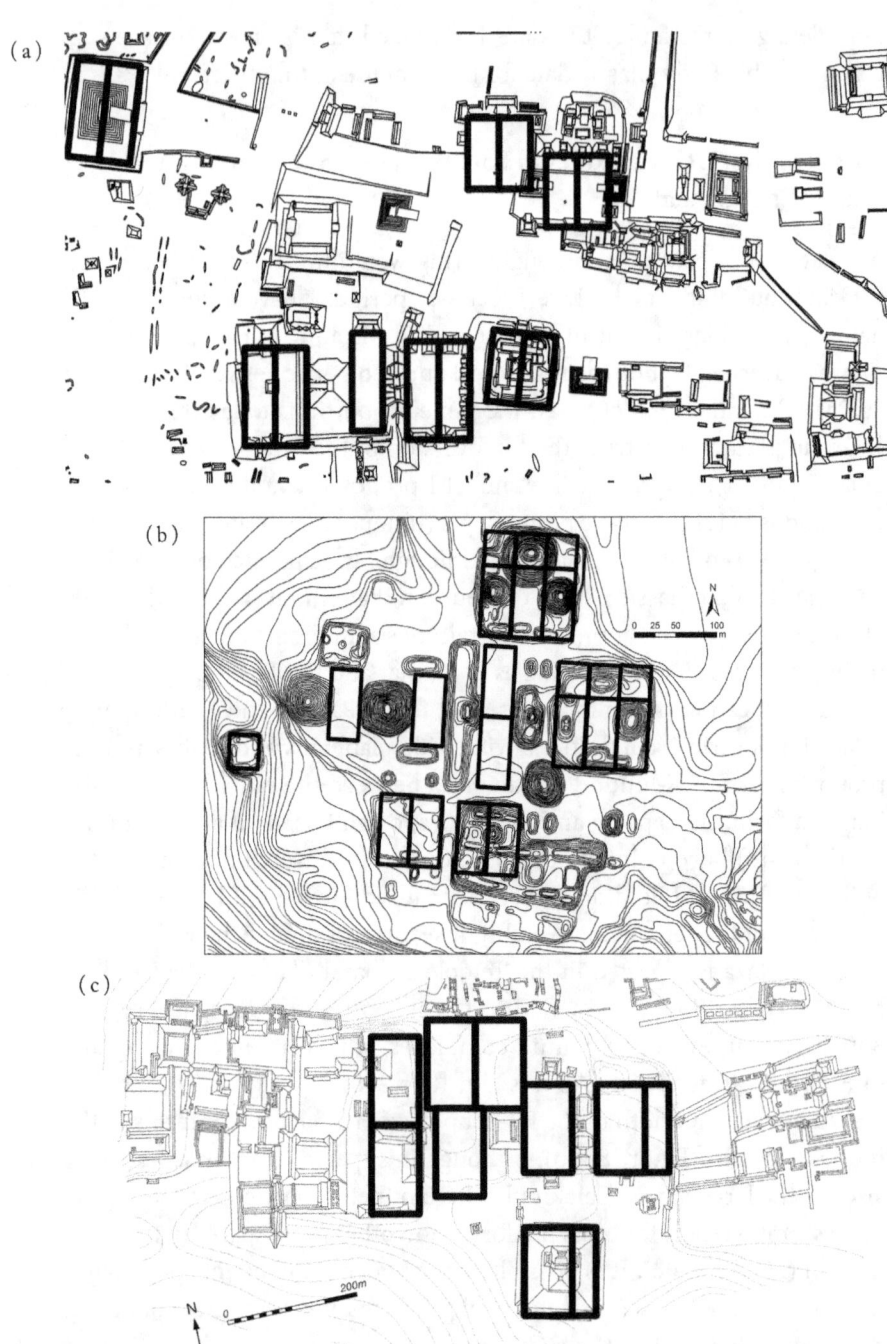

Figure 8.10. (a) Hypothetical replication of Mundo Perdido plaza dimensions across Tikal; (b) Yaxhá; (c) Calakmul.

of planning and expansion to be indirect evidence of emerging political authorities (Hansen 1998; McAnany 2010; Ringle 1999). The implications of the similar techniques riddled with dimensional idiosyncrasies noted above should be underscored. During the Late Preclassic, with respect to architectural and material evidence, no one site or group of sites held sway over others; in other words, Late Preclassic emerging dynasts drew their authority from generations of inherited practices in their own locally constructed ritual spaces. At present, it is still difficult for archaeologists to interpret the extent and diversity of Preclassic populations, however; thus the extent of any perceived boundaries between polities is unknown. Because of the geographic proximity of El Palmar and Tikal, these two Middle and Late Preclassic communities could serve in the future to clarify the origins of Maya politics.

In the phases after the final expansion of the radial pyramids at Tikal and El Palmar, however, we can observe distinct changes in the engagement of the residents with their respective E Groups. Most notably, the lack of any superstructure on the summit of Mundo Perdido's radial pyramid, Structure 5C-54-5, stands in clear contrast to the findings from El Palmar of floor resurfacings and standing masonry walls (Chapter 16 in this volume, for discussion of access to restricted spaces in E Groups). As mentioned, residents constructed the main building at the summit of Structure E4-1 during the Preclassic period but resurfaced the floor at least twice in later periods. There seems to be a third type of use for the summit of the E Group pyramid at Uaxactún, because the Ricketsons (1937:40) reported four postholes on the summit of E-VII-Sub, presumably for a perishable superstructure.

In both cases, it is clear that access from the eastern plaza was of paramount importance, because only the eastern staircase reached the summit of 5C-54. The staircases on each side are an oft-overlooked medium of expression; however, in deciding how to travel from the plaza floor to the top of a pyramidal building and back down again, the builders opted to break up the vertical movement by adding a multiplicity of access routes, interrupted by sculptural friezes or masks, best seen in the fully exposed, Late Preclassic E-VII-Sub at Uaxactún. Thus terracing and staircases create an aesthetics of "awe" (Monroe 2010) by affecting what the viewer sees by standing on various parts of the building and by altering the way that sunlight breaks over the surface of the building at different parts of the day (Chapter 16 in this volume). In other words, architectural forms specifically convey a particular idea through their relationship with the path of the sun at a specific moment or part of the day. Others have identified such hierophanies in the Maya area with respect to E Groups (Aveni et al. 2003:173) and architecture at Palenque (Méndez et al. 2005).

A final, parallel social action is evident in the remains of both the El Palmar and Tikal E Groups: reuse of the final Late Preclassic phase. As Laporte (translated from 1983:1-13–1-14) noted:

> On top of the remains of 54-5, as well as on top of the upper floor of the High Plaza, abundant ceramic material belonging to the Early and Late Classic was collected. This is important because it demonstrates that although there were no longer building episodes during the Late Classic, Structure 5C-54 continued playing a primordial and functional role within the religious context of Tikal.

Similarly, excavations on the east–west axis on the eastern pyramid-plaza interface recovered a complete Cubierta Impressed pot associated with a typically Early Classic chert biface (Zachary Hruby, personal communication, 2011).

More information about the manner in which the Late to Terminal Preclassic or Protoclassic (0–250 CE) population engaged with the E Group comes from the eastern platform, Structure E4-4. At least once after the final expansion of the group dating to approximately 390–190 BCE (2-sigma cal), builders added a staircase on the western side of the platform. An excavation unit produced two tetrapod cache plates produced with a reddish paste and a cream slip classified as part of the Flor Group (Figure 8.11). Although Culbert (1993, 1999) classifies similar tetrapod plates at Tikal as belonging to Cimi Phase, 150–250 CE, others (Brady et al. 1998) argue that these smaller mammiforms could occur in the Lowlands between 100/50 BCE and 50/100 CE (Takeshi Inomata, personal communication, 2013). Aside from a prismatic obsidian blade that had been intentionally broken, the plates did not contain any nonperishable associated offerings, but perhaps residue analysis of the differentially colored soil from the two plates will shed further light on this event. This offering represents one of the final construction-related rituals performed at El Palmar in the end of the Late Preclassic.

Because very few remains from the Terminal Preclassic were found at El Palmar outside of superficial contexts, it is difficult to interpret who was living at the site toward the end of the Late Preclassic, dedicating the plates, and building the final staircase to the eastern E Group platform. Further evidence for a continuous occupation comes from the several modifications

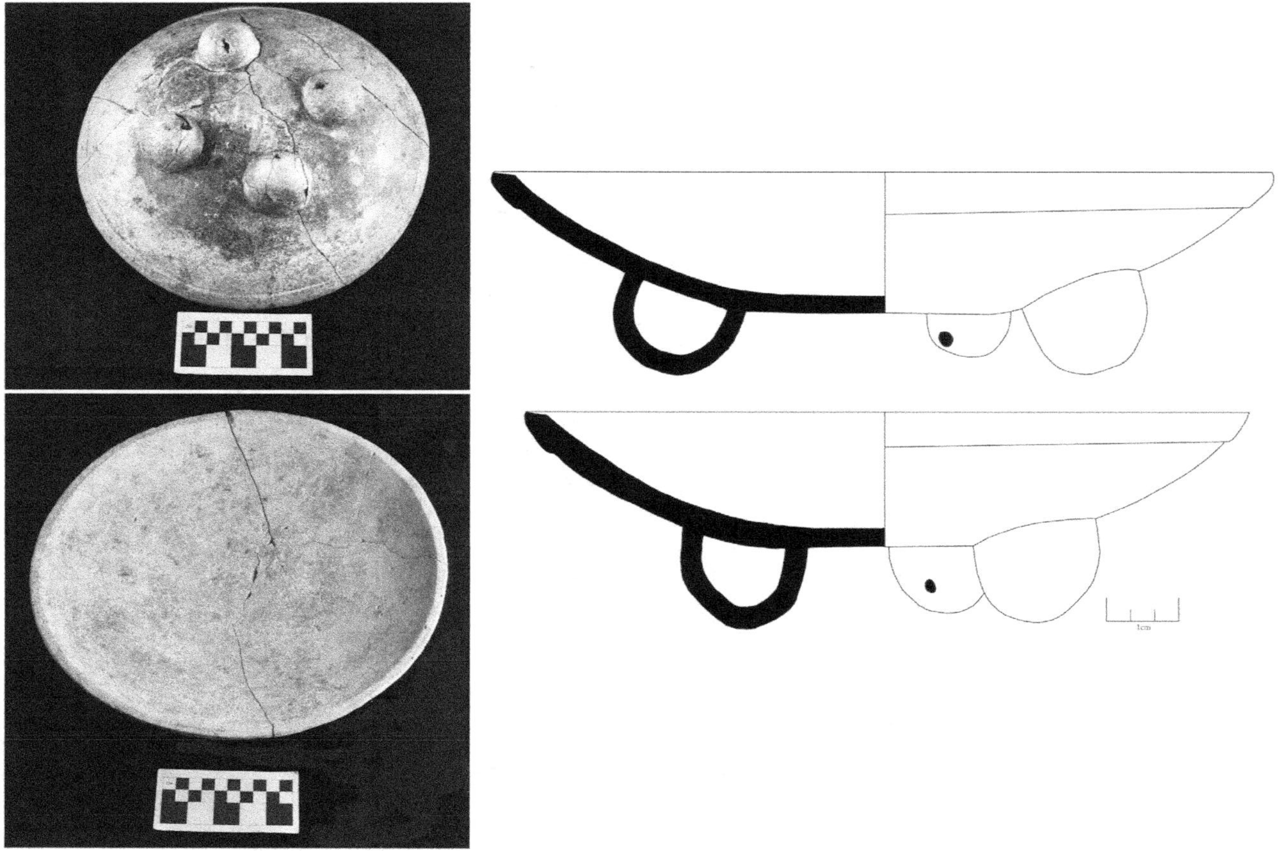

Figure 8.11. Tetrapod cache plates, Structure E4-4, El Palmar.

made by residents after the Late Preclassic boom, suggesting a possible reoccupation at a later date than the final staircase. Unlike post-150 CE modifications at nearby E Groups at Uaxactún and Tikal, the El Palmar E Group exhibits small, low platforms, with no apparent comparisons in the region (Doyle 2013b). Two lines of evidence indicate that these platforms were later than the staircase building event: (1) an intrusive burial on the east–west axis of Structure E4-4 of an individual with Early Classic ceramics of the Balanza and possibly Dos Arroyos polychrome groups (Doyle and Matute 2010:213–214; Scherer 2010:328–329); and (2) surface collections near the platforms that included Early Classic materials, the most diagnostic of which was a miniature eccentric made out of green obsidian, which likely came from the Pachuca source near Teotihuacán (Zachary Hruby, personal communication, 2010) and was commonly used in the Early Classic.

Discussion: Climbing Ruined Mountains

Several points deserve mention about the meanings behind Preclassic E Group expansions, especially the proliferation of stucco masks as a medium for mythological and religious expression. First, these masks all seem to appear in the same period, within a few generations in the late Middle Preclassic or early Late Preclassic, roughly 300–1 BCE (Estrada-Belli 2011; Freidel and Schele 1988; Hansen 1998). Second, they appear in public ceremonial space, at places of high visibility for both the participants in the ceremonies and the viewers. In fact the masks or the actual or natural characters that they represent could have been considered active participants in whatever activities transpired in these Preclassic plazas. In this way, these masks did not adorn the building as an extrinsic decoration but rather communicated to the viewers that this pyramid was actually a mythological mountain place and could be considered charged with the same power as the natural phenomenon (Freidel and Schele 1989; Stuart 1987; Taube 1998). It is possible that monumentalized E Groups with their deity heads pertain to Classic period concepts of "civilized spaces," specifically because of their symbolism as the unification of the four directions through rectangular plazas and radial pyramids (Stephen Houston, personal communication, 2012; Freidel et al. 1993:128–131; Hanks 1990; Taube 2003).

In a related vein, Laporte and Fialko (translated from 1995:56; see also Aimers and Rice 2006:90–92) also brought up a major question pertaining to the shelf life of E Groups in the Classic Period:

What phenomenon influenced the fact that the builders no longer practiced major reconstructions on the Great Pyramid? One interesting option is that the ritual associated with the E Groups fell into disuse, because of the advent of new ceremonies related to the *k'atun* endings (Coggins 1979). Some of the findings made in the E Group of Mundo Perdido, however, indicate that ritual aspects related to the ancient solar cult certainly persisted.

In the following discussion I briefly want to examine the engagement of populations with these constructions after the major expansion in the Late Preclassic to address the question: why did it become undesirable to continue building big in E Groups?

The evidence from El Palmar highlights a significant shift in building practices after the Late Preclassic: at some point, the residents only desired or only had the resources to refurbish, resurface, or make minor changes, such as add a new staircase. This clearly contrasts with the two prior major investments in Structures E4-1-2nd and E4-1-1st. I want to return to the observation at Mundo Perdido that the penultimate phase of the pyramid only existed with one phase of the plaza floor. One obvious interpretation of this is that the plaza floor (the corresponding layer at El Palmar was of considerable thickness) simply lasted for many generations without need to resurface. A second possibility is that a shift in the local political authority necessitated the expansion of the building rather than modification of Structure 5C-54. Laporte and Fialko (translated from 1993:37–38; see also Laporte and Fialko 1995:49) suggest another possibility:

> The new rebuilding of the pyramid in Chuen times, 5C-54-3 and the 5D-84/88-3 platform indicate the cyclic completion of a preestablished ritual, perhaps since Eb, according to which is seen the increase and definition of determined architectural features: the large radial pyramid 5C-54-3 presents more volume, including demarcated masks for auxiliary staircases. The deposition of Burials PNT-001 and PNT-004 is associated with this phase, the first of which was associated with the east–west axis of the pyramid and the second below 5C-54-Sub 1.

In other words, Preclassic calendrics played a role in the E Group rebuilding phases, also noted at other sites, such as Caracol, Belize (Chase and Chase 1995, Chapter 2 in this volume). Given the evidence for similar phasing over the Preclassic Period at two neighboring E Groups, it is highly possible that the periodic renewal of E Groups was part of grander cycles of ritual and expansion. Thus the evidence of extensive planning, although probably at the hands of a ruler or group of powerful people at Tikal and El Palmar, might have been mandated by a greater belief in ritual cycles that was shared across the Lowland Maya Late Preclassic.

If such cycles dictated action in the Preclassic, however, it is clear that both at Mundo Perdido and El Palmar the Terminal Preclassic and Early Classic actions did not conform to such periodic volume expansions. Laporte (translated from 1997:346) sums up his interpretation of the evidence:

> The apparent lack of renovation in the Late Classic may reflect different causes: from the partial abandonment of the E Group to the constructive aspect itself that avoided the potential accretion again of the size of the monument. This abandonment in the function of such an important building in the history of Tikal has been considered as a clear index of the transformation of an ancient concept. This action could have been in accordance with the reorganization, if not the abandonment, of a ritual linked principally to an ancient solar cult.

I would argue that triadic architecture became the new centers of communities, thus the focus of monumental building efforts, toward the end of the Late Preclassic (Doyle 2013b; MacLellan 2009; Saturno and Rossi n.d.; Chapter 10 in this volume). They supplanted the E Group axis as the central point on the landscape with which the communities identified.

At Tikal, of course, major burials of dynastic founders occurred in the Late Preclassic, not at Mundo Perdido, but at the North Acropolis, which is an early example of the triadic arrangement (Coe 1990; Hansen 1998; Velásquez 2014). The North Acropolis, and not the Mundo Perdido E Group, remained a major focus of monumental buildings throughout the Classic period.

Evidence from El Palmar also supports the hypothesis that Triadic Groups supplanted E Groups as central spatial and conceptual axes. Probably during the fourth century CE a group of residents constructed a small structure containing what was likely the tomb of an important individual. Looters pierced the small structure in the middle of the Triadic Group plaza, Structure E5-1, and encountered a sizable tomb (approximately 1 m by 3 m) with an intact vaulted ceiling (Doyle and Piedrasanta n.d.). The tomb was oriented north–south and had been looted in the late twentieth century. Found inside were only a few fragments of what was likely a jade and shell mosaic mask (probably part of a pectoral or belt). The placement of the small burial temple (slightly askew from the final central axis of the largest pyramid in the Triadic Group), the construction of the tomb and subsequent superstructure, and the meager artifacts left by the looters all suggest an Early Classic date. During the fourth century in the region, many similar tombs, including an intact tomb found at El Zotz (Román and Newman 2010), and looted tombs found at Bejucal (Garrison et al. 2013) contained important royal individuals, although these chambers lay below larger-scale pyramids.

Regardless of the exact timing of this entombment, the placement of the burial shows a distinct intent to reconnect with the major alignments of the Preclassic buildings, possibly as a nod to their ancestral connection with El Palmar. Also, it is significant that the builders placed the tomb and its small building on the east–west axis of the Triadic Group, and not on the east–west axis of the E Group as builders had done in the Early Classic at Tikal (Laporte and Fialko 1993, 1995). Perhaps the reoccupants of El Palmar were familiar only with the Late Preclassic concept of center, as it followed Late Preclassic rulers in performances in the newly erected Triadic Groups. A suggestive interpretation of the entombment would be that the Early Classic peoples from near El Palmar sought to return the body of a nobleperson to an important ancestral center.

Conclusion

The case study of Tikal and El Palmar presented here is a rich example of two communities that developed similar building practices in the Middle and Late Preclassic periods, perhaps due to shared beliefs in wider temporal cycles demanding renewal or expansion of existing E Group architecture. Despite similarities with Tikal in the Classic period engagement with the E Group radial pyramids, however, the population at El Palmar suffered a precipitous decline in the second and third centuries CE. Many factors led to this Preclassic "collapse" (Doyle 2013b; Estrada-Belli 2011; Grube 1995). Elsewhere I have emphasized the shifting political landscape as resulting from the growth at Early Classic Tikal (Doyle et al. 2012).

More recent evidence from El Palmar underscores the site's importance for understanding the role of the localized environment in the perceived population decline at the end of the Late Preclassic (Beach et al. n.d.; Doyle 2013b). Soil studies showed that Late Preclassic El Palmar suffered high rates of soil erosion, and preliminary results indicate that a relative dry period occurred at the end of the Late Preclassic, as noted across the Lowlands (for example, Kennett et al. 2012). Pollen evidence from a soil pit at El Palmar shows an initial decline in maize levels at the end of the Late Preclassic at the site but a distinct spike in maize pollen sometime in the Early Classic (Beach et al. n.d.). Recent research on modeling the agricultural potential around Tikal concluded that the area around the *bajo* areas close to El Palmar had a high probability of "sustained maize agriculture" (Balzotti et al. 2013:Figure 3).

Therefore it is plausible that the co-occurrence of political changes and environmental drying led to the cessation of monumental building at El Palmar in the early first millennium. The potential for maize agriculture, however, perhaps allowed certain individuals to reoccupy the ruined Preclassic platforms at El Palmar (Doyle and Piedrasanta n.d.). Evidence from a residential platform and a modest pyramidal building on the shore of the Laguna El Palmar supports the reoccupation hypothesis, dating to 230–410 CE (2-sigma cal). During this time, a massive deposit of ceramic vessels, faunal material, and other artifacts likely occurred as one event or at least over a short period during one generation (Doyle 2013b).

It is unclear whether the reoccupants who constructed the aforementioned tomb were the same as the ones who left the materials at the temple by the water. What is abundantly clear, however, is that the peoples who engaged with the center of El Palmar in the third to fifth centuries CE did not conduct large-scale building or engage in ritual behaviors in the E Group at the site. These Early Classic practices at El Palmar suggest that they had disconnected from the E Group gathering space and monumental buildings. This disconnect was the ultimate result of the reoccupations that happened for generations after authorities enacted the final monumental building plan.

Acknowledgments

I am grateful to the editors of this volume and Debra Walker for helpful comments that improved many ideas presented in this chapter. The Institute of Anthropology and History of Guatemala granted permits for the work at El Palmar as a part of the El Zotz Archaeological Project, directed by Stephen Houston and Edwin Román. Work at El Palmar was also supported generously by the U.S. National Science Foundation (BCES #1023274—Doctoral Dissertation Improvement Grant, Houston and Doyle, Principal Investigators (PIs); BCES #0840930—Landscape Succession in

Lowland Maya Archaeology, Houston and Garrison, PIs; the U.S. National Endowment for the Humanities (Grant #RZ-50680-07—Archaeology of El Zotz, Guatemala, Houston, PI); the Wenner-Gren Foundation for Anthropological Research (Dissertation Fieldwork Grant, Doyle, PI); and Brown University Graduate School and Department of Anthropology, the Brown University Dupee Family Professorship of Social Sciences (Houston, chair).

Notes

1. Estructura 5C-54-2, from Laporte (1983: 1-18–1-20):

Se trate de un basamento escalonado compuesto de cuatro cuerpos, siendo los Cuerpos 1 y 4 de menor altura que los intermedios. Los cuerpos intermedios no presentan moldura, mientras que los otros sí. La escalinata Oeste, única conocida de la posibilidad de ser radial, es saliente para los Cuerpos 1 y 2 y es remetida para los Cuerpos 3 y 4: de la base a la base del Cuerpo 3 es más ancha que para el propio Cuerpo 3; para el Cuerpo 4 se presenta una etapa individual del mismo ancho que la anterior. En relación a los aspectos decorativos es difícil precisar si tuvo mascarones pues estarían colocados en los sectores de mayor mutilación, pero considerando la posibilidad de ser radial también es posible que si los presentara.

Con respecto al Cuerpo 4 hay que agregar que se trata de una remodelación (2-B), pues en la plataforma superior se presentan pisos anteriores que juegan con la terminación de las escalinatas del Cuerpo 3. Ya el hecho de que este tramo de escalinata es más angosto que el inferior parece indicar que el Cuerpo 3 fue en un tiempo el superior de la estructura. Se menciona además la diferencia del estuco que recubre los cuerpos inferiores y el del Cuerpo 4. Esta estructura tiene un notorio asentamiento hacia el Norte. Las dimensiones generales son de 32.25 de longitud NS y 7.80 de altura. El relleno de 54-2 presenta abundancia de piedra pequeña con escasa tierra oscura en capas oblicuas, es suelto y proclive a asentamientos; a este relleno lo recubre un relleno compacto de tierra oscura y tierra caliza y piedra mediana y grande en gran cantidad. Se construyen muros de contención de piedras sin cantear, unidas por lodo, que siguen el contorno de la estructura de manera muy eficaz. Aparecen por vez primera los muros exteriores construidos de piedra canteada, secundados por muros "de construcción."

De los seis pisos de la plataforma superior, los cuatro superiores corresponden a cambios de nivel del último cuerpo, mientras que los dos más profundos representan una etapa en que el basamento tenía solamente tres cuerpos (54-2-A). Representa un cambio de la época anterior en que sus muros están construidos con bloques de piedra canteada (0.50 × 0.30), unidos por argamasa y no por lodo; los recubrimientos son de estuco calizo delgado, salvo el del Cuerpo 4 que es de barro calcinado, también de acabado excelente. Hay diversas desviaciones en los muros, lo cual le da una cierta asimetría. Se inicia la escalinata en dos etapas, lo que se repetirá en la siguiente fase constructiva. El fechamiento de 5C-54-2 se apoya en los Entierros MP-002 y 003 (Suboperación 50, Lote 6), cuales son uno sólo, colocados dentro del relleno del Cuerpo 3, bajo el Piso 6, es decir anteriores a la construcción del Cuerpo 4 . . . Este edificio se fecha para la fase Tzec, caso interesante al observar la continuidad arquitectónica entre la faceta Tardía de Eb y Tzec.

[Structure 5C-54-2: It is a stepped base consisting of four tiers, Tiers 1 and 4 of which are of lesser height than the intermediaries. The intermediate tiers do not have molding, while the others do. The west staircase, the only one known possibly to be radial, is extended for Tiers 1 and 2 and inset for Tiers 3 and 4: from the base [of the staircase] to the base of Tier 3 is wider than for the same on Tier 3; for Tier 4 it presents a single individual stage of the same width as the previous one. In relation to the decorative aspects, it is difficult to determine if it had masks, as they would have been located in the sectors with the most mutilation, but considering the possibility of being radial it is also possible that they would have been present. With respect to Tier 4, one must add that it is a remodeling event (2-B), as in the upper platform there are prior floors, which combine with the staircases of Tier 3. Now the fact that this stretch of staircase is narrower than the lower one seems to indicate that Tier 3 was at one time the top of the structure. Also, it should be mentioned that there was a difference in the stucco that covered the lower tiers and Tier 4. This structure has a notable foundation to the north. The overall dimensions are 32.25 m in length north–south and 7.80 m height. The fill of 54-2 presents an abundance of small stones with low levels of dark soil in slanted [sloped?] layers, which is loose and prone to settling; this filling is covered by a filling of dark soil and crushed limestone with a large quantity of medium and large stones. Retention walls were constructed of uncut stones, joined with mud, that follow the contour of the structure very effectively. For the first time, exterior walls composed of cut stones appear, supported by "construction" walls. Of the six floors of the upper platform, the four upper ones correspond to changes to the level of the final tier, while the two deepest ones represent a stage in which the basal level only had three tiers (54-2-A). This represents a change from the prior period in that its walls are constructed with cut stone blocks (0.50 m × 0.30 m), joined by mortar and not by mud; the coatings are of thin limestone stucco, except for Tier 4 which is of limey clay, also of excellent finishing. There are certain deviations in the walls, which gives it a certain asymmetry. The staircase begins in two stages, which repeats in the following construction phase. The dating of 5C-54-2 is supported by burials MP-002 and 003 (Suboperation 50, Lot 6), which are just one, located within the fill of Tier 3, below Floor 6, that is, before the construction of Tier 4. . . . This building dates to the Tzec Phase, an interesting case to observe the architectural continuity between the late Eb facet and Tzec.]

2. Estructura 5C-54-3-A, from Laporte (1983: 1-17–1-18):

Durante la fase Chuen se construye la plataforma de escasos 0.60 de altura, con orientación NO-SE, que debió funcionar en algún momento contemporáneo a 5C54-2 de fase Tzec. Fechándola se encuentra el Entierro MP-004 (Suboperación 36, Pozo 11) y es el primer elemento arquitectónico que limita los basamentos escalonados en el sector Oeste. Sobresale a 5C-54-5 hacia al Oeste, a lo cual se debe su mutilación.

Presenta una técnica constructiva de buena calidad, con un relleno compacto y uniforme compuesto de tierra oscura y clara sin intrusión de piedra. La poca altura de la plataforma no exige de muros de contención, aunque fueron localizados algunos de tipo "cajón," con una sola hilada. Se encuentra totalmente cubierta de estuco de material calizo de grano fino y de un espesor medio. Muestra remodelaciones de pisos debido posiblemente al desgaste sufrido durante su utilización. Su funcionalidad fue corta aparentemente, cubierta por los pisos y mutilada en parte por los rellenos de 5C-54-3-B.

[Structure 5C-54-3-A: During the Chuen Phase a platform was constructed of barely 0.60 m in height, with a northwest–southeast orientation, which must have functioned at some contemporary moment with 5C-54-2 in the Tzec Phase. Providing a date, Burial MP-004 (Suboperation 36, Unit 11) was found, and it is the first architectural element that delimits the tiered bases in the west sector. It protrudes to 5C-54-5 to the west, to which it owes its destruction.

It presents a good-quality construction technique, with a compact and uniform fill composed of dark and light soil without stone inclusions. The low height of the platform does not require retention walls, although some of the "drawer" type were located, with just one row. It was encountered totally covered in fine-grained limestone stucco of medium thickness. It shows remodeling of the floors, due possibly to the wear suffered during its use. Its functionality was apparently short-lived, covered by the floors and destroyed in part by the fills of 5C-54-3-B.]

3. Original Spanish text: "Son rellenos uniformes de tierra compacta y piedra de todo tamaño, con buena consistencia; solamente algunos sectores tienen rellenos más sueltos. Fueron detectados muros de contención. También hay muros de construcción en los cuerpos inferiores, marcando el límite o planta de la estructura y de su núcleo. Los muros exteriores están compuestos de piedra de tamaño mayor, canteadas y colocadas en forma de soga. . . . El edificio presenta un acabado tosco."

4. Estructura 5C-54-5, from Laporte (1983:1-11–1-14):

La estructura 54-4 fue ampliamente estudiada en el lado Sur, y en especial la esquina Sureste, en donde fueron descubiertos totalmente cuatro cuerpos de la misma, dando una altura de 21 metros. También fue localizada ésta en el lado Norte y en la esquina del segundo cuerpo Suroeste. Está ubicada inmediatamente atrás de 54-5 y según parece sus dimensiones son de proporciones enormes; aunque su forma no pudo ser definida exactamente debe ser bastante similar a la construida encima de ella.

Presenta un sistema de construcción diferente al estructura final, ya que durante esta fase de piedras se encuentra generalmente en posición de canto o de lado, existiendo una oapa de argamasa en la sisa de las mismas, así como restos de estuco encima de los muros y pisos estucados en la plataforma de cada uno de ello.

Existen evidencias de una remodelación o de una segunda fase constructiva, ya que fueron encontrados grandes muros que van de Esta a Oeste desde la esquina Sureste hasta una esquina saliente hacia el Sur; esto pertenece a la primer etapa, pero durante la segunda, fueron colocados muros adosados únicamente al muro original, que salen en dirección Sur. Estos muros forman al mismo tiempo una especia de "cajón" o de "nicho" de aproximadamente 3 metros de ancho. Al momento de ser colocados los muros de la segunda etapa, fueron destruidos los de la esquina Sureste y la esquina saliente, dejando únicamente en perfecto estado la parte central que volvió a ser reutilizada. Nos inclinamos a pensar que a estos muros salientes de la segunda etapa se les haya adosado también otros muros que correrían hacia sus respectivas esquinas reutilizando la piedra del o de los muros desmantelados; pero de esto no se encuentran evidencias ya que pudieron ser destruidos para poder construir 54-5, dejando únicamente los muros que no ocasionaban problemas para el nuevo diseño y que al mismo tiempo servían para dar una mayor fuerza y consistencia al relleno.

[Structure 5C-54-4: Structure 54-4 was amply studied on the south side, and especially in the southeast corner, wherein four complete tiers were discovered, reaching a height of 21 m. This was also located in the north side and in the southeast corner of the second tier. It is located immediately behind 54-5 and its dimensions seem to be of enormous proportions; although its form could not be defined exactly, it must be very similar to the pyramid constructed on top of it.

It presents a construction system different from the final structure, as during this phase the stones are encountered generally positioned on edge or sideways, with a coating of mortar in their seams, as well as remains of stucco on top of the stuccoed walls and floors in the platform of each of them.

There is evidence of a remodeling or a second construction phase, as large walls were encountered that go from east to west from the southeast corner to a corner protruding toward the south; this belongs to the first phase, but during the second, there were *adosado* walls located only to the original wall, which protrudes in the south direction. These walls form at the same time a type of "drawer" or "niche" approximately 3 m in width. At the moment when the walls of the second phase were placed, the walls of the southeast corner and the protruding corner were destroyed, leaving in perfect state only the central part that became reutilized. We are inclined to think that to these protruding walls of the second stage were attached other walls that followed to their respective corners, reusing the stone or that of the dismantled walls; but evidence of this was not found, as they could have been destroyed to construct 54-5, leaving only those walls that did not cause problems for the new design and at the same time served to give better force and consistency to the fill.]

5. Laporte and Fialko (1995:56) identified three constructive phases for 5C-54-5: A, B, and C. 5C-54-5B refers to the Early Classic addition of the ninth tier, and 5C-54-5C to the addition of the tenth.

6. Translated from Laporte (1983:1–50): "The east-west tunnel reached 67.46 m in length, which is the maximum dimension of the structure." This tunnel, Suboperation 32, was actually the continuation of tunnels begun by the University of Pennsylvania project in both the west and east faces that were never joined.

7. Original Spanish text:

Como era de esperarse, la más investigada fue la estructura 5C-54-5, que corresponde a la faceta exterior, o sea, la última etapa de construcción. Esta se presenta en un estado de conservación lamentable, ya que existen sectores completamente derrumbados. Se considera que es natural que esto haya sucedido, ya que el relleno empleado para la edificación de la misma es bastante malo. Este se compone de tierra café arenosa y con raras excepciones de piedra grande; además el sistema empleado arquitectónicamente sufre debilidades tremendas, ya que las piedras utilizadas para su construcción no llevan ningún amarre en el cruce de los muros, sino que solamente van adosados los unos a los otros, lo cual no da una resistencia suficiente a este enorme construcción. La estructura 54-5 se compone de diez cuerpos que presentan diferentes dimensiones, tanto el alto como en el ancho de sus plataformas. Su base mide 61.30 metros de largo desde la esquina (*noroeste a la esquina suroeste; y 56.25 mts. desde esta misma esquina)/hasta el extremo sureste. Pero si tomamos esta medida en el eje axial, se presentan con dimensión de 72 metros Norte–Sur y 66.50 metros Este–Oeste; esto es tomando en consideración las esquinas salientes del edificio. La altura de la misma tiene una dimensión de 30.70 metros.

Los lados Norte y Sur fueron diseñados de igual manera, siendo lo más curioso la existencia de "muros entrantes" o "nichos" localizados a nivel del piso y repitiéndose en línea recta ascendente, pero con diferente dimensiones hasta el cuarto nivel. Estos se encuentran cercanos a sus respectivas esquinas, o sea, tanto en el extremo Este como en el Oeste. El lado Oeste presenta verdaderos nichos decorativos cercanos a sus extremos Norte y Sur. Estos fueron encontrados en los primeros 4 niveles, así como también el nivel número 8, por lo que se cree que estuvieron presentes en toda la fachada del edificio. Estos no van en línea recta, sino van acercándose al centro de la estructura conforme sus cuerpos se reducen de tamaño. El resto de su base en este lado se compone únicamente de esquinas remetidas que se presentan con diferentes dimensiones.

Fueron localizadas escalinatas centrales en los 4 lados, pudiendo comprobarse que ni la Norte, ni la Sur, llegan hasta la superficie superior, sino que únicamente ascienden hasta el octavo cuerpo. En el lado Este esta situación no ha sido definida debido al desgarre producido el año 1979, pero podría ser semejante al sector Oeste, en que la escalinata central asciende hasta la cima de la estructura, contando con una inclinación de 45 grados y un número aproximado de 86 escalones.

Esta escalinata se encuentra flanqueada por enormes tableros, de los cuales sólo el Norte se presenta en buenas condiciones, así como también por mascarones que podrían representar reminiscencias de algunas de las estructuras preclásicas de la Acrópolis Norte o de la E-VII-Sub de Uaxactún.

En la parte superior de esta edificación, no fueron encontrados restos de edificio alguno construido en piedra, únicamente fueron localizados los restos de estuco. Se piensa que tampoco existió un templo construido con material perecedero, ya que si así fuera, habrían quedado amontonamientos o restos del derrumbe encima de los pisos, o alguna señal o huella de los postes que lo soportaban; al contrario de esto, la superficie fue encontrada sin ningún tipo de derrumbe que la recubriera; el piso superior ya sólo presenta restos de la grava que sirvió para su fundición, evidenciado así que estuvo expuesto a la intemperie por mucho tiempo. Por lo tanto la superficie superior de la estructura no soportó ningún tipo de templo y que su plataforma siempre fue lisa.

En el lado Sur, fueron localizadas do escalinatas auxiliares, una en la base de la estructura y otra en la parte intermedia, su función aún se desconoce; ambas se encuentran al Oeste de la escalinata central.

La estructura 54-5 sufrió remodelaciones hechas durante el Clásico Temprano, que pueden verse en el lado Oeste al sur de la escalinata central, en que fue eliminada una escalinata auxiliar, así como también en las esquinas noroeste del sexto y séptimo cuerpos en que fueron sustituidas unas de forma redondeada para dar lugar a esquinas rectas y con remetimientos.

References Cited

Aimers, James J., and Prudence M. Rice
2006   Astronomy, Ritual and the Interpretation of Maya "E-Group" Architectural Assemblages. *Ancient Mesoamerica* 17(1):79–96.
Ashmore, Wendy
2005   The Idea of a Maya Town. In *Structure and Meaning in Human Settlements*, edited by Tony Atkin and Joseph Rykwert, pp. 35–54. University of Pennsylvania Museum of Archaeology and Anthropology, Philadelphia.
Aveni, Anthony F., Anne S. Dowd, and Benjamin Vining
2003   Maya Calendar Reform?: Evidence from Orientations of Specialized Architectural Assemblages. *Latin American Antiquity* 14(2):159–178.
Balzotti, Chris S., David L. Webster, Tim M. Murtha, L. Petersen, Richard L. Burnett, and Richard E. Terry
2013   Modelling the Ancient Maize Agriculture Potential of Landforms in Tikal National Park, Guatemala. *International Journal of Remote Sensing* 34(164):5868–5891.
Beach, Timothy, Sheryl Luzzadder-Beach, S. Bozarth, J. Flood, Richard E. Terry, and James A. Doyle
n.d.   Soils and Water Chemistry and Paleoecology at El Zotz and Its Surroundings. In *An Inconstant Landscape: The Archaeology of El Zotz, Guatemala*, edited by Thomas G. Garrison and Stephen Houston. University Press of Colorado, Boulder, in press.
Brady, James E., Joseph Ball, Ronald L. Bishop, Duncan C. Pring, Norman Hammond, and Rupert A. Housley
1998   The Lowland Maya "Protoclassic": A Reconsideration of Its Nature and Significance. *Ancient Mesoamerica* 9:17–38.
Chase, Arlen F., and Diane Z. Chase
1995   External Impetus, Internal Synthesis, and Standardization: E Group Assemblages and the Crystallization of Classic Maya Society in the Southern Lowlands. In *The Emergence of Lowland Maya Civilization: The Transition from the*

Preclassic to the Early Classic, edited by Nikolai Grube, pp. 97–102. Saurwein, Möckmühl, Germany.

Coe, William R.
1990   *Tikal Report No. 14: Excavations in the Great Plaza, North Terrace, and North Acropolis of Tikal*. University Museum, University of Pennsylvania, Philadelphia.

Coggins, Clemency
1979   A New Order and the Role of the Calendar. In *Maya Archaeology and Ethnohistory*, edited by Norman Hammond, pp. 38–50. University of Texas Press, Austin.

Culbert, T. Patrick
1993   *Tikal Report No. 25 Part A: The Ceramics of Tikal*. University Museum, University of Pennsylvania, Philadelphia.
1999   La secuencia cerámica Preclásica en Tikal y la Acrópolis del Norte. In *XII Simposio de Investigaciones Arqueológicas en Guatemala, 1998*, edited by J. P. Laporte and H. L. Escobedo, pp. 63–74. Museo Nacional de Arqueología y Etnología, Guatemala City.

Doyle, James A.
2012   Re-Group on "E-Groups": Monumentality and Early Centers in the Middle Preclassic Maya Lowlands. *Latin American Antiquity* 23(4):355–379.
2013a Early Maya Geometric Planning Conventions at El Palmar, Guatemala. *Journal of Archaeological Science* 40:793–798.
2013b The First Maya "Collapse": The End of the Preclassic Period at El Palmar, Petén, Guatemala. Ph.D. dissertation. Department of Anthropology, Brown University.

Doyle, James A., Thomas G. Garrison, and Stephen D. Houston
2012   Watchful Realms: Integrating GIS Analysis and Political History in the Southern Maya Lowlands. *Antiquity* 86: 792–807.

Doyle, James A., and Stephen D. Houston
2012   A Watery Tableau at El Mirador, Guatemala. *Maya Decipherment: Ideas on Ancient Maya Writing and Iconography*. http://decipherment.wordpress.com/2012/04/09/a-watery-tableau-at-el-mirador-guatemala, accessed August 17, 2013.

Doyle, James A., and Varinia Matute Rodríguez
2010   Excavaciones y levantamiento topográfico de la temporada 2009 en El Palmar. In Proyecto Arqueológico "El Zotz": Informe No. 4, temporada 2009, edited by Edwin Román and Stephen D. Houston, pp. 209–248. Report submitted to the Instituto de Antropología e Historia, Guatemala City.

Doyle, James A., and Rony Piedrasanta
n.d.   The Preclassic Maya of El Palmar and the Buenavista Valley, Petén, Guatemala. In *An Inconstant Landscape: The Archaeology of El Zotz, Guatemala*, edited by Thomas G. Garrison and Stephen Houston. University Press of Colorado, Boulder, in press.

Estrada-Belli, Francisco
2006 Lightning Sky, Rain, and the Maize God: The Ideology of Preclassic Maya Rulers at Cival, Peten, Guatemala. *Ancient Mesoamerica* 17(01):57–78.
2011 *The First Maya Civilization: Ritual and Power before the Classic Period*. Routledge, New York.
2012 Early Civilization in the Maya Lowlands, Monumentality, and Place Making. In *Early New World Monumentality*, edited by R. L. Burger and R. M. Rosenswig, pp. 198–227. University Press of Florida, Gainesville.

Freidel, David A., and Linda Schele
1988 Kingship in the Late Preclassic Maya Lowlands: The Instruments and Places of Ritual Power. *American Anthropologist* 90(3):547–567.
1989 Dead Kings and Living Mountains: Dedication and Termination Rituals of the Lowland Maya. In *Word and Image in Maya Culture*, edited by W. F. Hanks, pp. 233–243. University of Utah Press, Salt Lake City.

Freidel, David A., Linda Schele, and Joy Parker
1993 *Maya Cosmos: Three Thousand Years on the Shaman's Path*. Morrow, New York.

García Barrios, Ana
2008 Chaahk, el dios de la lluvia, en el Periodo Clásico maya: Aspectos religiosos y políticos. Ph.D. dissertation. Departamento de Antropología de América, Universidad Complutense de Madrid.

Garrison, Thomas G., Stephen D. Houston, Andrew K. Scherer, David Del Cid, Ewa Czapiewska, and Edwin Román
2013 A Royal Maya Country House: Archaeology at Bejucal, Guatemala. *Journal of Field Archaeology* 41(5):532–549.

Grube, Nikolai (editor)
1995 *The Emergence of Lowland Maya Civilization: The Transition from the Preclassic to the Early Classic, a Conference at Hildesheim, Germany, November 1992*. Saurwein, Möckmühl, Germany.

Hammond, Norman
1986 New Light on the Most Ancient Maya. *Man* 21:399–413.

Hanks, William F.
1990 *Referential Practice: Language and Lived Space among the Maya*. University of Chicago Press, Chicago.

Hansen, Richard D.
1998 Continuity and Disjunction: The Pre-Classic Antecedents of Classic Maya Architecture. In *Function and Meaning in Classic Maya Architecture: A Symposium at Dumbarton Oaks, 7th and 8th October 1994*, edited by Stephen D. Houston, pp. 49–122. Dumbarton Oaks, Washington, D.C.

Henderson, Lucia Ross
2013 Bodies Politic, Bodies in Stone: Imagery of the Human and the Divine in the Sculpture of Late Preclassic Kaminaljuyú, Guatemala. Ph.D. dissertation. Department of Art and Art History, University of Texas at Austin.

Inomata, Takeshi
n.d. Emergence of Standardized Spatial Plans in Southern Mesoamerica: Chronol-

ogy and Inter-Regional Interaction Viewed from Ceibal, Guatemala. *Ancient Mesoamerica* 27, in press.

Inomata, Takeshi, Daniela Triadan, Kazuo Aoyama, Victor Castillo, and Hitoshi Yonenobu
2013   Early Ceremonial Constructions at Ceibal, Guatemala, and the Origins of Lowland Maya Civilization. *Science* 340:467–471.

Kennett, Douglas J., Sebastian F. M. Breitenbach, Valorie V. Aquino, Yemane Asmerom, Jaime Awe, James U. L. Baldini, Patrick Bartlein, Brendan J. Culleton, Claire Ebert, Christopher Jazwa, Martha J. Macri, Norbert Marwan, Victor Polyak, Keith M. Prufer, Harriet E. Ridley, Harald Sodemann, Bruce Winterhalder, and Gerald H. Haug
2012   Development and Disintegration of Maya Political Systems in Response to Climate Change. *Science* 338(6108):788–791.

Laporte, Juan Pedro
1983   *Informe de Mundo Perdido, Tikal*. INAH, Guatemala City.
1997   Exploración y restauración en la Gran Pirámide de Mundo Perdido, Tikal (Estructura 5C-54). In *X Simposio de Investigaciones Arqueológicas en Guatemala, 1996*, edited by Juan Pedro Laporte and Héctor Escobedo, pp. 332–359. Museo Nacional de Arqueología y Etnología, Guatemala City.

Laporte, Juan Pedro, and Vilma Fialko
1993   El preclásico de Mundo Perdido: Algunos aportes sobre los orígenes de Tikal. In *Tikal y Uaxactún en el Preclásico*, edited by Juan Pedro Laporte and Vilma Fialko, pp. 9–38. Universidad Nacional Autónoma de México, Mexico City.
1995   Un reencuentro con Mundo Perdido, Tikal, Guatemala. *Ancient Mesoamerica* 6:41–94.

McAnany, Patricia A.
2010   Ritual Works: Monumental Architecture and Generative Schemes of Power. In *Ancestral Maya Economies in Archaeological Perspective*, pp. 140–157. Cambridge University Press, New York.

MacLellan, Jessica
2009   Change and Continuity in the Preclassic Architecture of the Las Pinturas Group San Bartolo, Petén, Guatemala. B.A. thesis, Department of Archaeology, Boston University.

Méndez, Alonso, Edwin L. Barnhart, Christopher Powell, and Carol Karasik
2005   Astronomical Observations from the Temple of the Sun. http://www.mayaexploration.org/pdf/observations_temple_sun.pdf, accessed January 10, 2015.

Monroe, J. Cameron
2010   Power by Design: Architecture and Politics in Precolonial Dahomey. *Journal of Social Archaeology* 10(3):367–397.

Nelson, Zachary, and James Doyle
2008   Programa de mapeo y reconocimiento (Operación 7). In *Proyecto Arqueológico "El Zotz": Informe no. 1, temporada de campo 2008*. http://www.mesoweb.com/zotz/El-Zotz-2008.pdf, accessed January 10, 2015.

Ricketson, Oliver, Jr., and Edith Bayles Ricketson
1937   *Uaxactun, Guatemala: Group E-1926–1931*. Carnegie Institute of Washington, Washington, D.C.

Ringle, William M.
1999   Pre-Classic Cityscapes: Ritual Politics among the Early Lowland Maya. In *Social Patterns in Pre-Classic Mesoamerica*, edited by David C. Grove and Rosemary A. Joyce, pp. 183–223. Dumbarton Oaks, Washington, D.C.

Román, Edwin, and Sarah Newman
2010   Excavaciones en el Grupo El Diablo (Operación 5). In Proyecto Arqueológico "El Zotz": Informe no. 5, temporada 2010, edited by Jose Luis Garrido López, Stephen Houston, and Edwin Román, pp. 117–162. Report submitted to the Instituto de Antropología e Historia, Guatemala City.

Saturno, William A., and Franco Rossi
n.d.   Changing Stages: Royal Legitimacy and the Architectural Development of the Pinturas Complex at San Bartolo, Guatemala. Unpublished manuscript, Boston University, Department of Archaeology.

Scherer, Andrew K.
2010   Osteología de El Zotz, Bejucal, y El Palmar temporadas de campo, 2008–2009. In Proyecto Arqueológico "El Zotz": Informe no. 4, temporada 2009, edited by Edwin Román and Stephen D. Houston, pp. 321–333. Report submitted to the Instituto de Antropología e Historia, Guatemala City.

Stanton, Travis W., and David A. Freidel
2003   Ideological Lock-In and the Dynamics of Formative Religions in Mesoamerica. *Mayab* 16:5–14.

Stuart, David
1987   Ten Phonetic Syllables. *Research Reports on Maya Writing* 14:1–52.

Taube, Karl
1998   The Jade Hearth: Centrality, Rulership, and the Classic Maya Temple. In *Function and Meaning in Classic Maya Architecture*, edited by Stephen D. Houston, pp. 427–478. Dumbarton Oaks, Washington, D.C.
2003   Ancient and Contemporary Maya Conceptions about Field and Forest. In *The Lowland Maya Area: Three Millennia at the Human-Wildland Interface*, edited by Arturo Gómez-Pompa, Michael F. Allen, Scott L. Fedick, and Juan J. Jiménez-Osornio, pp. 461–492. Food Products, New York.

Urquizú, Mónica, and William A. Saturno
2004   Proyecto Arqueológico Regional San Bartolo: Resultados de la segunda temporada de campo 2003. In *XVII Simposio de Investigaciones Arqueológicas en Guatemala, 2003*, edited by Juan Pedro Laporte, Bárbara Arroyo, Héctor Escobedo, and Héctor Mejía, pp. 607–613. Ministerio de Cultura y Deportes, Instituto de Antropología e Historia, Asociación Tikal, Guatemala City.

Velásquez Fergusson, Laura
2014   El patrón triádico en el contexto urbano e ideológico de los antiguos asentamientos mayas. *Estudios de Cultura Maya* 43:13–40.

9

The History, Function, and Meaning of Preclassic E Groups in the Cival Region

FRANCISCO ESTRADA-BELLI

Solar observations framed by architecture and ritual offerings placed within the Cival E Group are evidence of the significance of these spaces for the ancient Maya who actively used them to celebrate their cosmovision. In the Late Preclassic period (350 BCE–0 CE), E Group architecture proliferated outside of the Cival hill-center into many smaller surrounding ceremonial sites. The comparison of a sample of accurately surveyed and dated complexes from the Cival region shows certain variability and some important common denominators that once again reject the notion that E Groups had no functionality in terms of solar observations (Aimers and Rice 2006) and at the same time have implications on the processes behind the seemingly nonrandom reproduction of E Group architecture at different sites. One important function that E Groups and, by extension, early Lowland ceremonial centers may have served is to tie claims of resident or nomadic groups to the landscape that they inhabited through geomancy (see also Ricketson 1928; Carlson 1981). Ultimately, I hope to be able to delineate a multiplicity of roles that these ceremonial complexes played in shaping Maya civilization in the Preclassic period.

Cival is an ancient Maya city located 55 km north of the modern town of Melchor de Mencos in the Petén district of Guatemala. It lies 35 km east of the city of Tikal and about 15 km west of the Guatemala-Belize border. The ceremonial center sits on a broad hill overlooking a sinkhole 500 m wide (which gives it the name *cival*). Vast tracks of low-lying land (*bajos*) surround the Cival hilltop center and are seasonally inundated by the Holmul River, which flows south-to-north toward its outlet in the Bay of Chetumal (Figure 9.1). A large residential settlement zone extends out from Cival for at least 2.5 km in every direction until eventually merging

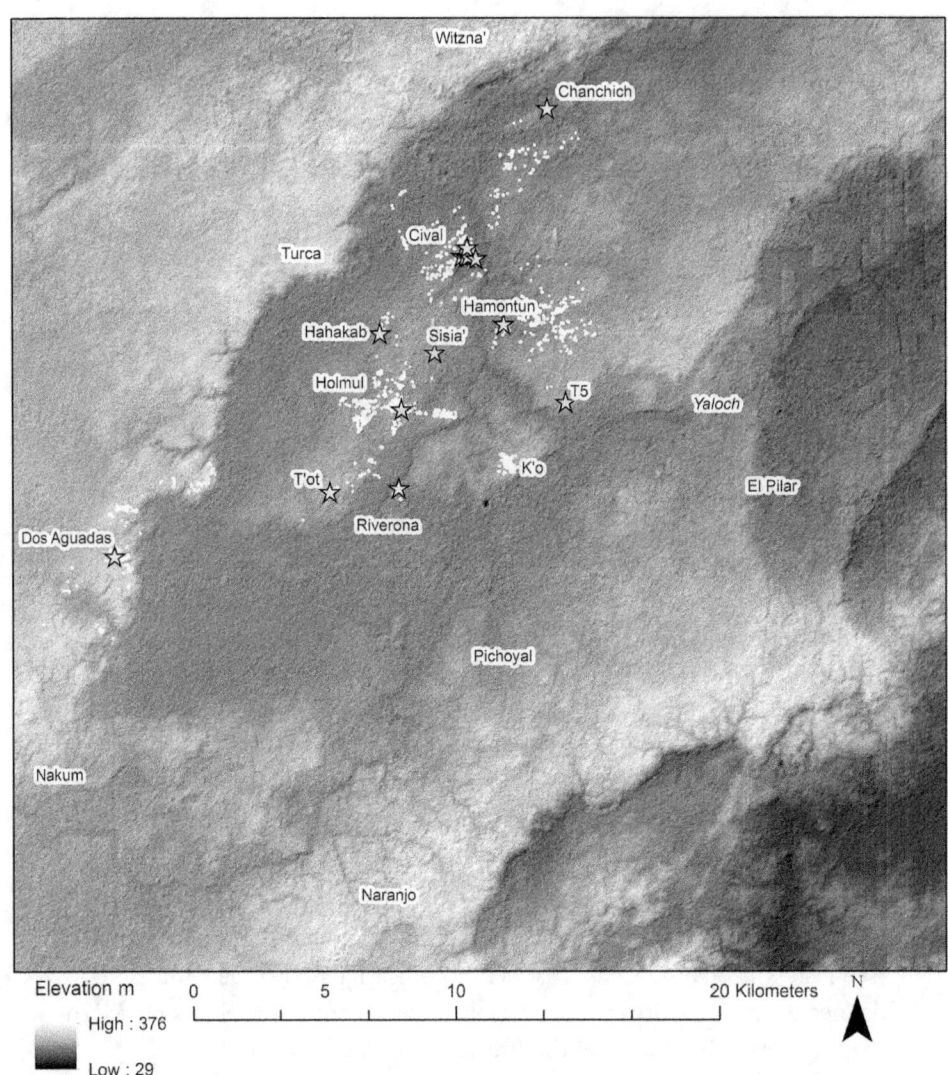

Figure 9.1. Map of the area surrounding the Cival region investigated by the Holmul Archaeological Project. Sites with E Groups are identified by star symbols. White dots represent mapped settlement structures. Neighboring sites are noted for reference. Topographic data courtesy of U.S. Geological Survey/Japan ASTER GDEM2 Program.

with the residential zones of adjacent ceremonial centers also occupied in the Preclassic period. The region studied by the Holmul Archaeological Project extends over approximately 200 km^2 centered on Holmul and including at least thirteen ceremonial centers located so far, including Cival, all occupied in the Preclassic period. Among the centers mapped by this project, nine feature at least one E Group for a total of twelve Preclassic E Group complexes recorded so far. Cival is unique in having five E Group complexes (see below). An additional site, Chanchich, is located 6.3 km to the north of Cival (not to be confused with a Classic period site of the same name in northwestern Belize: see Houk 2015) and features one of the largest E Groups in this region. This site was first reported by Fialko (2005) and was investigated by the Holmul Archaeological Project in the 2014 and 2015 seasons (Estrada-Belli 2014, 2015).

The site of Cival was first visited by archaeologist Raymond Merwin during the 1909–1911 Peabody Museum of Harvard University expeditions to the Classic Maya city of Holmul, located a short distance (7 km) to the south (Merwin and Valliant 1932). Merwin noted and photographed a stela with the carving of a striding human figure. The photo remained largely unnoticed in the archives of the Peabody Museum until another Peabody Museum's explorer, Ian Graham, saw it in the 1970s and attempted to locate it in subsequent visits to the area. On one occasion Graham drafted a preliminary map of the ceremonial center that he named Cival, which clearly showed Preclassic-style triadic and E Group architecture (Ian Graham, personal communication, 1992). The stela photographed by Merwin and the site remained effectively "lost" until 2001, when the Holmul Archaeological Project located the site and noticed a carved stela under the spoils of a looters' trench in the main plaza. In subsequent research campaigns, between 2001 and 2013, a full map of the ceremonial center and its settlement was completed with a total station. Numerous excavations were carried out in an effort to establish baseline data on the occupation and function of various parts of the settlement (see annual reports online at www.bu.edu/holmul/reports; Estrada-Belli 2002a, Estrada-Belli et al. 2003).

Surveys of the area around Cival and Holmul's main ceremonial centers between 2000 and 2015 located and mapped twelve additional medium-sized ceremonial centers within the 200 km^2 research area around Holmul. Excavations confirmed that all were occupied during the Preclassic period, suggesting that the region's population density was at its highest during that period. All the region's centers share certain characteristics, including E Group monumental architecture, a strategic position along access routes to Cival, access to upland and wetland terrain, and broad views of the surrounding areas. Only one site, K'o, lacked E Group architecture, although it had commanding views and is one of the largest centers in this region. The implication of these shared characteristics is that the sites were established with the same concerns about access to land, water, trade routes, and security in mind. Each of them presented evidence of Middle Preclassic occupation in the form of ceramics, some reaching back to 1000 BCE (Pre-Mamom ceramics: Estrada-Belli 2011; Neivens de Estrada 2014), while Cival is the only site with Middle Preclassic architecture, which is strictly its E Group plaza.

Among all the sites in this region (the Holmul study region), the site of Cival stands out for its size. Its ceremonial center is situated on a 500 × 500 m wide hill at the end of a ridge between the Holmul River to the east and a *tintal bajo* (swamp area) to the west. Numerous peripheral ritual complexes and residential house-platforms sprawl over nearby hilltops. An uninterrupted stretch of mound structures has been documented up to a distance of 7 km from Cival that may have been part of what appears to be the Cival greater settlement zone. At the northern end of this zone is the large ceremonial center of Chanchich mentioned above. Beyond it is a 200 m tall escarpment, which may have represented a natural boundary of the Cival settlement zone during the Preclassic period.

The Cival E Group Complex

Cival is unique in this region not only for the size of its monumental core and settlement zone but also for being the only center in which E Group architecture is documented at the onset of the Middle Preclassic period. Over time, as many as five E Group complexes were built within the site core. Cival's first E Group is situated at the central and highest point of the hilltop. Excavations in the western and eastern structures as well as in the plaza (Estrada-Belli 2006, 2011, 2014) have confirmed that the initial version of those buildings was not constructed but carved into the soft limestone. Both platforms only reached 1.5 m in height. The first version of the western pyramid was no more than a single-tier broad platform with radial stairways carved. The eastern platform was a modified limestone knoll into which the steps of a central stairway were carved. Clearly, the location was chosen not only because of the obviously fortunate situation of a broad hill with commanding views of the surrounding landscape, proximity to perennial water sources (river and sinkhole), and vast wetland terrain for

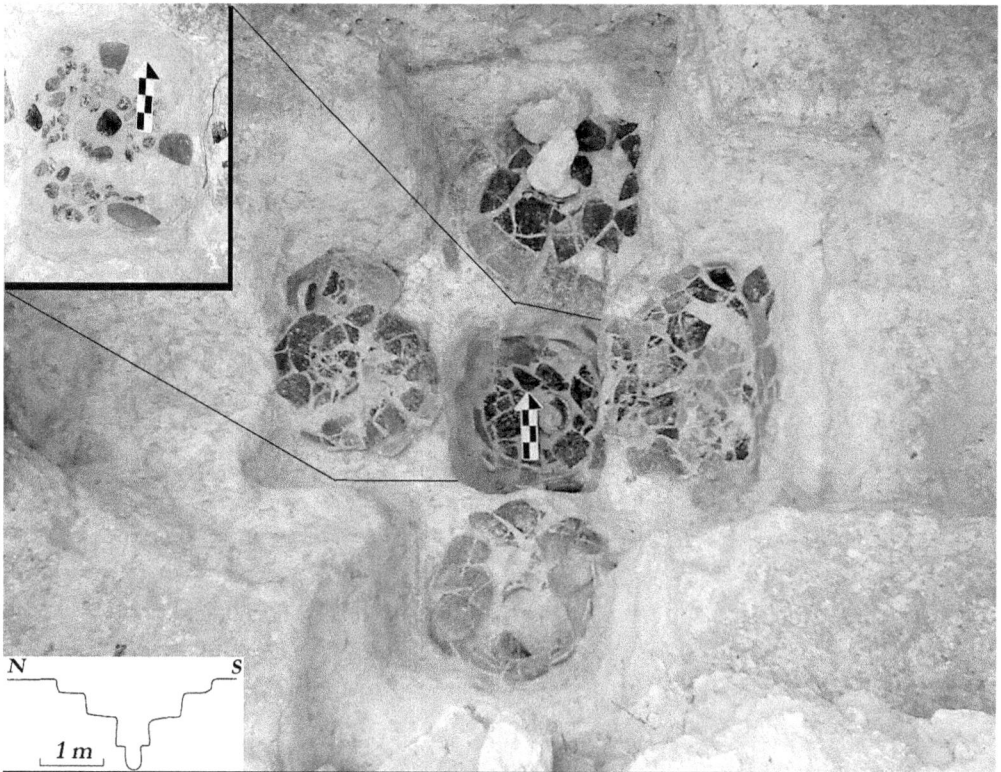

Figure 9.2. Photo and profile views of the Cival Cache 4 containing jade and ceramic jars from ca. 800 BCE.

subsistence but because the limestone on the hilltop was of a fine and soft kind, ideal for being modified into terraces and platforms.

Excavations at the margins of the E Group plaza and beyond documented a massive infilling project, up to 6 m deep in some spots, below the first plaster floor. Under the first floor of the North Plaza (Figure 9.4) was a multichamber *chultun* (humanmade underground cavity). Its construction and use predated the hilltop's infilling project. Within its main chamber were the well-preserved remains of an adult male. From the bone collagen of this individual we were able to secure Cival's earliest C^{14} date (840–800 BCE cal 1 sigma).[1] In the main plaza, a bit of charcoal from the capping of Cival Cache 4 (the "jade cache": see below), which was placed on the eastern edge of the E Group, provided a probable C^{14} date for the placing of the offering between 790 and 760 BCE (cal. 1 sigma).[2] Thus, the construction (carving) of the Cival E Group and the massive infilling effort by which the hill was expanded to form ample leveled space beyond its original limits occurred sometime between 750 and 800 BCE and therefore might be considered part of a single construction project (Estrada-Belli 2011). The proposed bracketing dates are consistent with the style of the ceramics of the construction fill, which can be placed in the Pre-Mamom ceramic phase (1000–850 BCE), and those of the jade offering, which lie at the intersection of the Pre-Mamom and Mamom phases (850–750 BCE, Figures 9.2, 9.4).

Subsequent to the stripping of the topsoil from the center of the hill, the infilling of the sides of the hill, and the carving of the east and west platform, the final act of this construction project was the activation of the E Group as a sacred landscape by placing a massive jade offering of axes, jade pebbles, and five ceramic water jars in a quincunx or k'an-cross pattern. The offering, much like the newly created spaces and volumes, reflects the basic pattern of Maya cosmovision. Within the $1 \times 1 \times 1$ m cross-shaped pit the offerings were placed in multiple layers. At the bottom and center of the idealized k'an cross was a narrow round hole no wider than 20 cm that contained the central and finest blue-green jade axe placed upright. Above it, a square pit contained the 103 pebbles of blue-green jade and the remaining 4 axes also placed cutting-edge up against each side of the pit. The axes may have represented green corncobs sprouting from the cross-shaped cleft in the earth, an image that is at the core of Maya cosmovision (Taube 2005). Further above, on the shelves created by the four arms of the k'an cross/cleft-in-the-earth pit were four large water jars. A fifth jar lay in the central pit, above the jades. These vessels likely symbolized the four directional and central Chaak rain gods invoked to fertilize the sprouting maize/axes symbols with the life-giving liquid substance. Similar directional jar offerings, sometimes tipped over as if in the act of pouring, are known not only in ancient Maya contexts but also elsewhere in Mesoamerica, including at Teotihuacán (Pyramid of the Moon: Sugiyama and López Luján 2007) and in the Aztec Templo Mayor (López Luján 2005), where they constitute ritual offerings associated with the inauguration of a new phase of the sacred pyramid.

Finally, in the last act of the Cival ritual offering the jars were smashed by throwing rocks onto them. Presumably this was intended to spill the liquid substance from the jars onto the jade/maize symbols. Then the pit was filled with soft marl and capped by a fresh layer of plaster matching the limestone surface of the plaza. At the same time, a wooden post was placed at the center of the pit, symbolizing a World Tree emerging from the buried maize seeds. As noted in earlier publications, this ritual reflects the most basic tenet of Maya cosmology, the maize/World Tree emerging from a cleft in the earth nourished by the gods of rain (Estrada-Belli 2006, 2011).

The western pyramid, with its radial stairways, forms a clear counterpart both in plan view and in elevation to the cross-shaped cleft-in-the-earth offering. In addition to the directional stairways, carvings along the main terraces often decorated these pyramids, at least in the Late Preclassic period. In the 2013 and 2014 field season, we uncovered two such reliefs on the northern and western sides of Cival's pyramid pertaining to its last, Late Preclassic period construction phase. Both appear to depict enormous head portraits. The northern relief had sufficient detail preserved in its otherwise eroded plaster coat to reveal shell-shaped ears on the sides of the face (Figure 9.5). This element clearly suggests that the masks depicted directional Chaak rain gods on the four sides of the pyramid. Originally, there may have been two identical head portraits in each side, for a total of eight. While no sign remains of a temple structure atop the pyramid, as Preclassic radial structures often lack these features, it is possible to speculate that an altar or structure of perishable material may have been dedicated to a rain god atop the pyramid, as well.

A carved stone depicting Chaak was found in 2014 just south of the main plaza and named Stela 3. The monument may originally have stood in front of or on the top of one of the E Group's structures and was probably dragged out of the site by looters in recent time. The carving depicts a figure in a contorted pose (Figure 9.3). The style and iconographic elements of this image suggest a Middle to Late Preclassic date (Estrada-Belli 2014).

As noted earlier, the initial version of the eastern platform of the E Group was no more than a modified limestone knoll 1.5 m tall and about 43 m in length. The western platform was located approximately 51 m from it across the plaza. This east–west distance was maintained throughout the history of the E Group, spanning over 1,000 years (not an uncommon characteristic of E Groups) in spite of several enlargements of the structures. This would suggest that this distance was crucial to the function of the complex and that it must have reflected a cosmological template with fixed and meaningful proportions (Estrada-Belli 2011; see also Chapter 8 in this volume).

An imaginary line can be traced from the center of the western pyramid across the plaza to the center of the eastern platform, passing through the jade cache and its post toward the eastern horizon (Figure 9.4). This line has a bearing of 86 degrees, which at Cival corresponds to the location of the sun at sunrise on the day of the equinox (correcting for magnetic drift),

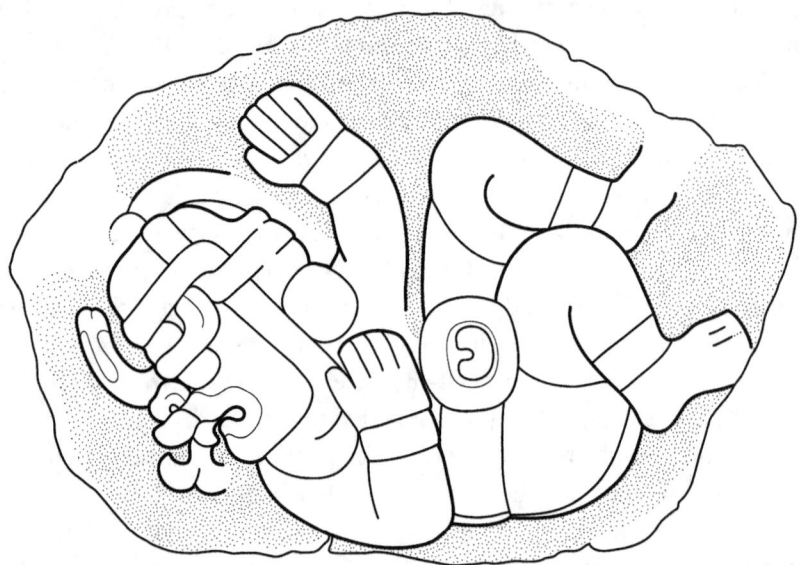

Figure 9.3. Stela 3 of Cival, depicting a Preclassic Rain God (Chaak) figure (Late Preclassic period, 350 BCE–200 CE), located on topsoil, 500 m southeast of the main plaza. Drawing by A. Tokovinine, Holmul Archaeological Project.

although due to uncertainties in our measurements this sight line may well be targeting the sunrise on two days prior to the equinox, on the so-called quarter days, which divide the year in four equal parts (Šprajc, personal communication, 2015; Šprajc and Sánchez 2013). A similarly imaginary line traced from the same central point on the western pyramid toward the northern edge of the eastern platform toward the horizon has a bearing or azimuth of 76 degrees, which corresponds to the sunrise point during the day of the passage of the sun by its zenith.

Finally, the line connecting the western pyramid with the southern corner of the eastern platform continues into the point of sunrise of the antizenith (106 degree azimuth), suggesting that the initial E Group plaza's function was tied to the observation of the sunrise in connection with those specific times of the year (Aveni et al. 2003; Estrada-Belli 2011). As noted by Aveni at al. (2003), the passage of the sun by its zenith, first in early May and again in early August, marks the beginning of the rains and of the growing season for maize, at least in the Petén and adjacent Lowland regions. The thematic links between the solar/agricultural calendar created by the arrangement of E Group platforms and the rain symbolism of the architecture, monuments, and the plaza offering are evident at Cival.

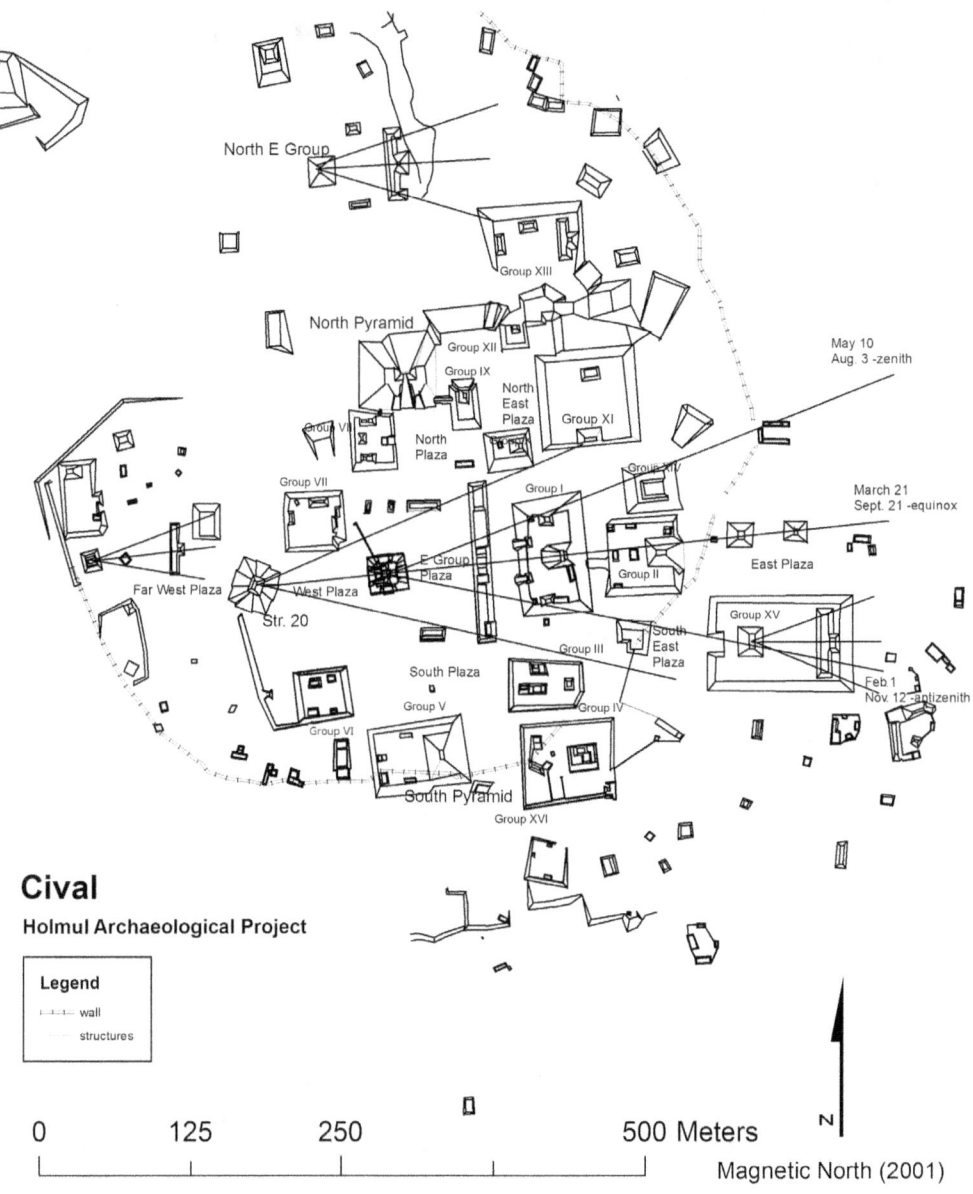

Figure 9.4. Map of Cival at the end of the Terminal Preclassic period (ca. 200 CE), highlighting the sunrise targets of each of the city's five E Groups.

Figure 9.5. Stucco mask on the northern façade of the Cival main E Group's western pyramid (Str. 9; Terminal Preclassic period, 0–200 CE). The carved head features, L-shaped eyes, shell ear, and beak or proboscis are consistent with the iconography of the rain god Chaak (Estrada-Belli 2014).

While E Groups should not be thought of as solar observatories in the western scientific sense, especially because of the impossibility of making exact observations using roughly shaped buildings, Aveni et al. (2003; see also Chapter 3 in this volume) have demonstrated with empirical data that they likely functioned as templates to commemorate important solar epiphanies and their corresponding dates in conjunction with ritual, meteorological, and agricultural periods (see also Aimers 1993). This is in agreement with the statements of Ricketson (1928) regarding Uaxactún and recent reviews of E Groups by Aimers (1993; Aimers and Rice 2006).

This basic architectural arrangement of Cival's first E Group and its function to celebrate solar dates continued unchanged for the remainder of the Middle Preclassic period, for over 400 years. At the beginning of the Late Preclassic period (ca. 350 BCE) new elements were introduced that reinforced and expanded the symbolic linkages of E Groups with calendar rituals as well as with the local landscape.

E Groups in the Late Preclassic Period at Cival and Beyond

Cival is so far unique among all known Preclassic ceremonial centers in featuring five separate E Group complexes within the confines of its monumental core. Each of these appears to have been built on bedrock by first stripping away the topsoil, as is the case in the main plaza. Later they were remodeled with multiple-tiered platforms with cut-stone and plaster facings over a stone and marl core that replicated the natural-bedrock appearance of the original version of the main plaza's E Group. Each of these additional complexes appears to have been built at the onset or during the Late Preclassic period. In some cases the structures were enlarged up to five times during the course of that lengthy period from 350 BCE to 200 CE. In only one case, in the North E Group, the monumental plaza and architecture were laid over preexisting buildings that apparently were residential in nature. In all other tested cases (Cival Far West, Holmul, and Hamontun), previously unoccupied locations were chosen or at least any preexisting architecture had been previously stripped away with the topsoil. In one case, in the East E Group, the actual floor and structures rested on an elevated fully artificial platform that stood 3–4 m above the natural ground (Figure 9.1).

The overall distribution of Cival's five E Groups follows an almost perfect directional arrangement except for a missing southern E Group. Four groups are located on the main hill, while the North E Group is on a separate hill, which is connected to the site center by a land bridge. Each of the E Groups appears to conform to the Cenote type (Chase and Chase 1995; see also Chapter 2 in this volume) with a wider and taller central structure set back from the main eastern platform. The new Central and North E Groups also feature outset platforms at the extremities of the main elongated structure, while all others only feature a central one (Figure 9.9).

Cival's central plaza underwent major changes at the onset of the Late Preclassic period (ca. 350 BCE). A Triadic Group (Group 1) was built at its eastern edge behind the eastern platform. The first version of the Triadic Group platform was no more than 3 m tall and its pyramidal structures likely only 2–3 m higher than that. Overall, then, the new Triadic Group created a more interesting backdrop to the eastern platform's simple horizontal line. Its central structure perfectly lined up with the center line of the eastern platform. The view of the sunrise from the west pyramid during the equinox was unaffected. Similarly, the two lateral pyramidal structures were small and lined up with the extremities of the eastern platform so as to maintain those sight lines to the zenith and antizenith sunrises unobstructed. Later the Uaxactún type of E Group recalled this triadic pattern in a condensed fashion with three temples built directly on the eastern platform.

Over time, the Triadic Group was expanded, in height and width, but the lateral sight lines with the E Group's pyramid were kept clear of obstructions. The view through the much higher central pyramid toward the equinox sunrise was compromised, however, because the observer on the west pyramid would have been somewhat lower than the top of the Triadic Group's central pyramid (18 m versus 33 m high). This would have hidden the sun as it emerged from the horizon for a few hours until it appeared off-angle. The architects of Cival resolved this problem with the construction of a new western pyramid further west of the original one. They also extended the sides of the eastern platform to a length of 129 meters. With these additions the architects created a larger E Group that fully contained the original complex while still allowing its original sight lines from the initial western pyramid to be functional. The new western pyramid was slightly taller (21 m high) than the old one thus allowing a sighting through the E Group's center and through the tip of the Triadic Group at a near-horizontal angle so as to view the equinoctial sunrise at the right date and time. The lateral sight lines of the new western pyramid went through the extended eastern platform searching for the sunrise during the December and June solstices.

It is difficult to date the expansion of the main Cival E Group exactly. The construction of the western pyramid was final (it was not subsequently remodeled). Ceramic material associated with its single-phase fill is Late Preclassic. The structure might thus have been built sometime near the end of the Late Preclassic period, most likely in the first century CE to match the last phase of the Triadic Group. The eastern platform was renovated one more time, however, in the Terminal Preclassic period, in the second or third century CE. It is therefore possible that by the beginning of the Common Era three types of solar horizon markers (the equinoxes [or the quarter days], the solstices, and the zenith passages) were venerated in the same architectural public space at Cival.

A clue to what might be the significance of combining these solar events into a single ritual template can be found in the pecked cross from Uaxactún (and elsewhere in Mesoamerica). Aveni et al. (2003; Chapter 3 in this volume) have pointed out that the number of days on those pecked crosses' concentric circles closely corresponds to the days separating the equinoxes

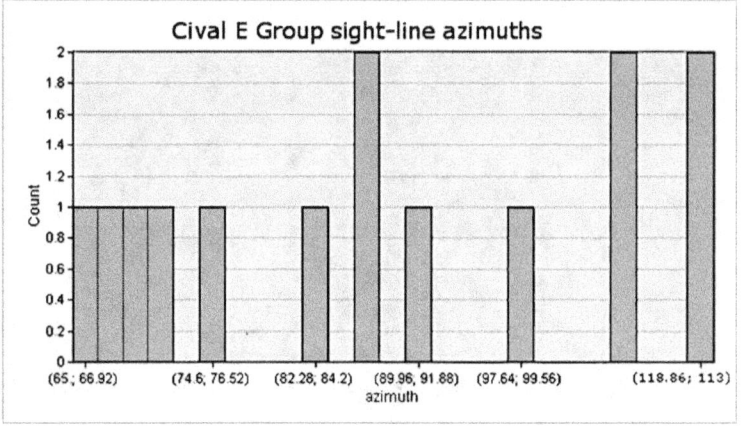

Figure 9.6. Histogram of sight-line azimuths (in degrees clockwise from north) pertaining to the five Cival E Groups.

from the solstices (outer ring) and the equinoxes from the days of zenith passages (inner ring). Moreover, those two counts of days closely correspond to the number of days in the solar Haab year cycle (360 + 5 days) and in the ritual/agricultural Tzolk'in (260 days) cycle. The intercalation of the 260 days of the Tzolk'in with a period of 105 days is still used today to regulate the yearly schedule of rituals during the growing and dry seasons by the Highland Maya (Girard 1962, 1966).

Among the Cival E Groups there is variability in sight-line orientation (Figure 9.6). The range of variation includes sunrises during solstices, zenith passages, and equinoxes or increments of 20 days prior to or after those solar events, as noted by Aveni et al. (2003). The north sight line of Cival's central E Group appears to be pointing to the sunrise on the day of the zenith. Two complexes, the Far West and the North E Groups, share the northern sight line (through the northern corner of their east platform) toward the June solstice (65–67 degrees).[3] Two other complexes, the Central and East E Group, share the center sight line to the equinox. Two others, the Central and West E Group (the larger central one), share the southern sight line to the sunrise on the day of the antizenith (107 degrees, November 12). Two complexes, the North and East E Groups, share a southern sight line to the December solstice (113 degrees, June 21). Finally, two others, the West and East E groups, have the same northern sight line (70 degrees, Z [Zenith] + 20 days and also JS [June Solstice]-20). In addition, the center line of the Far West E Group points to the sunrise on April 1, which corresponds to 40 days before the zenith passage (Z-40). Finally, the North

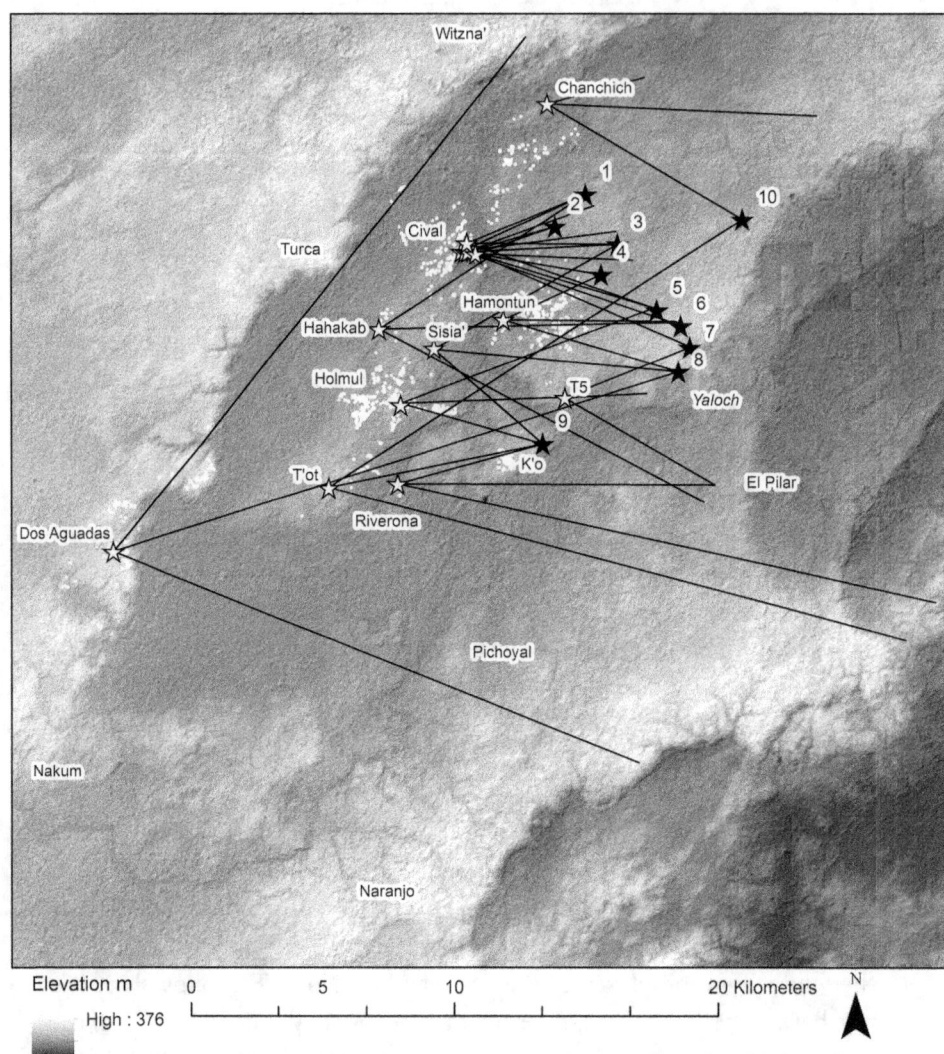

Figure 9.7. Location of the thirteen E Groups in the region surrounding Cival, with star symbols and hilltops targeted (red stars, numbered 1–9) by multiple E Group sight lines (red lines). Topographic data courtesy of U.S. Geological Survey and Japan ASTER GDEM program.

E Group's center line points to only 3 degrees south of the equinox line and would thus correspond to March 17, 55 days prior to the zenith passage (Z-55). This sight line is at odds with the consistency of 20 day increments in relation to major solar markers as described above and therefore requires further analysis (see below).

During the Late Preclassic period (350 BCE–0 CE) several additional E Groups were built outside of the Cival ceremonial center. As at Cival, each of these was constructed on bare ground after stripping the topsoil with stone and mortar faced by cut stones and stucco. Specifically, eight E Groups have been mapped at secondary ceremonial centers in the Cival region, for a total of thirteen including the five Cival E Groups. As at Cival, these complexes widely range in size and orientation while maintaining certain basic common characteristics, such as the western radial pyramid-eastern platform pair and fixed plaza width through time. Adjacent to the E Groups, ballcourts and palace-like platform groups were also added during the Late Preclassic period (ballcourts exist only at Dos Aguadas and Chanchich, the two largest sites, palaces at all others). Monumental Triadic Groups, another architectural hallmark of this period, are only documented at Cival so far in this region.

To improve the present analysis, all thirteen E Groups in the region, including those previously discussed within the Cival core, are discussed here as a single group. Even though each site may have constituted a separate political entity, it is likely that because of proximity and other factors these centers may have been politically and ritually related to the Cival center during the time in which E Groups were in use for public rituals. As noted elsewhere (Estrada-Belli 2002a, 2011, Estrada-Belli et al. 2003), ample archaeological evidence indicates that Cival was the main political center and therefore its architecture probably had a leading role in shaping ceremonialism in the entire region. What remains to be ascertained is whether the initial construction of E Groups was spontaneous and independent at each site or interconnected and planned as a whole from a single source. The limits of Cival's hypothesized region of influence are unknown, although it would be reasonable to assume that they might have extended halfway to three other neighboring major centers of the Preclassic period: Naranjo, Nakum, and El Pilar to the south (10 km), southeast (10 km), and east (7 km), respectively. Chanchich may have been the northernmost site affiliated with Cival. No major Preclassic site further to the north is known at this time. Chanchich's location is coincidentally at the same distance from Cival as Holmul (exactly 6.3 km). This would suggest that both these

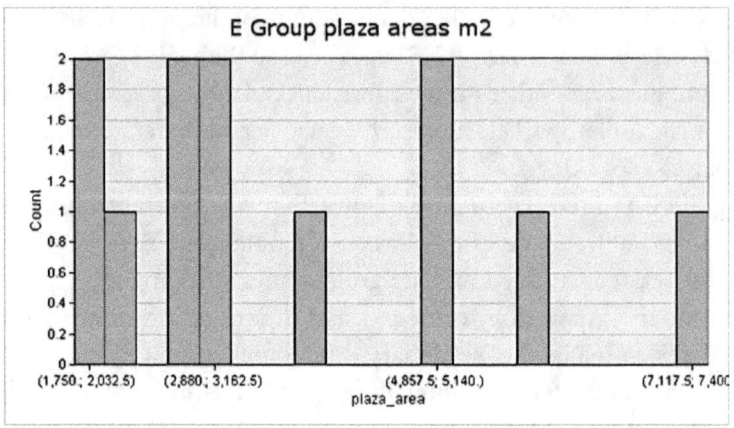

Figure 9.8. Histogram of E Group plaza areas at Cival and surrounding region in square meters.

centers, the two largest outside of Cival, served as hubs of political and ceremonial activity in the northern and southern sectors of Cival's domain. The recent finding of a causeway linking Cival to Holmul and remnants of a causeway/ramp on the southern edge of Chanchich leading in the direction of Cival support this hypothesis (Estrada-Belli 2015).

E Group Dimensions

Let me begin the comparison by noting that one measure of the size of each of these E Groups might be plaza area and that this metric appears to be roughly proportional to other dimensions of the surrounding ceremonial core, such as total volume of monumental architecture, ballcourts, and residential groups (Figure 9.8). The largest plaza associated with an E Group in this region, measuring 7,400 m^2, is at Cival, in the West E Group. Cival also had by far the largest volume of monumental architecture and residential settlement in the region during the Late Preclassic period (never surpassed in the Classic periods by any of the region's sites). As noted earlier, Cival's West E Group in turn incorporated an earlier E Group in its center, although only the western part of the plaza, which was built later in the Late Preclassic period, was included in the West plaza area calculation. Holmul's E Group plaza is second in size with 5,800 m^2, followed by Chanchich, reinforcing the hypothesis that these two centers served similar roles in the region, as secondary centers in relation to Cival. Further below in the plaza area size rankings are two plazas measuring 5,000 m^2, the Central E Group at Cival and the Dos Aguadas complex.

It is worth noting that a 5,000 m² plaza could accommodate a standing crowd of 5,000 to 10,000 people, which in many cases far exceeds the currently estimated population of each of these centers. Cival's population, considering even its vast rural settlement, probably only reached 10,000 according to the most optimistic estimate for its peak (the Late Preclassic period). The population of any of the other centers in the region would only reach a fraction of that figure. This apparent incongruity between the size of plazas and population estimates may have implications regarding the function of E Groups as monumental areas for the congregation of a population that at times may have included seminomadic groups and was widely dispersed over a region that was wider than its immediate settlement zone, as noted elsewhere in this volume (see Chapter 7 in this volume; see also Estrada-Belli 2011, 2012). Perhaps in the Late Preclassic period each of the larger E Groups in the region hosted ceremonies attended by the population of the entire region and beyond on a rotation basis.

Other dimensions to use in comparing the Cival region's set of 13 E Groups in search of consistencies and variability might be (1) plaza width, which is known in most cases to be maintained over the several centuries of use in spite of refurbishment of the adjoining structures, (2) length of the eastern platform, (3) footprint area of the western pyramid, and (4) azimuth of the three solar observations at sunrise potentially allowed through the center and extremities of the eastern platform by an observer on the western pyramid (Figure 9.9). The last measure of comparison is obviously dependent on the unique combination of the previous three factors determining the size and spacing of the architecture from and through which the solar observations were made.

The histogram of plaza widths shows a relative consistency in the distance between the western pyramid, the observation point for sunrises, and the eastern platform (Figure 9.10). Most E Groups appear to fit in a cluster that ranges from small (32 m) to large (63.5 m) with only one outlier, Cival's West E Group (162.2 m). There thus appears to be little variability in the width of E Group plazas, if we exclude Cival's West E Group as a bit of a singularity, at least for this region. It is worth noting that Cival's unusual set of nested E Groups is also present at Yaxhá in even larger size (Quintana et al. 2000). Moreover, the main Yaxhá E Groups also face a Triadic Group, which, as at Cival, provides a backdrop for the eastern horizon of the central and western E Groups. With this exception in mind, it appears that the width of E Groups in the Cival region at least in general terms follows a pattern of standardized units of measure, which, as noted by Doyle

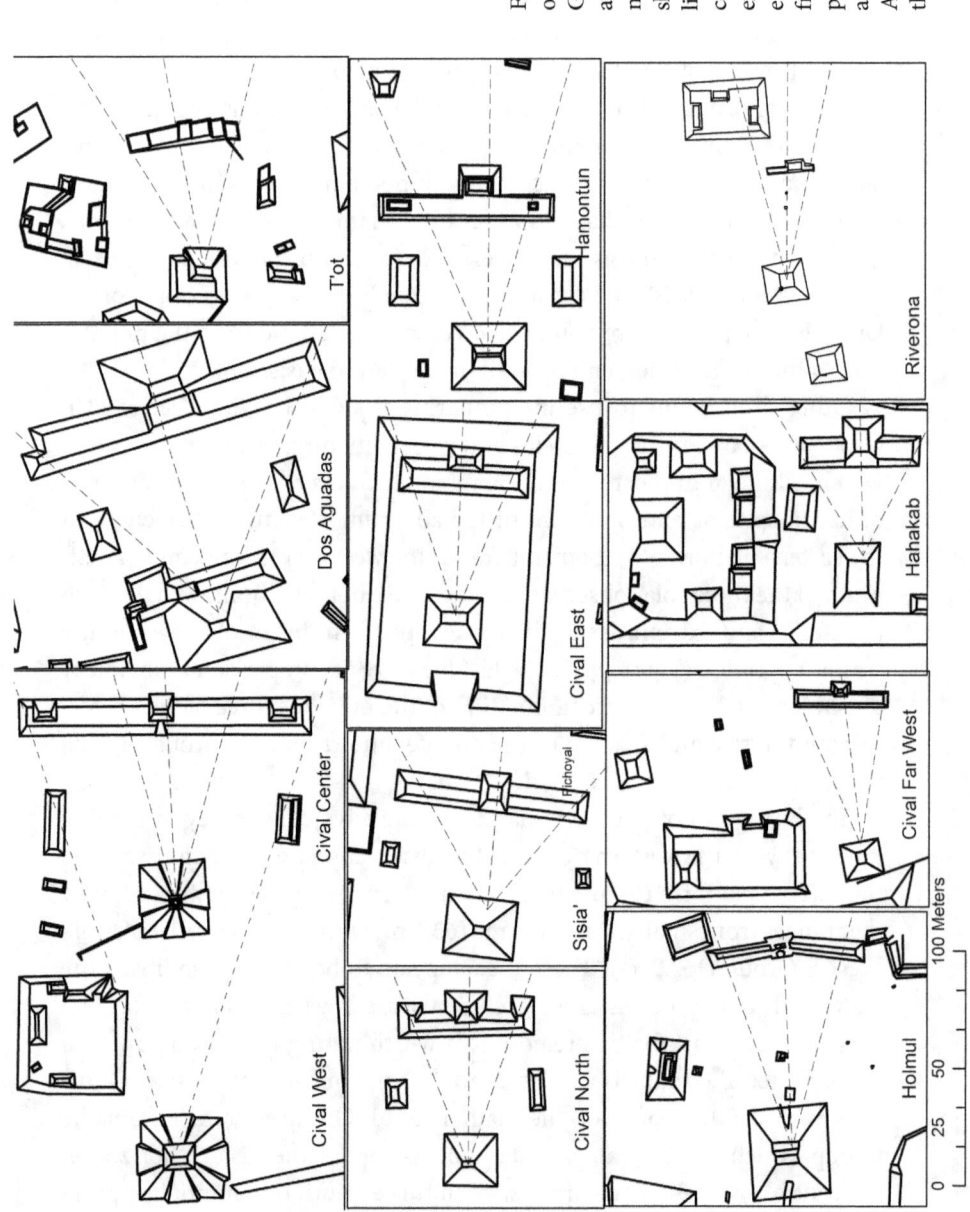

Figure 9.9. Maps of eleven E Groups mapped at Cival and nearby sites showing sight lines through center and extremities of the eastern platforms from the western pyramids as well as relative size. All maps are at the same scale.

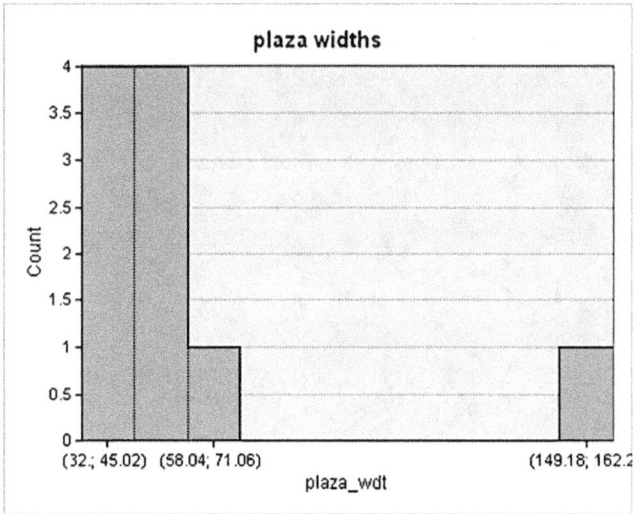

Figure 9.10. Histogram of E–W plaza width (m) of twelve of thirteen E Groups in the Cival region measured from the edge of the western pyramid to the edge of the eastern platform.

(2013, Chapter 8 in this volume), may have its origin in the use of cords of standard length for laying out agricultural fields.

The distribution of lengths of eastern platforms (Figure 9.11) and basal area (footprint) of western pyramids in our sample once again shows the Cival's West E Group as an outlier (1,258 m^2, Figure 9.12). It is not the only extreme case, however, since Holmul has a similarly large western pyramid (1,318 m^2). This is likely due to later Classic period enlargements, as is the

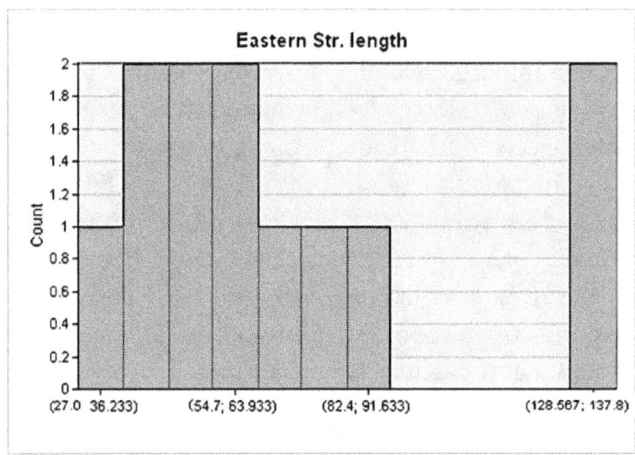

Figure 9.11. Histogram of length of eastern platform for twelve E Groups at Cival and nearby sites.

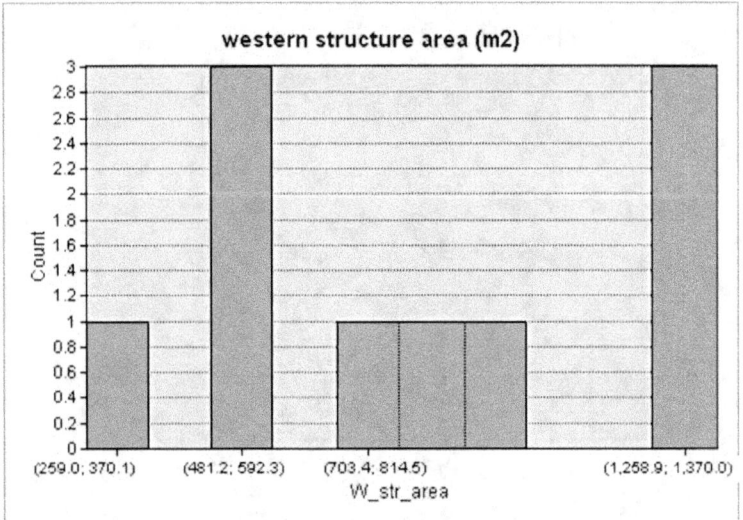

Figure 9.12. Histogram of footprint areas of western pyramid at Cival and nearby sites.

case at Dos Aguadas (1,370 m²). In terms of lengths of eastern platforms, both Dos Aguadas and Cival's West E Groups stand far from the rest of the sample at 137 m and 129 m in length, respectively. In the Dos Aguadas case there was at least one enlargement in the Early Classic period and one in the Late/Terminal Classic period, although it is unknown how much these remodeling efforts may have affected the length in addition to the height of the structure. All of the remaining cases in this sample appear to have been built and used only during the Late Preclassic period (350 BCE–0 CE). Even with these caveats in mind, these structures' parameters appear to vary more than other measures of comparison. Each of the three metrics might be affected by length of use and number of subsequent enlargements, in addition to the relative importance of the sites in the regional hierarchy throughout their use history. The three measures appear to be interrelated, however. Plaza width appears to be a good predictor of eastern platform length and western pyramid footprint area (R sq correlation coefficients = 0.77 and 0.74), while western pyramid and eastern platforms dimensions are also strongly related to one another (R sq. = 0.84). As might be apparent when we review the azimuth sight lines below, this relatedness in the dimensions of plazas and structures of E Groups may be in large part a function of the sightings that the architects were attempting to achieve on the horizon using these structures as viewing templates.

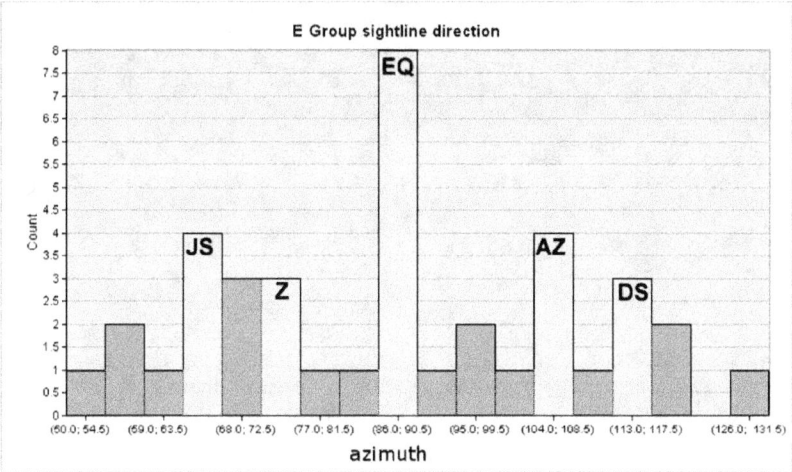

Figure 9.13. Histogram of azimuths for each of three sight lines for twelve E Groups at Cival and nearby sites. Cival E Group's sight lines are highlighted and the corresponding major solar events are identified by their initials, June Solstice, Zenith, Equinox, Antizenith, December Solstice ($n = 38$).

E Group Sight Lines

At first glance the distribution of E Group sight lines from all sites in the Cival region appears to be widely dispersed across the range between 50 degrees (the northern sight line of Dos Aguadas) to 131 degrees (the southern sight line of Sisia') (Figure 9.13). In either case, the overall orientation of the E Groups appears to be widely dispersed to the north and to the south of the equinox. The Dos Aguadas center line sights the zenith-day sunrise, for example. There are some clear recurrences within the whole sample, however. The equinox or quarter days sight lines are the most common. They occur five times, in each instance as an E Group center line. The second most common is the June solstice with four occurrences. The December solstice is targeted only two times (out of thirty-eight sight lines in the sample) while the antiazimuth is sighted only at three E Groups. But, as noted in the Cival case study, some of the other sight lines that do not correspond to this set of specific sunrise events do appear to mark the sun rising at evenly spaced intervals prior to or after one of those major events. For example, three E Groups (Cival West, Cival East, and Holmul) share the Z+20 (and JS-20) sight line. The Riverona and Cival Far West southern sight lines appear to approximate the Z-80 sunrise (99–101 degrees).

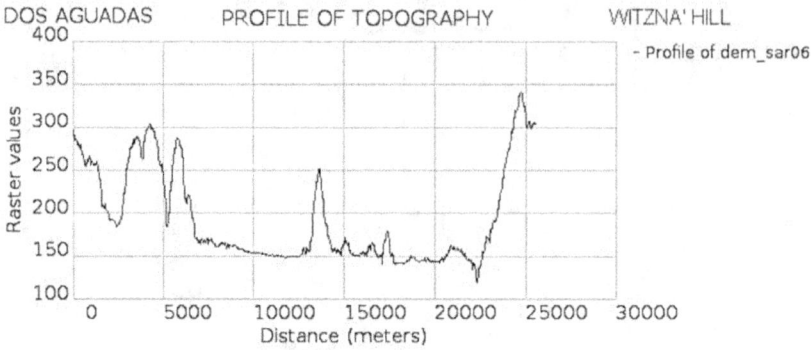

Figure 9.14. Profile of the topography along the Dos Aguadas northern sight line to a major hill in the vicinity of Witzná (see Figure 9.7). Topographic data courtesy of National Aeronautics and Space Administration AIRSAR 1999 mission.

The Riverona and Sisia' center lines in turn approximate the Z-60 sunrise on the horizon (96 degrees). In other words the majority of Cival region's E Groups' sight lines seem to conform to the pattern of solar events and regular 20-day intervals first noted by Aveni et al. (2003) and observed in the Cival site core sample above.

However, there are also some interesting discrepancies in the regional sample. The seemingly odd sight line of the Cival North E Group marking the sunrise on April 1 for the nonstandardized day-distance of Z-55 noted above also occurs at the sites of Hahakab and Hamontun, southeast and southwest of Cival. Also perplexing is the southern sight line of three E Groups (Hahakab, Hamontun, and T5) with azimuths of 118 degrees, well past the southernmost position of the sun on the horizon (December 21, 113 degrees). Likewise, at the other end of the range as many as four sight lines extend beyond the northernmost point of sunrise (65 degrees, June solstice). These outliers range from an extreme of 50 (Dos Aguadas northern line) to 57–58 (Hahakab and T'ot) and 60 degrees (Sisia'). It is presently unknown whether any or all of these uncommon sight lines might be related to a undetermined celestial body observed in the predawn sky on the horizon or to mapping error. Further analysis might perhaps elucidate this point. It is also perplexing to consider that all these nonsolar sight lines are widely distributed in the region. There is something other than celestial bodies on the horizon in each of these directions, however: a major landscape feature (hill). This is perhaps not coincidental in the case of the extreme Dos Aguadas northern line, which points to the most prominent

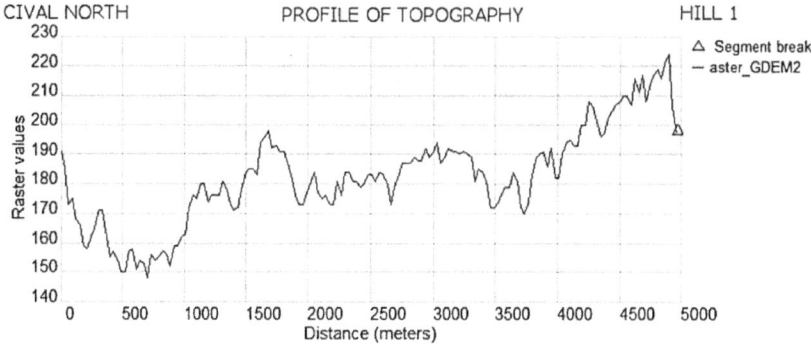

Figure 9.15. Profile of the topography of the Cival region along the northern sight line of the North E Group at Cival, targeting a major hill approximately 5 km away also targeted by two other E Groups (Hill 1; see Figure 9.7). Topographic data courtesy of U.S. Geological Survey/Japan ASTER GDEM2 program.

hill along the long escarpment that rings one side of the Cival basin. This very tall hill, which is located at 25 km away and is near the Classic period city of Witzná, is so prominent that it would have been visible on any clear day (Figure 9.14). The closeness of another important center might have had something to do with its sighting from the Dos Aguada's E Group, although little is currently known about Witzná's history. This hill is by far the most conspicuous rise in the region's horizon and might therefore have held special religious significance for the region's inhabitants.

In a similar fashion the northern sight line from Hahakab's E Group is the second most extreme in the sample at 58 degrees and points to a notable rise in the landscape at a distance of 9 km.

What's most striking, however, is that this hill was not targeted by Hahakab's E Group alone. Two other E Groups, Cival North and Far West, looked toward it through their northern sight line (Figure 9.15).

A glance at Figure 9.7 (in which sight lines for all the E Groups in the region are plotted against the natural topography) thus allows us to identify nine major hills that are targeted by more than one E Group. The visibility of each of the targeted hills from each of its connected E Groups was confirmed by drawing a profile similar to those in Figure 9.6 on the natural topography along the sight line. Here too the sample shows interesting patterns. When we consider that each E Group sight line may have had visual links not only with the sunrise but also with a significant point on the landscape's horizon, we realize that all E Groups in fact shared one or more hill-targets. Even Dos Aguadas, the most extreme and distant from all other E Groups, targeted through its center line a "shared" hill (Hill 8) that was also sighted by two other E Groups (Sisia' and Hamontun). Hills 3, 5, 8, and 9 all are sighted (shared) by three different E Groups (Figure 9.7).

Hill 3 is sighted by three E Groups (Cival Central, Cival North, and Sisia'). Cival's Center E Group sighting occurs through its center line toward the equinox and therefore might be considered an earlier choice, because it is associated with the earliest E Group in the region. If we look at which other hills were targeted by this first E Group, we find that its northern sight line (to the zenith passage) pointed to Hill 2, which is also targeted by Cival's East E Group on the day of the Z+20 interval. A further example of this pattern might be Hill 5, which is targeted by the southern sight line of the Central Cival E Group, pointing to the sunrise on the day of the antizenith and is also targeted by the North E Group at Cival (south sight line) and by the Holmul E Group (northern sight line). Based on these examples it is possible to hypothesize that the initial identification of significant points on the landscape in connection with solar events on the horizon may have been done in the Middle Preclassic and in the only E Group in use at that time in this region (Cival Center) and that the proliferation of E Groups at and around Cival may have been guided by the desire to tie the new E Groups to some of the hilltops originally sighted from that complex. As the number of E Groups and their dispersion on the landscape increased, other hills were added (up to a total of nine), in such a way as to maintain all E Groups interconnected not only by observations of related solar events but by marking significant features on the landscape shared by neighboring centers.

Beyond their selective visibility through E Group architecture, the nine shared hills appear to be significant in terms of a sacred landscape in a way similar to what has been described by Evon Z. Vogt (1981) for the sacred mountains around Zinacantán. To test this hypothesis, a set of trials using the Geographic Information Systems "viewshed" tool were run on high-resolution topographic data to determine which hills were generally visible from each of the E Groups without regard to specific sight lines (Madry and Rakos 1996; Estrada-Belli 2002b; Tourtellot et al. 2000). The viewshed maps showed that, with a few exceptions, the suspected sacred hills were prominently visible from all E groups. Interestingly, Cival's five E Groups had all nine hills within their view. This would suggest that the nine hills were first selected by the Civaleños as sacred features of the surrounding landscape sometime in the Late Preclassic period or, perhaps more likely, in the Middle Preclassic period during the construction of the first E Group. This pattern would also suggest that the construction of secondary E Groups was initiated and supervised by the Cival rulers. All other E Groups in the region, dating to the Late Preclassic period, were likely situated to allow visibility of as many of the nine sacred hills as possible.

The main focus of the architecture was to target the three most relevant hills specific to the E Group site location, but with special care to include at least one or more of the nine sacred hills that were also visible from other neighboring viewing locations, as noted above. Thus, outside Cival, six other E Groups had views of all but one hill. Two E Groups could see at least five hills and only one (Hahakab) was oriented so that only four of the nine sacred hills could be seen. Hill 1 was visible by all E Groups. The second most visible was Hill 2. Both are located in the extreme north sector of the region, but, surprisingly, not on the tall escarpment ridge that is most prominent on the far horizon.

Of the hilltop locations inspected, five had small structures. A low square platform was the most common type, but small range residential structures were present as well. No major pyramids have been noted in these locations, and no excavation data are presently available to support any hypothesis about the special function of these structures. It is possible however, as noted earlier, that each may have held special significance and as such would have been associated with altars, pyres, or other less conspicuous features that may currently be difficult to detect under the jungle undergrowth without proper excavation.

This discussion suggests that the process of assigning ritual significance to specific features in the horizon in addition to the cardinal directions and other cosmological divisions, also known as "geomancy," may have been a major element of E Group rituals since their inception in the Middle Preclassic period. Oliver Ricketson (1928) was the first archaeologist to suggest that geomancy, as well as observation of celestial bodies (the sun, as noted by Frans Blom in 1924), played a role in the function of E Groups. Later George Kubler (1958) reiterated the idea in his study of Maya architecture. In exploring Mesoamerican cities as expression of cosmological as well as local mythology, John B. Carlson (1981) drew upon the literature on Chinese geomancy as well as Maya ethnological and documentary data (especially codices) to show various ways in which geomancy may have played a role in the laying out of Maya ceremonial spaces and buildings, including E Groups. Radial pyramids such as the Postclassic period El Castillo of Chichén Itzá and Mayapán, according to Carlson, are especially clear examples of the materialization of primordial and widespread spatiotemporal cosmological constructs and geomancy that are specific to each site's mythological narrative.

Concluding Remarks

This chapter presents some data on E Groups from an unusual sample of thirteen neighboring architectural complexes recorded by a single team (the Holmul Archaeological Project, from 2000 to 2015; see annual reports at http://bu.edu/holmul/reports). Previous studies have benefited from larger and more widely distributed samples of E Groups (Aimers and Rice 2006; Aveni et al. 2003). This analysis, however, might have benefited not only from the size of the sample but also from the richness of contextual information available for each E Group. All but two were accurately mapped using GPS positioning and total stations. Several were excavated, some extensively (Cival Center, Dos Aguadas, Holmul, and Hamontun). All of the maps were complemented by surface and stratigraphic data obtained from excavation of structures and residential areas nearby. This enabled me to place the E Groups in a broader regional context during the time of their use. The nature of this sample may have helped remove some of the limitations of larger samples without stratigraphic data, such as lack of construction history, inconsistent mapping accuracy, and other variables that might mask commonalities in the way E Groups were built and used.

One of the most intriguing aspects of E Groups is that until recently they have defied definitions and interpretations because of a perceived wild variability in sizes, orientations, and architectural elements combined with the false assumption that Uaxactún's E Group was the prototype (Aimers 1993; Aimers and Rice 2006). Several interesting patterns have emerged from the current sample from Cival however. With the benefit of excavated data, we were able to observe the original size and orientation and to infer some of the religious meanings associated with one of the earliest E Groups in the Lowlands: Cival's Central E Group, which dates to the early part of the Middle Preclassic period (see also Inomata et al. 2013 and Chapter 7 in this volume). For example, it is clear that elements previously thought to be integral to E Groups such as the two ancillary structures that often frame an E Group plaza on the north and south sides are late additions. Likewise, the often-cited Eastern Triadic Structures arrangement is not as common as previously thought in well-documented examples from the Late Preclassic period. In its stead, there is most often only one addition to the flat eastern platform, a higher pyramidal platform in its center that is set back from the plaza (also known as the Cenote Style E Group). But first and foremost, the earliest E Groups, as others note (see Chapters 7, 11, 12, and 15 in this volume), were not built at all but were carved out of a soft limestone bedrock that had been previously stripped of topsoil. The stripping of topsoil is also a common feature of early residential patio groups and perhaps of the earliest Lowland architecture in general. Anyone who has had the misfortune of walking on Petén topsoil after a rain will agree that stripping it down to the soft limestone around a house might be a good idea.

Another important characteristic of the Cival Central E Group is that it formed an integral part of the foundation of the site as a ceremonial space, the first in this region. Prior to that time (roughly 800 BCE) the area had been occupied by sparsely distributed agriculturalist groups whose ritual activity can only be inferred from their sophisticated incised ceramics (Estrada-Belli 2011; Neivens de Estrada 2014). In many ways, the creation of the first E Groups in the Middle Preclassic period coalesced many elements of the preexisting multicultural and possibly multiethnic, widely dispersed, loosely integrated population into a new, more tightly integrated ethnic identity. This new identity, built around E Group rituals, is what we have been calling Maya culture. As I have suggested elsewhere (Estrada-Belli 2011) and as Inomata argues convincingly (Chapter 7 in this volume), the creation of E Groups may also have served as a magnet for the social interaction of surrounding sedentary and seminomadic populations of farmers and hunter-gatherers to coexist peacefully if not with mutual benefit. In that sense, E Groups provided tangible foci not only for human interaction and social integration but also for creating ties between people and landscape in more permanent ways than was previously possible.

Until the end of the Middle Preclassic period (from 800 to 400 BCE) the Cival Central E Group served its purpose as the only humanmade monumental space in its region. At the onset of the Late Preclassic period, roughly about 350 BCE, many things changed and improved in and around Cival. The stimulus for these changes may have originated at Cival itself or, in my view, more likely somewhere outside the confines of this small tract of the Maya Lowlands, but nevertheless within the Maya Lowlands. The changes affected various aspects of rituality, the use of sacred space, and the hierarchical relations among people and their places of residence and congregation. Verticality in architecture might reflect increased hierarchization in social relations.

The patterns observed in our sample of Late Preclassic period E Groups indicate that the way E Groups were built and used was indeed highly variable but not random. As Doyle has noted (Chapter 8 in this volume), no two (Preclassic) E Groups in the Lowlands are identical. This is borne out by our sample and warrants further explanation. In our sample we found the apparent variability to be masking many important commonalities among E Groups, large and small. As Doyle (2013) notes, there appear to be specific units of measure at work in the layout of E Groups. In addition to this, the proportions of plazas and buildings appear to be dependent on the observations that the architects intended to make from and/or through this architecture onto the eastern horizon.

My analysis shows that the pattern of solar observations according to fixed intervals of 20-day units in the yearly movement of sun on the eastern horizon first noted by Aveni et al. (2003) was a major concern of the Cival architects. In this region of fertile wetlands and generous rainfall, there is a close correspondence between solar events and meteorological and agricultural cycles, as noted by Aveni et al (2003). Closer inspection of the patterns of dates and calendar references has led to further inferences. The combination of celebration of the Haab cycle through the equinoxes and solstices with the concomitant celebration of zenith passages and equinoxes related to the Tzolk'in and the count of 20 days, as illustrated by the Early Classic Uaxactún pecked cross (Aveni et al. 2003), is also supported by the Cival data. At Cival, these distinct calendrical commemorations could have been enacted within the same space by the construction of two nested E Groups, one dedicated to the solstices (West E Group) and one to the zenith (Central E Group). Everywhere else, E Groups seem to have been dedicated to each of these sets of commemorations or cycles separately. Considering the relative ubiquity of E Groups in the Lowlands, it is possible that each community could have had access to both these types within a reasonable distance.

Furthermore, the inferred celebration of these calendar cycles (Haab and Tzolk'in) at Cival at the onset of the Late Preclassic period is significant in relation to the question regarding the adoption of the Long Count system. This calendar system was based on the count of days in groups of 20 as well as on the interplay of those two cycles. We have seen how several of the early E Groups demonstrate a focus not only on the zenith passage but also on the count of 20 days prior to or after that event (Aveni et al. 2003). These plazas in the Late Preclassic period were used to erect monuments (three at Cival: Figures 9.3, 9.16, 9.17; Estrada-Belli et al. 2003, Estrada-Belli 2006, 2011, 2015), which is also significant and has been noted at several other sites by Aimers and Rice (2006). In the Cival E Group, a low platform was

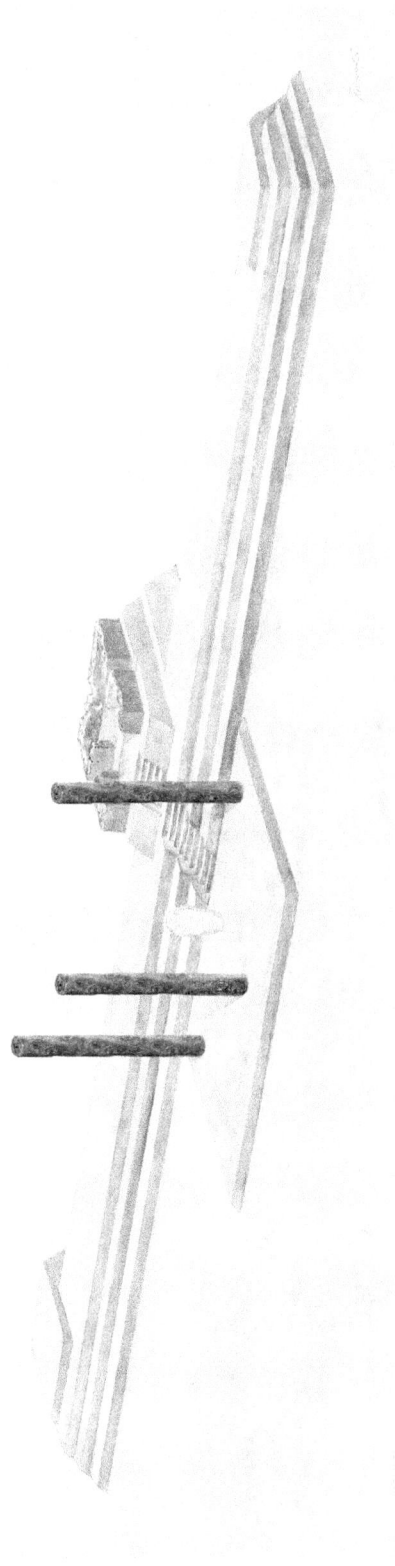

Figure 9.16. Artistic rendering of Cival Center E Group. After its latest Late Preclassic period expansion to 129 m in length, a low platform was built in the plaza against the stairway, on which Stela 2 and three tree-posts 1 m wide were erected. Drawing by Fernando Álvarez, Holmul Archaeological Project.

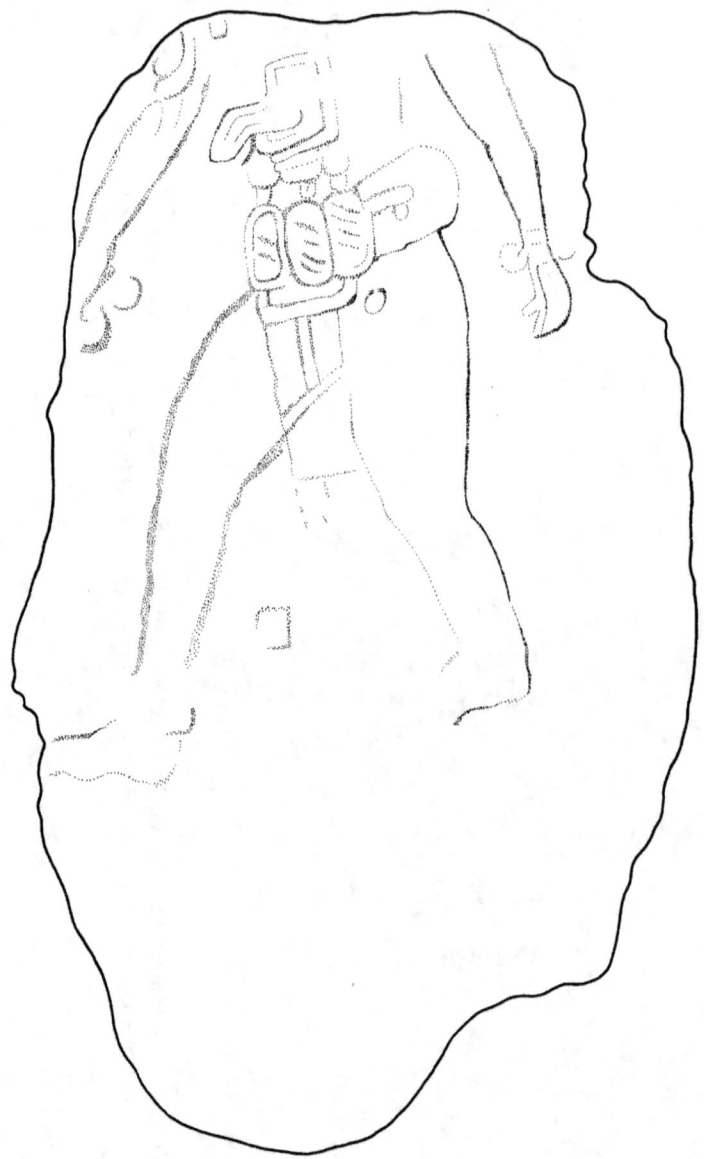

Figure 9.17. Drawing of low-relief carving on Cival Stela 2 of a dancing figure wearing a royal Principal Bird Deity head pectoral, ca. 200 BCE. Drawing by Nikolai Grube, Holmul Archaeological Project.

built in front of the eastern platform. Around 200 BCE Stela 2 was erected on it, depicting a bird-costumed ruler in a dance pose. It is tempting to suggest that these types of monuments, while lacking any text, were used to commemorate not only a ruler's action but specifically a Long Count cycle completion, as it was the norm in subsequent dated monuments erected in E Groups.

The subject of the function of these low platforms has been poorly explored in relation to E Groups. They are quite common in the Cival region's sample and have been documented at Cival, Holmul, Hamontun, and at other sites outside this area. It is possible that dance performances were an integral part of several rituals surrounding solar and meteorological events conducted in E Groups, as the iconography of Cival Stelae 2 and 3 seems to suggest.

In terms of the meaning of E Groups I found that from their foundation these sacred spaces were associated with images of maize/World Trees sprouting from a cleft in the earth and the life-giving role of rain gods. In addition to the obvious role that solar deities might have played in E Group rituals we now have many more elements of Maya cosmology reflected in the architecture, spaces, and ritual images within E Groups. Western radial pyramids in particular reflect the cosmic four parts plus center concept (see also Carlson 1981; Cohodas 1980). And the plaza itself may reflect the watery surface that separates the earth from the underworld. As the erection of ruler's portrait stelae demonstrates, this cosmic arena was soon to be appropriated by rulers to perform in their role as the community's spiritual and political leaders.

One final issue that may be illustrated by the Cival regional E Group sample is their proliferation during the Late Preclassic period. As in the case of the variability of E Groups, their proliferation could be either spontaneous and independent or relatively guided and dependent on a central place or idea. In the present analysis there appears to be one original place, at least in this region, for the specific rituals and architecture of the early Maya: the Cival Central E Group, which was used from 800 BCE through 200 CE, during much of the Middle and the Late Preclassic periods.

One interesting new element that emerged in the course of this analysis is the importance of hilltops as targets for the observation of sunrises from E Groups. This feature has multiple implications. On one hand, it would appear that the observations made from E Groups are best understood as being guided through a landscape, humanmade as well as natural. Both realms were home to primordial deities as mountains according to ethnographic and epigraphic data (Vogt 1969, 1981). On the other hand, the distant hilltops that were sighted from different locations on different calendar dates emerge as significant elements of E Group rituality in and of themselves. During the period in which E Groups proliferated, certainly to satisfy a more populous and more complex society, the primordial nine sacred hilltops in the Cival landscape served as points of reference to keep all ceremonial centers integrated with one another and with the "original" Cival center in a web of connections that featured solar events and landscape deities. What resulted was effectively a single ritual system on a regional level. The geographic extent of this system probably coincided with the extent of Cival's political reach as a seat of power in this region. The new E Groups appear not as spontaneous and independent creations but as projections of a uniform design to optimize the distribution of ritual services, with the concomitant hierarchical distribution of political power. At the same time, E Groups are not entirely a standardized phenomenon. Instead, each E Group is different in some peculiar ways, being dedicated to a unique combination of solar events, cosmological constructs, and local geomancy. These unique combinations of elements perhaps reflect underlying local identities as well as pan-Maya beliefs. Those local identities, manifested by outward-looking landscape rituals, may well have had their antecedent in the ethnic identities noted in the distribution of styles among the Lowlands' earliest ceramics (Estrada-Belli 2011; Neivens de Estrada 2014). All these local meanings, however, must have coexisted within the overarching function of E Groups as interconnected nested elements of a wide-ranging Lowland community.

Acknowledgments

The work presented here was made possible by research agreements issued by the Ministry of Culture of Guatemala. Academic support was provided by Boston University, Vanderbilt University, and Tulane University with the financial support of National Science Foundation, the Fundación Patrimonio Cultural y Natural Maya (PACUNAM), the National Geographic Society, the Alphawood Foundation, the Peabody Museum of Archaeology and Ethnology at Harvard University, the Maya Archaeology Initiative, Peter and Alexandra Harrison, ARB-USA, Toyota USA, Mary and Dennis Neivens, Summitracing, Debora and Pedro Aguirre, Mitchell Allen, and Michael Romero. I am grateful for the dedicated work of many U.S. and Guatemalan archaeology students.

Notes

1. Beta-234440, conventional radiocarbon age: 2670±40 BP, 2 sigma calibrated result: (95 percent probability) cal 900 to 790 BCE (cal BP 2850 to 2740), 1 sigma calibrated result: (68 percent probability) cal 840 to 800 BCE.

2. Beta-213528, conventional radiocarbon age: 2520±40 BP, 2 sigma calibrated result: (95 percent probability) cal 800 to 520 BCE, 1 sigma calibrated result: (68 percent probability) cal 790 to 760 BCE and cal 680 to 550 BCE.

3. Degrees measurements for Cival are to 2001 magnetic north, which that year had a declination of 2 degrees and 4 minutes to true north.

References Cited

Aimers, James J.
1993   Messages from the Gods: An Hermeneutic Analysis of the Maya E-Group Complex. M.A. thesis. Trent University, Anthropology Department, Peterborough, Ontario.
Aimers, James J., and Prudence M. Rice
2006   Astronomy, Ritual, and the Interpretation of Maya "E Group" Architectural Assemblages. *Ancient Mesoamerica* 17(2):79–96.
Aveni, Anthony F., Anne S. Dowd, and Benjamin Vining
2003   Maya Calendar Reform?: Evidence from Orientations of Specialized Architectural Assemblages. *Latin American Antiquity* 14(2):159–178.
Blom, Frans
1924   Report on the Preliminary Work at Uaxactún, Guatemala. *Carnegie Institution of Washington Year Book* 23:217–219.
Carlson, John B.
1981   A Geomantic Model for the Interpretation of Mesoamerican Sites: An Essay in Cross-Cultural Comparison. In *Mesoamerican Sites and World-Views*, edited by Elizabeth P. Benson, pp. 143–215. Dumbarton Oaks, Washington, D.C.
Chase, Arlen F., and Diane Z. Chase
1995   External Impetus, Internal Synthesis, and Standardization: E Group Assemblages and the Crystallization of Classic Maya Society in the Southern Lowlands. *Acta Mesoamericana* 8:87–101 (special issue edited by Nikolai Grube entitled *The Emergence of Lowland Maya Civilization: The Transition from the Preclassic to Early Classic*).
Cohodas, Marvin
1980   Radial Pyramids and Radial-Associated Assemblages of the Central Maya Area. *Journal of the Society of Architectural Historians* 39(3):208–223.
Doyle, James A.
2013   Early Maya Geometric Planning Conventions at El Palmar, Guatemala. *Journal of Archaeological Science* 40(2):793–798.
Estrada-Belli, Francisco
2002a   Anatomía de una ciudad Maya: Holmul. Resultados de investigaciones arqueológicas en 2000 y 2001. *Mexicon* 24(5):107–112.

2002b   Thinking Big: Designing the Ancient Maya Landscape of La Milpa, Belize. *Context* 17(1):9–11.
2006   Lightning Sky, Rain and the Maize God: The Ideology of Preclassic Maya Rulers at Cival, Peten, Guatemala. *Ancient Mesoamerica* 17(1):57–78.
2011   *The First Maya Civilization: Ritual and Power before the Classic Period*. Routledge, New York.
2012   Early Civilization in the Maya Lowlands, Monumentality, and Place Making: A View from the Holmul Region. In *Early New World Monumentality*, edited by Richard L. Burger and Robert M. Rosenswig, pp. 198–230. University Press of Florida, Gainesville.
2014   Investigaciones arqueológicas en la región de Holmul, Petén: Holmul y Cival. Informe preliminar de la temporada de 2014. Holmul Archaeological Reports, Boston University. http://www.bu.edu/holmul/reports, accessed July 2015.
2015   Investigaciones arqueológicas en la región de Holmul, Petén: Holmul y Cival. Informe preliminar de la temporada de 2015. Holmul Archaeological Reports, Boston University. http://www.bu.edu/holmul/reports, accessed October 2016.

Estrada-Belli, Francisco, Nikolai Grube, Marc Wolf, Kristen Gardella, and Claudio Lozano Guerra-Librero
2003   Preclassic Maya Monuments and Temples at Cival, Petén, Guatemala. *Antiquity*. http://www.antiquity.ac.uk/projgall/belli296, accessed July 2015.

Fialko, Vilma
2005   Diez años de investigaciones arqueológicas en la cuenca del río Holmul, región noreste de Petén. In *XVIII Simposio de Investigaciones Arqueológicas en Guatemala, 2004*, edited by Juan Pedro Laporte, Bárbara Arroyo, and Héctor E. Mejía, pp. 244–260. Museo Nacional de Arqueología y Etnología, Guatemala City.

Girard, Raphael
1962   *Los mayas eternos*. Libro Mex Editores, Mexico City.
1966   *Los mayas: Su civilización, su historia, sus vinculaciones continentales*. Libro Mex, Mexico City.

Houk, Brett A.
2015   *Ancient Maya Cities of the Eastern Lowlands*. University Press of Florida, Gainesville.

Inomata, Takeshi, Daniela Triadan, Kazuo Aoyama, Victor Castillo, and Hitoshi Yonenobu
2013   Early Ceremonial Constructions at Ceibal, Guatemala, and the Origins of Lowland Maya Civilization. *Science* 340(1126):467–471.

Kubler, George
1958   The Design of Space in Maya Architecture. In *XXXI Congreso Internacional de Americanistas, 1954, Miscelánea Paul Rivet, Octogenario Dicata*, Vol. 1, pp. 515–531. Universidad Autónoma de México, Mexico City.

López Luján, Leonardo
2005   *The Offerings of the Templo Mayor of Tenochtitlan*. University of New Mexico Press, Albuquerque.

Madry, Scott H., and Lynn Rakos
1996   Line-of-Sight and Cost-Surface Techniques for Regional Research in the Arroux River Valley. In *New Methods, Old Problems: Geographic Information Systems in Modern Archaeological Research*, edited by Herbert D. G. Maschner, pp. 104–126. Center for Archaeological Investigations, Occasional Papers No. 23. Southern Illinois University, Carbondale.

Merwin, Raymond Edwin, and George Clapp Vaillant
1932   *The Ruins of Holmul*. Memoirs of the Peabody Museum of American Archaeology and Ethnology, Vol. 3, No. 2. Harvard University, Cambridge, Massachusetts.

Neivens de Estrada, Niña
2014   A Tangled Web: Ceramic Adoption in the Maya Lowlands and Community Interaction in the Early Middle Preclassic as Seen in the K'awil Complex from Holmul, Peten, Guatemala. In *The Maya and Their Central American Neighbors: Settlement Patterns, Architecture, Hieroglyphic Texts, and Ceramics*, edited by Geoffrey E. Braswell, pp. 177–200. Routledge, London.

Quintana, Oscar, Wolfgang W. Wurster, and Bernard Hermes
2000   El Plano del sitio maya de Yaxhá, Petén, Guatemala. *Beiträge zur Allgemeinen und Vergleichenden Archaeologie* 20:261–286.

Ricketson, Oliver, Jr.
1928   Notes on Two Maya Astronomic Observatories. *American Anthropologist* 30:434–444.

Šprajc, Ivan, and Pedro Francisco Sánchez Nava
2013   Equinoxes in Mesoamerican Architectural Alignments: Prehispanic Reality or Modern Myth? In *Ancient Cosmologies and Modern Prophets: Proceedings of the 20th Conference of the European Society for Astronomy in Culture*, edited by Ivan Šprajc and Peter Pehani, pp. 319–338. Slovene Anthropological Society, Ljubljana.

Sugiyama, Saburo, and Leonardo López Luján
2007   Dedicatory Burial/Offering Complexes at the Moon Pyramid, Teotihuacan. *Ancient Mesoamerica* 18(1):127–146.

Taube, Karl A.
2005   The Symbolism of Jade in Classic Maya Religion. *Ancient Mesoamerica* 16(1):23–50.

Tourtellot, Gair, Marc Wolf, Francisco Estrada-Belli, and Norman Hammond
2000   Discovery of Two Predicted Ancient Maya Sites in Belize. *Antiquity* 74:481–482.

Vogt, Evon Z.
1969   *Zinacantán: A Maya Community in the Highlands of Chiapas*. Harvard University Press, Cambridge, Massachusetts.
1981   Some Aspects of Sacred Geography in Highland Chiapas. In *Mesoamerican Sites and World-Views*, edited by Elizabeth P. Benson, pp. 119–142. Dumbarton Oaks Research Library and Collections, Washington D.C.

10

Time to Rule

Celestial Observation and Appropriation among the Early Maya

WILLIAM A. SATURNO, BORIS BELTRÁN, AND FRANCO D. ROSSI

Between 300 and 200 BCE a San Bartolo *ajaw* oversaw the redesign of an E Group. The four-cornered plaza in which this group sat had long been a key public area for the social, ritual, recreational, and economic activities of surrounding inhabitants and had roots stretching perhaps as far back as the San Bartolo community itself. In the redesign, particular cultural symbols and beliefs likely long affixed to this place were made tangible—Maize God paintings in the eastern structure, avian-serpent solar deities sculpted on the radial pyramid, and a small ceremonial ballcourt at the radial pyramid's eastern base. But in addition to these modifications, the *ajaw* also saw that his role in "completing" temporal cycles was written in hieroglyphic text alongside the Maize God and that a painted marker seemingly featuring himself and an ancestor was rendered at the very center of the ballcourt alley, inscribing his own identity onto the community's public space in the same way a wealthy benefactor might do today. A century or so later, another *ajaw* (a descendant perhaps) would stand, distanced from the public far below, atop the central pyramid of an elevated Triadic Group, built over the E Group designed by his ancestor. Such monumental complexes, their features, and their changes through time can help us better perceive and understand not only the sociopolitical shifts that were under way at the start of the Late Preclassic period (350 BCE–0 CE) but the symbols and rituals in which these shifts were publicly couched and legitimized. This chapter offers one particularly informative case study in this regard from the Pinturas Group of San Bartolo, at which a scenario closely resembling that described above seems actually to have transpired during the Late Preclassic period.

The emergence of hierarchically stratified societies from what were initially more corporate forms of social complexity has been well documented across the ancient world (Blanton and Fargher 2008, 2011; Liu 2004; Parkinson and Galaty 2007). In Mesoamerica, recent discussions similarly emphasize these corporate social forms as preceding later political complexity, with early collective efforts tangibly made manifest through the creation of the earliest "public" or monumental spaces. The tendency on the part of the ancient Maya to preserve earlier architecture within later constructions permits us to explore these architectural expressions of shifting institutions of authority not otherwise evident.

E Groups are widely acknowledged as among the very first standardized architectural expressions of the ancient Maya. Such groups tell us much about the ways cosmologies, religion, ancestral veneration, political systems, and so forth were rendered architecturally tangible (Aimers and Rice 2006; Chase and Chase 1995; Estrada-Belli 2006; Guderjan 2006). E Groups, commonly linked to cosmological and public ritual, are often framed in opposition to Triadic Groups, expressly linked to dynastic ritual and ancestor veneration (Laporte 1995), though the archaeological data do not always support this dichotomy (see Chase and Chase 1995 for E Group links to dynastic ritual). Thus, while many of the shared meanings among E Groups are more or less well understood, it is important that ongoing research not only continues to underscore what is common but also parses local variants as well as changing and sometimes divergent uses and symbolic overlays through time. In her discussion on anthropological approaches and constructions of place, Margaret Rodman (2003:205) writes: "Places are not inert containers. They are politicized, culturally relative, historically specific, local and multiple constructions"—at any given moment in time. Thus, it is key that we try to understand the ongoing localized historical processes that shaped specific E Group assemblages—and simultaneously illuminate the broader social contexts particular to archaeological moments as snapshots in the "biographies" of these architectural assemblages (Ashmore 2002, 2009).

At the Pinturas Group of San Bartolo, seven phases of architecture were successively built, each subsuming the previous ones and all upon the same plaza space. Focusing specifically on the last incarnation of the Pinturas E Group (called Sub-5) before its transition to a Triadic Group, this chapter queries how architectural changes reflect on emergent forms of political authority. This question is explored through analyzing the ways in which long-standing ideologies were made innovatively tangible at Sub-5, the manner in which early rulers entered those long-standing ideological systems through these innovations, and the narratives of local history and mythological overlays that developed alongside "holy lordship" as a partial result.

Site Layout

San Bartolo is a medium-sized and predominantly Preclassic (1000 BCE–250 CE) city located in the currently uninhabited northeastern region of the Department of Petén, Guatemala (Figure 10.1). The site sits on roughly 4 square km of well-drained uplands bordering a tributary of the large Bajo de Azúcar (Garrison 2007). It is perhaps best known for its murals found within the penultimate architectural phase of the Las Pinturas group, which vividly reveal many of the foundational concepts that underlie dynastic kingship in the Maya Lowlands (Hurst 2009; Saturno 2009; Saturno et al. 2005; Taube et al. 2010). San Bartolo, however, is actually composed of four principal architectural groups in total situated along a roughly east to west axis containing more than 130 structures. Moving west to east, these groups are Jabalí, Ventanas, Pinturas, and Saraguate, which are briefly reviewed below (see Urquizú and Saturno 2002, 2003, 2004, 2005, 2006a, 2007, 2008; Runggaldier 2009; Griffin 2012; Garrison 2007; Hurst 2009; Davies 2012; Craig 2009).

The Jabalí complex, the westernmost of these groups, is also the smallest. Evidence suggests that the earliest layers of this Triadic Group, closely associated with emerging elite authority, date to the late Middle Preclassic (1000–350 BCE). Excavations revealed various mortuary and offertory events in the archaeological record as well as matching monumental stucco masks, which flank the stairs in a Late Preclassic construction (Pellecer et al. 2005; Pellecer et al. 2008; León et al. 2010). One of the earliest Maya royal burials, Tomb 1 (~300–100 BCE), was excavated within this group in 2006 (Saturno 2006; Urquizú and Saturno 2006b). San Bartolo Tomb 1 was roughly contemporary with the tomb recently discovered at the nearby site of K'o and with the high-status burials bearing royal symbols discovered at Cuello (Tomasic and Bozarth 2011; Hammond 1999:54–56). Funerary offerings at Jabalí Tomb 1 included an effigy vessel featuring an early form of the rain god Chaak in which a carved greenstone maize deity figure was placed, revealing early elites' developing associations with water and agricultural symbolism.

Las Ventanas is the largest of the four groups, named for the tall pyramid also called Las Ventanas (Structure 20) on its central plaza's northern side.

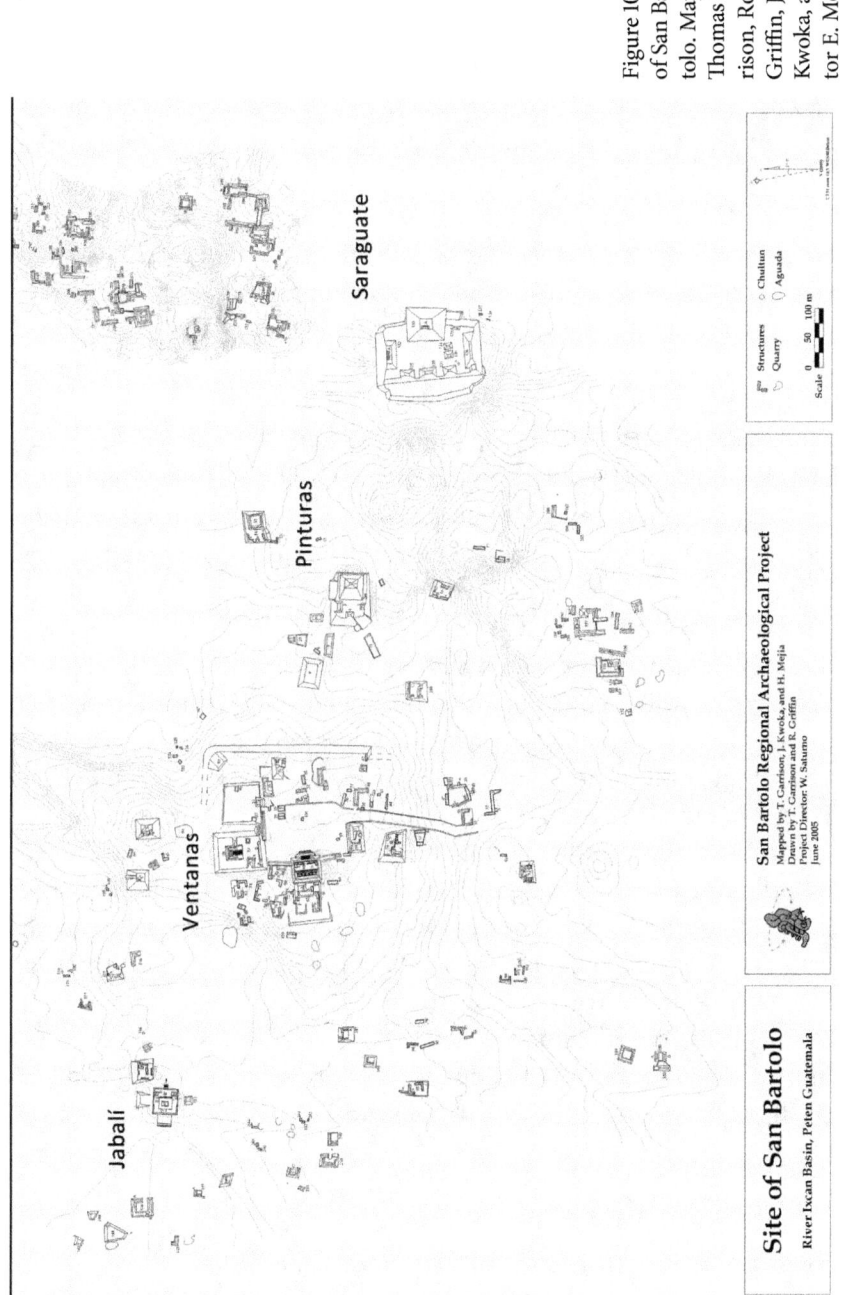

Figure 10.1. Map of San Bartolo. Mapped by Thomas G. Garrison, Robert E. Griffin, Joshua J. Kwoka, and Héctor E. Mejía.

The earlier substructure and platform of this pyramid also date to the late Middle Preclassic period (Urquizú 2003a, 2003b, 2003c:87). The central plaza zone of the Las Ventanas group additionally features a Late Preclassic ballcourt and a large administrative palace and is surrounded by residential groups. Las Ventanas seems to have served as the administrative center of San Bartolo's Late Preclassic population as well as the focal point of subsequent Late Classic period (550–800 CE) reoccupation and elaboration (Runggaldier 2009; Davies 2012).

The Saraguates group is the largest construction by volume thus far encountered at San Bartolo and dates to the Late Preclassic. The group consists of seven structures arranged around an open plaza space atop a massive platform. The hilltop on which Saraguates sits was modified and incorporated into the construction of this platform. It is the easternmost group at San Bartolo and is arranged as a kind of reverse E Group (Hurst 2006; Pellecer 2006; Urquizú and Menéndez 2006). This orientation as well as its location on a high point in the landscape allowed individuals within the Saraguates group to look westward over San Bartolo's other three architectural groups, underscoring intentional sight lines across the city as well as the site's Late Preclassic east–west orientation (see Šprajc et al. 2009).

Las Pinturas is the architectural group on which this chapter focuses. Structure 1, the temple pyramid and primary structure in the final phase, Late Preclassic Triadic Group, is the focal point of Pinturas, standing 26 m high. Initial archaeological investigations at Pinturas were focused on uncovering, documenting, and conserving the remarkably preserved Late Preclassic mural program. These early murals adorn the interior walls of a small structure (Sub-1A) built off the back (east face) of the buried penultimate phase (Sub-1 phase) of Structure 1 (Saturno 2009; Saturno et al. 2005).[1] These final architectural phases were preceded by at least seven earlier ones, stretching back into the late Middle Preclassic period (Escobedo 2002). The Pinturas Triadic Group sits on a 75 m by 90 m platform roughly 5 m high (Escobar and Runggaldier 2002). The Sub-5 E Group (discussed in more detail below) was first discovered deep within this large platform (Beltrán 2006, 2008, 2010, 2015; Beltrán and Saravia 2012).

Las Pinturas E Group

Excavations show that in its earliest three manifestations, Sub-7 (Ixkik), Sub-6 (Ixmucané), and Sub-5 (Ixbalamqué), the Pinturas group existed as an E Group complex.[2] The earliest ceramics belong to the widespread Mamom sphere (Rivera 2008, 2010, 2012), supporting the purported relationship between the Mamom and E Group phenomenon (Chapter 8 in this volume; 2012). The transition to a Triadic Group did not occur until sometime between 250 BCE and 100 BCE, when the entire Sub-5 E Group was covered over within the Sub-4 Triadic Group platform. The four subsequent architectural phases were all Triadic Groups and were oriented westward (like Sub-4), toward what had become the site center at Ventanas, as opposed to eastward like the earlier E Groups. Elsewhere we argue that this ostensible royal appropriation of monumental space at Pinturas represents a crucial step in emergent systems of authority (Saturno et al. n.d.). Over the course of the Late Preclassic, it seems that early rulers no longer required the same performative effort in entering ideologies dealing with forces of nature as represented in E Groups and instead became (along with dynastic ancestors) the focus of an ideology unto themselves (Chase and Chase 1995:100–101). Though this shift in monumental architecture constitutes rather dramatic evidence of the power of emerging political structures, it is clear that this institutional turn was already well under way at San Bartolo during the Sub-5 E Group phase and likely even before.

Sub-7, Ixkik Phase (600–300 BCE)

Sub-7 is the earliest construction phase of the Pinturas architectural group and was built as an E Group. The majority of its ceramics belong to the local San Bartolo Mamom variety—termed the Ixtab ceramic sphere, which consists of the Uaxactún Sin Engobe, Flores Ceroso, and Mars Naranja ceramic classes (Rivera 2010, 2012). Select ceramic samples conform to preceding ceramic classes (contemporary with Tikal's Early Eb sphere), however, showing that occupation in and around the site likely stretched considerably further back in time (see Rivera 2010, 2012).

During the Sub-7 phase, Pinturas consisted of the typical E Group components, a radial pyramid (Sub-7b) and a low linear platform (Sub-7a) directly east of that pyramid, which featured sloped terracing in its construction. A six-step stairway climbs the eastern façade of the central portion of Sub-7a, arriving at an initial flat area before one further step to the top of the platform. This area would have supported a perishable structure, as evidenced from the postholes discovered there, each roughly 0.3 m in diameter (Beltrán 2005:68).

Sub-6, Ixmucané (400?–300 BCE)

The second E Group phase is poorly defined both architecturally and ceramically due to its razing in preparation for building the subsequent phase. Floors from the linear platform Sub-6a and radial pyramid Sub-6b were encountered, however, as was a portion of a wall, which seems to have belonged to the superstructure. This wall was constructed with cut limestone blocks and plastered over, indicating that by this time masonry structures had replaced the perishable ones of the previous phase in Sub-7a (Beltrán 2008:68).

Sub-5 Ixbalamqué (300–200 BCE)

The use of masonry walls on the E Group's linear platform was continued in the subsequent phase, Sub-5, the last phase in which Pinturas held an E Group configuration and the focus of this chapter (Figures 10.2 and 10.3). The Sub-5 phase is the most thoroughly explored archaeologically and the most precisely dated of the Pinturas early architectural manifestations. The emphasis on this particular phase is due largely to Boris Beltrán's discovery of plastered limestone blocks bearing some of the earliest hieroglyphic inscriptions in the Central Lowlands (see Saturno et al. 2006).

The ceramics of the Sub-5 architectural phase constitute the San Bartolo Ixbalamqué ceramic complex, which corresponds to the earlier side of the larger Chicanel sphere at Uaxactún—specifically to the Chuen complex of Tikal and Barton Creek sphere of Barton Ramie (Rivera 2010). Five AMS carbon samples support this ceramic chronology. These were run from sealed deposits in phases Sub-6, Sub-5, and Sub-4 in order to bracket the dating for Sub-5 accurately. When evaluated together, these carbon samples date the Sub-5 phase and its early inscribed blocks to sometime between 300 and 200 BCE (see Saturno et al. 2006 for a full discussion).

The group's linear platform Sub-5a measures 26 m by 12 m and stands a little over 2 m high. Its three sections support three staircases—two built into the east side and one central stairway on the west side—and the whole structure is covered in well-preserved white plaster. Sub-5a's three sloping terraces constitute the main body of the structure, and an additional platform elevates its central section above the rest. There is reason to believe that the three masonry superstructures built atop Sub-5a held interior and perhaps exterior paintings and even writings. Several blocks recovered in the central superstructure of Sub-5a's three rooms were decorated with polychrome murals and hieroglyphic inscriptions (Beltrán 2005, 2006).

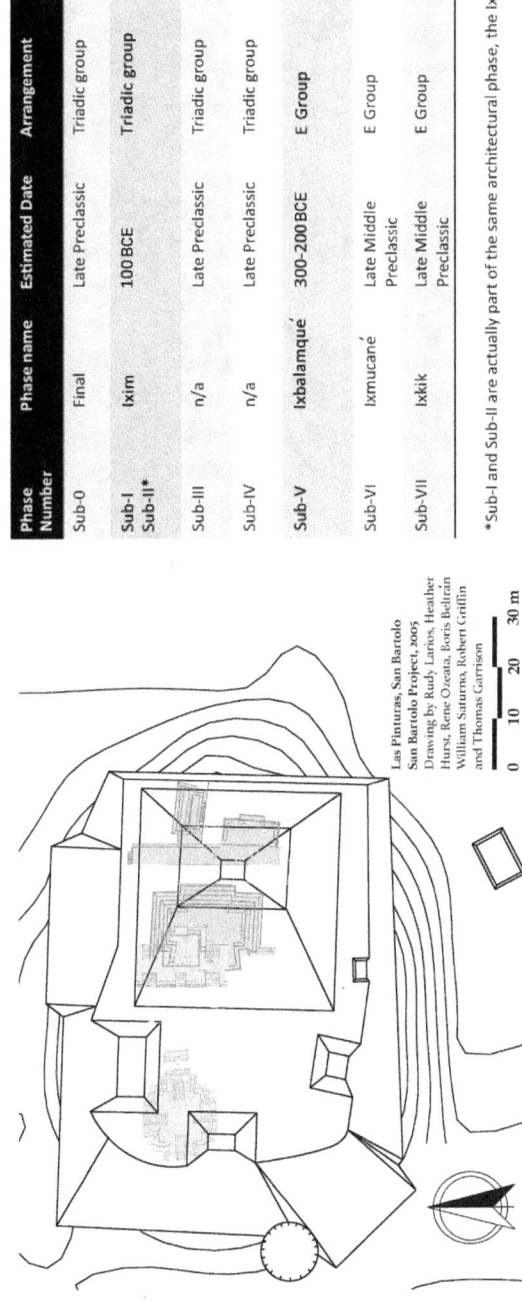

Phase Number	Phase name	Estimated Date	Arrangement	Key Named Structures
Sub-0	Final	Late Preclassic	Triadic group	Str. 1, 3, 4, and 5
Sub-I Sub-II*	Ixim	100 BCE	Triadic group	Sub-IA, Sub-IB, Yaxché Platform, Ixim Pyramid
Sub-III	n/a	Late Preclassic	Triadic group	n/a
Sub-IV	n/a	Late Preclassic	Triadic group	n/a
Sub-V	Ixbalamqué	300–200 BCE	E Group	Ixbalamqué, Hunahpu, ballcourt
Sub-VI	Ixmucané	Late Middle Preclassic	E Group	Ixmucané
Sub-VII	Ixkik	Late Middle Preclassic	E Group	Ixkik

*Sub-I and Sub-II are actually part of the same architectural phase, the Ixim phase

Figure 10.2. (*Left*) plan of Pinturas complex with Sub-1 and Sub-5 highlighted (by Rudy Larios, Heather Hurst, Rene Ozaeta, Boris Beltrán, William Saturno, Robert Griffin, Thomas Garrison); (*right*) chart of architectural phases of Pinturas.

Figure 10.3. Reconstruction of Sub-5 E Group. Illustration by Heather Hurst.

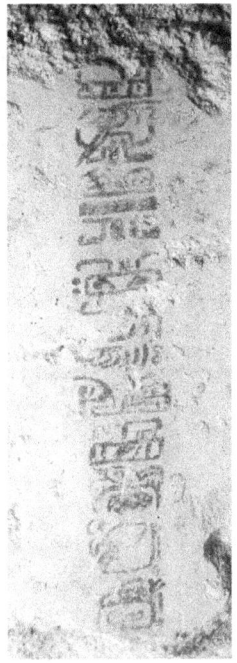
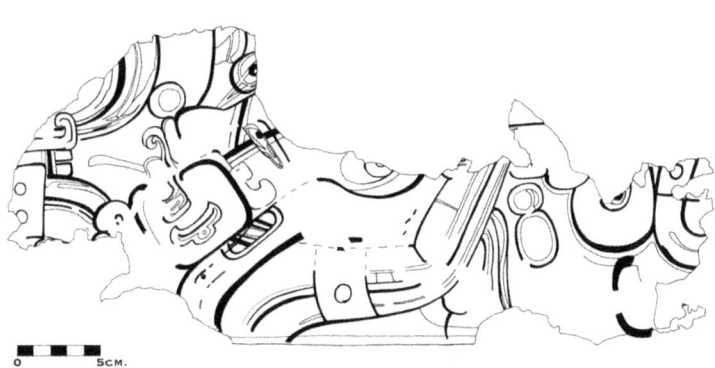

Figure 10.4. (*Left*) early painted hieroglyphic block from Sub-5 (photograph by Boris Beltrán); (*right*) Maize God from Ixbalamqué doorjamb (illustration by Heather Hurst).

Sub-5a's painted doorjamb held an especially early depiction of the Maya Maize God (Saturno et al. 2006; Taube et al. 2010:10), and various painted stucco fragments and stone blocks from the dismantled wall of the same room were also found (Beltrán 2005, 2008) (Figure 10.4). The aforementioned inscribed block is especially important and bears glyphic parallels to the famous Dumbarton Oaks jade celt. The text features hieroglyphs that may be referring to a distance number and a completion event (featuring the verb *tzutz*) possibly relating to a Preclassic K'atun-ending (see Giron-Ábrego 2012, 2013). Key to our discussion here, however, is a glyph on this block that clearly reads *ajaw* ("lord," "noble," or "ruler"), attesting to an especially early usage of the well-known Classic period (250–900 CE) royal title, between 300 and 200 BCE (Saturno et al. 2006).

The radial pyramid (Sub-5b) of the Sub-5 E Group lies 18 m west of linear platform Sub-5a. Matching sets of stucco masks flank each of the four central stairways of Sub-5b. Eight narrow, inset stairways ascend Sub-5b from the plaza floor to a small flat area immediately above the masks. These inset stairways are two to a side and are located between each mask and its corresponding corner of the pyramid (Beltrán 2010). The Sub-5b masks consist of an anthropomorphic avian face emerging from the sloped

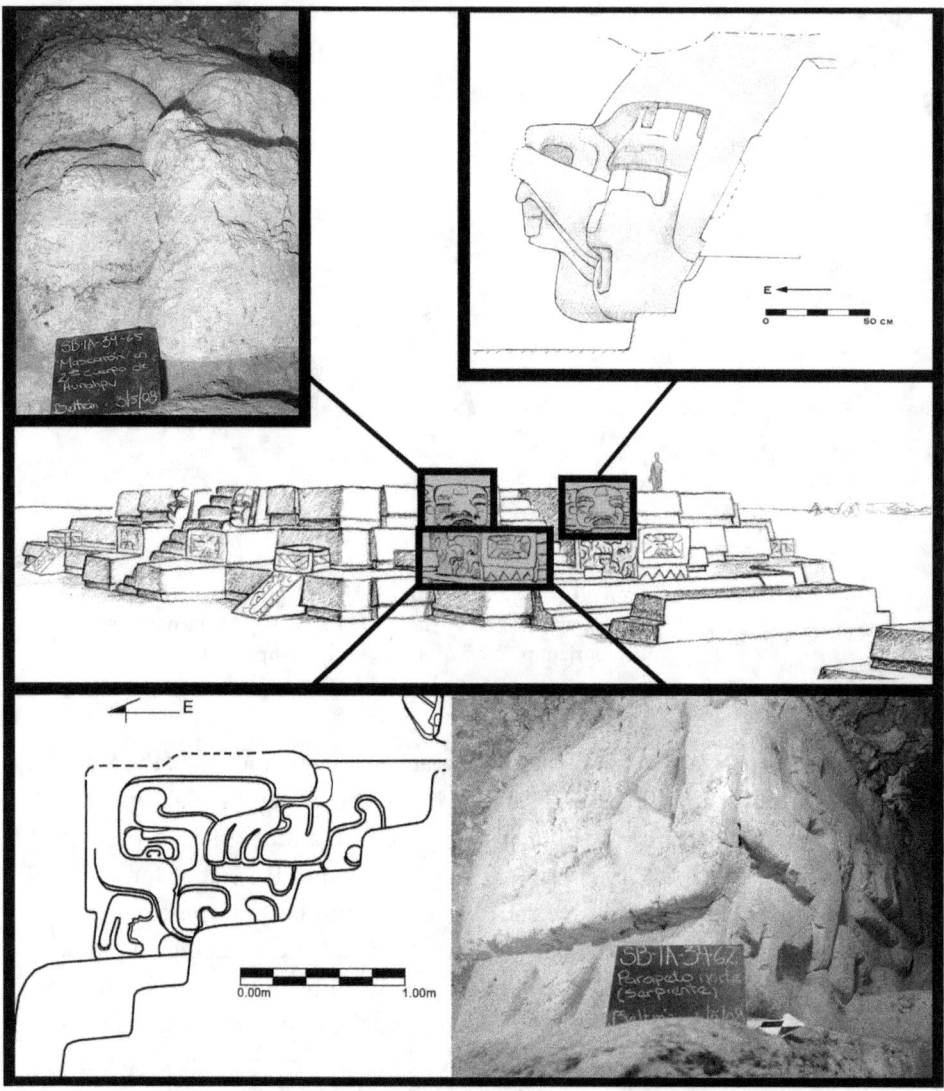

Figure 10.5. Reconstruction of Sub-5 "Hunahpu" radial pyramid with plaster masks and serpent balustrade adornments detailed. Illustrations by Heather Hurst; photos by Boris Beltrán.

terrace, resting atop a stylized Feathered Serpent. These serpent balustrades extend out from the base of each mask nearly 2.5 m, leaving considerable space for elaborate feather swirls and the double-pronged fang visible in profile. The front of this serpent depicts a rectangular frame containing a geometrically abstract form overlaying the center of an "X" (Figure 10.5).

A small ballcourt was built off the eastern stairway of Sub-5b ballcourt positioned between the Sub-5a linear platform and the Sub-5b radial pyramid. It incorporates the stairway and slope of Sub-5b into its west bank and is largely white with large sections painted red. Interestingly, the ballcourt is too small for actual competition, measuring only 6 m by 1.8 m and standing at 1.25 m tall. A small ballcourt marker was painted in the alley of the mini-ballcourt (Beltrán 2010; Hurst 2009) (Figure 10.6). In an event likely marking the termination of the E Group and the onset of the Sub-4 construction episode, ancient inhabitants left an offering consisting of human finger and rib bones, a jade axe fragment, and a large Late Preclassic Sierra Red sherd (Beltrán 2010).

E Groups

Before discussing the implications of the Pinturas E Group, it is important to explain our view on E Group complexes more broadly. As recent research demonstrates, the E Group emerged as an architectural form in its own right within the Maya area (Inomata et al. 2013). This emergence was the product not of one-directional influence from elsewhere but of autochthonous innovation in the midst of the intensified interregional interaction and competition occurring during the early Middle Preclassic period among emergent centers in the southern Maya region, the Pacific and Gulf coasts, and Chiapas (Inomata et al. 2013; Ringle 1999:213–215). Following Rosemary Joyce (2004:8), we see the earliest of E Groups as novel expressions of collective group identities that contributed to "the structuration of early societies that produced them [these monuments]." We draw on James Doyle's (2012:370) recent argument that these were multipurpose spaces from their inception and support the notion that "early E-Groups could represent the earliest large-scale places of community cohesion and political belonging in the Maya Lowlands" (like a town square: see Chapter 1 in this volume), centrally located both physically and cognitively in Middle Preclassic Maya communities and their immediate hinterlands.

Geometric planning practices for such quadrangular spaces are surprisingly consistent across much of the Maya area, involving the measurement of rectangular plots using stakes and cords (Hanks 1990:355–357; Landa in Tozzer 1941:96; Wilson 1972:121). Recently, the possibility of similar planning practices for monumental architectural spaces in use during the Preclassic has been cogently argued, based on a more or less standardized "golden rectangle" (48.5 m × 78.43 m) as a measurement base (Doyle 2013).

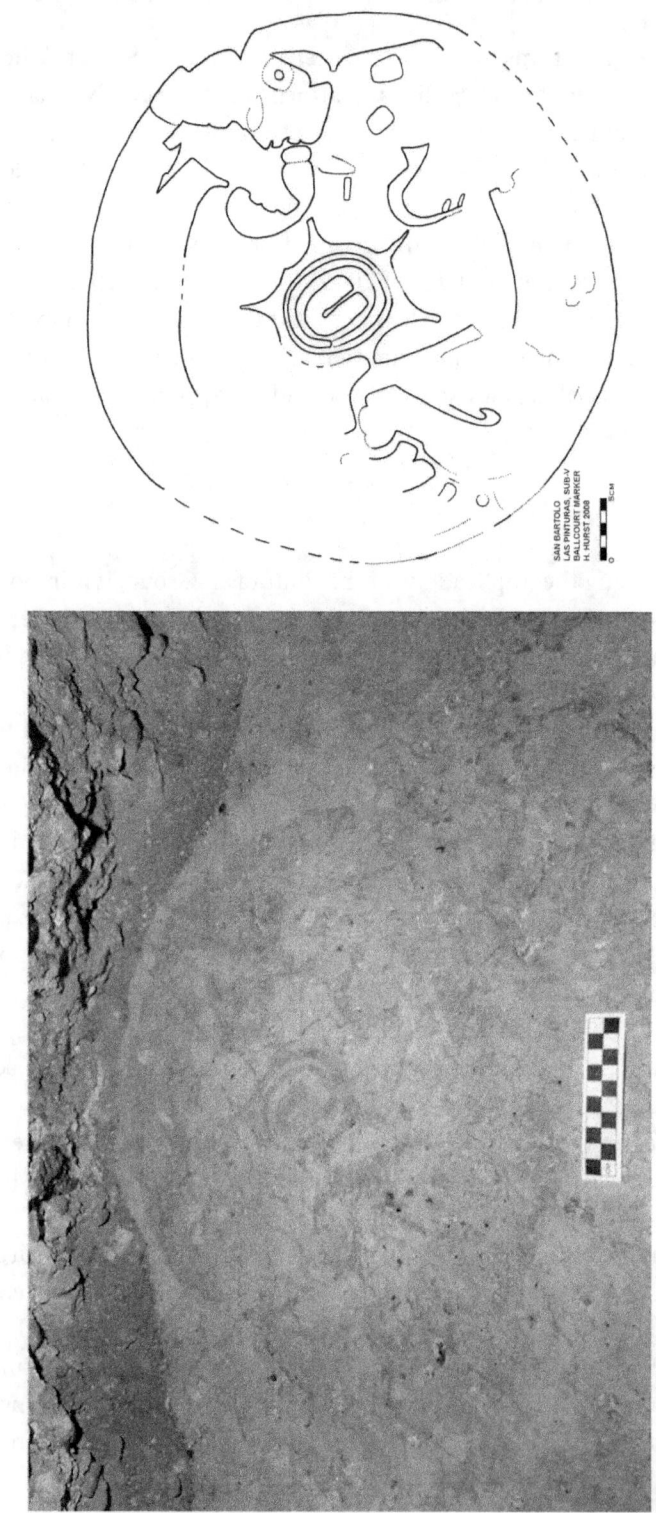

Figure 10.6. Painted marker on alley floor of Sub-5 "Hunahpu" ballcourt. Photo by Boris Beltrán; illustration by Heather Hurst.

According to this argument, the creation of monumental spaces during the Middle Preclassic largely mirrored the planning processes for agricultural and domestic spaces. These plaza, agricultural, and domestic spaces as well as the very settlement itself would have overlapped cognitively as four-cornered and socially constructed (Taube 2003).

Although public ritual was undoubtedly one important use of these spaces, we believe that a more vital driver in these groups' establishment and spread throughout the Maya Lowlands may have been the early E Group's place as a central locus for economic and other social activities as well as its potential role as an early "Maya civic requirement for sociopolitical units" (Doyle 2012:369). We do not focus on the origins of these groups in this chapter, however, but rather on a particular moment in the architectural evolution of these groups, what Joyce (2004:8) would call an "imagined landscape[s] whose realization . . . had both intended and unintended consequences." But this is not to say that there was no intent underpinning how and to what end this landscape was realized at Pinturas Sub-5. In the following discussion, we seek first to demonstrate intent in the architectural design of Sub-5 on the part of emerging political authorities and then to shed light on shifts in ideological narratives that were not necessarily intended. It should be emphasized that we do not see the broader community as passive receivers of monumental art and political rhetoric but instead as active participants in shaping how early rulers were able to enter into long-standing systems of ideology and governance.

Making Ideologies Tangible

The Sub-5 E Group architecturally and iconographically brings together many elements often discussed as characteristic of later E Groups. In addition to the radial pyramid in the west and linear three-sectioned platform in the east, Sub-5 elaborated upon the previous architectural forms of Sub-7 and Sub-6, inputting highly innovative and cosmologically evocative modifications on an already ritually, economically, and socially significant place in the landscape. E Groups' celestial and agricultural associations have been long argued in tandem with their role in commemorating the passage of time. At Sub-5, these entangled meanings were made tangible in a very real, permanent, and public way not only through the monumentality and intricate stucco mask and balustrade sculpture known from various other E Groups but through novel additions to the E Group complex, such as a mini-ballcourt built into the radial pyramid as well as painted texts and decorative art within the linear platform.

The plastered balustrade featuring Feathered Serpent and anthropomorphic bird deity imagery on the Sub-5b radial pyramid recalls a similar artistic program at Uaxactún E-7 Sub, the E Group par excellence. The avian mask at Sub-5b has been interpreted as a form of the Principal Bird Deity: a celestial and solar deity whose inevitable descent is preserved in mythological narratives of his death (Saturno et al. n.d.; Bardawil 1976; Christenson 2007:30–42; Taube et al. 2010:33). He is borne upon the back of a Feathered Serpent carved into the Sub-5b balustrade (Figure 10.5). The "X" in the mouth of the Feathered Serpent features prominently in later "skyband" imagery (as do Feathered Serpents) and seems to accent this deity as celestial as well. Radial pyramids and their imagery have often been discussed as referring to sun and sky imagery linked to the setting (dying) sun (Cohodas 1980; Saturno et al. n.d.), and these links are strongly supported at Sub-5.

The Maize God imagery in the central structure of the Sub-5a linear platform also supports well-attested associations with regard to the Maize God and agricultural metaphor implicit to the four-cornered, milpa-like plaza space and notions of the center (Taube 2003:465). Rendering the Maize God in the eastern structure was perhaps intentionally meant to evoke metaphorical links between his rising from the underworld and the sun's rising over the group and perhaps simultaneously liken the four-cornered E Group plaza to the four-sided agricultural plot where maize grows.

Alongside the Maize God imagery, the early text block features what appears to be a calendrical "completion" (Giron-Ábrego 2012). Mario Giron-Ábrego (2012) has argued that this "completion" may in fact refer to a K'atun or 20-year completion event—key calendrical and ritual celebrations which existed through subsequent historical periods. These K'atun periods have also been argued to be closely associated with Preclassic E Group rituals (Aimers and Rice 2006:90–92). As James Aimers and Prudence Rice (2006:91) note, however, "because carved and dated period-ending stelae were not erected in the lowlands until the Late Preclassic period, this k'atun-ending function cannot be recognized archaeologically in earlier periods." At Sub-5, this block suggests such connections existed as early as the very start of the Late Preclassic, between 300 and 200 BCE, well before the stelae monuments that later attest to this connection (Chase and Chase 1987; Valdés and Fahsen 1995:203–205).

The Sub-5 pyramid ballcourt is a particularly interesting innovation. Ballcourts have also been discussed as closely related and even integral to

E Group complexes (see Aimers and Rice 2006:89–90), but the Sub-5 E Group represents the only known example in which the ballcourt was actually appended to the east-facing side of an E Group's radial pyramid. This was a new addition in the Sub-5 phase, though a tangible symbolic overlay between ballcourts and these complexes must also already have existed for this ballcourt's placement to make sense for San Bartolo's inhabitants.

During the Classic period, the Maize God is often depicted in art as rising from the center of a ballcourt, just as the sixteenth-century Popol Vuh tells us that the Hero Twins' father, a later form of this Maize God, descended into the underworld via a ballcourt (Christenson 2007:60–71). Sacrifice is a key component of these narratives that many scholars argue was central to ballgame ritual. Associated sacrifices often incorporated a victim's grisly descent down a stairway (Miller and Houston 1987). At San Bartolo, these sacrificial connections are materially borne out by the ceramic and finger bone offering left in the Sub-5 ballcourt alley at the very base of the pyramid's eastern stairway. It is difficult to determine exactly how deep in time prior to Sub-5 these sacrificial associations stretch for the Pinturas Group and other early E Groups as well.

Ballcourts are also commonly aligned conceptually with the notion of "center." In imagery and myth, they often act as a point of both emergence and descent between the underworld and the human world and serve as the horizontal center in later cosmological diagrams. The Sub-5 ballcourt fits well with these notions of center, demonstrated through its placement between both the structures that frame the Sub-5 E Group's center point and through the featured imagery of two important deities, the Maize God and Principal Bird Deity, both of whom cyclically descend and emerge across worlds through a vertical center.

It is reasonable to suspect that these overlays are deeply seated in Maya society, stretching perhaps as far back as the very first sedentary and maize-dependent settlements in the Maya area—or at least as far back as the earliest "public" spaces. Doyle's (2012) argument for Middle Preclassic E Groups as early civic requirements and multifunctional centers is especially intriguing here, as any early ballgame activities would likely have transpired in these open, flat, public areas.

Competitive ballplay would further underscore the ballcourt as a center within the proverbial town center but would also significantly bind ballgame symbolism to the broader histories and cosmologies already overlaid in E Group complexes, just as we see at Sub-5.

Entering the Narrative

Monumentality often goes hand in hand with institutional authorities like kingship. As we see especially at Ceibal and elsewhere as well, however, some of the earliest E Groups and associated plazas were probably the result of coordinated labor efforts on the part of community members, as opposed to any centralized authority (Inomata et al. 2013; Doyle 2012). E Groups seem to have their roots as public and multifunctional spaces with particular symbolic and historical meanings for community members, likely related to cohesion and community identity. But clear changes in how E Groups were seen and used were under way during the Late Preclassic, as emerging dynasties began inscribing their own narratives onto these highly meaningful places in local thought. Patricia McAnany (2010:151) writes of this phenomenon that "the pathway to strengthened fields of political power and economic difference . . . appears not to have been paved with acts of self-aggrandizement, but rather with an adroit manipulation of cosmological precepts." Making the understood symbolic associations of E Groups physically tangible and monumental, as described above, is a strong testament to these processes as McAnany (2010) describes them. At Sub-5, however, the ways in which early rulers entered these cosmological narratives are suggestively and perhaps revealingly attested by key archaeological discoveries: the painted ballcourt marker and the early glyph block.

During the Classic period, Maya lords and other elites were commonly depicted in ballplay. A notable youth was sometimes called "he of the ballgame."[3] And the Early Postclassic (900–1200 CE) Popol Vuh casts Hunahpu ("first lord") and his twin brother as expert ballplayers. The cultural and chronological factors were of course variable from Middle Preclassic origins through the Postclassic, but the importance of the ballgame and the desire on the part of rulers to be seen as ballplayers remain surprisingly consistent. Without overanalyzing this phenomenon, it seems reasonable to posit that, throughout time, the physical prowess necessary for being a ballplayer was something with which lords and princes wished to identify themselves. In addition to this link with high-status individuals, the ballgame was also bound up in E Group symbolism, ritual sacrifice, and movement between the human world and the underworld (Aimers and Rice 2006; Schele and Miller 1986:241–253; Schele and Freidel 1991). These interwoven strands of meaning are key to understanding pyramid Sub-5b, its small ballcourt, and most importantly its ballcourt marker as entry points into the ideological narratives of early rulers at San Bartolo.

As mentioned, the Sub-5b ballcourt is too small for conventional ballplay and features a red painted circular ballcourt marker in its alley. The ballcourt marker depicts two inwardly facing figures with a rubber ball between them inscribed with an inverted "U" (Figure 10.6). The marker's layout is quite similar to those of the famous Mot-mot marker, the equally famous Tomb 1 peccary skull scene, and the Ballcourt IIa central marker, all of which were found in Early Classic period contexts (250–550 CE) at the site of Copán, Honduras (see Stuart 2004:221–232; Fash et al. 2004:70–71). We note here that the Sub-5 marker appears to depict a rubber ball between the portrayed figures, rather than a hieroglyphic text as we see on the Copán examples. Both the Mot-mot marker and IIA central floor marker were found in association with ballcourts. The former was installed in the Early Classic plaza floor as part of the same construction event as the nearby ballcourt, in commemoration of the 9th Bak'tun. The latter was installed as part of the ballcourt in its second phase. On the IIa central floor marker, the portrayed figures are depicted engaging in actual ballplay (Fash et al. 2004:71). It is important to mention that the Mot-mot marker depicts the Copán dynastic founder and his son and successor and was placed as the capstone over a young woman's tomb (Stuart 2004:231–232; Fash et al. 2004:71–73), and the peccary skull depicts what may be an early semimythical figure predating the Copán dynasty founder referenced on the Mot-mot (Stuart 2012:128). While the text on the central floor marker of Ballcourt IIa is highly eroded, it might be that this scene similarly depicts a Copán king and his successor, though it remains unclear whether or not it refers to the same founder and son depicted on the slightly earlier Mot-mot marker.

At San Bartolo, the Pinturas ballcourt itself would have denoted the conceptual center of the E Group, and this marker probably served to additionally underscore this centrality, even further emphasizing the alley as a ritual and conceptual center horizontally across San Bartolo and its immediate hinterland. At Early Classic Copán, the Mot-mot marker and Ballcourt IIa marker seem to have marked centrality in a similar way. The similarity in iconographic format for the Pinturas ballcourt marker suggests that these well-known Classic period associations concerning ballcourts—as places where the boundaries between the human world and underworld were permeable—were in fact quite ancient. It suggests that interactions with revered ancestors were possible at ballcourts during the Late Preclassic and that rulers could use such places as a nexus for engaging those ancestors publicly.

In a discussion on E Groups, Arlen and Diane Chase (1995:100) interpret elite burials at the Tikal E Group as "a conjoining of civic and dynastic ritual." The Sub-5 ballcourt marker suggests just that. As early rulers carved out their place within existing ideologies, dynastic ancestor rituals would have been performed in this setting, as the notions of firm dynastic bloodlines and patrilineal descent were increasingly solidified in a highly public way. The ballcourt marker was painted at what was perceived to be the crux of the earth and the underworld. What better place to commune with the dead and simultaneously enter dynastic history into the ritual narratives already associated with E Groups?

The second artifact shedding light on how early kings became bound up with Sub-5 E Group comes from the early text block that references a temporal "completion" event, possibly of a K'atun (20-year period). Following this "completion," a possible distance number leads into a statement featuring an *ajaw* as the primary actor (Giron-Ábrego 2012; Saturno et al. 2006). While the verb or pronoun associated with the *ajaw* glyph is currently undeciphered, the link with an early calendrical "completion" (*tzutz*) event is important.[4] K'atun-endings prominently feature in the hieroglyphic texts of Classic period monumental stelae and constitute the "endings" most cited with the *tzutz* verb during that time. It is important to note that these 20-year periods were key factors in the construction of Maya royal identity and are among the most commonly referenced acts overseen by Classic period Maya kings (*k'uhul ajaw*).

K'atuns constitute one of the Long Count period time units, and this particular calendar (younger than the Calendar Round, arising only in the Late Preclassic) has been convincingly argued to be specifically related to dynastic rhetoric—as a means to link kings to parallel events in deep time beyond the 52-year Calendar Round cycle (Gossen and Leventhal 1993). During the Classic period, K'atun periods were often incorporated into the titles that kings used to identify themselves to the public—as 3 K'atun Lord or 2 K'atun Suzerain,[5] demonstrating the cognitive link between accumulating these periods and dynastic legitimacy. The most notable example of this is Copán's ruler 12, K'ahk' Uti' Witz' K'awiil. On the well-known Altar Q, a monument of a much later Copán king (Ruler 16), Ruler 12 is not named on the monument like the other kings but is instead identified only by his tenure as king as related through 20-year periods: "5-K'atun Ajaw" or 80–100-year-old lord (Fash 1991:101–113; Martin and Grube 2008:203).

The passage of time is a well-attested component of E Group ritual and ideological underpinnings. At E Groups, however, time-based commemorations are more strongly linked (even if imprecisely) with the constantly changing path of the sun over the course of a given year—with reference to solstice points and equinoxes as well as zenith and nadir passages (Aveni and Hartung 1989; Aveni et al. 2003). Classic period placement of K'atun-ending stelae in various E Group complexes in the Maya area has already led some archaeologists to argue for a connection between these "completion" events and E Groups (Aimers and Rice 2006:90–92). But firm K'atun period associations with E Groups, while certainly existent, are far more archaeologically elusive than the other symbolic E Group overlays discussed in this chapter, especially the further backward we move in time. The evidence for this link mostly occurs in the form of period-ending or "completion" event stela monuments from the Terminal Preclassic or Protoclassic (ca. 50–200 CE), Early Classic, or later. Thus, wherever K'atun-endings and E Groups can be linked, the institution of dynastic kingship had already long been in place.

Like the imagery on the ballcourt marker, this text plays on what were likely extant themes already embedded within E Group ritual narratives—the passage of time over the course of a year. Whether 20-year periods were commemorated during the Middle Preclassic is difficult to say. But the explicit connections between these periods and later dynastic symbolism are clear, and the lack of K'atun periods being venerated outside royal narratives suggests that public commemoration of these periods at E Groups arose alongside early dynasties. The Sub-5 text thus not only serves as another form by which Late Preclassic kings entered E Group ritual narratives but also, and maybe more importantly, provides perhaps the earliest example in which a local sovereign was inserted into these narratives of time directly via textual reference.

Drafting a Local History

The scale of the political and social changes already under way during the Sub-5 phase at Pinturas is dramatically demonstrated in the following architectural phase, Sub-4. During the Sub-4 phase, a Triadic Group platform was constructed that engulfed the entirety of the earlier E Group complex—monumentally supplanting much of the associated cosmological symbolism embedded within its layout with another that underscored dynasty and difference (Saturno et al. n.d.; MacLellan 2009). Three remodeling phases later (Sub-1 phase), Pinturas was still a Triadic Group; and more importantly, it served as the location in which an elaborate mural was rendered. These Sub-1A San Bartolo murals offer a compelling and currently unique window into some of the mytho-historical consequences stemming from early dynasts entering prominent ritual narratives.

The San Bartolo murals were painted in a small room (Sub-1A) built off the back of the large Triadic Group platform called Yaxché. Interpreted by several scholars as a didactic space for highborn youth (Houston 2009; Saturno 2009), the mural room features narratives, which relate the foundational stories that underpin Maya dynastic rule. The scenes portrayed on the walls detail commonly expressed themes and mythical associations that we know quite well from later periods, including the ancestral cave emergence from flower mountain (Taube 2004), birth from the gourd (van Akkeren 2006), and the Maize God cycle, as well as the parallels of this cycle with dynastic rulership (Freidel et al. 1993; Fields and Reents-Budet 2006). A key narrative with particular relevance to this discussion, however, is the four-directional offering narrative featured on the southern half of the west wall.

There a figure interpreted as an early form of Hun Ajaw ("first lord") makes offerings at four directional trees, atop each of which sits the Principal Bird Deity (Taube et al. 2010:16–17; Bardawil 1976). As the name would suggest, this figure is the embodiment of "the office of human kingship" (Taube 2003:472). With each of Hun Ajaw's offerings, a piece of the bird falls away amid spirals of blood until it finally hangs, vanquished, from Hun Ajaw's back (Saturno 2009:121–123; Taube et al. 2010:19–20).

In a discussion on this particular mythological complex, Karl Taube (2003:472) writes that "the shooting of the monster bird from its tree may concern the mastery and domination of the forest." Looking at each of the four directional offering scenes, these collectively not only resemble with surprising similarity the very offerings portrayed in the New Year's pages of the Dresden Codex (Taube et al. 2010:27–28), but also recall the laying out of any quadrangular socially constructed human space throughout various Maya societies—be it a milpa, house, central plaza, or even settlement (García-Zambrano 1994; Taube 2003). As such, this scene represents an appropriation of what Andrea Stone (1995:15) calls "the wilderness, forest, or bush" for the creation of "the domestic center or community" (see also Saturno 2009)—a foundational narrative with clear cosmological and culturally deep-seated overtones throughout Mesoamerica.

This narrative holds highly localized relevance as well, however, and one of its underlying meanings may in fact concern the very founding of San Bartolo—infusing an extant local belief in this four-cornered founding (already rife with agricultural metaphor) with explicit dynastic symbolism. In one of its manifold ideological layers, this scene could also represent the establishment of four-cornered civic space like the very E Group on which its constituent architecture was built. This is not to suggest that Hun Ajaw historically founded San Bartolo but rather meant to emphasize that the west wall scene, usually discussed in terms of its much broader and widespread cosmological underpinnings, may in fact be the San Bartolo version of a highly common foundational tale as opposed to simply a tale of human creation on the whole.

As such, we believe the ruler being crowned in another of the mural's narratives that intentionally runs parallel to that of the revered Maize God is in fact an early historical king or mythical local dynastic founder—either way, a revered ancestor. We also believe that the north wall emergence and gourd births bear directly on the local mytho-historical foundation for this specific place and its citizens.

Middle Preclassic E Groups were among the earliest civic requirements for what made a Middle Preclassic Petén community a community—the product of what Inomata and colleagues (2013:470) have called "increasingly prescribed forms of interactions and shared notions of new social order"—the foundation of a community would have quite literally involved appropriating four-cornered space from the forest. Such space would have served as a central and uniting point for households in the surrounding hinterland and would likely have been the place where travelers first went when moving between towns and across the landscape. While we may never know what the Middle Preclassic foundational stories might have been, we do know that by around 150–100 BCE these narratives at San Bartolo clearly feature an *ajaw*, specifically "first" *ajaw*: the prototypical dynast who did not necessarily exist as such when these towns were first laid out.

On the murals, however, it is this protagonist who appropriates four-cornered space through sacrifice and defeats the dangerous and "wild" bird—thus establishing a place for civilization to thrive. We believe that it was only through the cumulative efforts of early leaders at San Bartolo over time, routinely entering extant ritual narratives tangibly at places like the Sub-5 E Group, that the eventual symbolic entrance of institutional kingship into these narratives became naturalized, as we see on the Sub-1 murals.

While we do not claim the Sub-5 E Group is representative of the moment at which institutional kingship emerged, we do believe that it was constructed at a time when institutionalized kingship was still relatively novel at San Bartolo, likely no more than a century or two old. At Jabalí, the royal burial discovered in 2006 provides further evidence of emergent dynastic ritual through the specialized construction of a mortuary chamber and interment of a rich offering linking the deceased with maize and fertility symbolism (Saturno 2006). This burial was more or less contemporary with the Sub-5 E Group (ca. 300–200 BCE). Its placement within the Jabalí Triadic Group at the far west of the site shows that early rulers were already interring their ancestors in a manner indicative of their elevated status in the community.

During the Sub-5 phase we see monumental additions to the previous E Groups, which strongly draw out the steadily increasing use of this longtime public space as a stage of sorts. These "stages" were conceivably employed by early kings for the public performance of rituals that underscored a shared identity and communal historicity for nearby inhabitants but also infused these performances with rhetoric that placed early kings at the very heart of this identity, the community, and its broader cosmology (Saturno et al. n.d.). The change at Pinturas to an elevated Triadic Group as at Jabalí is made all the more significant when considered in this light. It not only demonstrates a full imposition of explicitly royal imagery and architecture onto the earliest public space and its mytho-history but also suggests that governors no longer needed to validate their rule publicly to the governed in the same way. By the end of the Late Preclassic, San Bartolo's historical charter featured an *ajaw*.

Conclusion

In a discussion on commemorative ceremonies, Paul Connerton (1989:43) writes of his case study that "this narrative was more than a story told—it was *cult enacted*. It was a rite fixed and performed. Its story was told not unequivocally in the past tense but in the tense of a metaphysical present." We believe that at some point between the first Sub-7 E Group and the creation of the San Bartolo murals the actors and themes in these ritual enactments and foundational narratives shifted to include the incipient dynasties that were gaining sway throughout the Maya Lowlands. Through repeated performances playing on themes in San Bartolo's mytho-historical past, early kings were able to enter these narratives through sponsorship of construction that realized themes of this past in tangible and monumental form and through increasingly infusing performances of long-standing rituals with dynastic symbolism—ostensibly altering the narrative *enacted* through time.

Like the San Bartolo murals that were painted two centuries after, the Sub-5 E Group makes physically tangible many conceptual overlays and symbolic associations long acknowledged and debated by Maya archaeologists and anthropologists alike. It firmly demonstrates that a conceptual link existed among E Groups, ballcourts, and the notion of horizontal and vertical center. Furthermore, it shows how the Feathered Serpent/solar avian, the Maize God, the ballgame, the commemoration of time, dynastic rulership, glorified ancestors, local historicity, and ritual sacrifice were all overlaid in a four-cornered universe made manifest in a complex that began as a modest Maya community's "civic requirement."

Acknowledgments

The authors wish to thank IDAEH and the Departamento de Monumentos, Guatemala, for supporting the Proyecto Regional Arqueológico San Bartolo-Xultun research in Petén, Guatemala. We further express our appreciation to all the many members and collaborators of the San Bartolo Project through the years. Special thanks to Heather Hurst and Patricia Rivera Castillo for their aid and facilitation in this work. We also extend our gratitude to the conference hosts, David Freidel and Jerry Sabloff, and to the Santa Fe Institute for sponsoring the event from which this volume emerged. We would like to offer further thanks to Anne Dowd and to our anonymous reviewers for their insightful and helpful comments.

Notes

1. The Ixim phase is actually composed of Sub-1 and Sub-II phases, which were initially numbered as separate but actually existed at the same time.

2. Although each of these phases has both a name designation (such as Ixkik) as well as numerical phase number (such as "-Sub-7"), it should be mentioned that in this chapter we refer only to the numerical phase number in order to avoid confusion.

3. For glyphic decipherment of "ballgame/ballplay" (*pitz*), see Stuart 1987:25.

4. For glyphic decipherment of "to end/complete" (*tzutz*), see Stuart 2001.

5. Numbered K'atun titles were first pointed out by Proskouriakoff (1963, 1964).

References Cited

Aimers, James J., and Prudence M. Rice
2006   Astronomy, Ritual, and the Interpretation of Maya "E-Group" Architectural Assemblages. *Ancient Mesoamerica* 17(1):79–96.

Ashmore, Wendy
2002   Decisions and Dispositions: Socializing Spatial Archaeology. *American Anthropologist* 104(4):1172–1183.
2009   Biographies of Place at Quirigua, Guatemala. In *The Archaeology of Meaningful Places,* edited by Brenda J. Bowser and Maria Nieves Zedeño pp. 2–30. Foundations of Anthropological Inquiry Series. University of Utah Press, Salt Lake City.

Aveni, Anthony, Anne S. Dowd, and Benjamin Vining
2003   Maya Calendar Reform? Evidence from Orientations of Specialized Architectural Assemblages. *Latin American Antiquity* 14(2):159–178.

Aveni, Anthony, and Horst Hartung
1989   Uaxactun, Guatemala, Group E and Similar Assemblages: An Archaeoastronomical Reconsideration. In *World Archaeoastronomy,* edited by Anthony Aveni, pp. 441–461. Cambridge University Press, Cambridge, United Kingdom.

Bardawil, Lawrence
1976   The Principal Bird Deity in Maya Art: An Iconographic Study of Form and Meaning. In *The Art, Iconography, and Dynastic History of Palenque, Part III,* edited by Merle Greene Robertson, pp. 195–209. Precolumbian Art Research Institute, Robert Louis Stevenson School, Pebble Beach, California.

Beltrán, Boris
2005   Excavaciones en los primeros estadíos constructivos del conjunto arquitectónico de Las Pinturas. In *Proyecto Regional Arqueológico San Bartolo: Informe preliminar no. 4, cuarta temporada 2005,* edited by Mónica Urquizú and William A. Saturno, pp. 59–78. Instituto de Antropología e Historia de Guatemala, Guatemala City.
2006   SB-1A: Excavaciones en la estructura Ixbalamque (Pinturas Sub 6), San Bartolo, Petén. In *Proyecto Regional Arqueológico San Bartolo: Informe preliminar no. 5, quinta temporada 2006,* edited by Mónica Urquizú and William A. Saturno, pp. 1–18. Instituto de Antropología e Historia de Guatemala, Guatemala City.
2008   Excavaciones de la tercera etapa constructiva del complejo arquitectónico Las Pinturas (Pinturas Sub-6). In *Proyecto Regional Arqueológico San Bartolo: Informe preliminar no. 7, septima temporada 2008,* edited by Mónica Urquizú and William A. Saturno, pp. 42–60. Instituto de Antropología e Historia de Guatemala, Guatemala City.
2010   Hunahpu, una pirámide radial (Pinturas Sub 6). In *Proyecto Regional Arqueológico San Bartolo: Informe preliminar no. 9, novena temporada 2010,* edited by William A. Saturno and Luis Romero, pp. 6–19. Instituto de Antropología e Historia de Guatemala, Guatemala City.

2015 Hunahpu, un complejo conmemorativo del Preclásico Medio del sitio arqueológico San Bartolo, Flores, Petén. Ph.D. dissertation (Licenciado), Escuela de Historia, Universidad de San Carlos, Guatemala.

Beltrán, Boris, and Juan Francisco Saravia
2012 Investigación y consolidación de tuneles, Pinturas Sub-6B Hunahpu, sitio arqueológico San Bartolo. In *Proyecto Regional Arqueológico San Bartolo: Informe preliminar no. 11, temporada de campo año 2012*, edited by Patricia Rivera Castillo and William A. Saturno, pp. 15–30. Instituto de Antropología e Historia de Guatemala, Guatemala City.

Blanton, Richard E., and Lane E. Fargher
2008 *Collective Action in the Formation of Pre-Modern States*. Springer, New York.
2011 The Collective Logic of Pre-Modern Cities. *World Archaeology* 43(3):505–522.

Chase, Arlen F., and Diane Z. Chase
1987 *Investigations at the Classic Maya City of Caracol, Belize: 1985–1987*. Precolumbian Art Research Institute, San Francisco, California.
1995 External Impetus, Internal Synthesis, and Standardization: E Group Assemblages and the Crystallization of Classic Maya Society in the Southern Lowlands. *Acta Mesoamericana* 8:87–101 (special issue edited by Nikolai Grube entitled *The Emergence of Lowland Maya Civilization: The Transition from the Preclassic to Early Classic*).

Christenson, Allen
2007 *Popol Vuh: Sacred Book of the Ancient Maya*. Center for the Preservation of Religious Texts, Brigham Young University, Provo, Utah.

Cohodas, Marvin
1980 Radial Pyramids and Radial Associated Assemblages of the Central Maya Area. *Journal of the Society of Architectural Historians* 39(3):208–223.

Connerton, Paul
1989 *How Societies Remember*. Cambridge University Press, Cambridge.

Craig, Jessica
2009 Shifting Perceptions of Sacred Spaces: Ceremonial Reuse of Maya Architecture and Monuments at San Bartolo, Guatemala. Ph.D. dissertation, Department of Anthropology, University of Kansas, Lawrence.

Davies, Diane E.
2012 Past Identities, Present Legitimation: The Reuse of a Late Preclassic Residential Group at the Maya Site of San Bartolo, Guatemala. Ph.D. dissertation, Department of Anthropology, Tulane University, New Orleans.

Doyle, James
2012 Regroup on "E-Groups": Monumentality and Early Centers in the Middle Preclassic Maya Lowlands. *Latin American Antiquity* 23(4):355–379.
2013 Early Maya Geometric Planning Conventions at El Palmar, Guatemala. *Journal of Archaeological Science* 40(2013):793–798.

Escobar, Luisa, and Astrid Runggaldier
2002 SB 1B: Excavaciones en la parte posterior de la pirámide de Las Pinturas. In *Proyecto Regional Arqueológico San Bartolo: Informe preliminar no. 1, primera*

temporada 2002, edited by Mónica Urquizú and William A. Saturno, pp. 12–13. Instituto de Antropología e Historia de Guatemala, Guatemala City.

Escobedo, Héctor
2002 SB-1: Excavaciones en la pirámide de Las Pinturas. In *Proyecto Regional Arqueológico San Bartolo: Informe preliminar no. 1, primera temporada 2002*, edited by Mónica Urquizú and William A. Saturno, pp. 42–46. Instituto de Antropología e Historia de Guatemala, Guatemala City.

Estrada-Belli, Francisco
2006 Lightning Sky, Rain, and the Maize God: The Ideology of Preclassic Maya Rulers at Cival, Peten, Guatemala. *Ancient Mesoamerica* 17(1):57–78.

Fash, William L.
1991 *Scribes, Warriors and Kings: The City of Copan and the Ancient Maya*. Thames and Hudson, New York.

Fash, William L., Barbara Fash, and Karla L. Davis-Salazar
2004 Setting the Stage: Origins of the Hieroglyphic Stairway on the Great Period Ending. In *Understanding Early Classic Copan*, edited by Ellen E. Bell, Marcello A. Canuto, and Robert Sharer, pp. 65–84. University Museum of Archaeology and Anthropology, Philadelphia, Pennsylvania.

Fields, Virginia M., and Dorie Reents-Budet (editors)
2006 *Lords of Creation: The Origins of Sacred Maya Kingship*. Los Angeles County Museum of Art, Los Angeles, California.

Freidel, David, Linda Schele, and Joy Parker
1993 *Maya Cosmos: Three Thousand Years on the Shaman's Path*. HarperCollins, New York.

García-Zambrano, Angel J.
1994 Early Colonial Evidence of Pre-Columbian Rituals of Foundation. In *Seventh Palenque Round Table, 1989*, edited by Virginia M. Fields, pp. 217–228. Precolumbian Art Research Institute, San Francisco, California.

Garrison, Thomas
2007 Ancient Maya Territories, Adaptive Regions, and Alliances: Contextualizing the San Bartolo-Xultun Intersite Survey. Ph.D. dissertation, Department of Anthropology, Harvard University, Cambridge, Massachusetts.

Giron-Ábrego, Mario
2012 An Early Example of the Logogram TZUTZ at San Bartolo. *Wayeb Notes* 42:1–6.
2013 A Late Preclassic Distance Number. *PARI Journal* 13(4):8–12.

Gossen, Gary H., and Richard M. Leventhal
1993 The Topography of Ancient Maya Religious Pluralism: A Dialogue with the Present. In *Lowland Maya Civilization in the Eighth Century A.D.*, edited by Jeremy A. Sabloff and John S. Henderson, pp. 185–217. Dumbarton Oaks Pre-Columbian Symposia and Colloquia. Dumbarton Oaks Research Library and Collection, Washington, D.C.

Griffin, Robert E.
2012 The Carrying Capacity of Ancient Maya Swidden Maize Cultivation: A Case

Study in the Region around San Bartolo, Peten, Guatemala. Ph.D. dissertation, Department of Anthropology, Pennsylvania State University, State College.

Guderjan, Thomas H.
2006   E-Groups, Pseudo-E-Groups, and the Development of the Classic Maya Identity in the Eastern Peten. *Ancient Mesoamerica* 17(1):97–104.

Hammond, Norman
1999   The Genesis of Hierarchy: Mortuary and Offertory Ritual in the Pre-Classic at Cuello, Belize. In *Social Patterns in Pre-Classic Mesoamerica*, edited by David C. Grove and Rosemary Joyce, pp. 49–66. Dumbarton Oaks Research Library and Collection, Washington, D.C.

Hanks, William F.
1990   *Referential Practice: Language and Lived Space among the Maya*. University of Chicago Press, Chicago.

Houston, Stephen D.
2009   A Splendid Predicament: Young Men in Classic Maya Society. *Cambridge Archaeological Journal* 19(2):149–178.

Hurst, Heather
2006   SB 20C: Excavaciones en el grupo Saraguate, Estructura 132. In *Proyecto Regional Arqueológico San Bartolo: Informe preliminar no. 5, quinta temporada 2006*, edited by Mónica Urquizú and William A. Saturno, pp. 58–66. Instituto de Antropología e Historia de Guatemala, Guatemala City.
2009   Murals and the Ancient Maya Artist: A Study of Art Production in the Guatemalan Lowlands. Ph.D. dissertation, Department of Anthropology, Yale University, New Haven, Connecticut.

Inomata, Takeshi, Daniela Triadan, Kazuo Aoyama, Victor Castillo, and Hitoshi Yonenobu
2013   Early Ceremonial Constructions at Ceibal, Guatemala, and the Origins of Lowland Maya Civilization. *Science* 340:467–471.

Joyce, Rosemary
2004   Unintended Consequences?: Monumentality as a Novel Experience in Formative Mesoamerica. *Journal of Archaeological Method and Theory* 11(1):5–29.

Laporte, Juan Pedro
1995   Preclásico a Clásico en Tikal: Proceso de transformación en Mundo Perdido. In *The Emergence of Lowland Maya Civilization: The Transition from the Preclassic to the Early Classic*, edited by Nikolai Grube, pp. 17–34. Verlag Anton Saurwein, Möckmühl, Germany.

León Antillón, Mónica de, Julio Caal, Alejandro Garay, Juliana Fernández, Kathleen Scanlan, Holly Swanson, Srivatsa Dattatreya, and Jared Katz
2010   Nuevas investigaciones sobre la Cuarta etapa constructiva en la Plataforma 110, Grupo Jabalí. In *Proyecto Regional Arqueológico San Bartolo: Informe preliminar no. 9, novena temporada 2010*, edited by William A. Saturno and Luis Romero, pp. 20–54. Instituto de Antropología e Historia de Guatemala, Guatemala City.

Liu, Li
2004   *The Chinese Neolithic: Trajectories to Early States*. Cambridge University Press, Cambridge.

McAnany, Patricia
2010   *Ancestral Maya Economies in Archaeological Perspective.* Cambridge University Press, New York.

MacLellan, Jessica
2009   Change and Continuity in the Preclassic Architecture of the Las Pinturas Group San Bartolo, Peten, Guatemala. Senior thesis, Department of Archaeology, Boston University, Boston.

Martin, Simon, and Nikolai Grube
2008   *Chronicle of the Maya Kings and Queens.* 2nd ed. Thames and Hudson, New York.

Miller, Mary Ellen, and Stephen D. Houston
1987   The Classic Maya Ballgame and Its Architectural Setting: A Study of Relations between Text and Image. *Res: Anthropology and Aesthetics* 14:46–65.

Parkinson, William A., and Michael L. Galaty
2007   Primary and Secondary State in Perspective: An Integrated Approach to State Formation in the Prehistoric Aegean. *American Anthropologist* 109:113–129.

Pellecer Alecio, Mónica
2006   SB 20A Y 20H: Prospección al suroeste y en el juego de pelota, Grupo Saraguate. In *Proyecto Regional Arqueológico San Bartolo: Informe preliminar no. 5, quinta temporada 2006,* edited by Mónica Urquizú and William A. Saturno, pp. 37–41. Instituto de Antropología e Historia de Guatemala, Guatemala City.

Pellecer Alecio, Mónica, Luís Méndez Salinas, Joshua Feola, and Quincy Stevens
2008   Los nuevos hallazgos del grupo Jabali: Excavaciones en las Plataformas 110, 111 y 112. In *Proyecto Regional Arqueológico San Bartolo: Informe preliminar no. 7, septima temporada 2008,* edited by Mónica Urquizú and William A. Saturno, pp. 177–216. Instituto de Antropología e Historia de Guatemala, Guatemala City.

Pellecer Alecio, Mónica, Damaris Menéndez, Hugo Ortiz, and José Garrido
2005   SB12: Excavaciones al frente de la plataforma, en el patio central y las estructuras B y C del Grupo Jabalí. In *Proyecto Regional Arqueológico San Bartolo: Informe preliminar no. 4, cuarta temporada de campo año 2005,* edited by Mónica Urquizú and William A. Saturno, pp. 250–316. Instituto de Antropología e Historia de Guatemala, Guatemala City.

Proskouriakoff, Tatiana
1963   Historical Data in the Inscriptions of Yaxchilan, Part 1. *Estudios de Cultura Maya* 3:149–167.
1964   Historical Data in the Inscriptions of Yaxchilan, Part 2. *Estudios de Cultura Maya* 4:177–201.

Ringle, William M.
1999   Pre-Classic Cityscapes: Ritual Politics among the Early Lowland Maya. In *Social Patterns in Pre-Classic Mesoamerica,* edited by David C. Grove and Rosemary Joyce, pp. 183–223. Dumbarton Oaks Research Library and Collection, Washington, D.C.

Rivera Castillo, Patricia
2008   Análisis cerámico sitios: San Bartolo y Xultúb, temporada de campo 2008. *Proyecto Regional Arqueológico San Bartolo: Informe preliminar no. 7, septima temporada 2008*, edited by Mónica Urquizú and William A. Saturno, pp. 276–311. Instituto de Antropología e Historia de Guatemala, Guatemala City.
2010   Clasificación cerámica sitios San Bartolo–Xultún: Novena temporada de campo año 2010. In *Proyecto Regional Arqueológico San Bartolo: Informe preliminar no. 9, novena temporada 2010*, edited by William A. Saturno and Luis Romero, pp. 254–281. Instituto de Antropología e Historia de Guatemala, Guatemala City.
2012   Cronología preliminar de los sitios San Bartolo y Xultún: Estudios cerámicos. In *Proyecto Regional Arqueológico San Bartolo: Informe preliminar no. 11, temporada de campo año 2012*, edited by Patricia Rivera Castillo and William A. Saturno, pp. 467–516. Instituto de Antropología e Historia de Guatemala, Guatemala City.

Rodman, Margaret
2003   Empowering Place: Multilocality and Multivocality. In *The Anthropology of Space and Place: Locating Culture*, edited by Setha Low and Denise Lawrence-Zuniga, pp. 204–223. Blackwell, Oxford, United Kingdom.

Runggaldier, Astrid
2009   Memory and Materiality in Monumental Architecture: Construction and Reuse of a Late Preclassic Maya Palace at San Bartolo, Guatemala. Ph.D. dissertation, Department of Archaeology, Boston University, Boston.

Saturno, William A.
2006   The Dawn of Maya Gods and Kings. *National Geographic* 209(1):68–77.
2009   Centering the Kingdom, Centering the King: Maya Creation and Legitimization at San Bartolo. In *The Art of Urbanism: How Mesoamerican Kingdoms Represented Themselves in Architecture and Imagery*, edited by William L. Fash and Leonardo López Luján, pp. 111–134. Dumbarton Oaks Research Library and Collection, Washington, D.C.

Saturno, William A., Franco D. Rossi, and Boris Beltrán
n.d.   Changing Stages: Royal Legitimacy and the Architectural Development of the Pinturas Complex at San Bartolo, Guatemala. In *Pathways to Complexity: A View from the Maya Lowlands*, edited by M. Kathryn Brown and George J. Bey III. University Press of Florida, Gainesville.

Saturno, William A., David Stuart, and Boris Beltrán
2006   Early Maya Writing at San Bartolo, Guatemala. *Science* 311:1281–1283.

Saturno, William A., Karl A. Taube, and David Stuart
2005   *The Murals of San Bartolo, El Peten, Guatemala, Part 1: The North Wall*. Ancient America, No. 7. Boundary End Archaeology Research Center, Barnardsville, North Carolina.

Schele, Linda, and David Freidel
1991   The Courts of Creation: Ballcourts, Ballgames, and Portals to the Maya Otherworld. In *The Mesoamerican Ballgame*, edited by Vernon L. Scarborough and David R. Wilcox, pp. 289–316. University of Arizona Press, Tucson.

Schele, Linda, and Mary Ellen Miller
1986   *The Blood of Kings: Dynasty and Ritual in Maya Art*. George Braziller, New York.

Šprajc, Ivan, Carlos Morales-Aguilar, and Richard Hansen
2009   Early Maya Astronomy and Urban Planning at El Mirador, Peten, Guatemala. *Anthropological Notebooks* 15(3):79–101.

Stone, Andrea
1995   *Images from the Underworld: Naj Tunich and Tradition of Maya Cave Painting*. University of Texas Press, Austin.

Stuart, David
1987   *Ten Phonetic Syllables*. Research Reports on Ancient Maya Writing, 14. Center for Maya Research, Washington, D.C.
2001   *A Reading of the "Completion Hand" as TZUTZ*. Research Reports on Ancient Maya Writing, 49. Center for Maya Research, Washington, D.C.
2004   The Beginning of the Copan Dynasty: A Review of the Hieroglyphic and Historical Evidence. In *Understanding Early Classic Copan*, edited by Ellen E. Bell, Marcello A. Canuto, and Robert Sharer, pp. 215–249. University Museum of Archaeology and Anthropology, Philadelphia, Pennsylvania.
2012   The Name of Paper: The Mythology of Crowning and Royal Nomenclature on Palenque's Palace Tablet. In *Maya Archaeology 2*, edited by Charles Golden, Stephen D. Houston, and Joel Skidmore, pp. 116–142. Precolumbia Mesoweb Press, San Francisco, California.

Taube, Karl A.
2003   Ancient and Contemporary Maya Conceptions about Field and Forest. In *The Lowland Maya Area: Three Millennia at the Human-Wildland Interface*, edited by Arturo Gómez-Pompa, Michael F. Allen, Scott I. Fedick, and Juan J. Jiménez-Osornio, pp. 461–492. Food Products Press, New York.
2004   Flower Mountain: Concepts of Life, Beauty, and Paradise among the Classic Maya. *Res: Art and Aesthetics* 45:69–98.

Taube, Karl A., William A. Saturno, David Stuart, and Heather Hurst
2010   *The Murals of San Bartolo, El Peten, Guatemala, Part 2: The West Wall*. Ancient America, No. 10. Boundary End Archaeology Research Center, Barnardsville, North Carolina.

Tomasic, John J., and Steven Bozarth
2011   New Data from a Preclassic Tomb at K'o, Guatemala. Paper presented at the Society for American Archaeology Annual Meeting, Sacramento, California, April 2011.

Tozzer, Alfred M.
1941   *Landa's Relación de las cosas de Yucatan: A Translation*. Papers of the Peabody Museum of American Archaeology and Ethnology, No. 18. Harvard University Press, Cambridge, Massachusetts.

Urquizú, Mónica
2003a   SB 6A: Excavación en la plaza Las Ventanas. In *Proyecto Regional Arqueológico San Bartolo: Informe preliminar no. 2, segunda temporada 2003*, edited

by Mónica Urquizú and William A. Saturno, pp. 42–44. Instituto de Antropología e Historia de Guatemala, Guatemala City.

2003b   SB 7: Excavaciones en la Pirámide Las Ventanas. In *Proyecto Regional Arqueológico San Bartolo: Informe preliminar no. 2, segunda temporada 2003*, edited by Mónica Urquizú and William A. Saturno, pp. 45–50. Instituto de Antropología e Historia de Guatemala, Guatemala City.

2003c   SB 10A: Excavaciones en la sección posterior a la gran plataforma de Las Ventanas. In *Proyecto Regional Arqueológico San Bartolo: Informe preliminar no. 2, segunda temporada 2003*, edited by Mónica Urquizú and William A. Saturno, pp. 86–87. Instituto de Antropología e Historia de Guatemala, Guatemala City.

Urquizú, Mónica, and Damaris Menéndez

2006   SB 20B: Excavaciones en la Estructura 133 del grupo Saraguate, San Bartolo, Petén. In *Proyecto Regional Arqueológico San Bartolo: Informe preliminar no. 5, quinta temporada 2006*, edited by Mónica Urquizú and William A. Saturno, pp. 42–57. Instituto de Antropología e Historia de Guatemala, Guatemala City.

Urquizú, Mónica, and William A. Saturno (editors)

2002   *Proyecto Regional Arqueológico San Bartolo: Informe Preliminar no. 1, primera temporada 2002*. Instituto de Antropología e Historia de Guatemala, Guatemala City.

2003   *Proyecto Regional Arqueológico San Bartolo: Informe preliminar no. 2, segunda temporada 2003*. Instituto de Antropología e Historia de Guatemala, Guatemala City.

2004   *Proyecto Regional Arqueológico San Bartolo: Informe preliminar no. 3, tercera temporada 2004*. Instituto de Antropología e Historia de Guatemala, Guatemala City.

2005   *Proyecto Regional Arqueológico San Bartolo: Informe preliminar no. 4, cuarta temporada 2005*. Instituto de Antropología e Historia de Guatemala, Guatemala City.

2006a   *Proyecto Regional Arqueológico San Bartolo: Informe preliminar no. 5, quinta temporada 2006*. Instituto de Antropología e Historia de Guatemala, Guatemala City.

2006b   Resultados preliminares de la cuarta temporada de campo del Proyecto Arqueológico San Bartolo. In *XIX Simposio de Investigaciones Arqueológicas en Guatemala*, edited by Juan Pedro Laporte, Bárbara Arroyo, and Héctor Mejía, pp. 59–78. Instituto de Antropología e Historia de Guatemala y Museo Nacional de Arqueología y Etnología, Guatemala City.

2007   *Proyecto Regional Arqueológico San Bartolo: Informe preliminar no. 6, sexta temporada 2007*. Instituto de Antropología e Historia de Guatemala, Guatemala City.

2008   *Proyecto Regional Arqueológico San Bartolo: Informe preliminar no. 7, septima temporada 2008*. Instituto de Antropología e Historia de Guatemala, Guatemala City.

Valdés, Juan Antonio, and Federico Fahsen

1995   The Reigning Dynasty of Uaxactun during the Early Classic. *Ancient Mesoamerica* 6(2):197–219.

van Akkeren, Ruud
2006   Tzuywa: Place of the Gourd. In *Tzuywa: Place of the Gourd*, pp. 36–73. Ancient America, No. 9. Boundary End Archaeology Research Center, Barnardsville, North Carolina.

Wilson, M. R.
1972   A Highland Maya People and Their Habitat: The Natural History, Demography and Economy of the K'ekchi'. Ph.D. dissertation, Department of Geography, University of Oregon, Eugene.

11

Ordinary People and East–West Symbolism

CYNTHIA ROBIN

East–west symbolism is a key component of E Group complexes (Aimers 1993; Aimers and Rice 2006; Aveni and Hartung 1989; Chase and Chase 1995; Cohodas 1980; Freidel et al. 1993; Laporte and Fialko 1990; Ricketson 1928). It also a key component of a number of likely related ritual architectural complexes in the Maya area: east–west Twin Pyramid complexes (Ashmore 1991; Coggins 1980; Guillemin 1968), Eastern Triadic Structures (Chapter 13 in this volume), and eastern shrines (Chase and Chase 1996; Hanks 1990; Iannone 2005). The focal nature of the east–west axis in Maya architecture and thought is not surprising, as this axis represents the rising and setting of the sun, the birth and dawn of each new day. Cross-culturally, many groups recognize the east–west axis as a salient orientational system, although there is cultural variation in meaning and manifestation (for example, Kus and Raharijaona 1990; Pearson and Richards 1994). By placing monuments at eastern and western points within a city, community, plaza, or house, the Maya spatially marked the path of the sun and the location of the rising and setting of the sun as seen on the horizon. East and west were linked not only to the cycle of the sun but also to other natural sources of power such as the annual agricultural cycle (Aimers and Rice 2006).

The authors in this volume collectively demonstrate the antiquity of the E Group complex and some (for example, Dowd in Chapter 16) identify it as one of the earliest religious complexes in the Maya area, pointing to the early significance of east–west symbolism in Maya thought and urban planning. Some three thousand years later, at the other end of the temporal spectrum, contemporary Maya place eastern shrines in houses dedicated to the ancestors (Hanks 1990; Vogt 1965). In modern day Yucatán, Mexico, the *h-men* (shaman) places the returning spirit addressees to the east on the altar table facing west. The *santo* (saint) stands on the front of these altars' easternmost edge, also facing west. The shaman stands to the west of the altar facing east in prayer with the audience behind him, who also face east (Hanks 1990:338). The east and west directions situate the house altar, ritual practitioner and participants, and ancestors within the house, the world, and the cosmos. Contemporary Maya eastern shrines and east–west focused rituals may be vestiges of an enduring religious tradition that has both undergone great transformation and seen great tenacity through time (Robin 2015).

I develop this line of argument through an analysis of the religious complex at the Maya farming community of Chan in Belize, which has a 2,000-year history (800 BCE–1200 CE; Robin 2012, 2013). Chan's central religious complex, located in its Central Group, consists of a tripartite east structure (Structure 5) and a single west structure (Structure 7) (Robin et al. 2012a). The burials identified within Chan's central religious complex indicate that one of its primary functions was as an ancestor shrine (Novotny 2012), linking ancestor veneration, the east–west axis, the rising and setting of the sun, and the agricultural cycle. While the specific meanings attached to the association of the ancestors and the east–west axis across Chan's 2,000-year history changed through time (as discussed below), and these meanings may have also differed from those associated with the eastern ancestor shrines in modern Maya houses, there appears to be an enduring association between ancestors and the east–west axis in the lives of ordinary Maya people. This chapter proceeds with an overview of the Chan site, a discussion of the architectural history of Chan's central religious complex, and a discussion of the ancestral burials interred there.

The Maya farming community of Chan is located in the upper Belize Valley region of west-central Belize, in an upland area between the Mopán and Macal branches of the Belize River (Figure 11.1). Across Chan's undulating upland terrain, its ancient inhabitants constructed a productive landscape of agricultural terraces surrounding a community center. This agricultural base supported Chan's 2,000-year occupation (800 BCE–1519 CE), which spans the major periods of political change in Maya society: the Preclassic (1000 BCE–250 CE), Classic (250–900 CE), and Postclassic (900–1200 CE) (Tables 11.1 and 11.2). The scale of the Chan community provides a window into the lives of people who lived in what was a prehistoric Maya agrarian community. Chan's deep chronology provides a means to examine diachronically how farmers' lives were embedded within and significant for the construction of broader Maya society (Robin 2012, 2013).

The Chan community consists of 274 households and 1,223 agricultural terraces surrounding a community center (Figure 11.2; Robin et al. 2012c).

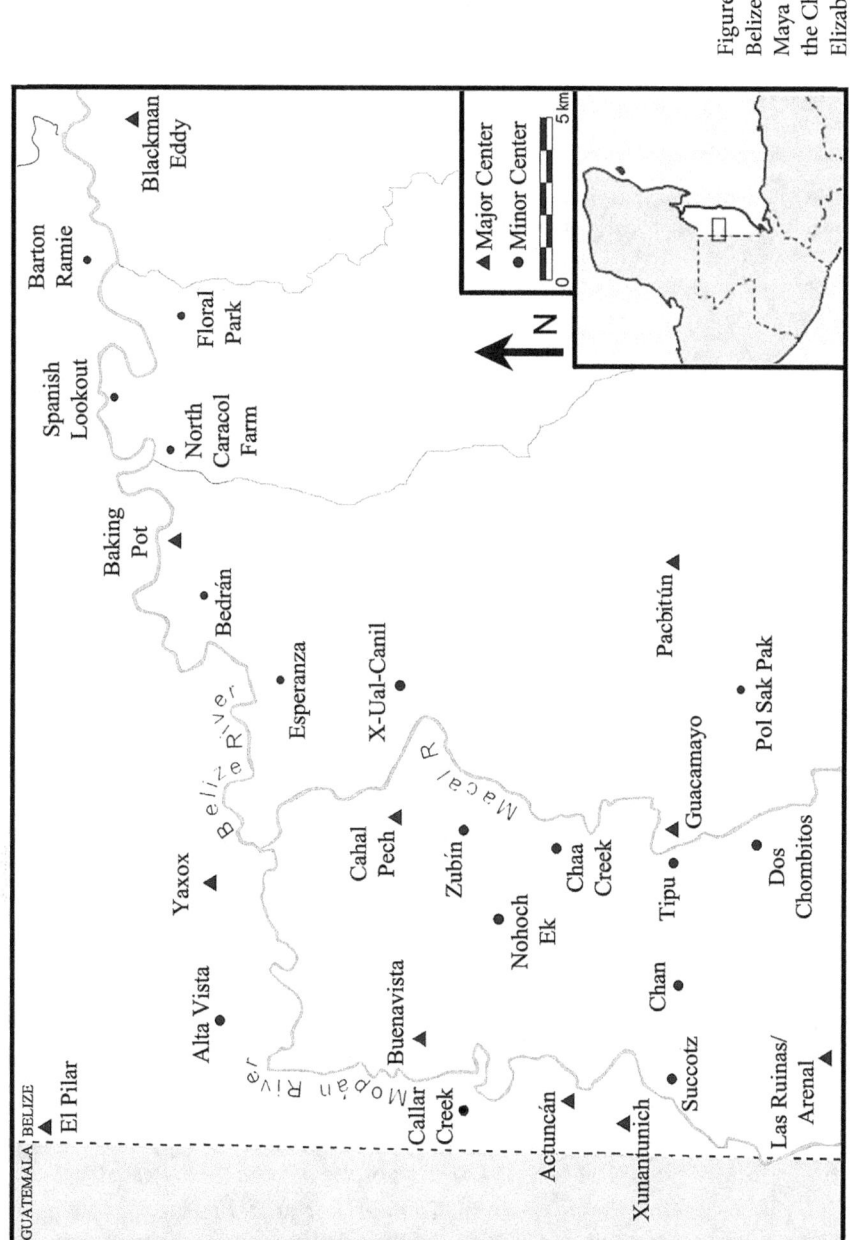

Figure 11.1. Map of the Belize River valley and Maya area showing the Chan site. Map by Elizabeth Shiffman.

Table 11.1. Chronology chart for the Chan site

	Calendar years[a]	Chan ceramic complexes[b]
Early Postclassic	900–1150/1200 CE	(Not a complete complex)
Terminal Classic	800/830–900 CE	Vieras
Late Late Classic	670–800/830 CE	Pesoro
Early Late Classic	600–670 CE	Jalacté
Early Classic	250–600 CE	Burrell
Terminal Preclassic	100/150–250 CE	Potts
Late Preclassic	350 BCE–100/150 CE	Cadlé
Middle Preclassic	650–350 BCE	Bodén
Early Middle Preclassic	1000/800–650 BCE	(Not a complete complex)

[a] Calendar years are approximate dates based on ceramic seriation in conjunction with twenty-four radiocarbon dates from Chan and correlation with other sites in the Maya Lowlands. See Table 11.2 for radiocarbon dates.
[b] Chan ceramic complexes are named for geographic bodies of water in and around the Belize Valley.

The majority of Chan's residents were farmers (Wyatt 2012). Some residents also produced chert bifaces (Hearth 2012) or limestone blocks (Kestle 2012), and leading residents were involved in the production and procurement of marine shell and obsidian objects (Keller 2012; Meierhoff et al. 2012).

Farmers' agricultural terraces are the most ubiquitous and substantial construction at Chan. Farmers constructed terraces up and down hillslopes and across channels. Agricultural terraces surround farmers' homes, making the farmsteads (or discrete residential and agricultural areas) the basic settlement unit at Chan. All of Chan's residents, from humblest farmer to community leader, lived in perishable buildings with thatch roofs constructed on stone substructures.

Chan's community center is located at the spatial and geographical center of the community on a local high point in the topography. It consists of two adjoining plazas, the Central Plaza and West Plaza (Figure 11.3). The Central Group is the largest architectural complex at Chan and was its main location for community-level political, ceremonial, administration, and adjudication events, housing a residence for Chan's leaders. The adjoining West Plaza is a largely open space used for political and ritual events (Cap 2012). On the east and west sides of the Central Group are the east and west shrines, Structures 5 and 7 (Figure 11.3). The east shrine, Structure 5, is a tripartite structure. The central building of the triad is the tallest structure at Chan, rising to a height of 5.6 m. The west shrine, Structure 7, is a single pyramidal structure. On the north side of the Central Group sits Chan's

Table 11.2. Summary of radiocarbon dates from the Chan site

Laboratory number	Provenience	Structure	Material	Context	Ceramic complex	Conventional date	Calibrated age	2-σ range
Beta-256798	1.AA.6	Structure 1	Carbonized wood	Fill	Bodén	2480±40 BP	740, 690, 660, 640, 550 BCE	780–410 BCE
Beta-256803	12.R.13	Structure 6	Carbonized wood	Fill	Bodén/Cadlé	2210±40 BP	350, 290, 220 BCE	390–170 BCE
Beta-256809	6.BBB.8	Structure 5	Carbonized wood	Fill	Bodén/Cadlé	2200±40 BP	350, 300, 210 BCE	380–170 BCE
Beta-256797	6.MMM.12	Structure 5	Carbonized wood	Burial 10	Cadlé	2270±40 BP	380 BCE	400–340 BCE; 320–210 BCE
Beta-256801	13.U.1	Structure 7	Carbonized wood	Burial 14	Cadlé	2180±40 BP	340, 330, 200 BCE	370–150 BCE; 140–110 BCE
Beta-256812	6.Y.27	Structure 5	Carbonized wood	Cache 8	Cadlé	2250±40 BP	370 BCE	400–200 BCE
Beta-256808	6.OOO.3	Structure 5	Carbonized wood	Burial 9	Cadlé	2290±40 BP	390 BCE	400–350 BCE; 290–220 BCE
Beta-278921	13.W.2	Structure 7	Human tooth	Burial 16	Cadlé	2440±40 BP	520 BCE	760–400 BCE
Beta-256802	13.W.3	Structure 7	Carbonized wood	Burial 16	Cadlé	2460±40 BP	720, 700, 540 BCE	770–410 BCE
Beta-278922	13.BB.2	Structure 7	Human tooth	Burial 17	Cadlé	2050±40 BP	50 BCE	170 BCE–30 CE
Beta-256805	13.BB.1	Structure 7	Carbonized wood	Burial 17	Cadlé	2540±40 BP	770 BCE	800–720 BCE; 700–540 BCE
Beta-256811	6.YY.30	Structure 5	Carbonized wood	Burial 8	Cadlé	1980±40 BP	20 CE	50 BCE–90 CE
Beta-256806	6.YY.23	Structure 5	Carbonized wood	Burial 6	Potts	2040±40 BP	40 CE	170 BCE–50 CE
Beta-256815	6.U.4	Structure 5	Carbonized wood	Burial 2	Potts/Burrell	1770±40 BP	250 CE	140–380 CE
Beta-278920	13.T.1–2	Structure 7	Human tooth	Burial 12	Burrell	1610±40 BP	420 CE	380–550 CE
Beta-278924	10.XX.4	Structure 8	Human tooth	Burial 20	Burrell	1550±40 BP	540 CE	420–600 CE
Beta-278919	6.KKK.16	Structure 5	Human tooth	Burial 7	Jalacté	1510±40 BP	560 CE	430–640 CE
Beta-278923	10.WW.3	Structure 8	Human tooth	Burial 19	Jalacté	1420±40 BP	640 CE	570–660 CE
Beta-278918	6.FFF.1–2	Structure 5	Human tooth	Burial 3.4	Jalacté/Pesoro	1350±40 BP	660 CE	640–710 CE; 750–760 CE
Beta-278917	6.FFF.1–2	Structure 5	Human tooth	Burial 3.2	Pesoro	1230±40 BP	780 CE	680–890 CE
Beta-256810	6.FFF.2	Structure 5	Carbonized wood	Burial 3.2	Pesoro	1170±40 BP	880 CE	770–980 CE
Beta-256813	6.J.6	Structure 5	Carbonized wood	Cache 17	Pesoro	1260±40 BP	720, 740, 770 CE	660–880 CE
Beta-256814	6.H.5	Structure 5	Carbonized wood	Terminal Deposit 3	Vieras	1150±40 BP	890 CE	780–980 CE
Beta-256804	12.U.1	Structure 6	Carbonized wood	Cache 22	Vieras	1170±40 BP	880 CE	770–980 CE

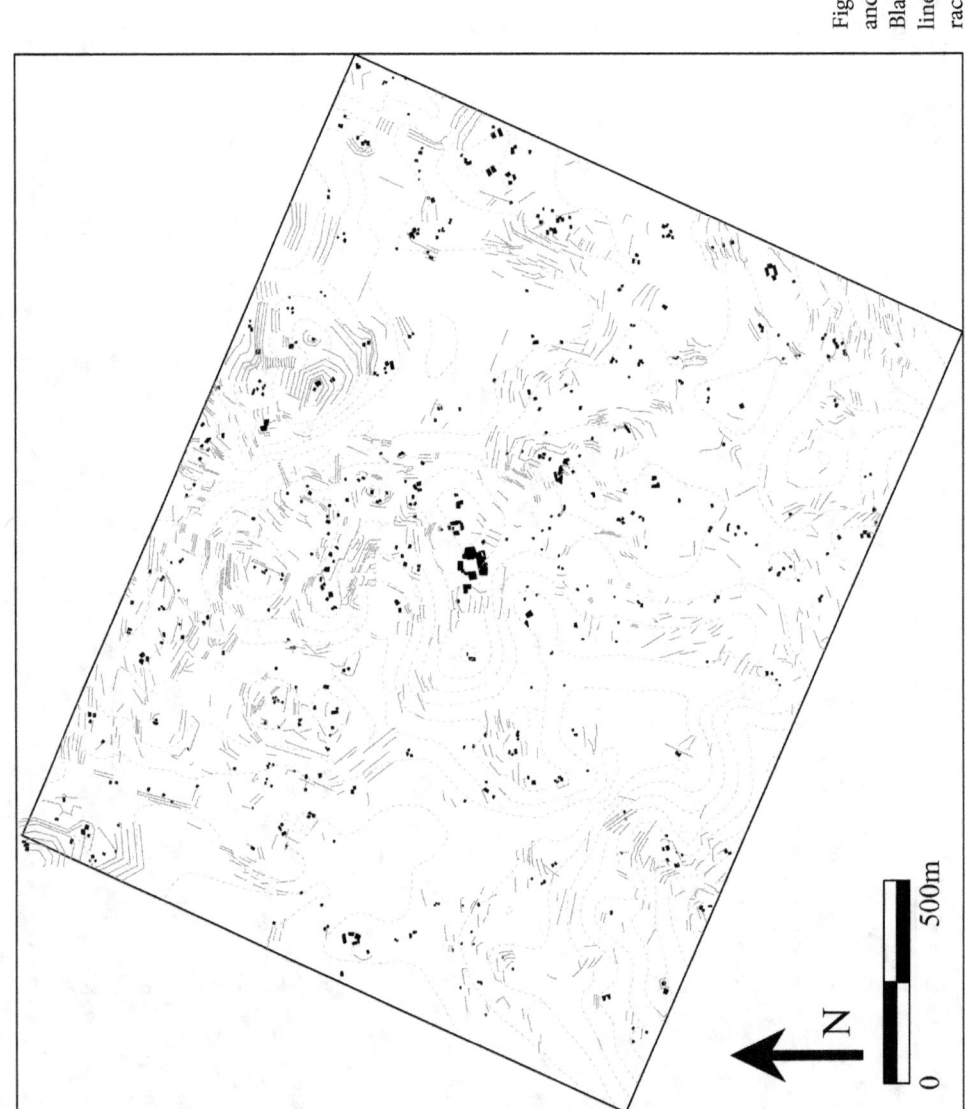

Figure 11.2. Topography, settlement, and agricultural terraces at Chan. Black squares are mounds; gray linear features are agricultural terraces; 10-meter contour interval.

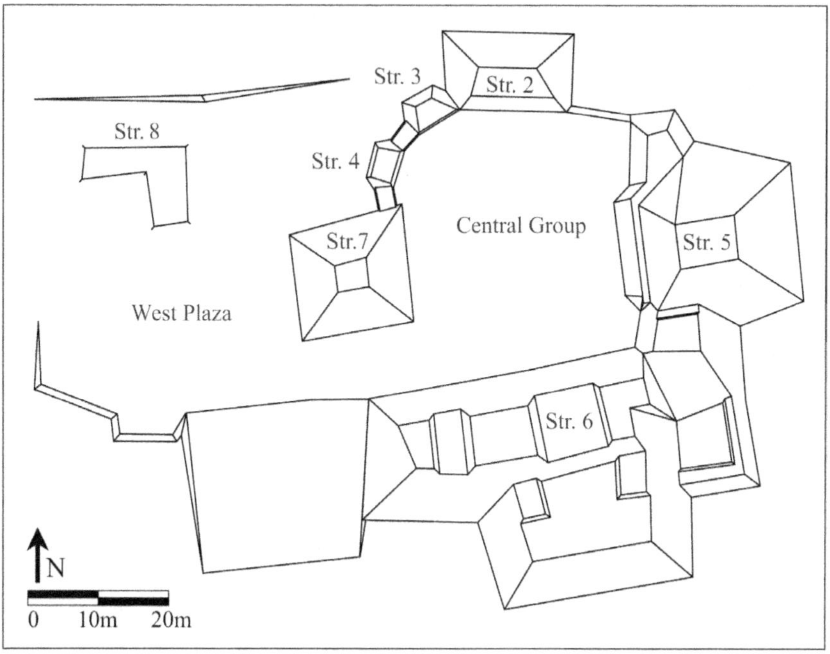

Figure 11.3. Chan's community center. Str. 5 and Str. 7 form the east and west structures of Chan's central religious complex.

leaders' residence (Structure 2) and two ancillary structures (Structures 3 and 4). The administrative building, Structure 7, is located on the south side of the Central Group.

Excavations were undertaken at Chan between 2002 and 2009 by a team of more than 120 archaeologists, botanists, geologists, geographers, chemists, computer scientists, artists, students, workers, and volunteers from Belize, the United States, England, Canada, and China (Robin 2012, 2013). The project team excavated a 10 percent sample of Chan's households (26 households) and associated agricultural terraces. This sample represents the temporal, socioeconomic, and vocational variability in households at Chan. The project also excavated all ritual, residential, and administrative buildings at Chan's community center.

One measure that Mayanists can use to judge site size is the height of the largest pyramidal structure. At Tikal, the largest Classic Maya regal center, located in the Petén area of Guatemala, the tallest temple (Temple IV) is 60 m high (Harrison 1999). At Xunantunich, the capital of the Late Classic polity that included Chan (which is considered a mid-sized Maya center), the tallest temple (El Castillo) is 43 m in height (LeCount and Yaeger 2010).

Chan, with its east temple only 5.6 m high, is not the smallest Maya site in terms of pyramidal structure height (Robin et al. 2012a). Bedrán, located 1 km southwest of Baking Pot, has an E Group with an east structure 2 m high (Conlon and Powis 2004). But Chan certainly represents a site at the smaller end of the spectrum in the Maya area.

The Belize Valley region where Chan is located was a peripheral and provincial part of the Maya world throughout most of its history. During the Preclassic, Early Classic, and early Late Classic periods (800 BCE–670 CE), numerous mid-sized centers jockeyed for power across the region. These centers were organized as competitive peers, but none became a paramount center in the region (Ashmore 2010; Ball 1993; Ball and Taschek 1991; Houston et al. 1992; Leventhal and Ashmore 2004; Reents-Budet 1994; Taschek and Ball 1992). Many of these centers have been the subject of extensive archaeological research or are currently under investigation so that their political histories can become understood. Among these mid-sized centers are Actuncán (LeCount 2004), Baking Pot (Audet and Awe 2004), Blackman Eddy (Garber et al. 2004), Buenavista (Ball and Taschek 2001; Yaeger et al. 2009), Cahal Pech (Awe 1992), Guacamayo (Ashmore 2010; Neff et al. 1995), Las Ruinas (Ball and Taschek 1991), and Xunantunich (Brown 2010; Leventhal and Ashmore 2004).

As documented by the Xunantunich Archaeological Project, at the end of the Late Classic (670–800/830 CE) this well-developed landscape was unified under the short-lived and late-flourishing Xunantunich polity capital (LeCount and Yaeger 2010; Leventhal and Ashmore 2004). Chan, located 4 km to the southeast of Xunantunich, is within a few hours' walk and was part of the late Late Classic Xunantunich polity during its heyday. Through time, Chan interacted with numerous Belize Valley centers in a set of complex and overlapping relations of influence and authority.

Construction History of Chan's Central Religious Complex

Archaeological investigations conducted in 2004 and 2005 investigated the architecture of Chan's central religious complex: the west shrine (Structure 7) and the north and central buildings of the tripartite east shrine (Structures 5-north and 5-center; Figure 11.3; Robin et al. 2012a). The south building of the tripartite east shrine was not excavated due to heavy looting. For clarity here I refer to the three buildings of the tripartite east shrine as the northern east structure, the central east structure, and the southern east structure. The single building of the west shrine is referred to here as the west structure.

The architecture of Chan's central religious complex was initially constructed in the Late Preclassic period (350 BCE–0 CE) and consists of a paired east and west shrine. At this time the east structure was a single, not a tripartite, structure. The Late Preclassic east structure was situated on a linear modified bedrock outcrop that ran north to south forming a platform for the east structure (Figure 11.4).

The modified bedrock platform extended beyond the east structure to the north and south, forming the platform upon which the northern and southern east structures would subsequently be built. It is not possible precisely to date the construction of the modified bedrock platform that sits stratigraphically below the east structure. It may have been constructed in the Late Preclassic, coeval with the construction of the initial Late Preclassic east structure. But it also may have been constructed before the Late Preclassic, in the Middle Preclassic, the period in which bedrock modification began at Chan (as discussed further in the ancestor veneration section below). Thus, while formal architecture may not have been constructed until the Late Preclassic, the modified bedrock outcrop may have a history extending back to the Middle Preclassic period, comparable to other modified bedrock outcrops associated with E Groups (Chapter 9 in this volume).

The Late Preclassic east structure rose 80 cm in height, including the height of the modified bedrock platform (Figure 11.4), and the west structure rose 50 cm in height (Figure 11.5). Each structure had a single step. Even though the east structure was a single construction in Late Preclassic times, an understanding of the tripartite nature of the eastern modified bedrock outcrop was inscribed in a nonarchitectural form into the modified outcrop: an upright stone, oriented along an east–west axis, and a cache containing a Candelario Appliquéd *incensario* (incense burner) fragment, charcoal, and two pieces of worked *Strombus* detritus marked the location on the modified bedrock outcrop upon which the northern east structure would be built in the subsequent Terminal Preclassic period (100/150–250 CE). The charcoal from the cache yielded a calibrated radiocarbon date of 400 to 200 BCE (2-sigma range; Kosakowsky et al. 2012; Table 11.2)

The east structure first took on its tripartite form in the Terminal Preclassic period, with three individual buildings being constructed along the modified bedrock outcrop. The northern east structure was first constructed at this time, elevated to a height of 50 cm. The Terminal Preclassic was also the period of greatest construction effort on the central east structure. At

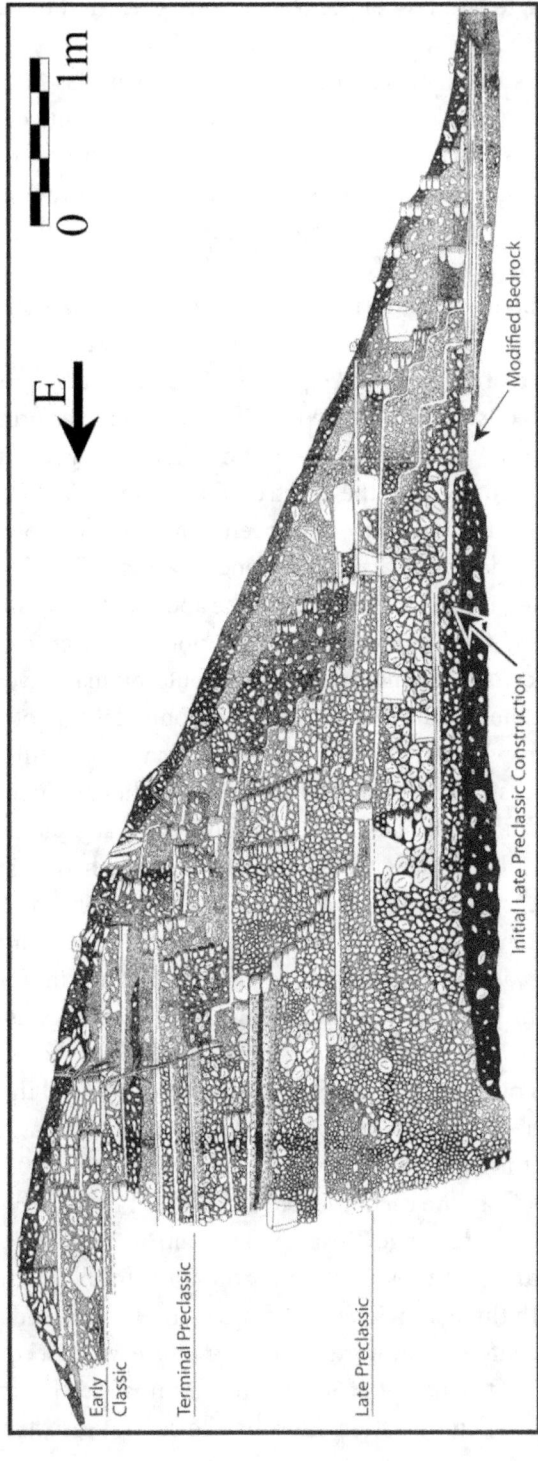

Figure 11.4. Profile of central east structure (Structure 5-center). Marked on the profile are the modified bedrock outcrop that underlies the structure and maximum structure heights through time. Illustration by Nasario Puc.

Figure 11.5. Profile of west structure (Structure 7). Marked on the profile are the maximum structure heights through time. Illustration by Carmen Ting.

the end of the Terminal Preclassic period the central east structure had reached a height of 4.3 m and was a multilevel structure with a lower and upper stair and frontal terrace (Figure 11.4). The west structure had reached a height of 2.7 m and was similarly a multilevel structure (Figure 11.5). The Preclassic was the period of most substantial construction at Chan's central religious complex, with the central east structure reaching 77 percent of its final height and the west structure reaching 55 percent of its final height. By the Early Classic, the central east structure had reached its final height and the west structure had reached 61 percent of its final height. Plausibly, more construction may have been undertaken on the west structure in the Classic period because in the Late Classic the West Plaza was expanded to the size illustrated in Figure 11.3, making the west structure both the western structure of Chan's religious complex and the central structure between two plazas of the Chan community center (the Central Plaza and West Plaza). While the heyday of architectural construction on Chan's religious complex was in the Preclassic, in the Late Classic the focus of architectural construction at the Central Group shifted from the religious complex to the northern leading family residence (Structure 2) and the southern administrative building (Structure 6).

In the Terminal Preclassic period, a cache of two lip-to-lip Pucte Brown or Balanza Black basal flange bowls was placed in the plaza area in front of the west structure (Kosakowsky et al. 2012). This cache contained a number of small jade, shell, and chert items at the base of which were five small figures placed in a quincunx pattern (Figure 11.6; Keller 2012). The central figure is slate. Around this are a yellowish and reddish *Spondylus* figure, a green jade figure, and a white shell profile face. The arrangement of the figures in this cache in a quincunx pattern initiates the marking of the west structure as associated with this cosmologically important pattern.

As the tripartite east structure and west structure were constructed and reconstructed across the Preclassic and Classic periods the two structures were constantly being remodeled in relation to one another. This indicates that these two ritual structures were not just situated opposite one another on the east and west sides of the Central Plaza but were also constructed as a related pair. At each remodeling of the tripartite east structure, as the structure grew in height and breadth, it extended further west into the Central Plaza (Figure 11.4). With each remodeling of the west structure, the structure grew in height and breadth as its front east-facing façade was cut back and its stairways were removed. Thus, the front façade of the west shrine did not extend further east into the plaza as the west structure grew

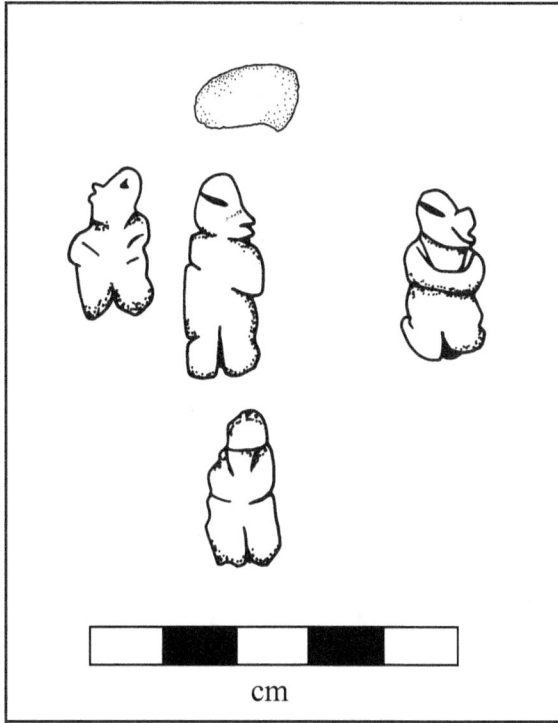

Figure 11.6. Cache 9 cutout figures. Figures were found face down in vessel. The view shown here is looking at the figures from the bottom of the vessel. The central figure is slate, the upper profile is white shell, the lower figure is jade, the left figure is reddish *Spondylus*, and the right figure is yellowish *Spondylus*. Illustration by Carmen Ting.

in size (Figure 11.5). Only in its final late Late Classic construction phase was the east-facing stair extended east into the plaza. This construction process allowed residents to maintain a relative distance between the tripartite east structure and west structure through time, until the late Late Classic. Maintaining a relative distance between the tripartite east structure and west structure through time may have been important in providing the space to accommodate the ritual participants who came to view the ceremonies enacted there. If one of the functions of the west structure was viewing the tripartite east structure, then maintaining a relative distance between the two structures could have been integral in maintaining lines of sight. The burial data discussed below suggest that the deceased ancestors interred in the west shrine may have looked east to the tripartite east structure, while the ancestors interred in the east shrine looked down to the earth. If the practitioners conducting rituals on the west structure looked east during their ceremonies, as the deceased did below their feet and as shamans do today in contemporary Yucatán, then their gaze would have paralleled the gaze of the deceased interred below their feet. It is intriguing to note that the tripartite east structure and west structure are the only structures at Chan constructed in relation to one another to maintain a distance between the two structures situated on opposite sides of a plaza. As all other excavated structures at Chan grew in height and breadth, each new construction phase extended the front façade of the structure into its plaza area, continually changing and reducing the space between structures constructed on opposite sides of plazas.

During the Classic period (250–900 CE), the tripartite east structure and the west structure continued to grow in size and elaboration. Each structure reached its maximum height in the late Late Classic period (670–800/830 CE). The central east structure was the tallest building at Chan, rising to a height of 5.6 m. The northern east structure was 2.2 m high, and the west structure was 4.9 m high. The east, west, and north façades of the west structure revealed remains of stairs associated with final phase construction. The south façade was not excavated. The presence of stairs on three sides of the west structure suggests that this single pyramidal structure may have been a radial structure with stairs on all sides.

Also in the late Late Classic Period, the northern east structure was extended to abut the central east structure, joining what had previously been individual buildings. Closing the open space between two buildings in the late Late Classic may be part of a broader construction process ongoing at the Central Group and not a practice solely associated with the ritual complex, as excavations identified a comparable abutting of Structure 2, the leading family residence, and the adjacent ancillary structure, Structure 3, also in the late Late Classic period.

Only the summit of the central east structure had a superstructure. Horizontal exposures of the ultimate- and penultimate-phase architecture of this superstructure identified that it had two tandem rooms. The rear room of the superstructure had a bench. The superstructure had partial masonry walls that rose 50 cm in height. The superstructure could have remained open to the air, or its walls could have supported a perishable building. Ritual practitioners placed terminal deposits dating to the Late and Terminal Classic periods that contained high concentrations of incense burner fragments and serving vessel sherds in the front room of the superstructure (Kosakowsky et al. 2012). Excavation supervisor Jim Meierhoff noted round burned patches across the floors of the front room and postulated that these were the locations of portable incense burners during ritual events. The burned patches corresponded with high levels of phosphorous on room floors, supporting Meierhoff's interpretation (Robin et al. 2012b).

The scorched floor traces of incense burners that once stood atop Chan's tallest shrine and the deposition of incense-burning and food-bearing vessels across a room floor are the lines of evidence that allow us to build a picture of the ritual use of Chan's central religious complex. Burning incense and serving food accompanied ritual events. The sight and smell of the incense rising from the ceremony would have been an integral part of the sensory experience of those events.

The architectural form, construction history, and chronology of Chan's central religious complex corresponded with those of an E Group, particularly the Cenote-style E Group defined by Arlen Chase and Diane Chase (Chapter 2 in this volume; Chase and Chase 1995). In the Cenote-style, as at Chan, the central building of the east structure is the largest of the three eastern buildings. Cenote-style E Groups were typically constructed in the Late Preclassic period, as is the case at Chan (Chapter 2 in this volume). At Cenote, Cival, and Chan, bedrock outcrops are incorporated into the architecture of the E Group complex as the foundation for the eastern linear platform at Cenote and Chan and the basis for the entire eastern tripartite structure at Cival (Chapters 2 and 9 in this volume).

Chan's west structure is more reminiscent of the archetypical E Group western structure from Uaxactún (Blom 1924; Ricketson 1928). With stairs on at least three sides (its south façade was not excavated, so the existence of a stair on that side is unknown), Chan's west structure was probably a radial structure that, as at Uaxactún, had no superstructure. The plan of a radial western structure is quadripartite, which like a quincunx would have five focal points arranged in a cross incorporated into its design: a point at the center of the structure and four points at the base of each stair. James Aimers and Prudence Rice (2006) and Clemency Coggins (1980) suggest that the radial form of the western E Group structure at Uaxactún represented a model of the Maya cosmogram, which is also oriented as a quincunx. The shape of Chan's west structure and its association with a quincunx cache similarly marks it as a cosmogram.

While Chan's E Group remained in use until the Terminal Classic period, in terms of its later chronology—and like E Groups discussed in other chapters in this volume—by the Late Classic period the focus of architectural construction at this site was away from the E Group to other constructions around the Central Plaza. In its final construction phase in the late Late Classic period, the northern east structure was extended to adjoin the central east structure, closing the space that existed for centuries between the two buildings, as part of a broader process of closing the space between structures around the Central Group at this time. Awe, Hoggarth, and Aimers (Chapter 13 in this volume) refer to this phase of construction as an Eastern Triadic Assemblage, as the three individual eastern structures were fused at this time. An Eastern Triadic Assemblage consists of an Eastern Triadic Structure, where all structures are connected, facing a single western structure. There should be no shared substructural platform underlying an Eastern Triadic Structure, although at Chan such a shared substructural platform existed in terms of a linear modified bedrock outcrop.

Ancestor Veneration

Like many other E Groups, Chan's E Group served as a focal point for burials and caches. Although the architecture of the E Group was initially constructed in the Late Preclassic period, this architecture enshrined and extended a practice of ancestor veneration that began in the Middle Preclassic period. Thus the antecedents of the ritual practices taking place in the E Group can be found in the burials and caches interred in the Central Plaza in the space that would later become the center of the E Group complex. In this chapter I focus on the practice of ancestor veneration (see also Brown's discussion in Chapter 12 in this volume).

In the Middle Preclassic period, a single individual was buried in the Central Plaza, presumably one of Chan's leading residents (Figure 11.7). This individual, an adult age 20–24 of unknown sex (Burial 1), was placed in a shallow grave cut into the underlying limestone bedrock (Novotny 2012). This grave was reentered for centuries across the Middle Preclassic and Late Preclassic periods (650 BCE–100/150 CE). At each reentry, the people visiting the grave deposited fragments of human bone, serpentine, jade, shell, and slate above the grave. These were either objects that people had originally placed with the deceased and later removed and replaced during the reentries or objects deposited later, at the time of the reentry, to commemorate visitation of the interred individual. In either case, residents remembered and revered the death and burial of this person for generations and in fact centuries, interring this individual with the most offerings of any ancestor or person buried at Chan and thus initiating a practice of remembering and revisiting ancestral burials across time at Chan.

Beginning with their construction in the Late Preclassic, Chan's east and west shrines became the community's primary location for ancestral

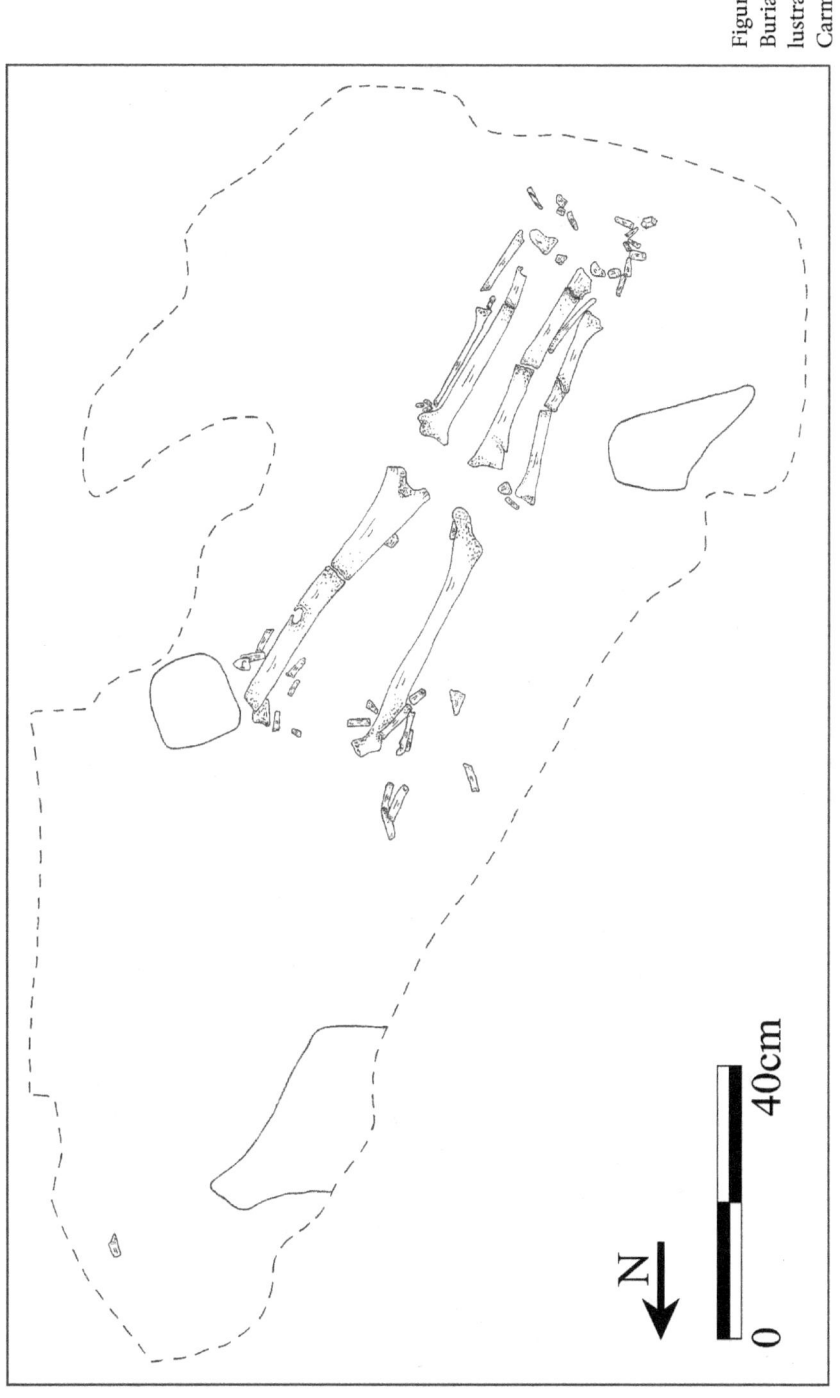

Figure 11.7. Burial 1. Illustration by Carmen Ting.

burials. Among the twenty individuals buried in fourteen graves that were excavated in these structures (Novotny 2012) were adults and children, both male and female.

While the E Group is a ritual architectural complex collectively dedicated to the veneration of select ancestors at Chan, there are differences between the burial rituals enacted in its east and west structures. The position of bodies in graves and ages of individuals interred in the east and west structures of the E Group contrast (Novotny 2012). Where the burial position of the individual could be discerned primary individuals in the east structure are all interred in an extended prone position with the head to the south. This is the most common burial position at sites throughout the Belize Valley (Healy 2004), showing a strong cultural affiliation between Chan and regional Belize Valley area residents. Only one individual buried in the west structure was interred in the standard Belize Valley position. One individual is interred in a flexed position with the head to the north and the cranium looking to the east (plausibly at the east structure). The other individuals are too poorly preserved to permit investigators to discern body position or contain only cranial material, but in all cases the heads of these individuals are located at the north end of the grave and may also have looked to the east (Kestle 2005). Interesting age differences between the individuals buried in the east and the west structures also occur: the only three children identified at Chan were all interred in the west structure of the E Group. Although more precise significance of the different patterns of ritual treatment of ancestors buried to the east and west in the E Group is not discernable at this time, there is a clear association between the east involving young adult ancestors and traditional Belize Valley burial practices. The west is associated with children and distinctive burial practices.

Just as ritual practices differed between the east and west structures of the E Group, the nature of ritual practices also changed through time. A focus on the individual ancestor as a part of ritual process was most marked at Chan in the Preclassic period, when ritual practitioners interred their dead in the Central Plaza and the east and west shrines with more grave offerings than their Classic period counterparts (Novotny 2012). Residents buried curated Middle Preclassic figurines (each with unique facial characteristics that may represent actual portraiture) with Late Preclassic ancestors, possibly to link the deceased with founding members of Chan (Kosakowsky et al. 2012; Chapter 5 in this volume). In terms of shell ornamentation, shell ornaments that marked individual identity accompanied only two shrine burials, Late Preclassic Burial 10 and Terminal Preclassic Burial 2 (Keller 2012).

In the Classic period, burial and caching in the shrines shifted from a focus on individual ancestors to a focus on the community as a whole (Robin et al. 2012a). This change is evidenced by a shift from burying ceramics and other material objects with individual ancestors to burying these items in caches and terminal deposits, foregrounding the community rather than the specific ancestor as the focus of ritual activity (Kosakowsky et al. 2012). Also, there is an increase in the number of multiple (over single) interment ancestor burials (Novotny 2012). These changes in Classic period rituals in the east and west shrines indicate a heightened focus on highlighting the community as a whole in ritual practices. It is perhaps important to note here that the growing focus on community-centered ritual over individual-centered ritual across the Classic period at Chan is the opposite of what we might expect during this period in the Maya area. Research across the Maya area from the Classic period suggests that it was a time of increasing focus on individuals and exclusionary power in ritual and politics, emblematic of the dominant political system of kingship (for example, Blanton et al. 1996). The data from Chan suggest the existence of alternative forms of ritual and politics in the Classic period that were more group- and community-centered and may have existed at smaller centers such as Chan during that period. The group-focused political strategies of the Postclassic period that emerged in the aftermath of the dissolution of the Classic Maya system of kingship may owe as much to the development of such strategies on the part of Classic period farming communities such as Chan as they do to the breakdown of the system of kingship (Robin 2015; Robin et al. 2012b; Robin et al. 2014).

Conclusion

The form, function, and chronology of Chan's E Group suggest a symbolic association between the path of the sun from east to west and the veneration of ancestors that has a 2,000-year history in the lives of farmers living in this community. The persistence of east–west symbolism in the house shrines that the contemporary Maya dedicate to the ancestors suggests continuity in these associations for ordinary people. The importance of east–west symbolism in Classic Maya religion is well attested in the elaborate ritual offerings, grand civic planning, and hieroglyphic writing of Classic

Maya elites (for example, Freidel et al. 1993). But the 2,000-year history of Chan is instructive, suggesting that many of the focal ideas of Maya religion were originally developed in the homes and communities of Maya farmers and later appropriated by society's elites.

Acknowledgments

I thank all the members of the Chan project and Belize Institute of Archaeology for their work on the Chan research, without which this chapter would not have been possible. The Chan project was funded by two National Science Foundation grants: a National Science Foundation Senior Archaeology Grant (2004:BCS-0314686) and a National Science Foundation International Research Fellowship (2003:INT-0303713); a National Endowment for the Humanities Collaborative Research Grant (2007:RZ-50804-07); a National Geographic Society Grant (2002); an H. John Heinz III Fund Grant for Archaeological Field Research in Latin America (2002); two anonymous donations; three University Research Grants from Northwestern University (2002, 2005, 2009); two Alumnae Foundation Grants from Northwestern University (2002, 2006); and an AT&T Research Scholar award (2005).

References Cited

Aimers, James J.
1993   An Hermeneutic Analysis of the Maya E-Group Complex. M.A. thesis, Anthropology Department, Trent University, Peterborough, Ontario, Canada.
Aimers, James J., and Prudence M. Rice
2006   Astronomy, Ritual, and the Interpretation of Maya "E-Group" Architectural Assemblages. *Ancient Mesoamerica* 17(1):79–96.
Ashmore, Wendy
1991   Site-Planning Principles and Concepts of Directionality among the Ancient Maya. *Latin American Antiquity* 2(3):199–226.
2010   Antecedents, Allies, Antagonists: Xunantunich and Its Neighbors. In *Classic Maya Provincial Politics: Xunantunich and Its Hinterlands*, edited by Lisa J. LeCount and Jason Yaeger, pp. 46–66. University of Arizona Press, Tucson, Arizona.
Audet, Carolyn M., and Jaime J. Awe
2004   What's Cooking at Baking Pot: A Report of the 2001 to 2003 Seasons. *Research Reports in Belizean Archaeology* 1:49–59.

Aveni, Anthony F., and H. Hartung
1989   Uaxactun, Guatemala, Group E, and Similar Assemblages: An Archaeoastronomical Reconsideration. In *World Archaeoastronomy*, edited by Anthony F. Aveni, pp. 441–461. Cambridge University Press, Cambridge.

Awe, Jaime J.
1992   Dawn in the Land between the Rivers: Formative Occupation at Cahal Pech Belize and Its Implications for Preclassic Development in the Central Maya Lowlands. Ph.D. dissertation, Anthropology Department, University of London, London.

Ball, Joseph W.
1993   Pottery, Potters, Palaces and Politics: Some Socioeconomic and Political Implications of Late Classic Maya Ceramic Industries. In *Lowland Maya Civilization in the Eighth Century*, edited by Jeremy A. Sabloff and John S. Henderson, pp. 243–272. Dumbarton Oaks, Washington, D.C.

Ball, Joseph W., and Jennifer T. Taschek
1991   Late Classic Lowland Maya Political Organization and Central-Place Analysis: New Insights from the Upper Belize Valley. *Ancient Mesoamerica* 2(2):149–165.
2001   The Buevanavista-Cahal Pech Royal Court: Multi-Palace Court Mobility and Usage in a Petty Lowland Maya Kingdom. In *Royal Courts of the Ancient Maya: 2. Data and Case Studies*, edited by Takeshi Inomata and Stephen D. Houston, 165–200. Westview Press, Boulder, Colorado.

Blanton, Richard E., Gary M. Feinman, Stephen A. Kowalewski, and Peter N. Peregrine
1996   A Dual-Processual Theory for the Evolution of Mesoamerican Civilization. *Current Anthropology* 37(1):1–14.

Blom, Frans
1924   Report on the Preliminary Work at Uaxactun, Guatemala. *Carnegie Institution of Washington Yearbook* 23:217–219.

Brown, M. Kathryn
2010   From Sunrise to Sunset: Preliminary Investigations of Preclassic and Postclassic Ritual Activity at Xunantunich, Belize. *Research Reports in Belizean Archaeology* 7:37–44.

Cap, Bernadette
2012   "Empty" Spaces and Public Places: A Microscopic View of Chan's West Plaza. In *Chan: An Ancient Maya Farming Community*, edited by C. Robin, pp. 150–172. University Press of Florida, Gainesville.

Chase, Arlen F., and Diane Z. Chase
1995   External Impetus, Internal Synthesis, and Standardization: E Group Assemblages and the Crystallization of Classic Maya Society in the Southern Lowlands. *Acta Mesoamericana* 8:87–101 (special issue edited by Nikolai Grube entitled *The Emergence of Lowland Maya Civilization: The Transition from the Preclassic to Early Classic*).
1996   The Organization and Composition of Classic Maya Society: The View from Caracol, Belize. In *Eighth Palenque Round Table*, edited by Martha J. Macri and Jan McHargue, pp. 213–222. Pre-Columbian Art Research Institute, San Francisco, California.

Coggins, Clemency
1980   The Shape of Time: Some Political Implications of a Four-Part Figure. *American Antiquity* 45(4):727–739.

Cohodas, Marvin
1980   Radial Pyramids and Radial-Associated Assemblages of the Central Maya Area. *Journal of the Society of Architectural Historians* 39(3):208–223.

Conlon, James M., and Terry G. Powis
2004   Major Center Identifiers at a Plazuela Group near the Ancient Maya Site of Baking Pot. In *The Ancient Maya of the Belize Valley: Half a Century of Archaeological Research*, edited by James F. Garber, pp. 70–85. University Press of Florida, Gainesville.

Freidel, David A., Linda Schele, and Joy Parker
1993   *Maya Cosmos: Three Thousand Years on the Shaman's Path.* William Morrow, New York.

Garber, James F., M. Kathryn Brown, Jaime J. Awe, and Christopher J. Hartman
2004   Middle Formative Prehistory of the Central Belize Valley: An Examination of Architecture, Material Culture, and Sociopolitical Change at Blackman Eddy. In *The Ancient Maya of the Belize Valley: Half a Century of Archaeological Research*, edited by James F. Garber, pp. 25–47. University Press of Florida, Gainesville.

Guillemin, George F.
1968   Development and Function of the Tikal Ceremonial Center. *Ethnos* 33(1–4):5–39.

Hanks, William F.
1990   *Referential Practice: Language and Lived Space among the Maya.* University of Chicago Press, Chicago.

Harrison, Peter D.
1999   *The Lords of Tikal: Rulers of an Ancient Maya City.* Thames and Hudson, New York.

Healy, Paul
2004   Preclassic Maya of the Belize Valley: Key Issues and Questions. *Research Reports in Belizean Archaeology* 3:13–30.

Hearth, Nicholas F.
2012   Organization of Chert Tool Economy during the Late and Terminal Classic Periods at Chan: Preliminary Thoughts Based upon Debitage Analysis. In *Chan: An Ancient Maya Farming Community*, edited by Cynthia Robin, pp. 192–206. University Press of Florida, Gainesville.

Houston, Stephen D., David Stuart, and Karl A. Taube
1992   Image and Text on the "Jauncy Vase." In *The Maya Vase Book*, edited by Justin Kerr, pp. 499–512. Kerr Associates, New York.

Iannone, Gyles
2005   The Rise and Fall of the Ancient Maya Petty Royal Court. *Latin American Antiquity* 16(1):26–44.

Keller, Angela
2012   Creating Community with Shell. In *Chan: An Ancient Maya Farming Com-*

munity, edited by Cynthia Robin, pp. 253–270. University Press of Florida, Gainesville.

Kestle, Caleb
2005 Operation 13, C-001: West Structure of E-Group. In The Chan Project: 2005 Season, edited by Cynthia Robin, pp. 33–44. Report submitted to the Belize Institute of Archaeology, Belmopan.
2012 Limestone Quarrying and Household Organization at Chan. In *Chan: An Ancient Maya Farming Community*, edited by Cynthia Robin, pp. 207–230. University Press of Florida, Gainesville.

Kosakowsky, Laura J., Anna C. Novotny, Angela H. Keller, Nicholas F. Hearth, and Carmen Ting
2012 Contextualizing Ritual Behavior: Caches, Burials, and Problematical Deposits from Chan's Community Center. In *Chan: An Ancient Maya Farming Community*, edited by Cynthia Robin, pp. 289–310. University Press of Florida, Gainesville.

Kus, Susan, and Victor Raharijaona
1990 Domestic Space and the Tenacity of Traditions among Some Betsileo of Madagascar. In *Domestic Architecture and the Use of Space: An Interdisciplinary Cross-Cultural Study*, edited by Susan Kent, pp. 21–33. Cambridge University Press, Cambridge.

Laporte, Juan P., and Vilma Fialko
1990 New Perspectives on Old Problems: Dynastic References for the Early Classic at Tikal. In *Vision and Revision in Maya Studies*, edited by Flora S. Clancy and Peter D. Harrison, pp. 33–66. University of New Mexico Press, Albuquerque.

LeCount, Lisa
2004 Looking for a Needle in a Haystack: The Early Classic Period at Actuncan, Cayo District. *Research Reports in Belizean Archaeology* 1:27–36.

LeCount, Lisa J., and Jason Yaeger
2010 *Classic Maya Provincial Politics: Xunantunich and Its Hinterlands*. University of Arizona Press, Tucson.

Leventhal, Richard M., and Wendy Ashmore
2004 Xunantunich in a Belize Valley Context. *The Ancient Maya of the Belize Valley: Half a Century of Archaeological Research*, edited by James F. Garber, pp. 168–179. University Press of Florida, Gainesville.

Meierhoff, James, Mark Golitko, and James D. Morris
2012 Obsidian Acquisition, Trade, and Regional Interaction at Chan. In *Chan: An Ancient Maya Farming Community*, edited by Cynthia Robin, pp. 271–288. University Press of Florida, Gainesville.

Neff, L. Theodore, Cynthia Robin, Kevin Schwartz, and Mary Morrison
1995 The Xunantunich Settlement Survey. In Xunantunich Archaeological Project: 1995 Season, edited by Richard Leventhal and Wendy Ashmore, pp. 164–192. Report submitted to the Belize Institute of Archaeology, Belmopan, Belize.

Novotny, Anna C.
2012 The Chan Community: A Bioarchaeological Perspective. In *Chan: An Ancient*

Maya Farming Community, edited by Cynthia Robin, pp. 231–252. University Press of Florida, Gainesville.

Pearson, Mike Parker, and Colin Richards
1994   Ordering the World: Perceptions of Architecture, Space, and Time. In *Architecture and Order: Approaches to Social Space*, edited by Michael Parker Pearson and Colin Richards, pp. 1–33. Routledge, London.

Reents-Budet, Dorie
1994   *Painting the Maya Universe: Royal Ceramics of the Classic Period*. Duke University Press, Durham, North Carolina.

Ricketson, Oliver G., Jr.
1928   Astronomical Observatories in the Maya Area. *Geographical Review* 18(2) (April):215–225.

Robin, Cynthia
2015   Of Earth and Stone: The Materiality of Maya Farmers' Everyday Lives at Chan, Belize. In *The Materiality of Everyday Life*, edited by Lisa Overholtzer and Cynthia Robin, 40–52. Archaeological Papers of the American Anthropological Association 26(1). Wiley Blackwell, Oxford, United Kingdom.

Robin, Cynthia (editor)
2012   *Chan: An Ancient Maya Farming Community*. University Press of Florida, Gainesville.
2013   *Everyday Life Matters: Maya Farmers at Chan*. University Press of Florida, Gainesville.

Robin, Cynthia, Laura Kosakowsky, Angela Keller, and James Meierhoff
2014   Leaders, Farmers, and Crafters: The Relationship between Leading Households and Other Households across the Chan Community. *Ancient Mesoamerica* 25(2):371–387.

Robin, Cynthia, James Meierhoff, Caleb Kestle, Chelsea Blackmore, Laura J. Kosakowsky, and Anna C. Novotny
2012a   Ritual in a Farming Community. In *Chan: An Ancient Maya Farming Community*, edited by Cynthia Robin, pp. 113–132. University Press of Florida, Gainesville.

Robin, Cynthia, James Meierhoff, and Laura J. Kosakowsky
2012b   Nonroyal Governance at Chan's Community Center. In *Chan: An Ancient Maya Farming Community*, edited by Cynthia Robin, pp. 133–149. University Press of Florida, Gainesville.

Robin, Cynthia, Andrew R. Wyatt, Laura T. Kosakowsky, Santiago Juarez, Ethan Kalosky, and Elise Enterkin
2012c   A Changing Cultural Landscape: Settlement Survey and GIS at Chan. In *Chan: An Ancient Maya Farming Community*, edited by Cynthia Robin, pp. 19–41. University Press of Florida, Gainesville.

Taschek, Jennifer J., and Joseph W. Ball
1992   Lord Smoke-Squirrel's Cacao Cup: The Archaeological Context and Socio-Historical Significance of the Buenavista Jauncy Vase. In *The Maya Vase Book*, edited by Justin Kerr, pp. 490–497. Kerr Associates, New York.

Vogt, Evon Z.
1965   Ceremonial Organization in Zinacantan. *Ethnology* 4(1):39–52.
Wyatt, Andrew
2012   Agricultural Practices at Chan: Farming and Political Economy in an Ancient Maya Community. In *Chan: An Ancient Maya Farming Community*, edited by Cynthia Robin, pp. 71–88. University Press of Florida, Gainesville.
Yaeger, Jason, Bernadette Cap, and Meaghan Peuramaki-Brown
2009   The 2007 Field Season of the Mopan Valley Archaeological Project: Buenavista del Cayo's East Plaza and Near-Periphery Settlement. *Research Reports in Belizean Archaeology* 6:209–217.

12

E Groups and Ancestors

The Sunrise of Complexity at Xunantunich, Belize

M. KATHRYN BROWN

The veneration of ancestors played a key role in the establishment of social hierarchies in the Maya Lowlands and was a central component of the institution of kingship (Schele and Miller 1986). The power and authority of ancient Maya rulers was legitimized through connections to important deities and ancestors, and these connections were clearly marked and performed within the built environment of ancient cities. Many monumental buildings and associated spaces were constructed to honor principal ancestors, to serve as the venues for activities that commemorated them, and to house their bones. This is especially evident in the Classic period (250–900 CE). In this chapter, I argue that these Classic period traditions were the outcome of historical processes that had their origins in the early Middle Preclassic period in the first public ritual complexes, E Groups.

As many scholars in this volume argue, early E Groups were constructed to celebrate the daily and the annual cycles of the sun and to undertake rituals required to ensure the continuity of those cycles. Annual solar cycles were particularly important, as they were intimately tied to the seasons, which in turn were the heart of early agricultural strategies and practices, including maize cultivation. Therefore, early E Group rituals likely revolved around both the sun and maize deities, and early E Group architectural complexes arguably began as monuments dedicated to these deities. Over generations, certain ritual practices included the selective and strategic use of the remains of particularly important ancestors. This presumably allowed the descendants of those ancestors to claim and commemorate privileged connections to the community's most important deities. That process thus provided both a pathway for social complexity and a way to legitimize the resulting social hierarchy.

Patricia McAnany (2001) observes that burial rituals that both emphasized the individual and commemorated a group's ancestors were becoming more elaborate over the course of the Preclassic period. Although the study of Maya burial practices has largely focused on primary interments, scholars have begun to recognize patterns of ritual behavior that involved the manipulation, removal, and redeposition of bones, presumably of important ancestors (Fitzsimmons 2009; Houston et al. 2006; McAnany 1995, 1998, 2001). While many burial rituals involved the primary interment of deceased individuals, McAnany (2001:133) argues that in the Late Preclassic "emphasis on ancestors culminated in the collection and reinterment of select ancestral bones at focal locales prior to building a nonresidential, monumental structure."

The placement of ancestors in E Group complexes exemplifies this process. Classic period E Group complexes were often important locales for royal burials and the redeposition of bones removed from other interments. Noting this pattern, Arlen Chase and Diane Chase (1995:100) argue that "the placement of deceased members of a ruling family in central civic architecture indicates the conjoining of civic and dynastic ritual." The data discussed in this chapter, however, suggest that burial of ancestors and the manipulation of ancestral bones within E Group complexes had already begun by the end of the Middle Preclassic period. Thus, E Groups appear to be one of the earliest public locations where these types of burial and commemorative rituals occurred. As noted above and as argued by David Freidel (Chapter 6) and others in this volume, Preclassic E Groups were locations for public rituals involving solar cycles and the maize cult. Therefore, the reburial of important ancestors and the primary interment of prominent individuals within the architectural features and plaza spaces of E Groups connected these individuals—and, indirectly by genealogical descent, their kin—to the sun and maize deities. Through such associations these sacred locations played a central role in the establishment and legitimization of hierarchical social institutions.

E Groups first appear in the Maya Lowlands during the early Middle Preclassic (Estrada-Belli 2011; Inomata et al. 2013). They have been suggested to be associated with large plazas, presumably where public rituals were conducted (Estrada-Belli 2011, Chapter 9 in this volume; Inomata et al. 2013, Chapter 7 in this volume). As Richard Hansen (1998:68) argues, "the unusual predominance and antiquity of the E Group complexes points to their central role in Maya ritual life." Arlen Chase and Diane Chase (1995) note, as do several of the authors of the chapters in this volume, that the rapid spread of early E Group complexes across the Southern and Central Maya Lowlands suggests the importance of this form of ritual architectural assemblage in the history of early Maya communities. Furthermore, ritual offerings in E Group plazas reveal a specialized ceremonial complex that emphasized the cosmos and solar cycles combined with ideological symbols related to maize and the hearth of creation (Estrada-Belli 2011). Although our knowledge of E Groups has increased significantly since they were first defined at Uaxactún (Ricketson and Ricketson 1937), we are just now beginning to get a better understanding of their origins, their functions, and their variability across time and space. The investigation of a Middle Preclassic E Group at Xunantunich, Belize, adds new data relevant to these issues and greatly expands our understanding of these important early ritual complexes. The new evidence from Xunantunich shows the importance of ancestor veneration in the Preclassic and the role of the physical remains of these ancestors in the strategies of their living descendants.

Early Xunantunich

The site of Xunantunich is best known for its Late Classic (550–800 CE) and Terminal Classic (800–900 CE) occupation. Most of what we know about the site comes from the Xunantunich Archaeological Project (XAP), directed by Richard Leventhal and Wendy Ashmore (see LeCount and Yaeger 2010). This project combined research in Xunantunich's site core with hinterland survey and excavations in a holistic investigation of the site's dynamic history during the Late (550–800 CE) and Terminal Classic (800–900 CE).

Little, however, was known about the Preclassic occupation of the area. Preclassic remains had been recovered in a few test pits in the site core; in tunnel excavations below El Castillo, the main acropolis in the Late Classic site core; and in test pits within a relatively small group 800 m to the east of the site core (LeCount and Yaeger 2010; Robin et al. 1994) (Figure 12.1). The dominant architectural features of this group, originally designated Group E, are two small pyramids framing the east and west sides of a large sloping plaza. Initial work at this location suggested that it dated predominately to the Middle Preclassic (Robin et al. 1994).

In order to understand more about the regional landscape of the Middle Preclassic in the Belize Valley, I initiated the Mopan Valley Preclassic Project (MVPP) and began investigations at Xunantunich in 2008, focusing

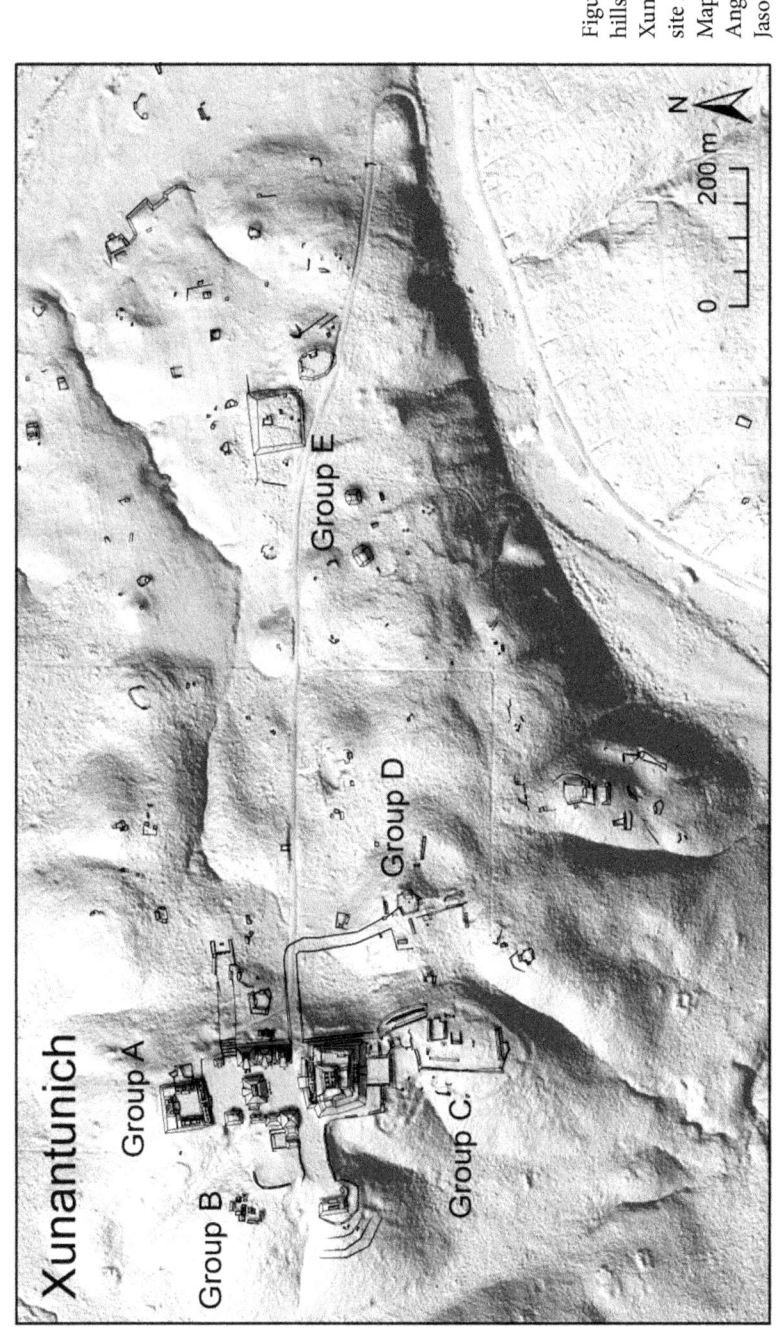

Figure 12.1. LiDAR hillshade image of Xunantunich with site map overlaid. Map courtesy of Angela Keller and Jason Yaeger.

primarily on Group E. Our work has revealed that the site of Xunantunich can actually be considered two distinct ceremonial centers, one dating to the Classic period and one dating to the Preclassic (Figure 12.1). For the purpose of this chapter and in order to differentiate accurately between the two separate ceremonial centers and their histories, I refer to the Late Classic site core as "Classic Xunantunich" and the Preclassic ceremonial center as "Early Xunantunich." Group E makes up the westernmost architectural complex of Early Xunantunich. Although the original designation of Group E was happenstance—it was the major architectural group mapped after Group D—our work has recently documented that this group is actually an early E Group. The Classic period site core of Xunantunich also exhibits an E Group architectural assemblage in the southern plaza of Group A (Aimers and Rice 2006; Jamison 2010; LeCount and Yaeger 2010; Figure 12.1) and should not be confused with the Preclassic E Group discussed in detail below (Chapter 13 in this volume). Although this is not the focus of this chapter, it is worth mentioning that the E Group at Classic Xunantunich was unusual: it is horizontally separated from the Early Xunantunich example and was initially constructed during the Late Classic period, like the other buildings in the Classic core (LeCount and Yaeger 2010). The fact that this E Group was constructed during the Late Classic is somewhat unusual, as E Groups typically date to earlier periods in Maya history. However, the presence of an E Group would have given the appearance of a long history on the landscape, and thus it may have been intentionally constructed to provide some legitimacy to the newly founded polity of Classic Xunantunich during the Late Classic period.

Intensive investigations at Early Xunantunich (Group E) began in 2008, focusing on the eastern pyramid (Structure E-2) and associated plaza. A recent LiDAR survey (Chase et al. 2014) showed that Group E was the westernmost architectural group of a larger ceremonial center with three plazas (Figure 12.2). Scholars are beginning to recognize that E Groups are the first identifiable ritual architectural complexes seen within the Maya Lowlands. Francisco Estrada-Belli (2011:74) points out that our current archaeological information "connects E-Group ritual complexes with the later emergence of monumentality and several other elements of what we recognize as hallmarks of Maya civilization." Our data from Xunantunich support this assertion, as the E Group appears to be the earliest documented architecture at the site to date.

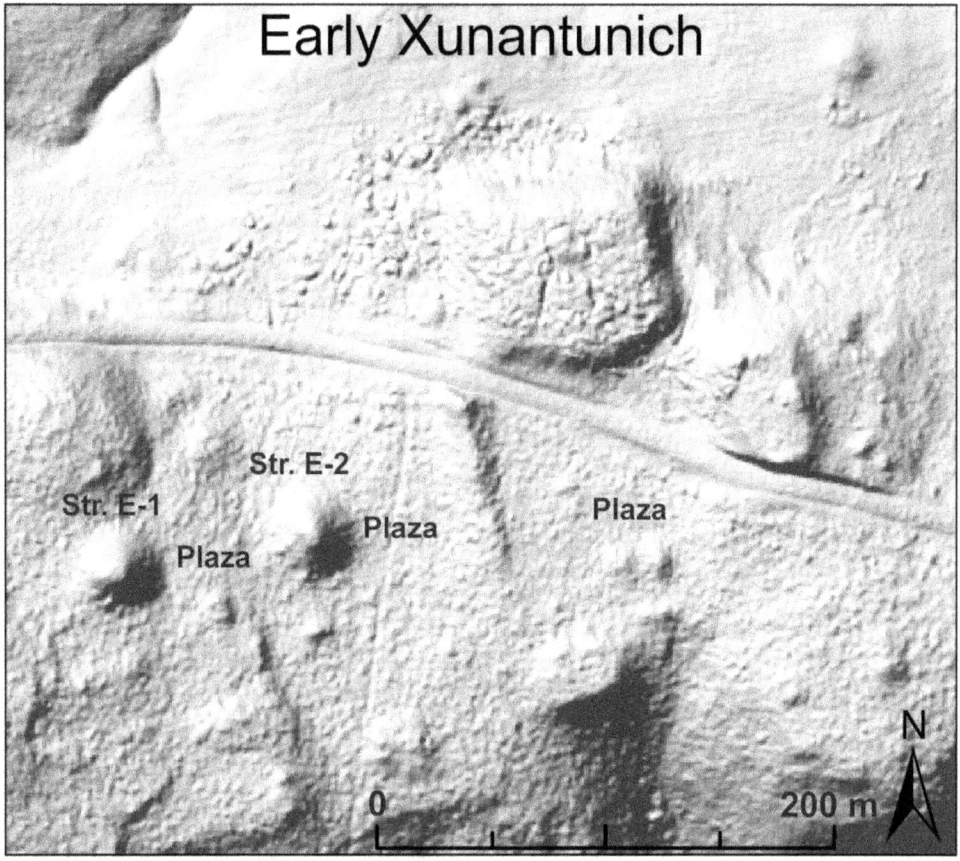

Figure 12.2. LiDAR hillshade image of Early Xunantunich.

Architectural History of Structure E-2

Our excavations of the eastern architectural complex of the early E Group, Structure E-2, have revealed that this structure had at least three construction phases and one subphase. The data collected to date suggest that the earliest two of these phases date to the Middle Preclassic. The earliest, Structure E-2-3rd, has been only partially investigated and appears to be a two to three tiered, rectangular platform approximately 3 m in height. This form coupled with the western pyramid (Structure E-1) suggests that this complex is an early E Group. Our excavations did not reveal a central staircase (or ramp) that would have provided access to the summit of Structure E-2-3rd from the west side, and it is likely that access was located on the back, eastern face of this building. In a similar fashion, at the site of Ceibal,

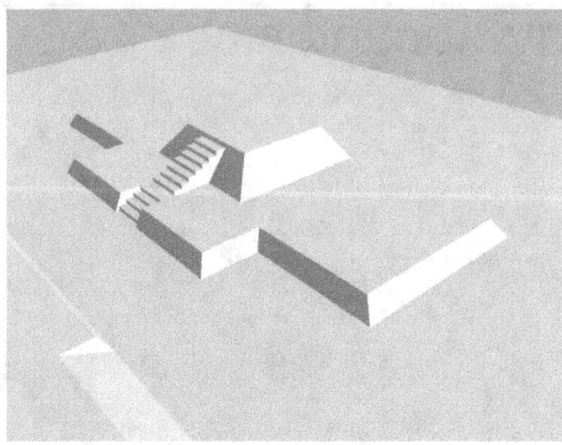

Figure 12.3. Isometric reconstruction of Structure E-2-2nd. Reconstruction by Leah McCurdy.

one of the earliest phases of the eastern component of the E Group was a single platform with an accessway off of the back side (Inomata et al. 2013, Chapter 7 in this volume).

Alternatively, there could have been side staircases or ramps outside the limits of our excavations. Nevertheless, the earliest phase appears to be a multitiered platform framing the eastern side of the plaza opposite the western structure. The ceramics from the construction fill of this phase date to the early Middle Preclassic period, suggesting an early date for this construction phase. We suspect that deeper penetrating excavations into Structure E-2-3rd will yield evidence of earlier construction sequences, possibly constructed of shaped bedrock, as is seen at both Ceibal and Cival (Estrada-Belli 2011, Chapter 9 in this volume; Inomata et al. 2013, Chapter 7 in this volume). We plan to investigate this possibility in the near future.

This multitiered platform (Structure E-2-3rd) was completely encased by a later construction phase, Structure E-2-2nd. With this construction phase, Structure E-2 takes a new form that consists of a small two-tiered pyramid set on top of a low platform with extended wings to the north and south (Figure 12.3).

This resembles the eastern complex of a Cenote Variant E Group (Chase 1983; Chase and Chase 1995) and is very similar in form to early versions of the Caracol E Group (Chase and Chase 1995, Chapter 2 in this volume). This phase had an inset staircase that was positioned in an outset frontal block and dates to the Middle Preclassic, quite possibly the early Middle Preclassic. The construction fill of both Middle Preclassic phases consisted almost entirely of pure white marl.

Above Structure E-2-2nd was a Late Preclassic construction phase (Structure E-2-1st-b) that appears to be of the same two-tiered pyramidal form set on top of a long, narrow platform. Although extensive stripping excavations were conducted on this phase, little of the original stonework remained. It appears that the Late Classic inhabitants of Classic Xunantunich borrowed most of the cut stones from this structure, resulting in extreme slumping of the construction fill. The fill of this phase was a mixture of white marl and dry laid rubble, allowing us to distinguish it from the earlier phases. Our excavations revealed evidence of at least one modification phase (Structure E-2-1st-a), although it was unclear if this was a completely new construction phase. We are currently interpreting this modification as a subphase; however, further investigations may modify this architectural sequence somewhat.

Rituals and Processions in the Early Xunantunich E Group

Most of what we know about the E Group at Early Xunantunich comes from Structure E-2-2nd, as this phase was the best preserved and most thoroughly investigated. It is interesting to note that a series of postholes was encountered in the plaza directly on centerline in front of the central staircase of Structure E-2-2nd, and I have interpreted these as the remains of a perishable altar/mesa feature (Brown 2013) (Figure 12.4).

The postholes were numerous (approximately forty) and consistent in size, roughly 10–15 cm in diameter. Most of the postholes were covered with a thin layer of marl, suggesting that a small perishable altar/mesa feature was erected in this location and rebuilt frequently, and new layers of marl placed to refurbish the marl surface of the plaza sealed the postholes of earlier versions of the feature. Excavations encountered a large piece of burned wood adjacent to a cluster of postholes that had not been patched with marl. This burned wood fragment was likely a portion of a burned post from the perishable feature. A sample of the burned post was analyzed and returned an AMS (UCIAMS 112169) date of 2435±20 BP, calibrated at the 2-sigma range to 746–407 BCE. The burned post was lying directly on the associated plaza surface, suggesting that the burning event was not swept away and may have been related to a final ritual associated with Structure E-2-2nd. The date securely places the structure within the Middle Preclassic. Additionally, this date corresponds nicely to an AMS date from a deposit of carbon and a partial Middle Preclassic vessel (Savanna Orange chocolate pot) that was found smashed on top of the plaza surface at the

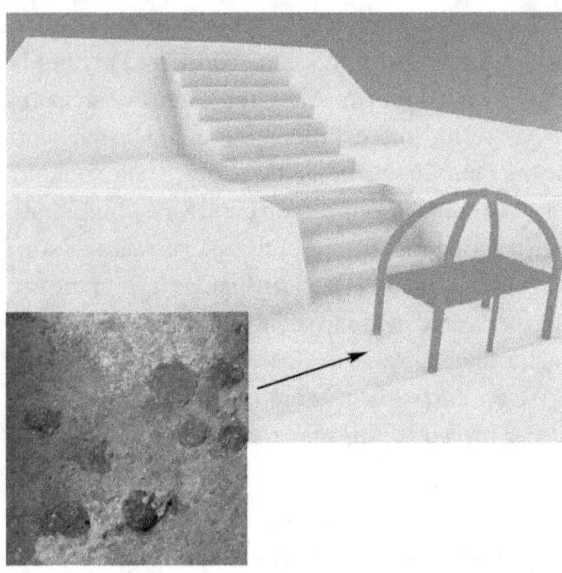

Figure 12.4. Isometric reconstruction of perishable altar in front of Structure E-2-2nd with insert showing sample of postholes. Reconstruction by Leah McCurdy.

base of the southern outset corner of the central pyramid of Structure E-2-2nd. This sample (UCIAMS 12168) yielded the very same age of 2435±20 BP. This suggests that the smashed partial vessel and burned debris near the corner were likely part of the same ritual event that terminated the perishable wooden structure located several meters away. Furthermore, the location of this burned patch and partial vessel at the outset corner of the structure is intriguing in light of several burned features discussed in more detail below. Burned wood from both areas was found directly on top of the associated plaza surface, which suggests that the dates reflect the final use of this phase of the eastern structure of the E Group and that a rebuilding event may have sealed the debris.

The presence of a wooden altar in the plaza directly in front of the central structure is suggestive of public ritual activities. Moreover, this altar was rebuilt numerous times, which supports the notion of cycles of rituals, quite possibly related to annual solar events like equinoxes and solstices. When we look at the overall plan of the E Group, the placement of this altar feature on the centerline of the structure in front of its central staircase is quite interesting.

As mentioned above, the plaza associated with the E Group was sloped from west to east. Excavations within the plaza showed that the space was heavily modified and included an enormous tiered platform feature

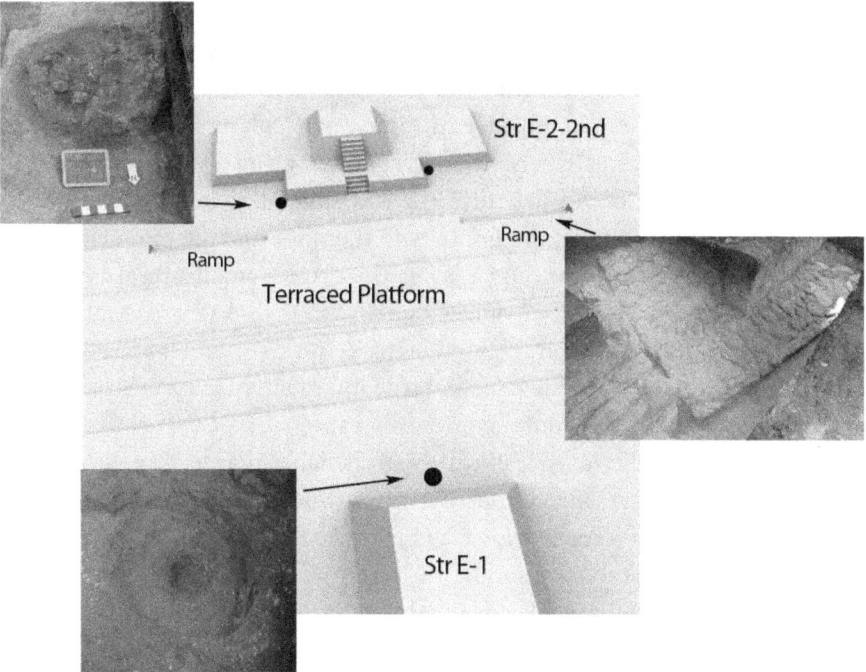

Figure 12.5. Isometric reconstruction of E Group at Early Xunantunich with inserts showing sample of fire features and paved ramp. Reconstruction by Leah McCurdy.

essentially extending across the entire plaza from north to south in front of the eastern structure. The eastern face of this platform consisted of a finely constructed stone wall slightly over a meter tall. Penetrating excavations revealed at least one earlier construction phase of this terraced platform that had a heavily plastered sloping frontal wall. This unusual architectural feature within the E Group plaza exhibited paved ramps (each over 6 m wide) leading to the northern and southern sides of the eastern architectural complex, limiting direct access to the central staircase and thus the wooden altar feature discussed above. In essence, the terraced plaza platform with ramps created a sunken space in front of the eastern architectural complex. The ramps were constructed of shaped and flattened stones that formed a fairly smooth paved surface (Figure 12.5).

The paved ramps would essentially funnel foot traffic to either side of the altar and central staircase of Structure E-2-2nd. The ramps appear to have functioned as pathways for ritual processions associated with both solstice and equinox events (Brown 2013). Additionally, the large size of the paved ramps would have accommodated not only large numbers of people in processions but also large volumes of water that would flow down the slope toward Structure E-2-2nd during the rainy season. In fact, we witnessed the practicality of these ramp features during a particularly heavy rainstorm in 2013. This event was especially striking: the roaring water encircled the exposed basal portions of Structure E-2-2nd, suggesting to us that this may have been an intentional function of both the slope and the ramp features. During certain days in the rainy season, the eastern architectural complex of the E Group essentially would be encircled with water, possibly representing the eastern watery sun (Chapter 6 in this volume; Stuart 2005) conflated with Yax Hal Witznal ("first true mountain of maize": Schele and Freidel 1993) emerging from the primordial sea.

In addition to the ramp features and perishable altar feature, three fire features were discovered in Group E: two in association with Structure E-2 and one in front of Structure E-1 (see Figure 12.5 for their location). These circular burned features are similar in size and shape to the remains of fire altars created by modern Mayan ritual practitioners for seasonal ceremonies (Brown 2012). Further investigation is necessary to tease out the chronology of these features at Early Xunantunich, but two were found in levels above the Structure E-2-2nd plaza. This placement suggests that they date to either the late Middle Preclassic or the Late Preclassic. These two small circular fire features were approximately 50 cm or less in diameter and were located near the north and south outset corners of the central pyramid of the eastern complex. The third fire feature is particularly interesting and was found dug into the plaza directly on centerline and in front of Structure E-1 (the western pyramid of the E Group). This feature was a larger circular pit filled with fire-cracked rock and ash. The base of this feature exhibited a basin shape cut into pure white marl with a post-like feature in the center (see Figure 12.5).

The date of this feature is uncertain, but evidence suggests that it is also Middle Preclassic or Late Preclassic in date. Moreover, this fire feature, when coupled with the watery symbolism associated with the eastern architectural complex discussed above, suggests that the western pyramid was symbolically linked to the fiery sun deity (Chapter 6 in this volume; Stuart 2005). Together these three fire features appear to represent the remains of ritual fires or fire altars, presumably lit at night. Rituals held at nighttime would make sense if the events were coordinated to watch the night sky and the rising sun (Chapter 6). It seems likely that rituals performed at early E Groups, although presumably public to a degree, may have been more orchestrated and therefore involved specific ritual specialists that oversaw the events. If these three fire features are roughly coeval in time, they may symbolically represent the three hearthstones of creation. Freidel et al. (1993) and others have suggested that particular triadic architectural arrangements may reflect the three stone place (Chapters 13 and 14 in this volume). Moreover, in-line triad architectural groupings, such as eastern complexes associated with later E Groups, may also symbolically reflect the three hearthstone place (Brown 2003; Stanton and Freidel 2003; Taube 1998). Alternatively, the two eastern fire features may represent fire altars that were placed in strategic locations to mark the spot on the horizon where the sun would rise on winter and summer solstices. This interpretation seems more likely because the southern fire feature was located further to the east, suggesting that the ritual events occurred at different times. Although these interpretations are preliminary and based on limited data, they do present interesting avenues for future investigation of ephemeral burned features associated with E Group complexes. Additionally, the small burned spot associated with the smashed partial vessel discussed above may represent a similar ritual event that left only traces of scattered carbon, as it may have been exposed for a period before a rebuilding episode. Further support for rituals involving perishable fire altars can be seen from our recent work at an early E Group at the nearby site of Buenavista del Cayo. There we uncovered numerous such circular burned features located on the centerline in front of the eastern structure, thus suggesting the possibility of similar ritual practices of lighting fires or creating fire altars at strategic places in E Group plazas.

In light of the three fire features found at the Early Xunantunich E Group, epigraphic data on Panel 18 from Dos Pilas Structure L5-49 is quite interesting. Although not part of a formal eastern architectural E Group complex, this panel does come from the central building of a three-temple platform located on the southern side of a plaza group (Houston 1993:23). Karl Taube (1998) notes the importance of this panel and its placement within the center of a three-temple platform as it relates to the central hearth of creation. Panel 18 mentions the 4 Ajaw 8 Kumk'u creation event and the green hearthstones. Furthermore, it has been suggested by David Stuart (in Taube 1998:468) that epigraphically this monument is labeled as a firestone and therefore may have been used in fire-making rituals. Although the Dos Pilas three-temple platform is much later in date, the epigraphic data complement the archaeological data from the E Group at Early Xunantunich. The presence of fire features in the Preclassic is significant and indicates, at least symbolically, continuity in ritual practices within architectural complexes emphasizing in-line triadic features and that these rituals may be related to the reenactment of creation.

It is not surprising that evidence of ritual activity would be encountered within the plaza of the E Group. The practice of placing caches and ritual offerings beneath E Group plazas has a long history, beginning in the early Middle Preclassic and continuing through the Classic period (Estrada-Belli 2011; Inomata et al. 2013). Numerous caches and offerings, including greenstone celts, were found at Ceibal beneath the E Group plaza beginning in the early Middle Preclassic, suggesting that "this space served as the primary stage of communal ritual throughout the Middle Preclassic" (Inomata et al. 2013:468, Chapter 7 in this volume). One of the best-known and early examples of this form of ritual caching is seen at the site of Cival in Guatemala (Chapter 9 in this volume). This elaborate offering contained five Middle Preclassic water jars placed in a quatrefoil pattern with four greenstone celts placed around the central ceramic vessel. Celts of this sort have been suggested to symbolize sprouting maize (Taube 2000). A single jade celt and 103 jade pebbles were placed beneath the central water jar (Estrada-Belli 2011). Francisco Estrada-Belli (2011:82) has interpreted this elaborate feature as an offering that represents a ritual dedicated to the ordering of the cosmos. It is quite interesting that this offering was placed within an E Group plaza, suggesting that early rituals at these locations celebrated themes related to water (Chapter 15 in this volume) and sprouting maize, both intricately tied to annual cycles of the sun (Chapter 6 in this volume), especially in light of the possible water symbolism at Early Xunantunich discussed above. Furthermore, this offering emphasized the importance of these cosmological themes during the Middle Preclassic, a time when maize becomes more important in the ancient Maya diet. Although Middle Preclassic caches of this sort have not been found to date at the Early Xunantunich E Group, further excavations may indeed reveal similar ritual patterns. The wooden altar and fire features do suggest that this location was utilized as ritual space during the Middle Preclassic.

Additionally, our excavations have uncovered a series of ritual deposits in this location dating to later periods, indicating that this sacred locality continued to be utilized for public rituals (Brown 2011, 2012). In fact, several ritual deposits date to a time after the E Group had been abandoned and was no longer in use, including Terminal Preclassic feasting debris and an early Postclassic (ca. 900–1,200 CE) altar on the centerline in front of Structure E-2 (Brown 2011).

Ancestor Veneration in the Early Xunantunich E Group

Although elaborate caches and offerings have been associated with Middle Preclassic E Group complexes, rituals and deposits involving human remains are more frequently associated with Late Preclassic and Classic period E Groups. These include both primary and secondary burials, as well as offerings and caches that include human skeletal elements, most commonly human skulls. The practice of bone manipulation, including placing heads in bowls so that they can be removed for procession and other rituals, is often associated with ancestor veneration and elaborate reburial rituals (Brown 2013; McAnany 1995; Robin et al. 2012). Moreover, human skulls placed within ceramic vessels seem to be a common theme associated with many E Groups, beginning in the Late Preclassic. In fact, Oliver Ricketson and Edith Ricketson (1937) first recorded this at Uaxactún. They documented lip-to-lip caches containing human skulls and bones within the eastern structures of the E Group complex (Ricketson and Ricketson 1937). Although rituals and burial rites involving human remains are more commonly found with later E Groups, they do have their origins in the Middle Preclassic. We see this pattern in the Belize River valley at Early Xunantunich and Chan (Robin et al. 2012) and quite possibly at the nearby center of Cahal Pech.

Buried beneath the plaza at the center of the Early Xunantunich E Group was a simple extended burial without grave goods placed in a thick lens of pure white marl. Skeletal analysis by Carolyn Freiwald suggests that the individual was an adult male. The individual was buried face up with his head to the north, an uncommon pattern for the Belize River valley, especially for later periods. This burial is one of only a handful of Middle Preclassic burials found to date in the Belize River valley, however, suggesting that burial placement may have been more variable during this early period. It is of special interest that the burial showed signs of reentry and that the head was completely removed in antiquity. Two teeth were present, providing strong evidence that the head was originally present but was removed at some point later in antiquity, presumably for ancestor ritual veneration practices. The Middle Preclassic burial placed at the center point of the E Group plaza is significant, as most early burials are found within or near residences. This individual was buried beneath a public, ritual space within the Early Xunantunich community, which indicates the commencement of a tradition that endured through the Classic period, a practice of placing important individuals in ceremonial spaces and the ensuing veneration of these individuals as prominent ancestors.

This pattern is also seen at the nearby site of Chan. In fact, an early Middle Preclassic burial from Chan, Burial 1, provides a clear parallel to the Early Xunantunich example, suggesting a pattern of burial placement and ritual veneration. Like the burial at Early Xunantunich, Burial 1 at Chan was intentionally placed at the center of the Chan E Group, the ceremonial heart of this early Maya community (Robin et al. 2012, Chapter 11 in this volume). Burial 1 from Chan was a simple crypt burial placed in a pit cut into bedrock (Robin et al. 2012). This burial shows signs of reentry at least twice: "body parts of this ancestor were removed from the grave and in some cases repositioned," including the removal of the skull (Robin et al. 2012:128). It is noteworthy that both the Early Xunantunich and Chan Middle Preclassic burials were the earliest interments found to date at these sites and were both placed at the center of E Group plazas. Moreover, both exhibited evidence of reentry and removal of the skull.

A third example from the nearby site of Cahal Pech, although somewhat later in date, may reflect similar burial practices and manipulation of bones for ancestor veneration. An early platform was encountered buried beneath Plaza B (Garber and Awe 2008). Although the platform was poorly preserved, it appears that ritual offerings were deposited in the four corners, including a crypt burial in the southeast corner. Although it is possible that the burial may have been intrusive to the platform, it is interesting to note that the burial was interred roughly in the center of Plaza B and may represent a similar placement to the Early Xunantunich and Chan examples. Though a recent AMS date of the skeleton itself suggests a Late Preclassic date (Jaime Awe, personal communication, 2016), this burial may reflect the continuation of a tradition of ancestor veneration established during the Middle Preclassic.

Furthermore, this plaza is bounded to the east by an architectural complex that greatly resembles an eastern architectural arrangement of an E Group. Although Jaime Awe, Julie Hoggarth, and James Aimers (Chapter 13 in this volume) suggest that this Eastern Triadic Structure group is not a formal E Group, the form is very similar; therefore, it may have served a similar function in the Middle Preclassic. It is also possible, although somewhat speculative, that this location may have been an E Group originally that was heavily modified in later times.

Nevertheless, the burial found within the center of this plaza was somewhat unusual: separate crypts were constructed for the head and body (Garber and Awe 2008). The head was placed within a red-slipped bowl with six jade beads. The placement of the head in a separate crypt and within a bowl has led James Garber and Jaime Awe (2008) to argue that the head of this specially treated individual may have symbolically represented the severed head of the Maize God. It is significant to note that the construction of two separate crypts, one for the body and the other for the head in a bowl, would facilitate reentry and removal of the head for later rituals without the disturbance of the other bones.

It is not known whether the heads of the Middle Preclassic Early Xunantunich and Chan burials were placed in bowls similar to the later burial found within Plaza B at Cahal Pech. It seems likely that the placement of heads in bowls may reflect a Late Preclassic tradition, as this practice is seen in other burials at Chan, Cahal Pech, and the E Group structures at Uaxactún, just to name a few. For example, a Late Preclassic burial at Chan, Burial 8, within the central eastern structure of the E Group contained a young adult male interred with six ceramic vessels, an exotic chert blade, and a jade pendant (Novotny 2012; Robin et al. 2012). The head of this individual was placed in a Sierra Red dish (Robin et al. 2012). This burial, much like the Middle Preclassic burials discussed above, showed evidence of reentry and manipulation of the bones. The placement of the head in a ceramic vessel may have allowed the descendants to reenter the burial and remove the head and vessel for ritual purposes (Robin et al. 2012). Therefore, the placement of heads in bowls may reflect a more formalized ritual practice within the Late Preclassic that emerged from an earlier tradition of reentry and bone retrieval beginning in the Middle Preclassic.

Another intriguing example of special treatment of disinterred remains in this fashion is seen from Cahal Pech. Awe (2013) uncovered an elaborate offering in a Late Preclassic construction phase of Structure B4 at Cahal Pech. Structure B4 is located on the southern side of Plaza B and is associated with the above-mentioned Eastern Triadic Structure assemblage (Chapter 13 in this volume). The central component of this offering was a skull in two ceramic bowls set lip-to-lip. It was surrounded by long bones that are possibly part of the remains of the body associated with the head, together with other offerings (Awe 2013).

Funerary rites that include placing heads in bowls were both symbolically and materially powerful, emphasizing the resurrection of a deceased ancestor in a fashion similar to the Maize God, while at the same time allowing this important ancestor to be present physically through the inclusion of the bones as part of ritual activities. These ritual practices are especially intriguing when they are found within E Group complexes, public places where presumably sun and maize deities were celebrated through ritual practices related to annual solar cycles and sprouting maize. The practices of burial reentry and removal of bones and presumably reburial of these skeletal elements at key locations show how later descendants manipulated the bones to link their ancestor symbolically to these important deities.

It is unclear when the local descendants reentered the Middle Preclassic burials at Early Xunantunich and Chan, but it seems most likely to have occurred at the end of the Middle Preclassic or most likely during the Late Preclassic, when we see the introduction of both primary and secondary burials into E Group structures. Primary and secondary burials placed within staircases or beneath the summit of E Group structures have been documented at a number of sites within the Belize River valley, including Chan (Robin et al. 2012), Actuncán (Lisa LeCount, personal communication, 2013; Donohue 2014), Cahal Pech (Chapter 13 in this volume), and Blackman Eddy (Brown et al. n.d.; Garber et al. 2004). In the Late Preclassic at Early Xunantunich, the eastern pyramid (Structure E-2-1st-a) was remodeled and expanded and a formal burial chamber was placed just under the pyramid's new summit as part of that expansion (Brown 2013). This tomb-like chamber was placed on centerline and measured approximately 1 m × 2 m (Figure 12.6). The chamber was most likely filled after the interment was placed inside and thus does not represent a formal tomb. Yet the burial chamber was more elaborate than a crypt.

Formal burial chambers and tombs dating to the Late Preclassic are uncommon, but burials of this sort increase in frequency by the Classic period, suggesting that "individuals of great stature were memorialized through monumental architecture" (McAnany 2001:133).

Our excavations showed that the Late Preclassic burial chamber was reentered in antiquity at least once and possibly additional times (Brown 2013). Also, the summit surface above the chamber was not patched, suggesting that the final reentry occurred after the structure was no longer in formal use, or that it marked the end of the structure's use, or that it represents postabandonment reentry. The contents of the burial chamber were removed in antiquity. Only a few scattered remains were present, allowing us to infer something about its original contents (Brown 2013). Three fragments of bone found within the chamber suggest that it was indeed a burial

E Groups and Ancestors: The Sunrise of Complexity at Xunantunich, Belize · 403

Figure 12.6. Photograph of burial chamber in Structure E-2-1st.

chamber. In addition, a single Middle Preclassic Savanna Orange miniature jar was found within the chamber itself. Given the identification of the vessel as a Middle Preclassic type, it predates the Late Preclassic context of the chamber. There are two possible explanations for this disjunction. The vessel may be an heirloom placed within the burial of a Late Preclassic individual. Alternatively, it is quite plausible that the chamber was made for a secondary reinterment of a Middle Preclassic ancestor, who was placed within the chamber along with items from his or her original burial. The fact that only three stray bone fragments were found lends support to this interpretation, as it seems likely that more bone fragments and teeth would have been present if a primary burial was reentered and removed. Of course, it is also possible that both an ancestor bundle and a primary burial were once present within the chamber. Radiocarbon dating of the bone fragments is necessary to shed light on the chronology and is planned for the future.

Following the final reentry, the chamber was filled in. After the chamber was filled, several large flat stones were laid on top, presumably to mark the location after the burial was removed. Placed at the center of these was a fairly large, irregularly shaped slate slab, incised on one face. The incised design was difficult to make out, as the slab had been placed with the incised side facing up. Due to the tendency of slate to fragment in layers, much of the incised design had peeled away, unfortunately. We can discern a figure in profile that appears to be wearing a headdress and a belt with some form of belt element, however. The figure appears to be holding something in front of his body, perhaps a staff or spear. Although we have been unable to ascertain more iconographic detail at this point, it is significant that the slab seems to be a portrait of an individual, possibly wearing some form of regalia. The placement of this slate slab above the reentered burial chamber may connect the portrait with the interred individual.

Our excavations next to the chamber uncovered fragments of a *Spondylus* shell ornament, possibly an earflare or chest pectoral. The close proximity to the burial chamber and the consistency of the fill suggest that this fragmented shell ornament was displaced when the contents and individual(s) were removed from the chamber. Many scholars have noted that *Spondylus* was highly valued by the ancient Maya and symbolized the watery underworld. *Spondylus* was an important part of royal regalia and appears to have been a symbol of power and authority for early Maya kings (Freidel et al. 2002:44). It is interesting to note that a Late Preclassic burial within the eastern structure of the E Group at Chan (Burial 10) contained several artifacts, including a *Spondylus* shell ornament as well as an heirloom Middle Preclassic figurine fragment (Novotny 2012).

The E Group at Early Xunantunich was abandoned at the end of the Late Preclassic. I have argued elsewhere that I believe that when the inhabitants abandoned this location they purposely retrieved the bones of the important individual buried in the eastern pyramid, quite possibly with the intention of reburying him or her at a new location (Brown 2013). Although slightly later in time, two recently discovered Early Classic (350–450 CE) elaborate burials within the plaza of the central E Group–like complex at the nearby site of Buenavista provide interesting parallels. The earliest of these burials was housed in a small crypt beneath the plaza directly in front of the eastern architectural complex. This burial featured an elaborate *Spondylus* and *Strombus* shell assemblage including elaborate earflares and a cut and incised marine shell pectoral that portrayed the image of an ancestor as well as a glyphic text bearing the term *ajaw* (Yaeger et al. 2015). Above this royal burial was a much larger rectangular chamber similar in form to the Late Preclassic chamber at Early Xunantunich. This burial chamber had been reentered in antiquity and the remains of the individual and most of the contents removed, leaving scattered bone fragments, *Spondylus* shell beads, fragments of a composite mosaic object, and several highly fragmented ceramic vessels (Yaeger et al. 2015). This burial chamber was then filled in, which is interesting in light of the reentered chamber at the E Group at Early Xunantunich, indicating a pattern of reentry and removal of bones of important individuals interred in E Groups within the Belize Valley, a practice that may have its roots in the Middle Preclassic. Additionally, the Early Xunantunich and Buenavista reentered chambers demonstrate that the Maya not only disinterred skulls for veneration but also sometimes exhumed entire skeletons of revered ancestors.

The removal of bones from ancestor graves coupled with the ritual reburial plays an important role in the rise of complexity in the Maya Lowlands. Robin et al. (2012:123) suggest that communicating with the ancestors through reentry into graves and utilizing their bones in ritual practices is deeply rooted in ancient Maya agrarian ideology. The removing and redepositing of the remains of certain important ancestors suggest that "bones of the ancestors 'paved the path' to the institutionalization of religious power represented by pyramid construction" (McAnany 2001:133). I would further argue that placement of ancestors in E Group complexes was part and parcel of this process. E Groups were early locations for public ritual emphasizing annual cycles of the sun. Additionally, as Freidel (Chapter 6) and others in this volume argue, rituals at E Groups are intricately tied to the maize cult. Therefore, the reburial of important ancestors coupled with the primary interment of prominent individuals within the architectural features and plazas of E Groups suggests an intentional practice that connects these ancestors and individuals to the watery and fiery sun and maize deities.

Conclusions

Recent investigations at Xunantunich show that the site was composed of two ceremonial centers, one dating to the Preclassic Period (Early Xunantunich) and one dating to the Late Classic. Current archaeological data indicate that Early Xunantunich was abandoned by the end of the Late Preclassic, prior to the construction of the Classic Period Xunantunich site core. Excavations within the Early Xunantunich E Group have shown that this architectural complex was first constructed during the early Middle Preclassic, suggesting that this may have been one of the earliest documented E Groups in Belize. The discovery of a Middle Preclassic E Group is significant. The fact that the Middle Preclassic community of Early Xunantunich focused its construction efforts on building an E Group indicates that early public ritual emphasized the daily east–west path of the sun and the annual cycle of solstices and equinoxes. The presence of a Middle Preclassic perishable wooden altar in front of the central staircase of the eastern central pyramid is suggestive of public ritual activities and further supports the importance of this central location to the community. Furthermore, this altar was rebuilt several times, which suggests a cycle of rituals, quite possibly related to annual solar events.

Investigations in the open space between the pyramids revealed a number of structures and features, dominated by a large platform with a series of terraces that rises up from the marl floor in front of the E Groups, eastern structure. Two broad ramps provided access up onto the platform, but it is interesting that their lateral positioning channeled movement (and possibly water during the rainy season) between the platform and the pyramid, resulting in no direct access between them. Instead, they suggest a ritual circuit, as people moved west and east, north and south, and up and down. Furthermore, there was no direct access to the wooden altar feature, a sunken location where presumably key rituals were conducted. Although early processions and ritual activities may have involved members of the community, aspiring rulers may have overseen rituals at this location, connecting themselves to important ancestors, supernaturals, and most specifically the maize deity. These cycles of rituals, presumably practices that helped ensure the continuity of solar cycles, may have been appropriated by elites by the Late Preclassic, as this is the time when we begin to see an increase in ancestor reburial and primary interments into the E Group structures.

We see this at the Early Xunantunich E Group with the construction of a formal burial chamber and presumably the remains of an important ancestor who was placed inside along with a Middle Preclassic vessel. I argue that the placement of an important ancestor—quite possibly several generations old—in the eastern structure of the E Group represents an attempt to merge certain ancestors with deities by the descendants of this ancestor. They chose the community's most sacred space, which had been the venue for generations of rituals celebrating the sun and its daily and annual cycles, and appropriated it for the veneration of one of their key ancestors. In doing so, they manipulated a long tradition of public ritual related to the rising sun to include the celebration of the rising or apotheosis of an important ancestor. This ideological two-step is one of the key steps in the larger process of the legitimizing of divine kingship.

This chamber was reentered at least once and possibly additional times, and the bones were retrieved. An incised slate slab depicting a male individual in profile was placed on top of the chamber. The timing of the final manipulation and removal of the bones appears to date to the abandonment of the E Group at the end of the Late Preclassic. The fact that the removal of the bones from the chamber—presumably retrieved for reburial at a new location—coincided roughly with the site abandonment is intriguing and strongly suggests that this particular ancestor was central to the community's identity. This illustrates both the importance of ritual ancestor veneration in the Preclassic period and the role of the physical remains of the ancestors in the strategies of their living descendants. As McAnany (1995:162) states, "The practice of ancestor veneration ultimately is not about the dead, but about how the living make use of the dead."

Acknowledgments

I am grateful to David Freidel, Arlen Chase, Anne Dowd, and Jerry Murdock for inviting me to participate in this volume and for all their hard work to see this volume through publication. I would like to thank James Aimers and Debra Walker for their insightful comments and suggestions. I am especially grateful to conduct archaeological research in the country of Belize and thank the Belize Institute of Archaeology for this opportunity. I would also like to thank all my staff members on the Mopan Valley Preclassic Project (MVPP). Leah McCurdy and Bernadette Cap deserve special recognition for their support and assistance with the illustrations for this chapter. I am grateful for the hard work and dedication of the MVPP Belizean archaeology team led by Anthony Chan and Louis Godoy. Jason Yaeger deserves acknowledgment for his comments on this chapter and for his continual support. Funding from the National Geographic Society Committee for Research and Exploration, Alphawood Foundation, Curtiss T. and Mary G. Brennan Foundation, Benedict and Trudy Termini, and University of Texas at San Antonio supported this research.

References Cited

Aimers, James J., and Prudence M. Rice
2006   Astronomy, Ritual, and the Interpretation of Maya "E-Group" Architectural Assemblages. *Ancient Mesoamerica* 17:79–96.

Awe, Jaime J.
2013   Journey on the Cahal Pech Time Machine: An Archaeological Reconstruction of the Dynastic Sequence at a Belize Valley Polity. *Research Reports in Belizean Archaeology* 10:33–50.

Brown, M. Kathryn
2003   Emerging Complexity in the Maya Lowlands: A View from Blackman Eddy, Belize. Ph.D. dissertation, Department of Anthropology, Southern Methodist University, Dallas, Texas, University Microfilms, Ann Arbor.
2011   Postclassic Veneration at Xunantunich, Belize. *Mexicon* 33:126–131.
2012   A Modern Maya Ritual at Xunantunich and Its Implications for Ancient Maya Ritual Behavior. *Research Reports in Belizean Archaeology* 9:195–205.
2013   Missing Persons: The Role of Ancestors in the Rise of Complexity. *Research Reports in Belizean Archaeology* 10:57–64.

Brown, M. Kathryn, Jaime J. Awe, and James F. Garber
n.d.   The Role of Ritual and Religion in the Foundation of Social Complexity in the Belize River Valley. In *Pathways to Complexity: A View from the Maya Lowlands*, edited by M. Kathryn Brown and George J. Bey III. University Press of Florida, Gainesville (forthcoming).

Chase, Arlen F.
1983   A Contextual Consideration of the Tayasal-Paxcaman Zone, El Peten, Guatemala. Ph.D. dissertation, Department of Anthropology, University of Pennsylvania, Philadelphia.

Chase, Arlen F., and Diane Z. Chase
1995   External Impetus, Internal Synthesis, and Standardization: E-Group Assemblages and the Crystallization of Classic Maya Society in the Southern Lowlands. *Acta Mesoamericana* 8:87–101 (special issue edited by Nikolai Grube entitled *The Emergence of Lowland Maya Civilization: The Transition from the Preclassic to Early Classic*).

Chase, Arlen F., Diane Z. Chase, Jaime J. Awe, John F. Weishampel, Gyles Iannone, Holley Moyes, Jason Yaeger, and M. Kathryn Brown
2014 The Use of LiDAR in Understanding the Ancient Maya Landscape: Caracol and Western Belize. *Advances in Archaeological Practice* 2(3):208–220.

Donohue, Luke
2014 Excavations at Structures 26 and 27 in Actuncan's E-Group. In Actuncan Archaeological Project: Report of the Sixth Field Season, edited by Lisa LeCount, pp. 131–154. Report submitted to the Institute of Archaeology, Belmopan, Belize.

Estrada-Belli, Francisco
2011 *The First Maya Civilization: Ritual and Power before the Classic Period*. Routledge, New York.

Fitzsimmons, James
2009 *Death and the Classic Maya Kings*. Linda Schele Series in Maya and Pre-Columbian Studies. University of Texas Press, Austin.

Freidel, David A., Kathryn Reese-Taylor, and David Mora Marín
2002 The Origins of Maya Civilizations: The Old Shell Game, Commodity, Treasure, and Kingship. In *Ancient Maya Political Economies*, edited by Marilyn Masson and David A. Freidel, pp. 41–86. AltaMira Press, Walnut Creek, California.

Freidel, David A., Linda Schele, and Joy Parker
1993 *Maya Cosmos: Three Thousand Years on the Shaman's Path*. William Morrow, New York.

Garber, James F., and Jaime J. Awe
2008 Middle Formative Architecture and Ritual at Cahal Pech. *Research Reports in Belizean Archaeology* 4:185–190.

Garber, James F., M. Kathryn Brown, and Jaime J. Awe
2004 Prehistory of the Central Belize Valley: An Examination of Architecture, Material Culture, and Sociopolitical Change at Blackman Eddy. In *The Ancient Maya of the Belize Valley: Half a Century of Archaeological Research*, edited by James F. Garber, pp. 25–47. University Press of Florida, Gainesville.

Hansen, Richard
1998 Continuity and Disjunction: The Preclassic Antecedents of Pre-Classic Maya Architecture. In *Function and Meaning in Classic Maya Architecture*, edited by Stephen D. Houston, pp. 49–122. Dumbarton Oaks Research Library and Collection, Washington, D.C.

Houston, Stephen
1993 *Hieroglyphs and History at Dos Pilas: Dynastic Politics of the Classic Maya*. University of Texas Press, Austin.

Houston, Stephen, David Stuart, and Karl Taube
2006 *Memory of the Bones: Body, Being, and Experience among the Classic Maya*. University of Texas Press, Austin.

Inomata, Takeshi, Daniela Triadan, Kazuo Aoyama, Victor Castillo, and Hitoshi Yonenobu
2013 Early Ceremonial Constructions at Ceibal, Guatemala, and the Origins of Lowland Maya Civilization. *Science* 340(6131):467–471.

Jamison, Thomas R.
2010 Monumental Building Programs and Changing Political Strategies at Xunantunich. In *Classic Maya Provincial Politics: Xunantunich and Its Hinterlands*, edited by Lisa LeCount and Jason Yaeger, pp. 122–144. University of Arizona Press, Tucson.

LeCount, Lisa, and Jason Yaeger
2010 *Classic Maya Provincial Politics: Xunantunich and Its Hinterlands*. University of Arizona Press, Tucson.

McAnany, Patricia
1995 *Living with the Ancestors: Kinship and Kingship in Ancient Maya Society*. University of Texas Press, Austin.
1998 Ancestors and the Classic Maya Built Environment. In *Function and Meaning in Classic Maya Architecture*, edited by Stephen D. Houston, pp. 271–298. Dumbarton Oaks Research Library and Collections, Washington, D.C.
2001 Cosmology and the Institutionalization of Hierarchy in the Maya Region. In *From Leaders to Rulers*, edited by Jonathan Haas, pp. 125–150. Kluwer Academic/Plenum Publishers, New York.

Novotny, Anna
2012 The Chan Community: A Bioarchaeological Perspective. In *Chan: An Ancient Maya Farming Community*, edited by Cynthia Robin, pp. 231–251. University Press of Florida, Gainesville.

Ricketson, Oliver G., Jr., and Edith Bayles Ricketson
1937 *Uaxactun, Guatemala: Group E 1926–1931*. Carnegie Institution of Washington, Washington, D.C.

Robin, Cynthia, James Meierhoff, Caleb Kestle, Chelsea Blackmore, Laura J. Kosakowsky, and Anna C. Novotny
2012 Ritual in a Farming Community. In *Chan: An Ancient Maya Farming Community*, edited by Cynthia Robin, pp. 113–132. University Press of Florida, Gainesville.

Robin, Cynthia, L. Theodore Neff, Jennifer J. Ehret, John Walkey, and Clarence H. Gifford
1994 Early Monumental Construction at Xunantunich: Preliminary Investigations of Group E and O/A2-1. In Xunantunich Archaeological Project: 1994 Field Season, edited by Richard M. Leventhal, pp. 101–107. Report on file at the Belize Institute of Archaeology, Belmopan, Belize.

Schele, Linda, and David A. Freidel
1993 Courts of Creation: Ballcourts, Ballgames and Portals to the Maya Otherworld. In *The Mesoamerican Ballgame*, edited by Vernon L. Scarborough and David R. Wilcox, pp. 289–316. University of Arizona Press, Tucson.

Schele, Linda, and Mary Miller
1986 *The Blood of Kings: Dynasty and Ritual in Maya Art*. Kimbell Art Museum, Fort Worth, Texas.

Stanton, Travis, and David Freidel
2003 Ideological Lock-In and the Dynamics of Formative Religions in Mesoamerica. *Mayab* 16:5–14.

Stuart, David
2005 *The Inscriptions of Temple XIX at Palenque.* San Francisco: Pre-Columbian Art Research Institute.

Taube, Karl
1998 The Jade Hearth: Centrality, Rulership, and the Classic Maya Temple. In *Function and Meaning in Classic Maya Architecture*, edited by Stephen D. Houston, pp. 427–518. Dumbarton Oaks Research Library and Collection, Washington, D.C.
2000 Lightning Celts and Corn Fetishes: The Formative Olmec and the Development of Maize Symbolism in Mesoamerica and the American Southwest. In *Olmec Art and Archaeology in Mesoamerica*, edited by John E. Clark and Mary Pye, pp. 297–337. National Gallery of Art, Washington, D.C.

Yaeger, Jason, M. Kathryn Brown, Christophe Helmke, Mark Zender, Bernadette Cap, Christie Kokel-Rodriguez, and Sylvia Batty
2015 Two Early Classic Elite Burials from Buenavista del Cayo, Belize. *Research Reports in Belizean Archaeology* 12:181–191.

13

Of Apples and Oranges

The Case of E Groups and Eastern Triadic Architectural Assemblages in the Belize River Valley

JAIME J. AWE, JULIE A. HOGGARTH, AND JAMES J. AIMERS

Ever since Frans Blom (1924) identified the first E Group assemblage at Uaxactún and proposed that assemblages of this type served as astronomical observatories, there has been controversy regarding the actual function(s) of these architectural assemblages. This situation is perhaps best reflected in the two most recent papers on the subject, published in the journal *Ancient Mesoamerica* in 2006. In the first article, James Aimers and Prudence Rice (2006:87) identified more than sixty possible examples of E Groups across the Maya Lowlands and proposed that their function transitioned from "celebrations of solar cycling" to "settings for valedictory ceremonies" such as K'atun-endings. In the second article, Thomas Guderjan (2006:97) argued for the presence of Late Classic pseudo–E groups in northern Belize and suggested that they were primarily "constructed to reinforce the identity of cities and the validity of their rulers." In an effort to test the validity of these and other hypotheses, this chapter provides a brief review of the hypothesized functions of E Groups in the Maya Lowlands and then examines data recovered from actual archaeological investigations of assemblages that have been called E Groups in the Belize River valley.

Definition of E Groups

In the original description of the E Group complex at Uaxactún, Blom (1924; also see Ricketson and Ricketson 1937; Ruppert 1940) defined this architectural assemblage as composed of three temples constructed in a north–south alignment atop a long substructural platform on the east side of a public plaza. Across the plaza, to the west of the triadic structure, is a "radial" or four-sided pyramid. At Uaxactún, the Eastern Triadic Structures are represented by Str. EI to the north, EII at center, and EIII to the south. The western pyramid (Str. EVII) is situated almost 90 degrees west of Str. EII. As Aimers and Rice (2006:79) note, ever since Blom identified the E Group arrangement at Uaxactún, they "have been identified, often in variant forms, throughout the lowlands" and in a few other regions of Mesoamerica. Excavation of Maya E Groups suggests that they had appeared by the beginning of the Middle Preclassic (ca. 900–750 BCE), with Inomata (Chapter 7 in this volume) dating the Maya E Group at Ceibal to 1000–900 BCE, and were constructed into the Terminal Classic period (ca. 800–900 CE) (Hansen 1998; Aimers and Rice 2006). The origins of the E Group are probably earlier and potentially non-Maya, however. Aimers and Rice (2006:80) noted similarities to structures at (Olmec) La Venta, and Inomata (Chapter 7 in this volume) links the origins of E Groups to interactions involving the Gulf Coast, Chiapas, and the Pacific Coast (see also Blake 2013).

At this point, we should clarify our definitions of E Groups, Eastern Triadic Assemblages (ETA), and Eastern Triadic Structures (ETS). Our definitions are purely morphological. We define an E Group as an architectural assemblage composed of a structure on the west side of a plaza across from a tripartite structure or set of three adjacent structures. In this chapter, we are focused on a particular variation of the E Group pattern that we call an Eastern Triadic Assemblage. An ETA is composed of an ETS facing a single structure to the west. Eastern Triadic Assemblages in our sample are exemplified by Group A at Pacbitún, in which a large central eastern structure is flanked by smaller structures to its north and south, facing a single structure to the west. In our definition of E Groups, the western structure does not have to be shown to be radial, but it must be present. When the western structure is not present, we simply refer to an ETS. We do not consider an isolated ETS to be an E Group although if a western structure had existed in the past, as at Cahal Pech, then the assemblage was an E Group in the past.

In a study of E Groups in the Petén, Arlen Chase (1983) divided the known examples into three morphological types. The first or Uaxactún Style, has the standard radial pyramid on the west side of the plaza and the three "linearly arranged buildings" on top of the long substructural platform to the east (Chase and Chase 1995:90). In the second type, designated the Cenote Style, the "eastern side of the assemblage is composed of a larger central structure . . . linked by wing-like platforms to low end structures" (Chase 1983:1245). The architecture of Chase's third type, the

Cenote Variant, is more anomalous and exhibits "significant morphological differences from the two more easily recognizable types described earlier" (Aimers and Rice 2006:81). ETAs could be placed in Chase's 1983 category of the Cenote Variant, but we are proposing the term "ETA" to highlight their somewhat more consistent layout. Informally, due to the frequency of caches and burials in ETS, we have called them Eastern Triadic Shrines, but we now prefer to use the functionally neutral term "Eastern Triadic Structures."

We hope that our definition of ETAs encourages more attempts to develop a more detailed typology of assemblages that have been called E Groups, ideally using a shared set of terms such as ETA, ETS, and so forth. Many published studies assume that all architectural complexes that have been called E Groups are morphologically similar, but Eastern Triadic Assemblages seem to represent a regional variation on the general E Group form. Furthermore, site-specific results are often generalized to the interpretation of the wide variety of architectural assemblages that have been called E Groups. We believe that this approach has contributed to the problem of determining the function of these assemblages and that more attention should be paid to variation in both form and meaning. This chapter takes a regional and morphologically specific approach in attempting to understand the function and meaning of Eastern Triadic Assemblages without extending this to all the assemblages that have been called E Groups in nearly a century of writing on the topic. While at first sight Eastern Triadic Assemblages may look similar to other architectural assemblages that have been called E Groups, we show below that the systematic recording of architectural data proves otherwise. Our interpretation stems from a clear definition of a particular architectural form combined with data derived from excavation.

Hypothesized Functions of E Groups

A review of the extant literature on E Groups indicates that at least six functional explanations have been proposed for these architectural assemblages. These include their use as astronomical observatories, for the scheduling of agricultural or trade activities, as settings for agricultural ritual, for use in geomantic systems, for the performance of ancestor rituals by an emerging ruling elite, and, more recently, as settings for "valedictory ceremonies" such as K'atun-endings. For the purposes of this chapter, we provide just a brief overview of these hypotheses. For more detailed discussions and information on the various hypotheses, refer to publications by Ricketson (1928a, 1928b), Ruppert (1940), Rathje (1972, 1978), Carlson (1981), Coggins (1983), Cohodas (1980), Laporte and Fialko (1990), Aimers (1993), Laporte (1993), Chase (1983), Chase and Chase (1995), Hansen (1998), Aylesworth (2002, 2004), Aimers and Rice (2006), and Guderjan (2006).

As indicated above, archaeologists working at Uaxactún in the early 1920s were the first to identify E Group architectural assemblages and to suggest that they functioned as astronomical observatories (Blom 1924, Ricketson 1928a). Not long thereafter, however, Ricketson (1928b:439–440) questioned this hypothesis and pondered whether the Uaxactún E Group actually functioned as "a true observatory, or planned to mark the already known directions of the four significant annual positions of the sun." Ricketson (1928b:439–440) even went so far as to suggest that "their erection is to be more closely associated with geomancy than with astronomy." Sixty years later, a study conducted by Aveni and Hartung (1989) noted that, while the Uaxactún assemblage accurately marked the position of the sun during the solstices, it was inaccurate for marking the passage of the sun during the equinox. They also suggested that subsequent architectural modification to the E Group "rendered useless their astronomical function" (1989:451). Aveni and Hartung (1989:452) thus concluded that "most E-Group complexes might have been non-functioning copies of the astronomically operational archetype at Uaxactún" and that their primary function may have been for "ritual and ceremony." In a more recent evaluation of the solstice hypotheses, Aimers and Rice (2006:86) confirmed Aveni and Hartung's observations. They too concluded that few of the "E-Group assemblages accurately marked the position of the sun at sunrise on the summer solstice": "These observations do not support the persistent belief that E-Groups were astronomically accurate markers of the solstices and equinoxes." Tests that Awe (2008) conducted on the E Group at Caracol in March and December of 2012 concur with these observations. They also suggest that any astronomical function that the assemblages may originally have had were completely altered by subsequent architectural modifications.

In a 2003 study of alignments at 31 E Groups, Aveni et al. (2003:162) reached the quite different conclusion that "it seems clear from the concentrations around June 21 and December 21 that the solar horizon extremes were significant with respect to the orientation of E Group complexes as a class." They also identified alignments related to the times of the passing of the sun along the zenith (May 10 and August 3 in the general area of study)

(Aveni et al. 2003:159). They further suggested that "this later [zenith] orientation calendar was derived from Teotihuacan during the Early Classic period (A.D. 278–593)" (see also Chapter 3 in this volume). In the present volume, most authors seem to follow Aveni et al. (2003) in accepting that E Groups marked solstices, equinoxes, and/or zeniths at least at some points in their period of use.

The use of E Groups for scheduling agricultural and trade activities was proposed by William Rathje (1972, 1978), who perceived E Groups as heuristic devices used in the scheduling of agricultural activities. As Aimers (1993; Aimers and Rice 2006) accurately noted, this hypothesis suffers from two inherent problems. First, it relies on the premise that all E Groups functioned accurately as observatories. Second, it assumes that Maya farmers were dependent on astronomers to schedule their agrarian activities. Surely no Maya farmers worth their salt would have ever needed to be told when to plant or harvest their crops. William Rathje (1972, 1978) can also be credited with the proposal that E Groups were developed for scheduling "trade activities effectively with population in areas which differed in specific production cycles, market schedules, or other features affecting their trade potential" (Rathje 1972:233). Here again, the problem derives from Rathje's assumption that E Groups were accurate timekeeping devices and that their primary function was to serve economic purposes.

An idea related to scheduling of agriculture is that E Groups were associated with the celebration of agricultural rituals. In a discussion of the western pyramids in E Group assemblages, Cohodas (1980:208) argued that these radial structures were like *k'in* signs and that their associated plazas were "designed for public participation in rituals regulated by the solar or agricultural calendar." This is reinforced by the observation that E Group plazas are often large, central, and located in "accessible and highly visible plazas of a likely ritual function" (Aimers 1993:93). Aveni et al. (2003:162) have more recently connected this idea to their solar zenith hypothesis: "From an agricultural perspective, the times leading up to the first zenith passage (May 10) would have been the most logical points to mark by orientations in specialized groups of buildings where rituals pertaining to the anticipation of the forthcoming crop might have been conducted (Aveni 1991:320). Indeed, Wisdom (1940) has documented one such set of festivals in the nine-month period encompassing the solar zenith passage among the Chorti."

In a paper on Mesoamerican sites and worldviews, John Carlson (1981:188) proposed that E Groups may have been sited using concepts of geomancy as well as astrology/astronomy. Geomancy can be considered the terrestrial equivalent of astrology. He suggested that, rather than being "astronomically operational," E Groups were constructed in alignment with culturally important topographic and/or celestial features ("cosmic geomancy"). This proposal harkens back to the suggestion made by Ricketson in the 1920s. The major problem with the hypothesis is that it is hard to prove under present conditions. In some cases we would need to cut down the forest around all the sites with E Groups to look for potential topographic or celestial features that the buildings could potentially be aligned with. In places where sites are located in regions with no discernible topographic features, such as the flat lowlands of the northeastern Yucatán and northern Belize, it would also be difficult to determine which celestial or landscape feature(s) may have been selected for alignment.

More detailed survey methods and landscape studies are now available through LiDAR data (Awe et al. 2015; Chase et al. 2011, 2012, 2014; Rosenswig et al. 2013) as well as through Geographic Information Systems (GIS) analyses of the natural and built environment in relation to site location (see Doyle 2012 and Estrada-Belli's use of a GIS viewshed tool in Chapter 9 in this volume). Michael Blake (2013:1) has examined about a dozen sites in Chiapas and neighboring regions of southeastern Mesoamerica using widely available tools:

> My main focus is on measuring solar alignments during equinoxes and solstices. I do this by using a relatively easy and widely accessible set of tools in Google Earth. I first overlay site maps on Google Earth satellite imagery in Google Earth and then use Google Earth's Sun feature, digital elevation model, and ruler tool to draw orientation lines from points on the site map to the horizon at sunrise and, in some cases, sunset. . . . it is also possible to explore sunrise/set locations at other specific dates or with site orientations other than equinoxes and solstices—such as major axes or alignments oriented to topographic features such as prominent mountains or volcanoes or to sun rise/set positions at the zenith.

Inomata and Estrada-Belli (Chapters 7 and 9 in this volume) link the orientation of E Groups to both celestial and terrestrial features (cosmic geomancy: see Aimers 1993:162; Carlson 1981:188).

In his study of E Groups in the Tayasal-Paxcaman area, Arlen Chase (1983) observed that there is an interesting shift in ritual activity between the Preclassic and Early Classic periods. He argued that E Groups served as the primary loci for community related rituals during the Preclassic. By the start of the Early Classic, this pattern had changed and public ritual began to focus more on ancestor veneration. Along these same lines, but based on their more recent study of caches and burials in the Caracol E Group, Chase and Chase (1995:100–101) argued:

> The transition from the Late Preclassic to the Early Classic Period in the Southern Maya Lowlands was a time of significant social change, which culminated in the reformulation of Preclassic Maya society into its Classic Period socio-political and dynastic patterns. The hallmark of this transition on an architectural level appears to have been the E-Group, which served as an architecturally standardized focal assemblage for integrating Late Preclassic and subsequently Early Classic Maya populations, first ritually and then dynastically.

In essence, Chase and Chase proposed that the primary function for Classic period E Groups was for the performance of ancestor rituals by emerging ruling elite. This perspective is supported, to some degree, by Laporte and Fialko's (1990) study of the E Group complex at Tikal. Laporte and Fialko (1990:65) report that the E Group was established during the Middle Preclassic and used predominantly for dedication ceremonies into the Late Preclassic period, but by Early Classic times E Groups are associated with "a change in the socio-political dynamics of the site."

In one of the two most recent studies of E Groups, Aimers and Rice (2006:92) suggest that during the Middle Preclassic period, and perhaps earlier, E Group assemblages were likely settings for astronomical observations, with stones and/or poles atop or in alignment with the architecture marking these important solar events. By Late Preclassic times, this function for observing solar cycles became obsolescent: E Groups began to be used as "settings for valedictory ceremonies" such as K'atun-endings.

> The fact that katun ending stelae were erected regularly in E-Groups in the lowlands—perhaps as early as the Late Preclassic and throughout the Classic period—and in twin-pyramid complexes in Late Classic Tikal prompts two observations (see Rice 2004). One is that katun endings were clearly important occasions for ritual celebrations for more than a millennium in the Maya Lowlands, and even early on they might have structured geopolitical activity in the same way they did in early Colonial-period Yucatan. The other is that during the Late Preclassic and Classic periods, the Maya built distinctive architectural

complexes that provided an appropriate frame for rituals related to calendrical cycling and their associated stone monuments. (Aimers and Rice 2006:92)

In sum, Aimers and Rice's (2006:87) proposal supports the idea that the function of E Groups likely changed at the end of the Preclassic and that, in the Classic period, "they came to be constructed to celebrate longer calendrical cycles known as katuns and, possibly, longer cycles of 13 katuns, or approximately 256 years, called the *may* (see Rice 2004)." A similar argument involving Bak'tuns has been put forth by Arlen and Diane Chase for Caracol (Chapter 2 in this volume).

While Aimers and Rice provide an interesting functional explanation for E Groups, there are potential problems with the proposal. Notably, it is almost impossible to test its validity in regions like the Belize Valley, where most stelae are plain. This lack of inscriptions precludes the accurate dating of monuments in public plazas and therefore does not allow us to determine whether the monuments were erected as part of K'atun-ending celebrations. However, we can begin to explore the hypothesis that monuments (carved or uncarved) are concentrated around these groups in ceremonial centers.

In a paper published in the same issue, Guderjan (2006:98) argues for the presence of Late Classic "pseudo-E-groups" in northern Belize, defined as consisting of

> two buildings sometimes linked by a common substructure that bound the east side of a large plaza. In addition, and unlike the central Peten version seen at Tikal and Uaxactún, these complexes do not have a western building to functionally complete the observatory. Instead, if they had a viewing position, it would be somewhere in midplaza. None, however, are known to exist and elsewhere they are unmarked.

Like others before him, Guderjan (2006:97) also suggests that the function of E Groups changed over time and that their original astronomical function was eventually replaced by rituals that reinforced "the identity of cities and the validity of their rulers." This suggestion does not really propose a new function, for in many respects it can be linked to the hypothesis previously proposed by the Chases (1995). The major problem with Guderjan's argument is that his "pseudo-E-Groups" look nothing like the original E Group assemblages identified in the Petén or proposed variants thereof.

His architectural assemblages lack the typical triadic eastern buildings, and the western radial temple is nonexistent. Although Guderjan recognized that his "pseudo-E-Groups" did not serve astronomical purposes in the Late Classic period, it is perplexing that he still tries to establish solar alignments between the two eastern pyramids and arbitrary points in the plaza to the west. This raises the question of whether the architectural assemblages from northern Belize should be referred to as "pseudo-E-Groups" or whether a new label should be used for these assemblages.

Architectural Analysis of "E Groups" or Eastern Triadic Assemblages in the Belize River Valley

Aimers and Rice (2006:81, Table 1) list sixty-four sites with E Groups or E Group variants in the Maya Lowlands. Of the sixteen sites identified in Belize, nine are in the Belize River valley. These include Actuncán, Las Ruinas de Arenal, Baking Pot, Barton Ramie, Blackman Eddy, Cahal Pech, El Pilar, Pacbitún, and Xunantunich. It is important to note that, as in the case of other sites in the Lowlands, the designation of these assemblages as E Groups was based primarily on the study of published site plans. Aimers (1993) had previously acknowledged that this approach was problematic and noted the need for greater scientific methodology in determining the function of E Groups. In an effort to apply this very type of systematic approach, this study purposely examines data derived from archaeological investigations. Specifically, it compares the architectural data and the excavated cultural remains from seven Eastern Triadic Structures in the Belize River valley: Cahal Pech, Pacbitún, Baking Pot, Xunantunich, Blackman Eddy, El Pilar, and Chan (Figure 13.1). The first six of these sites were included in the list of E Groups and E Group variants in Aimers and Rice (2006). With the exception of El Pilar, where limited excavations have been conducted, most of the centers used in this analysis have also been the focus of intensive archaeological research during the last twenty years.

The primary reason for examining architectural data from the triadic assemblages was to determine the morphology and construction sequence for each of the assemblages. To acquire this information, we first recorded architectural data for all the buildings and then produced north–south profiles for each assemblage. This information was subsequently used to compare and contrast the morphological features of the seven assemblages. The results of the study presented in Table 13.1 and Figure 13.2 indicate that, even within the relatively small Belize Valley subregion, there

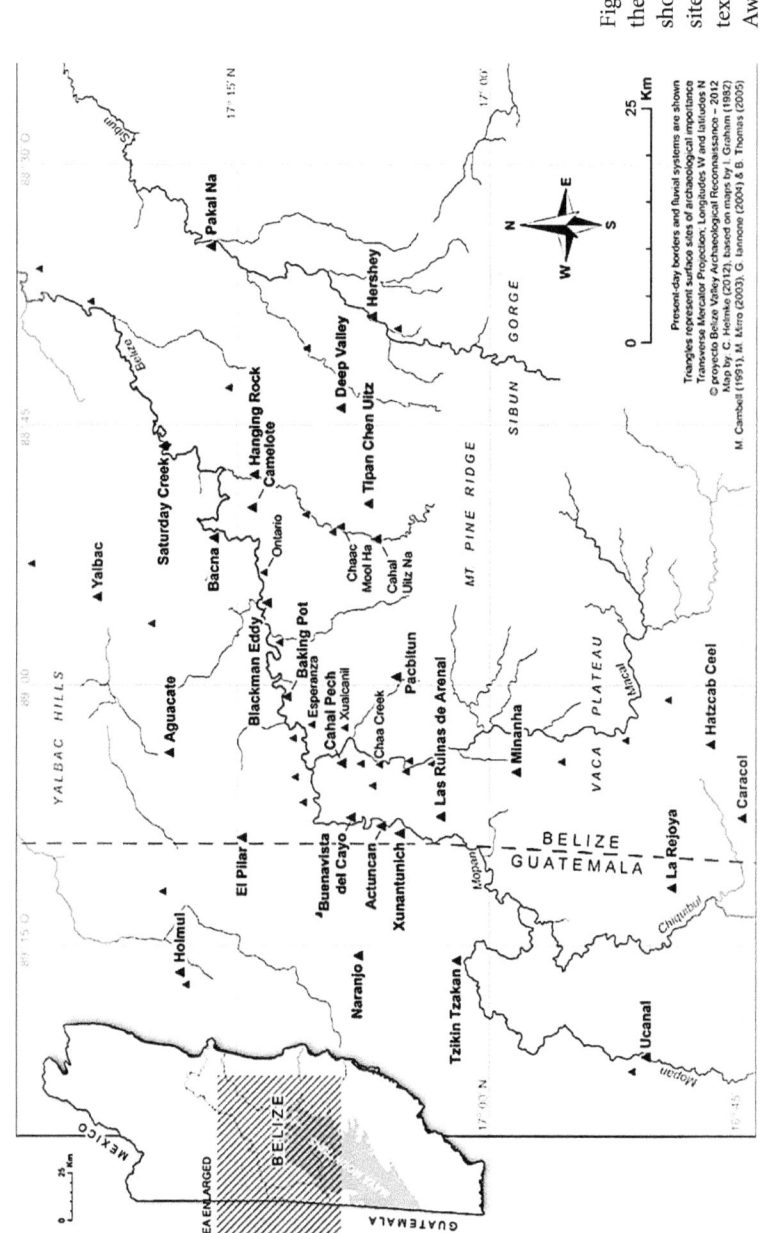

Figure 13.1. Map of the Belize River valley, showing location of sites discussed in the text (after Helmke and Awe 2012).

Table 13.1. Height measurements of Eastern Triadic Structures in the Belize River valley

Site name	North structure	Central structure	South structure
Cahal Pech	5.5 m	11.5 m	6.9 m
Pacbitun	10.5 m	15.4 m	11.0 m
Baking Pot	7.5 m	12.5 m	6.0 m
Chan	2.2 m	5.8 m	3.5 m
Xunantunich	13.0 m	11.8 m	11.0 m
Blackman Eddy	5.3 m	10.5 m	5.7 m
El Pilar	4.35 m	18.0 m	4.0 m

is considerable architectural variation from site to site. For example, while the central structure of most of the Belize Valley assemblages is substantially taller than the northern and southern structures, the central building is not the tallest in some cases, such as Xunantunich. When heights of the northern and southern structures are compared, it is also apparent that in several examples (Cahal Pech, Pacbitún, Chan), the southern structure is the taller of the two. In other cases (Baking Pot and Xunantunich), however, the northern building exceeds the height of the southern structure. The northern and southern buildings at El Pilar and Blackman Eddy are relatively similar in height. Indeed, minor height differences in these (and a few other) assemblages may simply reflect different levels of preservation between individual structures.

Another interesting pattern emerges when we examine the construction histories of those triadic assemblages that have been excavated. At Cahal Pech (Figure 13.3), for example, intensive excavations of all three structures (Awe 1992, 2013; Conlon 2013) indicate that the first architectural phase of Str. B1 (the central structure of the Eastern Triadic Structure) dates to the Late Middle Preclassic period. The first phase for the northern (Str. B2) and southern (Str. B3) buildings took place between the Late Middle and Late Preclassic periods. None of the structures, however, were connected to each other at this time. It was not until the end of the Late Preclassic period that all three structures became linked as a result of sequential modifications to the buildings. It is also interesting that only the southern and central structures underwent architectural modifications toward the end of the Late Classic. In the case of the southern building (Str. B3), the final modification adopted rounded terraces akin to that of Sr. B4 at Xunantunich and Str. B5 at Caracol. In their final form, therefore, the architecture of each of the structures that form the Eastern Triadic Assemblage at Cahal Pech (Figure

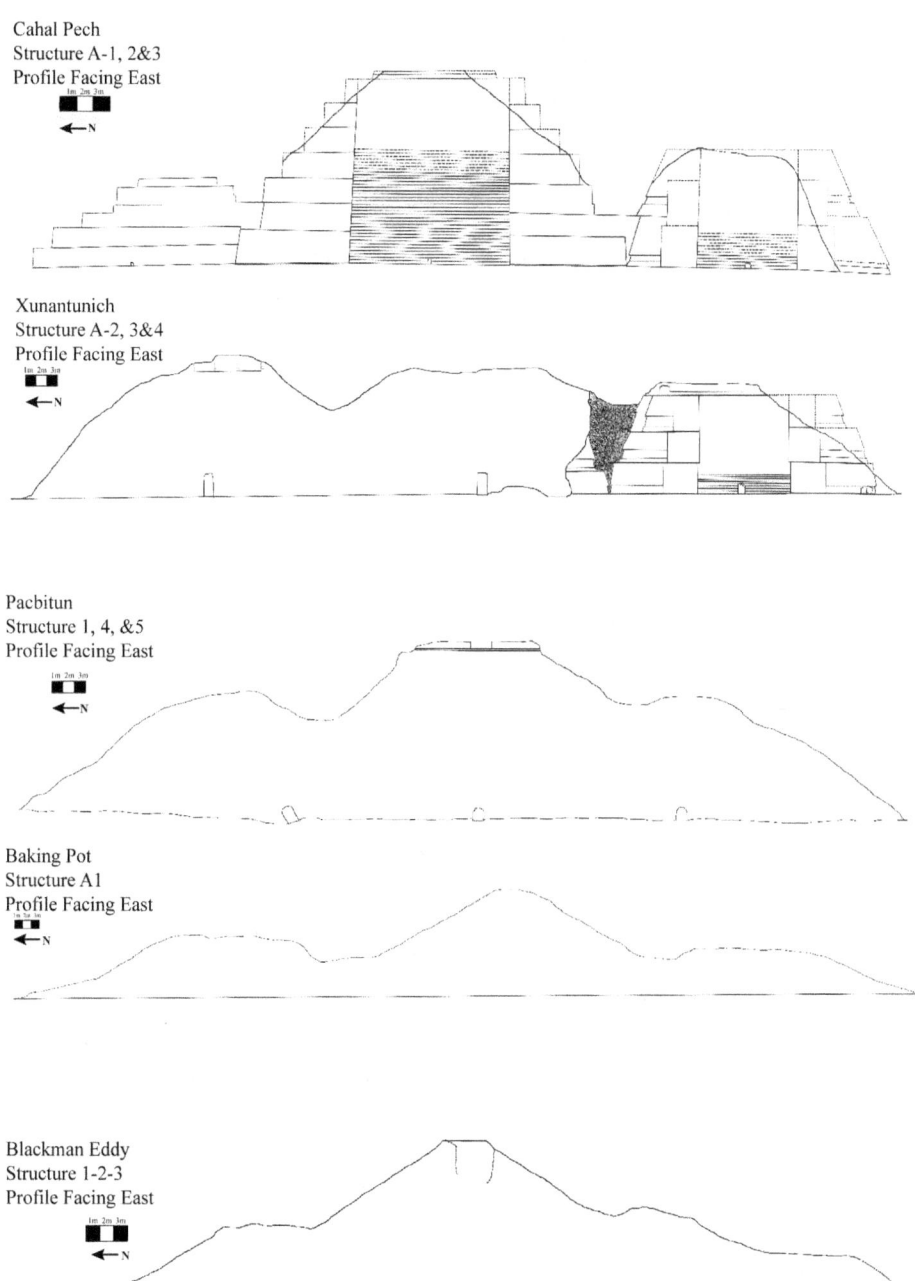

Figure 13.2. North–south profiles of Eastern Triadic Assemblages at selected Belize valley sites.

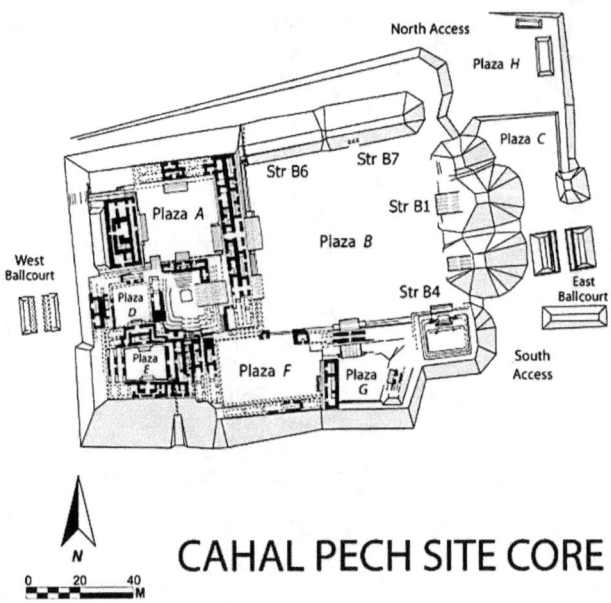

Figure 13.3. Plan of Cahal Pech site core.

13.4) was very different. Our excavations further indicate that this was also the case in earlier construction phases. Whether the same holds true for other sites in the valley has yet to be determined. Little is known of its form or function of the western building, for it was completely engulfed by the subsequent construction of a large Late Classic *audiencia* (administrative) style building.

Our examination of excavation data for Pacbitún and Chan reflects equally disparate construction histories for their triadic structures. At Pacbitún, Healy et al. (2004a:229) report: "From excavations of all three structures, it is apparent that each began as a separate structure but were joined by the Late Preclassic period into one massive architectural unit that dominated the entire end of Plaza A." In spite of this, Classic period modifications to individual structures in the assemblage do not appear to have been uniform.

At Chan, Cynthia Robin (2012) and her colleagues designated the Eastern Triadic Assemblage as Str. 5-central, 5-north, and 5-south. Their investigations of Str. 5 central established that it underwent ten major construction phases, the first dating to the Late Preclassic (350 BCE–100/150 CE) period (Meierhoff et al. 2004:37; Robin et al. 2008, 2012:119–120).

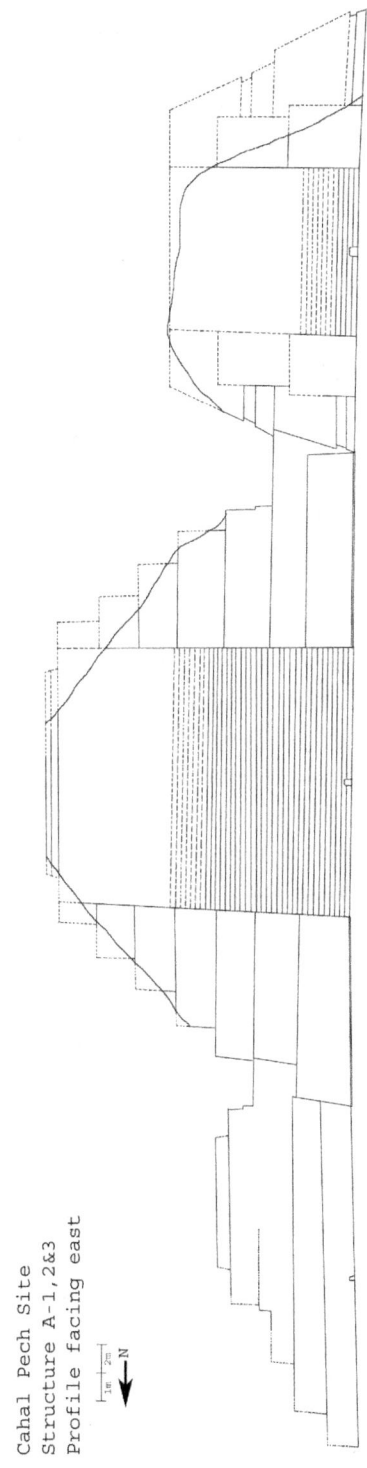

Figure 13.4. North–south profile of Eastern Triadic Assemblage at Cahal Pech.

Excavation of Str. 5-north recorded just four construction phases, reflecting "a shorter and less complex depositional history" than Str. 5-central (Robin et al. 2012:119–120). Str. 5-south was not excavated because it was severely looted. The investigations, nevertheless, revealed that Structure 5 at Chan did not attain its triadic form until the "Terminal Preclassic period (100/150–250 CE)."

At Xunantunich, excavations of the Eastern Triadic Structure in Plaza A revealed that the southern structure was erected in just two major construction phases, both in the Late Classic period. Surprisingly, the architectural morphologies of both phases are quite different. The first phase (A4-Sub) was represented by a low platform that supported a double vaulted building (Audet 2006:138–147). In contrast, the terminal phase of the structure was considerably taller than the first, but the summit of the pyramid was flat and supported no masonry superstructure. In the case of Structure A3, the central eastern building, excavations by Awe in 2015 revealed that it was primarily constructed in a single major construction episode, with only minor modifications to the original building. All major construction activity dated to the Late Classic period, with a few modifications dating to the Terminal Classic. Investigations of Str. A2, the northern structure, are still ongoing, but preliminary excavations also indicate that it may have been erected in no more than two construction phases dating to the Late Classic period.

Like most major sites in the greater Belize River valley, El Pilar also has an Eastern Triadic Structure with a pyramid to the west. The central structure of the eastern triadic group is designated as EP 7. Anabel Ford's (2004:253) investigation of looter's trenches in EP 7 recorded nine "major construction episodes" that spanned from the Middle Preclassic to the Terminal Classic. Interestingly, Ford (2004:253) reported that the first constructions of EP 7 faced east and then the structure was reoriented to face west in the Late Preclassic. Whether this also holds true for the northern and southern structures, and whether they share similar construction histories with EP 7, has yet to be determined.

At Blackman Eddy, considerable looting of the Eastern Triadic Assemblage also limited excavation efforts. In spite of this situation, Garber et al. (2004b) examined the central (Str. 1) and southern (Str. 4) structures and concluded that the two buildings were erected by at least Early Classic times and perhaps earlier. Height measurements of the architecture at Blackman Eddy also reflect similarities with Baking Pot, where the northern and southern structures are likely of similar height. What sets the Blackman

Eddy assemblage apart from all the other sites in the valley, however, is that a small structure was appended to both the northern and southern buildings of the triadic group.

When we review all this architectural information, several significant observations become apparent. First, the data indicate that the construction histories of buildings that form so-called E Group assemblages in the Belize River valley are not coeval and are not symmetrical. The data, in fact, clearly reflect considerable variation from site to site. The data further demonstrate that there are considerable differences between the Eastern Triadic Structures in the Belize Valley and the eastern structures of Uaxactún type E Groups. In the Belize River valley, for example, Eastern Triadic Structures were clearly constructed, or modified, independently of each other. This does not seem to be the case at Uaxactún. Second, and unlike the Uaxactún E Groups, the Belize Valley triadic buildings were not constructed on top of a shared substructural platform, and the three buildings eventually fuse into each other as a result of sequential increases in their size. Third, height measurements of the triadic structures in the Belize River valley vary substantially from site to site. This contrasts with the Uaxactún E Group and with others such as the E Group at Caracol (Chase and Chase 1987). Several other researchers have noted that there is considerable variation in the forms and size of E Groups across the Maya Lowlands (Aylesworth 2004). Aimers (1993) noted that most of them, particularly in the Belize River valley, simply do not perform well as observatories (for the accurate marking of solstices and/or equinoxes). It is therefore quite obvious that the forms of Eastern Triadic Assemblages in the Belize River valley are inconsistent with the architectural morphology of Uaxactún Style E Groups and that they likely never served as astronomical observatories in their terminal-phase constructions. Like many researchers working across the Maya Lowlands, however, we still lack chronological information for the first construction phases of most E Groups in the region.

Given the available data from the Belize Valley and other areas, we are skeptical of the astronomical function assigned a priori to these architectural assemblages by some researchers and find the equation of the functionally neutral term "E Group" with astronomical functions problematic. In fact, we are open to the argument that the assemblages we are discussing should not be called E Groups at all because of the baggage that the term has accumulated. This is why we also call them Eastern Triadic Assemblages when a western structure is present. But, given that the sites and buildings being discussed here are included in reviews of the E Group literature, we think that it is reasonable at this time to include these Eastern Triadic Assemblages as a type of E Group if we accept this as a purely morphological classification. We would also not be surprised if new excavations in other areas lead to new types of E Groups based purely on morphology. The possible astronomical alignment of many E Groups is still a question requiring excavation.

Monuments Associated with Eastern Triadic Structures in the Belize Valley

In their paper on E Groups, Aimers and Rice (2006:87) suggested that E Groups were used as settings for public celebrations of annual solar cycling (rather than as astronomically accurate observatories in a Western scientific sense) by the end of the Late Preclassic. "At some time thereafter, they came to be construed to celebrate longer calendrical cycles known as katuns and, possibly, longer cycles of 13 katuns, or approximately 256 years, called the *may* (see Rice 2004)." This conclusion was based on the observation that many K'atun-ending monuments in the Petén have been found in plazas containing E Group assemblages. In an effort to test whether this practice and tradition extended eastward, we examined the distribution of inscribed and plain monuments at several sites in the Belize River valley. Although the local traditions did not focus on carved monuments, uncarved stelae and altars are sometimes identified in public spaces in regional centers. This means that we do not have data available to test the hypothesis that these constructions were associated with ceremonies associated with K'atun-endings or other calendrical events. We would expect that if Eastern Triadic Assemblages served these purposes, as Aimers and Rice suggest, then monuments (carved or not) would be concentrated around these areas more so than in other public areas since K'atun-endings would be more frequent occasions than typical political events such as the birth, death, and ascension of rulers.

Plaza A at Blackman Eddy contains three stelae and one altar, but none of these were erected in front of the three eastern structures. Only one of the Blackman Eddy stelae is carved, which has an early 8th cycle date of 8.17.?.?.?. Unfortunately, the last three digits are poorly preserved, making it difficult to determine their actual numeric value. In spite of this, the eroded numbers look more like bars than zeros, so it is unlikely that the monument records a K'atun-ending (Christophe Helmke, personal communication, 2015). At Cahal Pech, there are plain stelae in front of the three structures in the triadic assemblage, but only the central and southern structures have stelae paired with altars. A fourth stela is located in front of a small temple (Str. B4) on the south side of the plaza. At Pacbitún, eight stelae and two altars were found in Plaza A (Healy 1990; Helmke et al. 2006b). Only one of the monuments, Stela 6, was carved, but it does not record a K'atun-ending date. Monuments in front of the three eastern buildings were all plain, and only the central structure had a stela-altar pair. A large fragment of another altar (Altar 3) was discovered cached in Str. 1. According to Helmke and Awe (2012:68), this monument "shows a standing ruler holding a bicephalic ceremonial bar across his chest, enclosed within the remains of a quatrefoil cartouche. The pose is rigid and the iconography stylized, a characteristic that places the monument somewhere in the latter half of the fifth century CE." Like Stela 6, Altar 3 at Pacbitún likely depicts a ruler but does not record a K'atun-ending event.

Nine stelae and three altars have been discovered in Plaza A (I-III) at Xunantunich (Helmke et al. 2006a, 2010). Three of these stelae and one of the altars are carved. The dates (820, 830, 849 CE) on the three inscribed stelae "all fall within a short period of three decades" (Helmke et al. 2010:107) and the Long Count dates on Stela 9 (10.0.0.0.0) and Stela 1 (10.1.0.0.0) suggest that they were likely erected to mark period-ending events. Interestingly, however, none of these period-ending monuments were erected in front of the triadic eastern structures. The three stelae and altars in front of the latter are all plain.

At Baking Pot, there are at least five plain monuments in the main plaza of Group A. Three of the monuments, all plain, are in front of the Eastern Triadic Structure. In contrast to Baking Pot and the other Belize River valley sites, no stelae were recorded in association with the Eastern Triadic Structures at El Pilar and Chan. The case of El Pilar is very intriguing, for this is a major center, much larger than several of the other Belize River valley sites. The absence of monuments at Pilar is therefore surprising, particularly given the size and monumentality of this site. Of course, it is possible that the site may have had carved monuments that were looted prior to their being recorded archaeologically. Alternatively, they may have been removed and redeposited in antiquity. As for Chan, the presence of an Eastern Triadic Assemblage and the absence of stelae reflect a pattern that appears to be typical at several medium and small Belize River valley sites. This is definitely the case at the Bedran group at Baking Pot (Figure 13.5), the BR 180 group at Barton Ramie (Figure 13.6; Willey et al. 1965:249–251, Figure 143), and Tzutziiy K'in outside Cahal Pech, all three small settlements (Figure

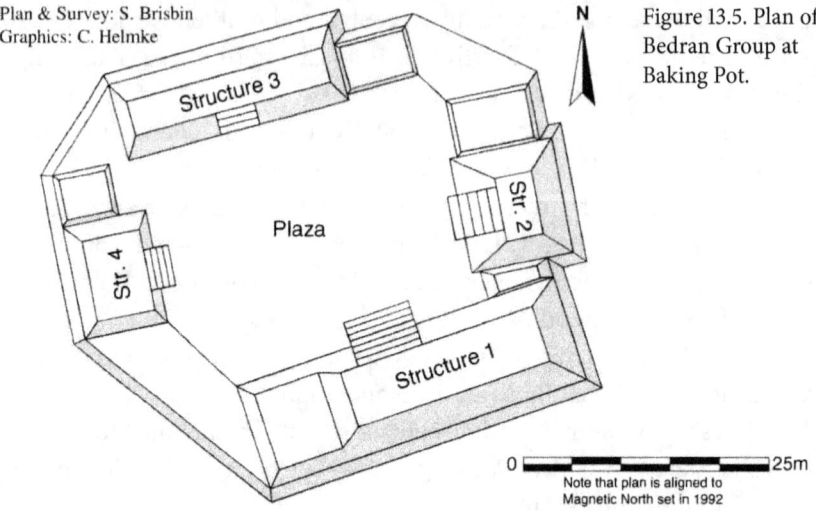

Figure 13.5. Plan of Bedran Group at Baking Pot.

13.2) in the peripheries of major centers in the Belize River valley. All three of these small settlements have Eastern Triadic Assemblages, but none have any stelae or altars. In spite of this, excavations on the central and northern triadic structures at Bedran (Conlon and Moore 2003; Conlon and Powis 2004; Colas et al. 2002) uncovered twelve burials and twenty-five caches. BR 180 at Barton Ramie was not excavated by Willey and his colleagues, so we have no burial data for that small settlement. Limited excavations at the Tzutziiy K'in settlement group west of Cahal Pech revealed one burial along the centerline of the central structure of the Eastern Triadic Group (Ebert and Fox 2015). An altar was identified directly above that burial and an additional uncarved altar in the plaza along the center-line in front of Str. 2. Investigations in the triadic structures at Zubin, however, another small settlement in the periphery of Cahal Pech, recorded thirteen burials and two caches in the central eastern structure (Iannone 1996).

Clearly, then, there are sites with Eastern Triadic Assemblages in the Belize River valley that completely lack plain or inscribed monuments but contain large numbers of burials and caches in their triadic architecture. Results of this study indicate that only four of the sites (Cahal Pech, Pacbitún, Baking Pot, and Xunantunich) in our sample have monuments in front of the buildings in the triadic assemblages. In a few cases, stelae were paired with altars, but this is the exception rather than the rule. These data do not offer sufficient support for the "valedictory" hypothesis, although admittedly a more thorough test would have been made possible by the presence/absence of calendar dates on associated monuments.

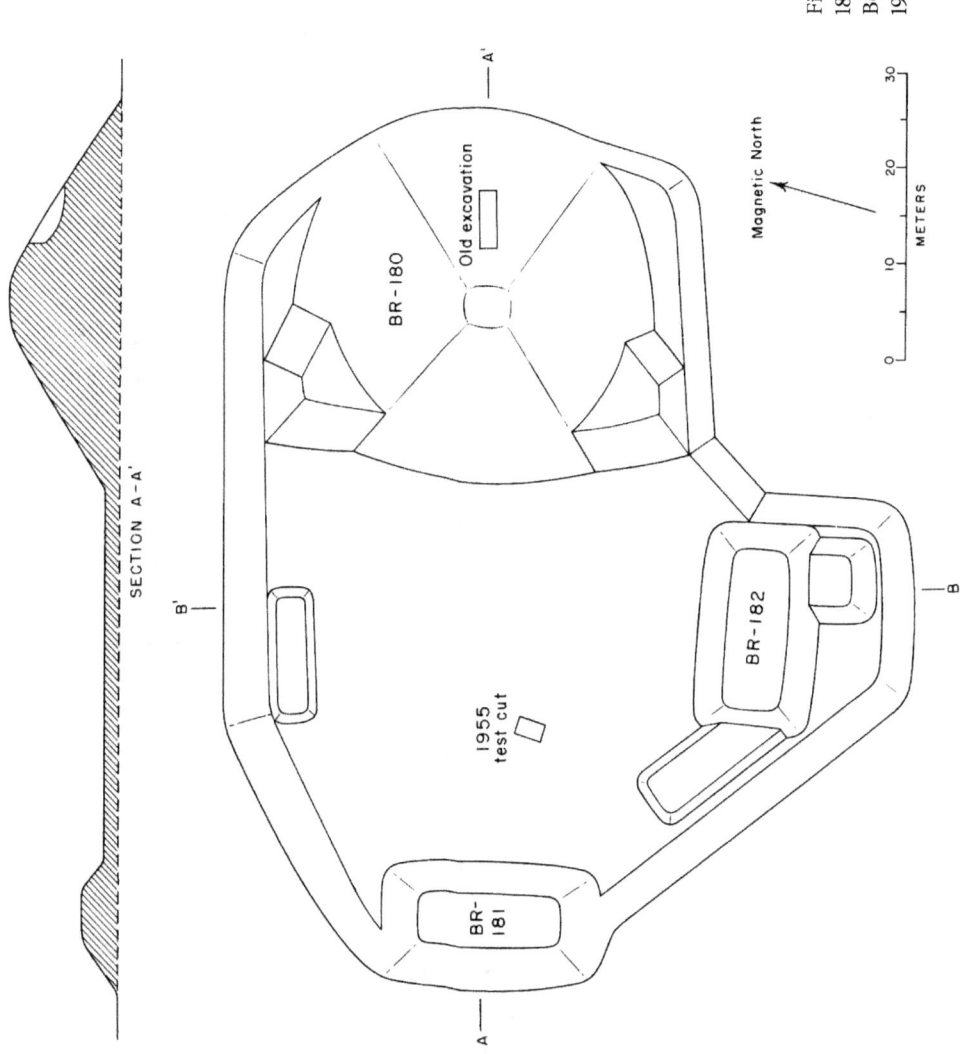

Figure 13.6. Plan of BR 180–182 at Barton Ramie, Belize (after Willey et al. 1965:Figure 143).

Burial and Cache Data from Eastern Triadic Assemblages in the Belize River Valley

The third part of the analysis explores the prospect of "E Group" architectural assemblages being associated with ancestor veneration rites, including burial of important personages and/or rulers. To do this, we focus attention on burial and cache data for each of the triadic structures of Belize River valley sites. Results of this study are provided in Table 13.2. After recording this information, the data were then compared with similar information from Uaxactún and Caracol, two sites with more typical E Group assemblages.

As Table 13.2 indicates, a total of eighteen burials and eight caches have been recovered in the three buildings of the Eastern Triadic Structure at Cahal Pech. Twelve of the eighteen burials, and six of the eight caches, were deposited along the primary axis of the central (Str. B1) building. The northern structure had two burials and the southern building had four burials and two caches. Examination of two looter's tunnels in the southern structure also indicates that the vandals may have located one, and possibly two, other burial(s) in this mound. The burials and caches in the Cahal Pech triadic assemblage ranged in date from the Late Middle Preclassic to the Terminal Classic period (Awe 2013). Interestingly, the two Terminal Classic burials were intrusive and associated with post abandonment activity at the site. Several of the Late Preclassic and Classic period burials were enclosed in vaulted tombs and contained exotic and high-quality grave goods. Inscriptions on three (deer antler, rings, and fragments of turtle shell, discovered in two separate tombs) bore royal titles that identified the name of the objects' owners (Santasilia 2012; Awe and Zender 2016). Because of the presence of these materials, plus the frequency of high-status burials and grave goods, Awe (2013) previously argued that most of the burials likely contained the remains of elite rulers and that the triadic buildings likely served as ancestral shrines.

Excavations at Pacbitún (Healy 1990 and personal communication, 2013; Healy et al. 2004a, 2004b) recovered thirty-seven burials and twenty caches. Twenty of the burials were discovered in the site's Eastern Triadic Assemblage. Six of these were found in the western, "radial" pyramid and fourteen were recovered in the Eastern Triadic Assemblage (nine in the central structure [Str. 1], three in the northern building [Str. 4], and two in the southern structure [Str. 5]). The fourteen burials ranged in date from the Late Preclassic to the Terminal Classic period. Eleven of the twenty

Table 13.2. Frequency of burials and caches in Eastern Triadic Structures in the Belize River valley site cores

Site name	Total # of burials/caches	Central structure	Northern structure	Southern structure
Cahal Pech	18 bur./8 caches	12 bur./6 caches	2 bur.	4 bur./2 caches*
Pacbitun	14 bur./11 caches	9 bur./9 caches	3 bur./1 cache	2 bur./1 cache
Baking Pot	4 bur./4 caches	4 bur./4 caches	NDA	NDA
Chan	9 bur./8 caches	8 bur./5 caches*	1 bur./3 caches*	NDA
Xunantunich	3 bur./5 caches	0 bur./2 caches	0 bur./0 caches	3 bur./3 caches
Blackman Eddy	4 bur./1 cache	1 cache*	NDA*	4 bur.*
El Pilar	NDA	NDA*	NDA	NDA

Note: "NDA" indicates no data available for site, and asterisk indicates that structure was looted.

caches discovered at the site were also found in the triadic buildings. Nine were recovered in the central (Str. 1) structure, and one each from the northern and southern buildings. In their discussion of the Pacbitún burials, Healy et al. (2004a) note that Burial BU 1-9, discovered in the central triadic structure, was the most impressive elite burial at the site. They also argue that this burial likely contained one of the Classic period rulers from Pacbitún and state: "The pattern of elite burials in Structure 1, virtually all on the central axis, provides another example of the use of ancestors to delineate an *axis mundi*" (2004a:229).

Fewer burials and caches have been recovered at Baking Pot for the simple reason that only limited investigations have been conducted on the triadic assemblage at this site. Notwithstanding this situation, two small excavations in the central eastern structure (Str. E central) recovered four burials and four caches, and an excavation on the western structure located a single large grave (Audet 2006:175–213). Two of the four burials found in Str. E-central were located at the summit of the mound, and the other two burials and four caches were recovered at the base of the building. The two summit burials (Burials 1 and 2) were both interred in vaulted tombs and contained the remains of a male and female, respectively, accompanied by a large number of sumptuous grave goods. The quantity and quality of these clearly indicate that both individuals were of very high rank. The deposition of Burial 1, between layers of chert flakes and obsidian blades, led Carolyn Audet (2006:180) to suggest that the deceased was symbolically "laid to rest in the watery underworld domain of the rain god." She further claimed: "This symbolic combination of water and human flesh. . . . made from maize were the essence of life, fertility and rebirth" (2006:180).

Investigations of Str. 5-central of the triadic structure at Chan recovered eight burials and eight caches. These deposits were all placed along the primary axis of the structure and were associated with "nearly every construction phase" (Meierhoff et al. 2004:37). The northern building contained one burial and three caches. The southern structure was not excavated because it had been severely looted. Excavations into the western structure of the assemblage recovered five burials. All contained the remains of juveniles, interestingly, oriented predominantly with their heads to the north (Robin et al. 2008). This orientation differs from the traditional head to the south position of Belize River Valley burials. In his discussion of the Chan burials, Kestle (2004:45) concluded: "The consistent and formal placement of burials and caches in Str. 5-north, like Str. 5-center, supports the identification of Str. 5 as a tripartite eastern ancestral shrine." Robin et al. (2012:122) reiterated this position, suggesting: "Like other E-Groups, Chan's E-Group served as a shrine for a select group of ancestors from the community."

The Eastern Triadic Assemblage at Xunantunich was the focus of archaeological investigations in 2002 and in 2015, both projects under the direction of Awe. Excavations of the southern building recovered three burials and four caches (Audet 2006:140–146). The most elaborate burial consisted of a crypt that contained the remains of a single male individual. Associated grave goods included polychrome ceramic vessels, several chert and obsidian eccentrics, and jade jewelry. After the deceased had been interred in the grave, the body and grave goods were blanketed with a layer of cinnabar. Based on the architectural context of the burial, the quality of the grave goods, and the treatment of the dead, Audet (2006:146) concluded that the grave most likely contained the remains of an elite male individual. Investigations of the central structure in 2015 yielded no elite burials, but two caches were recovered along the structure's primary east–west axis. The first cache contained eighteen eccentrics, nine made of chert and nine of obsidian. The second cache included a large jade bead, a stingray spine, a large marine shell, and sixty-two jute (*Pachychilus* sp.) shells.

At Blackman Eddy, James Garber designated the structures of the Eastern Triadic Structure as Str. 1 (central), Str. 2 (north), and Str. 4 (south) (Garber et al. 2004a). Because the buildings were heavily looted, Garber focused only limited research attention on them. On Str. 1, the investigations cleared out a looter's trench and recovered a single cache. Excavations on Str. 4, where another looter's trench and tunnel had gutted the building's primary axis, revealed a looted crypt and a single Early Classic ceramic vessel that the looters had missed. Further clearing of the looter's trench uncovered three more burials (Garber et al. 2004b:61–62). Two of these were secondary burials consisting of only skulls and long bones. Garber et al. (2004b:61) concluded that the presence of these secondary burials was very likely linked to the practice of "ancestor veneration" and that the axial location of the crypt and burials "may have been the primary reason for the construction of Structure A4."

In the case of El Pilar, only the central structure (EP 7) of the Eastern Triadic Structure has received limited archaeological attention. As indicated previously, this investigation (Ford 2004:253) focused on a looter's trench along the primary axis of the building and recorded nine "major construction episodes" spanning from the Middle Preclassic to the Terminal Classic period. Unfortunately, it appears that any burial or cache that the structure may have contained was discovered by the looters. Future investigations of the northern and southern buildings may provide information on special deposits in the triadic assemblage of this site.

In sum, extensive archaeological data from sites across the Belize River valley offer a great deal of support for the use of Eastern Triadic Assemblages in association with dynastic interment and ancestor veneration rites. In contrast with the available data on the architectural variability and locations of carved monuments in public areas, the ancestral shrine hypothesis has the strongest support in the archaeological record of Belize River valley sites. The lack of strong support for astronomical functions suggests that ancestor veneration was not a secondary function but rather the primary purpose of Eastern Triadic Assemblages in the Belize River valley.

Discussion

During the last ninety years, at least six functional explanations have been proposed for E Groups. Frans Blom's original suggestion that they were used as astronomical observatories was followed by other hypotheses arguing for their use in scheduling agricultural or trade activities, for agricultural celebrations, for use in geomantic systems, and more recently for the performance of ancestor rituals or settings for valedictory ceremonies associated with K'atun-endings.

The longest-lived and influential functional association of E Groups is that they served to mark and commemorate important annual positions of the sun: the solstices, equinoxes, and zeniths. Although many scholars, including most of those in this volume, support this idea, it has never been clear as a whole for the many assemblages identified as E Groups. In the sample discussed here, these astronomical alignments are problematic for a number of reasons, including the actual orientation of the buildings and their construction histories. Those studies that support this functional hypothesis often have not pursued sufficient excavations to test this proposition for early construction phases. As we noted above, several of the "E Groups" or Eastern Triadic Assemblages discussed here did not begin as unified structures at all. In other cases (such as Pacbitún), background hills or other structures appear higher than the structures themselves, making the postulated role of the architecture as markers problematic. Because there is so much variation in E Group morphology, truly firm conclusions about the astronomical orientations of E Groups are likely to have to be drawn on a site-by-site basis in conjunction with excavation.

Previous research by several scholars and the archaeological data presented above have also negated the agricultural and trade scheduling hypotheses. Evidence for the influence of a system of geomancy at some sites is increasing (see Chapters 7 and 9 in this volume; Blake 2013), but more work needs to be done. What remains to be tested further were the arguments that E Groups were likely used for ancestor rituals or for valedictory ceremonies associated with calendrical cycles.

Aimers and Rice (2006:92) argued: "The large number of katun monuments in E-Group plazas convinces us that E-Groups were early settings for valedictory ceremonies similar to those associated with the Late Classic twin pyramid complexes at Tikal and related sites." Critical to their argument is the presence or absence of K'atun-ending monuments in plazas with E Groups. As the authors point out, this is not an issue with some of the sites in the central Petén (those that have stelae with K'atun-ending dates). The problem becomes evident with sites in other Lowland Maya subregions that have E Group–like assemblages but no inscribed stelae. Of course, we could assume that plain monuments at these sites were originally carved, stuccoed, or painted, but even if so we would have no way to know what the inscriptions on the stelae might have referred to. We also cannot neglect sites such as Blackman Eddy and Pacbitún, which have carved stelae in plazas with triadic assemblages that do not refer to K'atun-ending events. The lack of monuments (carved or uncarved) around E Groups is also true for several sites in the Belize River valley, including large centers such as El Pilar, Saturday Creek (Runggaldier et al. 2013), and possibly Yalbac (Lucero 2008 notes that a large boulder in Plaza 3 might be a stela). In sum, the period-ending hypothesis of Aimers and Rice is not supported by carved monument data for Eastern Triadic Assemblages in the Belize River valley.

We should note, however, that K'atun-ending celebrations appear to have been manifested differently from region to region. For example, Tikal constructed Twin Pyramid Complexes, Caracol dedicated large Ahau altars, and other sites commemorated K'atun-ending periods by erecting stelae. These different practices are typical of the regionalism found in many artifact assemblages and practices across the Maya Lowlands (such as mortuary practices: Scherer 2015). Caches are one of the most common deposits that we find in Belize Valley ETAs. It is possible, therefore, that placing caches in ETSs may have occurred during K'atun-ending celebrations. This hypothesis is difficult to test, but worth noting. E Groups with numerous caches are also found in the Petén (for example, at Tikal and Uaxactún). Thus, although we cannot rule out the K'atun-ending hypothesis in the Belize River valley, it makes sense to look for alternative or possibly additional roles for these morphologically distinctive assemblages.

One such function is the ancestor veneration hypothesis proposed by Arlen Chase (1983) and by Chase and Chase (1995). The Chases (1995:100) contend that E Groups represent an architectural hallmark for the transition "of Preclassic Maya society into its Classic Period socio-political and dynastic patterns." The coeval and associated rise of the "stelae cult" at this time was also indicative of the growing importance of "rulership and centralized authority": "Nowhere . . . can this juxtaposition be more clearly seen than in the purposeful placement of important burials in the formal civic buildings of the E-Group assemblage" (Chase and Chase 1995:100). Aimers (1993:186–188) linked this to a changing emphasis on the nature of time from cyclical (in relation to agricultural cycles) to linear (in relation to dynastic history) (see also Aimers and Rice 2006:92) If we accept the Chases' argument that during the Late Preclassic to Early Classic transition E Groups began to be used as ancestral shrines and for publicly reflecting the authority of elite rulers, then we should expect these architectural assemblages to have certain characteristics. First, they should be located in public, open-access courtyards rather than in plazas with restricted access. Second, the plazas and triadic assemblages should contain or be associated with carved and uncarved monuments. Third, the buildings in the triadic assemblages should contain a significant number of elite burials.

In respect to the first criterion, there is not a single example of an Eastern Triadic Assemblage in the Belize River valley that delimits a restricted access plaza (see Awe 2008). Indeed, every site in our sample and all others listed by Aimers and Rice (2006) are located in public access plazas (see Aimers 1993:Table 3). This same pattern is evident in northern Belize and in the central Petén. Given this spatial configuration, it is obvious that activities conducted on or around Eastern Triadic Assemblages were for public participation.

When we examine the spatial distribution of monuments in Belize River valley sites, a similar pattern emerges. Plazas with Eastern Triadic Assemblages contain the largest number of carved and/or plain monuments. The same holds true for sites like Caracol and several others in the central Petén (Chase and Chase 1995). One of the few sites that diverges from this pattern is Tikal. But here again the majority of monuments are located in one of their most public plazas and, interestingly, the largest number of elite tombs and burials have been found within buildings encircling this courtyard (the great plaza).

Turning to burials, our study of triadic assemblages in the Belize River valley clearly demonstrates that, in comparison with other buildings, these structures contain a disproportionate number of elite graves. At Pacbitún, for example, twenty-one of the thirty-seven burials excavated at the site were discovered in the "E Group" (Healy, personal communication, 2013) and Str. 1 (the central building) had more interments than any other structure at the site. This same pattern is repeated at Cahal Pech and at Chan and also holds true for smaller sites like Bedran and Zubin. As we noted above, the central structure in the triadic assemblage at Cahal Pech alone contained twelve burials and several caches. At Chan, archaeologists found eight burials and five caches in the central structure, and this does not account for similar deposits that were likely looted from this building. The preponderance of special deposits in these assemblages may actually explain why looters target these buildings in their search for objects to supply the illegal antiquities market.

High frequencies of burials and caches have also been documented in E Groups outside of the Belize River valley. Chase and Chase (1995:93) report that this was certainly the case at the Petén site of Cenote. Here, too, the majority of burials and caches were located in the central structure of the E Group and included, among other things, lip-to-lip vessels with a skull inside. In their study of the Tikal Group, Laporte and Fialko (1990) noted that, while burials are not frequently discovered in central Petén E Groups, this is not the case for Tikal, where a series of important deposits and elaborate burials were recovered in the triadic buildings. In reference to the Tikal interments, Chase and Chase (1995:95) commented: "The high status" of the individuals in the burials "is evident both in their placement and in the grave goods that accompany them." Laporte and Fialko (1990:45) also noted that the most ostentatious chamber (and perhaps the earliest) in the E Group may be attributable to one of Tikal's early rulers, "Jaguar Paw III." Although Laporte and Fialko suggest that elite burials are rare at Uaxactún, it is important to point out that Ricketson and Ricketson (1937:49–58) did report on a number of burials and caches in this site's E Group. On Str. E1, they uncovered a cache containing pottery sherds and a cist containing lip-to-lip vessels encasing a skull with jadeite objects. Structure E2, the central building, had three cists. One contained the body of a child and a single ceramic vessel, the second had lip-to-lip vessels containing a skull, and the third had two lip-to-lip vessels encasing two obsidian blades. Structure E3 (southern) had three cists; two contained lip-to-lip vessels with skulls in them. The western radial structure (EVII) had one burial and three caches. While some archaeologists (Laporte and Fialko 1990; Aylesworth 2004) interpret the skulls encased in lip-to-lip vessels as examples of sacrificial victims, there is evidence to suggest that they more likely represent the exhumed and redeposited remains of venerated ancestors (see below and also McAnany 1995, 1998).

South of the Belize River valley, at Caracol, archaeologists discovered a number of special deposits in that site's E Group. In the north building (Str. A5), which was looted, a Terminal Classic tomb was located at the base of its central stairway, and "there were two distinct areas with human remains included in the fill at the building's summit" (Arlen Chase, personal communication, 2013). Structure A7, the southern building, had a large tomb dating to the late Early Classic. Two ancillary structures, A4 and A8, contained two tombs and a cache, respectively, and Structure A6, the central building, had two tombs at the base of the stairway and six caches along the primary axis.

In their explanation of the frequency of burials in the Eastern Triadic Assemblage at Chan, Robin et al. (2012:122) concluded that "the E-Group is a ritual architectural complex that is collectively dedicated to the veneration of select ancestors at Chan." Along the same line, Healy et al. (2004a:229) stated: "The pattern of elite burials in Structure 1 [at Pacbitún], virtually all on the central axis, provides another example of the use of ancestors to delineate an *axis mundi.*" This position echoes an earlier statement by McAnany (1998:271), who argued that the "incorporation of ancestors into monumental architecture" served "to establish a political and ritual *axis mundi*." If we apply these perspectives to our examination of the burial data from Eastern Triadic Assemblages in the Belize River valley, it becomes readily apparent that the data strongly support the Chases' contention that their primary function was related to ancestor rituals. More specifically, we contend that public rituals on Eastern Triadic Assemblages in the Belize River valley focused particularly on the burial and veneration of deceased rulers/ancestors. This observation is suggested not only by the significant number of burials in these buildings but particularly by the frequency of elaborate elite (royal) tombs and secondary burials, often represented by skulls encased in lip-to-lip vessels. With the exception of Blackman Eddy and El Pilar, which were either severely looted or minimally investigated, elaborate royal tombs were discovered in the triadic assemblages of Cahal Pech (Awe 2013), Pacbitún (Healy et al 2004a), and Baking Pot and Xunantunich (Audet 2006). Elite burials were also concentrated in the Eastern Triadic Structures at the smaller site of Chan. According to Healy et al. (2004a:235–236), the interment of rulers in triadic shrines ensured that:

> These powerful individuals continued to influence Classic Maya society well beyond their mortal life spans. The presence of their bodily remains housed in some of the most impressive and centrally located architecture at Maya centers likely became foci for numerous later elaborate rituals and commemorations. These entombed ancestors functioned to link new rulers to familial bloodlines and the inheritance of political power, status, and wealth (McAnany 1995). In this sense, Pacbitún BU 1-9 clearly reinforces the notion of a widely held Classic Maya "royal cult and kingship."

As for secondary burials, it is widely accepted that these interments primarily incorporate the remains of deceased ancestors that were exhumed from their original graves (see McAnany 1995, 1998, Awe 2013). When we examine the burial data from triadic assemblages in the Belize River valley and the Petén, it is readily apparent that one of the most common types of secondary burials in these structures is represented by skulls and bony fragments encased within lip-to-lip vessels. In a previous discussion of Middle and Late Preclassic examples of this type of interment at Cahal Pech, Garber and Awe (2008:187; also Awe 2013:38–40) suggested that this practice likely reflects an ideological concept that was closely connected to the Maya creation story and the myth of the Hero Twins. We argue that the skull is representative of the severed head of the Maize God, the deity whose persona was commonly appropriated by Late Preclassic and Classic period Maya rulers. The placement of skulls within lip-to-lip ceramic vessels is a symbolic representation of the Maize God's skull lying within the underworld. The burial of the skull encased in the lip-to-lip vessels within a temple is thus synonymous with the severed head of Hunapu lying in a cave within the sacred mountain. In the ancient Maya creation story, after the Hero Twins defeat the Lords of Death, they retrieve the severed head of their father. The head is then taken to the Three Stone Place of creation, where it is resurrected as the Maize God.

We further posit that a likely explanation for the triadic pattern of the so-called E Groups in the Belize River valley is that they were symbolic representations of the importance of the number three in Maya cosmology. The importance of "triads" in Maya ideology was likely tied to the mythical three hearthstone place described in the Popol Vuh. Creation and the rebirth of sacred ancestors take place at the three hearthstone place (Freidel et al. 1993; Taube 1998:432–446). Taube (1998:433) adds that "for the Classic Maya, the sacred hearth is also portrayed as a watery place and frequently fuses with the verdant ceiba, or *yax che*, also marking the world center." The concepts of creation and rebirth may also explain the reason for locating triadic ancestral shrines on the east side of the plaza. This tradition (see McAnany 1995:55) very likely reflects the belief or concept that, like the sun that is born or reborn everyday in the east, the spirits of deceased ancestors were interred within Eastern Triadic Assemblages. The regular placement of ruler tombs, and secondary burials, in Eastern Triadic Assemblages in the Belize River valley certainly lends support to this idea. This position is shared by Robin et al. (2012:122), who suggest: "The focal nature of the east structure is not surprising, as east represents the position of the rising sun and considered the dominant direction along the east-west axis." Assuming that this hypothesis is accurate, it may also explain why there is so much variation in the architecture of triadic assemblages. As Aimers and Rice (2006:82) note, "examination of site and structure plans provided little indication of strict rules regarding the morphology of the E-Group. Each site seemed to be a variation on a recognizable theme." Maintaining symmetry of the architecture for astronomical purposes does not, therefore, appear to have been a critical concern to the Maya. This is demonstrated by the variability in the heights, orientations of structures, and architectural disparities as identified from the E Groups of the Belize River valley. In contrast, locating the triadic structures on the eastern side of public plazas may have been far more important for ideological reasons than for astronomical or calendrical purposes. In the end, "Classic Maya royal ancestor veneration became an overtly political institution couched within a grand cosmological scheme" (McAnany 1998:281).

Conclusion

During the last two decades, several researchers have included a number of Belize Valley centers in lists of sites containing E Group complexes. In large part, this identification was based primarily on the study of published site plans. Actual archaeological investigation of these centers now suggests that what we are calling Eastern Triadic Assemblages differ substantially from the archetypal E Group identified at Uaxactún, that there is considerable variation in their architectural morphology, and that they did not accurately mark the solstices and equinoxes, although some more general solar symbolism may have been part of their original design or their modification. On the basis of these empirical data, we refer to them instead as Eastern Triadic Assemblages. Additionally, we propose that the central function for these buildings was as ancestor shrines.

Archaeological investigations in the Belize River valley have found that Eastern Triadic Assemblages have a long history of construction and use. Early examples, like those at Cahal Pech and Pacbitún, likely had their origins in the Middle Preclassic period. By Late Preclassic times, they had been established at Cahal Pech, Pacbitún, and Chan. During Early Classic times, they were present at all major and some minor centers and continued to be used into the Terminal Classic period (for example, Xunantunich).

Our study of triadic assemblages also reveals that none of the sites in the Belize River valley, except for Xunantunich, contain monuments that record K'atun-endings. Unfortunately, we will never know whether plain monuments at sites such as Cahal Pech, Baking Pot, and Pacbitún were actually erected to mark these events or whether the large number of caches discovered in Eastern Triadic Structures were deposited to mark the completion of K'atun cycles. Nevertheless, on the basis of available data, the hypotheses that Eastern Triadic Assemblages were used as settings for "valedictory ceremonies" is not clearly supported in the Belize River valley. What archaeological investigations there do establish is that significant numbers of elite burials were deposited in Eastern Triadic Assemblages by at least the Late Preclassic period. In addition to "royal" interments, a substantial number of these burials are represented by skulls encased in lip-to-lip vessels, a practice that we believe was ideologically related to the death and rebirth of the Maize God as described in the Popol Vuh. The frequency of tombs and elite graves and the symbolically laden lip-to-lip burials lead us to conclude that the primary function of these Eastern Triadic Structures was for the interment of elite rulers and for rituals associated with ancestor veneration.

Acknowledgments

The research reported herein could not have been accomplished without the support and assistance of a number of friends and colleagues. Particular gratitude is extended to the Tilden Family Foundation for their financial support to the Belize Valley Archaeological Reconnaissance (BVAR) project. A special thank you to Doug Tilden, Catharina Santasilia, Mark Zender, Reiko Ishihara, Ashley McKeown, Mat Saunders, Jim Conlon, and the BVAR crews who, over the years, worked tirelessly on the excavations of the triadic assemblage at Cahal Pech, Baking Pot, Bedran, and Xunantunich. Gratitude is certainly owed to Jorge Can, Josue Ramos, Jordan Smith, Gabe Bram, Toni Beardall, and Merle Alfaro for assisting us with the mapping of the triadic assemblages in the Belize River valley. Thanks as well to our colleagues Paul Healy, Arlen Chase, and Cynthia Robin for their collaboration and for sharing their site data. Finally, we want to thank our colleagues at the Belize Institute of Archaeology for their continued support of our research and thank John Morris for his constructive comments on our ideas.

References Cited

Aimers, James J.
- 1993 An Hermeneutic Analysis of the Maya E-Group Complex. M.A. thesis, Department of Anthropology, Trent University, Peterborough, Ontario, Canada.
- 1997 Preliminary Investigations of Architecture in Plaza 2 of Group 1 at Baking Pot, Belize. In A Report on the 1996 Field Season: The Belize River Valley Archaeological Project, edited by Jaime J. Awe and James M. Conlon, pp. 21–46. Department of Anthropology, Trent University, Peterborough, Ontario, Canada.

Aimers, James J., and Prudence M. Rice
- 2006 Astronomy, Ritual, and the Interpretation of Maya "E-Group" Architectural Assemblages. *Ancient Mesoamerica* 17:79–96.

Audet, Carolyn M.
- 2006 Political Organization in the Belize Valley: Excavations at Baking Pot, Cahal Pech and Xunantunich. Ph.D. dissertation, Vanderbilt University, Nashville, Tennessee.

Aveni, Anthony F.
- 1991 The Real Venus: Kukulkan in the Maya Inscriptions and Alignments. In *Sixth*

Mesa Redonda de Palenque 1986, edited by Virginia Fields, pp. 309–321. University of Oklahoma Press, Norman.

Aveni, Anthony F., Anne S. Dowd, and Benjamin Vining
2003   Maya Calendar Reform?: Evidence from Orientations of Specialized Architectural Assemblages. *Latin American Antiquity* 14(2):159–178.

Aveni, Anthony F., and Horst Hartung
1989   Uaxactún, Guatemala Group E and Similar Assemblages: An Archaeoastronomical Reconsideration. In *World Archaeoastronomy*, edited by Anthony F. Aveni, pp. 441–461. Cambridge University Press, Cambridge.

Awe, Jaime J.
1992   Dawn in the Land between the Rivers: Formative Occupation at Cahal Pech, Belize and Its Implications for Preclassic Development in the Maya Lowlands. Ph.D. dissertation, University of London, England.
2008   Architectural Manifestations of Power and Prestige: Examples from Classic Period Monumental Architecture at Cahal Pech, Xunantunich and Caracol, Belize. *Research Reports in Belizean Archaeology* 5:159–174.
2013   Journey on the Cahal Pech Time Machine: An Archaeological Reconstruction of the Dynastic Sequence at a Belize Valley Polity. *Research Reports in Belizean Archaeology* 10:33–50.

Awe, Jaime J., Claire E. Ebert, and Julie A. Hoggarth
2015   Three K'atuns of Pioneering Settlement Research: Preliminary Results of the Lidar Survey in the Belize River Valley. In *Breaking Barriers: Proceedings of the 47th Annual Chacmool Conference,* pp. 57–75. University of Calgary, Calgary, Alberta, Canada.

Awe, Jaime J., and Marc Zender
2016   K'awiil Chan K'inich, K'an Bahlam: Royal Titles and Symbols of Rulership at Cahal Pech, Belize. *Mexicon* 28(6):157–165.

Aylesworth, Grant R.
2002   Ancient Maya E-Group Architectural Complexes. Master's thesis, Department of Anthropology, Tulane University, New Orleans.
2004   Astronomical Interpretations of Ancient Maya E-Group Architectural Complexes. *Archaeoastronomy: The Journal of Astronomy in Culture* 18:34–66.

Blake, Michael
2013   Solar Orientations and Formative Period Site Layouts in Southeast Mesoamerica: Sunrise and Sunset Alignments during the Equinoxes and Solstices. Paper presented at the Society for American Archaeology 78th Annual Meeting, Honolulu, Hawaii, April 3–7, 2013.

Blom, Frans
1924   Report on the Preliminary Work at Uaxactún, Guatemala. *Carnegie Institution of Washington Yearbook* 23:217–219.

Carlson, John
1981   A Geomantic Model for the Interpretation of Mesoamerican Sites: An Essay in Cross-Cultural Comparison. In *Mesoamerican Sites and World-Views*, edited by Elizabeth P. Benson, pp. 143–215. Dumbarton Oaks, Washington, D.C.

Chase, Arlen F.
1983   A Contextual Consideration of the Tayasal-Paxcaman Zone, El Peten, Guatemala. Ph.D. dissertation, Department of Anthropology, University of Pennsylvania, Philadelphia.

Chase, Arlen F., and Diane Z. Chase
1987   *Investigations at the Classic Maya City of Caracol, Belize: 1985–1987.* Pre-Columbian Art Research Institute Monograph 3. Pre-Columbian Art Research Institute, San Francisco, California.
1995   External Impetus, Internal Synthesis, and Standardization: E-Group Assemblages and the Crystallization of Classic Maya Society in the Southern Lowlands. *Acta Mesoamericana* 8:87–101 (special issue edited by Nikolai Grube entitled *The Emergence of Lowland Maya Civilization: The Transition from the Preclassic to Early Classic*).

Chase, Arlen F., Diane Z. Chase, Jaime J. Awe, John F. Weishampel, Gyles Iannone, Holley Moyes, Jason Yaeger, Kathryn Brown, Ramesh L. Shrestha, William E. Carter, and Juan Fernández Díaz
2014   Ancient Maya Regional Settlement and Inter-Site Analysis: The 2013 West-Central Belize LiDAR Survey. *Remote Sensing* 6(9):8671–8695.

Chase, Arlen F., Diane Z. Chase, Christopher T. Fisher, Stephen J. Leisz, and John F. Weishampel
2012   Geospatial Revolution and Remote Sensing LiDAR in Mesoamerican Archaeology. *Proceedings of the National Academy of Sciences* 109(32):12916–12921.

Chase, Arlen F., Diane Z. Chase, John F. Weishampel, Jason B. Drake, Ramesh L. Shrestha, K. Clint Slatton, Jaime J. Awe, and William E. Carter
2011   Airborne LiDAR, Archaeology, and the Ancient Maya Landscape at Caracol, Belize. *Journal of Archaeological Science* 38(2):387–398.

Coggins, Clemency
1983   *The Stucco Decoration and Architectural Assemblage of Structure 1-SUB, Dzibilchaltun, Yucatan, Mexico.* Publication 49, Middle American Research Institute. Tulane University, New Orleans.

Cohodas, Marvin
1980   Radial Pyramids and Radial Associated Assemblages of the Central Maya Area. *Journal of the Society of Architectural Historians* 39(3):208–223.

Colas, Pierre R., Christophe Helmke, Jaime J. Awe, and Terry G. Powis
2002   Epigraphic and Ceramic Analyses of Two Early Classic Maya Vessels from Baking Pot, Belize. *Mexicon* 24(2):33–39.

Conlon, James
2013   Archaeological Investigations of Structure B-3, Cahal Pech: A Preliminary Report. In Belize Valley Archaeological Reconnaissance Project: Report of the 2012 Season, edited by Julie Hoggarth and Jaime J. Awe, pp. 60–70. Institute of Archaeology, Belmopan, Belize.

Conlon, James, and Allan F. Moore
2003   Identifying Urban and Rural Settlement Components: An Examination of Classic Period Plazuela Group Function at the Ancient Maya Site of Baking Pot, Belize. In *Perspectives on Ancient Maya Rural Complexity*, edited by Gyles

Iannone and Samuel V. Connell, pp. 59–70. Monograph 49. Cotsen Institute of Archaeology, University of California, Los Angeles.

Conlon, James, and Terry G. Powis
2004 Major Center Identifiers at a Plazuela Group near the Ancient Maya Site of Baking Pot. In *The Ancient Maya of the Belize Valley: Half a Century of Archaeological Research*, edited by James F. Garber, pp. 70–85. University Press of Florida, Gainesville.

Doyle, James
2012 Regroup on E-Groups: Monumentality and Early Centers in the Middle Preclassic Maya Lowlands. *Latin American Antiquity* 23(4):355–379.

Ebert, Claire E. and Steven Fox
2016 The 2015 Settlement Excavations at Cahal Pech, Belize: Continued Research at Tzutziiy K'in, the Zopilote Group, and the Martinez Group. In *The Belize Valley Archaeological Reconnaissance Project: A Report of the 2015 Field Season*, edited by Julie A. Hoggarth and Jaime J. Awe, pp. 80–112. Institute of Archaeology, Baylor University, Waco, Texas.

Ford, Anabel
2004 Integration among Communities, Centers, and Regions: The Case from El Pilar. In *The Ancient Maya of the Belize Valley: Half a Century of Archaeological Research*, edited by James F. Garber, pp. 238–256. University Press of Florida, Gainesville.

Freidel, David A., Linda Schele, and Joy Parker
1993 *Maya Cosmos*. William Morrow, New York.

Garber, James F., and Jaime J. Awe
2008 Middle Formative Architecture and Ritual at Cahal Pech. *Research Reports in Belizean Archaeology* 5:185–190.

Garber, James F., M. Kathryn Brown, Jaime J. Awe, and Christopher J. Hartman
2004a Middle Formative Prehistory of the Central Belize Valley: An Examination of Architecture, Material Culture, and Sociopolitical Change at Blackman Eddy. In *The Ancient Maya of the Belize Valley: Half a Century of Archaeological Research*, edited by James F. Garber, pp. 25–47. University Press of Florida, Gainesville.

Garber, James F., M. Kathryn Brown, W. David Brown, David M. Glassman, Christopher J. Hartman, F. Kent Reilly III, and Lauren A. Sullivan
2004b Archaeological Investigations at Blackman Eddy. In *The Ancient Maya of the Belize Valley: Half a Century of Archaeological Research*, edited by James F. Garber, pp. 48–69. University Press of Florida, Gainesville.

Guderjan, Thomas H.
2006 E-Groups, Pseudo-E-Groups, and the Development of the Classic Maya Identity in the Eastern Petén. *Ancient Mesoamerica* 17:97–104.

Hansen, Richard D.
1998 Continuity and Disjunction: The Pre-Classic Antecedents of Classic Maya Architecture. In *Function and Meaning in Classic Maya Architecture*, edited by Stephen D. Houston, pp. 49–122. Dumbarton Oaks Research Library and Collection, Washington, D.C.

Healy, Paul F.
1990 Excavations at Pacbitún, Belize: Preliminary Report on the 1986 and 1987 Investigations. *Journal of Field Archaeology* 17:242–262.

Healy, Paul F., Jaime J. Awe, and Herman Helmuth
2004a Defining Royal Maya Burials: A Case from Pacbitún, Belize. In *The Ancient Maya of the Belize Valley: Half a Century of Archaeological Research*, edited by James F. Garber, 228–237. University Press of Florida, Gainesville.

Healy, Paul F., Bobbi Hohmann, and Terry G. Powis
2004b The Ancient Maya Center of Pacbitún. In *The Ancient Maya of the Belize Valley: Half a Century of Archaeological Research*, edited by James F. Garber, 207–227. University Press of Florida, Gainesville.

Helmke, Christophe, and Jaime J. Awe
2012 Ancient Maya Territorial Organization of Central Belize: Confluence of Archaeological and Epigraphic Data. *Contributions in New World Archaeology* 4:59–90.

Helmke, Christophe, Jaime J. Awe, and Nikolai Grube
2010 Carved Monuments and Inscriptions of Xunantunich: Implications for Terminal Classic Sociopolitical Relationships in the Belize Valley. In *Classic Maya Provincial Politics: Xunantunich and Its Hinterlands*, edited by Lisa J. LeCount and Jason Yaeger, pp. 97–121. University of Arizona Press, Tucson.

Helmke, Christophe, Nikolai Grube, and Jaime J. Awe
2006a A Comprehensive Review of the Carved Monuments and Hieroglyphic Inscriptions of Xunantunich, Belize. In *The Belize Valley Archaeological Reconnaissance Project: A Report of the 2005 Field Season*, edited by Christophe Helmke and Jaime J. Awe, pp. 143–186. Institute of Archaeology, Belmopan, Belize.

Helmke, Christophe, Nikolai Grube, Jaime J. Awe, and Paul F. Healy
2006b A Reinterpretation of Stela 6, Pacbitún, Belize. *Mexicon* 28:70–75.

Iannone, Gyles
1996 Problems in the Study of Ancient Maya Settlements and Social Organization: Insights from the Minor Center of Zubin, Cayo District, Belize. Ph.D. dissertation, Institute of Archaeology, University College, London.

Kestle, Caleb
2004 Operation 6, Str. 5-North. In *The Chan Project, 2004 Season*, edited by Cynthia Robin, pp. 39–46. Northwestern University, Evanston, Illinois.

Laporte, Juan Pedro
1993 Architecture and Social Change in Late Classic Maya Society: The Evidence from Mundo Perdido, Tikal. In *Lowland Maya Civilization in the Eighth Century A.D.*, edited by Jeremy A. Sabloff and John S. Henderson, pp. 299–320. Dumbarton Oaks, Washington, D.C.

Laporte, Juan Pedro, and Vilma Fialko
1990 New Perspectives on Old Problems: Dynastic References for the Early Classic at Tikal. In *Vision and Revision in Maya Studies*, edited by Flora S. Clancy and Peter D. Harrison, pp. 33–66. University of New Mexico Press, Albuquerque.

Lucero, Lisa J.
2008 Plaza 1: Royal Rituals of Yalbac. *Research Reports in Belizean Archaeology* 5:219–226.

McAnany, Patricia
1995 *Living with the Ancestors: Kinship and Kingship in Ancient Maya Society*. University of Texas Press, Austin.
1998 Ancestors and the Classic Maya Built Environment. In *Function and Meaning in Classic Maya Architecture*, edited by Stephen D. Houston, pp. 271–298. Dumbarton Oaks Research Library and Collection, Washington, D.C.

Meierhoff, Jim, Caleb Kestle, and Ethan Kalosky
2004 Operation 6, Str. 5-Center. In *The Chan Project 2004 Season*, edited by Cynthia Robin, pp. 15–38. Northwestern University, Evanston, Illinois.

Rathje, William
1972 Trade Models and Archaeological Problems: The Classic Maya and Their E-Group Complex. In *XL Congresso Internazionale degli Americanisti*, Vol. 4, pp. 223–235. Kraus Reprint, Rome, Italy.
1978 Trade Models and Archaeological Problems: Classic Maya Examples. In *Mesoamerican Communication Routes and Cultural Contacts*, edited by Thomas A. Lee Jr. and Carlos Navarette, pp. 147–175. Papers of the New World Archaeological Foundation, No. 40. Provo, Utah.

Rice, Prudence M.
2004 *Maya Political Science: Time, Astronomy, and the Cosmos*. University of Texas Press, Austin.

Ricketson, Oliver, Jr.
1928a Astronomical Observatories in the Maya Area. *Geographical Review* 18:215–225.
1928b Notes on Two Maya Astronomic Observatories. *American Anthropologist* 30:434–444.

Ricketson, Oliver G., and Edith B. Ricketson
1937 *Uaxactún, Guatemala, Group E, 1926–1931. Part I: The Excavations; Part II: The Artifacts*. Carnegie Institution of Washington, Publication No. 477. Carnegie Institution of Washington, Washington, D.C.

Robin, Cynthia (editor)
2012 *Chan: An Ancient Maya Farming Community*. University Press of Florida, Gainesville.

Robin, Cynthia, James Meierhoff, Caleb Kestle, Chelsea Blackmore, Laura J. Kosakowsky, and Ana C. Novotny
2008 A 2000 Year History of Ritual in a Farming Community. Paper presented at the 2008 Society for American Archaeology Meetings, Vancouver, Canada, March 26–30, 2008.
2012 Ritual in a Farming Community. In *Chan: An Ancient Maya Farming Community*, edited by Cynthia Robin, pp. 113–132. University Press of Florida, Gainesville.

Rosenswig, Robert M., Ricardo López-Torrijos, Caroline E. Antonelli, and Rebecca R. Mendelsohn
2013   LiDAR Mapping and Surface Survey of the Izapa State on the Tropical Piedmont of Chiapas, Mexico. *Journal of Archaeological Science* 40(3):1493–1507.

Runggaldier, Astrid, Marieka Brouwer Burg, and Eleanor Harrison-Buck
2013   Hats Kaab: A Newly Discovered E-Group at the Closing of the 13th Baktun. *Research Reports in Belizean Archaeology* 10 (October 19):65–75.

Ruppert, Karl J.
1940   A Special Assemblage of Maya Structures. In *The Maya and Their Neighbors: Essays on Middle American Anthropology and Archaeology*, edited by Clarence L. Hay, Ralph L. Linton, Samuel K. Lothrop, Harry L. Shapiro, and George C. Valliant, pp. 222–231. D. Appleton-Century, New York.

Santasilia, Catharina E.
2012   The Discovery of an Elite Maya Tomb: Excavations at the Summit of Structure B-1, Cahal Pech, Belize. In Belize Valley Archaeological Reconnaissance Project, Progress Report of the 2011 Season, Vol. 16, edited by Julie Hoggarth, Rafael Guerra, and Jaime J. Awe, pp. 35–58. Institute of Archaeology, Belize.

Scherer, Andrew K.
2015   *Mortuary Landscapes of the Classic Maya: Rituals of Body and Soul.* University of Texas Press, Austin.

Taube, Karl
1998   The Jade Hearth: Centrality, Rulership and the Classic Maya Temple. In *Function and Meaning in Classic Maya Architecture*, edited by Stephen D. Houston, pp. 427–478. Dumbarton Oaks Research Library and Collection, Washington, D.C.

Willey, Gordon R., William R. Bullard, John B. Glass, and James C. Gifford
1965   *Prehistoric Maya Settlements in the Belize Valley.* Papers of the Peabody Museum of Archaeology and Ethnology, Vol. 64. Harvard University, Cambridge, Massachusetts.

Wisdom, Charles
1940   *The Chorti Indians of Guatemala.* University of Chicago Publications in Anthropology, Ethnological Series. University of Chicago Press, Chicago.

14

The Founding of Yaxuná

Place and Trade in Preclassic Yucatán

TRAVIS W. STANTON

It has long been known that E Groups were an integral part of early Maya centers as well as places where sky watching occurred (Chase 1983; Ricketson and Ricketson 1937; Ruppert 1940). Yet for many years they were only reported from the Southern Lowlands, where we know that they are much more numerous today (Aimers and Rice 2006; Chase and Chase 1995; Rice 2004). By the early 1980s only Dzibilchaltún stood as a site where possible, albeit dubious, Late Classic period (550–800 CE) E Groups might occur in the north (Coggins 1983; Coggins and Drucker 1988). The first Preclassic period (1000 BCE–250 CE) E Group to be identified in this region was at Yaxuná, where David Freidel recognized that the Carnegie archaeologists who first mapped the site drew the complex incorrectly (Brainerd 1958; O'Neill 1933). Although George Brainerd (1958; Thompson 1954) trenched the western radial structure and the associated Central Acropolis at Yaxuná, however, little was known about E Group complexes in the north until recently.

In this chapter I discuss the state of knowledge of the Preclassic period in northern Yucatán and how current data pertain to "external" contacts located in the Southern Lowlands. Examples of E Groups at a select number of sites in the Northern Lowlands contrast with triadic groups found at other early sites in the region (see Chapter 13 in this volume for a discussion of triadic groups). Artifactual evidence at one of the sites with an E Group, Yaxuná, suggests high levels of exchange with Southern Lowland sites and indicates that the E Group form may have been more than just a ritual complex, incorporating an important economic component as well. I argue that the presence of the E Group form in the Northern Lowlands indicates the existence of two inland trade routes connecting this region with the south during the Preclassic (Rathje 1971). Further, data indicating an early date for Southern Lowland contacts in the Yaxuná region are presented and discussed. The evidence indicates that Yaxuná was established as an early Middle Preclassic center with ties to the south. By at least the Late Preclassic this site utilized a solar calendar convention similar to those in the Southern Lowlands as a tool to aggregate farmers. By establishing this place, the people who created this E Group were able to draw the local population into new economic and social practices centered on the complex while providing access to nonlocal goods through an early version of the religious fair in Mesoamerica (Stanton and Freidel 2003).

The Preclassic in the Northern Lowlands

While the Northern Maya Lowlands form a subregion of the larger Maya area, the far north has always had a different feel for archaeologists compared to subregions like Petén and Belize. Scholars often focus on the use of architecture, writing, and ceramics dating to the Classic period (250–900 CE) as prime examples of this difference in the north (Ball 1993; Gendrop 1983; Lacandena 1995). Yet Preclassic origins have been portrayed as derived from the south through migrations of Lowland Maya who had already adopted a sedentary agricultural lifestyle and produced pottery (Andrews 1990). A series of data sets are changing this model. First, there is evidence to indicate that forest clearance and maize agriculture preceded pottery production in the north (Leyden 2002; Leyden et al. 1998; Zimmerman 2013) as elsewhere across the Lowlands (Islebe et al. 1996; Wahl et al. 2006). This hints at preceramic hunter-gatherer groups practicing horticulture. Second, the first northern pottery complexes date to 1000–800 BCE, on a par with Southern Lowlands sites (Ceballos and Robles 2012; Glover and Stanton 2010). Although the dating of early periods in the Northern Lowlands has been relatively scant until recently, evidence suggests that the Maya in this area lived in small sedentary villages by 1000 BCE (see the discussion of Yaxuná below).

Apart from the late Archaic period (2000–1000 BCE) pollen data indicating forest clearance and a limited number of Paleoindian period (11,000–7,500 BCE) skeletal remains that have become increasingly more common over the past ten years, however, there is little evidence of occupation prior to 1000 BCE. Although most of the Paleoindian remains have not been systematically reported in detail (but see Chatters et al. 2014; González et al. 2006, 2008), some scholars have argued that these early skeletons are not morphologically Maya (Terraza and Benavente 2006) and may represent an early Amerind migration that was later absorbed, pushed out, or replaced by later peoples that we view as Mesoamerican. Based on dental morphology, however, Andrea Cucina (personal communication, 2015) suggests that Naia at least shows some continuity with later Maya populations.

In light of these contrasting views of the Paleoindian data, it is unfortunate that we have practically no evidence of the Late Archaic occupation in the north that would shed light on who was cutting down the forest in the centuries leading up to the adoption of pottery technology. The data from Northern Lowlands and central Belize indicate continuity in lithics, food production, and resource exploitation from the Late Archaic to the Middle Formative (Iceland 2005; Lohse 2010). I suspect that the Late Archaic peoples in the north were the genetic ancestors of the Preclassic Maya (although for me they had not yet adopted a lifestyle that we could classify as culturally Maya), living a semisedentary lifeway akin to tropical horticulturalists in South America (see Chapter 7 in this volume for a discussion of Lowland Maya semisedentary peoples). Yet this period of extreme cultural transition so crucial for understanding early E Groups and their role as transformative agents in defining the emerging Preclassic Maya as a series of culturally similar peoples is still relatively unknown (Inomata et al. 2015), handicapping our understanding of how E Groups really changed the cultural landscape when they appeared.

With this caveat aside, around the time when the first ceramics were adopted it is clear that strategies for integrating people into more sedentary communities were implemented across the Lowlands. Early E Group complexes are some of the earliest if not the earliest examples of such integrative tools (Chapter 7 in this volume). As noted by many of the authors in this volume, the rapid spread and relative uniformity of E Groups signals a profound connection among early Maya communities in the Southern Lowlands that is also reflected in a wider range of strong ceramic homogeneity during the Preclassic; this may indicate high levels of interaction during the Late Archaic, with the E Group complex spreading along already established routes of social communication. Yet in the north there were other types of public spaces that may have had similar functions as integrative tools, possibly with calendrical associations. One type of in-line triadic structure with a tall central building and two wings on a large basal platform has been reported from several Middle Preclassic sites such as Poxilá and Xocnaceh. Middle Preclassic ballcourts and *sacbeob* have also been documented at many sites in northwest Yucatán (Anderson 2012; Medina and Lawton 2002).

The main problem with these data is that the dating of the construction phases is not well understood. The work of E. W. Andrews (1988) at Komchén relied on cross-dating with poorly dated sites in other regions of the Maya area. Since that time, little has been done to rectify problems with the original chronology in the north, still heavily based on the work of Robert Smith (1955, 1971) (Glover and Stanton 2010). Apart from the research of Fernando Robles Castellanos (Ceballos and Robles 2012) in the northwest portion of the peninsula, which to date has focused on ceramic complexes and not on their relation to public architecture, there are only a handful of published absolute dates from the Middle Preclassic. As has been reported by numerous scholars (Anderson 2005, 2010, 2011, 2012; Andrews et al. 2008; Bey 2006; Gallareta 2005; Hernández 2005; Hernández and Arias 2003; Hernández and Viana 2006; Stanton 2000, 2005a, 2012; Stanton and Ardren 2005), recent work in Yucatán over the past fifteen years has greatly increased our understanding of both the Middle and Late Preclassic. We are still far from understanding the pace and pattern of Preclassic developments in the north, however, as well as how sites socially and politically articulated across the region and beyond. Therefore, we do not yet know if Triadic Groups emerged around the same time as the E Groups or if they were slightly later.

With this problem in mind, it looks like there may have been small villages with stone architecture at around 1000 BCE. No clear dates for early monumental architecture have been reported for the Middle Preclassic, but if we follow the ceramic sequences of E. W. Andrews (1988) and Joseph Ball (1978a, 1978b), it appears that fairly sizable pyramids and other features such as ballcourts and causeways appeared by at least 400 BCE if not earlier. Around this time we see an increase in population, with very high levels being reached by around 200–100 BCE. By 200 CE there is a demographic collapse, and many sites are abandoned during the Terminal Preclassic or Protoclassic (0–250 CE) (Chase and Chase 2005; Glover and Stanton 2010), with the exception of Izamal and its hinterland, a region that experienced urban growth whose nature and scale can only be compared to Chichén Itzá in later times (Burgos et al. 2005, 2008, 2009). Presently none of the explored northern Lowland E Groups shows much evidence of construction during the Classic period, although some appear to have been used at this time (for example, stelae placed in the plaza at Santa Rosa Xtampak).

Northern E Groups and Their Relation to Early Trade

Regardless of the timing of Northern Lowland public architecture, E Group complexes are a rare occurrence in the north. Two Preclassic sites in the Northern Lowlands have clear E Group assemblages, San Antonio Chel and Yaxuná (Figure 14.1).

I discuss the Yaxuná example in more detail below, but it appears to be a heavily robbed of stone Uaxactún Style E Group that was abandoned during the Terminal Preclassic. The San Antonio Chel E Group was found relatively recently by Anthony Andrews and Fernando Robles (2004) in their survey of the northwest portion of the peninsula, a region with a high number of sites dating to the Preclassic. Although Robles (Ceballos and Robles 2012; Peniche 2012; Peniche et al. 2009) has been intensively excavating a number of the Preclassic sites around Ciudad Caucel and David Anderson (2010 and personal communication, 2012) undertook research at Xtobó for his dissertation, no member of the project has done more than excavate off-mound test pits at San Antonio Chel, which reveal intensive Middle and Late Preclassic occupations of the site. The complex has a radial pyramid on the west and a linear structure on the east, with several superstructures in the plaza in front of the linear structure. The orientation appears to be just east of north, which may indicate that it has a celestial alignment.

The presence of an E Group in the extreme northwest area is important, as James Aimers and Prudence Rice (2006) have noted, given the presence of a large number of Preclassic period ballcourts in this region (Anderson 2012; Medina and Lawton 2002). Few of the ballcourts have been excavated (only test pits), but surface evidence indicates that they are Middle and Late Preclassic. Although some sites, like Xtobó (Anderson 2010), are decent sized, most of the sites that have the ballcourts are small villages and hamlets, some with evidence of only a few households. In fact, Xtobó probably did not have more than 2,000 inhabitants at its apex, prompting some researchers to see Komchén as the regional center during the Middle Preclassic (Anderson 2012). The regional distribution of ballcourts here looks a bit like the intrasite distribution of ballcourts at Cantona, Puebla (600–900 CE), where the large domestic groups had an attached ballcourt (twenty-six in total: García and Merino 1998, 2000). The distribution at Cantona does not suggest that ceremonies were taking place at different "calendrical seats" (Rice 2004), but more likely that the ballcourts served social functions more focused on the relationships among important family groups. Regardless, it is interesting to note that the known Preclassic ballcourts in

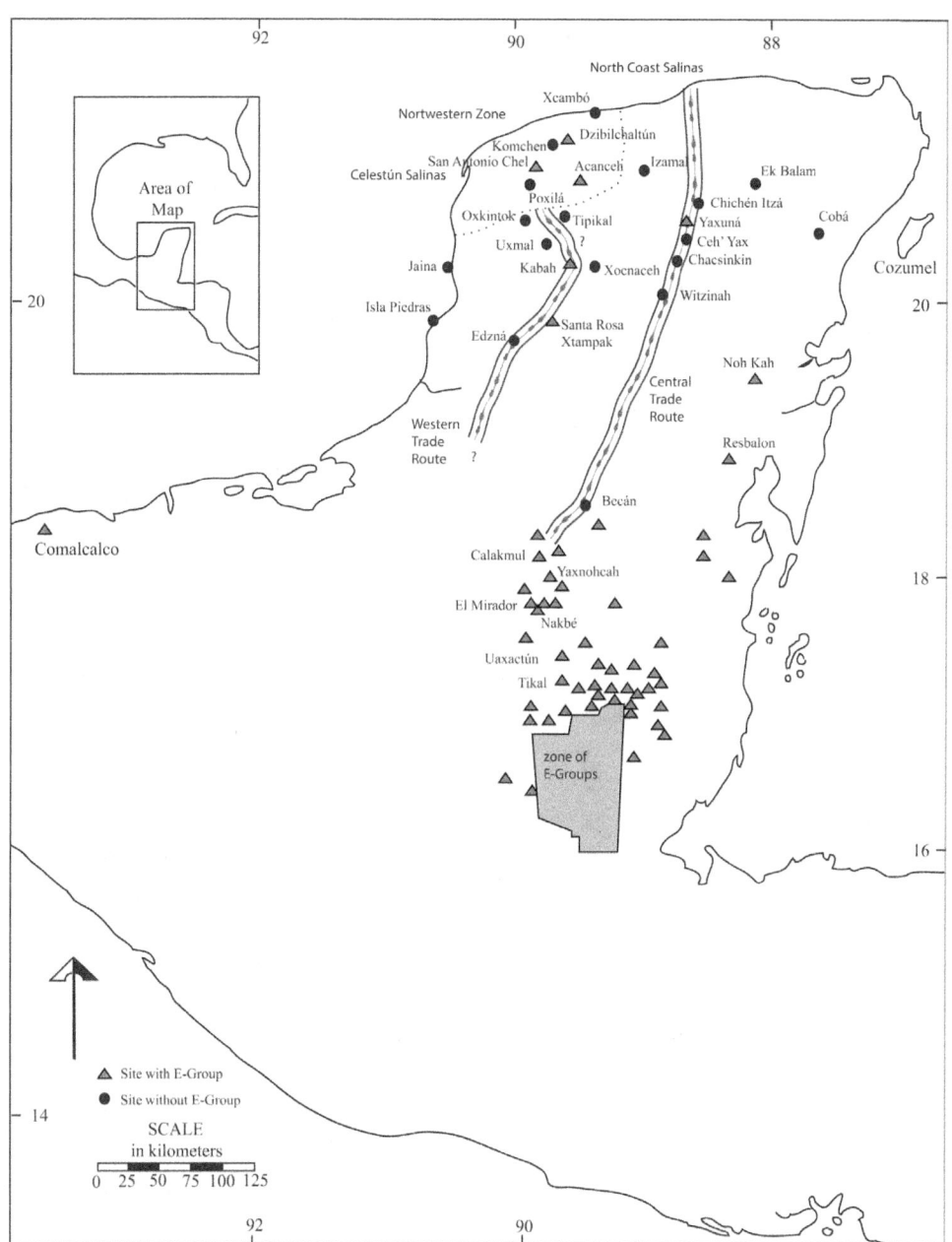

Figure 14.1. Map of the Maya area showing sites with E Groups and proposed Preclassic trade routes.

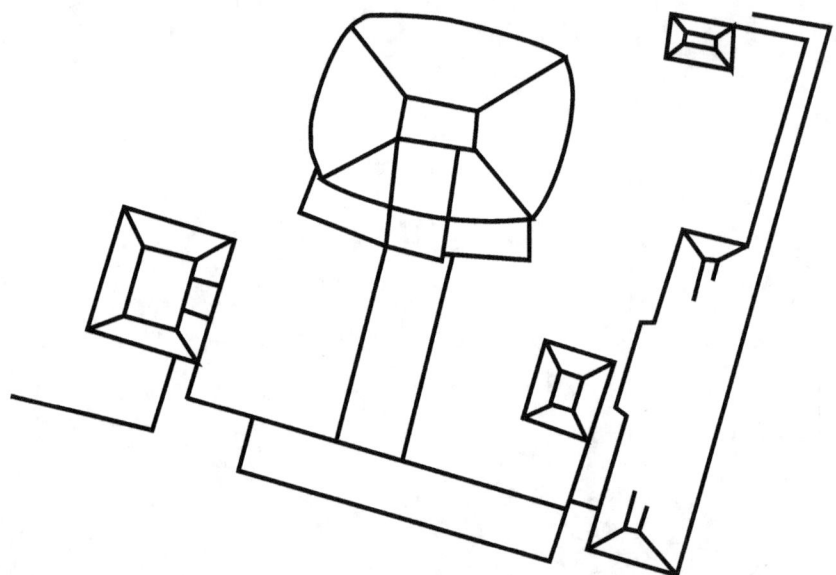

Figure 14.2. Maler-convention drawing of the possible E Group at Kabah (redrawn from Smith 1971).

the north are concentrated in this area, with one example known from the Puuc region (Tomás Gallareta, personal communication, 2002), the same area that I argue was connected by a western inland trade route.

The site of Acanceh, also located in the northwest portion of the peninsula but outside of the survey area of Andrews and Robles (2004), also appears to have an E Group (Coggins 1983:37–38). Excavated by Alicia Beatriz Quintal (1999; Quintal and Rodríguez 2006a, 2006b) over ten years ago, the radial structure has the typical look of a Preclassic E Group western building, replete with stucco masks interpreted as representations of gods including K'inich Ajaw. Little has actually been published from the excavations, but Quintal (2014) has reported both Middle and Late Preclassic construction episodes from this 12 m high structure oriented about north 17° east; no later construction has been reported. Unfortunately, most of the archaeological site has been destroyed by Colonial period (1519–1697 CE) and modern activity; if an eastern triadic group existed, it is no longer visible on the surface.

Two other Preclassic sites have probable E Groups, Kabah and Santa Rosa Xtampak. The possible E Group at Kabah is located in the Great Pyramid plaza, where a project directed by Lourdes Toscano has just begun work (Figure 14.2).

The Founding of Yaxuná: Place and Trade in Preclassic Yucatán · 457

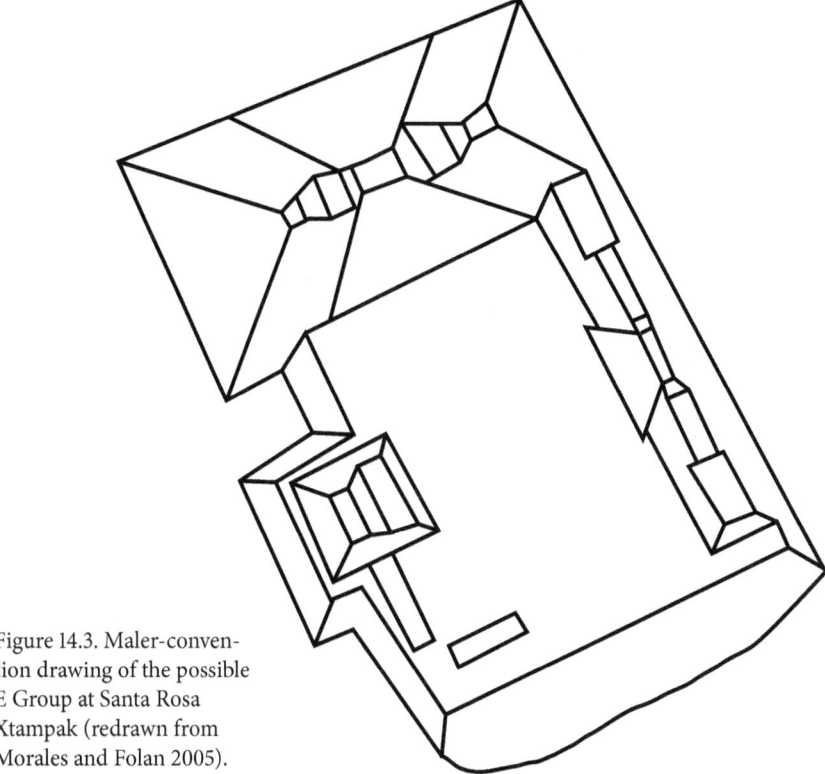

Figure 14.3. Maler-convention drawing of the possible E Group at Santa Rosa Xtampak (redrawn from Morales and Folan 2005).

Little is currently known about the group except that it is part of the "early" occupation of the site (Lourdes Toscano, personal communication, 2010). Brainerd (1958:232) reported Late Preclassic monochromes at Kabah but did not specify where they were located. He did, however, analyze ceramics from a few test trenches in this group. While they are not very well defined on the map, there is a linear structure on the east and a pyramidal structure on the west. Although I have not had a chance personally to inspect this group, the western structure does not appear to be radial on the map. But the orientation of the group is slightly east of north.

The last possible E Group is also on the western side of the peninsula at Santa Rosa Xtampak, an immense site located in the Chenes zone, not far from the Bolonchén District in the Puuc Hills. The Carnegie project dug test pits at the site, registered monuments, and made a map of its center; but apart from the map and the monuments, very little was published (Proskouriakoff 1950). What is evident is that one of the main plazas (Morales and Folan 2005), where the Carnegie archaeologists found Classic period carved stelae, is in the form of an E Group (Figure 14.3).

The orientation of the group is slightly west of north (possibly indicating a geographical rather than celestial alignment), but a surface inspection of the group in 1998 revealed an elongated eastern structure with what appeared to be three superstructures. The western structure does not seem to be radial, however. Interestingly the northern structure of the group is an immense triadic group very similar to the ones reported at Poxilá and Xocnaceh. The staircase leading to the E Group plaza from this structure has Preclassic-style megalithic blocks like those registered at Xocnaceh.

Assuming that the Acanceh, Kabah, and Santa Rosa Xtampak examples are valid, the distribution of known E Groups is rather clear; they tend to be located in the northwest portion of the peninsula and in a line toward the south through the Puuc and Chenes zones with one outlier in the central Northern Lowlands. As we have seen from San Bartolo and Xunantunich (Chapters 10 and 12 in this volume), other E Groups may be located at previously explored sites but have yet to be identified. There has also been little survey in the southern cone of Yucatán and western Quintana Roo, where other E Groups may occur. Noh Kah has the northernmost E Group that I have been able to identify on the eastern side of the peninsula (with Resbalón off to the south possibly heading off in another line toward the Dzibanché region). Recent salvage work in the southern cone of Yucatán has not reported this type of architecture.

I interpret the distribution of northern E Groups to be indicative of two early inland trade routes that connected the Northern and Southern Lowlands, for several reasons (Figure 14.1). First, the work of Jack Eaton (1978; Ball 1978b) and later projects along the Northern Lowland coasts (Inurreta 2002; Inurreta and Pat 2005; Robles 1987) has demonstrated that coastal sites in the northern area were not trading centers during the Preclassic but small fishing hamlets or even temporary camps. Coastal trade does not develop until the Early Classic period (Sierra 1999), reaching an apex during the Terminal Classic (800–900 CE) and Postclassic or Epiclassic (900–1,200 CE) (Andrews 1978). Yet obsidian, greenstone, foreign ceramics, and likely other products reached the Northern Lowlands during the Middle and Late Preclassic. Thus, the coastal data suggest inland trade at this time. If people were indeed living on the coast during the Preclassic, they would have had to trade for maize and other agricultural products that cannot be grown in this zone. Salt and marine products such as shells and fish are the logical trade items that coastal peoples may have traded to inland sites like Yaxuná and Acanceh, whose inhabitants may have passed these products off to the south; or alternatively the inland sites may have provided the labor to collect these products if the coastal sites were seasonal. While marine shells are found at Yaxuná as early as the ninth century BCE, no Preclassic fish remains have been reported at this or other Northern Lowlands inland sites in Yucatán; faunal data pertaining to this period are admittedly sparse, however.

Second, while little work has been done on the distribution and sourcing of Preclassic obsidian in the north, Olmec-style greenstone artifacts are reported from several sites. Interestingly, these sites have a spatial distribution similar to the E Group pattern. In the central portion of the peninsula, Andrews (1986, 1987) first reported Middle Preclassic greenstone at Chacsinkin, located directly south of Yaxuná. Although the artifacts are from a looted context, they are clearly Middle Preclassic Olmec style. Shortly after the Chacsinkin greenstones were reported, Suhler (1996) discovered Olmec-style greenstone artifacts in a late Middle Preclassic or early Late Preclassic cache located in a dance platform at Yaxuná. Furthermore, other Middle Preclassic Olmec-style greenstone caches have been reported in the western portion of the peninsula, including Xocnaceh, Poxilá, Tipikal, and sites in the vicinity of Ciudad Caucel (Peraza et al. 2002; Robles, personal communication, 2013), all located on the western trade route proposed here.

Moreover, Southern Lowland ceramics groups such as Muxunal and Pital appear in considerable numbers in these same areas (more than in other parts of the Northern Lowlands [Sara Dzul, personal communication, 2012]), as reported for Yaxuná (Stanton and Magnoni 2013) and in the northwest portion of the peninsula (Ceballos and Robles 2012). Of even more interest, Travis Stanton and Traci Ardren (2005) reported a foreign white-slipped ware at Yaxuná with motifs common on Middle Preclassic Olmec-style ceramics. These El Llanto Group ceramics were first defined in the Maya area at Edzná by Donald Forsyth (1983) and have also been found in the northwest portion of the peninsula (personal observation of the collections at Centro Instituto Nacional de Antropología e Historia [INAH], Yucatán). Christine Niederberger (1976:135–136, 186) first reported similar ceramic styles at Zohapilco (Zacatenco Phase, 800–400 BCE) in the Basin of Mexico, where they are very common. Ceramics with similar attributes are reported down the "Western Olmec Corridor" (Grove 1968, 1970:92) at sites such as Las Bocas, Chalcatzingo, and Teopanticuantitlán, probably including Oxtotitlán as well (Cyphers 1992). Small numbers of these ceramics have been found at Cuantinchán Viejo, Puebla (personal observation, 2006; Seiferle-Valencia 2007), but are very rare in the Puebla-Tlaxcala

Valley. They have only been reported at Yaxuná and the Puuc region, which suggests the existence of a series of intersite connections along the western and central portions of the peninsula that ultimately linked with more extensive exchange networks during the Middle Preclassic.

Together, these data indicate that one Preclassic trade route may have passed from the northwest portion of the peninsula through the Puuc region down the western portion of the peninsula, while the other may have passed from the north coast through Yaxuná and on toward Petén. Both of these trade routes would have accessed the two major zones of salt flats (Celestún and Río Lagartos) located in the Northern Lowlands (Andrews 1980, 1983), although other products were also likely to have flowed from the north to the south. While I discuss these routes in the context of the Preclassic, it is well known among archaeologists working in the north that several Classic period sites exhibit Southern Lowland traits. These sites, Oxkintok in the west (Varela 1998; Varela and Braswell 2003), Yaxuná in the center (Stanton 2005b), and Cobá and its port of Xelhá in the east (Canché 1992; Robles 1990) are commonly known as "Petenoid" sites. While little is known about the Preclassic and Early Classic at Cobá and Xelhá (Canché 1992; Robles 1990), Oxkintok and Yaxuná both exhibit Teotihuacanoid traits during the middle portion of the Classic period (Stanton 2005b; Varela and Braswell 2003), as do several sites in the northwest portion of the peninsula, including Chunchucmil, Caucel (Rodríguez et al. 2014), and Dzibilchaltún (Maldonado 2003), all areas located on the proposed Preclassic trade routes. In fact Teotihuacanoid traits are reported at both Xelhá (Berlo 1992; Toscano 1994) and Cobá (Karl Taube, personal communication, 2014) as well, but not in sufficient detail. These data indicate that these early trade routes may have had great longevity, surviving the rise and fall of particular centers, similar to trade routes in other places and times in Mesoamerica and around the world (Carballo and Pluckhahn 2007).

In the specific case of Yaxuná, high percentages of Southern Lowland–looking ceramics occur uninterrupted for over a thousand years. Many of these ceramics have modal similarities to the Becán and Calakmul areas: Middle Preclassic (Pital and Muxunal groups), Late Preclassic (Zapatista, Chunhinta, Sierra, and possibly Polvero groups), Terminal Preclassic (Zapatista, Dos Arroyos, and Sierra groups), Early Classic (Dos Arroyos Group), and Late Classic (Chinos, Zacatal, Saxché, and Chimbote groups). In fact Ball (1977) reports high instances of trickle designs during his Late Classic Bejuco Complex (630–750 CE), attributes that could tie it to the Yaxuná area, where trickle designs were more popular than elsewhere in the Northern Lowlands (Ball [1977] also reports slatewares for the Terminal Classic at Becán). The Late to Terminal Classic period distribution of sites with Puuc-style architecture (Xuenkal, Popolá, Yaxuná, and Ceh' Yax) along the proposed trade route, the Late Classic construction of the Cobá-Yaxuná *sacbé*, and the location of Chichén Itzá directly to the north of Yaxuná all indicate that there was continued interest in the control of trade along this inland route through the Terminal Classic (Loya and Stanton 2013, 2014; Stanton 2012).

In sum, evidence suggests two trade routes between the Northern and Southern Lowlands during the Preclassic that are marked by sites with E Group complexes; a third may be possibly identified on the eastern side of the peninsula with more regional survey. It is unclear whether these E Groups were constructed by early Northern Lowland Maya transitioning from a semisedentary Late Archaic lifestyle (Chapter 7 in this volume; Stanton 2000; Stanton and Ardren 2005) who adopted the Southern Lowland convention or by Southern Lowland Maya who migrated to the north looking to open trade routes toward the salt flats. Regardless, these complexes mark the inclusion of a very Southern Lowland tradition in the north and can be clearly related not just to ritual practice but to economic, and likely other social, activities as well. With this in mind I turn to a discussion of the Yaxuná data.

The Founding of Yaxuná

If we can accept the hypothesis that northern E Groups are a type of Southern Lowland ritual complex located at sites connecting the north to the south via early and long-lived inland trade routes, how would they have functioned as early integrative centers in relation to other more locally northern strategies to define early ritual places? It is not enough for us to say that these E Groups are evidence of "southern influence" or that they marked trade routes. These E Group places would have also been extremely important for the establishment of local ritual, economic, and social practices at early northern centers. Yet, how early are they? Do they follow material patterns similar to those of excavated E Groups in the Southern Lowlands? These are questions that we can begin to answer at Yaxuná.

Establishing the Center in the Middle Preclassic

Yaxuná has been known as an important Middle Formative center since the project directed by David Freidel in the 1980s and 1990s (Stanton 2000,

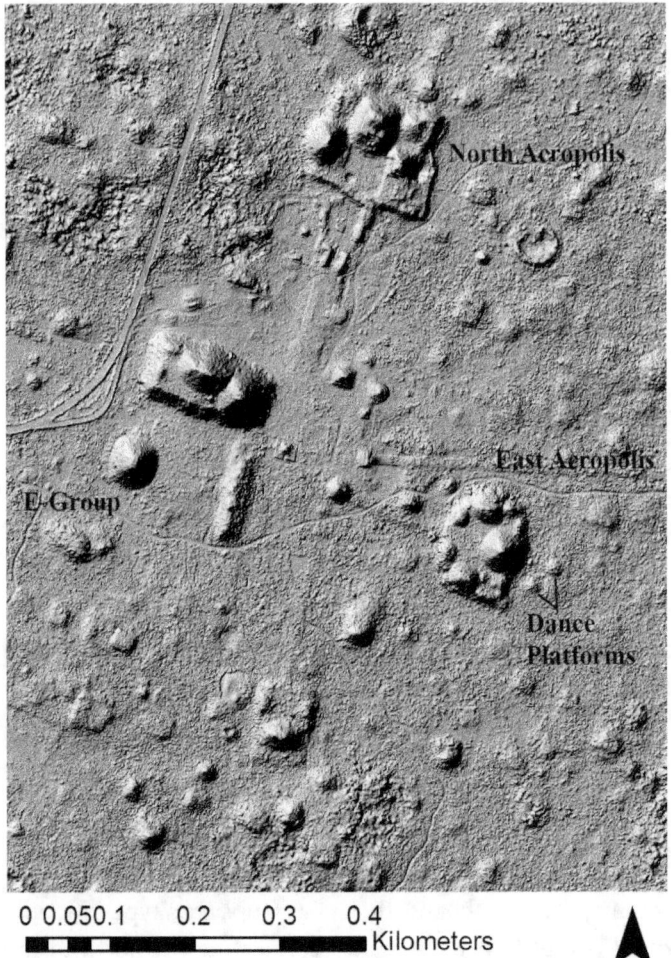

Figure 14.4. LiDAR hillshade image of central Yaxuná.

2005a; Stanton and Ardren 2005; Stanton et al. 2010; Suhler 1996). The size and age of the site, however, have been unclear until recently. In 2013 the Proyecto de Interacción Política del Centro de Yucatán (PIPCY), directed by Travis Stanton and Aline Magnoni, placed deep plaza excavations in the North Acropolis and East Acropolis (both triadic groups in their final form) to attempt to define the construction sequence of two of the more important monumental groups at the site (Figure 14.4).

Prior to the excavations, we hypothesized that the East Acropolis should have a Middle Preclassic component, given the location of two transitional

Figure 14.5. The two ceramic vessels and the Middle Formative greenstone from the cache in the dance platform at Yaxuná. Photographs by Vania Carrillo and Charles Suhler.

Middle/Late Preclassic dance platforms previously excavated by Suhler (1996) off to the east of the platform. AMS radiocarbon assays have been performed on three burned wood samples from one of those platforms, Structure 6E-120. Two of the samples came from below the sealed plaster floor and could predate the construction by some time; the ranges for these dates (all dates here are calibrated to two standard deviations) are 520–380 BCE (2360±40 BP, Beta-265026) and 382–186 BCE (2211±39, AA103490); the ceramics associated with these samples are Early Nabanché (650–350 BCE). A third sample was found associated with the floor but sealed within and sealed by the building's termination and follow-on roof collapse; 390–200 BCE (2250±40 BP, Beta-265025). Given that Suhler (1996) reports that the platform was intentionally burned when it was abandoned, the sample could be from the original wooden roof beams (possibly dating the original construction of the building) or could be from material brought in to burn the structure (thus dating its abandonment).

The only structural cache located in Structure 6E-120 was a lip-to-lip vessel cache (a trickle polychrome and an incised bichrome, both transitional Middle to Late Preclassic) with Olmec-style greenstone and a stone sphere (Figure 14.5) similar to those found in the plaza of the Yaxuná E Group (see below) and at other sites (Chapter 7 in this volume).

Given the radiocarbon dates, I suggest that the moment of construction of Structure 6E-120 dates to the third century BCE. Excavations elsewhere at Yaxuná suggest that the Early and Late Nabanché-style ceramics (Andrews 1988) overlap for some time at the site, and a third to fourth century BCE date would fit well with these data. The East Acropolis, however, does not show any evidence of Early Nabanché, indicating that the dance platforms stood alone in the eastern portion of the site core prior to the construction of the East Acropolis at some point during the Late Preclassic.

Stanton and Freidel (2005; Suhler 1996) interpreted the quatrefoil plan of the internal corridors of the dance platforms and the cache as evidence that they marked the birthplace of the Maize God in the geomantic plan of the site. In fact, Structure 6E-120 lines up directly with the line of sight from the radial structure of the E Group across the middle building of the range structure, placing the birthplace of the Maize God to the east of the E Group. Although we believed that a substructure of the East Acropolis would reveal a similar date and link an early form of the group to this east–west alignment, the earliest ceramics from our excavations in the Eastern Acropolis are exclusively Late Preclassic. The excavations at the North Acropolis, where Early Classic tombs have been reported (Suhler 1996; Suhler and Freidel 1998), revealed a similar pattern of Late Preclassic floors below the Classic Period overburden, indicating that Yaxuná looked quite different during the third century BCE, with an early version of the E Group plaza and the dance platforms taking a prominent role rather than the acropolis groups visible today.

Excavations beginning in 2013 at the E Group, however, revealed an even earlier chronology than found in the dance platforms. Excavating on the center line directly in front of the eastern building (badly robbed of stones during Prehispanic times) for his doctoral thesis, Ryan Collins came across a series of superimposed floors separated by fill. While Collins will present his work in more detail in other forums, it is important to mention our initial understanding of the stratigraphy, as it bears on the timing of the Yaxuná E Group and how the center was first defined. Two adjacent 2 × 2 m units were taken down to bedrock in front of the eastern structure and revealed intact stratigraphy with a series of four preserved or semipreserved floors (Figure 14.6).

While an occasional Classic period sherd was recovered in the upper levels where the floors were found in a fragmentary state, the majority of the material from above Floor 3 is Late and Terminal Preclassic. The fill from between well-preserved Floors 3 and 4 dates to the Middle Preclassic;

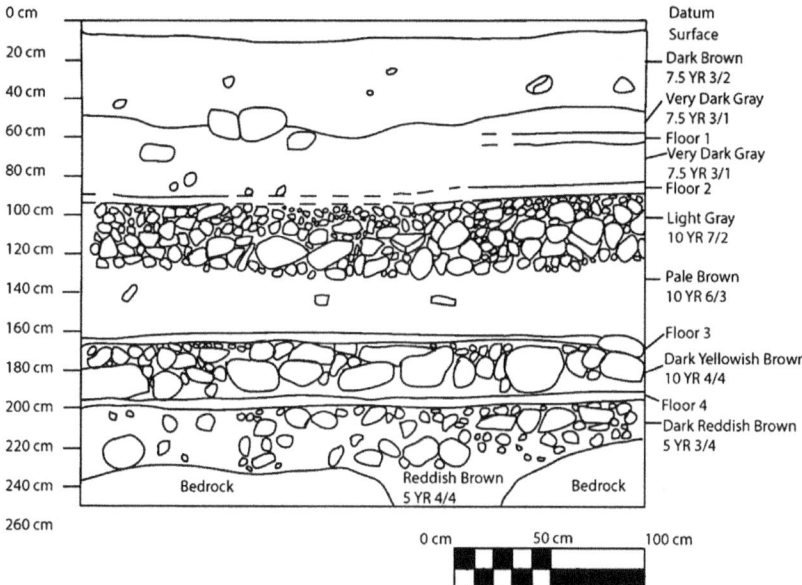

Figure 14.6. North profile of the center-line excavation into the plaza in front of Structure 5E-2. Drawing by Ryan Collins.

most of this material is Early Nabanché, but one Ek Complex sherd was recovered. Andrews et al. (2008; Ceballos and Robles 2012) have now redated the Ek Complex (1000–800 BCE) to the early portion of the Middle Preclassic, arguing that it is pre-Mamom, on par with Xe and Cunil materials in the south. While the majority of the ceramic material comes from fill, the only sherd found in direct association with Floor 3 was from a Middle Preclassic El Llanto Cream vessel, suggesting that Floor 3 is Middle Preclassic.

Unfortunately, no radiocarbon samples were recovered from the lower floors during the 2013 excavations. Excavations in the central portion of the plaza during the 2014 field season, however, revealed an even more complex floor sequence (at least eleven floors). One of the lowest floors (Floor 9) was heavily burned and a radiocarbon sample associated with this burning dates to 813–433 BCE (2543±59, AA103490) at two standard deviations (Table 14.1). A second date from the fill between Floors 9 and 10 has a range of 927 to 807 BCE (2720±35, AA103490). A final sample on bedrock below Floor 11, a tamped earth surface, yielded a date range of 979–824 BCE (2754±32, AA104923). While the lower two dates are not from ideal contexts, given these early dates, the presence of tamped earth floors, and the association of an Ek Complex sherd in the lower levels of the

Table 14.1. AMS radiocarbon dates mentioned in the text

Sample ID	Associated materials	$d^{13}C$ value	^{14}C age BP	$d^{14}C$ age	Calibrated 2-sigma	Context
YAX26DDLV1L2	Yaxuná IIb, Late Nabanché	-25	2250	40	390–200 BCE	Burned wood associated with the floor, but below the collapse of Str. 6E-120
YAX26GLV2L1	Yaxuná Ia, Early Nabanché	-23.4	2360	40	520–380 BCE	Burned wood between the earliest floor and bedrock of Str. 6E-120
YAX14-1-4.1	Yaxuná Ia, Early Nabanché		2900	120	1392–835 BCE	Burned wood on bedrock mixed in with midden context below earliest construction phase of Str. 6E-32
PIPCY 025	Yaxuná Ia, Early Nabanché	-25	2406	39	749–397 BCE	Burned wood in the midden material composing the fill of the first phase of construction of Str. 6E-32
PIPCY 026	Yaxuná Ia, Early Nabanché	-24.4	2211	39	382–186 BCE	Burned wood between the earliest floor and bedrock of Str. 6E-120
PIPCY037	Yaxuná Ia, Early Nabanché	-25.3	2543	59	813–433 BCE	Burned wood from burning directly on Floor 9 of the E Group
PIPCY043	Yaxuná Ia, Early Nabanché	-27.8	2754	32	979–824 BCE	Burned wood on bedrock below the E Group plaza
PIPCY045	Yaxuná Ia, Early Nabanché	-27.3	2720	35	927–807 BCE	Burned wood from the fill between floors 9 and 10 of the E Group plaza

plaza in front of the eastern structure, it appears that there was construction at the E Group very early in the history of Yaxuná and that some of the founding public architecture was built at this locality. Whether this early construction represents an early form of the E Group or not remains to be investigated. The fact remains that this Preclassic E Group is built at the place of the earliest known public architecture at Yaxuná.

Interestingly, bedrock at the 6E-30 Group, an early domestic platform at the site (and the largest compared across all periods), was cleaned of all soils and an extensive deposit of broken ceramics, nonlocal chert reduction flakes (the most found at Yaxuná at any period), shell reduction flakes, and malachite flakes was laid down on bedrock under the eastern structure, which has the form of an ancestor temple. The ceramics in the deposit are Early Nabanché and two carbon samples just above bedrock revealed ranges of 1392–835 BCE (2900±120, AA96529) and 749–397 BCE (2406±29, AA103489). I believe the first date to be derived from old carbon, but that the second date may represent the deposition of the deposit, a Middle Preclassic event that happened during the centuries following the initial construction of the E Group. Chase and Chase (1998, 2006:51) have mentioned that malachite flakes and pebbles were used to sanctify caches at Caracol, suggesting that this deposit may mark the consecration of the ancestor temple. Yet the chert and shell reduction flakes appear to indicate that artifacts, possibly the very symbols of power that early leaders would have used to set them apart, were manufactured during the consecration of this group. The resulting debitage may have been included as a consecration offering (see Chapter 8 in this volume for a Southern Lowland example of chert debitage in E Group buildings). This may have been done as the first settlers of Yaxuná attempted to define it as a place. It is easy to suggest that this midden deposit reflects early place-making activities at Yaxuná with the consecration of the earliest ancestor temple at the site. Yet the artifacts also suggest people-making activities. Defining these early places and the new roles of people went hand in hand and was extremely important for establishing the identities that were transformed and manipulated for millennia.

The discussion of the 6E-30 Group is relevant to the E Group for two reasons. First, the extensive presence of nonlocal materials in the deposit reinforces the idea that exchange networks were developing in the area of the Maya world relatively early in the sequence. Second, the superimposed floors located in front of the eastern structure of the Yaxuná E Group were associated with caches of fist-sized limestone spheres and a large quantity of chert debris in the Late to Terminal Preclassic upper levels. These patterns have also been noted at sites in the Southern Lowlands and indicate that the Yaxuná E Group was used in the same ways as Southern Lowlands complexes during the latter part of the Preclassic (Doyle 2013; Chapter 7 in this volume). Although we had originally speculated that the spheres could be hammerstones for lithic production, Inomata (personal communication, 2013) believes that they may have been used as tokens to mark the calendar. Again, it is interesting to note that one large limestone sphere was recovered in the Middle Preclassic dance platform cache. Returning to the idea of chert debris and people-making, it is probably not coincidental that the two largest chert scatters found so far at Yaxuná are at the 6E-30 Group and the E Group plaza. Once the E Group was established, early leaders may have used it as a place for people-making rituals, including investiture, and abandoned the practice of manufacturing leadership symbols in domestic contexts as reflected in the 6E-30 data.

Places where such types of leadership ceremonies took place during the Classic and Postclassic periods often followed the religious-fair model where religious ceremonies were undertaken in conjunction with market activities (Freidel 1979; Ringle et al. 1998). The Epiclassic Feathered Serpent cult centers would be a good example of this model, with some researchers arguing that these centers took over trade routes following the decline of Teotihuacán (Ringle et al 1998). In line with Rathje's (1971) model for the origin and development of Maya civilization, the spread of the E Group may reflect a very similar pattern in a very different cultural context. As Chase and Chase note (Chapter 2 in this volume), the distribution of E Groups to the southeast of Petén is along rivers, suggesting the spread of a cult complex along communication and trade routes much like the situation seen in the north. It is quite possible that the calendrical convention expressed by the E Group was first established in central Petén and quickly spread as cult centers along trade routes in and out of this area. It is likely that E Groups could have functioned as early places of exchange (not just nodes along a route), although I would not use the term "market" for this early period.

In fact, these new cult centers would have functioned to aggregate people not just through agricultural rituals important for an emerging sedentary society (one increasingly dependent on produced food as the years passed) but through the social and economic pull of the places that were created. As has been argued for many early ceremonial sites where hunters and gatherers met periodically, such as Poverty Point (Gibson 1998) and Göbekli Tepe (Banning 2011), people could come together for a wide variety of reasons, including exchange of spouses and trade. I think it is likely that these early E Groups created this type of environment where people would not only aggregate on a full-time basis (living at the sites) but would come in from other areas to participate in the rituals, creating a social and economic gravity through the temporary influx of outside populations (Inomata et al. 2015). In effect, although formal markets may not have existed, the foundations for linking calendrical ritual activity and markets so popular during later periods may have been laid at the dawn of Maya civilization, at least at sites participating in the E Group cult.

Discussion: The Ties That Bind

While much remains to be understood about E Group complexes in the Northern Lowlands, they appear to mark Preclassic trade routes between the Northern and Southern Lowlands. As Rathje (1971) hypothesized, salt was probably the primary resource that Southern Lowland populations would have been interested in, given its importance for a diet increasingly based on maize. Excavations at Acanceh and Yaxuná indicate Middle Preclassic construction at least at these two complexes, with at least the Yaxuná example extending back into the early Middle Preclassic. The significance of very early Southern Lowland architecture at a time when the entire Lowland area was transitioning from a semisedentary to a more fixed agricultural lifestyle is of extreme importance for understanding the ways in which Northern and Southern Lowland societies articulated. These data indicate that the social fabrics of these two areas were intricately entwined, despite some variation in the expression of what we consider Maya material culture. They also demonstrate that at least some people in the Northern Lowlands used the idea of the calendar to found important aggregation centers that would set the tone for later renegotiations of built landscape.

The future task for Maya archaeologists, however, is to gain a better understanding of the role of E Groups as integrative tools (Chase and Chase 1995). Beyond ritual, what other activities may have taken place at the E Group plazas and how other social and economic spaces benefited by the social pull of the E Group complex are important questions that have yet to be adequately answered. At Yaxuná there is little doubt of the early importance of the calendar and Maize God associations with the E Group. Yet, in the end, the E Group complexes at Yaxuná and Acanceh, and most likely San Antonio Chel, fell out of use at the end of the Preclassic. The Yaxuná E Group was robbed for stones during the Early Classic, and little evidence of later reuse of the complex has been found as yet in the excavations. This shift in the use of public space is reflective of immense social changes in the north. Settlement data indicate large-scale decrease of regional populations, with a concentration of settlement in the area of Izamal during the Terminal Preclassic and the specter of Teotihuacanoid traits in the same regions where the E Groups are found looming in the middle of the Classic period. While these changes are poorly understood, they mark a shift away from this Southern Lowland calendar convention and toward a more northern conception of how to define community identity and bring and keep people together.

Acknowledgments

I wish to thank Jerry Murdock, Murray Gell-Mann, and Jerry Sabloff for sponsoring the Santa Fe Institute workshops, which led to this volume, as well as my colleagues who participated in the fruitful discussions that molded all of the chapters. Funding for the excavations at the Yaxuná E Group came from Jerry Murdock, Bernard Selz, and Roberto Hernández and I wish to thank Pedro Sánchez Nava and Ángeles Olay Barrientos of the Consejo de Arqueología del Instituto de Antropología e Historia for their help in obtaining the permits for this work. Finally, I thank Ryan Collins, Aline Magnoni, Debra Walker, and an anonymous reviewer for providing comments on this chapter.

References Cited

Aimers, James J., and Prudence M. Rice
2006   Astronomy, Ritual, and the Interpretation of Maya "E-Group" Architectural Assemblages. *Ancient Mesoamerica* 17:79–96.
Anderson, David S.
2005   Preclassic Settlement Patterns in Northwest Yucatán. *Mono y Conejo* 3:13–22.
2010   Xtobo, Yucatan, Mexico: The Study of a Preclassic Community. Ph.D. dissertation, Department of Anthropology, Tulane University, New Orleans.
2011   Xtobo, Yucatan, Mexico, and the Emergent Preclassic of the Northern Maya Lowlands. *Ancient Mesoamerica* 22:301–322.
2012   The Origins of the Mesoamerican Ballgame: A New Perspective from the Northern Maya Lowlands. In *The Ancient Maya of Mexico: Reinterpreting the Past of the Northern Maya Lowlands*, edited by Geoffrey E. Braswell, pp. 43–64. Equinox Publishing, Bristol, Connecticut.
Andrews, Anthony P.
1978   Puertos costeros del Posclásico Temprano en el norte de Yucatán. *Estudios de Cultura Maya* 11:75–93.
1980   *Salt-Making, Merchants and Markets: The Role of a Critical Resource in the Northern Maya Lowlands.* University of Arizona Press, Tucson.
1983   *Ancient Maya Salt Production and Trade.* University of Arizona Press, Tucson.
Andrews, Anthony P., and Fernando Robles Castellanos
2004   An Archaeological Survey of Northwest Yucatan, Mexico. *Mexicon* 25:7–14.
Andrews, E. Wyllys, V
1986   Olmec Jades from Chacsinkin, Yucatan, and Maya Ceramics from La Venta, Tabasco. In *Research and Reflections in Archaeology and History: Essays in Honor of Doris Stone*, edited by E. Wyllys Andrews V, pp. 11–49. Middle American Research Institute, Publication 57. Tulane University, New Orleans.
1987   A Cache of Early Jades from Chacsinkin, Yucatan. *Mexicon* 9:78–85.

1988   Ceramic Units from Komchen, Yucatan, Mexico. *Ceramica de Cultura Maya* 15:51–64.

1990   The Early Ceramic History of the Lowland Maya. In *Vision and Revision in Maya Studies*, edited by Flora S. Clancy and Peter D. Harrison, pp. 1–19. University of New Mexico Press, Albuquerque.

Andrews, E. Wyllys, V, George J. Bey III, and Christopher Gunn

2008   Rethinking the Early Ceramic History of the Northern Maya Lowlands: New Evidence and Interpretations. Paper presented at the 73rd Annual Meeting of the Society for American Archaeology, Vancouver, Canada, 2008.

Ball, Joseph W.

1977   *The Archaeological Ceramics of Becan, Campeche, Mexico*. Middle American Research Institute, Publication 43. Tulane University, New Orleans.

1978a   *Archaeological Pottery of the Yucatan-Campeche Coast*. Middle American Research Institute, Publication 46. Tulane University, New Orleans.

1978b   The Rise of the Northern Maya Chiefdoms: A Socioprocessual Analysis. *Estudios de Cultura Maya* 10:209–222.

1993   Pottery, Potters, and Polities: Some Socioeconomic and Political Implications of Late Classic Maya Ceramic Industries. In *Lowland Maya Civilization in the Eighth Century CE*, edited by Jeremy A. Sabloff and John S. Henderson, pp. 243–272. Dumbarton Oaks, Washington, D.C.

Banning, E. B.

2011   So Fair a House: Göbekli Tepe and the Identification of Temples in the Pre-Pottery Neolithic of the Near East. *Current Anthropology* 52:619–660.

Berlo, Janet C.

1992   Icons and Ideologies at Teotihuacan: The Great Goddess Reconsidered. In *Art, Ideology, and the City of Teotihuacan*, edited by Janet C. Berlo, pp. 129–168. Dumbarton Oaks Research Library and Collection, Washington, D.C.

Bey, George J., III

2006   Changing Archaeological Perspectives on the Northern Maya Lowlands. In *Lifeways in the Northern Maya Lowlands: New Approaches to Archaeology in the Yucatán Peninsula*, edited by Jennifer P. Mathews and Bethany A. Morrison, pp. 13–37. University of Arizona Press, Tucson.

Brainerd, George W.

1958   *The Archaeological Ceramics of Yucatan*. Anthropological Records, Vol. 19. University of California, Berkeley.

Burgos Villanueva, Rafael, Miguel Cobarrubias Reyna, Sara Dzul Góngara, and Yoly Palomo Carrillo

2008   Investigaciones arqueológicas en la región costera y al interior de la provincia histórica de Ah Kin Chel, Yucatán. In *Investigadores de la Cultura Maya 16*, pp. 47–61. Universidad Autónoma de Campeche, Campeche, Mexico.

Burgos Villanueva, Rafael, Miguel Cobarrubias Reyna, and José Estrada Faisal

2005   Estudios en la periferia de Izamal: El área de transición entre una zona de producción agrícola y una zona limítrofe de ocupación humana al poniente del área urbana. In *Investigadores de la Cultura Maya 13*, pp. 425–444. Universidad Autónoma de Campeche, Campeche, Mexico.

Burgos Villanueva, Rafael, Miguel Cobarrubias Reyna, Yoly Palomo Carrillo, and Sara Dzul Góngara
2009   Estudios en un sitio intermedio en la ruta de comunicación entre dos grandes asentamientos prehispánicos: Izamal-Dzilam. In *investigadores de la cultura maya 17, tomo I*, pp. 299–318. Universidad Autónoma de Campeche, Campeche, Mexico.

Canché Manzanero, Elena M.
1992   *La secuencia cerámica de Xelhá, Q. Roo*. Licenciatura thesis, Facultad de Ciencias Antropológicas, Universidad Autónoma de Yucatán, Mérida, Mexico.

Carballo, David M., and Thomas Pluckhahn
2007   Transportation Corridors and Political Evolution in Highland Mesoamerica: Settlement Analyses Incorporating GIS for Northern Tlaxcala, Mexico. *Journal of Anthropological Archaeology* 26:607–629.

Ceballos Gallareta, Teresa, and Fernando Robles Castellanos
2012   Las etapas más tempranas de la alfarería maya en al noroeste de la península de Yucatán. *Ancient Mesoamerica* 23:403–419.

Chase, Arlen F.
1983   A Contextual Consideration of the Tayasal-Paxcaman Zone, El Peten, Guatemala. Ph.D. dissertation, Department of Anthropology, University of Pennsylvania, Philadelphia.

Chase, Arlen F., and Diane Z. Chase
1995   External Impetus, Internal Synthesis, and Standardization: E Group Assemblages and the Crystallization of Classic Maya Society in the Southern Lowlands. *Acta Mesoamericana* 8:87–101 (special issue edited by Nikolai Grube entitled *The Emergence of Lowland Maya Civilization: The Transition from the Preclassic to Early Classic*).
2005   The Early Classic Period at Caracol, Belize: Transitions, Complexity, and Methodological Issues in Maya Archaeology. *Research Reports in Belizean Archaeology* 2:17–38.
2006   Before the Boom: Caracol's Preclassic Era. *Research Reports in Belizean Archaeology* 3:41–57.

Chase, Diane Z., and Arlen F. Chase
1998   The Architectural Context of Caches, Burials, and Other Ritual Activities for the Classic Period Maya (as Reflected at Caracol, Belize). In *Function and Meaning in Classic Maya Architecture*, edited by Stephen D. Houston, pp. 299–332. Dumbarton Oaks Research Library and Collection, Washington, D.C.

Chatters, James C., Douglas J. Kennett, Yemane Asmerom, Brian M. Kemp, Victor Polyak, Alberto Nava Blank, Patricia A. Beddows, Eduard Reinhardt, Joaquin Arroyo-Cabrales, Deborah A. Bolnick, Ripan S. Malhi, Brendan J. Culleton, Pilar Luna Erreguerena, Dominique Rissolo, Shanti Morell-Hart, and Thomas W. Stafford Jr.
2014   Late Pleistocene Human Skeleton and mtDNA Link Paleoamericans and Modern Native Americans. *Science* 344(6185):750–754.

Coggins, Clemency C.
1983   *The Stucco Decoration and Architectural Assemblage of Structure 1-Sub, Dzibilchaltún, Yucatan, Mexico.* Middle American Research Institute Publication No. 49. Tulane University, New Orleans.

Coggins, Clemency C., and R. David Drucker
1988   The Observatory at Dzibilchaltún. In *New Directions in American Archaeoastronomy*, edited by Anthony F. Aveni, pp. 17–56. BAR International Series 454. British Archaeological Reports, Oxford, United Kingdom.

Cyphers Guillén, Ann
1992   *Chalcatzingo, Morelos: Estudio de cerámica y sociedad.* Universidad Nacional Autónoma de México, Mexico City.

Doyle, James A.
2013   The First Maya "Collapse": The End of the Preclassic Period at El Palmar, Petén, Guatemala. Ph.D. dissertation, Department of Anthropology, Brown University, Providence, Rhode Island.

Eaton, Jack D.
1978   *Studies in the Archaeology of Coastal Yucatan and Campeche, Mexico: Archaeological Survey of the Yucatan-Campeche Coast.* Middle American Research Institute, Publication 41. Tulane University, New Orleans.

Forsyth, Donald W.
1983   *Investigations at Edzna, Campeche, Mexico, Volume 1, Part 2: Ceramics.* Papers of the New World Archaeological Foundation No. 46. Brigham Young University, Provo, Utah.

Freidel, David A.
1979   Culture Areas and Interaction Spheres: Contrasting Approaches to the Emergence of Civilization in the Maya Lowlands. *American Antiquity* 44:36–54.

Gallareta Negrón, Tomás
2005   *Proyecto Xocnaceh: Segunda temporada de campo.* Informe Técnico al Consejo de Arqueología del Instituto Nacional de Antropología e Historia, Mexico City.

García Cook, Ángel, and B. Leonor Merino Carrión
1998   Cantona: Urbe prehispánica en el altiplano central de México. *Latin American Antiquity* 9:191–216.
2000   El Proyecto Arqueológico Cantona. In *Arqueología, historia, y antropología: En memoriam José Luis Lorenzo Bautista*, edited by Jaime Litvak and Lorena Mirambell, pp. 161–203. Instituto Nacional de Antropología e Historia, Mexico City.

Gendrop, Paul
1983   *Los estilos Río Bec, Chenes, y Puuc en la arquitectura maya.* Universidad Nacional Autónoma de México, Mexico City.

Gibson, Jon L.
1998   Broken Circles, Owl Monsters, and Black Earth Midden: Separating Sacred and Secular at Poverty Point. In *Ancient Earthen Enclosures of the Eastern Woodlands*, edited by Robert C. Mainfort and Lynne P. Sullivan, pp. 17–30. University Press of Florida, Gainesville.

Glover, Jeffrey B., and Travis W. Stanton
2010   Assessing the Role of Preclassic Traditions in the Formation of Early Classic Yucatec Cultures. *Journal of Field Archaeology* 35:58–77.

González González, Arturo H., Carmen Rojas Sandoval, Alejandro Terrazas Mata, Martha Benavente Sanvicente, and Wolfgang Stinnesbeck
2006   Poblamiento temprano en la Península de Yucatán: Evidencias localizadas en cuevas sumergidas de Quintana Roo, México. In *2° Simposio Internacional el Hombre Temprano en América*, edited by José C. Jiménez López, pp. 73–90. Instituto Nacional de Antropología e Historia, Mexico City.

González González, Arturo H., Carmen Rojas Sandoval, Alejandro Terrazas Mata, Martha Benavente Sanvicente, Wolfgang Stinnesbeck, Jerónimo Avilés O., Magdalena de los Ríos, and Eugenio Acevez
2008   The Arrival of Humans on the Yucatan Peninsula: Evidence from Submerged Caves in the State of Quintana Roo, Mexico. *Current Research in the Pleistocene* 25:1–24.

Grove, David C.
1968   Chalcatzingo, Morelos, Mexico: A Reappraisal of the Olmec Rock Carvings. *American Antiquity* 33:486–491.
1970   *Los murales de la cueva de Oxtotitlán, Acatlán, Guerrero: Informe sobre las investigaciones arqueológicas en Chilapa, Guerrero, noviembre de 1968*. Instituto Nacional de Antropología e Historia, Mexico City.

Hernández Hernández, Concepción
2005   La cerámica del periodo Preclásico Tardío (300 a.C.–350 d.C.) en el norte de la península de Yucatán. In *La producción alfarera en el México antiguo I*, edited by Beatriz L. Merino Carrión and Ángel García Cook, pp. 753–779. Instituto Nacional de Antropología e Historia, Mexico City.

Hernández Hernández, Concepción, and José Manuel Arias López
2003   Los entierros del conjunto habitacional de Ni'Chac: Un sitio del Preclásico Tardío en el norte de Yucatán. In *Los investigadores de la cultura maya 11*, pp. 279–301. Universidad Autónoma de Campeche, Campeche, Mexico.

Hernández Hernández, Concepción, and Leonid Viana Campos
2006   El sitio "Flor de Mayo": Aportaciones para la arqueología del norte de Yucatán. In *Los mayas de ayer y hoy: Memorias del Primer Congreso Internacional de Cultura Maya, tomo I*, edited by Alfredo Barrera Rubio and Ruth Gubler, pp. 104–131. Eugenia Montalván Proyectos Culturales SCP, Mérida, Mexico.

Iceland, Harry B.
2005   The Preceramic to Early Middle Formative Transition in Northern Belize: Evidence for the Ethnic Identity of the Preceramic Inhabitants. In *New Perspectives on Formative Mesoamerican Cultures*, edited by Terry G. Powis, pp. 15–26. BAR International Series 1377. Archaeopress, Oxford, United Kingdom.

Inomata, Takeshi, Jessica MacLellan, Daniela Triadan, Jessica Munson, Melissa Burham, Kazuo Aoyama, Hiroo Nasu, Flory Pinzón, and Hitoshi Yonenobu
2015   The Development of Sedentary Communities in the Maya Lowlands: Co-Existing Mobile Groups and Public Ceremonies at Ceibal, Guatemala. *Proceedings of the National Academy of Sciences* 112(14):4268–4273.

Inurreta Díaz, Armando Francisco
2002   *Uaymil: Un puerto de transbordo en la costa norte de Campeche*. Tesis profesional, licenciado en ciencias antropológicas en la especialidad de arqueología, Universidad Autónoma de Yucatán, Mérida, Mexico.

Inurreta Díaz, Armando, and Edgar Daniel Pat Cruz
2005   Isla Piedras: Asentamiento del Clásico Temprano en la costa norte de Campeche. *Los investigadores de la cultura maya 13*, pp. 255–266. Universidad Autónoma de Campeche, Campeche, Mexico.

Islebe, Gerald A., Henry Hooghiemstra, Mark Brenner, Jason H. Curtis, and David A. Hodell
1996   A Holocene Vegetation History from Lowland Guatemala. *Holocene* 6:265–271.

Lacandena García-Gallo, Alfonso
1995   Evolución formal de las grafías escriturarias mayas: Implicaciones históricas y culturales. Ph.D. dissertation, Universidad de Complutense de Madrid, Madrid, Spain.

Leyden, Barbara W.
2002   Pollen Evidence for Climatic Variability and Cultural Disturbance in the Maya Lowlands. *Ancient Mesoamerica* 13:85–101.

Leyden, Barbara W., Mark Brenner, and Bruce H. Dahlin
1998   Cultural and Climatic History of Coba, a Lowland Maya City in Quintana Roo, Mexico. *Quaternary Research* 49:111–122.

Lohse, Jon C.
2010   Archaic Origins of the Lowland Maya. *Latin American Antiquity* 21:312–352.

Loya González, Tatiana, and Travis W. Stanton
2013   The Impact of Politics on Material Culture: Evaluating the Yaxuná-Cobá Sacbé. *Ancient Mesoamerica* 24:25–42.
2014   Petrographic Analysis of Arena Red Ceramics at Yaxuná, Yucatán. In *The Archaeology of Yucatán: New Directions and Data*, edited by Travis W. Stanton, pp. 337–362. BAR International Series. Archaeopress, Oxford, United Kingdom.

Maldonado Cárdenas, Rubén
2003   El talud tablero remetido de Dzibilchaltún: ¿Desarrollo regional o de influencia teotihuacana? In *Los investigadores de la cultura maya 11*, pp. 484–492. Universidad Autónoma de Campeche, Campeche, Mexico.

Medina Castillo, Edgar, and Crorey Lawton
2002   El juego de pelota: Nuevos hallazgos en el noreste de Yucatán. In *Los investigadores de la cultura maya 10*, pp. 278–285. Universidad Autónoma de Campeche, Campeche, Mexico.

Morales López, Abel, and William J. Folan
2005   Santa Rosa Xtampak, Campeche: Su patrón de asentamiento del Preclásico al Clásico. *Mayab* 18:5–16.

Niederberger, Christine
1976   *Zohapilco: Cinco milenios de ocupación humana en un sitio lacustre de la Cuenca de México*. Colección Científica 30. Instituto Nacional de Antropología e Historia, Mexico City.

O'Neill, John
1933 Survey of Yaxuna. *Carnegie Institution of Washington Yearbook* 32:88–89.

Pagliaro, Jonathan B., Travis W. Stanton, and Donald Slater
2014 Is There an Ek Complex in Central Yucatan?: Evaluating Early Ceramics from Yaxuna and Aktun Kuruxtun. Paper presented at the 79th Annual Meeting of the Society for American Archaeology, Austin, Texas, 2014.

Peniche May, Nancy
2012 The Architecture of Power and Sociopolitical Complexity in Northwestern Yucatan during the Preclassic Period. In *The Ancient Maya of Mexico: Reinterpreting the Past of the Northern Maya Lowlands*, edited by Geoffrey E. Braswell, pp. 65–87. Equinox Publishing, Bristol, Connecticut.

Peniche May, Nancy, Mónica E. Rodríguez Pérez, and Teresa N. Ceballos Gallareta
2009 La función de un edificio del periodo Preclásico: La Estructura 1714 de Xaman Susulá. In *Los investigadores de la cultura maya 17, tomo II*, pp. 253–264. Universidad Autónoma de Campeche, Campeche, Mexico.

Peraza Lope, Carlos, Pedro Delgado Kú, and Bárbara Escamilla Ojeda
2002 Intervenciones en un edificio del Preclásico Medio en Tipikal, Yucatán. *In Los investigadores de la cultura maya 10*, pp. 262–276. Universidad Autónoma de Campeche, Campeche, Mexico.

Proskouriakoff, Tatiana
1950 *A Study of Classic Maya Sculpture*. Carnegie Institution of Washington, Publication 593. Carnegie Institution of Washington, Washington, D.C.

Quintal Suaste, Alicia Beatriz
1999 Los mascarones de Acanceh. *Arqueología Mexicana* 37:14–17.
2014 Cronología y asentamiento del sitio de Acanceh, Yucatán. In *The Archaeology of Yucatán: New Directions and Data*, edited by Travis W. Stanton, pp. 93–104. BAR International Series. Archaeopress, Oxford, United Kingdom.

Quintal Suaste, Beatriz, and Dehmian Rodríguez Barrales
2006a Ciclos de fuego: Análisis iconográfico de la Estructura 1 de Acanceh, Yucatán, México. *Los mayas de ayer y hoy: Memorias del Primer Congreso Internacional de Cultura Maya, tomo I*, edited by Alfredo Barrera Rubio and Ruth Gubler, pp. 175–202. Eugenia Montalván Proyectos Culturales SCP, Mérida, Mexico.
2006b Representaciones de entidades sobrenaturales en el friso del Palacio de los Estucos. *Los mayas de ayer y hoy: Memorias del Primer Congreso Internacional de Cultura Maya, tomo I*, edited by Alfredo Barrera Rubio and Ruth Gubler, pp. 156–173. Eugenia Montalván Proyectos Culturales SCP, Mérida, Mexico.

Rathje, William L.
1971 The Origin and Development of Lowland Classic Maya Civilization. *American Antiquity* 36:275–285.

Rice, Prudence M.
2004 *Maya Political Science: Time, Astronomy, and the Cosmos*. University of Texas Press, Austin, Texas.

Ricketson, Oliver G., and Edith B. Ricketson
1937 *Uaxactun, Guatemala, Group E*. Carnegie Institution of Washington, Publication 447. Carnegie Institution of Washington, Washington, D.C.

Ringle, William M., Tomás Gallareta Negrón, and George J. Bey III
1998	The Return of Quetzalcoatl: Evidence for the Spread of a World Religion during the Epiclassic Period. *Ancient Mesoamerica* 9:183–232.

Robles Castellanos, Fernando
1987	La secuencia cerámica preliminar de Isla Cerritos, costa centro-norte de Yucatán. In *Maya Ceramics*, edited by Prudence M. Rice and Robert J. Sharer, pp. 99–109. BAR International Series 345. British Archaeological Reports, Oxford, United Kingdom.
1990	*La secuencia cerámica de la región de Cobá, Quintana Roo.* Instituto Nacional de Antropología e Historia, Mexico City.

Rodríguez Pérez, Mónica, Teresa Ceballos Gallareta, and Rubén Chuc Aguilar
2014	Un enclave de Oxkintok en el norte de Caucel a inicios del Clásico Tardío: El desarrollo de la Estructura BU 17/26 011-006. In *The Archaeology of Yucatán: New Directions and Data*, edited by Travis W. Stanton, pp. 105–122. BAR International Series. Archaeopress, Oxford.

Ruppert, Karl
1940	A Special Assemblage of Maya Structures. In *The Maya and Their Neighbors: Essays on Middle American Anthropology and Archaeology*, edited by Clarence L. Hay, Ralph L. Linton, Samuel K. Lothrop, Harry L. Shapiro, and George C. Vaillant, pp. 222–231. D. Appleton-Century, New York.

Seiferle-Valencia, Ann C.
2007	Before the Eagle's Nest: The Formative Period Archaeology of Cuantinchan Viejo, Puebla, Mexico. Ph.D. dissertation, Department of Anthropology, Harvard University, Cambridge, Massachusetts.

Sierra Sosa, Thelma N.
1999	Xcambó: Codiciado enclave económico del Clásico maya. *Arqueología* 7(37):40–47.

Smith, Robert E.
1955	*Ceramic Sequence at Uaxactun, Guatemala.* Middle American Research Institute, Publication 20. Tulane University, New Orleans.
1971	*The Pottery of Mayapan.* Papers of the Peabody Museum of Archaeology and Ethnology, Vol. 66. Harvard University, Cambridge, Massachusetts.

Stanton, Travis W.
2000	Heterarchy, Hierarchy, and the Emergence of the Northern Lowland Maya: A Study of Complexity at Yaxuna, Yucatan, Mexico (400 BCE–CE 600). Ph.D. dissertation, Department of Anthropology, Southern Methodist University, Dallas, Texas.
2005a	Formative Maya Causeways: Incipient Internal Site Design at Yaxuná, Yucatán, Mexico. *Mono y Conejo* 3:32–34.
2005b	Taluds, Tripods, and Teotihuacanos: A Critique of Central Mexican Influence in Classic Period Yucatán. *Mayab* 18:17–35.
2012	The Rise of Formative Period Complex Societies in Northern Maya Lowlands. In *Oxford Handbook of Mesoamerican Archaeology*, edited by Deborah L. Nichols and Christopher A. Pool, pp. 268–282. Oxford University Press, Oxford.

Stanton, Travis W., and Traci Ardren
2005   The Middle Formative of Yucatán in Context: The View from Yaxuná. *Ancient Mesoamerica* 16:213–228.

Stanton, Travis W., and David A. Freidel
2003   Ideological Lock-In and the Dynamics of Formative Religions in Mesoamerica. *Mayeb* 16:5–14.
2005   Placing the Centre, Centring the Place: The Influence of Formative Sacbeob in Classic Site Design at Yaxuná, Yucatán. *Cambridge Archaeological Journal* 15:225–249.

Stanton, Travis W., David A. Freidel, Charles K. Suhler, Traci Ardren, James N. Ambrosino, Justine M. Shaw, and Sharon Bennett
2010   *Excavations at Yaxuná, 1986–1996: Results of the Selz Foundation Yaxuná Project*. BAR International Series 2056. Archaeopress, Oxford, United Kingdom.

Stanton, Travis W., and Aline Magnoni
2013   Informe Global: Proyecto de Interacción Política del Centro de Yucatán, temporadas 2007, 2008, 2009 y 2011. Global report to the Consejo de Arqueología del Instituto Nacional de Antropología e Historia, Mexico City.

Suhler, Charles K.
1996   Excavations at the North Acropolis, Yaxuna, Yucatan, Mexico. Ph.D. dissertation, Department of Anthropology, Southern Methodist University, Dallas, Texas.

Suhler, Charles K., and David A. Freidel
1998   Life and Death in a Maya War Zone. *Archaeology* 51(3):28–34.

Terraza Mata, Alejandro, and Martha E. Benavente Sanvicente
2006   Estudio preliminar de tres cráneos tempranos, procedentes de cuevas sumergidas de la costa de Quintana Roo. In *2º Simposio Internacional del Hombre Temprano en América*, edited by José C. Jiménez López, pp. 189–197. Instituto Nacional de Antropología e Historia, Mexico City.

Thompson, J. Eric S.
1954   *The Rise and Fall of Maya Civilization*. University of Oklahoma Press, Norman.

Toscano Hernández, Lourdes
1994   Secuencia arqueológica de la arquitectura pública de Xelhá, Quintana Roo. Licenciatura thesis, licenciado en ciencias antropológicas en la especialidad de arqueología, Universidad Veracruzana, Xalapa, Mexico.

Varela Torrecilla, Carmen
1998   *El Clásico Medio en el noroccidente de Yucatán*. Paris Monographs in American Archaeology, No. 2, BAR International Series 739. British Archaeological Reports, Oxford, United Kingdom.

Varela Torrecilla, Carmen, and Geoffrey E. Braswell
2003   Teotihuacan and Oxkintok: New Perspectives from Yucatán. In *The Maya and Teotihuacan: Reinterpreting Early Classic Interaction*, edited by Geoffrey E. Braswell, pp. 249–271. University of Texas Press, Austin, Texas.

Wahl, David, Roger Byrne, Thomas Schreiner, and Richard Hansen
2006   Holocene Vegetation Change in the Northern Peten and Its Implications for Maya Prehistory. *Quaternary Research* 65:380–389.

Zimmerman, Mario
2013   *La aparición de las plantas domésticas en el norte de la península de Yucatán.* Licenciatura thesis, licenciado en ciencias antropológicas en la especialidad de arqueología, Universidad Autónoma de Yucatán, Mérida, Mexico.

15

Founding Landscapes in the Central Karstic Uplands

KATHRYN REESE-TAYLOR

There are regions in which E Groups seem to cluster in great density. These clusters can basically be separated into two larger areas, the Central Karstic Uplands and the Southern Petén, including the Belize River valley, the Mopán River valley, the Holmul River valley, and the Petén Lakes region.

While other chapters in this volume (with the notable exceptions of Chapters 14 and 16) focus on sites with E Groups in the southern Petén, this chapter concentrates on the Central Karstic Uplands. Recent investigations in this region have demonstrated that most sites were densely populated from the Preclassic to the Terminal Classic (800–900 CE) periods (Braswell et al. 2004; Carrasco 1998; Carrasco and Boucher 1994; Carrasco and Colón 2005; Folan et al. 1995; Folan et al. 2001; Grube et al. 2012; Hansen 1992a, 1992b, 1998; Mejía 2008, 2009; Morales et al. 2008; Robichaux and Pruett 2008; Šprajc 2008). Many centers, such as El Mirador, Nakbé, Calakmul, and Yaxnohcah, however, also have unusually large Preclassic civic centers, suggesting that this region was of primary importance during this early period (Figure 15.1).

Therefore, in this chapter I discuss the central ideological concepts that shaped the early cities within this region. Specifically, I consider the E Group within the context of the broader Preclassic built environment in order to explain the precocious development of Maya urban centers within the Central Karstic Uplands.

Yaxnohcah, "the first great city," is located in southern Campeche, approximately 26 km northeast of El Mirador, 21 km southeast of Calakmul, and 15 km northwest of Naachtún. The settlement is situated in the heart of the Maya Lowlands in the Central Karstic Uplands. Excavations in 2011 and 2013 revealed that Yaxnohcah grew exponentially during the Preclassic period, like many other sites in the Central Karstic Uplands.

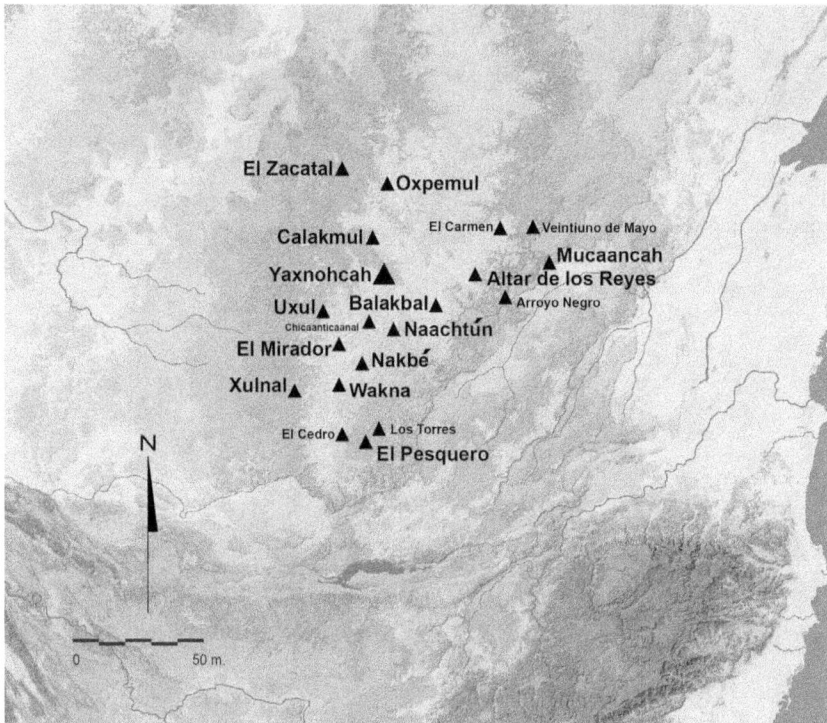

Figure 15.1. Map of Central Karstic Uplands showing sites with E Groups.

Even before the initiation of the Proyecto Arqueológico Yaxnohcah, scholars recognized that the scale of Yaxnohcah was remarkable. Ivan Šprajc and Carlos Morales (2007) originally recorded six large civic platform complexes spread over 7 km². Since then, through reconnaissance and LiDAR survey, the boundaries of greater Yaxnohcah have been extended to over 25 km² and include at least ten such platform complexes of varying sizes (Figure 15.2).

Yaxnohcah's E Group, the Brisa Complex, its associated residential compound, the Baalche' Group, and the adjacent reservoirs were the heart of this integrated landscape from the early Middle Preclassic (Macal Complex, 900–600 BCE) to the Postclassic (900–1519 CE) (Luch Complex, dating after CE 1000) (Figure 15.3; Table 15.1).

Multiple *sacbeob* have been mapped that link civic/ceremonial complexes and outlying residential zones with the Brisa Complex. One wide *sacbe* links the Alba Platform with the ballcourt adjacent to and immediately north of the Brisa Complex, establishing a strong north–south orientation to the main civic precinct. Other *sacbeob* run to the northeast and

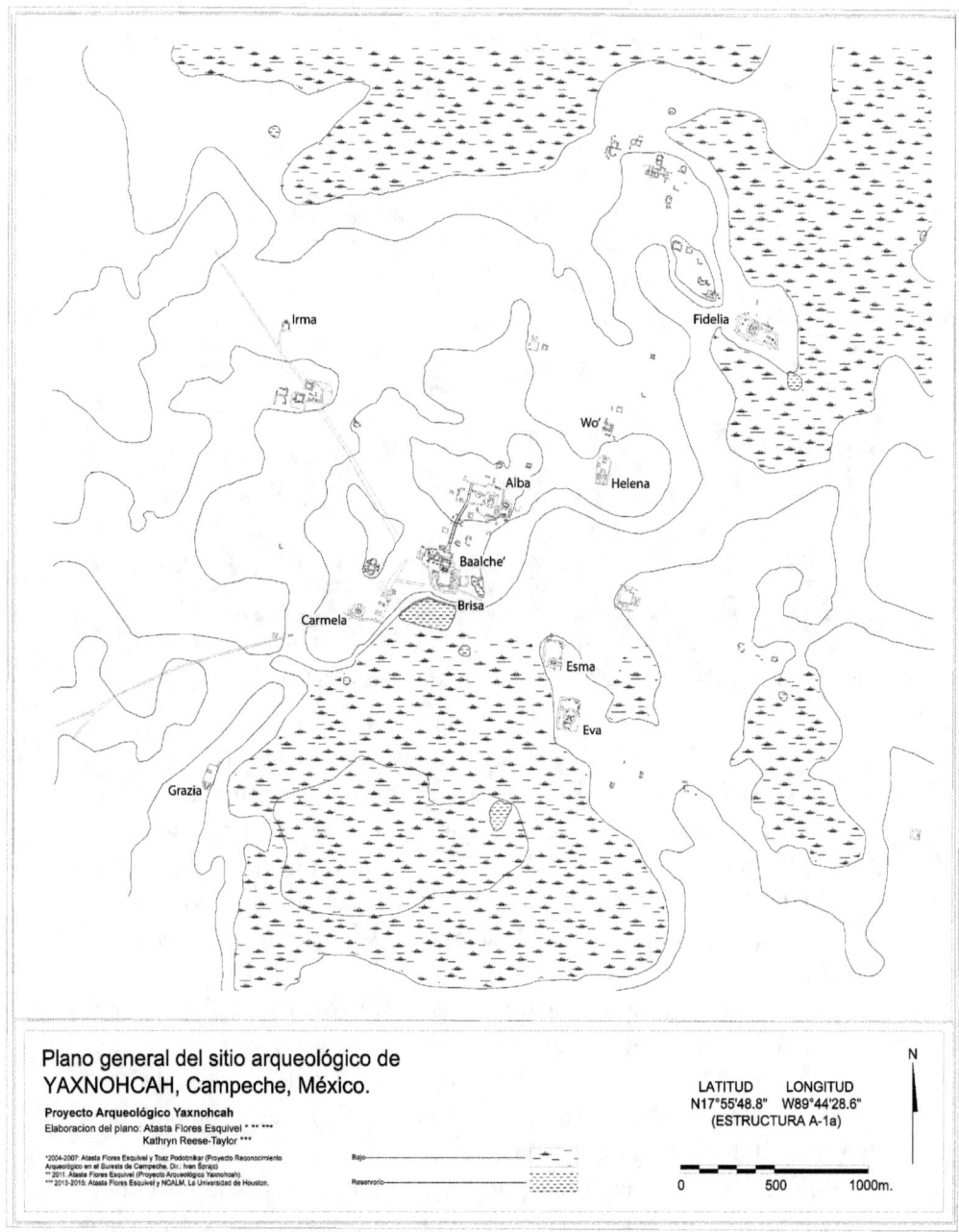

Figure 15.2. Map of Yaxnohcah.

Figure 15.3. Map of Yaxnohcah civic precinct.

Table 15.1. Yaxnohcah chronology based on ceramic complexes

Date estimates w/out C^{14}	Period name	Yaxnohcah ceramic complex	Meaning of complex name
After 1000 CE	Postclassic	Luch	Calabash tree
850–1000 CE	Terminal Classic	Xikinche'	Edible mushroom that grows in trees
650–850 CE	Late Classic	Late Tux	Cotton seed
500–650 CE	Middle Classic	Early Tux	
200–500 CE	Early Classic	Kiwi'	Achiote paste
100 BCE–200 CE	Terminal Preclassic	Wob	Pitaya
300–100 BCE	Late Preclassic	Chay	Chaya
600–300 BCE	Late Middle Preclassic	Um	Avocado
900–3000 BCE	Early Middle Preclassic	Macal	Cocoyam

the southwest, connecting the central precinct with distant civic structures and residential groups. Although we have not yet determined the original construction date of the road system, the buildings at the termini of the *sacbeob* date as early as the Middle Preclassic.

Not too surprisingly, the initial act of settling in the area of Yaxnohcah included bedrock leveling of rocky outcrops. To date, bedrock leveling that includes carving of the bedrock as well as filling in depressions with the mineral *sascab* to construct a level surface has been uncovered in several excavations. The Brisa E Group is one of these contexts.

Ceramics associated with early leveling events have been isolated stratigraphically and can be defined as a distinct functionally complete pre-Mamom complex. Of the >25,000 sherds so far recovered at Yaxnohcah, about 1,000 stem from this era, termed Macal Complex (900–600 BCE) (Walker 2016). Abelino Red bowls and jars, Huetche White bowls, and Crisanto Black bowls constitute the predominant types in the complex. Preslip incising and horizontal fluting are common. Based on cross-correlation with other sites, the complex dates to 900–600 BCE.

Besides sealed isolated contexts, Macal Complex sherds have been recovered in sealed contexts mixed with Late Middle Preclassic (Um Complex) ceramics, and in unsealed contexts mixed with later material. Macal Complex ceramics are prevalent in other contexts throughout the greater Yaxnohcah area. Archaeologists have recovered early ceramics from the fill found in agricultural fields, alluvial deposits from abandoned quarries, and of course construction fill. In general, pre-Mamom ceramics form a backdrop to almost all subsequent activity at Yaxnohcah, suggesting widespread settlement and substantive populations during the early Middle Preclassic.

Yaxnohcah continued to grow during the Middle Preclassic. The Brisa Complex was expanded during this period. and the plaza was extended to the north. In addition, a project of landscape modification that included the construction of a reservoir to the south of the E Group platform was realized. The Brisa Reservoir has an area of 30,125 m^2. Without excavations there is a 3 m height difference from the bottom of the land surface to the top of the surrounding berm, indicating that the Brisa reservoir has a capacity to hold 90,375,000 liters of water at a minimum. Test excavations in the berm of the reservoir yielded Middle Preclassic (Um Complex) ceramics exclusively, including waxy Joventud Red, Pital Cream, and Chunhinta Black types.

Middle Preclassic (Um Complex) ceramics have been recovered in isolated contexts in the Alba Complex, the Fidelia Platform, and the Helena Platform. Furthermore, Middle Preclassic ceramics are prevalent in mixed contexts in every excavation unit, including those in agricultural fields and water features, as well as in most *saqueos* (looter's trenches) examined. This leads us to suggest that the Middle Preclassic was one of the largest occupations at the site, extending from the southern Grazia Platform to north of Fidelia.

Unlike the Middle Preclassic, the Late Preclassic occupation has proven to be more elusive. At this time, we cannot isolate a Late Preclassic occupation based on sealed ceramic stratigraphy. Typical waxy Late Preclassic (Chay Complex) ceramic types such as Sierra Red have been recovered in relatively small numbers, generally mixed with earlier waxy types such as Joventud Red or later Terminal Preclassic or Protoclassic (0–250 CE) (Wob Complex) types, especially the lustrous, double-slipped Cabro Red.[1] Because Yaxnohcah is so large and to date our sample is relatively small, it is still unclear whether this is the result of sampling error or a true diminution in the Late Preclassic population.

Excavations in the Baalche' Group plaza immediately north of the Brisa Complex revealed a deposit of Preclassic water jars, marine shell, and projectile points, scattered throughout the lower lots of the platform construction. Several partial vessels were from the early Middle Preclassic, such as a Consejo Red jar, and the Middle Preclassic, such as Joventud Red, Dzudzuquil Variegated, and Chunhinta Black jars. Several additional partial vessels were also present, however, including a Sierra Red plate and a double-slipped red incurving bowl, indicating that the mixed deposit dated to the Late/Terminal Preclassic period. A carbon sample obtained from this context produced a date of 110 BCE–50 CE.

Excavations on a residential platform situated in the northern edge of the Baalche' Group also revealed occupation that occurred during this period. These higher-status residences are directly associated with the E Group and are indicative of the development of centralized authority.

Early Classic (250–550 CE) (Kiwi' Complex) occupation at Yaxnohcah also appears to have been widespread, although not very substantial. Evidence comes from the excavations in the residential platform of the Baalche' Group and from excavations in several structures throughout the settlement.

The Yaxnohcah residential zone grew significantly during the Late Classic (550–800 CE) (Tux Complex). Almost every residential group explored to date has evidence of a Late Classic component. Many of these data come from surface collections and *saqueos*, but excavations in the Wo' Group revealed substantive Late Classic occupations in all structures tested.

The Baalche' Group, too, has a notable Late Classic (late Tux Complex) presence. Several pottery types recovered from the platform fill had painted or incised glyphs, including Saxché Orange Polychrome, Zacatel Cream Polychrome, and Carmelita Incised. A concentration of broken ceramic figurines was also recovered from the fill of the Baalche' residential platform.

Long after the site was abandoned, Postclassic people returned to Yaxnohcah and dedicated a small stela in the centerline of the Brisa 3, the western structure of the E Group. The monument consisted of a large rectangular construction block from the Brisa 3, which was set into a small rectangular altar. Dedicatory offerings including a Navula Unslipped tripod cup, a Huhi Impressed widemouth jar, and several pieces of a Cehac-hunacti Composite spiked censer were scattered around the small monolith.

E Groups on the Central Karstic Uplands

Yaxnohcah is by no means the only site with a Preclassic E Group in this region (Table 15.2). Cenote style E Groups predominate in this region: of the 23 known sites with E Groups in the Central Karstic Uplands, 83 percent of the complexes are likely the Cenote type ($n = 19$). This may be because most of these E Groups date to the Preclassic period, although only a few have had their construction dates verified through archaeological investigations: Calakmul (Andrews 1995; Carrasco and Boucher 1994), El Mirador

Table 15.2. E Groups in the Central Karst Plateau

	Site name	West/East structures	Associated azimuth	Azimuth measurements	Dates	Type	Plaza width (E/W)[a]	Associated architecture[b]	Water feature[c]	References
1	Altar de los Reyes	Strs. 12 and 13	95°52'	E–W alignment from Str. 12 to Str. 13	ca. **Mar 7, Oct 6 (E)** ca. Apr 3, Aug 17 (W)	Cenote	61 m	Triadic Group (E) Ballcourt (N)		Flores and Šprajc 2008:25; Šprajc 2008
2	Arroyo Negro		99°36'		Mar 31, Sep 11 **Feb 26, Oct 16** Jan 26, Nov 11	Uaxac.?	40 m			Šprajc et al. 1997
3	Balakbal	Strs. VI and VIII	100° 100°15'/280°15'	E–W alignment from Str. VI to Str. VIII	May 6 **Feb 24, Oct 18** Aug 8 **Feb 23, Oct 19 (E)** Apr 14, Aug 29 (W)	Cenote	52 m	Ballcourt (W)		Aveni et al. 2003 Šprajc 2008
4	Calakmul	Strs. XI and IV	92°30'	E–W alignment from Str. XI to IVb	**Jun 21 (N)** Mar 15, Sep 29 (C)	Cenote	65 m	Triadic Group (N) Triadic Group (S)	Reservoir (NE)	Aveni et al. 2003; Folan et al. 1995
5	El Carmen					Cenote?				Šprajc 2008
6	El Cedro	Strs. 4 and 2				Uaxac.	50 m			Mejía 2009
7	Champerico	Strs. 13 and 15	103°40'/283°40'	E–W alignment of Str. 15a	**Feb 15, Oct 26 (E)** Apr 25, Aug 17 (W)	Cenote	30 m	Ballcourt (N)		Šprajc 2008
8	Chicaanti-caanal	Strs. 1 and 2	104°/284°	E–W alignment of Str. 1	**Feb 13, Oct 29 (E)** Apr 25, Aug 19 (W)	Cenote	50 m	Triadic Group (E) Ballcourt (E)		Šprajc 2008
9	El Mirador León	Strs. 5D2-1 and 5D1-1, 2, 4, 5	93° 95°34'/275°34'	E–W alignment from Str. 5D2-1 to Str. 5D2-2	**Jun 21 (N)** Mar 13, Sep 30 (C) **Dec 21 (S)** **Mar 7, Oct 6 (E)** Apr 3, Aug 17 (W)	Cenote	50 m	Triadic Group (N) Triadic Group (SE) Triadic Group (S) Ballcourt (NE)		Aveni et al. 2003; Šprajc and Morales 2007

(*continued*)

Table 15.2—Continued

	Site name	West/East structures	Associated azimuth	Azimuth measurements	Dates	Type	Plaza width (E/W)[a]	Associated architecture[b]	Water feature[c]	References
10	El Mirador Pava	Strs. 3A6-1 and 3A6-3	Group of 14°	N–S alignment of Strs. 3A6-1 and 3A6-3		Cenote	55 m	Triadic Group (NW) Triadic Group (NE) Triadic Group (E) Triadic Group (S)	Reservoir (E)	Šprajc et al. 2009:Fig. 2
11	Mucaancah[d]	Strs. 18 and 20				Cenote	60 m	Triadic Group (N) Ballcourt (N)		Šprajc 2008
12	Naachtún[e]	Strs. 20/22 and 23	92°21'	E–W alignment from Str. 20 to Str. 23b	Apr 19, Aug 24 (N) **Mar 15, Sep 29 (C)** Feb 9, Nov 3 (S)	Uaxac.	110 m / 45 m		Reservoir (S)	Aveni et al. 2003
13	Nakbé	Strs. 47 and 51	101°30' 100°26'	E–W alignment from Str. 47 to Str. 51	Apr 19, Aug 24 (N) **Feb 18, Oct 23 (C)** **Feb 19, Oct 22 (E)** Apr 19, Aug 25 (W)	Cenote	50 m	Triadic Group (E) Ballcourt (S)	Reservoir (S)	Aveni et al. 2003; Velásquez 1999; Šprajc and Morales 2007
14	Oxpemul[f]	Strs. 2 and 5	98°37'	E–W alignment from Str. 2 to Str. 5b	Apr 21, Aug 23 (N) **Feb 28, Oct 14 (C)**	Cenote?	55 m	Triadic Group (S) Ballcourt (E)		Aveni et al. 2003; Šprajc 2008
15	El Pesquero	Strs. 7 and 5				Cenote	60 m	Triadic Group (N)		Mejía 2009; Mejía et al. 2010
16	Las Torres	Strs. 27 and 45				Cenote	45 m			Mejía 2009
17	Uxul	Strs. XI and XIII	93°25' 93°25'/273°25'	E–W alignment from Str. XI to Str. XIIIb E–W alignment of Str. XI	Apr 14, Aug 30 (N) **Mar 12, Oct 2 (C)** Jan 15, Nov 30 (S) **Mar 12, Oct 2 (E)** Mar 28, Sep 15 (W)	Cenote	60 m	Ballcourt (SW)		Aveni et al. 2003; Šprajc 2008

	Site	Structures	Azimuth	Alignment	Dates	Water	Width	Associated Architecture	Reference
18	Veintiuno de Mayo								Šprajc 2008
19	Wakna	Plaza A, Strs. 6 and 2	92° ca. 6° E of N	E–W alignment from Str. 6 to Str. 2	Jun 21 (N) **Mar 25, Sep 18 (C)** Jan 27, Nov 16 (C1) Dec 21 (S) **Mar 7, Oct 6 (E)** Apr 3, Aug 17 (W)	Uaxac.? Cenote	53 m	Triadic Group (N) Triadic Group (S)	Reservoir (NW) Aveni et al. 2003; Mejía and Valle 2006
20	Xulnal	Strs. 3C6 and 3C8				Cenote	50 m	Triadic Group (E)	
21	Xulnal South	Group D				Cenote	65 m	Ballcourt (N)	Reservoir (NE)
22	Yaxnohcah	Brisa 1 and 3	100°40′/280°40′	E–W alignment from Brisa 1 to Brisa 3	**Feb 22, Oct 20 (E)** Apr 16, Aug 28 (W)	Cenote	52 m	Triadic Group (N) Ballcourt (N) Residential group (N)	Reservoir (NE) Reese-Taylor and Anaya 2013; Šprajc 2008
23	El Zacatal	Strs. 2 and 3				Cenote	48 m	Triadic Group (N) Ballcourt (NE)	Šprajc 2008

[a] With the exception of Wakna (Mejía and Valle 2006), all plaza width measurements are approximations based upon plan maps of the site.

[b] Refers to architecture adjacent to the E Group.

[c] Refers to water features adjacent to or within the E Group.

[d] Šprajc (2008) does not consider this complex to be an E Group. However, the arrangement of the structures and the dimensions of the plaza, as well as the associated architecture, fall well within the range of variation identified for Cenote-style E Groups.

[e] Str. 20 is a large structure measuring 38 m in height on the western edge of the plaza, while Str. 22 is a small radial pyramid 5 m in height in the middle of the plaza. Plaza measurements were taken from both structures: 110 m between Str. 20 and Str. 18 and 45 m between Str. 22 and Str. 18. It is quite likely that Str. 22 was the vantage point from which most astronomical observations were made. This could explain the minor discrepancy in dates at Naachtún compared to others in the Group of 11°.

[f] Šprajc (2008) questions this identification because of the height difference between the eastern and western structures, although Aveni et al. (2003) include Oxpemul in their sample of E Groups from throughout the May region. I include it because even though the eastern structure is the more elevated of the two, it is possible to mark the rising of astronomical bodies from a vantage point on the western structure.

León (Farley 2007; Matheny and Matheny 2011), El Mirador Pava (Howell 1989; Matheny and Matheny 2011; Suyuc et al. 2006), El Cedro, El Pesquero, and Las Torres (Mejía 2009), Naachtún (Rangel and Reese-Taylor 2005, 2013; Reese-Taylor et al. 2005), Nakbé (Morales et al. 2008), and Yaxnohcah (Reese-Taylor and Anaya Hernández 2013, 2014).

Dates for the earliest construction of E Groups in this region vary. Based on ceramics recovered from excavations, the Yaxnohcah Brisa E Group dates to the early Middle Preclassic (1000–600 BCE), while the Nakbé E Group is dated to the late Middle Preclassic (600–350 BCE) (Hansen 1992a:180; Morales et al. 2008). The initial phases of both the El Mirador León E Group (Farley 2007) and El Pesquero E Group (Mejía 2009) may also date to the late Middle Preclassic, although more excavations and radiocarbon dates are needed to confirm this tentative claim. During the Late Preclassic period, E Groups were constructed at Calakmul (Andrews 1995; Carrasco and Boucher 1994) and also in the Pava Complex at El Mirador (Demarest 1984; Howell 1989). Finally, the E Group at Naachtún was constructed initially during the Early Classic period; ceramics recovered from excavations and cleaning of looter's trenches in Structure 23 suggest that the initial phase dates to 150–300 CE (Rangel and Reese-Taylor 2005; Reese-Taylor et al. 2005).

The orientations of E Groups in the Central Karstic Uplands fall between 3° east of north to 14° east of north, yet astronomical alignments are often grouped in sets. For instance, Šprajc (2008) and Morales (Šprajc and Morales 2007) identified several clusters of alignments in the southeastern Petén and at El Mirador. Anthony Aveni, Anne S. Dowd, and Benjamin Vining (2003) identified an important alignment cluster, the Group of 14°, which demarcates the Tzolk'in calendar. There are several important factors to consider, however, when developing these clusters.

First, the azimuth measurements are imprecise. Even when the azimuths are measured in the field, as are the measurements for the E Groups from a number of sites in southern Campeche, the measurements are taken from unexcavated structures. Therefore, Šprajc (2008) estimates an accuracy of ±1°, while Aveni et al. (2003:162) suggest an accuracy of ±2°.

Second, while the azimuths are very interesting, especially when considering issues of city planning in general, what is specifically important regarding E Groups are the days on which the sunrises or sunsets are observed from within complexes. Determining the days is not a function of simple azimuths, but we must also consider declination angles and height of the structures. These are not available on rectified maps, so when reckoning which days are observed in these complexes, the range of variation is much greater. Šprajc (2008) states that variation can be as much as ±3 days.

Finally, what people choose to observe can also vary, which may affect azimuth measurements. Aveni (2001:66) gives an excellent example of this subjectivity: "The modern experimenter who tries to duplicate ancient solar observations is immediately beset with the problem of the definition of sunset." Because of horizon angles and declinations, the azimuth measurements for the setting sun taken from the center of the disk may differ from the azimuth measurements taken from the upper edge of the disk.

Therefore, azimuth measurements are not an end. They are heuristic tools for predicting the days that were venerated within these complexes. The azimuth groupings are useful in a very general sense, but the days being commemorated in the E Groups should be the focus of our studies. Therefore, based on the days being commemorated, I have classified the E Groups in the Central Karstic Uplands into four types.

Solstice Commemorative E Groups

One discernible pattern consists of E Groups that specifically commemorate the solstices. Only three of these types of E Groups have been identified because solstice days are normally observed when the sun rises over northern or southern architectural features, and only a few of these alignments have been recorded. E Groups that follow this pattern include Calakmul, El Mirador León, and Wakna.

Haab Commemorative E Groups

Days commemorated by these E Groups occur on either side of the summer solstice (SS) or the zenith passages (ZP) and are bundled into groups of twenty, as if they were months in the Haab. If we count in multiples of twenty from June 22, then the following sets of days were significant:

20 days = June 2/July 11
40 days = May 13/July 31
60 days = April 23/August 20
80 days = April 3/September 9
100 days = May 14/September 29
120 days = February 22/October 19.

Another set of commemorative days occurs in multiples of twenty on either side of zenith passage. According to Aveni et al. (2003), zenith passage falls between May 9–12 and August 2–5 in this region. Determining precise sets of days requires knowledge of the exact latitude of each site. Even with this information, however, allowances are given because precise zenith passage is difficult to identify with naked-eye astronomy (Aveni et al. 2003:175).

The latitudes of the sites in this study fall between 17°30' and 18°18'. According to the *American Ephemeris and Nautical Atlas* (U.S. Naval Observatory 1903), the zenith passage dates range from midday on May 10 to midday on May 13 and August 4 to August 1, respectively. We would expect to see a difference of two or three days between commemorative events when moving from south to north. The average of these days is May 12 and August 2 (rounding down from 2.5). Therefore, for purposes of this study, I use these dates with a range of variation of ±2 days. Significant sets of days include:

20 days = April 23/August 21
40 days = April 3/September 10
60 days = May 14/September 30
80 days = February 22/October 20
100 days = February 2/November 9
20 days = January 13/November 29.

What is noticeable right away is that in four out of six instances, these dates overlap almost exactly: April 23/August 20 (SS) and April 23/August 21 (ZP), April 3/September 9 (SS) and April 3/September 10 (ZP), May 14/September 29 (SS) and May 14/September 30 (ZP), and February 22/October 19 (SS) and February 22/October 20 (ZP). This suggests that the majority of the E Groups in this region would have been able to commemorate both summer solstice and zenith passages.

What is important about this type of E Group, however, is that it defines months of twenty days, the foundation of the Haab, the 365-day solar year. For example, at Yaxnohcah, the solar year is divided into four segments based on the days commemorated in the Brisa Complex E Group, February 22 and October 20.

February 22–June 21 = 120 days
June 22–October 20 = 120 days
October 21–December 21 = 63 days
December 22–February 22 = 62 days.

Each of the four segments is further partitioned into months of 20 days each with a period of 5 days (the Wayeb) falling immediately before and after the December solstice.

Haab Commemorative E Groups include Arroyo Negro, Balakbal, Calakmul, El Mirador León, Naachtún, Nakbé, Uxul, Wakna, and Yaxnohcah. The complexes from Calakmul, El Mirador León, and Wakna are also Solstice Commemorative E Groups. Their primary azimuths, however, from the center of the western structure to the center of the eastern structure, delineate months of 20 days on either side of the solstice or zenith passage. These E Groups, then, are members of both the Haab and Solstice Commemorative groups.

Tzolk'in Commemorative E Groups

Finally some E Groups specifically commemorate the Tzolk'in, the ritual calendar of 260 days.[2] For instance, from February 12 to October 30 is 260 days. E Groups from both Champerico and Chicaanticaanal commemorate dates that demarcate the Tzolk'in. The major alignment associated with this type of E Group is ca. 14° east of north, measured from the center of the western structure to the center of the eastern structure. While the commemorative dates are not given, Šprajc et al. (2009) also identify 14° east of north as the primary azimuth of the El Mirador La Pava E Group.[3]

The commemoration of the 260-day cycle, beginning on February 12 and ending on October 30, becomes common in Mesoamerica during the Classic period (CE 250–900), particularly among the Maya. According to Šprajc (2008), it is the predominant alignment of architectural complexes in southern Campeche. Aveni et al. (2003) have argued that alignments identifying these days were first established at Teotihuacán and then adopted by the Lowland Maya during the Early Classic period. If the El Mirador La Pava E Group indeed observes these days, as suggested by a 14° azimuth, then this practice may have originated in the Central Karstic Uplands.

E Groups Commemorating Unique Dates

The Altar de los Reyes E Group commemorates the days March 7 and October 6. This complex was measured in the field by Šprajc (Flores and Šprajc 2008; Šprajc 2008). While these dates do not seem to have an obvious significance to us, no doubt they were important to the people that built this E Group. Interestingly, these two dates occur 60 days on either side of May 6 and August 8: both May 6 and August 8 are commemorated in the northern and southern alignments of the Balakbal E Group (Table 15.2) (Aveni et al. 2003). Given the proximity of May 6 and August 8 to zenith passage dates in this region, it is likely that the events taking place on these days were related to zenith passage observations.

These days may also have been commemorated in two other E Groups: El Mirador León (Šprajc and Morales 2007) and Wakna (Mejía and Valle 2006). Šprajc (personal communication, 2013) has expressed a lack of confidence in the azimuth measurements on which the dates are based, however, because of the deteriorated condition of the architecture in the El Mirador León E Group. Héctor Mejía and Gendry Valle (2006) do not give their methodology for determining this azimuth at Wakna. Given that alternate azimuths for these groups were available (Aveni et al. 2003), these two alignments and their accompanying dates were not considered in this study. Nonetheless, they are given in the table so that a complete record of all measurements is available to scholars.

Finally, Oxpemul commemorates another unique set of dates, February 28 and October 14, with its primary alignment. These two dates do not establish bundles of 20 days on either side of a solstice or zenith passage, so they likely do not work to track the Haab. Also, they do not constitute a period of 260 days, so they do not demarcate the Tzolk'in; but the dates commemorated by the azimuth from the west to the northeastern structure of the E Group are April 21 and August 23, and they occur 20 days on either side of the zenith passage days. Therefore, it is possible that the Oxpemul complex should be included in the Haab Commemorative grouping.[4]

Architecture and Features Associated with E Groups

Triadic Groups

Triadic Groups are commonly in direct association with E Groups, complementing a majority of the E Groups in the Central Karstic Uplands (thirteen out of twenty-three E groups have associated triadic groups) (Table 15.2). Most of these triadic arrangements consist of three structures configured in a triangle form, with the largest structure situated at the apex of the triangle, flanked by two much smaller structures of equal size. This triad of structures was placed atop massive platforms; therefore, these architectural complexes constitute acropolises.

Triadic Groups located to the east of E Groups always amplify the astronomical alignments. Atasta Flores and Šprajc (2008) refer to these as Acropolis E Groups. Acropolis E Groups may be found at Altar de los Reyes (Flores Esquivel and Šprajc 2008), Chicaanticaanal, El Mirador León, El Mirador La Pava, Nakbé, and Xulnal. These acropolises provide several additional sight lines that would have allowed early astronomers to refine

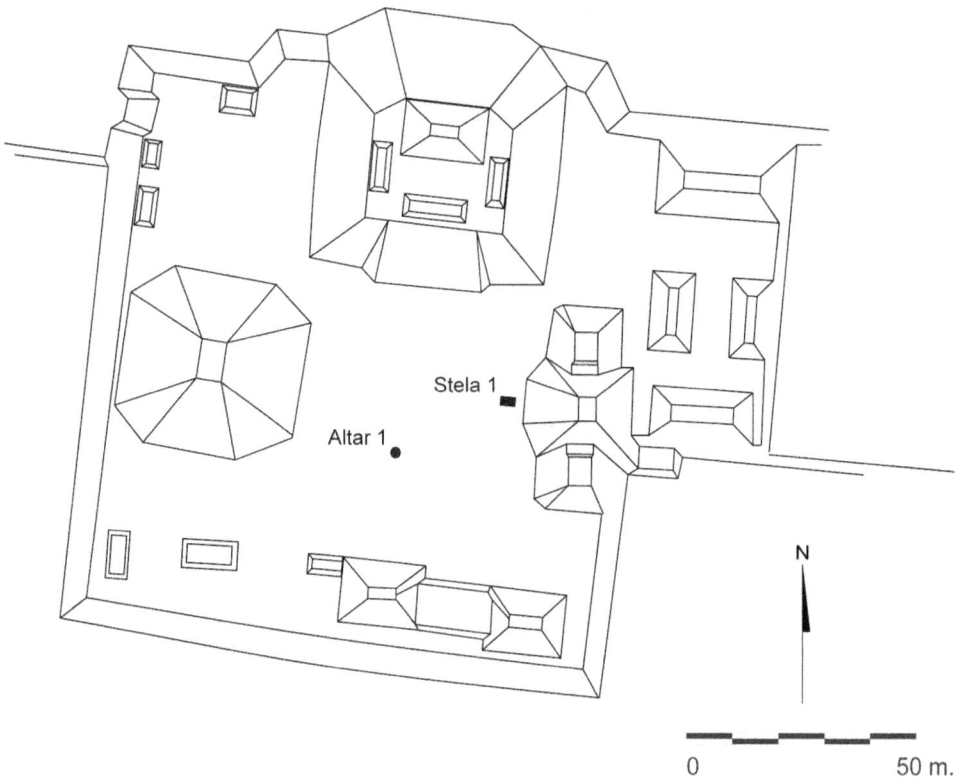

Figure 15.4. Map of El Zacatal (after F. C. Atasta Flores in Šprajc 2009:Figure 3.1).

calendric observations. For instance, an azimuth of 24° east of north is obtained when sighting from the western building in the Altar de los Reyes E Group to the northernmost structure associated with the acropolis to the east (Flores Esquivel and Šprajc 2008). This azimuth is commonly associated with the commemoration of solstices (Šprajc 2008). Therefore, the appendage of the triadic acropolis to the east augmented the number of ritual days that could be commemorated within the complex.

Triadic acropolises located directly north and south are also common within the Central Karstic Uplands. Northern acropolises can be found at El Zacatal and Mucaancah, while southern acropolises have been recorded at El Mirador León, El Mirador Pava, and Oxpemul. Acropolises in both the north and south have been identified at Calakmul, Wakna, and Yaxnohcah. These acropolises all provide a strong north–south alignment that complements the east–west alignment established by the E Groups.

The north–south alignment is commonly established from a vantage point in the center of the apex structure in the triad sighting to a feature, generally a building or a monument, on the opposite side of the E Group.[5] For instance, at El Zacatal, the north–south alignment is established from a northern vantage point in the center of the Structure 1 apex to the center of Structure 5 in the south. This sight line also bisects Altar 1 in the middle of the E Group (Figure 15.4). The north–south alignment, in most cases, is ca. 90° to the east–west alignment established by the E Group.[6] The objective, then, of these complexes seems to be the laying out of the four directions and centering the settlement (Stanton and Freidel 2005).

At El Mirador's León, a triadic group was also constructed in the southeast, and at El Mirador's Pava triadic groups were constructed in the northeast and northwest. At this time, however, the relationship between the E Group and triadic groups placed in the intercardinal directions is unclear.

Ballcourts

Another type of architecture closely associated with E Groups is the ballcourt (Table 15.2); ballcourts are found in association with twelve out of twenty-three E Groups (Aimers and Rice 2006:Table 3). In the Central Karstic Uplands, there seems to have been a preference for placing ballcourts to the north or south of E Groups as well.

The alignments of ballcourts are generally unavailable, and their small size, as rendered on maps, often does not allow for even an imprecise azimuth to be obtained. There is a general pattern of a north–south alignment in the Central Karstic Uplands, however, suggesting that ballcourts reinforced the north–south axis of the site. In the case of Champerico, Uxul, and Xulnal south, the ballcourt may have established the north–south axis. In the two cases, at Oxpemul (ballcourt to the east) and at Balakbal (ballcourt to the west), the ballcourts are oriented east–west and seem to follow the same azimuth as the E Groups.

The E Group, the triadic acropolis, and the ballcourt are in close physical proximity in many sites: Altar de los Reyes, Chicaanticaanal, El Mirador Leon, El Zacatal, Mucaancah, Nakbé, Oxpemul, and Yaxnohcah.

Reservoirs

Reservoirs are less commonly found in direct association with E Groups in the Central Karstic Uplands (Table 15.2). Sites with reservoirs near E Groups include Calakmul, El Mirador Pava, Naachtún, Nakbé, Wakna,

Xulnal, and Yaxnohcah. Because of the small number, no directional preference could be determined. Only Nakbé and Yaxnohcah, however, have civic complexes including an E Group, triadic acropolis, ballcourt, and reservoir in close association.

Residential Groups

Only Yaxnohcah has a residential group adjacent to the E Group. This residential group, the Baalche' Group, is a large multiroom palace on the northern edge of the Brisa plaza. The Baalche' palace was originally constructed during the Late Preclassic period.

The Ideological Constructs of Early Landscapes

E Groups were certainly central in Preclassic landscapes. In some cases, archaeological excavations suggest that they were the first structures built by the earliest settlers in the Central Karstic Uplands. At Yaxnohcah, the earliest civic structures uncovered so far include the Brisa E Group and the Helena platform, both of which date to the late Early to early Middle Preclassic (1000–600 BCE) in the standard chronology used in this volume. Two reservoirs are associated with the Brisa E Group (Figure 15.5). While no dates are available for the smaller reservoir to the west of the ballcourt (the Baalche' Reservoir), the massive Brisa Reservoir to the south of the E Group is early. Ceramics dating to the late Middle Preclassic were recovered in excavations placed into the berm that surrounded the tank. The ballcourt to the north of the Brisa E Group is one of four ballcourts at the site but is, arguably, the most significant because of its location at one southern end of the formal north–south avenue that connects the Alba triadic acropolis to the Brisa E Group.

The Nakbé E Group appears to have been initially constructed during the late Middle Preclassic (600–300 BCE) (Hansen 1992a, 1992b). The ballcourt just south of the E Group also dates to this time (Velásquez 1992). As at Yaxnohcah, a large reservoir lies just west of the Nakbé ballcourt. Structure 59, the triadic complex east of the E Group at Nakbé, is poorly reported; however, Gustavo Martínez (1994) notes that the earliest floor of this complex (Piso 4) dates to the Middle Preclassic.[7] Therefore, the sacred landscapes of Yaxnohcah and Nakbé appear to have encompassed all the architectural features embodying the Preclassic religious canon, as early as the late Middle Preclassic.[8]

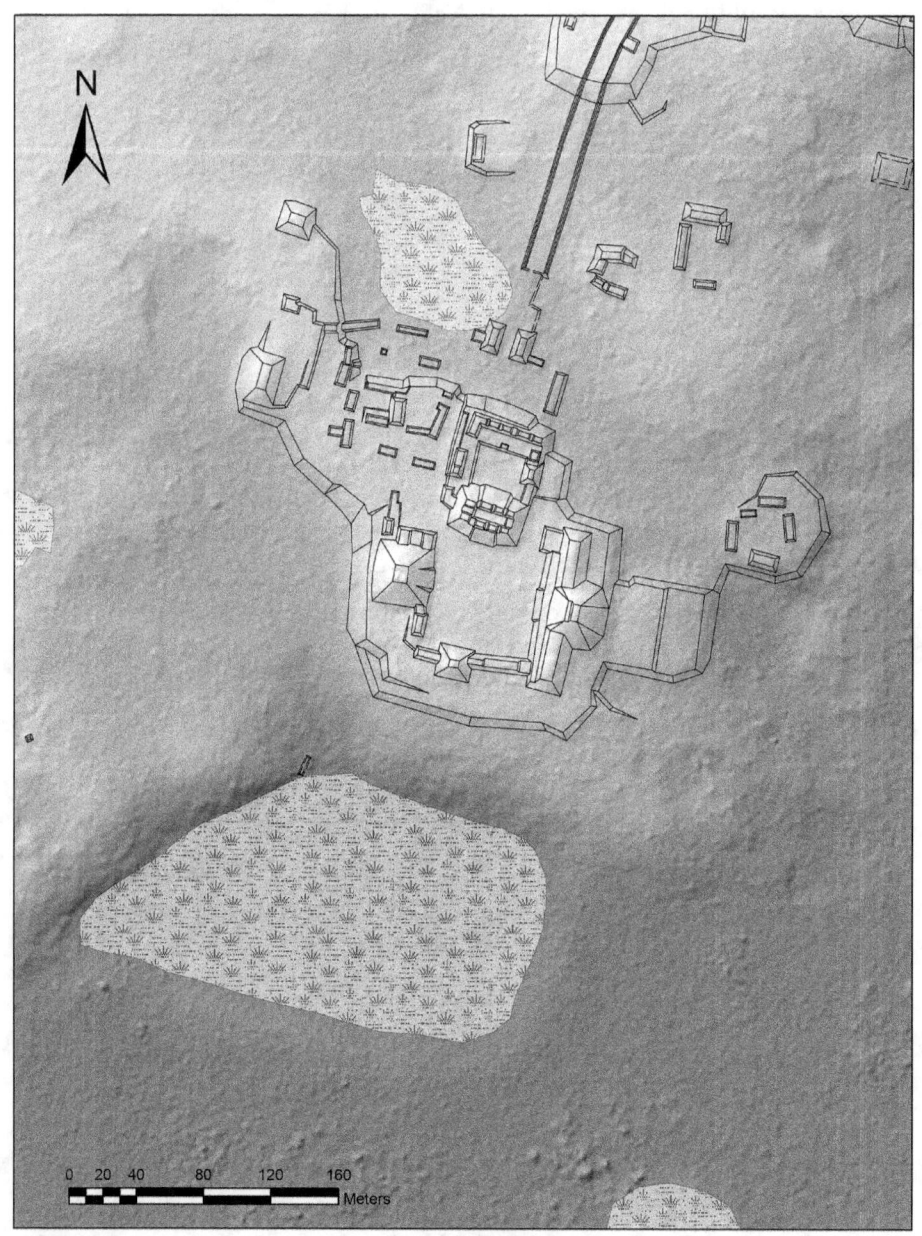

Figure 15.5. Map of Brisa E Group and reservoirs by F. C. Atasta Flores.

E Groups

The temporalization of space lies at the heart of Middle Preclassic landscapes. The construction of complexes designed to track the solar year established the Haab as the communal calendar shared across great distances. It also allowed dispersed colonists to schedule public ceremonies around important dates in the agricultural cycle. Sharing a common calendar and commemorative "feast" days helped to codify Maya religion and unify a worldview among early sedentary groups.

Early E Groups also delineated the known universe. The movement of the sun defined an important east–west axis, as well as the levels of the cosmos. The east–west axis reflected the duality of the world that permeated all aspects of daily life. For instance, among the Chortí the solar year is divided into two seasons, separated by the first solar zenith passage, which marks the beginning of the rainy season, and possibly the solar nadir in November that marks the beginning of the dry season (Girard 1962). The rainy season is associated with darkness and the dry season with light. The Tzotzil Maya also divide the year into two seasonal halves, with the right hand (also associated with the direction north) symbolic of the rainy season and the left hand (also associated with the direction south) symbolic of the dry season (Gossen 1974; Hopkins and Josserand 2001).

The constructs of zenith and nadir, implicit in the movement of the sun and other astronomical bodies, also laid out the levels of the cosmos. The sun's journey was viewed from the vantage point of the earthly realm, but with an understanding that the sun's zenith passage defined an upper realm and its nadir passage defined a lower realm. This principle of laying out the levels of the cosmos was also enacted in the public caching rituals and mortuary practices (Acuña 2007, 2009; Estrada-Belli 2006, Chase and Chase 1998; Chapter 7 in this volume; McAnany et al. 1999; Smith 1982).

Finally, E Groups may have defined the corners of the known universe by marking the rising and setting of the sun on the summer and winter solstices (Girard 1962; Köhler 1980; Villa 1945; Sosa 1985). While solstice observations were important in some early E Groups, it is difficult to determine whether Middle Preclassic E Groups in the Central Karstic Uplands commemorated these days because of the overlap discussed above and also because we lack the northern and southern azimuths that specifically demarcate solstice days.[9] Clearly, the E Groups at Calakmul, El Mirador León, and Wakna do observe the solstices, but this practice may have started during the Late Preclassic in this region. At Yaxnohcah, the Fidelia Complex, an enormous Middle Preclassic platform and its superstructures, is specifically oriented to 24° east of north, aligned to commemorate the winter solstice. Therefore, it is possible that solstice rituals were not celebrated in E Groups but in complementary civic complexes during the Middle Preclassic.

Three Stone Places

The E Groups at Yaxnohcah and Nakbé are associated with other types of architecture that further reified early Maya religious ideology. Triadic Groups are monumental structures symbolic of the three hearthstones found in Maya houses and the mythological three stones of creation (Taube 1998). These stones are significant in the Maya creation myth as recorded on Quiriguá Stela C. During the creation of the world, the three stones of the cosmic hearth were set. The Classic period inscription on Quiriguá Stela C is perhaps the most detailed account of these actions; yet the creation events were viewed through the lens of Late Classic kingship in the southeastern Maya region (Freidel et al. 1993; Looper 2003). On Stela C, each of the three stones is referred to as a specific stone throne, linking these important acts of creation with kingship. The earliest compelling evidence for kingship is found in the San Bartolo murals, however, dating to roughly 200 BCE. The Nakbé and Yaxnohcah triadic complexes predate these murals by 100–200 years, therefore suggesting that metaphorical references to the three stones embodied by the triadic complexes were not originally aspects of a royal charter but explicitly religious in nature.

But what exactly was the religious nature of the three stone symbolism? David Freidel, Linda Schele, and Joy Parker (1993) and Karl Taube (1998) argue that the three stones center the cosmos during the act of creation just as the three hearthstones center the house. While this may be true, it does not explain the relationship between triadic complexes and E Groups in early landscapes. One possible explanation can be inferred from the west wall of Pinturas Sub 1-A at San Bartolo.

In the first four scenes, an individual, who may be an early version of Hun Ajaw, is depicted making sacrifices at the foot of the World Tree (Taube et al. 2010). Taube et al. (2010:19) suggest a conceptual overlap between the Preclassic version of Hun Ajaw and the Classic period concept of the "Four Lords," a group of deities associated with period endings and calendar rites. Furthermore, David Stuart (2004) argues that the "Four Lords" were the Classic period counterparts to the yearbearers, best known from the codices.

Additionally, in each scene an animal was placed on a tripod and a group of smoking or flaming stones was inserted into the open cavity of each sacrifice. We understand that these were stones because of the *kawak* markings drawn on each.[10] The number of stones varies. In the first scene, five stones were placed in the cavity of a fish. In the second and third scenes, three stones were placed into the cavities of a deer and a turkey, respectively. The fourth scene depicts Hun Ajaw walking on bed of yellow flowers.

In all cases, the sacrifices were made at the base of the World Tree with the Principal Bird Deity perched in its upper branches. According to Taube et al. (2010), the Principal Bird Deity in the tree of each scene was also associated with a cardinal direction. The fifth scene, which follows the four sacrifices, portrayed the Principal Bird Deity descending from a sky band with a terminating serpent's head and attended by swirling black elements, probably denoting dark rain clouds (Taube et al. 2010:46).

The ground line on which Hun Ajaw walked in the first three scenes represented the three levels of the cosmos. In the first scene, he walked on a watery surface atop a crocodile and sacrificed a fish, both symbolic of the watery underworld. In the second scene, he was striding on a solid ground line and sacrificed a deer, both symbolic of the terrestrial realm. In the third scene, he floated several inches above the ground and sacrificed a turkey, depicting an aerial or heavenly realm (Taube et al. 2010).

Rituals based on this mythic narrative could have been enacted in the E Group and adjacent acropolis complexes. E Groups would have offered a temporal landscape based upon the Haab and manifested the four directions (east–west; zenith–nadir) as well as created the three levels of the cosmos. The three superstructures in the triadic arrangement atop the large truncated platforms created a symbolic three-stone place, serving to center the space and manifesting the hearth in which the sacrifices were made (Freidel et al. 1993; Taube 1998; Taube et al. 2010).[11]

Rain and the Resurrection of the Maize Deity

In both Nakbé and Yaxnohcah, the ballcourt and the reservoir are located immediately adjacent to each other, with the ballcourt to the east and the reservoir to the west. Their close proximity suggests that they are to be treated as a single ritual complex. The Colonial period (1519–1697 CE) Popol Vuh records that ballcourts were the location of the Maize God's resurrection, which occurred in the underworld (Tedlock 1996). The murals of San Bartolo also depict the resurrection of the Maize God, although the event is viewed through a quatrefoil portal, an opening to the underworld, which was located in the body of an earth turtle (Taube et al. 2010). During the Classic period, the Maize God is often depicted sprouting from the back of a crack in a turtle carapace or from a cleft in a mountain. Cross sections of ballcourts are also synonymous with mountain clefts in the Maya religious lexicon. Therefore, at least during the Classic period, there was considerable conceptual overlap between cracks in the earth's surface, metaphorically represented as a turtle or a mountain, and ballcourts.

Pools of water, quatrefoils, and mirrors are the window/portal between the three levels of the cosmos (Chapter 6 in this volume). Moreover, they are metaphorically equivalent in Maya imagery. For instance, a Middle Preclassic earthen quatrefoil from La Blanca was meant to contain water (Love and Guernsey 2007:926). Water imagery is also prevalent on the stucco quatrefoil from Aguacatal, Campeche (Houston et al. 2005). The quatrefoil on the West Wall at San Bartolo shows a Maize God dancing between two other deities sitting on either side. The deity to the south is Chaak, god of rain and lightning, while the deity to the north is the god of terrestrial water (Taube et al. 2010).

Quatrefoils and pools of water are also viewed as windows/portals to the underworld (Freidel et al. 1993; Tedlock 1992). As seen in the West Wall of the San Bartolo murals, the viewer in this realm can observe events transpiring in the underworld through the quatrefoil portal. Other examples of viewing events in the underworld through a quatrefoil portal include the carved Copán peccary skull and the three Copán ballcourt markers.[12] During the Preclassic, no entity is depicted as traveling through the portal in the Maya Lowlands, although in the Classic period the Maize God (Bonampak Stela 1), rulers (Copán ballcourt markers), and apparently sacrificial victims travel between realms (Tikal Altar 10).

Half sections of quatrefoils are depicted as the mouths of caves, which are also entrances to the underworld in both the San Bartolo murals and in the pictographs from Chalcatzingo Monument 1. The imagery from Middle Preclassic Chalcatzingo Monument 1 also portrays rain droplets and mist emerging from the mouth of the cave, as well as small plants growing from its corner (Grove 1968; Guzmán 1934). In the San Bartolo murals, the half-quatrefoil cave mouth on the North Wall has vegetation growing from its exterior.

Therefore, the ritual complex of ballcourt and reservoir at Nakbé and Yaxnohcah are clearly related to the resurrection of the Maize God in the underworld. The rains that filled the reservoir created the reflective surface through which to view this event in the underworld. Rains were also necessary for maize to sprout, the earthly equivalent to the resurrection of the Maize God. Thus, it is likely that the rituals held in this complex would take place during the rainy season and that their timing would be predicted by solar observations in the E Group.

The Orion Factor

Does the constellation Orion have anything to do with this? In a very general sense, yes. The western constellation Orion is actually composed of two Maya constellations: the Three Stone Place and the ballcourt/turtle. These two constellations were important during the Middle Preclassic period, when they rose approximately 10–15° east of north. Because of their prominence in the night sky during the Middle Preclassic, the two constellations of Orion were probably important in scheduling household rituals, much like the Pleiades among contemporary Maya.

Today many people observe the movement of the Pleiades to regulate the agricultural season (Milbrath 2000:38). Among the Lacandón, fields are burned when the Pleiades reaches the treetops at dawn (Thompson 1974:93). Among the Quiché, high-altitude maize is planted when the Pleiades set, while low-altitude maize is planted when the Pleiades are in conjunction with the sun in May. Conjunction with the sun also coincides with zenith passage and the onset of rains (Tedlock 1992:185, 189). The K'iche' burn undergrowth and turn soil when the Pleiades reach the meridian immediately after sunset in February. In Yucatán, the Pleiades rise at dawn on June 13, when the rains begin (Redfield and Villa 1962; Sosa 1985).

At 500 BCE from the location of Yaxnohcah, Orion crossed the meridian at sunset on February 22, which coincided with the sunrise date observed in the E Group at Yaxnohcah. Orion began to set at sunset on May 7 and completely disappeared by May 16, which may have signaled the time for the burning of the fields and turning of soil. Orion then reappeared just before dawn on June 3 and was completely above the horizon just before dawn on June 12. This corresponded with the onset of the rainy season and planting. Therefore, while religious practitioners could track the Haab and schedule rituals by observing the sunrise in the E Group, Middle Preclassic farmers could time agricultural practices by watching the movement of Orion (the ballcourt and the Three Stone Place). It was no coincidence that significant events in the creation narrative (and the agricultural cycle) were mapped onto the most prominent constellation in the night sky.

Conclusions

What can we conclude from this treatise about E Groups in the Central Karstic Uplands? Most of the Central Karstic Uplands E Groups were constructed in the Cenote style, which indicates a Preclassic date for 83 percent of the complexes in this region. The majority of the complexes that have been investigated archaeologically, however, are Late Preclassic in date. The Yaxnohcah E Group dates to the late Early to early Middle Preclassic (1000–600 BCE) using the standard chronology of this volume (see Chapter 1), based on ceramics recovered from beneath plaza floors. The Nakbé E Group has been dated to the late Middle Preclassic period (600–300 BCE), based on ceramics recovered from excavations (Operation 51) placed in the E Group plaza (Hansen 1992a:180). Excavations in El Mirador León also yielded late Middle Preclassic ceramics, but the context is far from clear. Further excavation and radiocarbon dates are needed to substantiate the dates of the E Group complexes in all of these sites.

E Groups in the Central Karstic Uplands overwhelmingly appear to track the Haab, commemorating days that fall in bundles of 20 days on either side of the summer solstice or zenith passage (Chapter 3 in this volume). Only three seem to demarcate the Tzolk'in. One of these three is the El Mirador La Pava E Group, which makes El Mirador the only site that has E Groups tracking both the Haab and the Tzolk'in. This seems fitting, as El Mirador was undoubtedly the most significant religious and political center in the Maya Lowlands during the Late Preclassic.

While E Groups likely did not originate in this region, the people of the Central Karstic Uplands quickly incorporated these complexes into a rich landscape, which included early manifestations of triadic acropolises, ballcourts, and reservoirs. Indeed, the full complement of architecture and features associated with E Groups was constructed very early at Nakbé and Yaxnohcah. These founding landscapes embody the basic tenets of Maya religion, such as centering space, defining the corners of the world, layering the realms, and temporalizing the cosmos. These canons are not only expressed through the rich story of the birth, death, and resurrection of the Maize God but are also conveyed in the daily practices of people as they move through the agricultural cycle.

At some point during the Late Preclassic, emerging elites appropriated communal ceremonies based upon the agricultural cycle and transformed them into ideologies for political legitimation. This is best exemplified at

Yaxnohcah, where a large palace was appended onto the E Group during the Late Preclassic. The juxtaposition of an elite residence with a public religious complex explicitly signified that the family living in the adjacent palace controlled the E Group and its concomitant ceremonies.

At this juncture, E Groups became more commonplace in the Central Karstic Uplands. They were constructed, along with associated architecture and features, to provide venues in which emerging rulers could oversee the ceremonies that incorporated them into the Maize God narrative, thereby substantiating their political authority. Moreover, in the Central Karstic Uplands triadic acropolises, ballcourts, and reservoirs were linked exclusively with Cenote style E Groups. Therefore, the religious ideology and ensuing political authority symbolized by the relationship among these architectural forms seems to have been a Late Preclassic phenomenon and did not endure in this specific form into the Classic period.

E Groups, in their pristine solar commemorative functions, remain emblematic of the Middle Preclassic period. The religious principles embodied within E Groups were first established during this time. And the formation of a uniquely Maya identity was revealed by the presence of E Groups in these early founding landscapes.

Acknowledgments

I would like to thank David Freidel, Arlen Chase, and Anne Dowd for organizing and editing this volume. I would also like to thank Debra S. Walker and James Aimers for their constructive comments on this chapter. I also want to acknowledge the work of Shawn G. Morton and Sarah Bednar on the excavations in the Brisa Complex at Yaxnohcah. This chapter could not have been written without their significant contributions in the field. Finally, I would like to thank the members of the Yaxnohcah Archaeological Project (2011–2015) for their contributions: Armando Anaya Hernández, Sarah Bednar, Jeffrey Brewer, Chris Carr, Nicholas P. Dunning, F. C. Atasta Flores Esquivel, Helga Geovannini Acuña, Shawn G. Morton, Meaghan Peuramaki-Brown, Alejandro Uriarte, Debra S. Walker, Ciriaco and Neri Requena, and the people from Constitución and Conhuas.

Notes

1. Cabro Red was first defined at Cerro Maya (Cerros) on Chetumal Bay in northern Belize (Robertson-Freidel 1980) but has links with contemporary types to the north in Quintana Roo and Yucatán (Robertson 2016). At Cerro Maya, Cabro Red was confined to the Terminal Preclassic period, dating no earlier than 100 BCE and continuing no later than about 200 CE.

2. The Tzolk'in is divided into groups of 20 days and 13 numbers, so technically the Haab commemorative E Groups might also demarcate the Tzolk'in. Only the Tzolk'in commemorative E Groups, however, define a period of 260 days.

3. The Mucaancah E Group may also have a primary azimuth of ca. 14° east of north (±1°).

4. As noted, the E Group at Oxpemul is unusual because the western structure is considerably shorter than the eastern structure. The measurements for this complex were derived from Aveni et al. (2003:167) and were likely made from the Ruppert and Denison (1943) map. Therefore, the horizon angle would not have been available, creating a problem for determining a precise declination. This would also result in an error in the identification of commemorative days.

5. This specifically is not the case at Yaxnohcah. The north–south alignment is ca. 90° to the east–west axis established by the lateral platforms on the triad in both the Alba and the Carmela acropolises.

6. The exception is Mucaancah. In this case, the structure atop the eastern platform of the E Group is skewed south of center. If the east–west azimuth is established from the center of the western structure to the center of the eastern platform, then a right angle (±3°) is created by the north–south and east–west alignments.

7. Martínez (1994:242) does not explicitly state the data on which he bases the dates for Structure 59; however, he *implies* that the Middle Preclassic date was based on the construction techniques.

8. It is interesting that the only two sites with the full complement of E Group, triadic complex, ballcourt, and reservoir have strong Middle Preclassic occupations. Although it is tempting, it would be premature to suggest that this suite of structures first appeared in full at either Nakbé or Yaxnohcah during the Middle Preclassic. At this time, there is no evidence the early Structure 59 substructure was triadic in form (Martínez 1994). Also, the Yaxnohcah E Group is not conclusively dated; nor are dates for the Yaxnohcah ballcourt conclusive.

9. See Francisco Estrada-Belli (Chapter 9 in this volume) for a discussion of solstice commemoration in the E Group at Cival.

10. Kawak is a day sign in the Tzolk'in. The glyph for Kawak includes specific motifs also found on the glyph for the word "stone."

11. Interestingly, the Acropolis E Groups, with acropolises to the east, all appear to have five or more superstructures and may represent a distinct, yet complementary, five-stone place.

12. At Izapa, on Stelae 5 and 27, events on the terrestrial plane are viewed through a quatrefoil from a vantage point in the heavenly sphere.

References Cited

Acuña, Mary Jane
2007 Ancient Maya Cosmological Landscapes: Early Classic Mural Paintings from Río Azul, Petén, Guatemala. M.A. thesis, Latin American Studies, University of Texas, Austin.
2009 Paisajes cosmológicos mayas: Las pinturas murales de Río Azul. In *XXII Simposio de Investigaciones Arqueológicas en Guatemala, 2008*, edited by Juan Pedro Laporte, Bárbara Arroyo, and Héctor Mejía, pp. 1233–1245. Museo Nacional de Arqueología y Etnología, Guatemala City.

Aimers, James J., and Prudence Rice
2006 Astronomy, Ritual, and the Interpretation of the Maya "E-Group" Architectural Assemblages. *Ancient Mesoamerica* 17:79–96.

Andrews, George
1995 Architectural Survey at Calakmul 1994/1995. George F. and Geraldine D. Andrews papers, the Alexander Architectural Archive, University of Texas Libraries, University of Texas, Austin.

Aveni, Anthony F.
2001 *Skywatchers: A Revised and Updated Version of Skywatchers of Ancient Mexico.* University of Texas Press, Austin.

Aveni, Anthony F., Anne S. Dowd, and Benjamin Vining
2003 Maya Calendar Reform?: Evidence from Orientations of Specialized Architectural Assemblages. *Latin American Antiquity* 14:159–178.

Braswell, Geoffrey E., Joel D. Gunn, Maria del Rosario Domínguez Carrasco, William J. Folan, Larraine A. Fletcher, Abel López Morales, and Michael D. Glascock
2004 Defining the Terminal Classic at Calakmul. In *The Terminal Classic in the Maya Lowlands: Collapse, Transition, and Transformation*, edited by Arthur A. Demarest, Prudence M. Rice, and Don S. Rice, pp. 162–194. University Press of Colorado, Boulder.

Carrasco Vargas, Ramón
1998 Metropolis of Calakmul Campeche. In *Maya*, edited by Peter Schmidt, Mercedes de la Garza, and Enrique Nalda, pp. 372–385. Rizzoli International, New York.

Carrasco Vargas, Ramón, and Sylviane Boucher
1994 Calakmul: Espacios sagrados y objectos de poder. *Arqueología Mexicana* 2(10):32–38.

Carrasco Vargas, Ramón, and Marinés Colón González
2005 El reino de Kaan y la antigua ciudad del Calakmul. *Arqueología Mexicana* 13(75):40–47.

Chase, Diane Z., and Arlen F. Chase
1998 The Architectural Context of Caches, Burials, and Other Ritual Activities for the Classic Period Maya (as Reflected at Caracol, Belize). In *Function and Meaning in Classic Maya Architecture*, edited by Stephen D. Houston, pp. 299–332. Dumbarton Oaks Research Library and Collection, Washington, D.C.

Demarest, Arthur A.
1984	Proyecto El Mirador de la Harvard University, 1982–1983. In *Mesoamerica 7*, pp. 1–160. Publicación del Centro de Investigaciones Regionales de Mesoamérica No. 368, Antigua, Guatemala.

Estrada-Belli, Francisco
2006	Lightning Sky, Rain, and the Maize God: The Ideology of Preclassic Maya Rulers at Cival, Peten, Guatemala. *Ancient Mesoamerica* 17(1):57–78.

Farley, Greg
2007	Grupo León, Plaza León: Operaciones 615a, 615b y 612 El Mirador, Petén. In Informe final temporada 2007: Investigación y conservación en los sitios arqueológicos de la zona cultural y natural Mirador, edited by N. M. López, pp. 606–609. Report submitted to Instituto de Antropología e Historia, Guatemala City.

Flores Esquivel, Atasta, and Ivan Šprajc
2008	Reconocimiento arqueológico en el sur de Campeche: Nuevos hallazgos y contribuciones para una visión regional. *Estudios de la Cultural Maya* 32:17–38.

Folan, William J., Joyce Marcus, Sophia Pinceman, María del Rosario Domínguez Carrasco, Larraine Fletcher, and Abel Morales López
1995	Calakmul: New Data from an Ancient Capital in Campeche, Mexico. *Latin American Antiquity* 64(4):310–334.

Folan, William, Abel Morales, Raymundo González, Lynda Florey, and María del Rosario Domínguez Carrasco
2001	Reconocimiento de los sitios arqueológicos de Oxpemul, El Laberinto, Pared de los Reyes, San Felipe, Flor de Cacao y Uxul en el Petén campechano. *Los Investigadores de la Cultura Maya* 9:239–266.

Freidel, David A., Linda Schele, and Joy Parker
1993	*Maya Cosmos: Three Thousand Years on the Shaman's Path*. William and Morrow, New York City.

Girard, Rafael
1962	*Los mayas eternos*. Libro México, Mexico City.

Gossen, Gary H.
1974	*Chamulas in the World of the Sun: Time and Space in a Maya Oral Tradition*. Harvard University Press, Cambridge, Massachusetts.

Grove, David C.
1968	Chalcatzingo, Morelos, Mexico: A Reappraisal of the Olmec Rock Carvings. *American Antiquity* 33:486–491.

Grube, Nikolai, Kai Delvendahl, Nicholaus Seefeld, and Beniamino Volta
2012	Under the Rule of the Smoke Kings: Uxul in the 7th and 8th Centuries. *Estudios de Cultura Maya* 40:11–49.

Guzmán, Eulalia
1934	Los relieves de las rocas del Cerro de la Cantera, Jonacatepec, Morelos. *Anales del Museo Nacional de Arqueología, Historia y Etnografía* 5(1):237–251.

Hansen, Richard D.
1992a	The Archaeology of Ideology: A Study of Maya Formative Architectural Sculp-

ture at Nakbe, Peten, Guatemala. Ph.D. Dissertation, Department of Anthropology, University of California, Los Angeles.

1992b El proceso cultural de Nakbe y el área nor-central de Petén: Las épocas tempranas. In *V Simposio de Investigaciones Arqueológicas en Guatemala, 1991*, edited by Juan Pedro Laporte, Héctor Escobedo, and Sandra Brady, pp. 68–83. Museo Nacional de Arqueología y Etnología, Guatemala City.

1998 Continuity and Disjunction: The Pre-classic Antecedents of Classic Maya Architecture. In *Function and Meaning in Classic Maya Architecture*, edited by Stephen D. Houston, pp. 49–122. Dumbarton Oaks Research Library and Collection, Washington, D.C.

Hopkins, Nicolas A., and J. Kathryn Josserand

2001 Directions and Partitions in Maya World View. Electronic manuscript, Foundation for the Advancement of Mesoamerican Studies. http://www.famsi.org/research/hopkins/DirectionalPartitions.pdf, accessed September 25, 2013.

Houston, Stephen, Zachary Nelson, Gene Ware, Cassandra Messick, Karl Taube, Ray Matheny, and Deanne Matheny

2005 The Pool of the Rain God: An Early Stuccoed Altar at Aguacatal, Campeche, Mexico. *Mesoamerican Voices* 2:37–62.

Howell, Wayne K.

1989 *Excavations in the Danta Complex at El Mirador, Petén, Guatemala*. Papers of the New World Archaeological Foundation 64. New World Archaeological Foundation, Brigham Young University, Provo, Utah.

Köhler, Ulrich

1980 Cosmovisión indígena e interpretación europea en estudios mesoamericanistas. In *La antropología americanista en la Aatualidad: Libro homenaje a Rafael Girard*, Vol. 1, pp. 583–596. Editores Mexicanos Unidos, México City.

Looper, Matthew G.

2003 *Lightning Warrior: Maya Art and Kingship at Quirigua*. University of Texas Press, Austin,.

Love, Michael, and Julia Guernsey

2007 Monument 3 from La Blanca, Guatemala: A Middle Preclassic Earthen Sculpture and Its Ritual Associations. *Antiquity* 81:920–932.

Martínez H., Gustavo

1994 Algunos aspectos arquitectónicos respecto a la Estructura 59 de Nakbé. In *VII Simposio de Investigaciones Arqueológicas en Guatemala, 1993*, edited by Juan Pedro Laporte and Héctor Escobedo, pp. 240–252. Museo Nacional de Arqueología y Etnología, Guatemala City.

Matheny, Ray T., and Deanne G. Matheny

2011 *Introduction to Investigations at El Mirador, Peten, Guatemala*. El Mirador Series, Part 1. Papers of the New World Archaeological Foundation No. 59. Brigham Young University, Provo, Utah.

McAnany, Patricia A., Rebecca Storey, and Angela K. Lockard 1999 Mortuary Ritual and Family Politics at Formative and Early Classic K'axob, Belize. *Ancient Mesoamerica* 10:129–146.

Mejía, Héctor E.
2008   Desarrollo y estructura de las ciudades al Sur de El Mirador, Petén. In *XXI Simposio de Investigaciones Arqueológicas en Guatemala, 2007*, edited by Juan Pedro Laporte, Bárbara Arroyo, and Héctor Mejía, pp. 647–671. Museo Nacional de Arqueología y Etnología, Guatemala City.

Mejía, Héctor E. (editor)
2009   Informe final de investigaciones 2008, tomo II: Investigaciones regionales. Report submitted to Instituto de Antropología e Historia, Guatemala City.

Mejía, Héctor E., Boris Aguilar, Julio Cotom, Hiro Iwamoto, and Antonio Portillo
2010   Rescate arqueológico en El Pesquero: Un sitio de rango intermedio en el límite sur de la Cuenca Mirador. In *XXIII Simposio de Investigaciones Arqueológicas en Guatemala, 2009*, edited by Bárbara Arroyo, Adriana Linares, and Lorena Paiz, pp. 564–578. Museo Nacional de Arqueología y Etnología, Guatemala City.

Mejía, Héctor E., and Gendry Valle
2006   Wakna: Una ciudad prehispánica al sur de Nakbé. In Investigación y conservación en los sitios arqueológicos El Mirador, La Muerta, Wakna, El Porvenir, El Güiro, La Iglesia, La Sarteneja, Chab Che' y La Ceibita: Informe final de la temporada 2005, Vol. 1, compiled by Edgar Suyus Ley and Richard D. Hansen, pp. 6–25. Report submitted to Instituto de Antropología e Historia, Guatemala City.

Milbrath, Susan
2000   *Star Gods of the Maya: Astronomy in Art, Folklore, and Calendrics.* University of Texas Press, Austin.

Morales Aguilar, Carlos, Richard D. Hansen, Abel Morales López, and Wayne K. Howell
2008   Nuevas perspectivas en los modelos de asentamiento maya durante el Preclásico en las Tierras Bajas: Los sitios de Nakbé y El Mirador, Petén. In *XXI Simposio de Investigaciones Arqueológicas en Guatemala, 2007*, edited by Juan Pedro Laporte, Bárbara Arroyo, and Héctor Mejía, pp. 198–213. Museo Nacional de Arqueología y Etnología, Guatemala City.

Rangel Guillermo, Martin, and Kathryn Reese-Taylor (editors)
2005   *Resultados de investigaciones arqueológicos en Naachtun, temporada 2004.* http://www.mesoweb.com/resources/informes/Naachtun2004.html, accessed December 29, 2005.
2013   *Proyecto Arqueologica Naachtun, 2004–2009: Informe no. 2, segundo temporada de campo en el sitio arqueológico Naachtun.* http://www.mesoweb.com/resources/informes/Naachtun2005.html, accessed February 1, 2013.

Redfield, Robert, and Alfonso Villa Rojas
1962   *Chan Kom: A Maya Village.* University of Chicago Press, Chicago.

Reese-Taylor, Kathryn, and Armando Anaya Hernández (editors)
2013   *Proyecto Arqueológico Yaxnohcah, 2011: Informe de la primera temporada de investigaciones.* http://www.mesoweb.com/resources/informes/Yaxnohcah2011.html, accessed July 1, 2013.
2014   *Proyecto Arqueológico Yaxnohcah, 2013: Informe de la segunda temporada*

de investigaciones. http://www.mesoweb.com/resources/informes/Yaxnohcah2013.html, accessed November 1, 2014.

Reese-Taylor, Kathryn, Peter Mathews, Marcelo Zamora Mejía, Debra Walker, Martin Rangel, Silvia Alvarado, Ernesto Arredondo, Shawn Morton, Alex Parmington, Roberta Parry, Baudilio Salazar, and Jeff Seibert
2005   Proyecto Arqueológico Naachtun: Resultados preliminares de la primera temporada de campo 2004. In *XVIII Simposio de investigaciones arqueológicas en Guatemala*, edited by Juan Pedro Laporte, Bárbara Arroyo, and Héctor E. Mejía, pp. 91–100. Ministerio de Cultura y Deportes, Instituto de Antropología e Historia, Asociación Tikal, and Foundation for the Advancement of Mesoamerican Studies, Guatemala City.

Robertson, Robin Alayne
2016   Red Wares, Zapatista, Drinking Vessels, Colonists and Exchange at Cerro Maya. In *Perspectives on the Ancient Maya of Chetumal Bay*, edited by Debra S. Walker, pp. 125–148. University Press of Florida, Gainesville.

Robertson-Freidel, Robin Alayne
1980   *The Ceramics from Cerros: A Late Preclassic Site in Northern Belize*. Ph.D. dissertation, Harvard University, Cambridge, Massachusetts; University Microfilms, Ann Arbor, Michigan.

Robichaux, Hubert R., and Candace Pruett
2008   Investigaciones epigráficas en Oxpemul, Campeche: Descubrimientos recientes. *Investigadores de la Cultura Maya* 16(1):89–106.

Ruppert, Karl, and John H. Denison
1943   *Archaeological Reconnaissance in Campeche, Quintana Roo, and Petén*. Publication 543. Carnegie Institution of Washington, Washington, D.C.

Smith, A. Ledyard
1982   *Major Architecture and Caches: Excavations at Seibal, Department of Peten, Guatemala, No. 1*. Memoirs of the Peabody Museum of Archaeology and Ethnology, Harvard University, Vol. 15. Harvard University Press, Cambridge, Massachusetts.

Sosa, John
1985   Maya Sky, the Maya World: A Symbolic Analysis of Yucatec Maya Cosmology. Ph.D. dissertation, Department of Anthropology, State University of New York at Albany.

Šprajc, Ivan (editor)
2008   *Reconocimiento arqueológico en el sureste del estado de Campeche, México: 1996-2005*. Paris Monographs in American Archaeology 19, BAR International Series 1742. British Archaeological Reports, Oxford, United Kingdom.

Šprajc, Ivan, Florentino García Cruz, and Héber Ojeda Mas
1997   Reconocimiento arqueológico en el sureste de Campeche, México: Informe preliminar. *Mexicon* 19(1):5–12.

Šprajc, Ivan, and Carlos Morales Aguilar
2007   Alineamientos astronómicos en los sitios arqueológicos de Tintal, el Mirador y Nakbé, Petén, Guatemala. In *Informe final temporada 2007: Investigación y conservación en los sitios arqueológicos de la zona cultural y natural mirador,*

edited by Nora María López, pp. 123–158. Report submitted to Instituto de Antropología e Historia, Guatemala City.

Šprajc, Ivan, Carlos Morales Aguilar, and Richard D. Hansen
2009   Early Maya Astronomy and Urban Planning at El Mirador, Peten, Guatemala. *Anthropological Notebooks* 15(3):79–101.

Stanton, Travis W., and David A. Freidel
2005   Placing the Centre, Centring the Place: The Influence of Formative Sacbeob in Classic Site Design at Yaxuná, Yucatán, Mexico. *Cambridge Archaeological Journal* 15(2):225–249.

Stuart, David
2004   New Year Records in Classic Maya Inscriptions. *PARI Journal* 5(2):1–6.

Suyuc, Edgar, Ana Luisa Arriola, and Enrique Hernández
2006   Excavaciones en El Grupo La Pava, Complejo Danta, Operación 402. In *Investigación y conservación en los sitios arqueológicos El Mirador, La Muerta, Wakna, El Porvenir, El Guiro, La Iglesia, La Sarteneja, Chab Che' y La Ceibita: Informe final de la temporada 2005*, edited by Edgar Suyuc Ley and Richard D. Hansen, pp. 490–522. Report submitted to Instituto de Antropología e Historia, Guatemala City.

Taube, Karl
1998   The Jade Hearth: Centrality, Rulership, and the Classic Maya Temple. In *Function and Meaning in Classic Maya Architecture*, edited by Stephen D. Houston, pp. 427–478. Dumbarton Oaks Research Library and Collection, Washington, D.C.

Taube, Karl, William A. Saturno, David Stuart, and Heather Hurst
2010   *The Murals of San Bartolo, El Petén, Guatemala. Part 2: The West Wall*. Ancient America 10. Boundary End Archaeology Center, Barnardsville, North Carolina.

Tedlock, Barbara
1992   *Time and the Highland Maya*. University of New Mexico Press, Albuquerque.

Tedlock, Dennis
1996   *Popol Vuh: The Definitive Edition of the Mayan Book of the Dawn of Life and the Glories of Gods and Kings*. Simon and Schuster, New York.

Thompson, J. Eric S.
1974   Maya Astronomy. *Philosophical Transactions of the Royal Society of London* 276:83–98.

U.S. Naval Observatory
1903   *American Ephemeris and Nautical Atlas*. Department of the Navy, United States, Washington, D.C.

Velásquez, Juan Luis
1992   Excavaciones en el Complejo 75 de Nakbé, Petén. In *V Simposio de Investigaciones Arqueológicas en Guatemala, 1991*, edited by Juan Pedro Laporte, Héctor Escobedo, and Sandra Brady, pp. 84–90. Museo Nacional de Arqueología y Etnología, Guatemala City.

Villa Rojas, Alfonso
1945   *Maya of East Central Quintana Roo*. Publication 559. Carnegie Institution of Washington, Washington, D.C.

Walker, Debra S.
2013   Notas preliminares sobre la cerámica recolectada en Yaxnohcah en 2011. *Proyecto Arqueológico Yaxnohcah, 2011: Informe de la primera temporada de investigaciones.* http://www.mesoweb.com/resources/informes/Yaxnohcah2011.html, accessed July 1, 2013.
2016   Notas sobre la secuencia cerámica en Yaxnohcah, 2013–15. In Proyecto Arqueológico Yaxnohcah, 2014–15: Informe de la tercera y cuarto temporadas de investigaciones, edited by Kathryn Reese-Taylor, Meaghan Peuramaki-Brown, and Armando Anaya Hernández. Report submitted to the Instituto Nacional de Antropología e Historia, Mexico City.

IV

Conclusion

16

More Than Smoke and Mirrors

Maya Temple Precincts and the Emergence of Religious Institutions in Mesoamerica

ANNE S. DOWD

By 3,000 years ago Lowland Maya centers such as El Mirador in Guatemala had formed as large nucleated communities. At the heart of these centers were standardized temple precincts. To date at least 176 have been identified and about 34 of these (20 percent) have been excavated. Presently the earliest Group E–type construction is at Ceibal (or Seibal), Guatemala, conservatively dated to 950 BCE at the beginning of the Real 1 Phase (1000–850 BCE). The time range for E Groups in the Maya region is about 1000 BCE to 1000 CE or 2,000 years (based upon Ceibal ^{14}C radiocarbon dates: for example, AA-95713, an accelerator mass spectrometry [AMS] date on charcoal in 17b soil, 2860±40, calibrated before present [cal BP], 1188–915 cal BCE, or about 1050 BCE) (Inomata et al. 2013:3, 4, Table S1). Recovering and analyzing additional samples that include burned annuals or perennials should help refine these dates. Single-grain optically stimulated luminescence (OSL) dating of ceramic temper is another dating technique that potentially offers greater precision.

For the Maya, both politics and religion relied on astronomy for divination, situating cosmological beliefs, charting calendar cycles, and influencing both human and natural forces, not only for ensuring successful agricultural harvests but also for commemorating ancestors, scheduling exchange markets or trade, and timing civic or ritual events. The Group E–type temple and platform arrangements around central plazas functioned as non-Western astronomical observatories for viewing the movements of the sun along the horizon (Aveni et al. 2003). Ritual and practical astronomy in E Groups is key to understanding beliefs and practices underlying Maya community life, governance, and religion.

Renewed anthropological attention to the material correlates of religious institutions accompanying primary (first-generation) and secondary (second-generation) state formation has identified temple precincts. Here priests, in service to a ruling elite, carried out their duties in sacred interior temple spaces where access was restricted, performed ceremonies in front of audiences in public enclosures (such as exterior plazas, platform stairways, or terraces), and were housed nearby in palaces, monasteries, communal residences, or cells, depending on their status or rank (Blanton et al. 1996; Burger and Salazar-Burger 1986; Clark 2007; DeMarrais et al. 1996; Earle 1997; Hughes 1997; Jarquín and Martínez 1982; Knight 1986; Kolb 1994; Kotkin 2007; Mumford 1968; Renfrew 1973, 1985; Trigger 1990:128; Valeri 1985; Wright 1995). In this chapter, I establish that the Maya built temple precincts encompassing Group E–type architectural complexes and that the spatial dimensions and number of temple interior rooms are one measure of sociocultural complexity underlying the religious institutions characterizing emerging states.

First I introduce some comparative examples of religious precincts. Especially compelling are those examples where astronomical observational practice in identifiable architecture is part of the overall priestly and scholarly activity. The purpose of bringing in a comparative framework is to show the usefulness of the hypothesis, which is that E Groups in prestate societies were centers for ideological performance that later became part of differentiated temple precincts in the service of state religion.

Comparisons with Priestly Precincts in Other Regions

In Europe, with its first church built in 326 CE and still in use today, the 108-acre Vatican in Italy is a well-known example of such a precinct. It has combined places of worship, spaces for an administrative bureaucracy, residences, grottos, and burials. Not only is partial access granted to large numbers of visitors for ceremony, confession, pilgrimage, worship, prayer, or meetings, but significant access restrictions to the most holy of sacred places within the compound exist.

Incidentally, the Vatican's Catholic Church owns a separate astronomical observatory in Arizona, purchased because light pollution from Rome rendered the Specola, an observatory built at the summer papal residence at Castel Gandolfo, functionally obsolete. Since 1817, four marble disks in St. Peter's Square touched by the shadow of an obelisk mark a meridian line and indicate the height of the sun at different points in the day (Papafava 1995:28). Gregory XIII, who was pope from 1572 to 1585, created the reformed Julian calendar using information gleaned from a seasonal solar marker in the tower Otaviano Mascherino, built in 1578–1580, in which astronomer Ignazio Dante showed how the vernal equinox no longer fell on March 21 but on March 11 (Papafava 1995:128–129). The points raised in this chapter demonstrate the considerable value of thinking about how religious institutions were centers of learning, book production, and even calendar reform, prior to the development of educational institutions such as universities and schools in our own society as well as in others.

In Mesopotamia, a temple on top of a mound, a ziggurat, was constructed at Uruk, ca. 2112–2095 BCE. The temple precinct there eventually occupied about a third of the city and showed increasing functional differentiation in religious architectural development over time (Adams 1966). At Mes Aynak, in the Gandhara region of eastern Afghanistan and northwestern Pakistan, the monks who occupied a Buddhist temple precinct guarded the world's most extensive copper production hub and mine during the third through eighth centuries CE (Bloch 2015). In Cambodia, the Khmer temple precinct at Angkor, at 2 km^2, is considered to be the largest in the world. Now a World Heritage Site, Angkor's succession of forty-one divine kings or *deva-raja* built eighty Hindu and Buddhist temples thought of as "Temple Mountains" between 879 and 1431 CE (Coe 2003; Evans et al. 2013; Mannikka 2000).

In North America, Mississippian sites such as Cahokia were constructed around ceremonial precincts surrounding central plazas to bring together people, ideas, and materials. The exact nature of sociopolitical development is still hotly debated. In other places, such as the Byzantine Middle East, temple precincts were outposts in pilgrimage areas where traders, religious specialists, military personnel, and nomads passed through for diverse purposes at a distance from the nearby settlements. Priests lived both close to and farther from centers of political power, framing intellectual accomplishments and leadership in unusual ways as well as changing the nature of settlement not only in urban but also in rural environments, as at Mount Nebo in Jordan, due east of Jerusalem (Dowd 2016). Such religious outposts still have iconic power, as exemplified by the Russian president Vladimir Putin's recent trip to the Orthodox Christian Simonopetra Monastery on the Mount Athos peninsula overlooking the Aegean Sea in northern Greece (Shuster 2016). New work on religious institution innovation and change around the world helps to situate these developments in the Americas. For example, at Çatalhöyük, in Turkey, religious institutions emerged first in the context of farming and settlement aggregation (Hodder 2010).

In Mesoamerica, the enclosed temple precinct in Central México's fourteenth–sixteenth century CE Aztec capital at Tenochtitlán contained multiple temples, which varied in size and elaboration depending on the importance of the god(s) they commemorated, and to some extent the hierarchy of the priests may have mimicked the deity hierarchy. There was also housing for priests and other religious personnel, space for large numbers of celebrants, the school (*calmecac*), a ballcourt, and sacred areas where only the most elite of the full-time religious leaders and the ruler were allowed entry (Anderson and Dibble 1951; Durán 1971; Redmond and Spencer 2013).

Eduardo Matos-Moctezuma recently discovered a sacrificial skull rack (*tzompantli*) behind the Templo Mayor (Structure II). This is the largest of the twin-stair temples, dedicated to two of the most important gods in the Aztec pantheon, Tlaloc and Huitzilopochtli. The Templo Mayor faces west, aligned with the equinox (about true north 97°00' east), and recalls symbolism embodied in the shrines on Mt. Tlaloc as well as the Hill of Tetzcotzingo sacred landscape (Aveni et al. 1988; Dowd 2015:212; Townsend 1992:144). The duality in the temple constructions was mirrored in the organization of the priesthood, whereby two high priests were directly under the ruler or Huey Tlatoani, possibly a reflection of an older moiety social division of cult responsibilities alternating with the dry and wet seasons (Townsend 1992:193–194). The twin temples atop the Temple Mayor, a water mountain (*atl tepetl*), had tandem room plans 97.9 m^2 in area, which had analogues at other Mesoamerican sites.

At Mitla, the Mixtec capital in Oaxaca, México, sixteenth-century religious precincts were composed of elevated two-room temples, altars, courtyards, and attached residences or ritual preparation spaces suitable for a priestly hierarchy (Byland and Pohl 1994; de Burgoa 1934 [1674]; de Córdova 1942 [1578]; Flannery and Marcus 1983; Marcus 1978). Monte Albán, Oaxaca, also had temple precincts exhibiting two-room standard temple floor plans: for example, one on the summit of Mound X, 41 m^2, and others across territory that the primary Zapotec state controlled during the Monte Albán II Phase (100 BCE–200 CE) (Fahmel Beyer 1991; Flannery and Marcus 1983:87, 2015; Marcus 1978; Redmond and Spencer 2008:257). El Magote's Structure 1 is an example of a temple with one room, 18.09 m^2, within an early religious compound used by part-time religious specialists who inhabited the Oaxaca chiefdom during the Early Monte Albán I Phase (500–300 BCE) (Redmond and Spencer 2008:245).

Four broad comparative frameworks have been recognized in examples of temple precincts in the service of a state's ruling elite, known either ethnographically or archaeologically, that may guide archaeological investigations of state or prestate level Maya examples (Adams 1966; Fahmel Beyer 1991; Carballo and Aveni 2012; Childe 1950; Flannery 1998; Flannery and Marcus 1983, 2015; Kirch 2004; Marcus and Flannery 2004; Redmond and Spencer 2008, 2013). These patterns include: (1) degrees of intersite design standardization; (2) divisions of space into segregated, often walled, enclosures delimiting or restricting access to the temple precinct with evidence of differentiated spatial functions within; (3) the presence of attached or nearby residences or ritual preparation areas for full-time specialists and their retinues; and (4) evidence of hierarchical organization in design, access, and elaboration of facilities and materials placed in them. Because political entities were fluid and changing, both through time and across space, a caveat raised by other scholars in reference to both prestate and state levels of sociopolitical organization also deserves mention (Schortman and Urban 2004; Suvrathan 2013).

The caveat is the variability in sociocultural organization that existed alongside urban centers, peripheral to them, or even within different social strata in a settlement. So, for example, Barbara Tedlock's (1992:51) perspectives on the interpenetrating categories of priest and shaman are worth noting here, making an analytical distinction between service to the community as priestly and service to individuals as shamanistic (Tomásková 2013). Returning to the case at hand, flexible behaviors and agencies may also be evidenced in the differences among Group E–type constructions, where a western structure typically faces three eastern structures on a long platform across a broad plaza—often beginning as a platform without stone masonry superstructures (Ricketson and Ricketson 1937). E Groups, forming the nuclei of ceremonial precincts in the Maya Lowlands, had parallels in other regions in Mesoamerica.

A Mesoamerican Temple Precinct

El Palenque, Oaxaca, México

I interpret the following example as an E Group–related astronomical complex or later Middle Formative Chiapas architectural pattern, even though it has not previously been identified as one. Between 2009 and 2011 in the Valley of Oaxaca, archaeologists excavated a 5,000 m² temple precinct at El Palenque, part of one of the independent Zapotec states emerging in the Ocotlán-Zimatlán subregion during the Late Monte Albán I Phase (300–100 BCE) (Redmond and Spencer 2008, 2013).

At El Palenque, archaeological data suggest that a full-time priesthood supervised religious activities in a set of three eastern temples facing an adjacent western plaza (Structures 16, 20, 29). Living quarters were behind and east of the temples in separate structures (Structures 27, 28), with distinctive proportions of serving wares suggesting that food was brought in from another location and with architectural features such as zigzag passages, steps into lowered main rooms, and east-facing entrances. One 2 cm incised and polished stone token was found in Structure 27. Small cells abutting the rear of the temples may have housed initiates or priests in training. On the west side of the plaza are two unexcavated mounds, K and J, one directly behind and to the west of the other. I argue that the plaza grouping strongly resembles Group E–type complex layouts in the Maya region and may also share functional similarities, including horizon-based astronomical alignments marking solar movements. The complex is oriented magnetic north 17° east or true north 12° east (Figure 16.1).

Excavations in the three eastern temples yielded artifacts and features suggestive of ritual activities (Redmond and Spencer 2013:E1710–E1714). In Room 1 of Structure 20 (the largest central room in the middle temple), two hearths, ornaments of exotic materials, effigy whistles and vessels, incense burners, obsidian and chert blades or perforators, and turkey, dove, and other faunal or human remains suggest auto-, animal, and possible human sacrifice. A cooking facility used for larger numbers of people than is normally found in a household was excavated on a terrace platform at the southeast (rear) corner of Structure 20. Middens associated with a firebox on the southeast side of the structure contained shell ornaments, mica, incense brazier or burner fragments, an anthropomorphic ceramic figurine wearing an opossum mask, an incised ground-stone celt, and food remains. Other firebox hearth features existed to the rear of the structure on the northeast and southeast sides. In addition, rectangular-shaped cells or small rooms abutted the temple's southeast base. The three main rooms total 227.80 m².

In Structures 16 and 29 (the adjoining north and south temples, respectively), shell ornaments, a deer bone awl, the left humerus of an ungulate such as a young deer, obsidian blades, chert perforators, grayware ceramics,

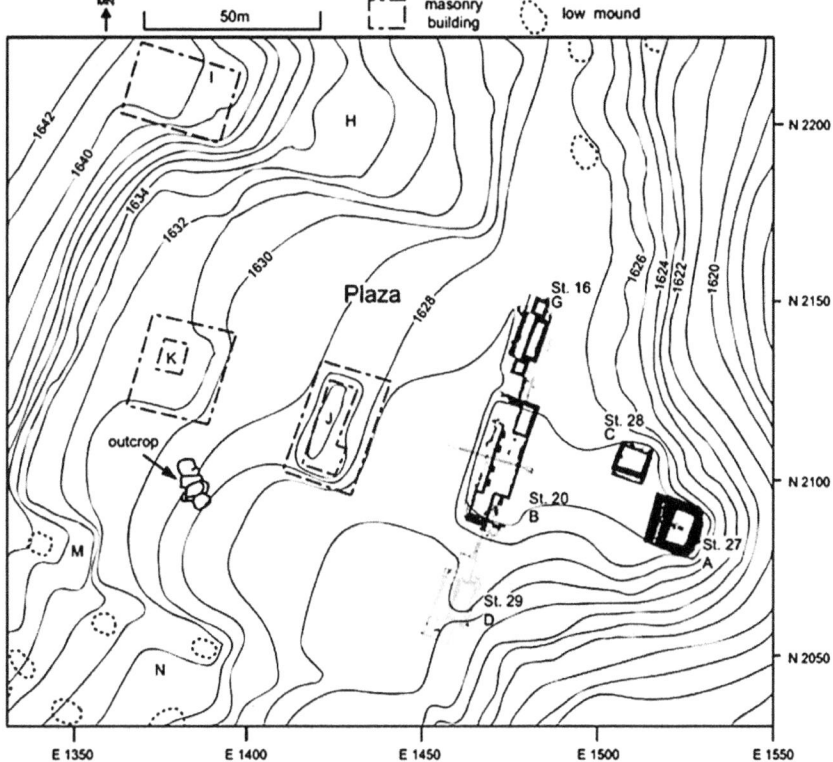

Figure 16.1. El Palenque temple precinct plan, Oaxaca, Mexico, topographic elevations are in meters above sea level (after Redmond and Spencer 2013:E1710). Courtesy of *Proceedings of the National Academy of Sciences.*

and ceramic incense brazier and effigy vessel fragments were found. Each of the three temples had rear, east-facing entrances accessed by stairways that would have permitted more private access by comparison to the main public, west-facing plaza entrances. In addition, a low wall connected the structures and restricted access to the precinct. In part, the destruction of the temples by fire may have accounted for the quality of the feature and artifact preservation. Structure 16's four rooms measure 64.42 m², and Structure 29's four rooms measure 94.35 m². Together the three temples (16, 20, 29) had 11 rooms with combined areas of 386.57 m².

Preliminary data from the westernmost Mound K indicate that the azimuth of the alignment to the north edge of the northeastern Structure 16 is true north 74° east and, if measured to the center doorway of the structure, true north 80° east (in line with 37 km distant Mitla). The date pairs for

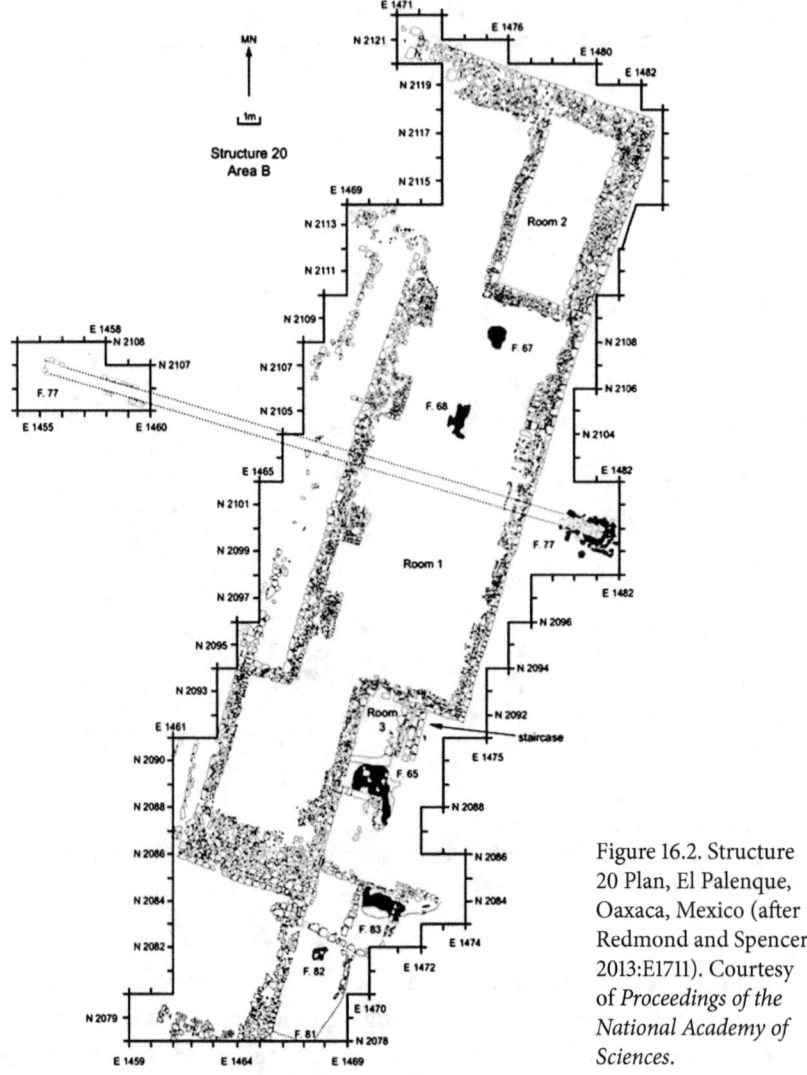

Figure 16.2. Structure 20 Plan, El Palenque, Oaxaca, Mexico (after Redmond and Spencer 2013:E1711). Courtesy of *Proceedings of the National Academy of Sciences*.

these alignments are May 3/August 11 and April 17/August 27 sunrise azimuth first gleam assuming a 5° horizon and using a magnetic declination of 5°. The alignment from Mound K to the south edge of the southeastern Structure 29 is azimuth true north 132° east, and, if the measurement is made to the center doorway, true north 124° east in line with 3,160 m high Cerro Vitache 2.6 km away. Both are outside of an observable solar event. The complex is at elevation 1,631 meters above sea level (masl).

Figure 16.3. Hun Ajaw Itzamnaj/One Maize Crocodile Tree or young Maize God emerging from a turtle carapace "Resurrection Plate," ca. 680–750 CE. Museum of Fine Arts, Boston, Massachusetts, Museum Catalog No. 1993.565, gift of Landon T. Clay (Vessel No. K1892). Copyright © 1998 Justin Kerr. All rights reserved.

A vaulted tunnel, Feature 77, with a rectangular masonry entrance began behind Structure 20, passed underneath the building along its midline, and ended in the central plaza 27 m away, aligned azimuth true north 101° east, corresponding with sunrise dates of October 20/February 22, assuming a 5° horizon, and appears to line up with a 2,560 m mountain named Vabiroa/Vachón 4–5 km in the distance. Elsa Redmond and Charles Spencer (2013:E1714) suggested that costumed impersonators secretly accessed the plaza during religious ceremonies and used this tunnel to emerge in front of Structure 20 (Figure 16.2). Although this is the Zapotec not the Maya region, and myths and rituals may have been altogether different, it is tempting to imagine the transubstantiated Maize God emerging from the plaza as though it were the turtle shell shown on the polychrome plate (K1892) exhibited at the Museum of Fine Arts, Boston (Figure 16.3).

At El Palenque, the presence of religious occupational specialists is documented archaeologically by the artifact and feature distributions in the three temples, two monastic residences, and a wall between the temples serving to limit access to the plaza (Redmond and Spencer 2008, 2013).

Variation in the size and layout of the three temples may relate to hierarchical organization within the priesthood. It is not yet known if there are temple rooms atop Mounds J or K.

This example from outside of the Maya area illustrates what Mayanists should look for in their E Group temples and adjacent platform terrace or plaza floor surfaces. Granted, portions of intact living surfaces were in a relatively good state of preservation at El Palenque, but such surfaces have also been discovered in the Maya region. For example, a burned palace and nearby priestly residences, M8-4 and M8-10, from Aguateca, Guatemala, provided a wealth of information on interior room living surfaces and activity areas (Inomata 1995).

I argue that in the Petén Lowlands there were full-time religious specialists, including astronomers and priests. Like sixteenth-century daykeepers described by Bishop Diego de Landa Calderón or Gaspar Antonio Chi (McAnany 2014:129; Tozzer 1941 [1566]:27–28), they were learned and literate, were hierarchically organized, and oversaw religious rituals within multiroom temples or on adjacent platform terraces and in plaza settings at Calakmul (*uxte' tuun* or three stone place), Campeche, Mexico. The latest multiroom temples constructed in the Calakmul E Group, perhaps known as turtle-stone *ahktuun* in an as yet unknown place *tz'i?-ni* but possibly an E Group (Stuart 2012–2015), appear to reveal the architectural footprint of a state-sponsored religion performed by full-time priests. Part-time religious specialists and emerging elites in prestate Maya polities before institutions had fully formed, or even after they devolved, may have used single-room temples on platforms or long platforms with or without gnomons on them. Gnomons are poles or upright standing stones used to mark solar or other astronomical positions. These E Group prototypes were founded on bedrock carved into platform terraces. An equation of square footage, number of interior temple rooms, and relative temple proportions may therefore correlate with degrees of religious and by extension sociocultural complexity.

A Maya Temple Precinct

Calakmul, Campeche, México

There is abundant hieroglyphic evidence that the snake or *kaan* dynasty was centered first at Dzibanché and then at Calakmul. Calakmul, now a World Heritage Site, was a large regional secondary state and possibly the center of a nascent empire (about 13,000 km² at its peak in 500–695 CE) in which social institutions such as religious, economic, political, and kinship practices, had developed (Beliaev 2000; Carrasco 1996; Carrasco et al. 1999; Demarest 1992; Grube 2004:117–118; Marcus 1987, 1995, 2014; Marcus and Folan 1994; Martin 2005; Martin and Grube 1995, 2000:103; Pincemin et al. 1998:310; Savage 2007; Stuart 2012–2015; Stuart and Houston 1994; Tokovinine 2013). In using the *kaan* imagery to symbolize their realm, *Boa constrictor* may have been the snake imagined as a polity predator based upon the species identified in an offering contained in jars beneath the floor in front of the cavity created for Stela 114 (Marcus and Folan 1994; Pincemin et al. 1998:319) (Figure 16.4). The centralized unitary societies

Figure 16.4. Stela 114, front face, 1.9 m high by 0.8 m wide by 0.3 m thick, deepest relief is 0.03 m, the ruler is shown dressed as GI. Using the 584,283 Goodman family correlation constant, the initial series date on the back of the monument is 8.19.15.12.13 8 Ben 6 Mol, September 14, 431 CE (Gregorian), a retrospective date on the monument erected to commemorate 9.0.0.0.0 or 435 CE. Copyright © 1994 Anne S. Dowd. All rights reserved.

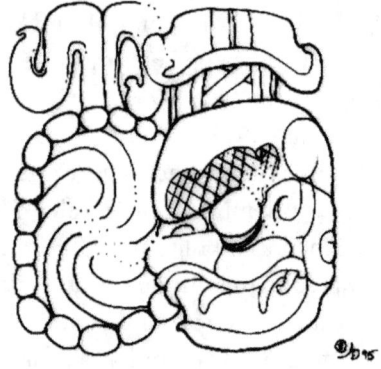

Figure 16.5. Calakmul's toponym or lineage name from Structure XIII, Calakmul, Mexico. Copyright © 1995 Anne S. Dowd. All rights reserved.

and multipolity networks under divine lords (*k'uhul ajawtaak*), such as in Calakmul's *kaanal* or *kaanul* dynasty, had emerged at least by the Early Classic (250–550 CE) to Late Classic (550–800 CE) transition (Figure 16.5). The first clearly identified monument that names Calakmul as the capital of the *kaan* dynasty did not appear until 635 CE (Stuart 2012–2015; Marcus 2014:104). Across the Lowlands, stelae with hieroglyphic inscriptions had reached their maximum area distribution by 534 CE (Marcus 1983:461).

Through the *kaanal* dynasty Calakmulqueños controlled a region encompassing Tikal, for a time, and other dependent, allied, or subjugated cities, such as Balakbal, Cancuén, Caracol, Champerico, Dos Pilas, El Palmar, El Perú–Waka', Holmul, La Corona, Los Alacranes, Moral-Reforma, Naranjo, Piedras Negras, Uxul, Yaxchilán, Y'okop, and Xultún for an estimated 330 years between 406 and 736 CE (Carrasco et al. 1999:49; Delvendahl 2008; Grube et al. 2012; Marcus 1973; Martin 2005:11; Pincemin et al. 1998:324) (Figure 16.6). An earlier *kaan* dynasty may have existed in the El Mirador basin by about 100–150 CE; in fact, Calakmul's rise to prominence did not begin until the Late Preclassic (350 BCE–0 CE) or Terminal Preclassic (0–250 CE), when El Mirador declined (Dahlin 1984; Hansen 1990; Marcus 2014:96). Like the Central Plaza containing the El León E Group at El Mirador, the Central Plaza forming Calakmul's temple precinct occupies 20,000 m² (Matheny and Matheny 2011:89).

The astronomical importance of the centrally located E Group complex has been discussed previously (Aveni et al. 2003; Chapter 3 in this volume; Dowd and Aveni 1998; Dowd at al. 1995; Dowd and Milbrath 2015). Briefly stated, the later interbuilding alignments coincide with a zenith-based set of calendar intervals, which was a shift from or an alternative to

Figure 16.6. Calakmul's Central Plaza view toward the southeast (after Folan et al. 2015:38 and Crisell 2000:21).

solstice-based calendar intervals, 20-day Winal "months" corresponding to festival dates. These alignments would have permitted an observer on the western structure (VI) to view astronomical phenomena rising and setting behind the profiles of the three eastern structures (IVa, IVb, IVc) along a low platform. Significant dates targeted by the 92°30' IVb center line are March 15/September 29 (Aveni et al. 2003:165) (Figure 16.7). A hierophany on June 21 at about 6:00 p.m. summer solstice sunset has been observed in the west entrance to Temple IVc, where full light aligns with the later-phase doorjambs at 294°00' or 0°02' of summer solstice last gleam 294°02', and an 115°30' alignment between VI and IVc's building edge has been identified as corresponding to within 0°21' of December 21 winter solstice sunrise, assuming a 3° horizon. Azimuths 64°30' and 128°30' of the corners of the north (IVa) and south (IVc) structures of the east platform as viewed from the west Structure VI were noted. Anthony Aveni, Ben Vining, and I (Aveni et al. 2003) have suggested that these dates corresponded with periodic rainy and dry season ceremonies.

A description of available excavation data from the buildings (IVa–c and VII, which are east and north, respectively) within Calakmul's temple precinct is provided in other sources (Braswell et al. 2004; Carrasco 1999) (Appendix A). The Cenote Style E Group and the overall site are oriented true north 13° east. It was at least used between about 350 BCE and CE 1400 CE.

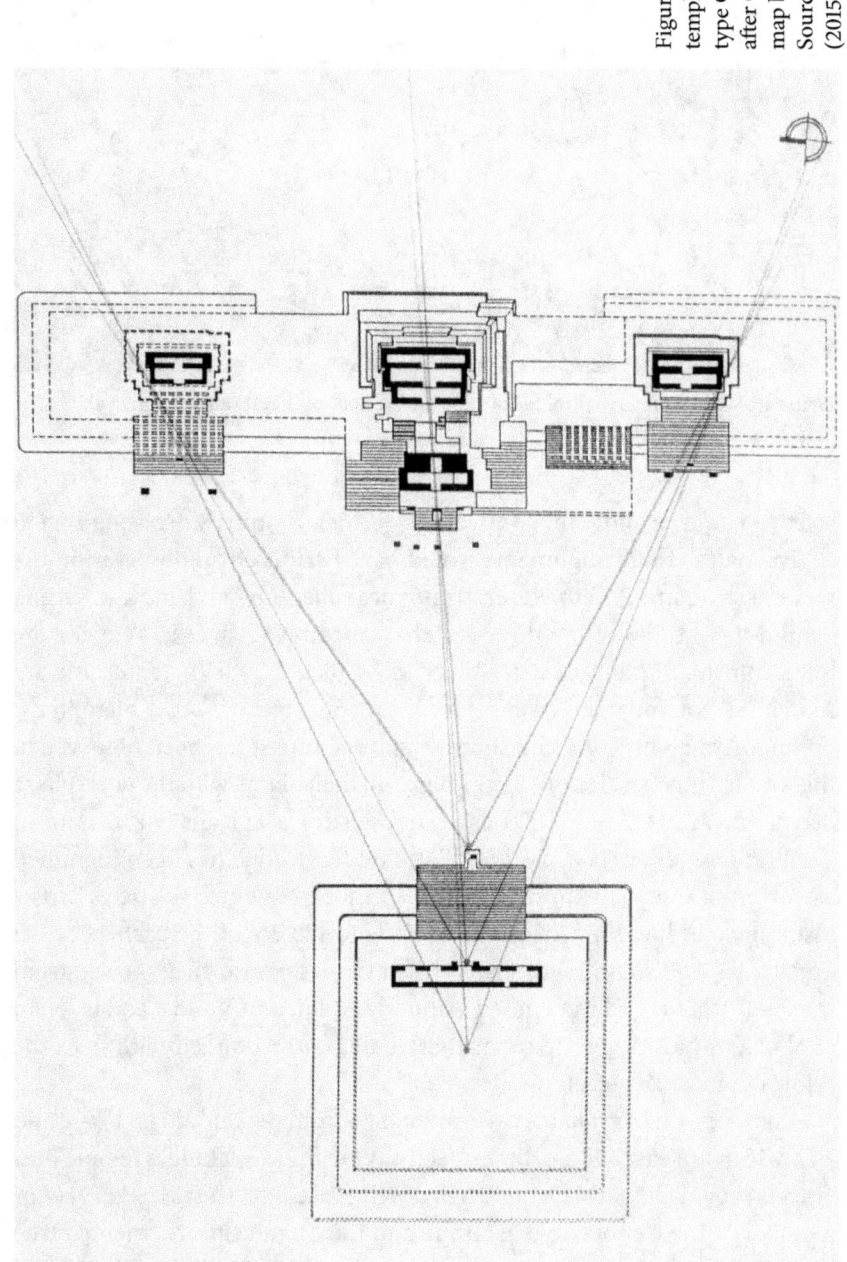

Figure 16.7. Calakmul temple precinct, Group E-type Complex (modified after Carrasco et al. 1995, map by Emyly González). Source: Dowd and Milbrath (2015:Figure 3.6a).

On the east side of the Central Plaza, Temple IV has three superstructures (Carrasco 1999) (Figure 16.8a–c). The northernmost, Temple IVa, is a two-roomed building with combined room floor areas of 17.15 m². The central Temple IVb is a three-roomed structure with two later rooms built below and in front of the substructure (Figures 16.9–16.11). The total estimated

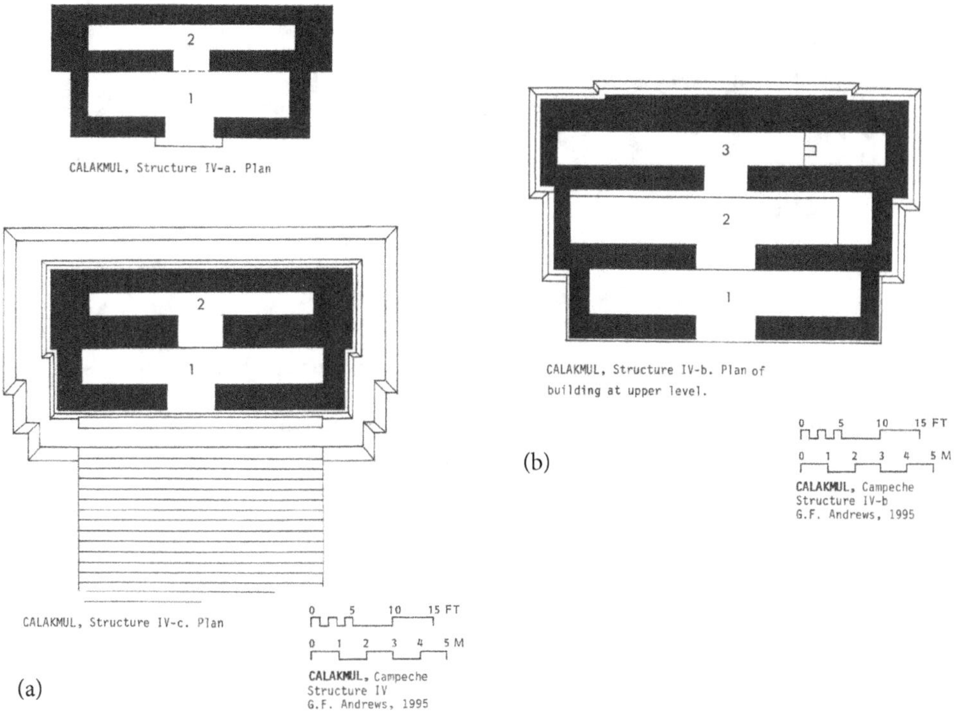

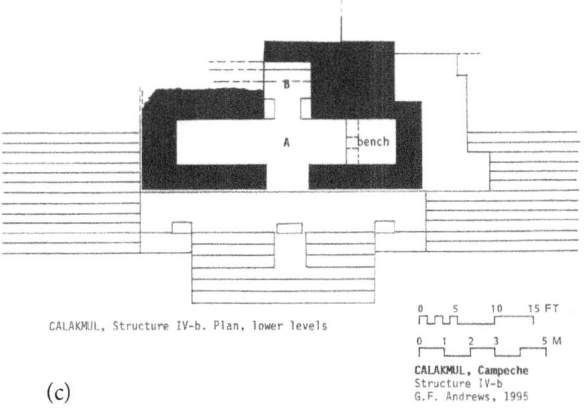

Figure 16.8. (a) Structure IVa and IVc plan details, Calakmul, Campeche, Mexico; (b) Structure IVb upper level; (c) Structure IVb lower level (after Andrews 1995:41, 51, 56). Courtesy of the George F. and Geraldine D. Andrews papers, Alexander Architectural Archive, University of Texas Libraries, University of Texas at Austin.

Figure 16.9. Reconstructed view northeast of Calakmul's Structure IVb, east side of Main Plaza (Benavides et al. 2007:59). Image courtesy of Grupo Azabache, S.A. de C.V., Mexico City; artwork by Omar Acero and Enrique Gutiérrez Barrios.

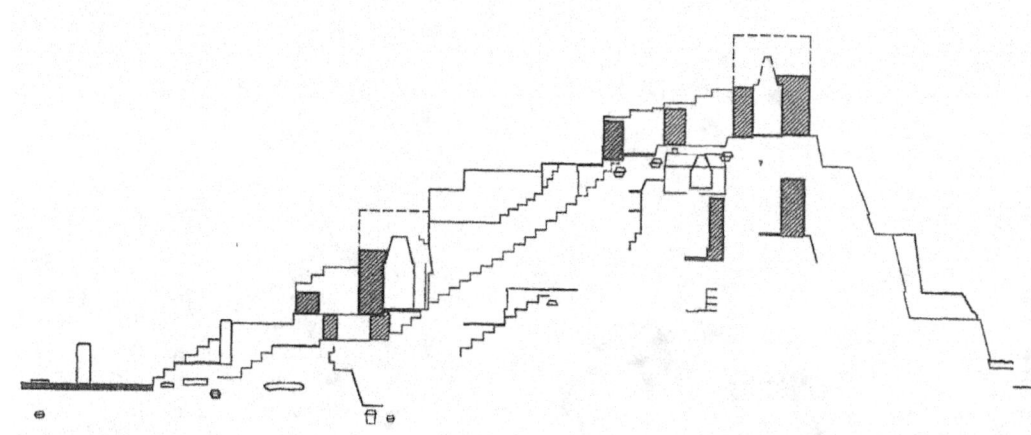

Figure 16.10. Profile of Calakmul Structure IVb (after Carrasco 1999:72, Figure 3, drawing by Emyly González).

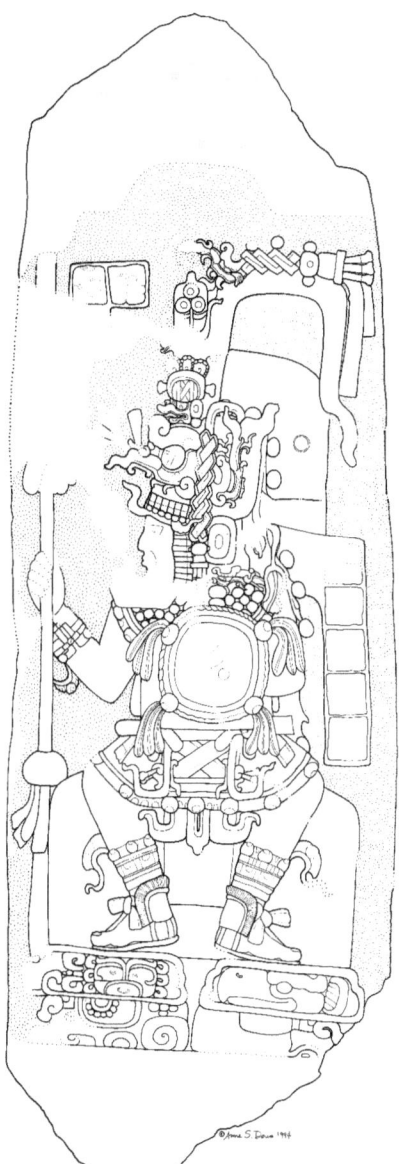

Figure 16.11. Lintel 1 found in Calakmul's Structure IVb, east side of Main Plaza. The individual portrayed is thought to be Tuun K'ab' Hix (a.k.a. K'altun Hix or Cu-Ix), who ruled Calakmul from 520 to 546 CE. Illustration by Anne S. Dowd. Copyright © 1994. All rights reserved.

area for the original three rooms is 54.88 m². As expanded to five rooms, the total estimated area is 84.54 m². The interior lower room was remodeled to make it smaller late in the construction sequence. The southernmost, Temple IVc, has two rooms and is angled to catch the afternoon sun, permitting a precisely lit area between the two doorjambs. The estimated floor areas of these rooms total 23.04 m². The first construction phase of

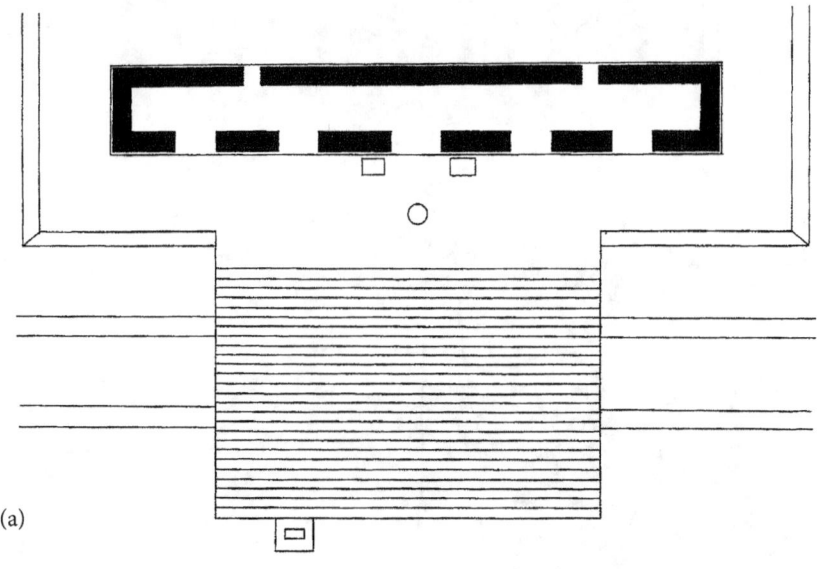

(a)

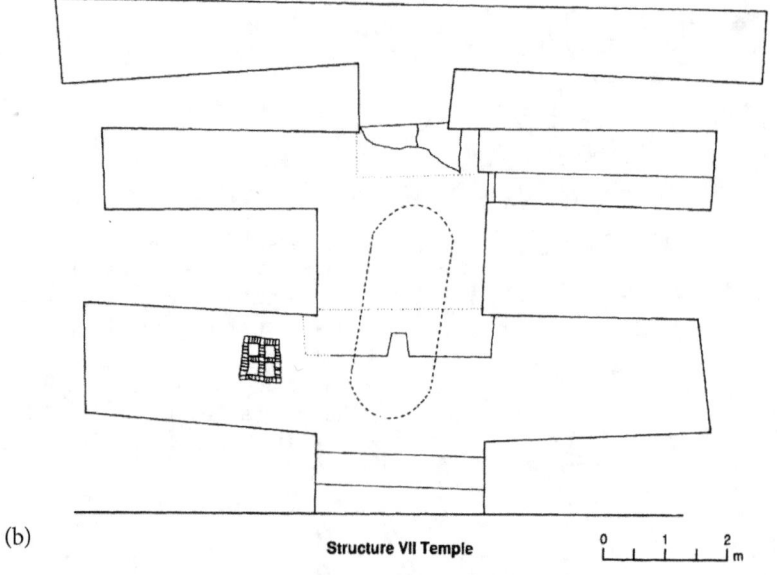

(b)

Structure VII Temple

0 1 2 m

Figure 16.12. Calakmul Structure VII (a), VI (b), and V (c) plans (after Andrews 1995:64, 73; Folan et al. 1995:Figure 8). Courtesy of Dra. María del Rosario Domínguez Carrasco at the Centro de Investigaciones Históricas y Sociales Universidad Autónoma de Campeche. Courtesy of Dr. William Folan at the Instituto Nacional de Antropologia y Historia, Mexico, and courtesy of the George F. and Geraldine D. Andrews papers, Alexander Architectural Archive, University of Texas Libraries, University of Texas at Austin.

all three temples on the east side of the plaza had single-roomed structures with floor areas totaling 22.31 m².

Structure VI on the west side of the main plaza has a long single room built of masonry on top of its broad platform (Figure 16.12a-c). It measures an estimated 23.16 m long × 1.85 m wide (42.85 m²) and has five east-facing doorways and two narrow west-facing ones. I suggest that the Structure VI summit, associated with Stelae 23 and 24 dated to 9.13.10.0.0 7 Ajaw 3 Kumk'u (or January 24, 702 CE, using the 584,283 correlation constant to convert the long count to a Gregorian date), was the platform upon which Yuknoom Tok' K'awiil danced to celebrate a major 360-day period ending of a reign that had begun in 698 CE and ended in 731 CE, as depicted on the newly discovered La Corona Element 55 panel (Stuart 2012–2015). Numerous stelae and altars are associated with the Calakmul E Group architecture.

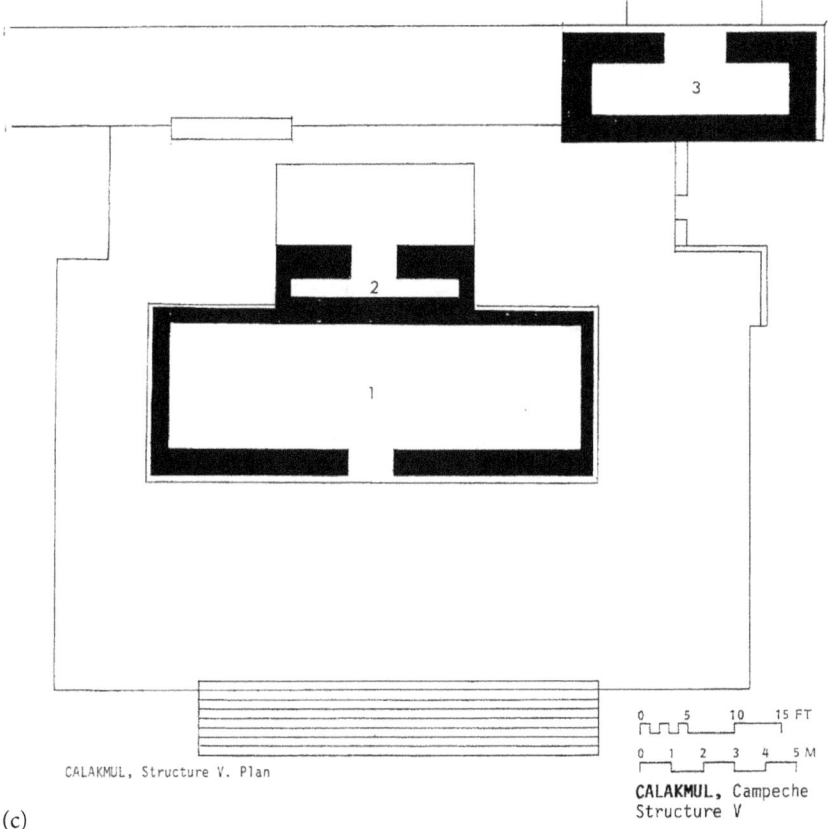

CALAKMUL, Structure V. Plan

CALAKMUL, Campeche
Structure V

(c)

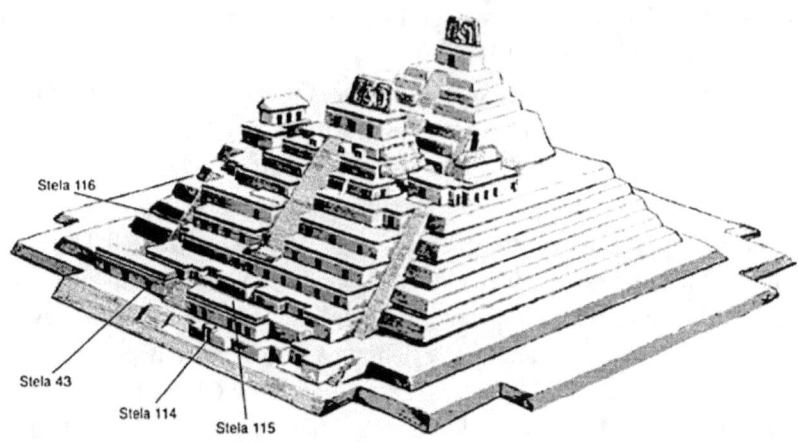

Figure 16.13. Calakmul's Structure II. Reconstruction drawing by Ernesto Tamay Segovia based on a photograph by Eldon Leiter (after Pincemin et al. 1998).

Some of the additional structures in the Group E or Central Plaza are to the north (VII), northeast (VIII), extreme northeast (IX), south (V), southeast (III), and extreme south (II). Southern Structure V has three rooms with a total of 31.43 m² interior floor space. Northern Structure VII has three rooms with interior floor areas totaling 47.79 m² (Domínguez 1992, 1994; Domínguez and Gallegos 1989–1990; Domínguez et al. 1998). At 55 m high, Structure II is the tallest monumental building at Calakmul, if not in the Maya world, and is located at the extreme southern end of the Central Plaza (Figure 16.13). There is a ballcourt (XI) west of the E Group. Ritual structures, palaces, and monastic cells or communal dormitories, or other buildings and specialized features, may have also formed a part of this important precinct and provided housing for religious personnel and space for ritual practice, preparation, or seclusion.

The presence or absence of increased space in E Group temples that could have accommodated larger religious bureaucracies may be illustrated at sites exhibiting varying E Group architecture, such as Uaxactún, Cenote, or Cenote Variant Styles. The first two have been described as follows: "In the Uaxactún E Group variant, the platform comprises a separate rectangular unit, usually about 70 m in length, supporting three buildings; in the Cenote E Group variant, the platform is much longer and narrower and the three buildings appear to be appended to it" (Chase 1983:191). The nomenclature used in this study is "Uaxactún Style E Group" or "Cenote Style

E Group," and "Cenote Variant Style E Group" to describe examples more like Cenote by comparison to the Uaxactún Style but not firmly in either category (Aimers and Rice 2006; Runggaldier et al. 2013:70).

Contextual information is available on Maya rituals recovered archaeologically from the architectural spaces where propitiation and sacrifice were repeatedly enacted in E Groups. Distinctive architectural plans, profiles, and concentrations of features such as altars, caches, burials, and *patolli* boards were left behind. Artifacts buried in E Group temples were also suggestive of ritual activity, including mosaic mirrors used for prophecy based on iconographic depictions on painted vases, censers for burning offerings, tokens, possible codices, perforators used for bloodletting, blades, lancets or eccentric flints, and human skulls.

The E Group: A Focus on Religious Function

As Bishop Diego de Landa (in Tozzer 1941 [1566]:27–28) noted:

> The natives of Yucatan were as attentive to the matters of religion as to those of government.... They provided priests for the towns when they were needed, examining them in the sciences and ceremonies, and committed to them the duties of their office, and the good example to people and provided them with books and sent them forth. *And they employed themselves in the duties of the temples and in teaching their sciences* as well as in writing books about them [emphasis added].

Bishop de Landa's observations (in Tozzer 1941 [1566]:27–28) written almost 450 years ago agree with Karl Ruppert's conclusion (1977:222) regarding Uaxactún's Group E written 75 years ago: "Since the small buildings on the east side of the plaza are definitely not domiciliary and the pyramid on the west does not support a building the arrangement must be ceremonial or esoteric in function."

As shown by concentrations of archaeological features such as altars or caches containing artifacts related to specialized ritual activities, as well as architectural alignment patterning corresponding to 20-day Winal months or *veintena* (20-day month)–like seasonal festival dates in the Maya calendar (Aveni et al. 2003), occupational specialists such as priests, scribes, daykeepers, and astronomers used these temple precincts to practice religion. This is not a new idea, because many early archaeologists, including Alfred V. Kidder (1950:8), Karl Ruppert (1977:222), A. Ledyard Smith (1950), and J. Eric S. Thompson (1970), took the E Group's religious function for granted. During the later twentieth century, religious explanations for cultural change were exaggerated to make them more vulnerable to attack by proponents of exclusively dynastic rule. Perhaps because of the paucity of information about priests or priesthood in the monumental hieroglyphic inscriptions, which is a public medium used to recount political events, the focus on religion practiced in temples has fallen out of favor lately.

An argument in support of integrating a more central role for occupational specialists who were priests in Maya urban centers may deserve to be resurrected, because religious architecture is distinguished from other functional classes by a number of important characteristics:

1. Cultural astronomers or archaeoastronomers have demonstrated their function for sky watching (Aveni and Hartung 1989; Aveni et al. 2003; Chapter 15 in this volume; Šprajc 2009);
2. Architectural design can be linked to calendar measurement and revision showing shifts from architectural alignments related to solstice- or zenith-based calendars and the distribution of Group E–type architecture and hieroglyphic texts recording calendar dates has significant overlap (Aveni et al. 2003; Milbrath 1999, 2013, Chapter 4);
3. Period-ending commemoration, or more specifically Bak'tun (400 years), half-Bak'tun (200 years), and the conjunction of a 256-year cycle with the Bak'tun ceremonialism, is evidenced by the dates on associated monuments (Chase and Chase 1995, 2006:54, Chapter 2 in this volume);
4. Ritual cache deposits, such as celts, stone spheres (residue analysis might assist with interpreting their function), and skulls, document references to cosmological underpinnings of sacred space, the center and the cardinal directions, counting, and offerings to sacred mountains (Chase and Chase 2006; Estrada-Belli 2011; Inomata et al. 2013; Chapter 7 in this volume; Smith 1950; Robin et al. 2012);
5. Mass ceramic figurine disposal, for example, in *chultuns* close to or beneath the Group E-type complex plaza floors, is possibly evidence of discard after large public ceremonies or secondary or tertiary deposits of accumulated debris from primary or secondary contexts (Rice 2015);

6. Burials show evidence of ancestor veneration, deity impersonation, and mythic or actual decapitation (Brown 2011, 2013, Chapter 12 in this volume; Robin et al. 2012);
7. Enclosed interior architecture was used by religious specialists for private ritual, preparation for public ceremonies, and private or public hierophantic displays and doorways and platform terraces were used for public performances related to sanctification, sacrifice, astronomy, or spectacle (Dowd 2015; Dowd and Milbrath 2015; Inomata et al. 2015);
8. Ethnographic analogies with other specialized religious structures meant to ensure subsistence success against drought or failure may be made (Redmond and Spencer 2008; Marcus and Flannery 2004); and
9. Connecting people to the universe took place through cosmology-inspired landscapes incorporating built and natural elements (Biehl 2012; Dowd 2015; Eddy 1974; Fowler 1996; Kelly and Brown 2014; Chapter 14 in this volume).

While there were undoubtedly multiple uses and polyvalic meanings for these central sacred places, with their broad plazas and space for large congregations of people, religious observance was the primary function, even if they had significant political overtones, such as the role of dynastic kings in Southern Lowland Maya societies. Public events related to rulership succession and to investiture ceremonies intended to give political recognition to allied leaders and to specific priestly castes undoubtedly also took place in these settings (Ringle 2004; Zender 2004). I argue in favor of both religious and political institutions, not one or the other.

Secular functions, residential, commercial, or recreational, may be eliminated for E Groups in part because we have identified locations for these activities elsewhere (for example, at acropolises, markets, and ballcourts). Functional overlap took place in some centers in which separate economic, recreational, or other facilities had not been constructed, however. For example, ballcourts may have been used for recreation in some instances and for ritual in others.

Ethnohistoric data reinforce the importance of religion to the Highland Maya, where a priestly title was diviner(s) (*aj q'iij*) or daykeeper(s) (*aj q'ijab'*) (Christenson 2003:7). Among the Classic Maya, priestly titles implying diverse religious duties included (1) prophet/teacher (*ti'sakhuun*),

Figure 16.14. *Aj k'uhuun* title from bench in Las Sepulturas Group, 9N-82, Copán, Honduras. Illustration by Anne S. Dowd (after Baudez 1994:Plate 111).

perhaps most similar to the *chilane* or *chilam* ("prophet") of Yucatán in the sixteenth century, (2) master of fire (*yajawk'ahk*) or master of the tree/woods (*yajawte'*); and (3) worshipper/venerator (*aj k'uhuun*) (Tedlock 1996:35–37; Zender 2004) (Figure 16.14). Priests' titles have been reported in texts from Early Classic times at Xultún to Late Classic times at Xcalumkín. God versus ancestor cult responsibilities may have further divided priestly orders. While I do not discuss the relative absence of E Groups north of the 18th latitude here, David Freidel (1986:424) has suggested that temples combined with palaces may be a substitute for E Groups in the northern region and hence another location where temple precincts developed.

Group E complexes functioned as or within temple precincts where religious occupational specialists, including astronomers, presided over ritual and practical observation of heavenly events (especially the movement of the sun along the horizon) and displayed their technological and aesthetic mastery to assembled audiences. Along with the rulers, Maya priests, skilled in astronomy and calendar reckoning, oversaw the ritual activities in E Groups. A conch shell trumpet with a set of large jadeite earflares found in Caracol E Group Structure A6-1st excavations near the southern interior doorway within collapse detritus well above the floor may be evidence of ritual paraphernalia originally stored above the beams in temple roofs or in niches high in the interior room walls (Chase and Chase 2006:53). Burned areas have been interpreted as loci of incense burners that once stood on the platform of Chan's tallest superstructure topping Structure 5. Incense burner and food vessel fragments were distributed on the interior temple floor, and a burner stand cache deposit was buried under the step leading to the second room, suggestive of the ritual activities (like burning copal incense and feasting) that took place there (Robin et al. 2012:120–122).

Increases in the number and floor plan area of temple rooms appear to have indicated the elaboration of institutions characterizing state-supported religion. These changes to architectural forms may correspond to transitions occurring in 350–550 CE, the period when the Maya and Teotihuacán cultures influenced one another (Aveni et al. 2003; Englehardt and Nagle 2011; Šprajc 2014). While Calakmul's exact leadership role at this time may have been in a state of flux given possible movements of early dynastic seats of power, E Group spatial data provide an important avenue for researching religious institutional developments.

Spatial Data on Maya Temple Precincts and Their Prototypes

In the past, scholars (Childe 1950:15; Flannery 1998; Flannery and Marcus 1983; Sanders 1974; Redmond and Spencer 2008:240, 254, 2013:E1707) have used the existence of standardized architecture in urban environments to conclude that state-level institutions had emerged. Likewise, I interpret the multiroom temples used by dedicated astronomer priests in precincts resembling Uaxactún's Group E, such as at Calakmul, as evidence for the formation of state-supported religious institutions. E Groups encapsulate degrees of religious specialization, which can presumably be measured.

Based upon the dates and changes in certain architectural details, such as when single-roomed temple superstructures were rebuilt into multiple rooms or other alterations to E Group architecture suggestive of calendar standardization or revision, stronger connections may be made between the timing of prestate to state shifts or the reverse based on presumed presence or absence of institutions. I have examined data from E Group examples with one-room structures, such as from San José, and interpret them as showing a lesser degree of religious institutionalization but a greater degree of religious "craft" specialization than E Groups with no interior space, such as those without temples at all on the eastern range structure, including Xunantunich (Benque Viejo), Hatz Kaab, and Ceibal's earliest constructions (Brown et al. 2011; Inomata et al. 2013; Runggaldier et al. 2013). Societies where institutional bureaucracies had not yet emerged may not have needed interior rooms within temples for private activities with access restrictions. This may be expected in relatively egalitarian situations where there was less occupational specialization, bureaucratic organization, and architectural elaboration or differentiation, such as when part-time rather than full-time specialists, or fewer specialists, worked and oversaw religious ceremonies in those E Group constructions without superstructures.

E Groups with multiroom temples may have coincided with a new degree of complexity, suggesting not only that states had formed but also that religious institutions involving numerous full-time specialists had developed. As these processes were evidently not unilineal, development was both from simpler forms to more complex ones and the reverse in places where institutions diminished and where remaining populations may have returned to smaller interior spaces in E Group temples or used portions of plazas. Increased floor area and number of rooms over time within the temples on top of Group E–type complex substructures may correlate with developing religious institutions. Differences in temple scale and elaboration may have indicated a hierarchical priestly organization or differently structured activities commemorated in the temples.

Maya site examples discussed below include Calakmul, as well as Cahal Pichik, Cenote, Hatzcap Ceel, San José, and Uaxactún (Appendix B). These multiroom and single-room temple complexes are described in order of size from largest to smallest. Additional information for E Groups from other sites is provided in tabular form (Table 16.1).

Precincts with Multiroom Temples

Beginning in the Late Preclassic period with single-roomed structures with an area of about 22.31 m^2, Calakmul by the Late Classic featured eight, nine, or ten rooms in its Group E, with an increase to roughly 167.58 m^2. Space was reduced in one of the lower IVb rooms late in the site's building sequence.

Multiroom examples of Group E temple architecture appeared at Uaxactún during the Early Classic (for example, eight rooms with a combined area 101.33 m^2) and expanded during the Late Classic (for example, nine rooms with a combined area of 136.43 m^2). These expanded room areas correlate with space for bureaucracies present in state-level religious institutions and with a greater degree of occupational specialization among the Maya.

Cenote, which is the type site for the Cenote Style E Groups with a larger central eastern structure by comparison to the two other eastern structures north and south of it, contains an estimated six rooms, with the front room in the east central temple having an approximate area of >15.00 m^2 during the Early Classic period. The other rooms were not well enough preserved or insufficiently excavated to measure. Interestingly, a late construction on

Table 16.1. Room counts/areas

Site name	West (area m²)	West (# rooms)	East 1 North (area m²)	East 1 North (# rooms)	East 2 Center (area m²)	East 2 Center (# rooms)	East 3 South (area m²)	East 3 South (# rooms)	Total (area m²)	Total (# rooms)
Acanceh	NA	NA	NA	NA	NA	NA	NA	NA	NA	NA
Cahal Pichik	64.8	1	NA	NA	NA	NA	29.58	2	94.38	3
Calakmul-early	42.85	1	17.15	2	54.88	3	23.04	2	137.92	8
Calakmul-late	42.85	1	17.15	2	84.54	5	23.04	2	167.58	10
Caracol	0	0	10.22	2	95.28	5	12.39	2	117.89	9
Cenote	NA	NA	NA	1?	15.0/NA	4	NA	1?	15	6
Chan	NA	0	0	0	2.7	2	0	0	2.7	2
Chanchich	NA	NA	NA	NA	NA	NA	NA	NA	NA	NA
Cival Center	NA	NA	NA	NA	NA	NA	NA	NA	NA	NA
Cival West	NA	NA	NA	NA	NA	NA	NA	NA	NA	NA
Cival Far West	NA	NA	NA	NA	NA	NA	NA	NA	NA	NA
Cival North	NA	NA	NA	NA	NA	NA	NA	NA	NA	NA
Cival East	NA	NA	NA	NA	NA	NA	NA	NA	NA	NA
Dos Aguadas	NA	NA	NA	NA	19.06	2	NA	NA	19.06	2
El Palmar	NA	2	NA	NA	NA	NA	NA	NA	NA	2
Hahakab	NA	NA	NA	NA	NA	NA	NA	NA	NA	NA
Hamontún	NA	NA	NA	NA	NA	NA	NA	NA	NA	NA
Hatzcap Ceel–early	N.A	>1	0	0	5.35	1	0	0	>5.35	>2
Hatzcap Ceel–late	N.A	>1	0	0	9.36	1	0	0	>9.36	>2
Hatz Kaab	NA	NA	NA	NA	0	0	NA	NA	0	0
Holmul	NA	NA	NA	NA	NA	NA	NA	NA	NA	NA

(*continued*)

Table 16.1—*Continued*

Site name	West (area m²)	West (# rooms)	East 1 North (area m²)	East 1 North (# rooms)	East 2 Center (area m²)	East 2 Center (# rooms)	East 3 South (area m²)	East 3 South (# rooms)	Total (area m²)	Total (# rooms)
La Técnica	NA	NA	NA	NA	NA	NA	NA	NA	NA	NA
Naachtún	NA	NA	19.20	3	20.60	3	14.80	3	54.60	3
Naranjo	60?	3?	0	0	0	0	0	0	60?	3?
Punto de Chimino	NA	NA	0	0	6.03	2	0	0	6.03	2
Riverona	NA	NA	NA	NA	NA	NA	NA	NA	NA	NA
San Bartolo	0	0	0	0	15.00	1	0	0	15.00	1
San José	NA	NA	0	0	NA	1	0	0	NA	1
Sisiá	NA	NA	NA	NA	NA	NA	NA	NA	NA	NA
Tikal	0	0	32.6	3	33.3	3	27.65	3	93.55	3
T'ot	NA	NA	NA	NA	NA	NA	NA	NA	NA	NA
Uaxactún-early	0	0	13.95	2	67.9	4	19.48	2	101.33	8
Uaxactún-late	0	0	13.95	2	103	5	19.48	2	136.43	9
Xunantunich	0	0	0	0	0	0	0	0	0	0
Yaxuná	NA	NA	NA	NA	NA	NA	NA	NA	NA	NA

NA = not applicable.

Table 16.2. Relative eastern temple proportions

Site name	East 1 North	East 2 Center	East 3 South	Levels of hierarchy	Style	Multiroom
Calakmul-early	18%	58%	24%	3	Cenote	X
Calakmul-late	14%	68%	18%	3	Cenote	X
Caracol	9%	81%	10%	3	Cenote	X
Naachtún	35%	38%	27%	3	Uaxactún	X
Tikal	35%	35%	30%	3	Uaxactún	X
Uaxactún-early	14%	67%	19%	3	Uaxactún	X
Uaxactún-late	10%	75%	14%	3	Uaxactún	X

the top of the east central temple during the end of the site's occupation shows a single-room construction postdating the multiple rooms that had been constructed during the Late Classic. This last construction phase may document a change from institutionalized religion to its reduced scale during the period when urban centers in the region collapsed or were in the process of doing so.

Another Cenote Style complex that has been excavated is at Cahal Pichik, with one room in the western structure and two rooms in the southeastern structure. These three rooms have a combined area of 94.38 m². By comparison with the single-roomed examples described below, sites like Calakmul show a 7.51 order of magnitude increase in interior temple space from the time when temples were single roomed examples compared to the time when they had multiple rooms. This implies that a social transformation—statehood—had taken place by the Terminal Preclassic/Early Classic transition (Table 16.2, Figure 6.15a–b).

Hatzcap Ceel has a Cenote Style complex with at least one room in the western structure (possibly more than one) and one room in the central eastern structure (>9.36 m²). Depending upon its number of rooms and their combined floor areas, it may have at least one multiroom temple and may therefore be transitional or on the lower end of architectural complexity in the sample of E Groups evaluated.

Prototypes with Single-Room Temples or Platforms

There are examples of E Group architecture with single-room temple architecture. San José has a Cenote Style complex with one room in the central eastern structure. Some sites, such as early phase Ceibal or Xunantunich,

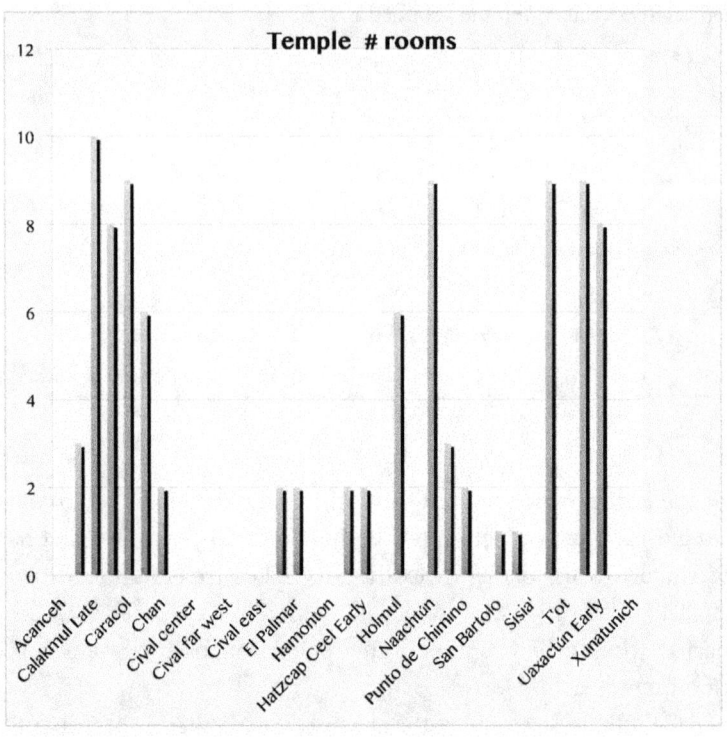

(a)

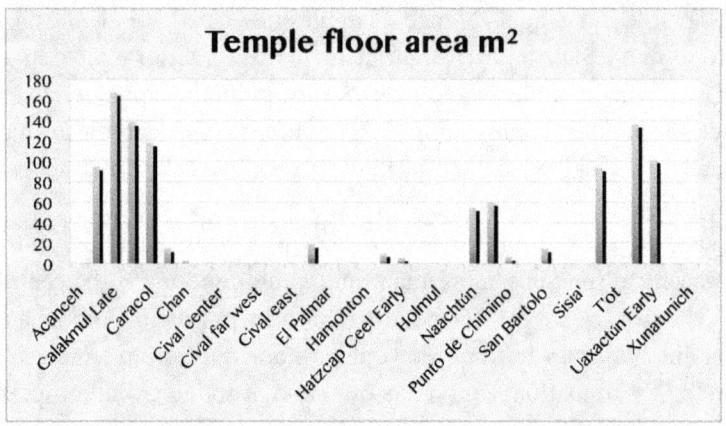

(b)

Figure 16.15. Graphs of (a) temple (#) rooms and (b) temple floor area (m^2).

have no temples on platforms (Brown et al. 2011; Inomata et al. 2013; Thompson 1939). Such variability may manifest the degree of religious specialization before, alongside, or at the point of declining institutionalization. Degrees of specialization with part-time rather than full-time specialists characterize prestate entities and groups exhibiting devolution in levels of complexity.

Final Observations

The thesis explored here is that, like other societies in Mesoamerica and elsewhere, the Maya had priestly precincts identifiable as architecturally and spatially anchored by unquestionably religious facilities, such as E Groups. E Groups were manifestly religious in nature and function. Far from being epiphenomenal, astronomy was important for the purposes of maintaining a precise calendar used for both practical and ritual purposes within the E Groups. Some researchers have assumed a lack of astronomical function in the absence of any explicit data collection or analysis that might account for variable operations from one complex to another.

Earlier in this chapter, I raised four general points concerning temple precincts that had developed to accommodate religious institutions. I discuss these below in terms of some of the data presently available for Maya Group E–type architectural complexes. Group E complexes existed at the onset of developing degrees of religious institutionalization and emerging sociocultural complexity, which in turn may have created the need for formal temple precincts, suggesting that religious ideology and its performance had a pivotal role in the growth and emergence of sociocultural complexity in the region (Baines and Yoffee 1998; Baudez 2004; Coe 1981; Freidel 1981, 1986; Geertz 1980; Schoenfelder 2003).

Theoretically, this explanation of the role that temple precincts played in emerging states is tied to the way in which religious institutions integrated technology and information for the purpose of organizing repetitive community ritual (Brumfiel 2011; Lemonnier 1986, 1992; Pfaffenberger 1988, 1992). Powerful elites spread religious doctrine through a region and unified efforts to grow crops successfully, defend land tenure from competitors, schedule trade, and perpetuate political systems through leadership continuity, competition, and warfare, all important to foster agriculture and relevant given that arable land is a finite resource (Carneiro 1970; McAnany 2014; Rathje 1971, 1973; Wittfogel 1957). New work on the life-cycle patterns of social and political change in the context of religions and nation states where few larger-scale polities are interspersed with more small units shows how this evolution occurs (Sabloff 1986; Sabloff and Marcus 2008; Salali et al. 2015; Spencer 2010, 2014). Educational systems interpenetrated religious institutions in these early states.

A valuable point of departure for investigating the topic of religious institutionalization is identifying what makes up a Maya temple precinct according to the four themes of architectural standardization, bounded spatial patterns, specialist residences or ritual seclusion zones, and evidence of hierarchical organization:

1. *Precinct or Temple Standardization.* Standardization is evident in the pattern of one western temple opposite a broad plaza from three eastern temples on a platform or a platform alone. Neither temple layouts nor whole architectural footprints of the complexes, however, are exactly the same. Standardization appears in the sets of principles for laying out astronomical azimuths that match festival dates in the solar and ritual calendars using 20-day Winal months, often varying from one site to another and over time. The presence of cord holders is patterned evidence for restricted access to the innermost temple chambers (for example, at Structures IVa, IVb, IVc, and VII) at Calakmul. Plaza proportions were standardized in Group E complexes (Chapter 8 in this volume).
2. *Delimited or Bounded Precinct.* While most of the Group E–type architectural groupings do not appear to have had walled enclosures, Calakmul has a wall north of the E Group behind Structure VII (as shown on the map by Folan et al. 1990, 1995:Figure 314). Many Cenote and Cenote-variant styles, for example, Group A at San José, have an element of access restriction in between the three eastern temples, which share a common platform. Both San José and Caracol have a drop-off or elevation change east of the E Group. At Ceibal, there is a development of adjacent structures that enclosed the southern and eastern edges of the plaza, channeling access through the west and northeastern sides. In the Northern Lowlands, Dzibilchaltún had a wall enclosing the Temple of the Seven Dolls (Structure 1-Sub) and associated buildings (Andrews 1968:42–43).
3. *Priest Residences.* To date specialized priestly residences and ritual preparation or seclusion spaces have not been explicitly identified

at Calakmul, although I excavated Structure XIX, a communal men's house west of the ballcourt (Dowd in Carrasco et al. 1995). The main palace acropolis is west of the Central Plaza, and a smaller but still impressive residential complex or acropolis exists east of the E Group. Among the artifacts found in the front room and on the stairs of the closer Structure III were Late Classic figurines that were also musical instruments suggestive of ceremonial activities (Braswell et al. 2004:175). The identification of specialized housing or ritual seclusion spaces for priests may involve the identification of features such as offset entrances creating more private and unusual access points (note Calakmul Structure III's angled passageway), multiple levels, and evidence that meals were cooked elsewhere and were brought in, as in Structures 27 and 28 at El Palenque. West facing 11-room Structure III and the small acropolis further east are possible candidates at Calakmul, but more information is needed to assess their respective functions.

4. *Hierarchical Organization of Priestly Duties.* Because there are temples of different sizes and levels of elaboration on top of pyramids within E Groups, priestly hierarchies may have corresponded to the three tiers first suggested by Joyce Marcus (1978:Table 1, 179) and supported by later studies (Zender 2004:368). By the last construction phase at Calakmul, there were at least three or four separate temple room configurations on the east side of the plaza that may be evidence of differentiated priestly duties (for example, to maintain the temples devoted to god cults) and levels of hierarchical organization. Calakmul's Phase II eastern three temples show proportions of interior space (E 58 percent, SE 24 percent, NE 18 percent) that compare favorably with those at El Palenque (E 59 percent, SE 24 percent, NE 17 percent) and may indicate a similar number of hierarchical divisions and relative priestly status.

As I have shown above, the Maya built temple precincts encompassing Group E–type architectural complexes, and the number (>1), floor area, and relative proportions of the temple interior rooms measure sociocultural complexity relating to religious institutions characterizing a state. In Maya E Groups that were developing into temple precincts functioning in the service of full-time state religious specialists—priests, rather than part-time shamans—archaeologists should expect to find shifts from platforms without temple architecture or single-roomed temples to multiroomed temples, paralleling the dramatic increase in interior space that I have documented here.

Relatively late in the overall developmental sequence and coincident with the Maya collapse, institutions degenerated. At Cenote in Guatemala, a multiroom temple was abandoned and a hastily constructed single-room temple took its place. Excavations in the central eastern Temple XV within the Dos Aguadas Group E may be another example of a temple remodeled into a smaller interior space late in the architectural sequence at the site (Estrada-Belli 2012:67). Calakmul had a late room in Structure IVb reconfigured into a smaller size.

Ritual practice should be evident in the astronomical alignments and in architectural renovations to improve hierophantic effects, such as are known from Calakmul as well as other sites (Dowd and Milbrath 2015:64). Evidence of sacrifice (including faunal and human remains, feasting), dance performances accompanied by musicians, divination, and offerings should be found on the floor surfaces, altars, and hearths extant in temple interiors and adjacent spaces as well as in buried contexts beneath floors or in walls or other specially constructed offering locations such as plaza centers. At Comalcalco, Mexico, in the Northern Lowlands, the 777 CE burial in Urn 26, with an accompanying hieroglyphic text on stingray spines, bone, and shell pendants, document Aj Pakal Tahn's priestly duties, as master of fire (*yajawk'ahk*), such as autosacrificial rites on the vernal equinox (for example, sunrise on 9.17.0.2.17 5 Kaban 10 Sip, March 20, 771 CE, using the 583,283 correlation constant, Gregorian [Zender 2004]). Burial 26 was inside a platform between northern structures II and IIa enclosing Comalcalco's North Plaza E Group.

Specialized architectural features such as tunnels or caverns recalling Xibalba ("Place of Fear") that may have been restricted for specialist use during ceremonies should be anticipated. Such examples are already known at Yaxuná, where two dance platforms, Structures 6E-53 and 6E-120 (dated to 550–600 CE), incorporate lobed interior subterranean chambers (Suhler et al. 1998). The tunnel Sergio Chávez Gómez and colleagues discovered in 2003 under the main plaza at Teotihuacán, Mexico, is where a sacred "Underworld" nexus may ultimately have married space designed for ritual seclusion with above-ground religious public performances. Its location, along the central west–east axis of a plaza within an E Group–like complex, recalls the relative tunnel position and layout at El Palenque. Multiple examples of artifacts linked to divination, esoteric knowledge, and ceremony have been found in E Groups, such as pyrite mosaic mirrors and remains of what are thought to have been codices, incised *patolli* boards, tokens, stick dice, bloodletting implements, incense braziers, and even a conch shell trumpet stored in one of the temple roofs at Caracol. Another conch shell trumpet, painted red, was found in Burial 8 under the plaza floor near Structures E, F, and G near the corner of the Uaxactún Group E (Ricketson and Ricketson 1937:120).

In some burial contexts, containers or bags for holding ritual paraphernalia have been surmised, based upon patterns of artifact deposition. Masks (some used to blur the distinction between human or divine) and elements of costume (such as a jaguar cloak) have been found in burials at Calakmul. More examples of these distinctive artifact classes and feature concentrations should be expected. With this foreknowledge, archaeologists should stand ready to preserve these fragile remains.

Intact floors and living surfaces with artifact distributions left in situ are relatively rare in the archaeological record, such as the example that I have introduced from the temple precinct at El Palenque, Oaxaca, México (772 km west southwest of Calakmul). But anticipating the former presence of such remains changes the way in which archaeologists excavate, interpret, and preserve data. More precision in excavation techniques above structure floors is warranted to discern material remains from floor assemblages in addition to trample zones above these floors that may have been left by postabandonment remnant groups or pilgrims when institutions and urban infrastructure had collapsed.

An example of good preservation of an interior living surface is found in Structure 6, Room 2, at Chan, occupied between 670 and 900 CE (Cynthia Robin, personal communication, 2015, and Chapter 11 in this volume). Religious activities were evidenced by distributions of artifacts that included jute, a spindle whorl, deer antler, a *patolli* board etched into the floor, graffiti on the walls, specialized architectural features like a quincunx or five-part pattern of postholes possibly used for an altar, changing floor levels by the use of benches or steps, and wall partitions. Perhaps Chan's Structure 6 was a two-story communal residence and workspace for priests at the E Group's southern end.

Kent Flannery (1998) has written extensively about the emergence of standardized temple and priestly residential compounds in both primary and secondary states. One idea, which may have analogies with the Maya region, is that in some cases priestly residences share the same astronomical orientation as the temples. If triadic complexes in the Maya region adjacent to some E Groups were used for housing priests, this might provide a parallel example of shared astronomical orientation.

An example is at Cival, where a triadic complex is east of and shares the central alignment with the largest centrally located E Group at the site (Chapter 9 in this volume). Another is at San Bartolo, with the didactic function of the Pinturas shrine in the Triadic Group modifying the earlier E Group (Chapters 10 and 13 in this volume). At El Perú–Waka', east of the in-line triadic design main city temple Structure M13-1 (the central temple in the possible E Group), Structure O14-04 has an apsidal "turtle" carapace plan and a Teotihuacán-style frontal platform containing a seventh-century tomb, Burial 39. Artifacts in the burial assemblage were characteristic of ritual tools and symbolic paraphernalia for a priestess (David Freidel and Michelle Rich in Dowd and Milbrath 2015). Connected to the in-line Triadic Group at El Perú–Waka' with a ramp leading southeast into the Chok Group, Structure M13-12's Burial 38 contained analogous grave goods suggestive of a priest's specialized ritual tool kit (Eppich 2007:317–325). Freidel (personal communication, 2015) suggests that additional space for priestly palaces may be in the northeast sector of the city near Plaza 1.

Scraped-down bedrock plazas and sculpted platforms form the earliest Group E constructions (Doyle et al. 2011; Estrada-Belli 2006:58; Hansen 2002; Inomata et al. 2015; Laporte and Fialko 1995; Prufer et al. 2011; Robin et al. 2012; Salazar 2005:113), where it looks as though the Maya planted their communities as they planted their milpas. A comparison is Freidel's (personal communication, 2012, and Chapter 6 in this volume) description of the image of a convex turtle's shell and an analogy with the earth's stone "shell." Through unifying religious ideology, the earliest subtractive sculpted bedrock (rather than additive stone masonry) E Group features (stepped temples, platforms, and quadripartite clefts in bedrock) would seem to reinforce the idea of the earth's surface being compared to a turtle shell and a place to center, anchor, plant, or "seat" the maize stalk, god, and ruler and ultimately each community.

These platform/temple/plaza complexes became increasingly differentiated as architectural space was redesigned to accommodate a hierarchical bureaucracy administering what had become a state religion. As discussed in this chapter, (1) standardized plans follow alignment principles based upon *veintena*-like dates for festivals at 20-day Winal month divisions in the ritual or solar calendars; (2) access to the precinct's exterior and interior spaces became more controlled; (3) residential or seclusion areas for priests were added; and (4) variation in temple size and elaboration suggests a

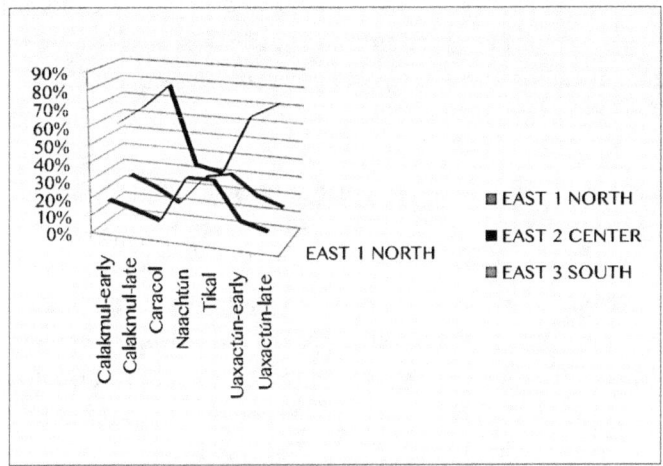

Figure 16.16. Relative eastern temple proportions.

hierarchy of religious specialists. Three important new patterns have been recognized in this study.

The first is that of a profoundly transformational process of change where multiroom temple interior space increased up to 751 percent or within 1-σ standard deviation 49.83 (m²) over single-room examples when statehood had emerged to accommodate religious institutions with full-time specialists at Calakmul, Mexico. Using room dimensions to calculate available space within temples provides proximal data for expanding and contracting priestly bureaucratic scales. The second pattern is late reductions in temple floor plans during the end of the late Terminal Classic (800–900 CE) or the Early Postclassic or Epiclassic period (950–1200 CE), for example at Cenote, Dos Aguadas, and Calakmul, indicating smaller spatial requirements for religious personnel. The third pattern is proportional differences in temple scale that are suggestive of hierarchical divisions and relative status within those orders in the priesthood.

Moreover, I have made a credible case for how Group E–type architectural complexes functioned within temple precincts, such as at Calakmul in Mexico; at Naachtún, Tikal, and Uaxactún in Guatemala; and at Caracol in Belize, which display a suite of characteristics comparable to religious compounds in known primary and secondary states from other parts of the world. The relative proportions of the sets of eastern temples' interior spaces are presented in Table 16.2 and Figure 16.16. Additional examples where expanded bureaucracies existed are Cahal Pichik, Chan,

Dos Aguadas, El Palmar, Hatzcap Ceel, Naranjo, and Punto de Chimino. Several sites have issues of preservation or insufficient excavation, which make their degree of elaboration difficult to ascertain (for example, Cahal Pichik or Dos Aguadas); but as excavation continues, new information will become available.

Prototypes of these religious compounds are evident at San José and San Bartolo, with single-room temples, as well as Hatz Kaab and one E Group at Xunantunich, which does not presently have evidence of stone temple architecture on top of the masonry-faced platforms. Additional excavation revealing previously unexposed temple rooms in these complexes could potentially modify these categories and provide more information about how the religious buildings were used. A possible school has been identified at San Bartolo in Sub IA behind the Pinturas Triadic Group platform. Quarters for astronomers may have been constructed close to the E Groups, given that certain activities, such as sky watching, took place at night. El Palenque demonstrates the existence of an early ceremonial center with clear evidence of priestly residences or ritual seclusion structures adjacent to the temples on the main east–west axis, broadly confirming Wendy Ashmore's (1991) ideas about directionality and Mesoamerican community planning principles.

The temple precinct model presented here should help guide research designs for future excavations in Maya centers to refine anthropological archaeologists' understanding of how and when degrees of religious specialization or its lack contributed to ebbs and flows in Mesoamerican sociocultural complexity whereby centralization and specialization distinguishing statehood co-occurred (Wright 1977). Along with emerging religious institutions, it is reasonable to expect that innovations in education, codex production, and calendar development took place as the spaces for ritual and learning expanded to accommodate full-time occupational specialists. The rulers and priests, including astronomers and daykeepers, devoted information technology to the observation of seasonally timed ceremonies using solar and other astronomical movements framed against the backdrop of sacred architecture and distant points on the horizon.

Maya priests choreographed nuanced sacred spectacles to enact a ritually charged vortex where natural forces from the sky, earth, and underworld collided in their temple precincts. They meant to shock and awe their audiences. The sheer quantities of copal incense burner (*incensario*) fragments and reflective pyrite mosaics from backed mirror-like divination devices left in these religious centers convey the impression that it was all done with smoke and mirrors. But priests and penitents must have been supremely gratified when nature cooperated by providing a blood-red lunar eclipse corroborating an astronomical codex prediction, a sheet of water flowing across a plaza floor reflecting the stars, or a bolt of lightning illuminating obsidian blades used for seasonally timed blood offerings burnt on bark paper ties. With bright sun and shadow to dramatize where a deity impersonator danced to chants and music of increasing poetic density signaling the approach of a ceremonial/calendrical crescendo, Maya religious temple precincts resonated as effective axes for the natural, human, and cosmic forces of continuity and change.

Acknowledgments

This chapter provided background information for a guided discussion and PowerPoint presentation titled "Maya Group E–Type Architectural Complexes: Their Formation and Development in Mesoamerica (Notebook 2)" at the second Santa Fe Institute working group on the topic "Early Maya E Groups, Solar Calendars and the Role of Astronomy in the Rise of Lowland Urbanism," held August 23–25, 2013. It was one of four planned Santa Fe Institute working groups organized by David Freidel, myself, and Arlen Chase and sponsored by Jerry Murdock. I am especially grateful to Jerry Murdock, who has supported this series of Santa Fe Institute working groups; Jerry Sabloff, who has been both our host and enthusiastic colleague; and David Freidel and Arlen Chase for their able leadership and organizational skills. Thanks go to M. Kathryn Brown, Francisco Estrada-Belli, and Franco Rossi, who assisted me with data from the E Groups in their regions. I also thank Lic. Ramón Carrasco Vargas, director of the Calakmul team for the opportunity to work together at Calakmul and at Balamkú, Mexico. I am grateful to two peer reviewers for their helpful comments. Wendy Ashmore, Anthony F. Aveni, David A. Freidel, John S. Justeson, Jeremy A. Sabloff, and Mary Beth D. Trubitt all graciously read and commented on a draft of this chapter. I dedicate this chapter to George Kubler, with whom I studied ancient architecture. Finally, I would like to thank Susan Milbrath, who first invited me to join this talented and diverse group of scholars.

Appendix A: Supplemental Calakmul Excavation Data from E Group Architecture

Structures IV–c, VI, and VII (Central Plaza)

As noted previously in Dowd et al. (1995:7–8) and subsequently reported in Carrasco (1996, 1999) as well as Dowd and Aveni (1998):

> Proyecto Arqueologico de la Biosfera Calakmul excavations have shown that there were at least three Late Classic construction phases:
> a) The first placed single rooms on top of Temples IVa, b and c. The temple on top of Structure VI was not yet constructed.
> b) The second phase added the second chambers to the front of temples on IVa, b and c. At this point the two stelae may have been positioned on top of Structure VI.
> c) Lastly, the third chamber was added to the front of Structure IVb and the superstructure on top of Structure VI was completed. An interesting feature of IVa is that the inner doorway was rebuilt to narrow the entrance by about 20 cm on either side. We tested the hypothesis that this renovation may have been a correction used to adjust the alignment of the two doorjambs to insure that on the winter solstice the exterior doorway shadows lined up with the inner passage, with negative results.
>
> The three dates Marcus (1987) uses for her dynastic history at the site may roughly correspond to these three construction phases, i.e. A.D. 672, A.D. 702 and A.D. 721.
>
> Structure IVb, the largest of the three temples, had changes made in the form of a lower chamber. What had been an inner room was filled in to create a smaller chamber. Above this level, in front of the superstructure, is a projecting platform that is skewed somewhat from the orientation of the front facade. There was no evidence of a substructure in VI, although IVb did have evidence of earlier constructions. Within IVb were found a broken lintel, ca. A.D. 500, and an altar. The lintel shows a ruler sitting on a throne and the altar, much eroded except for the center, displays a quatrefoil design.

Ramón Carrasco (1999:74) describes the front rooms added on to the lower platform of Structure IVb as Río Bec in style, while the rear of the platform is constructed in Petén masonry style, as is shown by the way the stone is cut and by the presence of a large basal molding. Northern

Belize-style Late Postclassic or Protohistoric period (1200–1519 CE) modeled anthropomorphic incense burners were recovered in Structure IVb. In the lower level front room were burned offerings dating to between the thirteenth through the fifteenth centuries that included fallen stucco decorations from the then deteriorating exterior (Carrasco 1996). Prior to the Late Classic constructions and modifications corresponding with IVa, IVb, and IVc, there were a series of four building episodes labeled Substructures 1–4 dating to the Early Classic (Carrasco 1999:74) (Figure 16.15).

Structure IVb

Caches

Caches and burials were found in the course of excavating Structure IVb and cleaning out looters' trenches (Carrasco 1999). For example, Cache 1 appears to have been associated with the earliest Substructure 1's stairway fill. It contained a female human cranium inside two plates of Early Classic Águila Orange (ca. fifth century) placed lip to lip.

Cache 2, dating to the last Late Classic construction phase, was found 0.77 m beneath Stela 11 (the central one of the three stelae in front of Structure IVb: 10, 11, and 12) and contained an obsidian knife, jadeite and shell beads, and two *Spondylus* shells. Four ceramic vessels, of which three were monochromatic orange and one polychromed Early Classic Águila pottery style, were in double lip-to-lip positions. One set of vessels held a human tooth, all that remained of a poorly preserved cranium.

Cache 3 was found beneath the altar associated with Stela 15 in a hole in the plaza construction fill. Two Águila Orange plates were positioned one on top of another and held jadeite and shell beads as well as fragments of anthropomorphic figurines decorated with shell.

Cache 4 was destroyed in the process of building a tomb in the center of the second room of the Structure IVb temple's second level during the Late Classic. The original receptacle was a four-sided, mat-impressed, calcified surface containing the remains of pottery vessels (one polychrome and the other an Águila Orange platter) and painted stucco fragments such as may have adorned a ceramic or wooden object in addition to some jadeite beads.

Cache 5, located at the foot of the second room wall in the second level of Structure IVb, was also disturbed. It originally contained more than eight Águila Orange plates, all broken but one.

Cache 6, possibly the earliest, contained seven Late Preclassic vessels, including examples of the Sierra Rojo, Polvero Negro and Flor Crema types. One was an Águila Orange cylindrical bucket, which contained a female cranium wrapped in red-stained cloth and capped by an Águila Orange plate.

Cache 7 contained three offerings collected on Águila Orange plates above a burial. The first held interior utilized flakes or scrapers of obsidian, some stuccoed cylinders painted red, blue, and yellow and shell fragments. The second and third held two infant skeletons in flexed positions (possibly sacrificed twins).

Cache 8 was found in the center of Room 1 of the second or upper level and contained five vessels (one polychrome), two plates, and one jug, besides a large platter holding five eccentric flints (debitage was also in the fill), pumice stone, shell, coral, and polychrome stucco-covered ceramic cylinders.

Burials

Burials from Structure IVb included Burial 1, located under the floor of Substructure 1 and containing a flexed burial of an adult woman. Burial 2 also contained the remains of an adult woman in a flexed position. This individual was buried under the front stairway of Substructure 1 with two Águila Orange plates, stingray spine and obsidian perforators, and jadeite and shell beads. Burial 3 was under the base of the rear wall of the second interior room, accompanied by three offerings in a location suggestive of an association with the next to last construction phase of Structure IVb. Green and red painted stucco and wood were the remains of a possible funerary mask, as well as jadeite beads, buried with the individual, who was in a flexed position.

Tombs

Two tombs were located in Structure IVb. The first was under the second upper room of the temple and was oriented east–west. The few materials left in situ suggest that the tomb had been robbed in antiquity. A small Olmec-style jadeite figurine was found in the tomb, which Carrasco (1999:82) suggests was a shaman.

Tomb 2 was under the first. Portions were also vandalized. Left in the tomb, however, was a funerary mask and eighteen vessels, most of which were Balanza Black type with an estimated date of about 450–600 CE (possibly contemporaneous with Stela 114 or slightly later). The human remains were that of an older individual. The Principal Bird Deity and a long-lipped supernatural adorn some of the ceramic vessels (Carrasco 1999).

Structure IVc

Caches

Two caches were under the plaza floor in front of Temple IVc. Cache 1 contained two Águila plates enclosing offerings of jadeite, pyrite, and marine shell fragments in addition to anthropomorphic ornaments decorated with jadeite, shell, and pyrite mosaic pieces. Similarly Cache 2 contained jadeite, shell, and pyrite items.

Burial

Burial 1 in Structure IVc was about 1 m under the floor of the temple's front room and appeared to have been placed there during the temple's last construction phase. Rather than being a prepared crypt, the male individual was buried in a semiextended position directly on the construction fill.

Structure VII

Supplemental data from Structure VII at Calakmul, Mexico, are described in detail below. At the north side of the Central Plaza, Structure VII has three superstructures in a triadic arrangement, or alternatively one superstructure and two platforms, on top of a 24 m high platform; the central building has three rooms (Braswell et al. 2004:177; Delvendahl 2008; Domínguez 1992, 1994; Domínguez and Gallegos 1989–1990; Domínguez et al. 1998; Folan et al. 1995:319–320). Begun in the Late Preclassic, the central superstructure is Late Classic; the last construction phase is Terminal Classic in date. On the west side of the floor in the outermost room is an incised *patolli* board. Floor assemblages included *incensario* fragments and examples of Late Classic Chen-Mul Modeled Mayapán-style incense burners distributed along the central axis of the three-roomed building. Terminal Classic cooking vessel fragments were found in the east side of the outer room.

Tomb 1

At about 780 CE an adult male was buried in the central Structure VII temple under an Río Bec–style altar containing a niche. Wrapped in burned matting and containing remains of a jaguar skull, claws, and tail, the body interred in Tomb 1 may have been wearing or bundled in a jaguar skin cape (Braswell et al. 2004:177; Coyoc 1985; Domínguez 1992; Folan et al. 1995:319). Within the tomb were over 2,147 pieces of jadeite, including a mosaic mask, as well as shells, a pearl, ten Late Classic ceramic vessels of Tepeu 2 (700–800 CE) date, and six El Chayel obsidian blades. The mask featured pieces of pyrite used to fashion the eyebrows. Shell corneas and obsidian pupils accentuated the eyes. Previously I have interpreted the mosaic mask and its context from Tomb 1 in Structure VII as evocative of God H or the Wind God (Dowd 1998). Among the jadeite artifacts were four large earflares, a ring, over 1,000 beads, an Ik'-shaped plaque, and two lip plugs carved with hieroglyphs. One hieroglyph is a possible day sign with the prefix number nine. The ten vessels included four Pedregal Modeled dishes under the burial, one Infierno Black dish, one small Botifela Orange flat-based bowl, one Cambio Unslipped vase, two Infierno Black tripod vessels with straight sides, and one Carmelita Incised tripod *cajete* with a postfire scratched motif. The burial was laid on a bed of seeds of *Metopium brownei* (che chem or poisonwood), which is used for making ceremonial incense. *Bursera* spp. (*chaka'*, gumbolimbo, or *indio desnudo*) seeds were also present. In addition, resin from the *Bursera simaruba* (*chaka'*) tree was in two of the vessels accompanying the burial. The two species grow in the vicinity of one another; while the first is toxic, the second is its antidote. An additional group of fifty-eight obsidian blades and four chert eccentrics was found in an associated cache. Many of the obsidian blades, the type commonly used for bloodletting, appeared to have been struck from the same core.

Other Associations

Behind Structure VII is a *chultun* filled with figurines and other ceramic objects, as Prudence Rice (2015, Chapter 5 in this volume) has discussed in association with E Groups.

Comparative Material

Calakmul's Structure VII has interior artifact and feature distributions that are similar to those found at Caracol's Structure A-3, also in the northern position in an E Group, which contained censer fragments, two *patolli* boards incised into the surface of an interior bench, and a burned zone in a rear chamber dated to 693±60 CE (Beta-18062). At Caracol, there was also a high-status burial in a tomb under the Structure A-3 floor with a reconstructed capstone date of 9.13.3.15.16 13 K'ib 9(10) K'ayab (or January 11, 696

CE, using the 584,283 correlation) (Chase and Chase 1987:13–15). As in the burial at Calakmul, obsidian and chert offerings are included among the grave goods. The co-occurrence of *patolli* boards and censer fragments suggests comparable northern E Group structure functions. The *patolli* boards may have been used for casting tokens, such as with divinatory games of chance and the censers employed for burning sticks of copal incense and offerings of blood-soaked paper ties.

Appendix B: Examples of Group E–Type Architectural Complexes Excavated at Other Maya Sites

Uaxactún Style E Group at Uaxactún

Uaxactún, Petén, Guatemala

At Uaxactún Group E's west side, Stela 20 was found in front of the pyramid's east stairway and was dated to 9.3.0.0.0 2 Ajaw 18 Muwan, January 28, 495 CE, using the 584,283 correlation (Smith 1950:63). The E-VII platform never supported a stone temple on its summit, although plastered over postholes indicated a temporary perishable superstructure (Ricketson and Ricketson 1937:43; Smith 1950:63). Uaxactún's east side displays Stelae 18 and 19, each dated 8.16.0.0.0 3 Ajaw 8 K'ank'in or February 1, 357 CE, using the 584,283 correlation (Smith 1950:63). Temple E-I contained two rooms (front: 4.5 m long × 1.4 m wide and back: 5.1 m long × 1.5 m wide), and the rear room had a built-in altar (0.6 m high, 2.4 m long, and 1.1 m long) (Ricketson and Ricketson 1937:47–49). Ceramics (for example, polychrome: Ricketson and Ricketson 1937:Plate 86) provide additional diagnostic information. A skull in a cache offering was found below the floor in front of the altar.

Temple E-II was originally a four-roomed structure that at a later date was expanded to five rooms with the addition of a lower front room (Ricketson and Ricketson 1937:50, 53). The areas of the four rooms total 67.90 m^2; with the addition of the later fifth room, the total is 103.00 m^2. Temple E-III contains two rooms, the front one measuring 5.2 m long × 1.7 m wide, and the rear one 5.6 m long × 1.9 m wide (Ricketson and Ricketson 1937:57). While construction had begun in the Preclassic and was finished in the Early Classic period, the last room in front of Temple E-II may have been built in the Late Classic period. Use of the complex continued into the Late Classic, even as the site was falling into ruin and abandoned, much as at Caracol. Uaxactún's alignments match solar solstice and equinox dates of June 21/December 21 and September 22/March 20 (Aveni et al. 2003: Table 1).

Cenote Style E Group at Cenote and Hatzcap Ceel

Cenote, Petén, Guatemala

At the west side of the Cenote Group E-type complex in Guatemala, Structure C5 was not excavated (Chase 1983). The northeastern structure C108 was not excavated but likely contained at least one room (Chase 1983). The central eastern Structure C1 building associated with the C1-1st construction phase probably originally enclosed four rooms with perishable walls and roof during the Early Classic. Measurements are only available for the 5.0 m long × 3.0 m wide front chamber (15.00 m^2) (Chase 1983:107). Structure C1-2nd A had a two-roomed building at its summit. The ultimate construction phase at C1 consisted of a freestanding shrine built on the ruined C1-1st construction in the Late Classic, Terminal, or Postclassic period (Chase 1983:137). By comparison to C1-1st's more elaborate construction, perhaps this represents a less organized sociopolitical effort, signaling devolution when institutions faltered. While the southeastern Structure C109 was not excavated, Chase (1983:167) reported that the temple was about 9.0 m long × 7.0 m wide (or less than 63 m^2 taking into consideration wall widths). Like C108, it probably had at least one room inside. Cenote's alignments match June 21/—and March 11/October 4 dates (Aveni et al. 2003:Table 1).

Hatzcap Ceel, Cayo, Belize

In Belize, Hatzcap Ceel's Group E west Pyramid A, 10.4 m high, had the remains of a small multiroom structure, which was destroyed by a landslide during excavation (three stucco floors were in evidence: Thompson 1931:249). The group had a northeastern Structure I flanking a central eastern Pyramid F, which was not excavated. Pyramid F, 10 m high, had a small stone masonry one-roomed temple on top with a floor plan measuring 5.35 m long × 1.75 m wide (9.36 m^2). It covered an earlier temple construction with a single room measuring 5.35 m long × 1.0 m wide (5.35 m^2). Below was a third stucco floor, under which was Votive Cache 3, containing a lidded urn made of sandy red slipped paste containing a second vessel with shell beads, jadeite beads, shell figurines, cephalopods or mollusks, and an iron pyrite mirror made of at least thirty-two squares of iron pyrite resting on a 6.5 cm square ceramic back (Thompson 1931:251, 275). The cache dates to no later than Late Classic Holmul V (600–830 CE), based on the presence of red and black on yellow painted ring-bowl ware sherds (Thompson 1931:276). Thompson (1931) did not excavate the southeastern Structure E. Hatzcap Ceel's interbuilding alignments match dates of June 21/—and February 26/October 16 (Aveni et al 2003:Table 1).

Cenote Variant Style E Group at Cahal Pichik and San José

Cahal Pichik, Cayo, Belize

At Cahal Pichik in Belize, on Group E's west side, Thompson (1931:239–248, 276) excavated portions of Group I in 1928–1929. It is Cenote Variant Style. The top of the western Structure B (42 m^2 base, 13 m high) features a one-room partial masonry, partial wattle-and-daub structure (about 8 × 8.10 m (64.80 m^2), with a 5 × 1 m, 1.05 m high stuccoed altar or bench along the rear or west wall, built in two construction phases). Among the stucco sculpture fragments that were found at the site was a Cauac glyph, reportedly stored in the British Museum (Thompson 1931:243). A cached offering (Votive Cache 4) was found "below the center of the back wall of the temple behind the altar" (Thompson 1931:276). Thompson (1931:276–77, Plate XXXVI) describes Votive Cache 4 as "placed in a low flat-bottomed bowl with everted lip, on top of which was placed a second bowl of exactly similar size (height 6.5 cm, diameter 17 cm), shape and texture. These vessels are of a rather coarse ware of a deep red color, unslipped and unpainted." Inside were a jadeite bead and perforated amulet (carved with a head). On the east side, the northeast Structure D in Group I was not excavated. The central eastern Structure E was excavated, but no evidence of a temple placed on top of the pyramidal mound was reported, even though there was a west-facing staircase leading to the summit. The southern Mound F had a *jacal* (adobe)-type two-room temple on top (Thompson 1931:245, Figure 10d). The front room dimensions were 5.4 m long × 4.5 m wide (24.30 m^2), and the rear with dressed stonewalls 4.8 m long × 1.1 m wide (5.28 m^2). Overall, the 1.5 m high basal structure located on top of the 3 m high Terrace L faces west-northwest. A refuse dump reportedly was under the floor of the back room, containing bones, ash, broken pottery, and a few whole vessels, including one with three internal handles in organic rich soil. The front room had two floor rebuilding episodes. Cahal Pichik's interbuilding alignments match dates of April 1/September 12 and February 9/November 3 (Aveni et al. 2003:Table 1).

San José, Cayo, Belize

At San José, also in Belize, the Group E-type complex was Cenote Variant Style, composed of Group A Structures 7 on the west and Structures 2, 3, and 4 on the east. Minimally excavated, Mound 7 was described as having a razor-backed summit, 9.5 m high, and a possible stairway in front (Thompson 1939:47). On the east side of the plaza, Mound A2 was a long mound, never faced with stone, 5.4 m high. The central Mound A3, 12 m high, had a floor 1.4 m below its summit, suggesting to Thompson (1939:46) that there had been a one-roomed temple on top. Six stucco floors suggested rebuilding or repair episodes of construction or refurbishment. Sherds of San José Phase I (350 BCE–250 CE) and Phase IV (700–850 CE) ceramics were identified in the layers of intervening fill below Floor 5. On Floor 6 were walls 1.71 m apart exposed for a length of 2 m, suggesting that the first construction phase also had included a room at the summit. Mound A4 behind Stela 1, 10 m high, may have had a stairway leading to a flat summit without a superstructure. Burials and caches were found in this mound (Caches A1 and A2 and Burials A1, A5, A6, A8). Burial A1 contained San José III (550–700 CE) ceramics and was under Floor 1 (Thompson 1939:68). Above Floor 1 were burials and caches containing San José III materials, and above these was a cache with San José IV materials. Current dating of these materials is Preclassic.

As at Uaxactún, Caracol, and Calakmul, the elaboration and angled orientation of the southeast structures is also noticeable at both San José and Cahal Pichik. San José's interbuilding alignments are true north 52°30' east (north Structure 2 edge), true north 89°30' east (Structure 3 centerline), and true north 118°30' east (south Structure 4 edge). The northeastern Structure 2's centerline, true north 62°30' east, is 2°30' from the summer solstice sunrise date, which corresponds to about 65°, assuming a 0° horizon line. The Structure 3 centerline is aligned with the equinoxes and can be converted to March 20/September 22 dates, assuming a 0° horizon, or within a day of those dates if the horizon is slightly elevated. The southeastern Structure 4's southern building edge is a few degrees south of the December 21 solstice sunrise. Its center doorway location, true north 113°30' east, nearly aligns with the winter solstice, which is about 114°30'at a 0° horizon. These are preliminary estimates, pending more precise horizon elevation data or additional on-site survey data.

References Cited

Adams, Robert M.
1966 *The Evolution of Urban Society: Early Mesopotamia and Prehispanic Mexico.* Aldine, Chicago.

Aimers, James J., and Prudence M. Rice
2006 Astronomy, Ritual, and the Interpretation of Maya "E-Group" Architectural Assemblages. *Ancient Mesoamerica* 17(1):79–96.

Anderson Arthur J. O., and Charles E. Dibble
1951 *Florentine Codex: Book 2. The Ceremonies.* School of American Research, Santa Fe, New Mexico.

Andrews, E. Wyllys, IV
1968 Dzibilchaltun: A Northern Maya Metropolis. *Archaeology* 21:36-47.

Andrews, George F.
1995 1994–1995 Architectural Survey at Calakmul. Unpublished manuscript. George F. and Geraldine D. Andrews papers, Alexander Architectural Archive, University of Texas Libraries, University of Texas at Austin.

Ashmore, Wendy
1991 Site-Planning Principles and Concepts of Directionality among the Ancient Maya. *Latin American Antiquity* 2(3):199–226.

Aveni, Anthony, Edward Calnak, and Horst Hartung
1988 Myth, Environment, and the Orientation of the Temple Major of Tenochtitlan. *American Antiquity* 53:287–309.

Aveni, Anthony F., Anne S. Dowd, and Benjamin Vining
2003 Maya Calendar Reform? Evidence from Orientations of Specialized Architectural Assemblages. *Latin American Antiquity* 14(2):159–178.

Aveni, Anthony F., and Horst Hartung
1989 Uaxactún, Guatemala, Group E, and Similar Assemblages: An Archaeoastronomical Reconsideration. In *World Archaeoastronomy*, edited by Anthony F. Aveni, pp. 441–461. Cambridge University Press, Cambridge, United Kingdom.

Baines, John, and Norman Yoffee
1998 Order, Legitimacy, and Wealth in Ancient Egypt and Mesopotamia. In *Archaic States*, edited by Gary M. Feinman and Joyce Marcus, pp. 199–261. School of American Research Press, Santa Fe, New Mexico.

Baudez, Claude-François
1994 *Maya Sculpture of Copán: The Iconography.* University of Oklahoma Press, Norman, Oklahoma.
2004 *Una historia de la religión de los antiguos mayas.* Centro de Estudios Mexicanos y Centroamericanos, Mexico City.

Beliaev, Dmitri
2000 Wuk Tsuk and Oxlahun Tsuk: Naranjo and Tikal in the Late Classic. *Acta Mesoamerica* 10:63–81.

Benavides C., Antonio, Ramón Carrasco Vargas, Roberto García Moll, Carlos Pallán Gayol, Agustín Peña Castillo, Juan Pablo Sereno Uribe, and Renée Lorelei Zapata
2007   *Mayas en Campeche: Calakmul, Edzná y otros sitios*. Ciudades Prehispánicas 4. Grupo Azabache, Mexico City.

Biehl, Peter F.
2012   Meanings and Functions of Enclosed Places in the European Neolithic: A Contextual Approach to Cult, Ritual, and Religion. *Archeological Papers of the American Anthropological Association* 21(1):130–146.

Blanton, Richard E., Gary M. Feinman, S. A. Kowalewski, and Peter N. Peregrine
1996   A Dual Processual Theory for the Evolution of Mesoamerican Civilization. *Current Anthropology* 37(1):1–14.

Bloch, Hannah
2015   Rescuing Mes Aynak. *National Geographic* 228(3):110–129.

Braswell, Geoffrey E., Joel D. Gunn, María del Rosario Domínguez Carrasco, William J. Folan, Larraine A. Fletcher, Abel Morales López, and Michael D. Glascock
2004   Defining the Terminal Classic at Calakmul, Campeche. In *The Terminal Classic in the Maya Lowlands: Collapse, Transition, and Transformation*, edited by Arthur A. Demarest, Don S. Rice, and Prudence M. Rice, pp. 162–194. University Press of Colorado.

Brown, M. Kathryn
2011   Postclassic Veneration at Xunantunich, Belize. *Mexicon* 33:126–131.
2013   Missing Persons: The Role of Ancestors in the Rise of Complexity. *Research Reports in Belizean Archaeology* 10:57–64.

Brown, M. Kathryn, Jennifer Cochran, Leah McCurdy, and David Mixter
2011   Preceramic to Postclassic: A Brief Synthesis of the Occupation History of Group E, Xunantunich. *Research Reports in Belizean Archaeology* 8:209–219.

Brumfiel, Elizabeth M.
2011   Technologies of Time: Calendrics and Commoners in Postclassic Mexico. *Ancient Mesoamerica* 22(1):53–70.

Burger, Richard L., and Lucy Salazar-Burger
1986   Early Organizational Diversity in the Peruvian Highlands: Huaricoto and Kotosh. In *Andean Archaeology: Papers in Memory of Clifford Evans*, edited by Ramiro Matos M., Solveig A. Turpin, and Herbert H. Eling Jr., pp. 65–84. Monograph 27. Institute of Archaeology, University of California, Los Angeles.

Byland, Bruce E., and John M. D. Pohl
1994   *In the Realm of 8 Deer: The Archaeology of the Mixtec Codices*. University of Oklahoma Press, Norman.

Carballo, David M., and Anthony F. Aveni
2012   Los vecinos del Preclásico en Xoxhitécatl y la institucionalización de la religión. *Arqueología Mexicana* XIX(117):52–57.

Carneiro, Robert L.
1970   A Theory of the Origin of the State. *Science* 169:733–738.

Carrasco Vargas, Ramón
1996   Arqueologia de una "superpotencia" Calakmul. *Arqueologia Mexicana* 3(18):46–51.
1999   Actividad ritual y objetos de poder en la Estructura IV de Calakmul, Campeche. In *Land of the Turkey and the Deer*, edited by Ruth Guber, pp. 69–84. Labyrinthos, Lancaster, California.
Carrasco Vargas, Ramón, Sylviane Boucher, Paula Alvarez González, Viera Tiesler Blos, Valeria García Vierna, Renata García Moreno, and Javier Vázquez Negrete
1999   A Dynastic Tomb from Campeche, Mexico: New Evidence on Jaguar Paw, a Ruler of Calakmul. *Latin American Antiquity* 10(1):47–58.
Carrasco Vargas, Ramón, Sylviane Boucher, Anne S. Dowd, Armando Paul, María Elena García, and Emyly González G.
1995   *Informe preliminar del Proyecto Arqueológico de la Biosfera de Calakmul*. Instituto Nacional de Antropología e Historía, Mérida, Yucatán, Mexico.
Carrasco Vargas, Ramón, Verónica A. Vázquez López, and Simon Martin
2009   Daily Life of the Ancient Maya Recorded on Murals at Calakmul, Mexico. *Proceedings of the National Academy of Sciences (PNAS)* 106(46):19245–19249.
Chase, Arlen F.
1983   *A Contextual Consideration of the Tayasal-Paxcaman Zone, El Petén, Guatemala*. Ph.D. dissertation, Department of Anthropology, University of Pennsylvania, Philadelphia, University Microfilms/ProQuest, Ann Arbor, Michigan.
Chase, Arlen F., and Diane Z. Chase
1987   *Investigations at the Classic Maya City of Caracol, Belize: 1985–1987*. Pre-Columbian Art Research Institute, Monograph 3. San Francisco, California.
1995   External Impetus, Internal Synthesis, and Standardization: E-Group Assemblages and the Crystallization of Classic Maya Society in the Southern Lowlands. *Acta Mesoamericana* 8:87–101 (special issue edited by Nikolai Grube entitled *The Emergence of Lowland Maya Civilization: The Transition from the Preclassic to Early Classic*).
2006   Before the Boom: Caracol's Preclassic Era. *Research Reports in Belizean Archaeology* 3:41–57.
Childe, V. Gordon
1950   The Urban Revolution. *Town Planning Review* 21(1):3–17.
Christenson, Allen J. (translator)
2003   *Popul Vuh: Sacred Book of the Quiché Maya People*. http://www.mesoweb.com/publications/Christenson/PopolVuh.pdf, accessed September 11, 2013.
Clark, John E.
2007   In Craft Specialization's Penumbra: Things, Persons, Action, Value, and Surplus. *Archaeological Papers of the American Anthropological Association*, 17(1):20–35.
Coe, Michael D.
1981   Religion and the Rise of Mesoamerican States. In *The Transition to Statehood in the New World*, edited by Grant D. Jones and Robert R. Kautz, pp. 157–171. Cambridge University Press, Cambridge, United Kingdom.
2003   *Angkor and the Khmer Civilization*. Thames and Hudson, London.

Coyoc Ramírez, Mario A.
1985   Entierro de la tumba I de la estructura 7 de Calakmul, Campeche. *Informacion* 9:99–131.

Crisell, Rob
2000   Uncovering the Maya Metropolis of Calakmul. *American Archaeology* 4(3):19–23.

Dahlin, Bruce
1984   A Colossus in Guatemala: The Preclassic City of El Mirador. *Archaeology* 37(5):18–25.

de Burgoa, Francisco
1934 [1674] *Geografica descripción* Vols. 25–26. Publicaciones del Archivo General de la Nación, Mexico City.

de Córdova, Juan.
1942 [1578] *Vocabulario castellano-zapoteco*. Instituto Nacional de Antropología e Historia, Mexico City.

Delvendahl, Kai
2008   *Calakmul in Sight: History and Archaeology of an Ancient Maya City*. Unas Letras Industria Editorial, Mérida, Mexico.

Demarest, Arthur A.
1992   Ideology in Ancient Maya Cultural Evolution: The Dynamic of Galactic Polities. In *Ideology and Pre-Columbian Civilizations*, edited by Arthur A. Demarest and Geoffrey W. Conrad, pp. 135–157. School of American Research Press, Santa Fe.

DeMarrais, Elizabeth, Luis Jaime Castillo, and Timothy K. Earle
1996   Ideology, Materialization, and Power Strategies. *Current Anthropology* 37:15–31.

Domínguez Carrasco, María del Rosario
1992   *El recinto superior del Edificio VII de Calakmul, Campeche: Una interpretación diacrónica de su desarrollo desde el punto de vista de la arquitectura y el material cerámico*. Licenciatura thesis, Escuela Nacional de Antropología e Historia, Instituto Nacional de Antropología e Historia, Mexico City.
1994   *Calakmul, Campeche: Un análisis de la cerámica*. Colección arqueología 4. Centro de Investigaciones Históricas y Sociales, Universidad Autónoma de Campeche, Campeche, Mexico.

Domínguez Carrasco, María del Rosario, and Miriam Judith Gallegos Gomora
1989–1990 Informe del trabajo del Proyecto Calakmul, 1984: Estructura VII. *Información* 14:56–84.

Domínguez Carrasco, M. R., Dorie Reents-Budet, Ronald L. Bishop, and William J. Folan
1998   La cerámica de Calakmúl: Un análisis químico y sociopolítico. In *Los investigadores de la cultura maya*, Vol. 6, pp. 361–375. Universidad Autónoma de Campeche, Campeche, Mexico.

Dowd, Anne S.
1998   What the Best-Dressed Maya Wore on Their Way to the Underworld. Invited research paper presented at the 31st Society for Historical Archaeology Annual Meeting, Atlanta, Georgia, January 8, 1998.

2016   *Archaeological Feasibility Study and Scope of Work for Mount Nebo, Jordan.* ArchaeoLOGIC USA, LLC, Vail, Colorado.

Dowd, Anne S. (editor)

2015   Cosmovision in New World Ritual Landscapes. *Cambridge Archaeological Journal* 25(1):211–297.

2017   Mesoamerican Cultural Astronomy and the Calendar Special Section. *Ancient Mesoamerica* 28(2).

Dowd, Anne S., and Anthony F. Aveni

1998   The Maya Space-Time Continuum: Calakmul's Group E-Type Complex. Paper presented at the 63rd Annual Meeting of the Society for American Archaeology, Seattle, March 26, 1998.

Dowd, Anne S., Anthony F. Aveni, and Ramón Carrasco Vargas

1995   Solar Observatory or Allegory?: Calakmul's Group E-Type Complex. Paper presented at the 60th Annual Meeting of the Society for American Archaeology, Minneapolis, Minnesota, May 4, 1995.

Dowd, Anne S., and Susan Milbrath (editors)

2015   *Cosmology, Calendars, and Horizon-Based Astronomy in Ancient Mesoamerica.* University Press of Colorado, Boulder.

Doyle, James A., Stephen D. Houston, Thomas G. Garrison, and Edwin Román

2011   ¿Alcance de la vista de Mundo Perdido?: La planicación urbana y el abandono abrupto de El Palmar, Petén, Guatemala. In *XXIV Simposio de Investigaciones Arqueológicas de Guatemala, 2010*, edited by Bárbara Arroyo, Lorena Piaz Aragón, Adriana Linares Palma, and Ana Lucía Arroyave, pp. 45–56. Ministerio de Cultura y Deportes, Guatemala City.

Durán, Diego

1971   *Book of the Gods and Rites and the Ancient Calendar.* Translated and edited by Fernando Horcasitas and Doris Heyden. University of Oklahoma Press, Norman.

Earle, Timothy K.

1997   *How Chiefs Come to Power: The Political Economy in Prehistory.* Stanford University Press, Stanford, Palo Alto, California.

Eddy, John A.

1974   Astronomical Alignment of the Big Horn Medicine Wheel. *Science* 184(4141):1035–1043.

Englehardt, Joshua D., and Donna M. Nagle

2011   Variations on a Theme: Dual-Processual Theory and the Foreign Impact on Mycenaean and Classic Maya Architecture. *American Journal of Archaeology* 115:355–382.

Eppich, Evan Keith

2007   WK13: Investigations in the Grupo Chok. In *Proyecto Arqueológico El Perú-Waka': Informe no. 4, temporada 2006*, edited by Hector Escobedo and David Freidel, pp. 306–364. Informe Entregado a la Dirección General del Patrimonio Cultural y Natural de Guatemala, Guatemala City.

Estrada-Belli, Francisco
2006   Lightning Sky, Rain and the Maize God: The Ideology of Preclassic Maya Rulers at Cival, Petén, Guatemala. *Ancient Mesoamerica* 17(1):57–78.
2011   *The First Maya Civilization: Ritual and Power before the Classic Period*. Routledge, New York.

Estrada-Belli, Francisco (editor)
2012   *Investigaciones arqueológicas en la región de Holmul, Petén: Holmul y Dos Aguadas*. Informe preliminar de la temporada 2012. Proyecto Arqueológico Holmul. Boston University, Archaeology Department. http://bu.edu/holmul/reports, accessed April 23, 2016.

Evans, Damian H., Roland J. Fletcher, Christophe Pottier, Jean-Baptiste Chevance, Dominique Soutif, Boun Suy Tan, Sokrithy Im, Darith Ea, Tina Tin, Samnang Kim, Christopher Comarty, Stéphane De Greef, Kasper Hanus, Pierre Bâty, Robert Kuszinger, Ichita Shimoda, and Glenn Boornazian
2013   Uncovering Archaeological Landscapes at Angkor using LiDAR. *Proceedings of the National Academy of Sciences of the United States of America* 110(31):12595–12600.

Fahmel Beyer, Bernd
1991   *La arquitectura de Monte Albán*. Universidad Nacional Autónoma de México, Mexico City.

Flannery, Kent V.
1998   The Ground Plans of Archaic States. In *Archaic States*, edited by Gary M. Feinman and Joyce Marcus, pp. 15–57. School of American Research Press, Santa Fe, New Mexico.

Flannery, Kent V., and Joyce Marcus
1983   The Earliest Public Buildings, Tombs, and Monuments at Monte Albán, with Notes on the Internal Chronology of Period I. In *The Cloud People: Divergent Evolution of the Zapotec and Mixtec Civilizations*, edited by Kent V. Flannery and Joyce Marcus, pp. 87–91. Academic Press, New York.
2015   *Excavations at San José Mogote: 2. The Cognitive Archaeology*. Memoirs, 58. University of Michigan Museum of Anthropology, Ann Arbor.

Folan, William J., Jacinto May Hau, Rogerio Cohouh Muñoz, and Raymundo González Heredia
1990   *Calakmul Campeche, México: Su mapa, una introducción*. Centro de Investigaciones Históricas y Sociales, Universidad Autónoma de Campeche, Campeche, Mexico.

Folan, William J., Joyce Marcus, Sophia Pincemin, María del Rosario Domínguez Carrasco, Larraine Fletcher, and Abel Morales López
1995   Calakmul: New Data from an Ancient Maya Capital in Campeche, Mexico. *Latin American Antiquity* 6(4):310–334.

Folan, William J., Maria del Rosario Domínguez Carrasco, Joel D. Gunn, Abel Morales López, Raymundo González Heredia, Gerardo Villanueva García, and Nuria Torrescano Valle
2015   Calakmul: Power, Perseverance, and Persistence. In *Archaeology and Bioarchaeology of Population Movement among the Prehispanic Maya*, edited by Andrea Cucina, pp. 37–50. Springer Briefs in Archaeology, New York.

Fowler, Melvin L.
1996   The Mound 72 and Woodhenge 72 Area of Cahokia. *Wisconsin Archeologist* 77(3/4):36–59.
Freidel, David A.
1981   Civilization as a State of Mind: The Cultural Evolution of the Lowland Maya. In *The Transition to Statehood in the New World*, edited by Grant D. Jones and Robert R. Kautz, pp. 188–227. Cambridge University Press, Cambridge, United Kingdom.
1986   Terminal Classic Lowland Maya: Successes, Failures, and Aftermaths. In *Late Lowland Maya Civilization: Classic to Postclassic*, edited by Jeremy A. Sabloff and E. Wyllys Andrews V, pp. 409–430. School of American Research Press, Santa Fe, New Mexico.
Geertz, Clifford
1980   *Negara: The Theater State in Nineteenth-Century Bali*. Princeton University Press, Princeton, New Jersey.
Grube, Nikolai
2004   El origen de la dinastía Kaan. In *Los cautivos de Dzibanché*, edited by Enrique Nalda, pp. 117–131. Instituto Nacional de Antropología e Historia, Mexico City.
Grube, Nikolai, Kai Delvendahl, Nicolaus Seefeld, and Beniamino Volta
2012   Under the Rule of the Snake Kings: Uxul in the 7th and 8th Centuries. *Estudios de Cultura Maya* 40:11–49.
Hansen, Richard D.
1990   *Excavations in the Tigre Complex, El Mirador, Petén, Guatemala*. Papers of the New World Archaeological Foundation, No. 62. El Mirador Series, Part 3. New World Archaeological Foundation, Brigham Young University, Provo, Utah.
2002   *The Architectural Development of an Early Maya Structure at Nacbé, Petén, Guatemala*. FAMSI Report. http://www.famsi.org/reports/95113/95113Hansen01.pdf, accessed September 12, 2015.
Hodder, Ian
2010   *Religion in the Emergence of Civilization: Çatalhöyük as a Case Study*. Cambridge University Press, Cambridge, United Kingdom.
Hughes, Timothy B.
1997   The Evolution of Political and Religious Structure in Early State Level Societies: Ideology in Archaeological Method and Theory. M.A. thesis, Department of Anthropology, University of Montana, Missoula.
Inomata, Takeshi
1995   Archaeological Investigations at the Fortified Center of Aguateca, El Petén, Guatemala: Implications for the Study of the Classic Maya Collapse. Ph.D. dissertation, Department of Anthropology, Vanderbilt University, Nashville, Tennessee.
Inomata, Takeshi, Jessica MacLellan, Daniela Triadan, Jessica Munson, Melissa Burham, Kazuo Aoyama, Hiroo Nasu, Flory Pinzón, and Hitoshi Yonenobu
2015   Development of Sedentary Communities in the Maya Lowlands: Coexisting Mobile Groups and Public Ceremonies at Ceibal, Guatemala. *Proceedings of the National Academy of Sciences* 112(14):4268–4273.

Inomata, Takeshi, Daniela Triadan, Kazuo Aoyama, Victor Castillo, and Hitoshi Yonenobu
2013   Early Ceremonial Constructions at Ceibal, Guatemala, and the Origins of Lowland Maya Civilization. *Science* 340:467–471.

Jarquín Pacheco, Ana María, and Enrique Martínez Vargas
1982   Las excavaciones en el conjunto 1D. In *Memoria del Proyecto Arqueológico Teotihuacan 80-82, Volumen 1*, edited by Ruben Cabrera Castro, Ignacio Rodríquez G., and Noel Morelos G., pp. 89–126. Colección Científica 132. Instituto Nacional de Antropología e Historia, Mexico City.

Kelly, John E., and James A. Brown
2014   Cahokia: The Processes and Principles of the Creation of an Early Mississippian City. In *Making Ancient Cities: Space and Place in Early Urban Societies*, edited by Andrew T. Creekmore III and Kevin D. Fisher, pp. 292–336. Cambridge University Press, Cambridge, United Kingdom.

Kidder, Alfred V.
1950   Introduction. *Uaxactun, Guatemala: Excavations of 1931–37*, by A. Ledyard Smith. Publication 588. Carnegie Institution, Washington, D.C.

Kirch, Patrick V.
2004   Temple Sites in Kahikinui, Maui, Hawaiian Islands: Their Orientations Decoded. *Antiquity* 78(299):102–114.

Knight, Vernon J.
1986   The Institutional Organization of Mississippian Religion. *American Antiquity* 51:675–687.

Kolb, Michael J.
1994   Monumentality and the Rise of Religious Authority in Precontact Hawai'i. *Current Anthropology* 34(5):521–547.

Kotkin, Joel
2007   *The City: A Global History*. Modern Library, New York.

Laporte, Juan Pedro, and Vilma Fialko
1995   Re-encuentro con el Mundo Perdido, Tikal, Guatemala. *Ancient Mesoamerica* 6(1):41–94.

Lemonnier, Pierre
1986   The Study of Material Culture Today: Toward an Anthropology of Technological Systems. *Journal of Anthropological Archaeology* 5:147–186.
1992   *Elements for an Anthropology of Technology*. Museum of Anthropology Anthropological Papers, No. 88. University of Michigan, Ann Arbor.

Mannikka, Eleanor
2000   *Angkor Wat: Time, Space, and Kingship*. University of Hawaii Press, Honolulu.

Marcus, Joyce
1973   Territorial Organization of the Lowland Classic Maya. *Science* 180:911–916.
1978   Archaeology and Religion: A Comparison of the Zapotec and Maya. *World Archaeology* 10(2):172–191.
1983   Lowland Maya Archaeology at the Crossroads. *American Antiquity* 48(3):454–488.
1987   *The Inscriptions of Calakmul: Royal Marriage at a Maya City in Campeche, México*. Museum of Anthropology Technical Report 21. University of Michigan, Ann Arbor.

1995   Where Is Lowland Maya Archaeology Headed? *Journal of Archaeological Research* 3:3–53.
2014   Maya Political Cycling and the Story of the *Kaan* Polity. In *The Ancient Maya of Mexico: Reinterpreting the Past of the Northern Maya Lowlands*, edited by Geoffrey E. Braswell, pp. 88–116. Routledge, New York.

Marcus, Joyce, and Kent V. Flannery
2004   The Coevolution of Ritual and Society: New ^{14}C dates from Ancient Mexico. *Proceedings of the National Academy of Sciences* 101(18):257–261.

Marcus, Joyce, and William. J. Folan
1994   Una stela más del siglo V y nueva información sobre Pata de Jaguar, gobernante de Calakmul, Campeche, en el siglo VII. *Gaceta Universitaría* 4(15–16):21–26. Universidad Autónoma de Campeche, Campeche, Mexico.

Martin, Simon
2005   Of Snakes and Bats: Shifting Identities at Calakmul. *PARI Journal* 6(2):5–13.

Martin, Simon, and Nikolai Grube
1995   Maya Superstates? *Archaeology* 48(6):41–46.
2000   *Chronicle of Maya Kings and Queens: Deciphering the Dynasties of the Ancient Maya*. Thames and Hudson, London.

Matheny, Ray T., and Deanne G. Matheny
2011   *Introduction to Investigations at El Mirador, Petén, Guatemala*. Papers of the New World Archaeological Foundation, Number 54. Brigham Young University, Provo, Utah.

McAnany, Patricia A.
2014   *Living with the Ancestors: Kinship and Kingship in Ancient Maya Society*. University of Texas Press, Austin.

Milbrath, Susan
1999   *Star Gods of the Maya: Astronomy in Art, Folklore, and Calendars*. University of Texas Press, Austin.
2013   *Heaven and Earth in Ancient Mexico: Astronomy and Seasonal Cycles in the Codex Borgia*. University of Texas Press, Austin.

Mumford, Lewis
1968   *The City in History: Its Origins, Its Transformations, and Its Prospects*. Harvest Books, New York.

Papafava, Francesco
1995   *Vatican*. Tipografia Vaticana, Vatican City.

Pfaffenberger, Bryan
1988   Fetished Objects and Humanized Nature: Towards an Anthropology of Technology. *Man* 23:236–252.
1992   Social Anthropology of Technology. *Annual Review of Anthropology* 21:491–516.

Pincemin, Sophia, Joyce Marcus, Lynda Florey Folan, William J. Folan, María del Rosario Domínguez Carrasco, and Abel Morales López
1998   Extending the Calakmul Dynasty Back in Time: A New Stela from a Maya Capital in Campeche, Mexico. *Latin American Antiquity* 9(4):310–327.

Prufer, Keith M., Holley Moyes, Brenden J. Culleton, Andrew Kindon, and Douglas J. Kennett
2011   Formation of a Complex Polity on the Eastern Periphery of the Maya Lowlands. *Latin American Antiquity* 22(2):199–223.

Rathje, William
1971   The Origin and Development of the Classic Maya Civilization. *American Antiquity* 36:275–285.
1973   Trade Models and Archaeological Problems: The Classic Maya and Their E Group Complex. *International Congress of Americanists* 4:231–235.

Redmond, Elsa M., and Charles S. Spencer
2008   Rituals of Sanctification and the Development of Standardized Temples in Oaxaca, Mexico. *Cambridge Archaeological Journal* 18:239–266.
2013   Early (300–100 B.C.) Temple Precinct in the Valley of Oaxaca, Mexico. *Proceedings of the National Academy of Sciences* 110(19):E1707–E1715.

Renfrew, Colin
1973   Monuments, Mobilization and Social Organization in Neolithic Wessex. In *Explanation of Culture Change: Models in Prehistory*, edited by Colin Renfrew, pp. 539–558. University of Pittsburgh Press, Pittsburgh, Pennsylvania.
1985   *The Archaeology of Cult: The Sanctuary at Phylakopi*. British School at Athens and Thames and Hudson, London.

Rice, Prudence M.
2015   Middle Preclassic Interregional Interaction and the Maya Lowlands. *Journal of Archaeological Research* 23(1):1–47.

Ricketson, Oliver G., Jr., and Edith Bayles Ricketson
1937   *Uaxactún, Guatemala, Group E, 1926–31*. Carnegie Institution of Washington, No. 477. Carnegie Institution of Washington, Washington, D.C.

Ringle, William M.
2004   On the Political Organization of Chichen Itza. *Ancient Mesoamerica* 15(2):167–218.

Robin, Cynthia, James Meierhoff, Caleb Kestle, Chelsea Blackmore, Laura J. Kosakowsky, and Anna C. Novotny
2012   Ritual in a Farming Community. In *Chan: An Ancient Maya Farming Community*, edited by Cynthia Robin, pp. 113–132. University Press of Florida, Gainesville.

Runggaldier, Astrid, Marieka Brouwer Burg, and Eleanor Harrison-Buck
2013   Hats Kaab: A Newly Discovered E-Group at the Closing of the 13th Baktun. *Research Reports in Belizean Archaeology* 10:65–75.

Ruppert, Karl
1977   A Special Assemblage of Maya Structures. In *The Maya and Their Neighbors: Essays on Middle American Anthropology and Archaeology*, edited by Clarence L. Hay, Ralph L. Linton, Samuel K. Lothrop, Harry L. Shapiro, and George C. Vaillant, pp. 222–231. Dover Publications, New York.

Sabloff, Jeremy A.
1986   Interaction among Classic Maya Polities: A Preliminary Examination. In *Peer Polity Interaction and Socio-political Change*, edited by Colin Renfrew and

John F. Cherry, pp. 109–116. Cambridge University Press, Cambridge, United Kingdom.

Sabloff, Jeremy A., and Joyce Marcus (editors)
2008 *The Ancient City: New Perspectives on Urbanism in the Old and New World.* SAR Press, Santa Fe, New Mexico.

Salali, Gul Deniz, Harvey Whitehouse, and Michael Hochberg
2015 A Life-Cycle Model of Human Social Groups Produces a U-Shaped Distribution in Group Size. *PLoS ONE* 10(9):e0138496.

Salazar, Baudilio
2005 Prospección de saqueos, Estructuras 20 y 23, Grupo A (Operación 7). In *Proyecto Arqueológico Naachtún, Informe no. 1, primera temporada de campo, febrero–abril de 2004*, edited by Martin Rangel and Kathryn Reese-Taylor, pp. 113–118. Instituto de Antropología e Historía de Guatemala, Guatemala City.

Sanders, William T.
1974 Chiefdom to State: Political Evolution at Kaminaljuyú, Guatemala. In *Reconstructing Complex Societies: An Archaeological Colloquium*, edited by Charlotte B. Moore, pp. 97–116. Supplement to the Bulletin of the American Schools of Oriental Research 20. Harvard University, Department of Anthropology, Cambridge, Massachusetts.

Savage, Christopher T.
2007 Alternative Epigraphic Interpretations of the Maya Snake Emblem Glyph. Master's thesis, Department of Interdisciplinary Studies, University of Central Florida, Orlando.

Schoenfelder, John W.
2003 Negotiating Poise in a Multi-hierarchical World: An Archaeological Exploration of Irrigated Rice Agriculture, Ideology, and Political Balances in the Coevolution of Intersecting Complex Networks in Bali. Ph.D. dissertation, Department of Anthropology, University of California, Los Angeles.

Schortman, Edward M., and Patricia A. Urban
2004 Modeling the Roles of Craft Production in Ancient Political Economies. *Journal of Archaeological Research* 12:185–226.

Shuster, Simon
2016 Putin's Pilgrimage: With Visits to One of Greece's Holiest Places, the Russian President Casts Himself as Protector of the Faith. *Time* 188(10-11):62–69.

Smith, A. Ledyard
1950 *Uaxactún, Guatemala: Excavations (1931–1937).* Carnegie Institution of Washington, No. 588. Carnegie Institution of Washington, Washington, D.C.

Spencer, Charles S.
2010 Territorial Expansion and Primary State Formation. *Proceedings of the National Academy of Sciences* 107(16):7119–7126.
2014 Modeling the Evolution of Bureaucracy: Political-Economic Reach and Administrative Complexity. *Social Evolution and History* 13(1):42–66.

Šprajc, Ivan
2009 Astronomical and Cosmological Aspects of Maya Architecture and Urbanism. In *Cosmology across Cultures*, edited by J. A. Rubiño-Martín, José Alberto Bel-

monte, Francisco Prada, and Antxon Alberdi, pp. 303–314. ASP Conference Series, Vol. 409. Astronomical Society of the Pacific, San Francisco.

2014   Teotihuacan Architectural Alignments in the Central Maya Lowlands? In *Archaeoastronomy and the Maya*, edited by Gerardo Aldana y Villalobos and Edwin L. Barnhart, pp. 41–56. Oxbow Books, Oxford.

Stuart, David

2012–2105   *Maya Decipherment: Ideas on Ancient Maya Writing and Iconography* (Web-blog). https://decipherment.wordpress.com/2012/06/30/notes-on-a-new-text-from-la-corona, accessed October 11, 2013.

Stuart, David, and Stephen Houston

1994   *Classic Maya Place Names*. Studies in Pre-Columbian Art and Archaeology, 33. Dumbarton Oaks, Washington, D.C.

Suhler, Charles K., David A. Freidel, and Traci Ardren

1998   Northern Maya Architecture, Ritual, and Cosmology. In *Anatomía de una civilización: Aproximaciones interdisciplinarias a la cultura maya*, edited by Andrés Ciudad Ruiz, Yolanda Fernández M., José Miguel García C., María Josepha Iglesias Ponce de León, Alfonso Lacadena G.-G., and Luis Tomás Sanz C., pp. 253–273. Sociedad Española de Estudios Mayas, Madrid, Spain.

Suvrathan, Uthara

2013   Complexity on the Periphery: A Study of Regional Organization at Banavasi, c. 1st–8th Century A.D. Ph.D. dissertation. Department of Anthropology, University of Michigan, Detroit.

Tedlock, Barbara

1992   *Time and the Highland Maya*. University of New Mexico Press, Albuquerque.

Tedlock, Dennis

1996   *Popol Vuh: The Mayan Book of the Dawn of Life*. Simon and Schuster, New York.

Thompson, J. Eric S.

1931   Archaeological Investigations in the Southern Cayo District British Honduras. *Field Museum of Natural History Anthropological Series, Publication 301*, 17(3):215–362.

1939   *Excavations at San Jose, British Honduras*. Carnegie Institution of Washington, No. 58. Carnegie Institute of Washington, Washington D.C.

1970   *Maya History and Religion*. Civilization of the American Indian Series, 99. University of Oklahoma Press, Norman.

Tokovinine, Alexander

2013   *Place and Identity in Classic Maya Narratives*. Studies in Pre-Columbian Art and Archaeology 37. Dumbarton Oaks, Washington, D.C.

Tomásková, Silvia

2013   *Wayward Shamans: The Prehistory of an Idea*. University of California Press, Oakland.

Townsend, Richard

1992   *The Aztecs*. Thames and Hudson, London.

Tozzer, Alfred M.
1941 [1566] *Landa's Relación de las Cosas de Yucatan.* Papers of the Peabody Museum of American Archaeology and Ethnology, Harvard University, Vol. 18. Peabody Museum, Cambridge, Massachusetts.

Trigger, Bruce
1990 Monumental Architecture: A Thermodynamic Explanation of Symbolic Behavior. *World Archaeology* 22(2):119–132.

Valeri, Valerio
1985 *Kingship and Sacrifice: Ritual and Society in Ancient Hawaii.* University of Chicago Press, Chicago.

Wittfogel, Karl
1957 *Oriental Despotism.* Yale University Press, New Haven, Connecticut.

Wright, Henry T.
1977 Recent Research on the Origin of the State. *Annual Review of Anthropology* 6:379–397.

Wright, James C.
1995 The Archaeological Correlates of Religion: Case Studies in the Aegean. In *Politeia: Society and State in the Aegean Bronze Age*, edited by Robert Laffineur and Wolf-Dietrich Niemeier, pp. 341–348. Université de Liège, Liège, Belgium.

Zender, Marc
2004 A Study of Classic Maya Priesthood. Ph.D. dissertation, Department of Archaeology, University of Calgary, Calgary, Alberta, Canada.

17

Epilogue

E Groups and Their Significance to the Ancient Maya

DIANE Z. CHASE, PATRICIA A. MCANANY,
AND JEREMY A. SABLOFF

E Groups are emerging as the earliest replicated public architecture in the Maya Lowlands. "Replicated" refers to the repetitive construction of a similar architectural form across parts of the Maya Lowlands. As earlier chapters indicate, there is no longer any doubt that E Groups were built (and rebuilt) as early as 1000 BCE (particularly at Ceibal) and that they continued to be built through the Early Classic period.

Contributors to this book point out, however, that the long duration of E Group construction and use can be contrasted with significant change and elaboration in E Group complexes. Regardless of this dynamism, there remains consensus that E Groups were linked to ground and horizon-based astronomy.

Although E Groups were invented in the Isthmian area to the west, their centrality in the Maya region—initially for community integration and place-making and later for performative activities linked to dynastic concerns and the long count—hints at their significance to understanding *both* the initial formation and subsequent development of Maya civilization. The rapid expansion during the Preclassic period of this highly patterned architectural form—complete with elaborative ground preparation, caching practices, and artifacts indicative of ritual activities—is unique within Maya history. The many archaeological contexts of Preclassic E Groups reviewed in the preceding chapters indicate that the expression, elaboration, and replication of this architectural form in the Maya Lowlands became thoroughly indigenous and, over time, entangled with an emerging ethos of rulership.

As with any highly patterned manifestation of what appear to have been deeply seated concepts girding this architectural form, contributors to this volume are compelled to attend to the definitional elasticity of E Groups and criteria for inclusion.

On this front, there is broad consensus about the basic form of E Groups. True E Groups contain both a western pyramid and an opposing long eastern structure. Architectural assemblages lacking a visible western pyramid are not considered to be E Groups unless excavation shows that a western structure did in fact exist at one point.

Development of E groups over time also is evident in low-lying Cenote-style structure assemblages that predate the initially identified Uaxactún forms. This earlier form exhibits variation in the length and superstructural composition of the eastern building. Middle and Late Preclassic period Cenote-style eastern platforms tend to be longer, measuring from 90 to 172 m, contain a larger central superstructure, and may or may not be flanked by smaller buildings. In contrast, the eastern structure of Early Classic E Groups tends to be shorter, measuring around 70 m in length (see Chase 1983, 1985).

The most famous E Group—that of Uaxactún—can be considered an example of a derived form. From the initial discovery and description of E Groups based on work at Group E at the site of Uaxactún in Guatemala (Ricketson and Ricketson 1937), archaeologists and archaeoastronomers have suggested that this architectural assemblage was constructed in order to permit detailed observations of the sky and the movement of the sun, moon, and stars. This explanation fits very well with mid-twentieth-century ideas about Classic Maya preoccupations with astronomy and calendrical reckoning.

Although the Uaxactún E Group indeed does conform to celestial alignments, testing of E Group–like architectural complexes at other sites and from earlier time periods confirmed a range of alignment solutions for celestial reckoning (Aveni and Hartung 1989; Aveni et al. 2003). The more general association of E Groups with tracking the passage of the sun has passed the test of time, however, and can be inferred from symbolic associations and temporality of construction and modification efforts. Furthermore, while the western pyramid size and function varied, the eastern structure, with its unvarying north–south alignment, always formed a horizon-based solar structure. As a structure complex from which changes in the movement of the sun could be detected as well as nocturnal patterns of lunar and stellar progression, E Groups must have been linked with celebratory ideas of renewal. As some volume contributors discuss, Preclassic E Groups occasionally yield associated ceramic assemblages that feature elaborate surface decoration, possibly indicative of communal ritual activities.

Classic period caches and stone monuments associated with E Group plazas and buildings mark the particular way in which this architectural form was indigenized within the Maya Lowlands. An architectural form that had worked to integrate fluid and perhaps not fully sedentary communities during the early centuries of the Preclassic period was harnessed to dynastic concerns with centrality and permanence during the Classic period. Not only were dated monuments focused on K'atun-ending cycles found within E Group plazas, as is the case with the Group E plaza at Uaxactún, but excavations at sites such as Caracol confirm that construction and renovation episodes were undertaken in association with larger temporal cycles such as Bak'tuns. Despite change in the manner in which these timescapes were deployed, caches located in front of and within E Group constructions confirm the highly charged cosmological function of these spaces, regardless of when they were constructed. Whether viewing the placement or content of ritual deposits, it is apparent that locations of E Groups continued to emphasize directionality and layering, effectively materializing Maya views of the world and time.

The location of ritual deposits associated with E Groups varied tremendously over the course of Maya history. Early on, a key ritual locus occurred in the open plaza space in front of the eastern structure (as at Ceibal); but later ritual deposits are found within the structures themselves (as at Uaxactún and Caracol). Excavations of Preclassic E Groups at Cenote and Xunantunich indicate clearly that founding these public structures required scraping off the black soil and exposing the white limestone bedrock. The base of these early constructions directly contacts bedrock, which conjures notions of purification or the conceptual necessity of firmly grounding a structure that was to be used for horizon-based astronomy.

Naturally, the lion's share of attention has been paid to the astronomical and cosmological function of E Groups. Often overlooked is the association between these architectural assemblages and water and the underworld. Reservoirs frequently were located nearby; and, in some cases, mechanisms that encouraged water pooling may have been created in place of formal reservoirs. Water symbolism is evident in cached objects that include the remains or likenesses of water creatures (such as shells, coral, or turtles). When combined with evidence for water pooling, turtle representations and turtle metaphors suggest the liminality of E Group structures that were simultaneously located in the current world and rooted in the underworld. At Caracol, Classic period tombs built at the base of the eastern E Group structure fill with water on a seasonal basis, creating a place where human remains and offerings are literally placed within the underworld. When this use is combined with their astronomical functions, it is apparent that these complexes operated on several registers and incorporated the totality of existence.

Thus, E groups were imbued with both cosmological and temporal significance; however, specific aspects of their focus and function changed over time. Spreading quickly over a broad swath of the southern Maya Lowlands in tandem with or slightly preceding the first signs of settled farming communities, early E Groups can be understood as an experiment engaged in by self-organizing communities settling novel terrain. The efficacy of these constructions to knit together kin groups and smaller communities is indicated by their longevity. Contributors to this volume take pains to note that the distribution and spread of E Groups conform to coeval systems of communication and trade, a further argument for the integrative capacity of E Groups.

While initially serving to focus and establish place, E Groups spread across the Lowlands and can be found in small communities in relatively close proximity to each other. But as time went on, E Groups became concentrated in politically dominant places, suggesting the shift in function from community integration to a focus on broader political strategies of power consolidation. Change in E Group distribution can be interpreted as proxy evidence of enlarged polities over time. In the Caracol polity, for instance, only the epicentral A Plaza E Group continued to be the locus of building and ritual efforts during the entirety of the Classic period.

During the Preclassic, the distribution of E Groups in the southeast Petén and Belize is more dense than elsewhere in the Maya Lowlands. This distribution provides a clue to systems of communication and trade as well as to changes in the political landscape. In the southeast Petén, for instance, E Groups initially can be found at sites of varying sizes that were located within 3 to 5 km of each other along a southern trade route that connected the Pasión River to the Caribbean Sea via the Belize River. Elsewhere in the Maya Lowlands, however, distances between E Group sites are much greater. Thus, the rapid spread in construction of E Groups did not take place in a vacuum of settlers preoccupied with marking time but aligned with emerging routes of trade and communication that linked the Petén with Belize. Mechanisms for replication conform to the imitation and emulation behaviors commonly expected among small peer polities (Renfrew 1986).

Yet, later in time, construction and renovation of E Groups took place predominantly in regional capitals. Established as physical expressions of Maya temporality and cosmology, E Groups continued to provide a structuring metaphor of place-making and renewal. But the ritual activities performed at Classic period E Groups changed dramatically; and, in some cases, the places that marked time also housed the corporeal remains of ancestors. In a remarkable way, E Groups changed radically while retaining the same highly patterned form—a classic characteristic of resilience. As this volume shows, a close examination of the many and varied archaeological contexts in which these architectural chameleons occur provides a rich window into the ancient Maya past.

References Cited

Aveni, Anthony F., Anne S. Dowd, and Benjamin Vining
2003   Maya Calendar Reform? Evidence from Orientations of Specialized Architectural Assemblages." *Latin American Antiquity* 14(2):159–178.

Aveni, Anthony F., and Horst Hartung
1989   Uaxactun, Guatemala, Group E, and Similar Assemblages: An Archaeoastronomical Reconsideration. In *World Archaeoastronomy*, edited by Anthony F. Aveni, pp. 441–446. Cambridge University Press, Cambridge.

Chase, Arlen F.
1983   A Contextual Consideration of the Tayasal-Paxcaman Zone, El Peten, Guatemala. Ph.D. dissertation, Department of Anthropology, University of Pennsylvania, Philadelphia.
1985   Archaeology in the Maya Heartland: The Tayasal-Paxcaman Zone, Lake Peten, Guatemala. *Archaeology* 38(1):32–39.

Renfrew, Colin
1986   Introduction: Peer Polity Interaction and Socio-political Change. In *Peer Polity Interaction and Socio-political Change*, edited by Colin Renfrew and John Cherry, pp. 1–18. Cambridge University Press, Cambridge, United Kingdom.

Ricketson, Oliver, Jr., and Edith B. Ricketson
1937   *Uaxactun, Guatemala, Group E, 1926–1931*. Publication 477. Carnegie Institution of Washington, Washington, D.C.

Contributors

James J. Aimers is associate professor of anthropology at the State University of New York at Geneseo. His M.A. thesis at Trent University was on E Groups.

Anthony F. Aveni is Russell Colgate Distinguished University Professor of Astronomy, Anthropology, and Native American Studies at Colgate University, where he has taught since 1963, and one of the founders of cultural astronomy. He has researched and written about Maya astronomy for more than four decades. He has been awarded the H. B. Nicholson Medal for Excellence in Research in Mesoamerican Studies by Harvard's Peabody Museum. Aveni was voted National Professor of the Year by the Council for Advancement and Support of Education in Washington, D.C., and named one of the ten best professors in the United States by *Rolling Stone* in 1991. At Colgate he has received, among other teaching awards, the Balmuth Teaching Award (2011), the Alumni Award for Excellence in Teaching (1997), and the Phi Eta Sigma National Honor Society's Distinguished Teaching Award voted by the Freshman Class of 1990. In 2013 the Society for American Archaeology awarded him the Fryxell Medal for Interdisciplinary Research (Earth Sciences).

Jaime J. Awe is assistant professor in the Department of Anthropology at Northern Arizona University. He was previously the director of the Institute of Archaeology in Belize.

Boris Beltrán, Lic., is a member of the San Bartolo–Xultun Regional Archaeological Project.

M. Kathryn Brown is associate professor in anthropology at the University of Texas at San Antonio. Dr. Brown's research focuses on the rise of complexity in the Maya Lowlands and the role of ritual and ceremonial architecture in the Preclassic period. She is currently the director of the Mopan Valley Preclassic Project and associate director of the Mopan Valley Archaeological Project. Brown has focused her recent investigations at the site of Xunantunich, Belize. She is the coeditor of *Ancient Mesoamerican Warfare* and has published several recent articles in *Mexicon*, *Latin American Antiquity*, and *Research Reports in Belizean Archaeology*.

Arlen F. Chase is professor of anthropology at Pomona College, Claremont. He was formerly a professor at the University of Nevada, Las Vegas, as well as a Pegasus Professor and associate dean in the College of Sciences at the University of Central Florida. His research interests focus on archaeological method and theory in the Maya area, with particular emphasis on contextual, settlement, and ceramic analysis and secondary interests on urbanism, ethnicity, and epigraphic interpretation. For more than thirty years, he has co-directed excavations at Caracol, Belize; before that he worked on a seven-year project at Santa Rita Corozal in the same country. He has authored over 160 articles and book chapters as well as *The Lowland Maya Postclassic* (edited with Prudence M. Rice), *Investigations at the Classic Maya City of Caracol, Belize* (with Diane Z. Chase), *A Postclassic Perspective* (with Diane Z. Chase), *Mesoamerican Elites: An Archaeological Assessment* (edited with Diane Z. Chase), *Studies in the Archaeology of Caracol, Belize* (with Diane Z. Chase), and *The Resilience and Vulnerability of Ancient Landscapes* (edited with Vernon Scarborough). His writings may be found at www.caracol.org.

Diane Z. Chase is vice president for academic innovation, student success, and strategic initiatives at Claremont Graduate University. She was formerly provost and executive vice-president at the University of Nevada, Las Vegas, as well as a Pegasus Professor and vice provost for academic program quality in academic affairs at the University of Central Florida. Her primary focus of research is on the ancient Maya of Central America. Her research interests focus on archaeological method and theory in the Maya area, with particular emphasis on complex societies and hermeneutics, ethnohistory, and osteological and mortuary analysis. For more than thirty years, she has co-directed excavations at Caracol, Belize; before that she directed a seven-year project at Santa Rita Corozal in the same country. She has authored over 150 articles and book chapters, as well as *Investigations at the Classic Maya City of Caracol, Belize* (with Arlen F. Chase), *A Postclassic Perspective* (with Arlen F. Chase), *Mesoamerican Elites: An Archaeological Assessment* (edited with Arlen F. Chase), and *Studies in the Archaeology of Caracol, Belize* (with Arlen F. Chase). Currently, she is working on a book with Arlen F. Chase entitled *Maya Archaeology: Reconstructing an Ancient Civilization*. Her writings may be found at www.caracol.org.

Anne S. Dowd is an archaeologist with the National Park Service. Combining her interests in art and science, she earned her Ph.D. at Brown University's Department of Anthropology with a specialization in archaeology. Building on her accomplishments excavating and recording freestanding or architectural sculpture at sites such as Balamkú and Calakmul in Mexico and Copán in Honduras, she uses decorated stucco or stone façades and architectural design to understand building function, iconography, and art symbolism in the Maya region. Examples of her publications include "La decoración del Templo XVIII" with Claude-François Baudez and *Cosmology, Calendars and Horizon-Based Astronomy in Ancient Mesoamerica* (with coeditor Susan Milbrath). Recently, she guest-edited a special section of the *Cambridge Archaeological Journal* titled "Cosmovision in New World Ritual Landscapes." Dowd is also a stone tool specialist interested in lithic technology, quarrying, and raw material procurement, including jade sources from Guatemala's Río Motagua region. She has served as the chair of the Society for American Archaeology's Prehistoric Quarries and Early Mines Interest Group (2010–2014). Dowd won the Eben Demarest Trust Award for excellence in archaeology in 1998, Brown University's Watson Smith Prize Honorable Mention in 1998, the Geochron Research Award in 1996, and the Daryle Bogenreif Award in 2010.

James A. Doyle is assistant curator for Art of the Ancient Americas at the Metropolitan Museum of Art. He held a postdoctoral appointment in Pre-Columbian Studies at Dumbarton Oaks Research Library and Collection in Washington, D.C., to work on the catalogue of the art from Central America and Colombia. He has also taught a variety of courses at Georgetown University, including Environmental History of Pre-Columbian Latin America, in the Science, Technology, and International Affairs program in the Edmund A. Walsh School of Foreign Service, and a seminar on Pre-Columbian Art and Architecture in the Department of Art and Art History. He was educated at Vanderbilt University and Brown University, where he wrote a dissertation on the art and architecture of the Preclassic period (1,000 BCE–250 CE) in the Maya Lowlands. The National Science Foundation and the Wenner-Gren Foundation funded dissertation field research in and around the E Group at the site of El Palmar, Petén, Guatemala, with practical support provided by the Casa Herrera of the Mesoamerica Center, University of Texas at Austin.

Francisco Estrada-Belli is an Italian-born Guatemalan archaeologist. He received a Ph.D. in archaeology from Boston University in 1998. He teaches archaeology and geographic information systems at Tulane University in New Orleans, having previously held positions at Harvard University, Boston University, and Vanderbilt University. He is the author of *The First Maya Civilization: Ritual and Power before the Classic Period*, the first book on the origins of Maya civilization since 1977. He is an active field researcher and directs a multidisciplinary archaeological project in the Holmul region of Petén, Guatemala. Estrada-Belli has research appointments with Universidad San Carlos de Guatemala and the American Museum of Natural History and is a fellow of the Society of Antiquaries of London and a National Geographic Explorer. In 2010 he co-founded the Maya Archaeological Initiative, a U.S. nonprofit organization that promotes research and youth education on Maya heritage as well as cultural site preservation.

David A. Freidel is professor of anthropology at Washington University in St. Louis. He has directed research at the site of Cerros (Cerro Maya) in Belize, at Yaxuná in Yucatán, Mexico, and at El Perú–Waka' in Petén, Guatemala. His interest in archaeoastronomy dates from his collaboration with Linda Schele in the writing of *Maya Cosmos, Three Thousand Years on the Shaman's Path* (with Joy Parker). He has coauthored or edited six books and 115 book chapters and articles, including *A Forest of Kings* (with Linda Schele). Freidel has focused on settlement patterns, monumental architecture, and material symbol-systems and presently is interested in the correlation of textual ancient history and the archaeological record of the Classic Maya and in the relationship among Maya religion, politics, and economics.

Julie A. Hoggarth is assistant professor of anthropology at Baylor University. She completed her Ph.D. at the University of Pittsburgh, where her research focused on household and community adaptation in response to the collapse of political systems at the end of the Classic period. Her main research interests center on the intersection of demography, subsistence systems, and political organization in Maya society. Her current research is focused on the effects of climate on the collapse and regeneration of complex societies. Hoggarth conducts archaeological fieldwork in Belize, where she is the codirector for the Belize Valley Archaeological Reconnaissance project.

Takeshi Inomata is professor and Agnese Nelms Haury Chair in Environment and Social Justice at the School of Anthropology, University of Arizona. He earned his Ph.D. from Vanderbilt University. Through archaeological excavations at Aguateca and Ceibal, Guatemala, Inomata has been examining social change, political organization, warfare, and households in Maya society.

Patricia A. McAnany is Kenan Eminent Professor of Anthropology at the University of North Carolina–Chapel Hill, external faculty at the Santa Fe Institute, and a senior fellow of the Pre-Columbian Program at Dumbarton Oaks in Washington, D.C. She has been the recipient of research awards from the National Science Foundation and the Archaeological Institute of America and of fellowships from the Guggenheim Foundation, the National Endowment for the Humanities, the Radcliffe Center for Advanced Study at Harvard University, Dumbarton Oaks, and the Institute for the Arts and Humanities at UNC–Chapel Hill. A Maya archaeologist, she is coprincipal investigator of Proyecto Arqueológico Colaborativo del Oriente de Yucatán, a community archaeology project focused on the Preclassic through Colonial community of Tahcabo, Yucatán. As executive director of the nonprofit InHerit: Indigenous Heritage Passed to Present, McAnany works with Indigenous communities throughout the Maya region to provide opportunities for dialogue about cultural heritage. She is the author/coeditor of several books, including *Ancestral Maya Economies in Archaeological Perspective*; *Questioning Collapse: Human Resilience, Ecological Vulnerability, and the Aftermath of Empire* (coedited with Norman Yoffee); and *Living with the Ancestors: Kinship and Kingship in Ancient Maya Society*.

Susan Milbrath is curator of Latin American Art and Archaeology at the Florida Museum of Natural History and an affiliate professor of anthropology at the University of Florida. She received her Ph.D. from Columbia University in art history and archaeology and has curated a number of major exhibits, including two traveling exhibits funded by the National Endowment for the Humanities. Her long-term research on the Mesoamerican worldview has demonstrated links between astronomy and seasonal ceremonies, identifying a number of important religious images related to astronomy. The results of this research are published in numerous articles and in her books *Star Gods of the Maya: Astronomy in Art, Folklore, and Calendars* and *Heaven and Earth in Ancient Mexico: Astronomy and Seasonal Cycles in the Codex Borgia*. Her recent research focuses on the archaeology and ethnohistory of Mayapán, the last Maya capital in Mexico, a site that provides an ideal opportunity to study the interface between the archaeological data and the historical records of the early Colonial period. She is currently conducting continuing research on Mesoamerican astronomy, with a focus on comparative imagery linking central Mexico and the Maya area.

Jerry Murdock is a co-founder of Insight Venture Partners. His many investments include Twitter, Snapchat, Nest, and Flipboard. He is a board member of Aspen Institute, Santa Fe Institute, and Aspen Center for Environmental Studies.

Kathryn Reese-Taylor is associate professor in the Department of Archaeology at the University of Calgary. She specializes in the origins and development of complexity during the Maya Preclassic period. Reese-Taylor has directed several archaeological projects in the Maya region at important sites, such as Naachtún in Petén, Guatemala, and is currently the director of the Yaxnohcah Environmental and Archaeological Research Project in southern Campeche, Mexico. The project focuses on environmental changes, human-environment interaction, and the development of urbanism in the tropical Maya Lowlands. Reese-Taylor is the coeditor of *Landscape and Power in Mesoamerica* and has written numerous articles and chapters based on her research.

Prudence M. Rice earned her doctorate in anthropology at the Pennsylvania State University and began teaching at the University of Florida in 1976. While in the Anthropology Department, she also held a courtesy appointment at the Florida Museum of Natural History. In 1991 she moved to Southern Illinois University, Carbondale (SIUC), where she served as chair of the Department of Anthropology from 1993 to 1999 then moved to the Office of Research Administration. She was associate vice chancellor for research from 2003 until her retirement from SIUC in 2011. Besides doing fieldwork in central Petén, she directed a historical archaeology project in Moquegua, Peru. She has authored, edited, and coedited ten books, including *The Kowoj: Identity, Migration, and Geopolitics in Late Postclassic Petén*,

Guatemala (with Don S. Rice); *Space-Time Perspectives on Early Colonial Moquegua*; and *The Terminal Classic in the Maya Lowlands: Collapse, Transition, and Transformation* (with Arthur A. Demarest and Don S. Rice).

Cynthia Robin is professor of anthropology at Northwestern University. Her research focuses on the ancient Maya and the meaning and significance of everyday life. She studies the everyday lives of ordinary people in society to illustrate how people make a difference in their societies and were not the mere pawns of leaders in history or prehistory. In the ancient Maya world she is interested in understanding how people created socially and environmentally sustainable communities through their daily practices. She currently directs the Aventura Archaeology Project, which is examining the 6,000-year history of an ancient Maya city and its Archaic predecessors. Between 2002 and 2010 she directed the Chan project in Belize, which explored the 2,000-year history of an ancient Maya farming community. She is the author of *Everyday Life Matters: Maya Farmers at Chan* and *Preclassic Maya Burials at Cuello, Belize*, editor of *Chan: An Ancient Maya Farming Community*, and coeditor of *Gender, Households, and Society: Unraveling the Threads of the Past and the Present* and *Spatial Theory and Archaeological Ethnographies*. Her major articles appear in *Current Anthropology, Journal of Archaeological Research, Journal of Social Archaeology*, and *Proceedings of the National Academy of Sciences*.

Franco D. Rossi is a visiting researcher at Boston University. He is an archaeologist and epigrapher specializing in the pre-Columbian Americas, with a focus on politics of literacy, art, and architecture of the Ancient Maya. His most recent work investigates broader questions of how writing, expertise, and science education were managed in ancient Mesoamerican statecraft.

Jeremy A. Sabloff is external professor and past president (2009–2015) of the Santa Fe Institute. Before coming to the Santa Fe Institute, he taught at Harvard University, the University of Utah, the University of New Mexico, the University of Pittsburgh, and the University of Pennsylvania (where he was the Williams Director of the University of Pennsylvania Museum from 1994 to 2004 and Christopher H. Browne Distinguished Professor of Anthropology). He is a member of the National Academy of Sciences (elected in 1994) and the American Philosophical Society (elected in 1996) and a Fellow of the American Academy of Arts and Sciences (elected in 1999).

He also is a Fellow of the Society of Antiquaries, London, and the American Association for the Advancement of Science. He was the American Anthropological Association's Distinguished Lecturer in 2010. He received the Society for American Archaeology's inaugural Award for Excellence in Latin American and Caribbean Archeology in 2011 and the Society's Lifetime Achievement Award in 2014. He also received the Lucy Wharton Drexel Medal from the University of Pennsylvania Museum in 2014. He is the author or coauthor of nine books and monographs as well as the editor or coeditor of twelve books. His principal scholarly interests include ancient Maya civilization, preindustrial urbanism, and the rise of early states, settlement pattern studies, archaeological theory and method, the history of archaeology, and the relevance of archaeology in the modern world.

William A. Saturno is assistant professor at Boston University and the director of the San Bartolo–Xultun Regional Archaeological Project.

Travis W. Stanton is associate professor in the Department of Anthropology at the University of California, Riverside. Conducting field research in the state of Yucatán since 1995, Stanton graduated with his doctorate from Southern Methodist University in 2000. He currently co-directs the Proyecto de Interacción Política del Centro de Yucatán. His publications include *Ancient Mesoamerican Warfare* (coedited with M. Kathryn Brown) and *Ruins of the Past* (coedited with Aline Magnoni).

Index

Page numbers in *italics* refer to illustrations; tables are noted with *t*.

Abaj Takalik: early calendar and monuments at, 104, 105
Abelino Red bowls and jars: at Yaxnohcah, 484
Acanceh (Mexico), 456, 469; coastal trade items and, 458; E Groups at, 10; temple room counts/areas, 543*t*
Accelerator Mass Spectrometry (AMS) dating, 145, 517; burned post, Early Xunantunich E Group, 393; Ixbalamqué ceramic complex, 334
Accession spaces, 186
Achiotes unslipped ceramics, 259, 263, 267, 269
Acropolises: E Groups in Central Karstic Uplands, 494–96, 504; secular functions at, 539
Actuncán (Belize), 237, 420; burials placed within staircases at, 402; as mid-sized center, 368
Acumal (Mexico): E Groups at, *14*
Acuña, Mary Jane, 206
Agency, 7; mindful, self-aggrandizing leaders, and, 179; performance and, 18
Agrarian ideology: ancient Maya, ritual reburial, and, 405
Agrarian year: 20-day periods and, 99
Agricultural cycles: Classic period architecture and phases of, 98; 260-day calendar and, 119; E Groups and celebration of, 10; 20-day periods and, 99
Agricultural season: movement of the Pleiades and regulation of, 503
Agricultural symbolism: early elites' developing associations with, 330
Agricultural terraces: at Chan, 362, 364, *366*
Agriculture: astronomical knowledge, E Groups, and, 85, 87; E Groups and scheduling of agricultural activities, 414, 416, 435, 436; first solar zenith passage (May 10) and, 81; maize life cycle celebrations, 154; religious doctrine and fostering of, 547. *See also* Maize agricultural cycles
Aguacatal, Campeche: water imagery on stucco quatrefoil from, 502
Aguateca, Guatemala: burned palace and nearby priestly residences at, 526
Aimers, James, 15, 87, 88, 203, 342, 375, 400, 412, 454
Aj k'uhuun title: from bench in Las Sepulturas Group, 9N-82, Copán, Honduras, *540*
Alliterative connections between words, Maya and use of, 195
Almanacs: divinatory, 149–51; planting, 104; sacred, 181; Venus, 117. *See also* Calendars
Altar de los Reyes: Acropolis E Groups at, 494, 495; ballcourts at, 496; in Central Karst Plateau, 487*t*; unique dates commemorated by E Groups, 493
Altars, 550; at Blackman Eddy, 428; at Cahal Pech, 429; Calakmul E Group architecture, 535; at Cenote, 47, 49; early Postclassic, Structure E-2, Xunantunich, 399; E Group temples, 537; fire, 396, 397; Giant Ahau, 62; at Pacbitún, 429; perishable wooden, Early Xunantunich E Group, 393, 394, *394,* 396, 406; Río Bec–style, Calakmul Structure VII, 559; Structure E-2, Xunantunich, 394, *394;* Uaxactún Style E Group at Uaxactún, 561–62; at Xunantunich, 429. *See also* Religion; Temple precincts
Altún Ha (Belize): great jade orb of, 200
American Ephemiris and Nautical Atlas, 492
Ancestor rituals: E Groups, emerging

ruling elite, and, 414, 418. *See also* Ancestor veneration
Ancestors: ballcourts and interactions with, 345; eastern shrines dedicated to, 361; north as home of, 140
Ancestor veneration, 443, 539; bone manipulation and, 399, 400, 401, 407; Chan's E Group and, 376, 378–79; in Early Xunantunich E Group, 399–407; east–west axis in Chan and, 362, 373; figurines and, 153; as primary purpose of Eastern Triadic Assemblages, Belize River valley, 435; social hierarchies in Maya Lowlands and, 386; ultimate goal of, 407
Ancestor veneration hypothesis: Chases' contention about E Groups and, 437, 440
Ancestral cave emergence from flower mountain theme: San Bartolo murals and, 348, 349
Ancestral shrine hypothesis: in archaeological record, Belize River valley, 432, 435
Ancestral shrines, 437; Chan's central religious complex, 362; placement on east side of plazas and, 441
Ancient Mesoamerica, 412
Anderson, David, 454
Andrews, Anthony, 454
Andrews, E. A., 453
Angkor, Cambodia: Khmer temple precinct at, 519
Animal figurines, 163n13
Anonal, 230
Anthropomorphic figurines: early contexts in Maya E Groups, 135–37; ending of production of, 160
Anthropomorphic heads, in Classic Maya hieroglyphic script, 148–49
Antiazimuth: Cival E Group sight lines and, 313
Antonio Chi, Gaspar, 526
Áquila Orange dishes and plates: Calakmul Structure IVb caches, 557, 558; Uaxactún E Group deposits, 45
Archaeology: of E Groups, 43, 45, 47, 49–50, 52–54, 56, 58–60, 62–65; historiography of E Group research, 8–10, 12–17; social complexity and, new interpretations in, 7–8. *See also various sites*
Archaic period: in Maya Lowlands, 219
Architectural decoration: cosmology and, 63
Architecture, 7; aesthetics of "awe" and, 275; analysis of E Groups or Eastern Triadic Assemblages in Belize River Valley, 420, 422, 424, 426–28; ancestor veneration, Chan, 376, 378; building narratives in the Preclassic, 187–91; Calakmul E Groups, *529, 530, 531, 532, 534,* 535, *535,* 536, *536*; ceremonialism in Cival and, 307; changes in Maya calendar in relation to, 119–21; Chan's central religious complex, 368–69, 372–76; Classic period, tracking of seasonal cycle and, 98; east–west axis in, focal nature of, 361; E Groups in Central Karstic Uplands, 494–97, *495,* 504; Las Pinturas Sub-5 E Group, 341–43; Mayapán, solar orientations in, 118; Middle and Late Preclassic period expansion episodes, 267, *268, 269*; middle to late Mamom Phase, at El Palmar and Tikal, 260, 263; monumental, 6, 308; mounded buildings, 217–18; plaza politics and, Late Preclassic site planning, 273, *274,* 275–76, 278; Puuc-style, 461; religious, distinctive characteristics of, 538–39, 547; replicated public, E Groups as, 578; sacred hills, Cival E Groups, and focus of, 317; solar and stellar alignments in early E Groups, 96–99; solar hierophanies and, 88, *89,* 91; spatial data on Maya temple precincts and their prototypes, 541–47, 550; triadic, new centers of communities and, 280; Triadic Groups, 98–99; verticality in, 319. *See also* Astronomical observatories; Ballcourts; E Groups; Plazas; Public architecture; Pyramids; Radial pyramids; Superstructures; Triadic Groups
Ardren, Traci, 459
Arroyo, Bárbara, 218
Arroyo Negro: in Central Karst Plateau, 487t; Haab Commemorative E Groups at, 493
Arroyo Pesquero: deposition of greenstone axes in watery features at, 239
Art, 7. *See also* Architecture; Ceramics; Figurines; Pottery; Stelae
Artifacts: breakage and deposition of, interpretive framework for, 135–36; elite, 154; Tikal, 139; Uaxactún, 138. *See also* Caches; Ceramics; Figurines; Pottery
Ashmore, Wendy, 388, 554
Astro-calendrics: early rituals and, 152
Astrology, 417
Astronomers, 554; assessing role of, 88; El Palenque, 526; overseeing of ritual activities

in E Groups and, 540; temple precinct duties and, 537
Astronomical events: Long Count inscriptions and, 112
Astronomical knowledge: uses of, 85, 87–88, 91
Astronomical observations: radial pyramids and, 116
Astronomical observatories, Maya: discovery of, 8; E Groups and questioning of hypothesis related to, 414, 415; meaning of, discussed, 87–88; Uaxactún Group E as archetype of, 79–82
Astronomy: enclosed interior architecture and, 539; ground- and horizon-based, E Groups and, 578; importance of, within E Groups, 547; Maya politics and religion and, 517; origin of Group E astronomical connection, 75–79; solar-based, Uaxactún Group E and, 152; Teotihuacán-type pecked cross-circles and, 79, 83. *See also* Calendars; Cosmology, Maya; Solar observations
Atlas arqueológico de Guatemala, 34, *55*, 56, 66n2
Authority: *Spondylus* as symbol of, 404
Authority systems: royal appropriation of monumental space at Pinturas and, 333. *See also* Kingship; Rulership
Autochthonous innovation: E Group emergence and, 339
Autonomous communities: during Middle and early Late Preclassic periods, 255
Aveni, Anthony, 10, 12, 59, 79, 96, 490, 529
Avian figurines, 163n13
Avian mask: Las Pinturas Sub-5b, 337, 342
"Awe": aesthetics of, terracing and staircases and, 275
Awe, Jaime, 203, 206, 400, 401
Axis mundi: elite burials and, 433, 439–40
Aylesworth, Grant, 15
Azimuth measurements: E Groups and, 490–91; El Palenque, Oaxaca, Mexico, 523–25
Azimuths: histogram, for Cival E Group's sight lines, *313*; of solar observations at sunrise, Cival region's set of 13 E Groups, 309
Aztec yearbearers system, 106

Baalche' Group, at Yaxnohcah, 497
Bajo de Azúcar, 330
Baking Pot (Belize), 420, 442; early excavation of triadic shrine at, 10; E Groups reported at, 10, *14*; elaborate royal tombs in triadic assemblages of, 440; frequency of burials and caches, Eastern Triadic Structures in, 433, 433*t*; Group A at, 429; height measurements of, Belize River valley, 422, 422*t*; as mid-sized center, 368; north–south profiles of, Belize River valley, *423*; plan of Bedran Group at, 429, *430*
Bak'tun ceremonialism: religious architecture and, 538
Bak'tun cycles, 63, 419, 580; Caracol's epicentral E Group buildings and, 60; Long Count calendar and, 102; numerology and starting point of, 123n7
Balakbal (Mexico): ballcourts at, 496; Calakmulqueños, *kaanal* dynasty, and control of, 528; in Central Karst Plateau, 487*t*; E Groups at, 10, *14*; Haab Commemorative E Groups at, 493
Balanza ceramics, 278; Balanza Black, Calakmul Structure IVb tomb, 558; Balanza Black basal flange bowls, Chan, 372
Ball, Joseph, 453
Ballcourts, 539; Calakmul, 536; Cival E Group dimensions, 308; Cival region, 307; Copán examples, 345; depictions of Maize God and, 343; E Groups, Central Karstic Uplands, 496, 497, 504; Las Pinturas Sub-5, 342–43; Las Pinturas Sub-5b, 339; Las Pinturas Sub-5 "Hunahpu" ballcourt, *340*; Las Ventanas group at San Bartolo, 332; Maize God's resurrection and, 501; Middle Preclassic, at northwest Yucatán sites, 452–53; Northern Lowlands, 453, 454; notion of "center" and, 343, 351; Tenochtitlán, 520; Yaxnohcah, 481
Ballcourt/turtle constellation, Orion factor and, 503
Ballplay: Maya lords and elites depicted in, 344. *See also* Ballcourts
Bar and dot positional numeration: calculation of calendar time and, 18
Barrel caches: at Cahal Pichik, 50; epicentral Caracol E Group, 54
Barton Ramie, 420; plan of BR 180-182 at, 429, *430*, *431*
Basalt, colossal heads of, 135
Beards: in Preclassic Maya fashion, 191; trilobe, with three dots, Cerros, 193

Bedrán: height of east structure in, 368
Bedrock: Chan's central religious complex, 369, *370*; early E Group construction and carving of, 220; modification of, 16
Belize: dense distribution of E Groups in, 581, 582; early Maya civilization centered in, 65; northern, Late Classic pseudo-E-Groups in, 412, 419–20; Preclassic calendrics and E Group rebuilding phases at, 279; western, triadic eastern buildings in, 66n1
Belize Red ceramics: southeast Petén and distribution of, 58
Belize River valley: architectural disparities and variations in E Groups of, 441; burial and cache data from Eastern Triadic Assemblages in, 432–35; burials and triadic assemblages in, 399, 438; burials placed within staircases at, 402; construction histories of E Group assemblages in, 424, 426–27; dense E Group clusters in, 480; Eastern Triadic Assemblages in, architectural analysis of, 420, 422, 424, 426–28; frequency of burials and caches in Eastern Triadic Structures in, 433*t*; height measurements of Eastern Triadic Structures in, 422, 422*t*; map of, *363, 421*; mid-sized centers in, 368; monuments associated with Eastern Triadic Structures in, 428–30; most common burial position in, 378; north–south profiles of Eastern Triadic Assemblages at selected sites in, *423*; plain stelae in, 419; spatial distribution of monuments in, 438
Beltrán, Boris, 188, 334
Bichrome rim treatments: early Mamom ceramics, El Palmar, 259
Birth from the gourd theme: San Bartolo murals and, 348, 349
Blackman Eddy, 420, 440; burials placed within staircases at, 402; carved stelae not referring to K'atun-ending events at, 436; construction histories of triadic assemblages at, 426–27; Eastern Triadic Structures at, 141; frequency of burials and caches, Eastern Triadic Structures at, 433*t*, 434–35; height measurements of, in Belize River valley, 422, 422*t*; as mid-sized center, 368; north–south profiles of, Belize River valley, *423*; Plaza A at, 428
Black-slipped jars: Ceibal caches, 223
Blake, Michael, 12, 179, 234, 235, 417

Blom, Frans, 8, 75, 76, 77, 79, 317, 412, 435; Uaxactún Group E plan illustration by, *78*
Blood: snakes as conduits of, Cerros West Wall, 194
Bloodletting instruments: Calakmul Structure VII tomb, 560; E Group temples, 537, 551
Blue Creek (Belize): pseudo-E-Groups at, 15
"Blue" jadeite: in Middle Preclassic deposits and contexts, 260
Board games: *patolli* beans and, 180
Body: Classic, Postclassic, and Lowland Maya views of, 136
Bone manipulation: ancestor veneration, burial/reburial rituals, and, 387, 399, 400, 401
Botifela Orange bowl: Calakmul Structure VII tomb, 560
Brainerd, George, 450
Breakage of objects: intentional, 135–36, 139, 141
Breath (*ik'*), 149
Bricker, Harvey, 117
Bricker, Victoria, 117
Brisa Complex E Group, Central Karstic Uplands: ideological constructs of, 497; map of reservoirs and, *498*; solar year and, 492
Brunton compass, 77
Buenavista: burials at, 405; as mid-sized center, 368
Buenavista del Cayo: rituals, perishable fire altars, and work at, 397
Buenavista–Nuevo San José: figurines at, 143
Building narratives: in the Preclassic, 187–91
Bullard, William, 6
Burials, 7, 278, 414; Belize River valley, 399; Buenavista, 405; Cahal Pech, 400–401; Calakmul, 551; Calakmul Structure IVb, 558; Calakmul Structure IVc, 559; Caracol E Group, 60, 418; Caracol Structure A-3, 560; Cenote, 49; Cenote E Group and locations of, *46*; chamber, Early Xunantunich Structure E-2-1st, 402–4, *403*; Chan, 400; at Chan's central religious complex, 361; Chan's E Group as focal point for, 376, *377*, 378; at Comalcalco, Mexico, 550; data from Eastern Triadic Assemblages, Belize River valley, 432–35; in Early Ritual Areas, recovery of, 158; Early Xunantunich E Group, 399; eastern platforms and, 60; E Group temples, 537; elaborate rituals, Preclassic period and, 387; elite, Tikal E Group, 346; high-status,

at Cuello, 330; at Jabalí, 350; King Chak Tok Ich'aak of Waka' as K'an Nahb Isimte', 184, *185*; Plaza B at Cahal Pech, 140; religious architecture and, 539; royal, Classic period E Group complexes, 387; ruling elites, 19–20; at San José Cayo, Belize, 564; secondary, 440, 441; triadic assemblages in Belize River valley and, 438. *See also* Ancestor veneration; Tombs

Bursera simaruba (chaka') tree resin: Calakmul Structure VII tomb, 560

Bursera spp. seeds: Calakmul Structure VII tomb, 560

Byzantine Middle East: temple precincts in, 519

Caban yearbearer, 101

Cabro Red ceramics: double-slipped, Wob Complex, Yaxnohcah, 485; first defined, at Cerro Maya (Cerros), 506n1

Caches, 7, 154, 414, 580; in Belize Valley ETAs, 437; at Cahal Pichik, Belize, 563; Calakmul Structure IVb, 557–58; Calakmul Structure IVc, 559; Caracol E Group, 54, 418; Caracol Structure A6, *51*; at Ceibal, 223; at Cenote, 49; Cenote E Group and locations of, *46*; centering with, 19; Chan, 140; Chan's central religious complex, 369; Chan's E Group as focal point for, 376; Cival, jade and ceramic jars, *297*, *298*; Classic period at Chan, 379; core of Structure of E-II at Uaxactún, *44*; cosmic, Cival, 141; cosmic, Plaza B at Cahal Pech, 140; cruciform, 238–39; dance platform at Yaxuná, *463*; data from Eastern Triadic Assemblages, Belize River valley, 432–35; in Early Ritual Areas, recovery of, 158; eastern platform at Uaxactún, *42*; eastern platforms and, 60; E Group temples, 537; figures in quincunx pattern, Chan, 372; greenstone axes, 217, 223, *224*, *225*, 227, 228, 229, 230, 233, 238, 239; greenstone celts, 398; at Hatzcap Ceel, Cayo, Belize, 562–63; Katun rituals and, 62; limestone spheres, Yaxuná E Group and, 467; material symbol-systems and, 17–18; MFC pattern, E Groups, and ritual practices related to, 227; Olmec-style greenstone, 459; placement beneath E Group plazas, 398; Protoclassic, at Ceibal, 231, *231*, 232, *232*; quadripartite motifs and, 239; at San José Cayo, Belize, 564; small stone spheres, 231; symbolisms in, 238–39; tetrapod plates, 276, *277*. *See also* Celt caches; Skull caches

Cahal Pech (Belize), 420, 442; anthropomorphic figurines and fragments at, 139–40, 153; burial practices at, 400–401; construction histories of triadic assemblages at, 422; E Groups excavated at, 12, *14*; elaborate royal tombs in triadic assemblages of, 440; frequency of burials and caches, Eastern Triadic Structures at, 433*t*, 438; height measurements of, in Belize River valley, 422, 422*t*; local spatial symbolism at, 237; as mid-sized center, 368; north–south profile of Eastern Triadic Assemblage at, *425*; north–south profiles of, Belize River valley, *423*; plan of site core, *424*; Plaza B, 139, 140; special treatment of disinterred remains at, 401; stelae at, 428–29; triadic shrines at, 12

Cahal Pichik (Belize): archaeology of E Groups at, 50; Cenote Style complex at, 545; Cenote Variant Style E Group at, 563; E Groups from, *48*; excavations in E Groups at, 9, 10, *14*; interbuilding alignments at, 563; temple precincts and expanded bureaucracies at, 553; temple room counts/areas, 543*t*

Cahokia, North America: ceremonial precincts in, 519

Calakmul (Mexico), 16, 486, 553; acropolises in both north and south at, 495; additional structures in Group E or Central Plaza, 536; architectural solar hierophanies at, 91; astronomical importance of centrally located E Group complex at, 528–29; burials at, 551; in Central Karst Plateau, 487*t*; Central Plaza view toward the southeast, *529*; delimited or bounded temple precinct at, 548; early and late, relative eastern temple proportions, 545*t*; early and late, temple room counts/areas, 543*t*; E Group excavated and reconstructed in, 12, *14*; E Groups at, *14*; figurines and fragments from, 141; Group E–type complex at, *90*; Haab Commemorative E Groups at, 493; lintel 1, Structure IVb, east side of Main Plaza, *533*; map of, showing Chiik Nahb market complex, *86*; market scene murals, Chiik Nahb market complex at, 85, *87*; Maya temple precinct at, 526–37; Phase II eastern three temples at, 549;

Calakmul—*continued*
plaza dimensions at, 273, *274*; precincts with multiroom temples in, 542; priest residences at, 549; profile of Structure IVb, *532*; reconstructed view northeast of Structure IVb, east side of Main Plaza, *532*; religious specialists at, 526; reservoirs near E Groups at, 496; Stela 114, front face, at, 527, *527*; Structure II, reconstruction drawing, *536*; Structure IVa and IVc plan details, *531*; Structure IVc north doorjambs at summer solstice sunset, 88, *89*; Structure VII, VI, and V plans, *534*; Structure VI summit, 535; Structure V plan, *535*; temple precinct, Group E-type complex at, *530*; toponym from Structure XIII at, *528*; unusually large Preclassic civic centers at, 480

Calakmulqueños: region controlled by, through *kaanal* dynasty, 528

Calakmul supplemental excavation data, 556–61; burial, Structure IVc, 559; burials, Structure IVb, 558; caches, Structure IVb, 557–58; caches, Structure IVc, 559; *chultun*, Structure VII, 560; comparative material, Structure VII, 560–61; Structures IVc, VI, and VII (Central Plaza), 556–57; Structure VII, 559–61; tomb 1, Structure VII, 559–60; tombs, Structure IVb, 558–59

Calendar Round: contemporary use of, 95; yearbearer type of, 101

Calendars: architectural design and, 538; calendrical commemorations at Cival, 304–5, 320; changes in Maya calendar, relative to architecture, 119–21; earliest known Long Count records and, 108–9, 111–13; early Classic Maya, 113–14, 116; early Mesoamerican, 99–102; Gregorian, 112, 113; Julian, 112, 113, 519; local solar-based, question of, 83–85; markets and calendrical ritual activity, 468; origin of the Haab and Tzolk'in, 102–6; Postclassic changes in, 117–19; solar alignments and Terminal Classic changes in, 116–17; solar observations, 260-day agricultural cycle, and, 106–8; 20-day Winal months in, 537; Uaxactún Group E, Terminal Preclassic–Early Classic transition, and, 75, 80. *See also* Almanacs; Long Count calendar; Stelae; Yearbearers

Calendrics: Preclassic, E Group re-building phases and, 279–80

Calendric system of Maya: unique achievement in perfection of, 76

Cambio Unslipped vase: Calakmul Structure VII tomb, 560

Cambodia: Khmer temple precinct at Angkor, 519

Cancuén: Calakmulqueños, *kaanal* dynasty, and control of, 528

Candelaria Peninsula: Mound ZZ1 and Operation 1 trench on, 143, *144,* 145

Candelario Appliquéd *incensario:* in Chan's central religious complex cache, 369

Cansís River: E Groups around, 13

Cantona, Puebla: ballcourts at, 454

Cantón Corralito, 218

Caobal, 230

Caracol (Belize), 16, 580; archaeology of, 49–50, 52–54, 56; artifact and feature distributions, Structure A-3, 560–61; cosmological representation of world order at, 63; E Groups at, 10, 12, *14,* 96, 415; E Groups from, epicenter, *48*; founder deities or "triad gods" of, *62, 63*; large Ahau altars at, 437; late Early Classic tombs at, 20; Preclassic calendrics and E Group rebuilding phases at, 279; relative eastern temple proportions, 545t; temple room counts/areas, 543t; temporal principles and, 17; water symbolism and tombs at, 581

Caracol E Group: aerial photo of, looking north, *51*; architectural development of eastern platform of, *52*; caches, *51*; caches and burials in, 418; deep religious meaning and central buildings of, 65; epicentral investigation, 53–54; expanded view, upper and lower plans of SD C8B-3, *53*; Structure E-2, Xunantunich compared with earlier versions of, 392; trade route from Río Pasión to the Caribbean Sea and, *55*

Caracol of Chichén Itzá: astronomical alignment studies at, 76

Cardinal directionality, 233, 235; cruciform caches and, 238–39; of Maya, vs. modern Western model of space, 239; sacred space and, 538; three stone symbolism and, 501. *See also* Geomancy

Carlson, John B., 186, 317, 416
Carmelita Incised pottery type: late Tux Complex, Baalche' Group, Yaxnohcah, 486
Carmelita Incised tripod *cajete:* Calakmul Structure VII tomb, 560
Carnegie Institute of Washington: Department of Terrestrial Magnetism, 75, 76, 77
Carr, Robert, 10
Carrasco, Ramón, 556
Cartouches: *k'in* glyph, Kohunlich composition and, 197; lower west mask, at Cerros, 196; Pinturas west wall mural, 192; profile head-variant glyphs, 150
Caso, Alfonso, 100
Castel Gandolfo: summer papal residence at, 518
Castillo radial pyramid: solar alignments and, 116–17
Çatalhöyük, Turkey: emergence of religious institutions at, 520
Cauac glyph: at Cahal Pichik, Belize, 563
Cauac Phase: flanges in ceramics during, 269
Caucel: Teotihuacanoid traits reported at, 460
Caves and caverns, 550; half sections of quatrefoils depicted as mouths of, 502; in Maya cosmology, 237
Ceh' Yax: Puuc-style architecture at, 461
Ceibal or Seibal (Guatemala), 16, 240, 541, 578, 580; anthropomorphic figurines at, 141; Cache 103, dating to 50–125 CE, *232*; Cache 128 of, dating to 50–125 CE, *231*; ceramics, 228; construction of Structure Ajaw, 220, 223; cruciform caches tied to cardinal directionality at, 238; dating of E Group at, 96, 413; delimited or bounded temple precinct at, 548; earliest known E Group assemblage at, 215; early architecture made of clay at, 227; E Group and trade route from Río Pasión to the Caribbean Sea, 55; E Groups at, 10, 12, *14, 48*; greenstone axe caches at, 217; greenstone axes, Cache 118, *224*; greenstone axes in cruciform pit, Cache 160, *225*; greenstone axes in flower-petal-like arrangement at, Cache 138, *225*; greenstone celts caches at, 398; Group A, map of, *222*; Late Preclassic transformation in, 230–31; Middle Formative Chiapas (MFC) pattern at, 220,
236–37; Protoclassic caches at, 231, *231,* 232, *232;* speculation on divining tokens at, 180; Structure Saqpusin, 223; Structure Xa'an, 223; water jars placed in cruciform caches at, 239
Celestial cycles: in Mesoamerican 260-day divinatory almanacs, 149
Celestial Monster: Milky Way depiction and, 200; Milky Way as living being glossed as, 183; Quadripartite Badge on tail of, 198; on Structure 10L-22, Copán, *199*
Celt caches: Middle Preclassic E Groups and, 18; sacred space and, 538
Cenote (Petén, Guatemala), 553; E Groups at, 12, *14;* interbuilding alignments at, 562; multiroom temple precinct at, 542, 545; stelae, 8; temple remodeled to smaller space at, 550; temple room counts/areas, 543*t*
Cenote E Group: archaeology of, 47, 49; deep religious meaning and central buildings of, 65; early Maya monuments and skull cache in, 19; eastern platform of, Structures C1, C108, and C109, *46;* trade route from Río Pasión to the Caribbean Sea and, 55
Cenote Style E Groups, 32, *33,* 34, 59, 319, 413; at Calakmul, 529; at Cenote, Petén, Guatemala, 562; in Central Karstic Uplands, 486, 504, 505; Chan's central religious complex compared with, 375; characteristics of, 10, 230; dating of, 34; at Hatzcap Ceel, Cayo, Belize, 562–63; isometric reconstruction of, *11;* perspective of center of Ixtontón, *57;* precincts with multiroom temples and, 542, 545; shown on map of Yaxhá, *61;* spacing of, 62
Cenote Variant Style E Groups, 414; at Cahal Pichik, Belize, 563; at San José Cayo, Belize, 564; Structure E-2, Xunantunich compared with eastern complex of, 392
Censer fragments: Caracol Structure A-3, 560, 561
Cente (Guatemala): E Groups reported at, 10
Centering: Caracol caches and, 60; principles, Early Classic period, 19
Centipede snake conflation: Cerro Maya 5C-2nd façade, 194
Central America: bedrock modification in, 16. *See also* Mesoamerica

Central Karstic Uplands: dense E Group clusters in, 480; E Groups commemorating unique dates in, 493–94; E Groups in, 486, 490–94, 499–500, 504, 505; E Group sites in, map of, *481*; Haab commemorative E Groups in, 491–93; ideological constructs of early landscapes in, 497, 499–503; orientations of E Groups in, 490; Solstice commemorative E Groups in, 491; Triadic Groups in, 494–96, *495*; Tzolk'in commemorative E Groups in, 493

Central Karst Plateau: E Groups in, 487*t*–489*t*

Central Park (New York), Olmsted's design for, 5

Central Petén Lakes region: figurines and fragments in, 142–43

Centro de Investigaciones Regionales de Mesoamérica (CIRMA), 259

Cephalopods: at Hatzcap Ceel, Cayo, Belize, 562

Ceramics, 319; Achiotes unslipped, 259, 263, 267, 269; Águila Group, 269; Balanza, 278; Brisa E Group, Yaxnohcah, 497; broken, bedrock at Yaxuná, 466; Buenavista–Nuevo San José, 143; Calakmul Structure IVb caches, 557–58; Calakmul Structure IVb tomb, 559; Calakmul Structure VII tomb, 560; Ceibal, 228; Chan ceramic complexes, 364*t*; Chay Complex, Yaxnohcah, 485; Chiapan, 228; in *chultun* behind Calakmul Structure VII, 560; Chunhinta Black, *258*, 259, 267; Cival E Group, 304; Cival region, 296; Classic period at Chan, 379; construction fill sequences, El Palmar, 260; cross-dating, at La Venta, 226; from dance platform at Yaxuná, *463*; Dos Arroyos polychrome groups, 278; Early Mamom, from El Palmar Structure E4-1, *258*; Early Nabanché, Yaxuná, 463, 464, 467; El Llanto Group, 459; El Palmar Structure E4-1-4th, 263; flanged plates/bowls at Chuen Complex (Tikal), 266; Flor Cream, 267, 269; grayware, 522; Indeterminate, 267, 269; jars, Cival Cache 4, *297*, 298; Joventud Red, *258*, 259; Las Pinturas E Group (San Bartolo), 333; Las Pinturas Group, Sub-7, 333; Late Chicanel, 269; Late Mamom, El Palmar, 263, 265; Macal Complex, 484; Mamom effect in Central Lowlands, 255, 257, 259–60, 263, 265–66; Muxunal Group, 459; Pinturas Sub-5 phase, 334; Pital Group, 459; Polvero Black, 267; Protoclassic caches, at Ceibal, 231, *231*, 232; at San José Cayo, Belize, 564; Sapote Striated, 269; Sierra Red, 267, 269, 339; southeast Petén and distribution of, 58; tetrapod plates, 276, *277*; Tikal, 139; trickle designs, Yaxuná, 460; Tzec collection, 265; Uaxactún Style E Group at Uaxactún, 561–62; Um Complex, Yaxnohcah, 485; Variegated Indeterminate, *258*, 259, 267, 269; Yaxnohcah chronology based on ceramic complexes, 484*t*. *See also* Figurines; Pottery

Ceremonial centers: Cival region, mapping by Holmul Archaeological Project, 295

Ceremonialism: early, E Group as proxy for, 31

Ceremonial spaces: Cival Central E Group and, 319; geomancy and laying out of, 317

Cerros (Cerro Maya): Eastern Triadic Structure at, 203; east side of Structure 5C-2nd, *192*; iconography of façade of Structure 5C-2nd at, 192–96; Structure 29 at, description of platforms, 203; Structure 29 at, preserved masks on platforms, *204*; Structure 29 at, viewed from the west, *204*; west side of Structure 5C-2nd, *193*

Cerros Project: small stone balls found, 180

Chaak Rain God, 191, 298, 299, 502; funerary offerings at Jabalí Tomb 1 and early form of, 330; mask at Mundo Perdido, 267; stucco mask, Cival, consistent with iconography of, *302*

Chak Chel: Quadripartite Badge carried on back of, 198

Chak Tok Ich'aak of Waka' (King): as K'an Nahb Isimte', burial 37, 184, *185*

Chalcatzingo: ceramics at, 459; Monument 1, pictographs from, 502

Chamfered plates: early Mamom, at Palmar, 259

Champerico: ballcourts at, 496; Calakmulqueños, *kaanal* dynasty, and control of, 528; in Central Karst Plateau, 487*t*; Tzolk'in Commemorative E Groups at, 493

Chan (Belize), 16, 442; agricultural terraces at, 362, 364, *366*; bedrock outcrops at, 375; Burial I at, *377*, 400; burials placed within staircases at, 402; Central Group at, 364,

367; Central Plaza at, 364, 372; central religious complex in, 362; chronology chart for site at, 364*t*; community center and east–west structures of central religious complex at, *367*; construction histories of triadic assemblages at, 424, 426; construction history of central religious complex at, 368–69, 372–76; Eastern Triadic Assemblage at, 376; Eastern Triadic Structures at, 429; E Groups excavated at, 12, *14*; elite burials at, 440; excavations undertaken at, 367; figurines at, 140, 153; frequency of burials and caches, Eastern Triadic Structures at, 433*t*, 434, 438, 439; height measurements of, in Belize River valley, 422, 422*t*; incense burners found at, 540; within Late Classic Xunantunich polity, 368; local spatial symbolism at, 237; overview of site, 362, *363*; profile of central east structure (Structure 5-center), *370*; profile of west structure (Structure 7), *371*; ritual use of central religious complex at, 375; Structure 6, Room 2 at, 551; summary of radiocarbon dates from, 365*t*; temple precincts and expanded bureaucracies at, 553; temple room counts/areas, 543*t*; topography, settlement, and agricultural terraces at, *366*; triadic shrine at, 16; West Plaza at, 364, 372; west structure shape, marked as cosmogram, 375

Chanchich (Belize), 308; ballcourts at, 307; E Group plaza at, 308; E Groups at, 295, 296; pseudo-E-Groups at, 15; temple room counts/areas, 543*t*

Chapman, John, 135

Charcoal: in Chan's central religious complex cache, 369

Charlie Chaplin figures: Caracol E Group, 54, 56

Chase, Arlen, 10, 12, 80, 230, 287, 346, 413, 417, 419, 437

Chase, Diane, 230, 287, 346, 419

Chávez Gómez, Sergio, 550

Cherla phase: Pacific coastal region, 218

Chert biface production: in Chan, 364

Chert debitage: in E Group buildings, 263, 467

Chert fragments: Nixtun-Ch'ich', 145

Chert reduction flakes: deposits at Yaxuná, 466

Chiapa de Corzo (Mexico): caching of small stone spheres at, 231; cruciform caches tied to cardinal directionality at, 238; greenstone axe caches at, 217, 227; linear mound-plus-platform arrangements at, 96; maps of MFC-pattern sites, *221*; MFC arrangements at, 226, 234; Middle Preclassic development at, 220; Middle Preclassic examples of E Groups at, 12; Stela 2 from, Long Count dates, and, 111

Chiapan centers: early MFC site plans at, 233

Chiapas, 4, 240, 417; caching of small stone spheres in, 231; greenstone axe caches at, 229

Chiapas Grijalva River valley: political decline or reorganization in, 229

Chiapas Pacific piedmont center: MFC pattern and, 226

Chicaanticaanal: Acropolis E Groups at, 494; ballcourts at, 496; in Central Karst Plateau, 487*t*; Tzolk'in Commemorative E Groups at, 493

Chichén Itzá, 453; astronomical alignment studies at Caracol of, 76; El Castillo at, geomancy and, 317–18; solar alignments and Terminal Classic at, 116–17

Chiik Nahb market complex (Calakmul): detail of, *86*; murals showing market scenes, 85, *87*

Chilane or *chilam* ("prophet"), 540

Children: burial practices in Chan and, 378

Chin paintings: Cerro Maya Structure 5C-2nd, 193

Chiquibul, Bajo and Alto: E Groups of, 36*t*–37*t*

Chortí: division of solar year among, 499; maize cycle, 260-day count, and, 106

Chuen ceramic phase: Tikal collection, North Acropolis, 265

Chuen Complex (Tikal): flanged plates and bowls at, 266

Chultuns (deep pits), 138, 139, 153, 159, 161–62n5; behind Calakmul Structure VII, 560; Cival, 297; figurine disposal in, 538

Chunchucmil: Teotihuacanoid traits reported at, 460

Chunhinta Black: Fine Inclusions paste variety: Tzec ceramics, 265

Chunhinta Black ceramics, *258*, 259, 263, 267, 485

Chunhinta Black jars: Baalche' Group plaza, Yaxnohcah, 485

Ciudad Caucel, 454; Olmec-style greenstone caches in vicinity of, 459
Cival (Guatemala), 16; bedrock outcrops at, 375; Cache 4, containing jade and ceramic jars, *297,* 298; Center E Group, artistic rendering of, *321;* Central E Group, significance of, 323; ceremonial center at, 293; Cival Center, temple room counts/areas, 543*t*; cruciform caches tied to cardinal directionality at, 238; dimensional relatedness in E Groups at, 312; E Group and Eastern Triadic Structures Group at, 141; E Group complex at, 296–300, 302; E Groups at, 12, *14*; E Groups built outside ceremonial center, 307; E Group sight-line azimuths, *305*; E Groups in Late Preclassic period at, 303–5, 307–9, 311–18; emerging patterns from E Group sample at, 318–19; first reporting of site at, 295; greenstone axe caching at, 228; histogram of E–W plaza width of E Groups in, *311*; location of thirteen E Groups in region surrounding, *306*; location and topography of, 293; as main political center, 307; major changes of central plaza at, Late Preclassic, 303–4; map of, at end of Late Preclassic period, *301*; maps of eleven E Groups mapped at, and nearby sites, *310*; Maya E Groups in Middle Preclassic at, 96, 97; Middle Preclassic cache at, 18; overall distribution of five E Groups at, 303; peak population at, 309; profile of topography along northern sight line of North E Group at, 315, *315*; ritual caching at, 398; Stela 2, dancing figure wearing Principal Bird Deity head pectoral, *322,* 323; Stela 3, depicting Preclassic rain god, 299, *300*; triadic complex at, 552; uniqueness of, among all known Preclassic ceremonial centers, 303; variability in sight-line orientation among E Groups, 305, 307; water jars placed in cruciform caches at, 239; West E Group, 308, 309
Cival region: discrepancies in E Group sight line sample, 314–16; E Group dimensions in, 308–9, 311–12; E Group sight lines in, *313, 313*–18; histogram of E–W plaza width of E Groups in, *311*; map of, investigated by Holmul Archaeological Project, *294*; proliferation of E Groups in, 323
Civic ritual: royal burials and conjoining of dynastic ritual and, 387

"Civilized spaces": Classic period concepts of, 278
Clark, John, 179, 217, 226
Classic Xunantunich E Group, 406; unusual characteristics of, 390
Clay architecture: at Ceibal, 227
Clay figurines, 135; agricultural rituals and, 154; Calakmul, 141. *See also* Figurines
Clay pastes: enchainment and variability in, 155
Cleared space: as sky-watching space, 182
Coastal trade: development of, 458
Cobá: Teotihuacanoid traits reported at, 460
Codices: geomancy and, 317
Coeval residential structures: at Ceibal, 141
Coggins, Clemency, 10, 103, 375
Cohodas, Marvin, 10, 12, 85
Cohune, 50; E Groups at, *14*
Collective group identities: E Group emergence and, 339
Collins, Ryan, 464
Comalcalco, Tabasco, E Groups at, 4
Comalcalco (Mexico), burials at, 550
Commemorative ceremonies and rituals: burials, E Groups, and, 387; cult-enacted, 350–51
Commemorative days, E Groups in Central Karstic Uplands: E Groups commemorating unique dates, 493–94; Haab commemorative E Groups, 491–93; solstice commemorative E Groups, 491; Tzolk'in commemorative E Groups, 493
Communal ceremonies: E Group plaza, Ceibal, 223
Communication: E Groups and coeval systems of, 581. *See also* Trade
Community-centered ritual: Classic period at Chan, 379
Community identity: E Groups and, 344
Conchas Phase: emergence of La Blanca during, 220
Conch shell trumpets, 540, 551
Connerton, Paul, 350
Consejo Red water jars: Baalche' Group plaza, Yaxnohcah, 485
Construction methods: fill sequences, at Mundo Perdido and El Palmar, 260; Lowland Maya architecture and, 228–29
Copán (Honduras): *aj k'uhuun* title from bench in Las Sepulturas Group, 9N-82, *540*; Celestial Monster on Structure 10L-22,

199; Mot-mot marker, Tomb 1 peccary skull scene, and Ballcourt IIa central marker at, 345

Coral: water symbolism and, 580

Corn: rituals and economic importance of, 154. *See also* Maize agricultural cycles

Corporate social forms: in Mesoamerica, 329

Cosmic celebrations, 152

Cosmic geomancy, 417

Cosmic order: structures and plazas of Early Ritual Areas and, 158

Cosmograms: Chan's west structure, 375

Cosmology, Maya, 582; architectural decoration and, 63; ballgame symbolism and, 343; cardinal directionality of Maya vs. modern Western model of space, 239; caves, hills, and water bodies in, 237; celestial symmetries in, 82; directional concepts of the earth and sky, 233–38; importance of number three in, 441; landscapes, connecting people to the universe, and, 539; maize/World Trees and, 298, 299, 323

Cosmos: E Group and interpreting Maya fascination with, 31; laying out the levels of, 499; ritual offerings in E Group plazas and, 388

Cosmovision, Maya: Cival E Group architecture and celebrations of, 293; Cival jade offering and basic pattern of, 298

Counting devices, 180

Creation cosmology: turtle imagery and, 122n2

Creation narratives, 178

Crisanto Black bowls: Yaxnohcah, 484

Crowns: Pinturas, 192

Cruciform caches: cardinal directionality and, 238–39; Real-Escoba transition and, 223–24; water jars placed in, 239

Cuadros Phase: Pacific coastal region, 217, 218

Cuantinchán Viejo, Puebla: ceramics at, 459

Cucina, Andrea, 452

Cuello: figurines recovered at, 141; high-status burials at, 330

Cu-Ix. *See* Tuun K'ab' Hix (a.k.a. K'altun Hix or Cu-Ix)

Culbert, T. Patrick, 265

Cult-enacted commemorative ceremonies, 350–51

Cult of the ruler rituals: anthropomorphic figurines and, 136

"Cult places," 158

Dahlin, Bruce, 10

Dance and dancing, 152, 323

Dance platforms: cache from, Yaxuná, *463*; Middle Formative, at Yaxuná, *188*; Middle/Late Preclassic, Yaxuná, 463; at Yaxuná, 550

Dante, Ignazio, 519

Day counts, 180, 181; Long Count system and, 181, 320, 323; rulership and, 201

Daykeepers (*aj q'ijab'*), 526, 537, 539, 554

Day-names: divinatory almanacs, 149, 150

Dead, disposal of. *See* Burials

Decapitation: anthropomorphic figurines and, 136, 161n1; mythic or actual, 539

Deep mythic time: Maya belief in, 8

Deity impersonation, 539, 555

Diablo complex of El Zotz: myriad of Sun Gods depicted at, 200

Dillon, Brian, 105

Dimensional idiosyncrasies: E Group buildings, Late Preclassic period, 273, 275

Directional concepts, of earth and sky, 233–38. *See also* Cardinal directionality

Directional jar offerings: in Mesoamerica, 298

Disinterment: ancestor veneration and, 405; special treatment of remains at Cahal Pech, 401

Dividable human body, embodiment theory and, 136

Divination practices and rituals, 554; caches and, 18; evidence of sacrifice and, 550

Divinatory almanacs, 149–51

Divine kingship: beginnings of, 160; as institutional reality, in Preclassic Maya world, 19; legitimizing through ancestor veneration and sun cycle rituals, 407; sacrifice of the Principal Bird Deity and, 189; Triadic Groups and, 98–99. *See also* Kingship

Diviners (*aj q'iij*), 539

Divining tokens, 180

Dos Aguadas, 315, 553; ballcourts at, 307; eastern platform lengths at, 312; E Groups mapped at, *310*; northern sight line, profile of topography along, *314*, 314–15; plaza measurements at, 308–9; sight lines of, 313; temple precincts and expanded bureaucracies at, 554; temple remodeled to smaller space at, 550; temple room counts/areas, 543*t*

Dos Arroyos polychrome groups, 278

Dos Pilas: Calakmulqueños, *kaanal* dynasty, and control of, 528
Dowd, Anne S., 490
Doyle, James, 181, 339
Dramas: masked, 152
Dresden Codex, 117, 348
Dry laid rubble fill: Structure E-2, Xunantunich, 393
Dumbarton Oaks collection: greenstone figure in squatting position in, 190–91
Dumbarton Oaks jade celt: Las Pinturas Sub-5 inscribed block and glyphic parallels to, 337
Dunning, Nicholas, 13
Dynamic ancestors, 333
Dynastic ancestor rituals: Las Pinturas Sub-5 ballcourt marker and, 346
Dynastic founding and development: E Groups, elaborate early burials, and, 20
Dynastic interment: Eastern Triadic Assemblages, Belize River valley, 435
Dynastic kingship: K'atun-endings, E Groups, and, 346; Las Pinturas murals and concepts of, 330
Dynastic ritual: royal burials, conjoining of civic ritual, and, 387
Dynastic rule: San Bartolo murals and stories underpinning, 348
Dynastic symbolism: cult-enacted commemorative ceremonies and, 350–51; San Bartolo foundational tale and, 348–49
Dynasties: emerging, Late Preclassic E Group changes and, 344
Dzibanché: snake (or *kaan*) dynasty centered first at, 526
Dzibilchaltún (Mexico), 450; E Groups at, 10, 12; Teotihuacanoid traits reported at, 460; wall enclosing Temple of the Seven Dolls at, 548
Dzibilnocac (Mexico): E Groups at, 10
Dzudzuquil Variegated ceramics: Baalche' Group plaza, Yaxnohcah, 485

Earflares: Calakmul Structure VII tomb, 560
Early Mamom ceramics, El Palmar, *258*, 259
Early Nabanché ceramics: Yaxuná, 463, 464, 467
Early Ritual Areas, 157, 158, 159, 160

Early Xunantunich E Group, 390, 406; abandonment of, 404–5, 406, 407; ancestor veneration in, 399–405; burial chamber in Structure E-2-1st, 402–4, *403*; intensive investigations at, beginning of, 390; isometric reconstruction of E Group at, with inserts showing sample of fire features and paved ramp, 395, *395*; LiDAR hillside image of, *391*; rituals and processions in, 393–99
Earth: directional concepts of sky and, 233–38; symbolisms of maize agriculture and broad notion of, 233
Earthen fills: Lowland Maya architecture and, 229
Eastern platforms: at Cahal Pichik and Hatzcap Ceel, 50; Caracol E Group, architectural development, *52*; of Caracol E Group, investigation of, 54; Caracol epicentral E Group, *51*; at Cenote, 47; of Cenote E Group, Structures C1, C108, and C109, *46*; Cenote Style E Group, *33*, 34, 59; extended, as first hallmark of an E Group, 32; histogram of length, twelve E Groups in Cival region, *311*; length, in comparison of Cival region's set of 13 E Groups, 309; Paxcamán E Group, 47; Uaxactún Style E Group, 32, *33*, 34, 59; upper Grijalva River area, Chiapas, 32; at Yaxhá, 62
Eastern shrines: east–west symbolism and, 361, 362
Eastern Triadic Assemblages (ETA): ancestor veneration, focal nature of the east, and, 441; in Belize River valley, architectural analysis of, 420, 422, 424, 426–28; burial and cache data from, Belize River valley, 432–35; at Chan, 376; definitions of, clarifying, 413–14; north–south profiles of, at Belize valley sites, *423*; origins and establishment of, 442; rationale behind use of term, 427–28
Eastern Triadic Structures (ETS): at Cerros (Cerro Maya), 203; definitions of, clarifying, 413, 414; east–west symbolism and, 361; frequency of burials and caches in, Belize River valley, 433*t*; height measurements of, in Belize River valley, 422, 422*t*; monuments associated with, in Belize River valley, 428–30; Pacbitún, 140, 141; primary function of, 443; at Uaxactún, 412–13
East Mound, Uaxactún: solar course and, 80

East–west axis: ancestor veneration in Chan and, 362
East–west construction/reconstruction: ritual structures, Chan Central Plaza, 372–73
East–west direction: cosmology of Mesoamerica and, 234
East–west symbolism: ancestor veneration in Chan and, 376, 378, 379; as key component of E Group complexes, 361
Eaton, Jack, 458
Eb yearbearer, 101
Economic policy: language of royal practice and, 202. *See also* Agriculture; Trade
Educational systems: religious institutions and, 548, 554
Edzná: El Llanto Group ceramics at, 459; origin of the Haab and, 102–3
E Group complexes: broadened functional definitions of, 15; distribution and significance of, 17–20; placement of ancestors in, 387
E Group plan variants: Cenote Style, *33*, 34, 59; Uaxactún Style, 32, *33*, 34, 59. *See also* Cenote Style E Groups; Uaxactún Style E Groups
E Group research, historiography of, 8–17; current research, 16–17; 1924–1954, 8–10, *14*; 1955–1984, 10, 12, *14*; 1985–2016, 12–15, *14*
E Groups: agriculture and, 85; alignment patterns analysis for, 15; as architectural chameleons, 582; background to, 5–8; in Belize River valley, architectural analysis of, 420, 422, 424, 426–28; celebration of agricultural cycles, 10; in Central Karstic Uplands, 486, 490–94, 499–500, 504, 505; changing focus and function of, over time, 581; cohesion, community identity, and, 344; complexes as formal Maya places in Late Preclassic, 17; as core of early Maya communities, 65; correlation with archaeoastronomical alignments, 3, 12; cultural standardization centered on, 8; definitional elasticity of, 579; definitions of, 412–14; derivation of term, 43; distribution of, in Middle Preclassic, 96–97; distribution of E-Group-type complexes, *13*; as earliest replicated public architecture in Maya Lowlands, 578; early, delineation of known universe and, 499; early, solar and stellar alignments in, 96–99; as early hallmarks of Maya public architecture, 59, 63, 64; early versions of complexes, Middle Preclassic period, 17; eastern structures and development of, 579; emergence of, as an architectural form, 339; establishment of ruling elites and, 20; extended eastern platforms as first hallmark of, 32; first appearance in Middle Preclassic Maya Lowlands, 387–88; as first standardized architectural expressions of ancient Maya, 329; geomancy and, 293, 414, 415, 417; geometric planning practices for, 339; Haab form of, 98; hypothesized functions of, 414–20; insights into interpretation of, 16; integrative capacity of, 581; as integrative tools, need for future research on, 469; Lowland Maya Early Ritual Areas, spatial distribution of, 151–52; as maize theaters, 12, 91; in Maya region, time range for, 517; meanings behind Preclassic expansions, 278–81; Middle Preclassic, in Central Southern Lowlands, *256*; nonastronomical ritual functions, debate over, 15; plaza politics and roles of, 273, 275–76, 278; plazas as cultural hallmarks, 20; plaza space dimensions, 14–15; religious function of, 537–41, 547; reported from Maya region, *14*; ritual and practical astronomy in, 517; shelf life of, in Classic Period, 278–79; significance of, to ancient Maya, 578–82; as solar commemorative structures, 203; of Southeastern Lowlands, 35t–41t; as timescape, 135–63; trade routes and locations of, 16, 17; transitions in functions of, 412; triadic pattern of, and number three in Maya cosmology, 441; true, 579; unified belief system in, 32. *See also* Isthmian origins of the E Group; Triadic Groups
Eight stone: origin of term, 76
El Achiotal (Guatemala): turtle mask at, 206
El Baúl: early calendar and monuments at, 104; Stela 1, Long Count dates and, 109
El Carmen: in Central Karst Plateau, 487t
El Castillo, 388; Chichén Itzá, geomancy and, 317–18; height of, 367
El Cedro, 490; in Central Karst Plateau, 487t
Elite authority: emerging, Jabalí complex (San Bartolo) and, 330. *See also* Kingship; Political power; Rulership
El Llanto Group ceramics, 459

El Manatí: greenstone axe caches at, 217, 223, 238
El Mirador (Guatemala), 7, 10, 98, 486; E Groups reported at, 10, *14*; Pava Complex at, 490; site planning at, Late Preclassic, 273; unusually large Preclassic civic centers at, 480
El Mirador La Pava: Acropolis E Groups at, 494
El Mirador León: Acropolis E Groups at, 494; ballcourts at, 496; in Central Karst Plateau, 487*t*; dating E Group at, 490; Haab Commemorative E Groups at, 493; southern triadic acropolises at, 495; unique dates commemorated by E Groups at, 494
El Mirador Pava, 490; in Central Karst Plateau, 488*t*; reservoirs near E Groups at, 496; southern triadic acropolises at, 495
El Palenque, Oaxaca, Mexico, 549, 554; Hun Ajaw Itzamnaj/One Maize Crocodile Tree or young Maize God emerging from turtle carapace "Resurrection Plate," *525*; religious specialists archaeologically documented at, 525–26; Room 1, Structure 20 at, 522; Structure 20 plan, *524*; Structures 16 and 29 at, 522–23; temple precinct at, 521–26; temple precinct plan, *523*; tunnel position and layout at, 550; vaulted tunnel, Feature 77 at, 525; westernmost Mound K at, 523–24
El Palmar (Petén, Guatemala), 16, 253; Calakmulqueños, *kaanal* dynasty, and control of, 528; comparison of Late Preclassic E Groups at Tikal and, *254*; construction fill sequences at, 260; dismantling of prior buildings at, 269; earliest structure encountered at, 259–60; Early Late Preclassic ceramics, Structure E4-1 at, 266–67; Early Mamom ceramics from Structure E4-1, *258*; Early Mamom or Late Eb/Early Tzec architecture at, 259; E Groups reported at, *14*; exterior walls of Structure E4-1-2nd, *270*; features of Mamom ceramics at, 259; hypotheses on similar architectural trends at Tikal and, 265–66; late Chicanel ceramics at, 269; Late Mamom ceramics at, 263, 265; Late Preclassic expansion episodes at, 267, 269; major sites near, map of, *254*; middle to late Mamom Phase architecture at, 260, 263; north profile of Late Preclassic expansion episode, Structure E4-1, *268*; Preclassic "collapse" at, 281; radial pyramid, final enlargement of, 272–73; radial pyramids at, 267, 275; reuse of final Late Preclassic phase at, 276; shift in building practices after Late Preclassic at, 279; similarities between Mamom or Late Eb/Tzec buildings at, 265; site planning at, Late Preclassic, 273; soil erosion, Late Preclassic, 281–82; Structure E4-1-4th, 260, *262*, 263; temple precincts and expanded bureaucracies at, 554; temple room counts/areas, 543*t*; tombs, 280–81
El Paraíso (Guatemala): E Groups at, *14*
El Perú–Waka': burial assemblage at, 552; Calakmulqueños, *kaanal* dynasty, and control of, 528
El Pesquero: in Central Karst Plateau, 488*t*; dating E Group at, 490
El Pilar, 307, 420, 440; construction histories of triadic assemblages at, 426; Eastern Triadic Structures at, 429; frequency of burials and caches, Eastern Triadic Structures at, 433*t*, 435; height measurements of, Belize River valley, 422, 422*t*
El Portón: caching of small stone spheres at, 231
El Zacatal: ballcourts at, 496; in Central Karst Plateau, 489*t*; map of, *495*; northern triadic acropolises at, 495; north–south alignment at, 496
El Zotz: tomb at, 281
Embodiment theory, on human bodies as partible and relational, 136
Enchainment: defined, 135, 155; figurine fragments and, 155–56; "presencing" through, 153
Epigraphy: Panel 18 from Dos Pilas Structure L5-49, 397–98; symbolism of hill, for Lowland Maya, 236
Epi-Olmec dating system: Long Count in, 111
Equinoxes, 394; Cival E Group sight lines and, 305, 307, 313; time-based commemorations, E Groups, and, 347; Uaxactún complex and Maya observance of, 31, 58; Uaxactún's Late Preclassic E Group and, 97
Esoteric knowledge, 550. *See also* Cosmology, Maya; Priests
Estrada-Belli, Francisco, 18, 182, 228, 237, 398
Exchange: of figurine fragments, 155; networks, Yaxuná E Group, 467. *See also* Trade
Eyes: lower masks at Cerros, L-shaped vs. oval-eyed variant discussion, 196

Face caches: Kat'un rituals and, 62
Face glyphs on Pomona earflare: human form Sun God example, 196
Fahsen, Federico, 83
Farmers and farming communities: in Chan, 362, 364, 379, 380. *See also* Agriculture
Feasting, 152; debris, Terminal Preclassic, Early Xunantunich E Group, 398; deposits, Blackman Eddy, 141
Feathered Serpent: balustrades, Las Pinturas Sub-5b, 338, *338,* 342; Epiclassic cult centers, religious-fair model and, 468
Female terracotta figurines, 135
Fertility: celebrations, figurines and, 153–54; symbolisms of maize agriculture and broad notion of, 233
Fetal life cycle: 260-day period and, 103–4
Fialko, Vilma, 58, 265
Fidelia Complex, at Yaxnohcah, 499–500
Figurines, 161; as ancestor images, 155–56; animal, 163n13; anthropomorphic, 135–37, 160; astro-calendrics and, 152; Cahal Pech, 139–40; Calakmul Structure IVb cache, 557; Calakmul Structure IVb tomb, 558; Central Petén Lakes region, 142–43; Chan, 140; Chan burials, 378; in *chultun* behind Calakmul Structure VII, 560; clay, 135, 141, 154; continuing debates over functions of, 156–57; dating of, 135; "decapitation" of heads from, 136, 161n1; disposal in *chultuns*, 538; Early Maya E Groups and, 137–40; Early Ritual Areas and, 158, 159, 160; El Palenque, Oaxaca, Mexico, 522; El Palmar Structure E4-1-4th, 263; greenstone, 135; hand-modeled, 136; at Hatzcap Ceel, Cayo, Belize, 562; heads of, in hieroglyphic script, 148–49; Ixlú and Nixtun-Ch'ich', 143, 145, *146, 147,* 148, 150, 151; Japanese Jomon, 153, 155; late Tux Complex, Baalche' Group, Yaxnohcah, 486; Olmec-style bearded figure in birthing pose, 190, *190,* 191; other Early Ritual Areas and, 140–42; possible functions/meanings, Early Ritual Areas, 151–57; pregnant, 154; sexual ambiguity of, 136–37, 154; socially mediated identities of, 157; Tikal, 138–39; traits of, 136; Uaxactún, 138. *See also* Ceramics; Pottery
Finca Acapulco: desertion of, 229; MFC pattern and, 224

Finca Arizona (Mexico): Middle Preclassic examples of E Groups at, 12
Fire: snakes as conduits of, Cerros West Wall, 194
Fire altars, 396, 397
Fire features: Early Xunantunich E Group, *395,* 396–97, 398
Fishing, 233
Flanged plates and bowls: Chuen Complex (Tikal), 266
Flannery, Kent, 6, 180, 551
Floors: preserved/semipreserved, at Yaxuná E Group, 465, *465*
Flor Cream ceramics, 267, 269; Calakmul Structure IVb cache, 558
Flores Ceroso ceramics class, 333
Flores Island, figurine heads recovered at, 142
Fluting: horizontal, Macal Complex ceramics, Yaxnohcah, 484
Foliated World Tree (Palenque): embellishment of, 184
Foreheads: dotted disk on, figurine heads, *147,* 150
Forsyth, Donald, 459
Founder deities: of Palenque, Tikal, and Caracol, *62,* 63, 64
Four-directional offering narrative: San Bartolo murals and, 348–49
"Four Lords," 500. *See also* Yearbearers
Fragmentation: exchange and enchainment and, 155–56; of objects, 135–36
Freidel, David, 12, 18, 85, 91, 287, 405, 450, 500, 540
Freiwald, Carolyn, 399
Funerary mask: Calakmul Structure IVb tomb, 558
Funerary offerings: at Jabalí Tomb 1, 330

Gaming boards: use of, 180
Garber, James, 187, 401, 434
Geographical latitude: 260-day intervals and, 104
Geographic Information Systems (GIS): landscape studies and, 417; "viewshed" tool, 316, 417
Geoh Shih, 181
Geomancy: Chinese, 317; Cival E Group rituals and, 317–18, 324; E Groups and, 293, 414, 415, 417, 435, 436

Geometrical planning practices: for E Groups, consistency of, 339
Giant Ahau altars, 54, 62
GI deity: dedication of the Temple of the Cross to, 186
Girard, Raphael, 106
Giron-Ábrigo, Mario, 342
GI Watery Sun: possible rise of, 191
Glyphs: head-variant, 149, 150
Gnomons, 526
God C Sun God: image of Foliated World Tree at Palenque and, 184
God H: mosaic mask evocative of, 560
"Golden rectangle" measurement base: for E Groups, 339
González, Rebecca, 226
Google Earth, 417
Graffiti on walls: Chan's Structure 6, 551
Graham, Ian, 295
Graham, John, 109
Grave offerings: Chan burials, 378
Grayware ceramics: El Palenque, Oaxaca, 522
Great Plaza Quadrangle map, for Tikal, 10
Greenstone: celts, 154, 398; Chan, 140; figurines, 135; Middle Formative, from dance platform at Yaxuná, 463; Olmec-style artifacts, 459
Greenstone axe caching, 233; Cache 118 of Ceibal, 224; Ceibal, 223, 224, 225; Chiapa de Corzo, 227; Cival, 228; emergence of E Group and, 217; near cessation of, late Middle Preclassic period, 230; San Isidro, 227; watery features and, 239
Gregorian calendars: Long Count date equivalencies, 112, 113
Gregory XIII (pope), 519
Grijalva River valley (Chiapas), 235, 236; Middle Formative Chiapas (MFC) pattern in, 220, 224
Group E astronomical connection: origin of, 75–79
Group of the Cross (Palenque): as architectural Creation Hearth, 186
Guacamayo: as mid-sized center, 368
Guatemala: Highlands, caching of small stone spheres in, 231; Pacific Slope of, Maya Long Count dates found on, 109
Guderjan, Thomas, 15, 412

Guenter, Stanley, 182
Guernsey, Julia, 189

Haab (h'ab), 501; calendar cycles at, 304, 320; dating of, 100; 365-day solar year foundational to, 492; description of, 95; establishment of, 499; Long Count inscriptions and, 114, 120; month patrons and 20-day periods of, 120; origin of, 102–6
Haab commemorative E Groups: Central Karstic Uplands, 491–93, 504
Haab form of E Group: 20-day intervals and, 98
Hahakab: E Group sight lines, 314; E Groups mapped at, 310; temple room counts/areas, 543t; viewing of sacred hills and, 317
Hairdos and headdresses: figurines, 146, 147, 148, 151; Preclassic figurine heads and Classic head-variant glyphs, 150; types of, 148
Hamontún: E Group sight lines, 314; E Groups mapped at, 310; low platforms at, 323; temple room counts/areas, 543t
Hansen, Richard, 59, 226, 387
Hartung, Horst, 12, 59, 79
Hatzcap Ceel, Cayo, Belize: archaeology of E Groups, 50; Cenote Style E Group at, 545, 562–63; early and late, temple room counts/areas, 543t; E Groups from, 48; excavations in E Groups at, 8, 10, 14; interbuilding alignments at, 563; temple precincts and expanded bureaucracies at, 554
Hatz Kaab, 554
Hauberg Stela, 124n15
Hazard, James, 10
Headbands, 156; leadership, 148, 151; monumental masks, Cerros, 192; plaited, 148; tied, 146
Head forms (or head variants): in Classic Maya hieroglyphic script, 149
Head portraits: enormous, Cival Late Preclassic period construction, 299
Heads: anthropomorphic, at Cahal Pech, 139, 140
Hearthstones of creation: fire features, Early Xunantunich E Group, and, 397; ritual offerings in E Group plazas and, 388
"He of the ballgame": notable youths and, 344
Hero Twins: secondary burials and myth of, 440, 441; Xbalanque, patron of number 9, 150

Hierarchically stratified societies: emergence of, Late Preclassic period, 328–29
Hierarchical social institutions: burial rituals, sacred locations, and legitimization of, 387
Hieroglyphic block: early painted, from Las Pinturas Sub-5, 337, *337*
Hieroglyphic inscriptions and writing: anthropomorphic heads used in, 148–49; calendrics in, dating, 101; of Classic Maya elites, east–west symbolism and, 379–80; Maya divinatory almanac and, 149–50; Pinturas, Sub-5, 334
Hieroglyphic stairway: Naranjo E Group, 60
Hierophanies. *See* Solar hierophanies
Highland Maya: day counts, growing/dry seasons, and, 305
Highlands of Guatemala: Tzolk'in and 365-day calendar used in, 95
Hills and hilltops: in Maya cosmology, 237; Saraguates group (San Bartolo), 332; solar observations and, 315–18, 323–24
H-men (shaman): modern east–west focused rituals and, 361
Hoggarth, Julie, 203, 400
Holmul, 307, 308; Calakmulqueños, *kaanal* dynasty, and control of, 528; E Group plaza, 308; E Group sight lines, 313; E Groups mapped at, *310*; large western pyramid, 311; low platforms at, 323; temple room counts/areas, 543*t*
Holmul Archaeological Project: ceremonial centers mapped in Cival region by, 295; map of area of Cival region investigated by, *294*
Holmul River valley: dense E Group clusters in, 480
Holtún: E Groups reported at, *14*
"Holy lordship": last incarnation of Pinturas E Group (Sub-5) and, 330
Household rituals: Pleiades and scheduling of, 503
House shrines: contemporary Maya, persistence of east–west symbolism and, 361–62, 379
Houston, Stephen, 200
Huetche White bowls: Yaxnohcah, 484
Huitzilopochtli: twin-stair temples dedicated to, 520
Human-form gods: emergence of Sun Gods, 196–97; partnership between Principal Bird Deity and, 191
Humus: early E Group construction and scraping of, 220
Hunahpu: twin brother and, cast as ballplayers, 344
"Hunahpu" ballcourt: painted marker on alley floor, Las Pinturas Sub-5, 339, *340*
Hun Ajaw ("first lord"), 500, *501*; four-directional offering narrative and, 348–49
Hunter-gatherers, 180, 233
Hun Yeh Winik (One Tooth Person), 178, *179*, 203

Iconicity: Preclassic figurine heads and Classic head-variant glyphs, 150–51
Iconography: anthropomorphic heads in hieroglyphic script, 148–49; ballcourts, 345; of façade of Structure 5C-2nd at Cerros, 192–96; Las Pinturas Sub-5 E Group, 341–43; Maize God, 154; Olmec-style bearded figure in birthing pose, 190, *190*, 191; Principal Bird Deity, at Late Preclassic Izapa, 189; symbolism of hill, for Lowland Maya, 236
"Identity tokens" (or "icons of identity"): figurine fragments as, 156
Ik' yearbearer, 101
Incense burners (*incensarios*), 540–41, 554; anthropomorphic, Calakmul Structure IVb, 557; Chen-Mul Modeled Mayapán-style, Calakmul Structure VII, 559; scorched floor traces of, at Chan, 374–75
Indeterminate ceramics, 267, 269
Infant skeletons: Calakmul Structure IVb cache, 558
Infierno Black dish and tripod vessels: Calakmul Structure VII tomb, 560
Initial Series Introductory Glyph (ISIG): early Classic Maya calendar and, 113; Long Count records and, 111, 112
Initiation ceremonies, 152
Inomata, Takeshi, 18, 180, 255, 413
Instrumental Neutron Activation Analysis (INAA): fragment enchainment as evidenced by, 155
Interior architecture: enclosed, religious functions, and, 539
Interments. *See* Burials

Investiture ceremonies, 539
Iron pyrite mirrors: at Hatzcap Ceel, Cayo, Belize, 562
Isthmian interaction sphere, 215, *216*, 240
Isthmian origins of the E Group, 215–41; changing symbolism and, 232–39; constant invention/re-creation of new traditions and, 241; directional concepts of the earth and sky, 233–38; early Preclassic antecedents, 217–19; Late Preclassic transformation, 229–32, 240–41; maize agriculture symbolisms, 233; map of Maya area and the Isthmian region, *216*; Middle Preclassic development, 220, 223–24, 226–29; political effects and, 240; symbolisms in caches, 238–39
Itz'aat (scribe), 177
Itzamnaaj: animal avatar of, 177; Principal Bird Deity as avatar of, 178, 189, 191
Ix Ek': archaeological investigation of, 58; E Groups reported at, *14*
Ixkún (Guatemala): archaeological investigation of, 58; E Groups at, *14*
Ixlú: figurines at, 143, 145, 151; Twin Temple complexes, 62
Ixtab ceramic sphere, 333
Ixtontón: archaeological investigation of, 58; E Groups reported at, *14*; perspective of center of, showing Cenote Style E Group, *57*
Izamal, 453
Izapa: alignment with Tacaná volcano, 235; Group A at, 230; MFC arrangements at, 233, 234; origin of the Tzolk'in at, 104
Izapa narrative: Pinturas narrative and, 189

Jabalí complex (San Bartolo), 330, *331*
Jabalí Triadic Group: royal burial within, 350
Jacal (adobe)-type two room temple: on top of southern Mound F, Cahal Pichik, 563
Jade and jadeite, 6; artifacts, Calakmul Structure VII tomb, 560; beads, Calakmul Structure IVb burials, 558; beads, Hatzcap Ceel, 562; beads cache, Calakmul Structure IVb, 557; Cival, offerings in quincunx or k'an-cross pattern, 298; cosmic cache placed into cruciform, Cival, 141; figures, cache at Chan, 372; jade celt offering at Cival, 398; jars, Cival Cache 4, *297*, 298; offerings, Calakmul Structure IVc, 559; Uaxactún E Group deposits, 45

Jaguar Claw II: Leiden Plaque and, 114
Jaguar Paw III, 439
Japanese Jomon figurines, 153, 155
"Jester God": white paper headband with jewels for, 148
Jeweled beards: Cerros Principal Bird Deity faces, 192, 193
Jewel ornaments: in depictions of rulers and some gods, 191
Jocotal Phase: mound building during, 218; Ojo de Agua abandoned at end of, 220
Joventud Red ceramics, *258*, 259, 263; Baalche' Group plaza, Yaxnohcah, 485; Chay Complex, Yaxnohcah, 485; waxy, Um Complex, Yaxnohcah, 485
Joyce, Rosemary, 339
Julian calendar: Long Count date equivalencies, 112, 113; reformed, 519
June solstice: in Round Temple, 121
Justeson, John, 103, 181

Kaan (or snake) dynasty: centered at Dzibanché, then at Calakmul, 526–27
Kaanal (or *kaanul*) dynasty, Calakmul, 528
Kabah: possible E Group at, 456, *456*
K'ahk' Uti' Witz' K'awiil (Copán ruler), 346
K'altun Hix. *See* Tuun K'ab' Hix (a.k.a. K'altun Hix or Cu-Ix)
Kaminaljuyú: caching of small stone spheres in, 231
Kan Bahlam (divine king), 184; depicted in Panel of the Cross, 200
K'ante'el (Maize World Tree), 184
K'atun-endings, 279, 580; E Groups as settings for, 412, 414, 418–19, 435; hieroglyphic texts of Classic period monumental stelae and, 346; Late Classic Maya inscriptions and, 114
K'atun monuments: at Tikal, 114
K'atun periods: Preclassic E Group rituals and, 342; stone stelae and ceremonies marking, 62
K'atuns, 419; Long Count calendar and, 102; rituals commemorating cycle of, 98; 20-year, time and celebration of, 60
K'atun short count, 121
Kawak: glyph for, 506n10; markings, 501
K'axob: E Groups reported at, *14*; figurines recovered at, 141
K'iche': agriculture season and movement of the Pleiades among, 503

Kidder, Alfred V., 537
Kingship, 6; dynastic, K'atun-endings, E Groups, and, 346; early, Las Pinturas Sub-5 E Group and, 346; institutionalized, Las Pinturas Sub-5 E Group and, 349–50; monumentality and, 344; performance and, 18–19; sacrifice of the bird, absorption of divine powers, and, 189; systemic breakdown of, 379; three stone symbolism and, 500. *See also* Divine kingship; Dynastic kingship
K'inich: as royal epithet in glyphic texts, 197
K'inich Ajaw (fiery sun), 178, 197, 203, 456
Kohunlich (Quintana Roo): ambiguity of masks uncovered at, 197
Komchén, 454
K'o site, Cival region, 296
Kovacevich, Brigitte, 202
Kubler, George, 317
Kurjack, Edward B., 10

Labial flanges, plates and bowls: Chuen Complex (Tikal), 266; El Palmar, Structure E4-1, 266–67
La Blanca: alignment with Tajumulco volcano, 235; earthen quatrefoil from, 502; emergence of, 220; Mound 1 pyramid at, 220
Lacandón: agriculture season and movement of the Pleiades among, 503
La Corona: Calakmulqueños, *kaanal* dynasty, and control of, 528
La Corona Element 55 panel, Calakmul, 535
Laguna Manatee: formal celt caches at, 18
Lake Petén-Itzá: figurines, 142; significance of clustering of E Groups in area of, 34
Lake Sacpuy: E Group at, 143
La Lagunita: caching of small stone spheres in, 231
La Libertad: abandonment of, 229; maps of MFC-pattern sites, *221*; MFC-pattern site at, 226
Lamanai (Belize): E Groups reported at, 10, *14*
La Merced: deposition of greenstone axes in watery features at, 239; greenstone axe caches at, 217, 223, 238
La Mojarra Stela 1 (Veracruz): epi-Olmec Long Count recording, 111–12
La Muneca (Mexico): E Groups at, *14*
Landa (Calderón), Diego de, 526, 537
Landscapes: cosmology-inspired, 539; Middle Preclassic, temporalization of space at heart of, 499; ritual practices and, 158; sacred, Cival E Groups, hilltops, and, 316–17, 324
Land tenure: religious doctrine and defense of, 547
Laporte, Juan Pedro, 13, 14, 56, 58, 151, 228, 259, 265
Las Bocas: ceramics at, 459
Las Pinturas E Group (San Bartolo), 330, *331,* 332–34, 337–39; architectural phases of, 335*t*; drafting a local history, 347–50; entering the narrative and, 344–47; focal point of, 332; making ideologies tangible, 341–43; painted marker on alley floor, Sub-5 "Hanahpu" ballcourt, *340*; plan of complex with Sub-1 and Sub-5 highlighted, *335,* 335*t*; reconstruction of Sub-5, *336*; reconstruction of Sub-5 "Hunahpu" radial pyramid, *338*; seven phases of architecture built at, 329–30; Sub-5, Ixbalamqué, 334, *335,* 335*t, 336, 337,* 337–39, *338*; Sub-6, Ixmucané, 334; Sub-7, Ixkik Phase, 333; Sub-4 phase, political and social changes, 347
Las Ruinas: as mid-sized center, 368
Las Ruinas de Arenal, 420
Las Torres, 490; in Central Karst Plateau, 488*t*
Las Tustlas Statuette (Veracruz): epi-Olmec inscription, 112
Las Ventanas group (San Bartolo), 330, *331,* 332
La Ténica: temple room counts/areas, 544*t*
La Unión: Group E-type complexes, 13
La Venta (Tabasco), 215, 413; celt caches and formally arranged deposits at, 18; collapse of, 229; cruciform caches tied to cardinal directionality at, 238; greenstone axe caches at, 229; linear mound-plus-platform arrangements in, 96; maps of MFC-pattern sites, *221*; MFC arrangements at, 233; MFC pattern and, 226–27, 236; spatial plan of, 236; Stela 13, Justeson's recent dating of, 122n3
Leaders: self-aggrandizing, mindful agency, and, 179
Leadership ceremonies: religious-fair model and, 468
"Learned persons" (*itz'aat*), 156
Leiden Plaque: early Classic Maya calendar and, 113–14, *115*
Leventhal, Richard, 388
Lévi-Strauss, Claude, 202

LiDAR data, 417
Life-cycle celebrations: figurines and, 153–54
Limestone block production: at Chan, 364
Limestone spheres: caches, Yaxuná E Group, 467; Protoclassic caches, Ceibal, 231, *232*
Lime stucco: Lowland Maya architecture and, 228–29
Linear mounds: Middle Preclassic, 96
Linear platforms: Pinturas, Sub-5, 334; Pinturas, Sub-7 phase, 333; Pinturas Sub-5a, 339
Lip plug: with hieroglyphs, Calakmul Structure VII tomb, 560
Lip-to-lip caches: basal flange bowls, at Chan, 372; human skulls in, at Uaxactún, 399; Plaza B at Cahal Pech, 140; red cache bowls, at Cenote, 49; vessel cache, Yaxuná, 463
Lip-to-lip vessels: skulls encased in, 439, 440–41, 442
Local history: drafting, Sub-5 phase at Pinturas and, 347–50
Locona Phase: Pacific coastal region, 217, 218
Long Count calendar: Late Preclassic and transition to, 99; Tzolk'in-Haab Calendar Round notation as subset of, 102
Long Count system, 578; astro-calendrics and, 152; calendrical commemorations at Cival and, 320, 323; counts of days and, 181; inscriptions, 365-day cycle first documented in, 95; period time units, K'atuns, and, 346; records, earliest known, 108–9, 111–13
Looper, Matthew, 178
Los Alacranes: Calakmulqueños, *kaanal* dynasty, and control of, 528
Los Lagos: E Groups of, 40*t*
Lost World Complex, 10, 182
Love, Michael, 220
Lowe, Gareth, 12, 32, 226
Lowlands, Maya. *See* Maya Lowlands
Low platforms: Cival Center E Group, Late Preclassic period expansion, *321*; function of, Cival E Groups, and, 323
Lunar records: early Trecena cycles and, 113

Macal Complex ceramics, 484
Machaquilá River: E Groups around, 13
MacNeish, Richard S., 180
Macri, Martha, 112, 148
Madrid Codex, 117, 118
Magic birds: radiant lords and, 191–202

"Magic latitude": astro-calendrics and, 152; early Lowland Maya E Groups concentrated along, 96
Magnoni, Aline, 462
Maize: ritual offerings in E Group plazas and, 388; sprouting, ritual offerings at Cival and, 398; three-stone kitchen hearth and, 159; types of, recovered in early Preclassic, 162n10
Maize agricultural cycles, 157; annual solar cycles, E Groups, and, 386; celebrations of, 154; disappearance interval of Orion and, 97; Mesoamerican, cycle of 260 days and, 106; 20-day periods in Middle Preclassic and, 99; 20-day sets in Maya calendar and, 96
Maize agriculture, 6; E Group and symbolism of, 233; El Palmar, 281
Maize cult: E Group rituals and, 405; Preclassic E Groups and public rituals involving, 387
Maize deities: ancestral connections, burial practices, and, 405; burial/reburial practices and links to, 402; early E Group rituals and, 386
Maize field metaphor, 182
Maize God, 91, 154, 158, 186; burial rituals and severed head of, 401; Classic period and depiction of, 343, 502; cosmic shark and, in Classic Maya corpus, 191; from Ixbalamqué doorjamb, *337*; Las Pinturas Sub-5a linear platform, 342; Late Preclassic, derivation of, 189; Olmec-style Late Preclassic to Early Classic evolution of, 197; patron of number 8, 150; Principal Bird Deity preempted by, 188–89; quatrefoil plan for dance platform, Yaxuná and birthplace of, 464; rain and resurrection of, 501–3; skulls encased in lip-to-lip vessels and death/rebirth of, 440–41, 442
Maize God cycle: San Bartolo murals and, 348
Maize God Prototype King: Olmec iconography of, 19
Maize theaters: E Groups as, 12, 91
Maize/World Tree: Maya cosmology and, 298, 299, 323
Malachite flakes: deposits at Yaxuná, 467
Malinalco (Mexico): Aztec rock sanctuary at, 16
Malmström, Vincent, 102, 103, 104
Mamom effect, in Central Lowlands, 255, 257, 259–60, 263, 265–66
Mamom-type ceramics: social mechanisms during Middle Preclassic and, 266

Index · 611

Manik yearbearer, 101
Marcus, Joyce, 156, 160, 181, 549
Marine shell objects/fragments: Calakmul Structure IVc, 559; procurement of, in Chan, 364
Marriages: fragment enchainment and, 155
Mars Naranja ceramic class, 333
Martin, Simon, 19
Martínez, Gustavo, 497
Mascherino, Otaviano, 519
Masks: burials at Calakmul and, 551; funerary, 558; mosaic, 560; shell mosaic, 281; snarling mouthed, 196, 203; Structure 29, at Cerros, 203, *204*; stucco, 278, 330, 337–38, 341, 456; stucco, northern façade of Cival main E Group's western pyramid, *302*; Tikal, Structure 5C-54-5, 272; turtle, 206
Masks, monumental: Cerros Structure 5C-2nd, iconography of, 192–96; at Kohunlich (Quintana Roo), 197; lower, feline sun-faced or radiant Maize God, Cerros, 191; upper, Principal Bird Deity, Cerros, 191, 192
Masonry techniques: Lowland Maya architecture, 228–29
Master of fire (*yajawk'ahk*), 540
Master of tree/woods (*yajawte'*), 540
Material culture: Middle-to-Late Preclassic transition and, 160
Material symbol-systems: caches and, 17–18
Mathews, Peter, 183
Matos-Moctezuma, Eduardo, 520
May, 419
May (or 256-year cycles): time and, 60
Maya area: chronological overview of, *4*
Maya city or town centers: organization of, 3
Maya civilization: E Group and rise of, 31; fascination with time, 8
Maya Cosmos (Freidel, Schele, and Parker), 200
Maya culture: E Group rituals and, 319
Maya Divinatory Almanac: and script, 149–51
Maya lords: depicted in ballplay, 344
Maya Lowlands, 253; ancestor veneration and social hierarchies in, 386; Archaic period in, 219; Central, Mamom effect in, 255, 257, 259–60, 263, 265–66; Central Southern, map of possible or confirmed Middle Preclassic E Groups in, *256*; Cival E Groups as interconnected nested elements of, 324; dynamic kingship in, 330; E Group assemblages in, 228, 230; E Groups and political belonging in, 339; examples of E Groups across, 412; foundational narratives and incipient dynasties gaining sway throughout, 350; Isthmian origins of the E Group and its adoption in, 215, 217, 228–29, 240–41; Late Preclassic changes in Cival and, 319; Middle Preclassic and first appearance of E Groups in, 387–88; regionalism in artifact assemblages and practices across, 437; ritual reburial and rise of complexity in, 405; sites with E Groups or E Group variants in, 420; symbolisms in caches of, 238–39
Mayan Long Count, 108
Mayapán, 317
Mayapán's Castillo: Postclassic calendar changes and, 118, 121
Maya region: reported E groups from, *14*
Maya thought: east–west symbolism and, 361
McAnany, Patricia, 202, 344, 387
Medial flanges: Cauac Phase ceramics, 269
Meierhoff, Jim, 374
Meléndez, Juan Carlos, 184
Merwin, Raymond, 295
Mes Aynak temple precinct (Afghanistan/Pakistan), 519
Mesoamerica: bar and dot positional numeration in, 18; commemoration of 260-day cycle in, 493; corporate social forms in, 329; directional jar offerings in, 298; earliest known E Group assemblage in, 119, 215; early states in, 7; maize agriculture in, 233; unique 260-day calendar in, 95
Mesoamerican calendar: early, 99–102
Mesoamerican temple precinct: El Palenque, Oaxaca, 521–26
Mesopotamia: temple precinct in, 519
Metopium brownei (che chem or poisonwood) bed of seeds: Calakmul Structure VII tomb, 560
Metztli (20-day months), 113
Middle Formative Chiapas (MFC) pattern, 217, 218, 240; at Ceibal, 220; directional concepts of earth and sky and, 233–34; Grijalva River valley sites, 224; maize agriculture and, 233; maps of sites, *221*; Pacific coastal societies and symbolism of, 235
Milbrath, Susan, 202
Milky Way: Celestial Monster and, 183, 200

Miller, Arthur, 194
Milpa preparation: first solar zenith passage (May 10) and, 81
Mindful agency: self-aggrandizing leaders and, 179
Mirador: MFC-pattern site at, 226
Mirrors: iron pyrite, 562; mosaic, 537, 551, 554; three levels of the cosmos, Maya imagery, and, 502
Mitla, Oaxaca: sixteenth-century religious precincts in, 520
Mixe-Zoque language: monuments with Cycle 7 Long Count dates and, 109
Mollusks: at Hatzcap Ceel, 562
Monkeys: as gods exemplifying *itz'aat,* 177
Monte Albán: emergence of, 7; temple precincts at, 520; yearbearers, 100
Month names, Maya: development of, 100
Monumental buildings and architecture, 6; ancestor veneration and construction of, 286; "individuals" of great stature memorialized through, 402; performance and, 18; triadic architecture toward end of Late Preclassic, 280
Monumentality, Maya: evolving, development of Preclassic lifeways and, 253; kingship and, 344
Monuments: associated with Eastern Triadic Structures in the Belize River valley, 428–30; bar and dot inscriptions on, 18; east–west axis in, focal nature of, 361; Izapan, 104; K'atun-ending, 428; Olmec, 104–5
Moon: cosmological landscape of E Groups and, 12
Moon Goddess: patron of number 1, 150
Mopán: maize cycle, 260-day count, and, 106
Mopán River valley: dense E Group clusters in, 480
Mopan Valley Preclassic Project (MVPP), 388
Morales, Carlos, 481
Morales, Paulino, *261*
Moral-Reforma: Calakmulqueños, *kaanal* dynasty, and control of, 528
Morley, Sylvanus G., 31, 75, 76
Mosaic mask: Calakmul Structure VII tomb, 560
Mosaic mirrors, 537, 551, 554

Mottled color palate: early Mamom ceramics, El Palmar, 259
Mound buildings: Cival region, 296; emergence of E Group and, 217; Pacific coastal societies, 235; Paso de la Amada, 217–18
Mountain Cow region (Belize): significance of clustering of E Groups in, 34, 43
Mountains: central axes of ceremonial centers and, 235; symbolism of, 235, 237. *See also* Volcanoes
Mount Athos peninsula: Orthodox Christian Simonopetra Monastery on, 519
Mount Nebo, Jordan, 519
Mucaancah: ballcourts at, 496; in Central Karst Plateau, 488*t*; E Groups reported at, *14*; northern triadic acropolises at, 495
"Mud-men," 159
Multipolity networks under divine lords (*k'uhul ajawtaak*), Calakmul, 528
Multi-room temples: development of religious institutions and, 542; precincts with, 542, 545
Mundo Perdido (Tikal), 228, 269; best preserved mask in, 267; building practices shift after Late Preclassic, 279; construction fill sequences at, 260; E Group at, 138–39; late Eb ceramics recovery, 255; plaza dimensions, 273, *274*; radial pyramid, earliest phase of, 259; Structure 5C-54, plan view of excavations in, *257*
Murals: Pinturas, 187, 191–92, 332, 334; San Bartolo complex, 101, 330, 348, 350, 351, 500, 501; traders depicted in, Chiik Nahb market complex, Calakmul, 85, *87*
Muxunal ceramic groups, 459

Naachtún (Guatemala), 490; in Central Karst Plateau, 488*t*; dating E Group at, 490; E Groups at, *14*; Haab Commemorative E Groups at, 493; relative eastern temple proportions, 545*t*; reservoirs near E Groups at, 496; temple room counts/areas, 544*t*
Nadir construct: Chortí, solar year, and, 499
Nadir passages: time-based commemorations, E Groups, and, 347
Nadzca'an (Mexico): E Groups at, 12, *14*
Naia: continuity with later Maya populations, 452

Nakbé (Guatemala): Acropolis E Groups at, 494; ballcourts at, 496; in Central Karst Plateau, 488*t*; civic complexes at, 497; dating E Group at, 490, 504; E Groups at, 12, *14*; Haab Commemorative E Groups at, 493; initial construction of E Group at, 497; Maya E Groups in Middle Preclassic at, 96, 97; Middle Preclassic buildings at, 260; reservoirs near E Groups at, 496; resurrection of Maize God and ballcourt/reservoir complex at, 501–2; unusually large Preclassic civic centers at, 480

Nakum (Guatemala), 307; E Groups at, 12, *14*

Naranjo, 307; Calakmulqueños, *kaanal* dynasty, and control of, 528; E Groups at, 12, *14*; founder deities of, 63; hieroglyphic stairway set in E Group at, 60; temple room counts/areas, 544*t*

Natural cycles: 260-day period and, 103

New England town squares: Maya centers compared with, 3

New Year pages, of the codices, 96

New York City, gridded street plan, 5

Niederberger, Christine, 459

Night sky: as revolution of watery underworld into the sky, 183–84

Nine Lords of the Night, 62; of Maya lunar series, 104

Nixtun-Ch'ich': figurines, 143, 145, *146, 147,* 148, 150, 151; pregnant figurine at, 154; site of, *144*; siting of Mound ZZ1 at, 162n12

Noh Kah, 458

North Acropolis: major burials of dynastic founders at, 280

Northern E Groups: early trade and, 454, 456–61

Northern Lowlands: contrasting views of Paleo-indian data in, 451–52; E Groups along trade routes in, 16; Preclassic in, 451–53; two trade routes between Southern Lowlands and, 458, 461, 469; zones of salt flats in, 460

North–south alignment: E Groups, Central Karstic Uplands, 496

North–south axis: Isthmian site plans and emphasis on, 234, 235

Number cycles: in Mesoamerican 260-day divinatory almanacs, 149

Numbers: supernatural patrons of, 150

Nuttall, Zelia, 103

Obsidian, 458, 459; blades, Calakmul Structure VII tomb, 560; blades, El Palenque, 522; fragments, Nixtun-Ch'ich', 145; objects procurement, Chan, 364; trade, 6

Ocozocoautla: MFC-pattern site at, 226

Ojo de Agua, 235; abandonment of, 220; earliest-known pyramids in, 218; map of, *219*

Olmec-style: bearded figure in birthing pose, iconographic analysis, 190, *190,* 191

Olmec 260-day calendar, 99–100

Olmsted, Frederick Law, 5

One Tooth Person, *179, 203*

Open plaza spaces: as sacred landscape, in ancient Maya thought, 183; sky watching and, 182

Optically stimulated luminescence (OSL) dating: single-grain, of ceramic temper, 517

Orion, 159; agricultural practices and movement of, 503; early E Groups and observations of, 119; equinox orientation of Uaxactún linked to, 97; turtle imagery and three "hearthstone" stars in, 122n2

Oxkintok: Teotihuacanoid traits reported at, 460

Oxpemul (Mexico): ballcourts at, 496; in Central Karst Plateau, 488*t*; E Groups at, *14*; southern triadic acropolises at, 495; unique dates commemorated by E Groups at, 494

Oxtotitlán, 459

Pacbitún (Belize), 420, 442; carved stelae not referring to K'atun-ending events at, 436; construction histories of triadic assemblages at, 424; E Groups excavated at, 12, *14*; elaborate royal tombs in triadic assemblages of, 440; elite burials in Structure 1 at, 439; figurines recovered at, 140; frequency of burials and caches, Eastern Triadic Structures at, 432–33, 433*t*; Group A at, 413; height measurements of, Belize River valley, 422, 422*t*; north–south profiles of, Belize River valley, *423*; Plaza A at, 429

Pacific Coast: southern, new architectural and spatial forms of, 218

Pakal the Great, Sarcophagus of, 194
Palaces: Cival region, 307; Las Ventanas group at San Bartolo, 332
Palenque, 8; architectural solar hierophanies at, 91; founder deities or "triad gods" of, 62, 63; Panel of the Foliated Cross at, 184; Panel of the Sun at, 203, *205*
Palenque Sarcophagus: quadripartite badge, pakal, and double-headed serpent from, 195, *195*
Panel of the Cross: Quadripartite Badge and, 200, *201*
Panel of the Foliated Cross (Palenque): primordial sprouting of maize in, 184
Panel of the Sun (Palenque), 203, *205*
Parker, Joy, 183, 200, 500
Parte Aguas Oriente-Occidente: E Groups of, 37*t*
Partibility: bodily, anthropomorphic figurines and, 136; exchange and enchainment and, 155
Paso de la Amada: mounded buildings, 217–18
Patolli beans: divinatory practices and, 180
Patolli boards: Calakmul Structure VII, 559; Caracol Structure A-3, 560, 561; E Group temples, 537, 551
Paved ramps: Early Xunantunich E Group, *395*, 395–96
Paxcamán (Guatemala): E Groups at, 10, 12; mapping of E Groups at, 47
Pecked cross: Uaxactún (and elsewhere in Mesoamerica), 304–5
Pecked cross-circles: quadripartite, carved into Temple Court floor, UAX 1, *84*; Teotihuacán-type, astronomy and, 79, 83
Pedregal Modeled dish: Calakmul Structure VII tomb, 560
Pendergast, David M., 10
People-making activities: chert debris and, at Yaxuná, 467–68
Performance: agency and, 18
Performance spaces: death and resurrection, 186; Preclassic public architecture and, 187–88, *188*
Period-ending commemoration: religious architecture and, 538
Personification heads: in Maya iconography, 198
"Personifications" signs: in Classic Maya hieroglyphic script, 149
Petén: central and west, E Groups of, 39*t*;
early open plaza spaces in, 182; E Groups clustered in, 3, 12, 13; E Groups with numerous caches in, 437; Lakes region, dense E Group clusters in, 480; mid-Petén latitudes, seasonal rainfall distribution, *81*; mid-Petén latitudes, sun watching circumstances in, 82; southeast, archaeology of, 56, 58; southeast, dense distribution of E Groups in, 581–82; southeast, early Maya civilization centered in, 64, 65; three morphological types of E Groups in, 413–14
"Petenoid" sites, 460
Piedras Negras: Calakmulqueños, *kaanal* dynasty, and control of, 528
Pilgrimage fairs, 85
Pilgrimage model, 266
Pinturas: royal appropriation of monumental space at, 333; Triadic Group, 332
Pinturas Complex, architecture in, 18
Pinturas Group (San Bartolo), 328
Pinturas murals: building murals at San Bartolo, performance depicted in, 18; key episodes depicted in, 191–92
Pinturas narrative: Izapa narrative and, 189
Pital ceramics groups, 459
Pital Cream ceramics, 259, 263, 485
Place: anthropological approaches and constructions of, 329
Place-making, 578, 582; Maya rituals of, 157–58; scraped-down bedrock plazas and sculpted platforms and, 552; at Yaxuná, 467
Planetary observations: patterning of K'atun-ending records at Tikal and, 114
Planting almanacs, 104
Plaster, construction phases and, 260
Plaza politics: E Group roles in Late Preclassic site planning and classic engagement, 273, 275–76, 278
Plazas, 539; Cival E Group dimensions, 308, 309; Classic Maya references to space in, 183; east–west axis in, focal nature of, 361; large, E Groups in Maya Lowlands and, 387; solar observations and, 186, 187; symbolisms in caches and, 238; water symbolism of, 239; as watery place, 184
Plaza width: in comparison of Cival region's set of 13 E Groups, 309; histogram of E-W plaza width, Cival region E Groups, *311*

Pleiades: scheduling of household rituals and, 503
Political institutions: religious institutions and, 539
Political power: Cival E Groups and, 324; E Groups and emergence of political authority, 151. *See also* Kingship; Rulership
Political systems: religious doctrine and perpetuation of, 547
Politics: Classic period at Chan and, 379
Polity growth: distribution of E Groups during Early Classic period and, 64
Polvero Black (Polvero Negro) ceramics, 267, 269, 558
Pope, Kevin, 226
Popolá: Puuc-style architecture at, 461
Popol Vuh, 158, 159, 343, 441, 442, 501
Postfire incisions: early Mamom ceramics, El Palmar, 259
Postholes: at Early Xunantunich E Group, 393, *394,* 395
Pottery: Chan, 140; Cival, 141; Cubierta Impressed, 276; first northern pottery complexes, dating of, 451; late Tux Complex, Baalche' Group, Yaxnohcah, 486; sherds of unslipped, Nixtun-Ch'ich', 145; Uaxactún, 43, 138. *See also* Ceramics; Figurines
Poverty Point, 468
Power: E Groups and consolidation of, 581; *Spondylus* as symbol of, 404. *See also* Political power
Power centers, Maya: autonomous nature of, 82
Poxilá, 458; in-line triadic structure at, 452; Olmec-style greenstone caches at, 459
Pregnant figurines, 154
"Preparing the Way" (Freidel), 177
Preservation of data: precision in excavation techniques and, 551
Preslip incising: Macal Complex ceramics, Yaxnohcah, 484
Prestate Maya polities: part-time religious specialists in, 526
Priestly precincts: comparative examples of, 518–21
Priestly titles: among Classic Maya, 539–40
Priests, 537; El Palenque, 526; hierarchical organization of duties for, 549; interpenetrating categories of shamans and, 521; overseeing of ritual activities in E Groups and, 540;

paucity of information about, 538; residences of, 548–49; ritual seclusion spaces for, 549; sacred spectacles and, 554
Principal Bird Deity, 192; as avatar of Itzamnaaj, 178, 189, 191; avian mask at Las Pinturas Sub-5b as form of, 342; with beard, San Bartolo West Wall, 193; ceramic decoration, Calakmul Structure IVb tomb, 559; depictions on west wall, Structure 5C-2nd Cerro Maya, 193; four-directional offering narrative and, 348; great jade orb of Altún Ha and, 200; Las Pinturas Sub-5 ballcourt and, 343; macaw-based, 189–90; partnership between human-form gods and, 191; pectoral worn by dancing figure, Cival Stela 2, *322, 323*; perched in Panel of the Cross, 200, *201*; preempted by Maize God, 188–89; in Quadripartite Badge composition, 198; three stone places and, 501
Processions: at Early Xunantunich E Group, 393–99, 406
Profile head-variant glyphs: distinguishing elements of, 149–50
Prophet/teachers *(ti'sakhuun),* 539
Proskouriakoff, Tatiana, 148
Proyecto Arqueologico de la Biosfera Calakmul excavations: Late Classic construction phases, 556
Proyecto Arqueológico Yaxnohcah, 481
Proyecto de Interacción Política del Centro de Yucatán, 462
Pseudo-E-Groups: lacking western and central eastern structure, Belize sites, 15; Late Classic, in northern Belize, 412, 419–20
Public architecture, Maya, 6; complex social organization and, 64; Preclassic, performance space for public ritual and, 187–88, *189*; replicated, E Groups as, 578
Pucte Brown basal flange bowls: cache at Chan, 372
Punto de Chimino: E Groups at, 12, *14*; temple precincts and expanded bureaucracies at, 554; temple room counts/areas, 544*t*
Pusilhá River: E Groups around, 13
Putin, Vladimir, 519
Puuc-Maya sites: median 14° alignments for, 107–8
Pyramid of the Sun, Teotihuacán: alignments at, 107

616 · Index

Pyramids: Cival E Group complex, 296, 299; Cival Triadic Group, 303–4; directional concepts of earth and sky and, 235; El Palmar Structure E4-1-4th, 260, *262*, 263; at Hatzcap Ceel, Cayo, Belize, 562; height of largest, judging site size and, 367; La Blanca, 220; La Venta, 236; Northern Lowlands, 453; true E Groups and, 579; Xunantunich, 388, 391. *See also* Radial pyramids

Pyrite offerings: Calakmul Structure IVc, 559

Quadripartite Badge: analysis of, 186; Classic contexts and occurrence of, 198; evolution of severed head image and, 198; iconography of, 198, 200; Panel of the Cross and depiction of, 200, *201*

Quadripartite Badge Dawn Bowl: double-headed serpent and, Palenque sarcophagus, 195, *195*

Quadripartite motifs: caches and, 239

Quam Hill: pseudo-E-Groups at, 15

Quarter days: orientations to, 126n23; sight lines, Cival E Groups, and, 313

Quatrefoil pattern: ritual caching at Cival and, 398

Quatrefoil plan: dance platform, Yaxuná, 464

Quatrefoils: images of plaza space and, 183, *183*; three levels of the cosmos, Maya imagery, and, 502; as windows/portals to underworld, 502

Quetzalcoatl, 189

Quiché: agriculture season and movement of the Pleiades among, 503; maize cycle, 260-day count, and, 106; yearbearers in Calendar Round of, 101

Quillarumiyoc: Inca sites at, 16

Quincunx cache: shape of Chan's west structure and association with, 375

Quintal, Alicia Beatriz, 456

Quintana Roo: widespread nature of 14° orientation and, 107

Quiriguá Stela C: Maya creation myth recorded on, 500

Raab, Mark, 226

Radial pyramids, 278; astronomical observations and, 116; cosmic four parts plus center concept and, 323; El Palmar, final enlargement, 272–73; geomancy and, 317–18; Las Pinturas Sub-5b, 337, 339; Las Pinturas Sub-5 E Group, 341; Las Pinturas Sub-5 "Hunahpu," reconstruction of, *338*; Mundo Perdido, 259; Pinturas, Sub-6, 334; Pinturas, Sub-7 phase, 333; San Antonio Chel, 454; solar alignments and, 116–17, 119; at Tikal and El Palmar, 267, 275

Radial stairways: Uaxactún Group E Structure E-VII, 45

Radiant lords: composite human form Maize-Sun God and, 197; magic birds and, 191–202

Radiocarbon dates: for E Groups in Maya region, 517; summary of, Chan site, 365*t*

Rain gods, 178

Rain/rainfall: onset of rainy season, in Maya area, 106, 124n10; resurrection of the Maize Deity and, 501–3; seasonal distribution, mid-Petén latitudes, *81*; snakes as conduits of, Cerros West Wall, 194; water metaphor of plaza and, 183

Rappaport, Roy, 188

Rathje, William, 85, 416

Real-Escoba transition: cruciform caches and, 223–24

Rebuilding phases: Preclassic calendrics and, 279–80

Reburial rituals: bone manipulation and, 399. *See also* Burials

Redmond, Elsa, 525

Reforma Incised ceramics: Tzec collection, 265

Registro de sitios arqueológicos del sureste y centro-oeste de Petén, 66n2

Reilly, Kent, 18, 190, 191

Relational human bodies: embodiment theory and, 136

Relation lines: astronomically based, 83

Religion: central buildings of E Groups and, 65; importance of, to Highland Maya, 539–40; Middle Preclassic Olmec and Maya, syncretism between, 191; state-supported, elaboration of institutions and, 541; Zapotec, 525. *See also* Altars; Priests; State-sponsored religion; Temple precincts

Religious architecture: important characteristics of, 538–39

Religious centers: European, as centers of learning, 519

Religious-fair model: leadership ceremonies and, 468
Religious function of E Groups, 537–41, 547
Religious ideology: three stones of creation in, 500–501
Religious institutions: political institutions and, 539
Religious occupational specialists, 549; at El Palenque, archaeological documentation of, 525–26; in Maya urban centers, 538; overseeing of ritual activities in E Groups and, 540; prestate entities and degrees of specialization, 547. *See also* Priests
Religious precincts: comparative examples of, 518–21. *See also* Temple precincts
Resbalón, 458
Reservoirs, 183, 184, 580; Brisa E Group, Yaxnohcah, 497; E Groups in Central Karstic Uplands and, 496–97, 504
Residential buildings: at Chan, 364; groups at Yaxnohcah, 497
Resurrection: motif, funerary rites with heads placed in bowls and, 401–2; sacrifice as means to, 200
Rice, Prudence, 15, 60, 87, 88, 100, 342, 375, 412, 454, 560
Ricketson, Edith, 9, 43, 79, 399
Ricketson, Oliver, 9, 43, 58, 76, 78, 79, 317, 399
Río Bec II (Mexico): E Groups at, *14*
Río Bec III (Mexico): E Groups at, *14*
Río Machaquilá y Santa Amelia: E Groups at, 39*t*
Río Mopán, Alta: E Groups at, 36*t*
Río Mopán, Bajo: E Groups at, 35*t*
Río Mopán, Medio: E Groups at, 35*t*
Río Poxte: E Groups at, 39*t*
Río San Juan, Alta: E Groups at, 38*t*
Río San Juan, Bajo: E Groups at, 38*t*
Río San Juan, Media: E Groups at, 38*t*
Río San Martín: E Groups at, 37*t*
Río Subín: E Groups at, 37*t*
Rites of passage, 152
Ritual areas: early, and figurines, 140–42; figurines and, possible functions/meanings, 151–57
Ritual deposits: symbolisms in caches and, 238–39; variation in location of, 580. *See also* Caches

Ritual offerings: placement beneath E Group plazas, 398
Rituals: at Early Xunantunich E Group, 393–99, 406; E Groups and interpretation of, 20
Riverona: E Group sight lines, 313, 314; E Groups mapped at, *310*; temple room counts/areas, 544*t*
Robin, Cynthia, 424
Robles, Fernando, 454
Robles Castellanos, Fernando, 453
Rodman, Margaret, 329
Román, Edwin, 200
Rosario 1: Group E–type complexes, 13
Rosenswig, Robert, 226
Rossi, Franco, 188
Royal appropriation: four-directional offering narrative and, 348–49; of monumental space at Pinturas, 333
Royal burials: Classic period E Group complexes, 387. *See also* Burials; Ruling elites; Tombs
"Royal cult and kingship" notion: interment of rulers in triadic shrines and, 440
Royal identity: K'atun-endings and construction of, 346
Royal tombs: plates designating location in, 184, 200
Rulers: depicted as ballplayers, 344; early, as focus of ideology unto themselves, 333
Rulership: Preclassic E Groups and emerging ethos of, 578; public events related to succession, 539; "stelae cult" and, 437; time reckoning with, 18. *See also* Divine kingship; Kingship
Ruling elites: burials in central civic architecture and, 387; E Groups and establishment of, 20; temple precincts and priests in service to, 518. *See also* Political power
Ruppert, Karl, 8, 34, 59, 62, 79, 537
Rust, William, 226

Sacbeob: Middle Preclassic, at northwest Yucatán sites, 452–53; multiple, Yaxnohcah, 481, 484
Sacred almanacs, 181
Sacred calendar, 95
Sacred geography, 88

Sacred hearth: portrayal of, for Classic Maya, 441

Sacred landscape: Cival E Groups, shared hills, and, 316–18, 324; open plaza space in ancient Maya thought and, 183

Sacred mountains: ritual cache deposits and offerings to, 538

Sacred places: multiple uses and polyvalic meanings for, 539

Sacrifice, 550; ballgame ritual and, 343; enclosed interior architecture and, 539; as global phenomenon, complexity of, 189; as means to resurrection, 200

Sages: conceptual tools of, 179; day counting by, 180, 181; role of, 177; self-aggrandizing leaders and, 179

Saints' relics: fragment enchainment analogous to, 155

Salsipuedes: E Groups at, 37*t*

Salt trade, 6

San Antonio Chel, 454, 469

San Bartolo (Guatemala), 16, 458, 554; *ajaw* featured in Late Preclassic historical charter of, 350; E Groups at, 12, *14*; ideological narratives of early rulers at, 344; map of, *331*; murals, 101, 330, 348, 350, 351, 500, 501; performance in Pinturas building murals at, 18; Pinturas shrine in Triadic Group at, 552; quatrefoil on West Wall at, 502; single-room temples at, 554; site layout, 330; temple room counts/areas, 544*t*; Tomb 1, 330; Ventanas pyramid at, 263; west wall of Pinturas Sub 1-A at, 500–501; yearbearer dates in murals of, 101. *See also* Las Pinturas E Group (San Bartolo)

San Bartolo Ixbalamqué ceramic complex, 334

San Bartolo Mamom ceramics variety, 333

Sánchez Nava, Pedro Francisco, 99

Sanctification: enclosed interior architecture and, 539

Sanders, William, 31

San Isidro (Mexico): cruciform caches tied to cardinal directionality at, 238; greenstone axe caches at, 217, 227; maps of MFC-pattern sites, *221*; MFC-pattern site at, 226; Middle Preclassic examples of E Groups at, 12; spatial plan of, 236

San Jerónimo, Escuintla: Early Preclassic mounds at, 218

San José, Cayo, Belize: Cenote Style complex with one room at, 545; Cenote Variant Style E Group at, 564; excavations in E Groups at, 10, *14*; interbuilding alignments at, 564; pseudo-E-Groups at, 15; single-room temples at, 554; temple room counts/areas, 544*t*

San Lorenzo: decline of, 215; greenstone axe caches at, 217

San Lorenzo Phase, 218

Santa Ana-Zamir: Group E–type complexes, 13

Santa Rosa Xtampak: possible E Group at, 456, *457*, 457–58; stelae in plaza at, 453

Santo (saint): modern east–west focused rituals and, 361

Sapote Striated ceramics, 269

Saraguate group (San Bartolo), 330, *331*, 332

Saturno, William, 188, 200

Savanna Orange ceramics, 259, 263; jar in burial chamber, Early Xunantunich Structure E-2-1st, 403; Tzec collection, 265

Savoie, Gary, 15

Saxché Orange Polychrome: late Tux Complex, Baalche' Group, Yaxnohcah, 486

Saywite: Inca sites at, 16

Scarlet Macaw, 177

Schele, Linda, 183, 200, 500

Scribes (*ts'ib, k'uhun*), 156, 537. *See also* Writing

Seasonality: market scheduling, timekeeping role of E Groups, and, 85; in Mesoamerica, clocking, 180

Secondary burials, 440, 441

Secular order: development of, 65

Seibal. *See* Ceibal or Seibal (Guatemala)

Serpent balustrades: feathered, Las Pinturas Sub-5b, 338, *338*, 342

Serpent Rain Gods, 191

Serpents: Cerros Principal Bird Deity faces vs. Pinturas Principal Bird Deity images and, 194; as conduit of wind and rain, 178. *See also* Snakes

Serving vessel sherds: at Chan, 374

Settlement pattern archaeology, 6

Settlement patterns, 7

Seven Temples Plaza: Tikal, 139

Severed head image: Quadripartite Badge as artistic evolution of, 198

Shallow fluting: early Mamom ceramics, El Palmar, 259
Shamans: interpenetrating categories of priests and, 521
Shark: cosmic, in Classic Maya corpus, 191
Shark's tooth: human form Classic Sun God and, 197
Shell beads: Calakmul Structure IVb cache, 557; at Hatzcap Ceel, Cayo, Belize, 562
Shell items: cache at Chan, 372
Shell ornaments: El Palenque, Oaxaca, México, 522; shrine burials, Chan, 378–79
Shell reduction flakes: deposits at Yaxuná, 466–67
Shells: Chan, 140; Nixtun-Ch'ich', 145; Tikal, 139; Uaxactún, 138; water symbolism and, 580
Shook, Edwin, 79
Shrine burials: Chan, shell ornaments and, 378–79
Shrines: east–west symbolism and, 361
Sierra Red ceramics, 263, 267, 269, 339; Baalche' Group plaza, Yaxnohcah, 485; Chay Complex, Yaxnohcah, 485
Sierra Rojo ceramics: Calakmul Structure IVb cache, 558
Siete Orejas volcano: Takalik Abaj alignment with, 235
Sight-line azimuths: Cival E Groups, *305*
Sight lines: Acropolis E Groups in Central Karstic Uplands and, 494–95, 496; of Cival E Groups, *313,* 313–18, 324; Saraguates group (San Bartolo), 332
Single-roomed temple superstructures, 541
Single-room temples or platforms: prototypes with, 545, 547, 554
Sisia': E Groups mapped at, *310*; sight lines of, 313, 314; temple room counts/areas, 544*t*
Sisson, Edward, 226
Site-formation processes: ethnoarchaeological studies of, 135
Site planning: Late Preclassic, E Groups, plaza politics, and, 273, 275–76, 278
Site size: judging, 367–68
Skull caches: ancestor veneration in Early Xunantunich E Group, 399; at Cenote, 49; Cenote E Group and, 19; core of Structure E-II at Uaxactún, *44*; in eastern buildings in Uaxactún E Group, 63; E Group temples, 537; encased in lip-to-lip vessels, 439, 440–41, 442; placed within ceramic vessels, 399, 401, 439; sacred space and, 538; Uaxactún E Group and, 19; Uaxactún Style E Group at Uaxactún, 561
Skull modification: agricultural rituals and, 154
Sky: directional concepts of earth and, 233–38
"Skyband" imagery: Feathered Serpents and, 342
Sky watching, 554; agricultural fields and, 182; religious architecture and, 538; synthesized ritualistic/scientific perspectives on, 87–88
Slatewares: Becán, 461
Slip colors: early Mamom ceramics, El Palmar, 259
Smashed jars: Cival ritual offering and, 298
Smith, A. Ledyard, 537
Smith, A. V., 43
Smith, Robert, 453
Smoke: snakes as conduits of, Cerros West Wall, 194
Snake (or *kaan*) dynasty: centered at Dzibanché, then at Calakmul, 526–27
Snake-cord frames: in later Maya art, 195
Snake-headed sky frames: in Late Preclassic compositions, 195
Snakes: Cerros Principal Bird Deity faces vs. Pinturas Principal Bird Deity images and, 193–94; in trees, in Preclassic and Classic compositions, 195–96. *See also* Serpents
Snarling mouthed masks: Cerros Structure 5C-2nd, 196; Structure 29, at Cerros, 203
Social complexity: new directions in topic of, 7
Social hierarchies: ancestor veneration in Maya Lowlands and, 386
Social order: new, Middle Preclassic E Groups and, 349
Social ranking: emergence of, 153
Societal development: E Groups and shaping of, 17
Sociocultural complexity: religious specialization and ebbs/flows in, 554; temple precincts and, 526, 547
Sociocultural organization, 7
Sociopolitical complexity: distribution of E Groups during Early Classic period and, 64
Sociopolitical organization, Maya: E Groups and transformations in, 34
Sociopolitical relations: Middle-to-Late Preclassic transition and, 160

Solar alignments, 234; in early E Groups, 96–99; Terminal Classic calendar changes and, 116–17
Solar-based astronomy: Uaxactún Group E and, 152
Solar calendars: local, question of, 83–85; wide use of, at time of European encounter, 180–81
Solar commemorative structures: E Groups as, 203
Solar course: East Mound, Uaxactún, and encapsulation of, 80
Solar cycles: annual, agricultural practices, and, 386; Preclassic E Groups and public rituals involving, 387, 406
Solar epiphanies: E Groups and commemoration of, 302
Solar events: Cival region's E Groups' sight lines and, 313–16, 324; east–west symbolism and, 361. *See also* Equinoxes; Solar observations; Solstices
Solar fixes, timed, 79
Solar hierophanies: aesthetics of "awe" and, 275–76; architectural, 88, *89*, 91; Calakmul, 529; orientation of the Castillo and, 117
Solar observations: hilltops and, 315–18, 323–24; as major concern of Cival architects, 320; plazas and, 186, 187; time-based commemorations, E Groups, and, 346–47; 260-day agricultural cycle and, 106–8, 123–24n9
Solar zenith–based alignments: agricultural calendrical function and data on, 83–85, 91
Solar zenith hypothesis: E Groups and, 416
Solar zeniths: E Groups and 20-day Winal intervals around, 59
Solstice commemorative E Groups: Central Karstic Uplands, 491, 493
Solstice/equinox building alignments, during Middle Preclassic, 82
Solstice hypotheses: E Groups and evaluation of, 415–16
Solstices, 394; Cival E Group sight lines and, 305, 313; Cival West E Group and, 320; fire altars, Xunantunich E Group, and, 397; time-based commemorations, E Groups, and, 347; Uaxactún complex and Maya observance of, 31, 58; Uaxactún's Late Preclassic E Group and, 97. *See also* Summer solstices; Winter solstices
Song, 149, 152

South America: bedrock modification in, 16
Southeastern Lowlands: co-occurrence of Cenote Style E Groups in, 60, 62; eastern platform, but no west structure in, 40*t*; E Groups of, 35*t*–41*t*; identified, but probably not E Groups in, 40*t*–41*t*; site status and spacing of E Groups in, 34
Southern Lowlands, 467; E Groups along trade routes in, 16; E Groups and rise of complexity in, 31–66; two trade routes between Northern Lowlands and, 458, 461, 469; Uaxactún Group E and crystallization of Maya culture in, 31; ubiquity of E Groups in, 3
Southern Petén: dense E Group clusters in, 480
Space: Middle Preclassic landscapes and temporalization of, 499
Spatial plan: standardized, emergence of E Group and, 217
Spatiotemporal cosmological constructs: radial pyramids and, 318
Specola: at Castel Gandolfo, 518
Spectacle: enclosed interior architecture and, 539; performances, buildings on plazas, and, 187
Speech: royal, 149
Spencer, Charles, 525
Spondylus: figures, Chan cache, 372, *373*; watery underworld symbolized by, 404
Spondylus shells and shell ornaments: Calakmul Structure IVb cache, 557; Caracol E Group, 53; Early Xunantunich burial chamber, 404; shell assemblage, Buenavista burial site, 405
Šprajc, Ivan, 99, 481
Stairways and staircases: aesthetics of "awe" and, 275; directional, Cival pyramid, 299; Las Pinturas Sub-5b, 337; perishable altar, Structure E-2, Xunantunich, 394, *394*; Pinturas, Sub-5, 334; Pinturas, Sub-7 phase, 333; primary and secondary burials placed within, 402; radial, Uaxactún Group E Structure E-VII, 45; sacrifice, ballgame ritual, and descent down, 343
Stanton, Travis, 12, 91, 187, 459, 462
"Star-gazing priests" model, of Maya civilization, 152
Stark, Lauren, 112
Starry Deer Crocodile, 183–84
Statehood: multiroom temples and, 545, 553
State-sponsored religion, 6; elaboration of

temple buildings and, 541; full-time priests and, 526; multiroom temples and, 541; platform/temple/plaza complexes and, 552
Stelae: astro-calendrics and, 152; Belize Valley, 419; Blackman Eddy, 428; Cahal Pech, 428–29; Calakmul E Group architecture, 535; Cival, 295; Cival Stela 2, dancing figure wearing Principal Bird Deity head pectoral, *322, 323*; dedicatory offerings and, at Yaxnohcah, 486; earliest, Uaxactún and Cenote, 8; earliest known Long Count records and, 109, *110, 111*; with hieroglyphic inscriptions, Lowlands, 528; K'atun-ending, 347, 418, 436; Pacbitún, 429; Santa Rosa Xtampak, 453; site of Uaxactún named in honor of, 31; Stela 9, early Bak'tun 8 date recorded on, 76; Uaxactún Style E Group, Tayasal, 47; Uaxactún Style E Group at Uaxactún, 561–62; Xunantunich, 429
Stellar alignments: in early E Groups, 96–99
Stick dice: gaming boards with, 180
Stirling Acropolis (La Venta), 227, 236
Stone: later Lower Maya architecture and use of, 227–28
Stone, Andrea, 348
Stone balls: as offerings in Late Preclassic plates, Ceibal, 180
Stone geode: Caracol E Group, 53
Stone spheres: caches, at Ceibal, 231, 232, *232*; sacred space and, 538
Stone stelae: temporal ritual and, 62; Uaxactún Style E Group, Tayasal, 47
Stone tool production debitage: El Palmar Structure E4-1-4th, 263
Story-telling, 152
Stratigraphy: Caracol caches, 60; Cenote, extending to other examples, 59; ceramics associated with leveling events, Yaxnohcah, 484; Cival region E Groups, 318; Early Mamom/Late Mamom division of ceramics from El Palmar, 257, 259; El Palmar Structure E4-1-4th, 263; Hatzcap Ceel, 50, 52; Yaxuná E Group, 464
Strombus beads: Caracol E Group, 53
Strombus detritus: in Chan's central religious complex cache, 369
Strombus shell assemblage: Buenavista burial site, 405
Stross, Brian, 148

Stuart, David, 18, 99, 101, 177, 397, 500
Stucco masks, 278; at Acanceh, 456; Jabalí complex (San Bartolo), 330; Las Pinturas Sub-5b, 337; Uaxactún Group E Structure E-VII, 45
Subsistence-based celebrations, 152
Suhler, Charles, 187
Summer solstices: commemorating, Haab Commemorative E Groups and, 491, 504; E Groups and marking of winter solstices and, 499
Sun: cosmological landscape of E Groups and, 12
Sun cartouches on cheeks: deities marked with, 196
Sun deities, burial/reburial practices and connection to, 402, 405
Sun God(s), 178; cosmic shark and, in Classic Maya corpus, 191; human form, emergence of, 196–97; patron of number 4, 150
Sunrises: Cival E Groups, sight-line orientation variability, and, 305
Supernatural heads: in Classic Maya hieroglyphic script, 149
Superstructures, 230; Calakmul, 531; Chan, 374; Fidelia Complex, at Yaxnohcah, 499–500; Lowland Maya and, 230; Pinturas, Sub-5, 334
Symbolism: in caches, 238–39; directional concepts of the Earth and sky, 233–38; maize agriculture, 233

Tableros: Tikal, Structure 5C-54-5, 272
Tacaná volcano: Izapa alignment with, 235
Tajumulco volcano: La Blanca alignment with, 235
Takalik Abaj: alignment with Siete Orejas volcano, 235; Altar 46, 105, *105*; caches of ceramic vessels and stone spheres at, 232; caching of small stone spheres at, 231; early calendar and monuments at, 104, 105; Maya E Groups in Middle Preclassic at, 96; Stela 5, Long Count dates and, 109, *110*
Taube, Karl, 193, 348, 397, 500
Tau-tooth: human form Classic Sun God and, 197
Tayasal (Guatemala): E Groups at, 10, 12
Tayasal-Paxcamán Zone: central Petén lakes district, three E Groups in, 47; E Groups studied in, 417–18
Tedlock, Barbara, 106, 521

Temple of the Cross: dedication of, 186
Temple of the Seven Dolls, Dzibilchaltún, 548
Temple precincts: access restrictions in, 541, 548, 552; astronomical orientation, priestly residences, and, 551–52; Calakmul, Campeche, Mexico, 526–37; comparative examples of, 518–21, 553; delimited or bounded, 548; El Palenque, Oaxaca, Mexico, 521–26; four comparative frameworks in examples of, 521, 547; graphs of temple # rooms and temple floor area (m^2), *546*; at heart of Maya nucleated communities, 517; multiroom temples, 542, 545, 550, 553; primary and secondary state formation and, 518; relative eastern temple proportions, 545*t*; religious functions practiced in, 537; religious occupational specialists and, 540; room counts/areas, 543*t*–544*t*; single-room temples or platforms, 545, 547, 550, 553; sociocultural complexity and, 526, 549; spatial data on, and their prototypes, 541–47, 553; standardization of, 548; Uaxactún Style E Group at Uaxactún, 561–62. *See also* Altars; Priests; Religion
Templo Mayor (Aztec): directional jar offerings at, 298; twin temples atop, 520
Temporal ritual: emphasis on, for ancient Maya, 62–63
Tenochtitlán: temple complex at, 520
Teopanticuantitlán: ceramics at, 459
Teotihuacán, 7, 493; directional jar offerings at, 298; 260-day cycle and Pyramid of the Sun at, 107
Teotihuacán-Maya connection: Uaxactún alignments, pecked cross, and, 83–85, *84*
Terracing: aesthetics of "awe" and, 275; terraced plaza platform, Structure E-2, Xunantunich, 395, *395*
Terracotta figurines: female, 135
Terrestrial cycles: in Mesoamerican 260-day divinatory almanacs, 149
Test pits: southeast Petén, 56
Tetrapod cache plates: El Palmar, Structure E4-4, 276, *277*
Tetrapod vessels: at Cenote, 49
Thompson, J. Eric S., 6, 8, 105, 538
Three: as a focus, in Maya art and iconography, 19; in Maya cosmology, importance of, 441
Three Stone Place, 159, 503

Three stone symbolism: religious nature of, 500–501
Tikal (Guatemala), 17, 418; Calakmulqueños, *kaanal* dynasty, and control of, 528; ceramic collection, North Acropolis, 265; comparison of Late Preclassic E Groups at El Palmar and, *254*; dismantling of prior buildings at, 269; Early Mamom or Late Eb/Early Tzec architecture at, 259; E Groups at, 12, *14*; elaborate burials and E Group at, 19–20; elaborate burials in triadic buildings at, 438–39; final expansion, Structure 5C-54-5, 271–72; founder deities or "triad gods" of, *62, 63*; Great Plaza Quadrangle map for, 10; height of Temple IV at, 367; hypotheses on similar architectural trends at El Palmar and, 265–66; K'atun monuments at, 114; major burials of dynastic founders at, 280; major sites near, map of, *254*; Maya E Groups in Middle Preclassic at, 96, 97; middle to late Mamom Phase architecture at, 260, 263; Mundo Perdido E Group complex at, 138–39, 228; plaza dimensions, *274*; pregnant figurine at, 154; radial pyramids at, 267, 275; relative eastern temple proportions, 545*t*; reuse of final Late Preclassic phase at, 276; similarities between Mamom or Late Eb/Tzec buildings at, 265; Stela 29, ISIG Long Count for, 113; Structure 5C-54-2, west elevation, *261*; Structure 5C-54-3B, west elevation, *264*; temple room counts/areas, 544*t*; tetrapod plates at, 276; Twin Pyramid Complexes at, 437; Twin Temple complexes at, 62
Time: ancient Maya and importance of, 17; Maya and fascination with, 8, 31; patron supernatural deities and, 150. *See also* Calendars
Time-based commemorations: solar observations, E Groups, and, 346–47
Time reckoning, with rulership, 18
Timescape of creation: Early Ritual Areas and early E Groups as, 158; Early Ritual Area spaces and re-creations of, 159
Tipikal: Olmec-style greenstone caches at, 459
Tlaloc: twin-stair temples dedicated to, 520
Tokens: positional patterning of, 180
Tombs: Calakmul Structure IVb, 558–59; Calakmul Structure VII, 559–60; at Caracol, water symbolism and, 581; Caracol E Group,

54, 56; E Groups, establishment of ruling elites, and, 20; El Palmar, 280–81; royal, plates designating location in, 184, 200. *See also* Burials

Tonalpohualli (count of days), 95

Toniná: founder deities of, 63

Topography: directional concepts of earth and sky and, 234; Lowland Maya E Groups, symbolisms, site planning, and, 237. *See also* Hills and hilltops; Mountains

Topoxté Islands: figurine fragments on, 142

Topsoil stripping: early residential patio groups and, 319

Toscano, Lourdes, 456

T'ot: E Groups mapped at, *310*; temple room counts/areas, 544*t*

Town squares: E Groups likened to, 3, 339

Trade: coastal, development of, 458; early, northern E Groups and relation to, 454, 456–61; E Groups and coeval systems of, 581; E Groups and scheduling for, 414, 416, 435, 436; religious doctrine and scheduling of, 547

Trade routes: distribution of northern E Groups and, 458; E Group locations and, 16, 17, 64; E Groups recorded by Guatemalan *Atlas* project and, *55*; Preclassic, map of Maya area and, *455*; southeast Petén, 58

Trecena (13-day month) cycles: early, lunar records and, 113

Trees: snakes and, metaphorical use of, 196

Tres Zapotes Stela C (Veracruz): Long Count dates and, 111

Triad gods: of Palenque, Tikal, Caracol, *62*, 63

Triadic architecture: new centers of communities and, 280

Triadic Groups, 273; in the Central Karstic Uplands, 494–96, *495,* 504; Cival, Late Preclassic period, 303–4; divine kingship and, 98–99; E Groups as central spatial/conceptual axes supplanted by, 280–81; E Groups framed in opposition to, 329; emergence of, 230; functions of, 186; Las Pinturas E Group transition to, 333; monumental, Cival region, 307; Pinturas, 332; three stone symbolism and, 500; Yaxhá E Groups and, 309

Triadic shrines, 16; Baking Pot, 10; Cahal Pech, 12; "royal cult and kingship" and interment of rulers in, 440

"Triads": importance of, in Maya ideology, 441

Tun: Long Count calendar and, 102

Tun-Ajaw, 121

Tunnels: costumed impersonators and, 525; "Underworld" nexus and, 550

Tun signs, 112, 113, *147*

Turtles: imagery, three "hearthstone" stars in Orion and, 122n2; masks, 206; water symbolism and, 580–81

Tuun K'ab' Hix (a.k.a. K'altun Hix or Cu-Ix): depiction Lintel 1, Calakmul, *533*

Tuxtla Mountains, 236

Twin Pyramid complexes: east–west, 361; at Tikal, 437

Twin Temple complexes: at Tikal, 62

Twisted cord iconography: Izapa and Tulum comparison and, 194

260-day agricultural cycle: solar observations and, 106–8, 123–24n9

Tzec plate collection: Tikal collection, North Acropolis, 265

Tzeltal maize cycle: description of, 154; 260-day count, and, 106

Tzolk'in: calendar cycles at, 304, 320; day names, 100; division into 20-day sets, 96; origin of, 102–6

Tzolk'in commemorative E Groups: Central Karstic Uplands, 493, 504, 506n2

Tzolk'in-Haab Calendar Round: use in Classic Period, 95

Tzolk'in sacred calendar: coining of term, 95; Group of 14° and demarcation of, Central Karstic Uplands and, 490

Tzompantli: discovery of, behind Templo Mayor, 520

Tzotzil Maya: division of solar year among, 499

Tzutziiy K'in, outside Cahal Pech, 429, 430

Tzutzuculi: abandonment of, 229; early MFC site plans at, 224, 233

UAX 1: pecked cross-circle measurements at, 83–85

Uaxac Canal (Guatemala): E Groups at, *14*

Uaxactún (Guatemala), 5, 98, 302, 388, 580; burials and caches at, 439; celestial alignments and, 579; Chan's west structure and archetypical E Group western structure from, 375; earliest stelae at, 8; early and late, relative eastern temple proportions, 545*t*;

Uaxactún—*continued*
early and late, temple room counts/areas, 544*t*; interbuilding alignments at, 561–62; Late Preclassic E-VII-Sub at, 275; multiroom examples of Group E temple architecture at, 542; pecked cross from, 304–5; quadripartite pecked cross-circle carved into Temple Court floor, Structure AV, *84*; stelae and naming of, 31

Uaxactún Group E, 10; annual calendar and Terminal Preclassic–Early Classic transition in, 75, 80; archaeology of, 43, 45, 47; as archetype of the Maya astronomical observatory, 79–82; building of, 230; caches from core of Structure E-II at, *44*; Early Classic buildings centered with caches at, 19; eastern platform at, with locations of caches, *42*; horizon-based solar astronomy and, 152; "index-fossil" Group E, 138; original description of, 412; plan illustration by Frans Blom, *78*; plan of, *77*; plan of latest (Early Classic) version of, *9*; prototype, Ricketson's excavating work, 8; reexamination of investigations for, 47; Ruppert on function of, 537; temples, 536; term "E Group" derived from, 43. *See also* Uaxactún Style E Groups

Uaxactún Sin Engobe ceramics class, 333

Uaxactún Style E Groups, 32, *33*, 34, 59, 413, 561–62; characteristics of, 10; confusion with triadic eastern building, western Belize, 66n1; construction histories of buildings in, 427; dating of, 34; shown on map of Yaxhá, *61*; spacing of, 62

Uayeb, 95

Ucanal, 63

Umbilicus cords: snakes symbolizing, 194

Um Complex ceramics: Yaxnohcah, 485

Underworld: quatrefoils and water pools as windows/portals to, 502; water symbolism and, 580–81

Urbanism and urban planning: autochthonous innovation, E Group complexes, and, 339; community identity, emerging dynasties, and, 344; corporate social forms and, 328–29; east–west symbolism and, 361, 379; E Group clusters in Central Karstic Uplands and Southern Petén, 480; foundational establishment of E Group architectural complexes and, 64–65; geometric planning practices, 339. *See also* Plazas; Public architecture; Trade

Urcid, Javier, 108

Uruk, Mesopotamia: temple precinct at, 519

Use-lives: ethnoarchaeological studies of, 135

U-shaped helmet-like hairdo: on figurines, *146, 148, 150*

Uxmal: E Groups reported at, 13

Uxul (Mexico): ballcourts at, 496; Calakmulqueños, *kaanal* dynasty, and control of, 528; in Central Karst Plateau, 488*t*; E Groups at, *14*; Haab Commemorative E Groups at, 493

"U yol ahk K'inich Bahlam in the head of the turtle," Altar 1 El Perú–Waka' (quatrefoil), *183*

Vadala, Jeffrey, 107, 202

Valdés, Juan Antonio, 83

Valedictory ceremonies: E Groups as settings for, 412, 414, 418–19, 435, 436

Variegated color palette: early Mamom ceramics, El Palmar, 259

Variegated Indeterminate ceramics, *258*, 259, 263, 267, 269

Vatican (Italy), 518–19

Vegetation: plaza space images in quatrefoil form with, 183

Veintena (20-day month) cycles, 537, 552

Veintiuno de Mayo: in Central Karst Plateau, 489*t*

Veneration of ancestors. *See* Ancestor veneration

Venus: Terminal Classic solar alignments and horizon positions of, 117; 260-day period and visibility of, 103

Venus almanac: Dresden Codex and, 117

Venusian cycles: in Mesoamerican divinatory almanacs, 149

Venus observations: in Late Classic period, 125n19

Veracruz: early calendar inscriptions in, 99

Veracruz/Tabasco Lowlands, 7

Viewshed maps: of sacred hills, Cival E Groups, 316

Vigesimal notation (Winal): time cycles and, 99

Vining, Benjamin, 490, 529

Vistahermosa: MFC-pattern site (possibly) at, 226

Vogt, Evon Z., 316

Volcanoes, 217; central axes of ceremonial centers and, 235; Isthmian region, *216*, 217; ritually significant, Takalik Abaj's proximity to, 105
Von Nagy, Christopher, 226
Voorhies, Barbara, 180

Wakna: acropolises in both north and south at, 495; in Central Karst Plateau, 489*t*; E Groups at, 12, *14*; Haab Commemorative E Groups at, 493; reservoirs near E Groups at, 496; unique dates commemorated by E Groups at, 494
Walker, Debra, 202
Watanabe, John, 239
Water bodies: in Maya cosmology, 237
Water jars: in quatrefoil pattern, ritual caching at Cival and, 398
Waterlilies: plaza space images in quatrefoil form with, 183
Waterlily Monster, 184
Waterlily serpent: patron of number 13, 150
Water metaphor: of plaza, rains, and, 183
Water pools: three levels of the cosmos, Maya imagery, and, 502; as windows/portals to underworld, 502
Water symbolism: early elites' developing associations with, 330; of maize agriculture and broad notion of, 233; of the plaza, 239; Structure E-2, Xunantunich, 396; underworld and, 580–81
Watery deities: burial practices and connection of ancestors to, 405
Watery features: greenstone axes deposition and, 239
Watery underworld: *Spondylus* as symbol of, 404
Western model of space: cardinal directionality of Maya vs., 239
"Western Olmec Corridor": ceramics, 459
Western pyramid footprint: in comparison of Cival region's set of 13 E Groups, 309; histogram of footprint areas, Cival region, 311, *312*
Western pyramids, 60; Caracol E Group, 50, 53, 60; Cenote E Group, 47; in E Group assemblages, 416; Uaxactún E Group, 43. *See also* Eastern platforms
White marl fill: Structure E-2, Xunantunich, 392, 393
Willey, Gordon, 6

Winals (Maya months), 15; derivation of word, 113; Long Count Calendar and, 102; time cycle calculations and, 99
Wind God: mosaic mask evocative of, 560
Winter solstices: E Groups and marking of summer solstices and, 499; Fidelia Complex and commemoration of, 499–500; Haab cycle and, 103; hierophany in the Castillo and, 121
Witzná hill: profile of topography along Dos Aguados northern sight line in vicinity of, *314*, 314–15
Wob Complex ceramics: Yaxnohcah, 485
World Tree, 298, 299, 323, 500, 501
Worship: Pinturas murals and sequence of, 189
Worshipper/venerator (*aj k'uhuun*), 540
Writing: Maya, emergence and development of, 160–61; as prestige technology, 88. *See also* Scribes

Xbalanque (Hero Twin), 150
Xcalumkin: priest's titles reported in texts from, 540
Xelhá: Teotihuacanoid traits reported at, 460
Xe Phase figurines, 142
Xibalba ("Place of Fear"), 550
Xocnaceh, 452, 458; Olmec-style greenstone caches at, 459
Xok Shell girdle: female rulers wearing, 198
Xtobó, 454
Xuenkal: Puuc-style architecture at, 461
Xulnal: Acropolis E Groups at, 494; ballcourts at, 496; in Central Karst Plateau, 489*t*; reservoirs near E Groups at, 497
Xulnal South: in Central Karst Plateau, 489*t*
Xultún: Calakmulqueños, *kaanal* dynasty, and control of, 528; priest's titles reported in texts from, 540
Xunantunich (Belize), 17, 420, 442, 458, 541, 554; architectural history of Structure E-2, 391–93; construction histories of triadic assemblages at, 426; E Groups at, 10, *14,* 223; elaborate royal tombs in triadic assemblages of, 440; frequency of burials and caches, Eastern Triadic Structures at, 433*t,* 434; height measurements of, in Belize River valley, 422, 422*t*; height of El Castillo at, 367; isometric reconstruction of perishable altar in front of Structure E-2-2nd, with

Xunantunich—*continued*
  inset showing postholes, *394*; isometric reconstruction of Structure E-2-2nd, *392*; Late Classic and Terminal Classic occupation, 388; LiDAR hillside image of, with site map overlaid, *389*; as mid-sized center, 368; north–south profiles of, Belize River valley, *423*; partial excavations of E Groups at, 12; Plaza A (I–III) at, 429; temple room counts/areas, 544*t*. *See also* Classic Xunantunich E Group; Early Xunantunich E Group
Xunantunich Archaeological Project (XAP), 368, 388

Yakalxiu: E Groups at, 13
Yaxché: San Bartolo murals painted at, 348
Yaxchilán: architectural solar hierophanies at, 91; Calakmulqueños, *kaanal* dynasty, and control of, 528
Yaxhá (Guatemala): E Groups at, 12, *14*, 80; E Groups facing Triadic Group at, 309; map of, *61*; plaza dimensions, 273, *274*; Twin Temple complexes, 62
Yax Hal Witznal, 396
Yaxhom: E Groups reported at, 13
Yaxnohcah (Mexico), 17; acropolises in both north and south at, 495; Baalche' Group at, 481, 485–86; ballcourts at, 496; Brisa Complex at, 481, 484, 485, 497; Brisa Reservoir at, 485; in Central Karst Plateau, 489*t*; Chay Complex ceramics at, 485; chronology based on ceramic complexes, 484*t*; civic complexes at, 497; civic precinct, map of, *483*; dating Brisa E Group at, 490; dating of E Groups at, 504; E Groups at, *14*; Fidelia Complex at, 499–500; Helena platform at, 497; map of, *482*; movement of the Pleiades and agricultural practices in, 503; remarkable scale of, 480–81; reservoirs near E Groups at, 497; residential group adjacent to E Group at, 497; resurrection of Maize God and ballcourt/reservoir complex at, 501–2; solar year at, 492; Tux Complex at, 486; unusually large Preclassic civic centers at, 480; Wob Complex ceramics at, 485
Yaxuná (Mexico), 17; AMS radiocarbon assays, burned wood samples, 463, 466*t*; central, LiDAR hillside image of, *462*; Central Acropolis at, 450; ceramic vessels and Middle Formative greenstone from cache in dance platform at, *463*; coastal trade items and, 458; dance platforms, 550; East Acropolis at, 462, *462*, 464; E Group assemblages at, 454; E Groups at, *14*; founding of, 461–68; as important Middle Formative center, 461; Middle Formative dance platforms at, *188*; North Acropolis at, 462, *462*, 464; north profile of center-line excavation into plaza in front of Structure 5E-2, *465*; performance platforms at, 187; Puuc-style architecture at, 461; Southern Lowland–looking ceramics at, 460–61; temple room counts/areas, 544*t*; Teotihuacanoid traits reported at, 460
Yearbearer dates: Postclassic Aztec system vs. Postclassic Maya system, 101
Yearbearers, 100, 119–20, 500; Aztec system of, 106; defined, 122n4; Monte Albán, 100; in Postclassic period, 96; use in Highlands of Guatemala, 95. *See also* Calendars
Yik'in Chan K'awiil (King), 182
Y'okop: Calakmulqueños, *kaanal* dynasty, and control of, 528
Yucatán: Bishop de Landa's observation on religion in, 537; modern day, east–west focused rituals and, 361–62, 373; movement of the Pleiades and agricultural practices in, 503
Yuknoom Tok' K'awiil, 535

Zacatel Cream Polychrome: late Tux Complex, Baalche' Group, Yaxnohcah, 486
Zapotec: month glyphs, at Monte Albán, 100; religion, 525; "Type II" yearbearer dates, 101
Zapotec state: emergence of, 7
Zenith dates: origin of the Tzolk'in and, 105
Zenith passages: and building alignments during Late Preclassic, 82; Chortí, solar year, and, 499; Cival E Groups and, 305, 307, 320; Haab Commemorative E Groups and, 491–92, 493, 504; time-based commemorations, E Groups, and, 347
Zero: spatial positioning and concept of, 181
Zinacantán: sacred mountains around, 316; small mound in ceremonial center and Tzotzil Maya speakers of, 5
Zohapilco: ceramic styles at, 459
Zoomorphic heads: in Classic Maya hieroglyphic script, 149
Zoomorphic mask: Structure 29, at Cerros, 203
Zubin, 430

MAYA STUDIES

Edited by Diane Z. Chase and Arlen F. Chase

Salt: White Gold of the Ancient Maya, by Heather McKillop (2002)
Archaeology and Ethnohistory of Iximché, by C. Roger Nance, Stephen L. Whittington, and Barbara E. Borg (2003)
The Ancient Maya of the Belize Valley: Half a Century of Archaeological Research, edited by James F. Garber (2004; first paperback edition, 2011)
Unconquered Lacandon Maya: Ethnohistory and Archaeology of Indigenous Culture Change, by Joel W. Palka (2005)
Chocolate in Mesoamerica: A Cultural History of Cacao, edited by Cameron L. McNeil (2006; first paperback edition, 2009)
Maya Christians and Their Churches in Sixteenth-Century Belize, by Elizabeth Graham (2011)
Chan: An Ancient Maya Farming Community, edited by Cynthia Robin (2012; first paperback edition, 2013)
Motul de San José: Politics, History, and Economy in a Classic Maya Polity, edited by Antonia E. Foias and Kitty F. Emery (2012; first paperback edition, 2015)
Ancient Maya Pottery: Classification, Analysis, and Interpretation, edited by James John Aimers (2013; first paperback edition, 2014)
Ancient Maya Political Dynamics, by Antonia E. Foias (2013; first paperback edition, 2014)
Ritual, Violence, and the Fall of the Classic Maya Kings, edited by Gyles Iannone, Brett A. Houk, and Sonja A. Schwake (2016; first paperback edition, 2018)
Perspectives on the Ancient Maya of Chetumal Bay, edited by Debra S. Walker (2016)
Maya E Groups: Calendars, Astronomy, and Urbanism in the Early Lowlands, edited by David A. Freidel, Arlen F. Chase, Anne S. Dowd, and Jerry Murdock (2017; first paperback edition, 2020)
War Owl Falling: Innovation, Creativity, and Culture Change in Ancient Maya Society, by Markus Eberl (2017)
Pathways to Complexity: A View from the Maya Lowlands, edited by M. Kathryn Brown and George J. Bey III (2018)
Water, Cacao, and the Early Maya of Chocolá, by Jonathan Kaplan and Federico Paredes Umaña (2018)
Maya Salt Works, by Heather McKillop (2019)
The Market for Mesoamerica: Reflections on the Sale of Pre-Columbian Antiquities, edited by Cara G. Tremain and Donna Yates (2019)
Migrations in Late Mesoamerica, edited by Christopher S. Beekman (2019)
Approaches to Monumental Landscapes of the Ancient Maya, edited by Brett A. Houk, Barbara Arroyo, and Terry G. Powis (2020)

www.ingramcontent.com/pod-product-compliance
Lightning Source LLC
Chambersburg PA
CBHW070740020526
44114CB00042B/2032